Harry Ballan

SYMBOLS
OF THE
KABBALAH

PHILOSOPHICAL AND
PSYCHOLOGICAL PERSPECTIVES

SANFORD L. DROB

JASON ARONSON INC.
Northvale, New Jersey
Jerusalem

The author gratefully acknowledges permission to reprint portions of the following:

S. Drob. "The Metaphors of Tikkun Haolam: Their Traditional Meaning and Contemporary Significance" in *Jewish Review* 3:6. Reprinted by permission of the Jewish Review, Inc. Copyright © 1990.

S. Drob. "The Sefirot: Kabbalistic Archetypes of Mind and Creation" in *Cross Currents* 47. Copyright © 1997. Reprinted by permission of the publisher.

S. Drob. "Tzimtzum: A Kabbalistic Theory of Creation" in *Jewish Review* 3:5. Reprinted by permission of the Jewish Review, Inc. Copyright © 1990.

R. Elior. *The Paradoxical Ascent to God:The Kabbalistic Theosophy of Habad Hasidism.* Reprinted by permission of the State University of New York Press. Copyright © 1993. All rights reserved.

M. Idel. *Hasidism: Between Ecstasy and Magic.* Reprinted by permission of the State University of New York Press. Copyright © 1995. All rights reserved.

M. Idel. *Kabbalah: New Perspectives.* Copyright © 1988 by Yale University Press. Reprinted by permission of the publisher.

D. Meltzer. *The Secret Garden: An Anthology in the Kabbalah.* Copyright © 1976, 1998 by David Meltzer. Reprinted by permission of the publisher.

R. Nozick. *Philosophical Explanations.* Copyright © 1981. Reprinted by permission of the publisher.

D. Wilder Menzi and Z Padeh. *The Tree of Life: Chayyim Vital's Introduction to the Kabbalah of Isaac Luria.* Copyright © 1999. Reprinted by permission of the publisher.

I. Robinson. *Moses Cordovero's Introduction to Kabbalah: An Annotated Translation of His Or Ne'erav.* Copyright © 1994. Reprinted by permission of the publisher.

I. Tishby and F. Lachower. *The Wisdom of the Zohar,* Vols., I, II, and III. Reprinted by permission of The Littman Library of Jewish Civilization. Copyright © 1989.

S. Zalman. *Likutei Amarim-Tanya.* Copyright © 1983. Reprinted by permission of the publisher.

This book was set in 10 pt. Galliard by Alabama Book Composition of Deatsville, AL, and printed and bound by Book-Mart Press, Inc. of North Bergen, NJ.

Library of Congress Cataloging-in-Publication Data

Drob, Sanford L.
   Symbols of the kabbalah: philosophical and psychological perspectives /
by Sanford L. Drob.
      p.   cm.
   Includes bibliographical references and index.
   ISBN 0–7657–6126–2
   1. Cabala—Terminology. I. Title
BM526 D765 2000
296.1'6—dc21   99–048145

Printed in the United States of America on acid-free paper. For information and catalog, write to Jason Aronson Inc., 230 Livingston Street, Northvale, NJ 07647-1726, or visit our website: www.aronson.com

For
Liliana Rusansky Drob

Contents

Preface

This work provides a philosophical and psychological interpretation of the major symbols and metaphors of the theosophical Kabbalah. The opening chapter explores a number of factors that have inhibited others from undertaking a philosophical interpretation of the Kabbalah in the past and explores the methodological and conceptual issues involved in providing an analysis of the theosophical Kabbalah from a philosophical and psychological point of view. Chapters Two through Nine each focus upon a major kabbalistic symbol and provide an interpretation of these symbols and the Kabbalah as a whole that strives to be comprehensible and relevant to the contemporary reader. Several of the chapters were originally written as separate essays and appeared (in different form) in *The Jewish Review* and *Crosscurrents*.[1]

I am indebted to a number of authors whose works have opened the world of the Kabbalah to those such as myself who are nonspecialists in Hebraic studies; first to Gershom Scholem, whose immense oeuvre has

---

1. See Sanford Drob, "Tzimtzum: A Kabbalistic Theory of Creation," *Jewish Review*, Vol. 3, No. 5 (April–May 1990); Sanford Drob, "The Metaphors of Tikkun Haolam: Their Traditional Meaning and Contemporary Significance," *Jewish Review*, Vol. 3, No. 6 (June 1990); Sanford Drob, "The Sefirot: Kabbalistic Archetypes of Mind and Creation," *Crosscurrents* 47 (1997):5–29.

literally defined the field of kabbalistic studies to the general reader; to Isaiah Tishby and Fischel Lachower, whose arrangement and commentary on the Zohar made that work accessible; to Immanuel Schochet, whose commentary on Schneur Zalman's *Tanya* and essay on the "Mystical Concepts of Chasidism" first brought me into the world of Lurianic thought; and to many other scholars, such as Moshe Idel, Rachel Elior, and Elliot Wolfson, whose works are cited herein.

On a more personal note I am indebted to the late Professor John Findlay whose works on Hegel and Plato, whose original Neoplatonic philosophy, and whose personal inspiration have constantly informed my efforts at a rational understanding of the Kabbalah. I would also like to thank Rabbi Shimmon Hecht for teaching me *Tanya*, and Rabbi Joel Kenney for guiding my exploration of Vital's *Sefer Etz Chayyim* and sharing with me his knowledge of kabbalistic and Hasidic symbolism.

Introduction:
The Kabbalistic Metaphors

This is an ambitious book. Its purpose is the interpretation of the main symbols of the theosophical Kabbalah from a perspective that is accessible and relevant to the contemporary reader. The essays that follow each focus upon a particular kabbalistic symbol, and on the relationship between the Kabbalah and some aspect of ancient or modern thought, and were all written with the conviction that the Kabbalah, particularly as it is expressed in the school of Isaac Luria (the Lurianic Kabbalah), provides a coherent and comprehensive account of the cosmos, and humanity's role within it, that is intellectually, morally, and spiritually significant for contemporary man. It is my view that the Lurianic Kabbalah provides us with a fundamental mythology or "basic metaphor," which organizes *everything* around itself in a manner that is strikingly original, illuminating, and vital for us today.

Although much of this book is an attempt to articulate the philosophical and psychological ideas that are implicit in the Kabbalah's myths, metaphors, and speculations, it is not a work of philosophy or psychology per se. While contemporary philosophy and psychology can provide a vocabulary that will enable us to understand the Kabbalah in a manner that is, from our perspective, perhaps "better" than the Kabbalists understood it themselves, the Kabbalah cannot be exhaustively described in rational terms. This is because the Kabbalah, as will soon become evident, is an approach to the world that is at once poetical and philosophical, symbolic and conceptual, mystical and logical, prescriptive and descriptive; and any attempt to define it through the categories of traditional philosophy, psychology, ethics, religion, etc., will of necessity miss part of the Kabbalah's essence. This is not only because the Kabbalah transcends the boundaries of these categories but because it is ultimately deconstructive of these categories as well. The conceptual schemes that I utilize in explicating the kabbalistic symbols, while extremely useful, must ultimately be discarded in favor of those symbols themselves.

It is curious that a serious philosophically and psychologically minded effort at explicating the Kabbalah has yet to be undertaken.[1] I am aware of no English-language attempt to treat the Kabbalah comprehensively from a contemporary philosophical point of view, and no work that could properly be called an effort at contemporary kabbalistic philosophy.[2] While both Elliot

---

1. Two works, one quite old, another much more recent, may be noted in this context: Maurice Fluegel's *Philosophy, Qabbala and Vedenta* (Baltimore: H. Fluegel & Company, 1902) and Edward Hoffman's *The Way of Splendor: Jewish Mysticism and Modern Psychology* (Northvale, NJ: Jason Aronson, 1981). Fluegel's work is remarkable for its positive reception of the Kabbalah during a period when scholars tended to regard it as a repository of superstition. Hoffman's is representative of contemporary popular accounts of mysticism and psychology. Neither work provides much in the way of the philosophical or psychological *analysis* and each is notable for an absence of any sustained discussion of theosophical themes.

2. Several contemporary authors have, however, made philosophical use of kabbalistic ideas. David Birnbaum's *God and Evil* (Hoboken, NJ: Ktav, 1989), for example, makes impressive theological use of the Lurianic concept of *Tzimtzum* (divine contraction). Birnbaum refers to his work as "a unified theodicy/theology/ philosophy" and draws upon a wide range of historical and contemporary Jewish sources to reach what is essentially a kabbalistic view of God and man. Still the points of contact with kabbalistic texts and theory are quite minimal. Among contemporary philosophers, Robert Nozick in *Philosophical Explanations* (Cambridge, MA: Harvard University Press, 1981) places the kabbalistic notion of *Ein-Sof* (without limit) in the context of a sophisticated analysis of the foundations of meaning. Nozick's entire philosophical thrust and style is extremely broad-minded, and as such he is open to the significance of kabbalistic (and other mystical) conceptions and symbols; yet his specific involvement with the Kabbalah is even more limited than Birnbaum's. Harold Bloom's *Kabbalah and Criticism* (New York: Continuum, 1983) applies kabbalistic notions to the criticism of literary texts. Bloom refers to himself as a "Jewish gnostic."

Wolfson[3] and Rachel Elior[4] explicate certain kabbalistic sources in a philosophical idiom, neither have attempted to articulate or defend a kabbalistic philosophy or ethic.

The few efforts in this direction have either been popularizations of kabbalistic ideas that simply represent kabbalistic themes with little interpretation and analysis, or books that treat the Kabbalah as a sort of precursor to "New Age" psychology.[5] The reasons for this situation, I believe, are to be found in the history of Kabbalah scholarship rather than in the nature of the Kabbalah itself.

Originally a discipline that was transmitted orally from master to only a few select disciples, the Kabbalah never became an explicit part of yeshiva study or rabbinical training. While the Hasidim adapted the Lurianic Kabbalah for the masses, they diluted and psychologized its symbolism to such an extent as to obscure many of its more interesting features. Taught in

---

None of these authors, however (and no others as far as I can gather), have attempted the task I have set for myself in this volume, that of providing a thoroughgoing philosophical and psychological interpretation of a number of key kabballistic symbols and ideas. There has yet to be written a contemporary kabbalistic response to the philosophical and psychological issues of our time.

3. See, for example, Elliot R. Wolfson "Woman—The Feminine as Other in Theosophic Kabbalah: Some Philosophical Observations on the Divine Androgyne," in *The Other in Jewish Thought and History: Constructions of Jewish Identity and Culture*, ed. L. Silberstein and R. Cohn (New York: New York University Press, 1994), pp. 166–204; Elliot R. Wolfson, *Along the Path: Studies in Kabbalistic Myth, Symbolism and Hermeneutics* (Albany: State University of New York Press, 1995); Elliot R. Wolfson, *Through a Speculum That Shines: Vision and Imagination in Medieval Jewish Mysticism* (Princeton, NJ: Princeton University Press, 1994); *Circle in the Square: Studies in the Use of Gender in Kabbalistic Symbolism* (Albany: State University of New York Press, 1995).

4. See, for example, Rachel Elior, "Chabad: The Contemplative Ascent to God," in *Jewish Spirituality: From the Sixteenth-Century Revival to the Present*, ed. Arthur Green (New York: Crossroads, 1987), pp. 157–205; "The Concept of God in Hekhalot Mysticism," in *Binah: Studies in Jewish Thought*, ed. J. Dan, (New York: Greenwood Publishing Group, 1989), pp. 97–120; and *The Paradoxical Ascent to God: The Kabbalistic Theosophy of Habad Hasidism*, trans by J. M. Green (Albany: State University of New York Press, 1993).

5. Among the more interesting recent popularizations of the Kabbalah are Herbert Weiner's, *9½ Mystics: The Kabbalah Today* (New York: Macmillan, 1986), Aryeh Kaplan's *Jewish Meditation: A Practical Guide* (New York: Schocken, 1985), and Adin Steinsaltz's *The Thirteen-Petalled Rose* (New York: Basic Books, 1985). Many other works of mostly dubious quality line the shelves of "Esoteric" bookshops.

its pure form only in the most intimate of master/pupil relationships, buried in unpublished manuscripts, or obscured in the teachings of Hasidism, Kabbalah failed to reveal itself as an integral part of the Judaism that was to interact with the wider intellectual world of the enlightenment. As such the Kabbalah never came under the serious scrutiny of those who would subject Judaism to the scientific and philosophically critical outlook of the eighteenth and nineteenth centuries. Those practitioners of *Wissenschaft des Judentums* who considered the Kabbalah, based their opinion on very limited data, and frequently regarded the Kabbalah with utter disdain—in Graetz's words, "the babble of a semi-idiot."[6]

It was not until the 1930s and 1940s that a group of scholars led by Gershom Scholem, Isaiah Tishby, and others pulled the Kabbalah out of academic obscurity and disrepute by providing the wider intellectual world with a catalogue of manuscripts and texts, and, more significantly, synopses and critiques of the Kabbalah's major doctrines. Scholem's immense oeuvre indeed provides the starting point for any intellectual or scholarly approach to the Kabbalah,[7] and a widening circle of his followers have created, both in Israel and America, an academically respectable, if somewhat narrowly

---

6. For a brief but very useful discussion of the historiography of the Kabbalah, see Moshe Idel, *Kabbalah: New Perspectives* (New Haven: Yale University Press, 1988), pp. 1–16. Idel points out that even in the early part of the nineteenth century, there were scholars of *Wissenschaft des Judentums*, such as Adolphe Franck and Adolf Jellinek, who were sympathetic to the Kabbalah. However, the most influential nineteenth century scholars were negative in their evaluations. Heinrich Graetz (1817–1891), whose *History of the Jews* (first published in 1887) remained the standard reference (in both German and English) well into this century, spoke of Isaac Luria's "fantastic mysticism" and "the absurdities" of the Zohar and concluded that "the Lurian cabala wrought great mischief to Judaism" and "had a deteriorating effect upon morals." Heinrich Graetz, *Popular History of the Jews*, fifth ed. (New York: Hebrew Publishing, 1937), Vol. 4, pp. 442–450.

7. For works by Scholem, see References. Works on Scholem include David Biale's *Gershom Scholem: Kabbalah and Counter-History*, 2d ed. (Cambridge, MA: Harvard University Press, 1982), Joseph Dan, *Gershom Scholem and the Mystical Dimensions of Jewish History* (New York: New York University Press, 1987), Eliezer Schweid, *Judaism and Mysticism According to Gershom Scholem: A Critical Analysis and Programmatic Discussion*, trans. David Weiner (Atlanta: Scholars Press, 1983), and Susan Handelman, *Fragments of Redemption: Jewish Thought and Literary Theory in Benjamin, Scholem & Levinas* (Bloomington and Indianapolis: Indiana University Press, 1991).

conceived,[8] area of Jewish studies, the study of Jewish mysticism. The history of Kabbalah, though not beyond controversy, is now fairly well documented, and several of its most important texts, which had hitherto either been completely unavailable or available only in poor translations, have been published, translated, and annotated in a manner that makes their ideas accessible for the very first time to the nonspecialist and general intellectual community.[9]

Still, in spite of the proliferation in Kabbalah scholarship, the Kabbalah has yet to be taken seriously as philosophy. There are, perhaps, several reasons for this. The first is that the Kabbalah is still only studied in departments of Jewish studies, where it continues to be *contrasted* with Jewish philosophy. A related and perhaps more important reason is that while the founder of modern Kabbalah scholarship, Gershom Scholem, dealt at great length with the symbols of the theosophical Kabbalah, he held almost as a matter of dogma that these symbols were essentially impenetrable to the rational mind. As such, neither he nor any of his disciples have attempted to interpret the Kabbalah from a contemporary philosophical or even psychological point of view. While a new generation of Kabbalah scholars, (e.g., Moshe Idel, Elliot Wolfson) have rejected many of Scholem's premises and methods, they have either focused on the ecstatic (meditational) aspects of the Kabbalah or have continued to hold, in their own fashion, that there is little of cognitive or rational interest in the theosophical symbols.

The result of this has been a significant lacuna in our understanding of what is one of the most powerful spiritual and intellectual movements in history. As I believe will become increasingly clear in the following pages, an intellectual approach to the Kabbalah yields numerous insights into theological, philosophical, and psychological issues. There is hardly an important philosophical problem about which the Kabbalah does not have something

---

8. Moshe Idel has been critical of an overly philological and historical approach to the study of Kabbalah and Hasidism. He writes, for example, that "phenomenology, psychology, anthropology and the comparative study of religions, intellectual history, and cultural history should all supplement the textology and historiography that reign supreme in modern Hasidic studies." Moshe Idel, *Hasidism: Between Ecstasy and Magic* (Albany: State University of New York Press, 1995), p. 28.

9. The most important of these is Isaiah Tishby and Fischel Lachower, *The Wisdom of the Zohar*, trans. David Goldstein (Oxford: Oxford University Press, 1989), a three-volume anthology of Zohar texts, translated and annotated with extensive introductions and commentary by Tishby.

very significant to say. The problems of good and evil, the creation and structure of the universe, the nature of being and nonbeing, the essence of thought and language, and the meaning of human existence are but a few of the issues with which the Kabbalah is concerned. Indeed, when the problems of philosophy are looked at from a kabbalistic perspective, they are, as I will attempt to show, completely transformed, in a manner that not only provides us with insight into our philosophical puzzles, but that dissolves our conviction that these problems must have unique solutions.

The kabbalistic ideas to be discussed in the following pages clearly have affinities to other systems of thought in both the Orient and the West. With respect to the former, the affinities between the Kabbalah and the Tao will be readily evident to anyone familiar with the Taoist conception of the "complementarity of opposites." In addition, there are many parallels (as well as important differences) between the Kabbalah and the various Vedic, Jainist, and Buddhist traditions of India. With regard to Western thought, it should be noted that even Scholem (who otherwise rejected the notion that there is philosophical significance to the kabbalistic symbols) acknowledged a relationship between the Kabbalah and idealism, particularly the dialectical idealism of Hegel.[10] Further, the deep affinities between the Kabbalah and Platonism, Neoplatonism, Gnosticism, and the theosophies of such thinkers as Boehme and Swedenborg are suggestive of historical as well as conceptual connections. Finally, there are important affinities between the Kabbalah and certain trends in twentieth-century thought; psychoanalysis and Jungian psychology in particular, as well as existentialism and deconstructionism.[11] Indeed, it is my view that it is only by being equipped with the nonlinear concepts of dialectical, psychoanalytic, and deconstructive thought that we

---

10. See Gershom Scholem, *Kabbalah* (Jerusalem: Keter, 1974) where Scholem exclaims with regard to the Lurianic Kabbalah, "we find a most astonishing tendency to a mode of contemplative thought that can be called 'dialectical' in the strictest sense of the term used by Hegel" (p. 143). Scholem points out that the later Christian Kabbalah, with its melange of kabbalistic and alchemical symbolism, has a discernible influence on the work of Schelling and Hegel, through their reading of the books of F. C. Oetinger (1702–1782), ibid., p. 200. See Chapter Seven in the present volume and my book, *Kabbalistic Metaphors: Jewish Mystical Themes in Ancient and Modern Thought* (Northvale, NJ: Jason Aronson, 2000) for a fuller discussion of Kabbalah and Hegelian thought.

11. Readers interested in a detailed study of the relationship of the Kabbalah to other spiritual, philosophical, and psychological systems of thought are referred to my *Kabbalistic Metaphors*.

can even begin to make sense of the kabbalistic symbols in our own time. So equipped, we are today probably in a better position to understand the philosophical aspects of the Kabbalah than were the Kabbalists themselves.

It is, of course, somewhat misleading to speak of the Kabbalah as if it were a single, unified set of symbols or ideas. Idel, for example, holds that three basic models can be discerned as operating and competing throughout the history of Jewish mysticism. These models can be readily distinguished according to the their basic *intent* with respect to God: the *theosophical* Kabbalah, embodied in the Zohar and the followers of Isaac Luria, seeks to *understand and describe* the divine realm; the *ecstatic* Kabbalah, exemplified in Abraham Abulafia and Isaac of Acre, strives to *achieve a mystical union* with God; and the *magico-theurgical* Kabbalah, present in a wide range of kabbalistic literature, endeavors to *alter* both God and the world.[12] It is the theosophical Kabbalah, with its descriptions of the nature and vicissitudes of the Godhead in relation to the world, that will be the major focus of this book. While one finds major differences in doctrine even amongst the theosophical Kabbalists, this Kabbalah, as Scholem has pointed out, possesses a common range of symbols and ideas that clearly constitute a discernible tradition.

Scholem distinguishes two main stages in the development of the theosophical Kabbalah. The first, which focused upon the theory of the ten divine archetypes known as the *Sefirot,* included all of the Kabbalists through Moses Cordovero (mid-sixteenth-century Safed). The second, though basing itself in the sefirotic doctrine and symbols, went beyond the early Kabbalah in its emphasis on such dynamic conceptions as divine catharsis and contraction and the shattering (*Shevirah*), repair, and restoration of the world (*Tikkun*). This second stage, which is identified with Isaac Luria and his followers, also involves a unique elaboration upon the symbols of *Partzufim,* the "faces," aspects, and personalities of God and man. Nevertheless, these two stages in the theosophical Kabbalah also have a great deal in common. As Idel writes:

If we disregard academic rhetoric . . . Lurianism and zoharic Kabbalah are much closer than we expect. . . . The fascination with a complex theology haunted by syzygies, sexual couplings, emanations, and questions

---

12. Idel, *Hasidism: Between Ecstasy and Magic,* p. 31.

of good and evil, is common to the two forms of Jewish theosophy. They are two forms or versions, of one basic structure.[13]

The present work, though it takes as its field the entire kabbalistic tradition, is essentially about the Lurianic theosophy, and its development in the hands of both the later Kabbalists and Hasidim. While I have also drawn extensively upon the Zohar and have consulted texts and commentaries relating to the period prior to the Zohar, as well as the works of Cordovero, the main perspective in this volume is derived from such works in the long Lurianic tradition as Chayyim Vital's *Sefer Etz Chayyim*[14] and Schneur Zalman's *Tanya*.[15]

My goal in this book is to show how ideas derived from the theosophical Kabbalah can provide a coherent and satisfying view of the cosmos and humanity's role within it. Underlying the kabbalistic ideas and symbols is a "basic metaphor" that provides insight into fundamental questions about the existence of the world and the meaning of human life. This metaphor, which is expressed most fully in the Kabbalah of Isaac Luria, integrates a variety of symbols into what superficially appears to be a purely mythological account of the creation and the ultimate destiny of the world, but which will be revealed to embody a fundamental philosophical and psychological perspective on these same matters.

I am under no illusion that my interpretations of the kabbalistic symbols constitute anything like a definitive reading of Jewish mysticism. In the first place, the very idea of a "definitive interpretation" violates the Kabbalist's own principle of the indefinite reinterpretability of texts. Second, as the following pages will reveal, my own interpretations of the kabbalistic symbols are frequently filtered through the writings of Scholem and other contemporary authors whose own scholarship is unavoidably as creative as it is

---

13. Idel, *Hasidism: Between Ecstasy and Magic*, p. 234.

14. Donald Wilder Menzi and Zwe Padeh, trans., *The Tree of Life: Chayyim Vital's Introduction to the Kabbalah of Isaac Luria* (Northvale, NJ: Jason Aronson, 1999). This is an English translation of the first "Gate" of Vital's *Sefer Etz Chayyim*, a work that was composed by Isaac Luria's most important disciple shortly after Luria's death. It is, according to many, the *locus classicus* of the Lurianic Kabbalah.

15. Schneur Zalman, *Likutei Amarim-Tanya*, bilingual edition (Brooklyn, NY: Kehot Publication Society, 1981), written by the first Lubavitcher rebbe in the eighteenth century and which is itself a nearly scriptural foundation for one of today's most prominent Hasidic sects, the Lubavitcher or Chabad Hasidim, whose members continue to this day to live their lives within the Lurianic metaphors.

historical.[16] While on the one hand my reading of the Kabbalah is greatly influenced by the writings of the Chabad Hasidim, on the other hand it is also influenced by Hegelian, Freudian, and Jungian thought. I make no apologies for this and indeed regard the interplay between kabbalistic and contemporary ideas the very strength and purpose of this work.

Still, "interpretation" can never, in my view, be an end unto itself. Understanding is valuable only to the extent that it makes a difference to life. There are those, of course, who question whether the kabbalistic metaphors can actually be "lived" (as opposed to merely "understood") outside the context of a Jewish form of life, outside the context of the language, law, and ritual in which these metaphors have their original home. While my purpose in these pages is to provide an understanding of these metaphors, it would, as will become apparent, go against the very spirit and even the very meaning of these metaphors if they were *only* understood. While it is the plan of this book to uncover a "truth" behind the myths of the Zohar and the Lurianic Kabbalah (and it is certainly my conviction that the Kabbalah has a very significant cognitive content), the value of these myths may well be not quite so much in their cognitive "truth" as in the impact they have upon the lives of those who participate in them. It is my hope that the kabbalistic myths I discuss herein will have something of an impact on those who read this work, both those who live their lives within and outside the framework of traditional Judaism.

16. Harold Bloom has called Scholem's work an emergent Jewish Gnostic theology "masking as historical scholarship." Harold Bloom, "The Pragmatics Of Contemporary Jewish Culture," in *Post-Analytic Philosophy*, ed. J. Rajchman and Cornel West (New York: Columbia University Press, 1985), p. 126.

Interpreting the Theosophical Kabbalah

INTRODUCTION: PHILOSOPHICAL MYTHOLOGY

In this book I propose a general model for understanding the theosophical Kabbalah, one that sees the Kabbalah as a wellspring of ideas and insights into philosophical and psychological questions. In this chapter, which serves as methodological introduction to the rest of this work, I provide a brief introduction to Lurianic theosophy, and defend a philosophical and psychological approach to the Kabbalah against those such as Gershom Scholem who hold that kabbalistic symbols are impenetrable to the rational mind. In addition I survey several vehicles, including deconstructive and dialectic thought, psychoanalysis, Jungian psychology, and comparative religious studies, through which a philosophical and psychological interpretation of the Kabbalah is made possible. Finally, I make some general remarks about myth, truth, and knowledge and offer a general view on the nature of kabbalistic symbolism.

As will become clear in the following pages, it is my view that the metaphors of the Kabbalah that have been brought to light by contemporary scholarship[1] can and should be interpreted in a manner that places them into a dialogue with contemporary philosophy and psychology. Indeed, the

---

1. See works by Scholem, Idel, Wolfson, Elior, Tishby, and Liebes in References.

unique blend of reason and myth, philosophy and mysticism, which is evident, for example, in the Kabbalah of Luria and Vital, is ideally suited to an era that recognizes both the rational and *irrational* as well as the constructive and the *deconstructive* as significant elements of a meaningful worldview. While a number of Kabbalists themselves attempted to understand the Kabbalah in rational/philosophical terms,[2] such an approach has not been favored by contemporary scholars of either Jewish mysticism or philosophy.[3]

One reason for this is the problematical nature of recent philosophy itself. With metaphysics discredited (through various linguistic analyses) and traditional philosophical concepts and vocabulary deconstructed to the point where "system building" was, by the third quarter of the twentieth century, considered absurd, students of philosophy were left with very little in the way of substantive philosophical options. For the most part those who continued to pursue clear-cut criteria for substantive philosophical agreement arrived at a form of scientism, in which philosophy is simply conceived as a vehicle for clearing away conceptual obstacles to the acknowledgment of scientific truths. Others, who held even scientific ideas subject to the sweep of linguistic deconstruction (e.g., Wittgensteinians), continued to conduct analyses that might be regarded "philosophical" but without any hope or even interest in achieving the worldview that for millennia had been regarded as the philosophical quest. They regarded such a philosophical *Weltanschauung* impossible because the questions that such a worldview is meant to answer rest on misleading assumptions about the very language with which they are asked.[4]

A third group, who have given up any hope of philosophical agreement

---

2. Idel points to what he refers to as the "philosophization of Kabbalah, including Lurianic Kabbalah" in the writings of such authors as R. Abraham Kohen Herrera and R. Joseph Rofe' del Medigo who, under the impact of medieval and Renaissance philosophy, interpreted Kabbalistic theosophy in Neoplatonic terms. Moshe Idel, *Hasidism: Between Ecstasy and Magic*, p. 233.

3. As I have indicated, exception to this is the contemporary philosopher Robert Nozick who, although by no means a scholar of the Kabbalah, has utilized a number of Kabbalistic notions in his philosophical writings. See Robert Nozick, *Philosophical Explanations* (Cambridge, MA: Harvard University Press, 1981).

4. More recent developments in contemporary Anglo-American thought have begun to loosen some of the constraints on "philosophizing" that had become the hallmark of academic philosophy. See, for example, Rajchman and West, *Post-Analytic Philosophy*.

through logical argument, but who still retain the urge to philosophize, have attempted to find the satisfaction of their philosophical urges (their drive for a *Weltanschauung*) in myth, poetry, and metaphor: in manners of thought and expression that have traditionally been held to be quite distinct from philosophy itself. The rationale for this approach is derived not so much from a critique of philosophical concepts or language, but rather from a growing sense that the products of philosophical speculation do not (and cannot) satisfy the urges that prompt philosophers in the first place. It is indeed characteristic of our own age that many have turned to myth, to the spontaneous productions of the human psyche—its symbols and archetypes, as expressed in poetry, art, literature, music, and cinema—as the food to satisfy their philosophical cravings.[5]

The Kabbalah itself was a reaction of the emotional and symbolical against the conceptual, and it has always flourished in times when the rational has become obsessional and rigid. Yet while the Kabbalists certainly opposed themselves to the purely rational tradition in Judaism (some even going so far as to declare that the Kabbalah begins where philosophy ends),[6] they also respected the rational enough to place it at the apex of their theosophical system, above even the spiritual, ethical, and aesthetic aspects of the Godhead. For the most part, their approach was to include within their purview both mythical and rational aspects of their symbols. The Kabbalah, as we shall see in the following pages, points to a fourth option for satisfying our contemporary philosophical desires: the application of philosophically critical reason and argumentation to the symbolic, mythical and mystical consciousness.[7] Such a "philosophical mythology" and "rational mysticism"[8] holds out the promise of retaining the logical sophistication of contemporary

---

5. This is the view of many who follow C. G. Jung, but it has become increasingly prevalent among what might be termed "postanalytic" philosophers as well.

6. The Kabbalist Rabbi Moses of Burgos (late thirteenth century) declared: "You ought to know that these philosophers whose wisdom you are praising end where we begin." Quoted in Gershom Scholem, *Major Trends In Jewish Mysticism* (New York: Schocken, 1941), p. 24.

7. This is the method used by psychoanalysis on the level of psychology, and it will be our task to apply such a method to the problems of philosophy as well.

8. "Rational mysticism" is a term utilized by J. N. Findlay and others to describe the work of philosophers such as Hegel who attempt to analyze and even derive the conclusions of mysticism through philosophical, intellectual means. "Philosophical mythology" as I am using this term seeks to (1) understand the philosophical

thought without abandoning the very urge to create a worldview, which has largely been surrendered by contemporary philosophers. The application of philosophy to mysticism, myth, and metaphor is based on the assumption that the "truth" that philosophy seeks is only accessible through an act of symbolization, which springs forth simultaneously from affective, connative, and cognitive aspects of man's psyche.

"Philosophical mythology" was indeed the preferred method of several theosophical Kabbalists (like Moses Cordovero and Moses Chayim Luzzatto) who held that the emotional and spiritual must always be integrated with the rational, but who lacked the conceptual apparatus to fully comprehend their own myths and symbols. Their symbols cried out for a dialectical, even deconstructed, view of reason, yet all the Kabbalists had was an Aristotelian model of thought. Their symbols required a dynamic psychology, yet such a psychology was still centuries beyond their own horizon. It will be our task in the pages ahead to set the kabbalistic symbols, particularly those of the Lurianic Kabbalah, against the background of ideas that can do them fuller justice.

HISTORICAL BACKGROUND

The history of the Kabbalah, although not without considerable controversy, is now reasonably well documented.[9] A general outline of the historical development of the theosophical Kabbalah, along with a review of the major kabbalistic sources that inform the present work appears in Table 1–1. English translations and commentaries are cited where available. (Full references to works cited in the table are found in References.)

Contemporary scholarship understands the Kabbalah to have developed out of a mixture of early Jewish (*Merkaveh*) mysticism, Neoplatonism, and Gnosticism. The Kabbalists themselves traced their theories to biblical descriptions of God's revelation, going back to the revelations to Moses at

---

implications of myth and (2) show how myth and metaphor can satisfy our philosophical urges and cravings.

9. See, for example, Gershom Scholem, *Origins of the Kabbalah*, trans. R. J. Zwi Werblowski (Princeton, NJ: Princeton University Press, 1987), originally published in 1962; Scholem, *Major Trends*; Scholem, *Kabbalah*, pp. 8–86; Idel, *Kabbalah: New Perspectives*; Mark Verman, *The Books of Contemplation: Medieval Jewish Mystical Sources* (Albany: State University of New York Press, 1992).

Table 1-1:

Historical Survey of the Theosophical Kabbalah

Historical Phase	Original Source	Available English Translation	Major Secondary References
Merkavah Hekhalot Mysticism	Book of Enoch, *Hekhalot Rabbati* (The Greater Palaces), *Hekhalot Zutari* (The Lesser Palaces) and *Merkaveh Rabbah* (The Great Chariot) 1st to 2nd century C.E.	N. Janowitz, *The Poetics of Ascent.* Trans. of *Merkaveh Rabbah* (The Great Chariot)	Schaefer, *The Hidden and Manifest God* Scholem, *Jewish Gnosticism, Merkabah Mysticism and Talmudic Tradition.* Scholem, *Major Trends,* pp. 40–79.
	Shi'r Koma (Measure of the Body) prior to the 6th century C.E.	D. Meltzer, *The Secret Garden,* pp. 23–40.	Scholem, *Origins of the Kabbalah,* pp. 20–24.
Pre- or proto-kabbalistic	*Sefer Yetzirah* 3rd to 6th century C.E.	D. Meltzer, *The Secret Garden,* pp. 41–45. A. Kaplan, *Sefer Yetzirah, The Book of Creation.*	Scholem, *Origins of the Kabbalah,* pp. 24–35.
The Early Kabbalah	*Sefer ha-Bahir* c. 1175–1200 C.E.	D. Meltzer, *The Secret Garden,* pp. 49–96. J. Dan & R.C. Kiener, *The Early Kabbalah,* pp. 57–70.	Scholem, *Origins,* Ch. 2, pp. 49–148.

Table 1–1: (*continued*)

Historical Survey of the Theosophical Kabbalah

Historical Phase	Original Source	Available English Translation	Major Secondary References
	School of Isaac The Blind c. 1175–1200	"The Mystical Torah—Kabbalistic Creation" and "The Process of Emanation," in *The Early Kabbalah*, pp. 71–86.	Scholem, *Origins*, Ch. 4, pp. 248–330.
	The School of Gerona Early 13th century: Azriel of Gerona Ezra ben Solomon Jacob ben Sheshet Moses ben Nachman (Nachmanides)	Azriel, "Explanation of the Ten Sefirot," and "Commentary to Talmudic Legends," in *The Early Kabbalah*, pp. 89–109. Ben Sheshet, "The Book of Faith and Reliance" and "Response of Correct Answers," in *The Early Kabbalah*, pp. 111–151.	Scholem, *Origins*, Ch. 4, pp. 365–475.
	c. 1230 The 'Iyyun' Circle: Sefer ha-Iyyun (The Book of Contemplation). Ma'yan ha-Chochmah (The Fountain of Wisdom).	M. Verman, *The Books of Contemplation*.	M. Verman, *The Books of Contemplation*. Scholem, *Origins*, Ch. 4, pp. 309–347.

Zohar	c. 1286, The Zohar is distributed by Moses deLeon, d. 1305. Traditionally attributed to Shimon bar Yochai (2nd century C.E.). More recently attributed to deLeon and his circle in 13th-century Spain.	Simon and Sperling, *The Zohar* (5 volumes, comprehensive but incomplete). Tishby & Lachower, *The Wisdom of the Zohar* (3 volumes, translations arranged by topic with extensive commentaries).	Commentaries in Tishby, *The Wisdom of the Zohar*. Scholem, *Major Trends In Jewish Mysticism*, Lectures 5 & 6, pp. 156–244. Yehuda Liebes, *Studies In The Zohar*.
	c. 1290, Joseph Gikatilla (1284–1325), *Sha'are Orah*	Gikatilla, *Gates of Light*, trans. Avi Weinstein.	Moshe Idel, Historical introduction to *Gates of Light*, pp. xxiii–xxxiv.
Christian Kabbalah	1517 Johannes Reuchlin (1455–1522) publishes *De Arte Cabalistica*, an early work of the Christian Kabbalah.	Reuchlin, *On the Art of the Kabbalah*, trans. by M. and S. Goodman.	Moshe Idel, Introduction to *On the Art of the Kabbalah*, pp. v–xxix.
Safedian Kabbalists	c. 1550, Moses Cordovero (1522–1570), *Pardes Rimmonim* (The Orchard of Pomegranates), Safed.		J. Ben-Shlomo, "Moses Cordovero" in Scholem, *Kabbalah*, pp. 401–404.
Lurianic Kabbalah	c. 1569 Isaac Luria (1534–1572) arrives and begins teaching in Safed.		Scholem, Major Trends, Lecture 7, pp. 244–286. I. Schochet, "Mystical concepts in Chasidism."

Table 1–1: (*continued*)

Historical Survey of the Theosophical Kabbalah

Historical Phase	Original Source	Available English Translation	Major Secondary References
	c. 1620, Chayyim Vital's (1542–1640) works, including those that will later be edited as *Sefer Etz Chayyim*, begin to circulate in manuscript form.	Menzi and Padeh (trans.), *The Tree of Life.* English translation of the first of seven chapters or "Palaces" of *Sefer Etz Chayyim.*	Menzi and Padeh, Introduction to Vital, *The Tree of Life.* Scholem, "The Basic Ideas of the Kabbalah," in *Kabbalah,* pp. 87–189 (covers pre-Lurianic and Lurianic theosophy). L. Fine, "The Contemplative Practice of Yihudim in Lurianic Kabbalah," in A. Green, ed., *Jewish Spirituality II,* pp. 64–98. L. Jacobs, "The Uplifting of Sparks in Later Jewish Mysticism," ibid., pp. 99–126.
	1666, Sabbatai Sevi (1626–1676), a Lurianic Kabbalist from Smyrna, and his "prophet" Nathan of Gaza, declare Sabbatai to be the Messiah.		Scholem, Sabbatai Sevi, *The Mystical Messiah.*

	Event	Primary Source	Secondary Sources
	1730s, Moses Chayyim Luzzatto (1707–1746) writes *Kelab Pithei Chochmah*, a succinct outline of Lurianic Kabbalah.	Luzzatto, *General Principles of the Kabbalah*, trans. P. Berg.	
Chasidism	1760 (d. 1772), Dov Baer of Mezhirech assumes leadership of early Chasidic movement after the death of the Baal Shem Tov. Author of *Maggid Devarev le-Ya'aqov*.		On Hasidism, see Rivka Schatz-Uffenheimer, *Hasidism as Mysticism*, and M. Idel, *Hasidism, Between Ecstasy and Magic*.
	1797, Schneur Zalman of Lyady (1745–1813), the first Lubavitcher rebbe (Chabad) publishes *Likutei Amarim-Tanya*.	Zalman, *Likutei Amarim-Tanya* (Hebrew-English Edition).	Elior, *The Paradoxical Ascent to God*. Mindel, *The Philosophy of Chabad*.
	1821 Aharon Halevi Horowitz of Staroselye (1766–1828), Chabad theorist, publishes *Sha'arei ha-Avodah* (Gates of Worship).		Elior, *The Paradoxical Ascent to God*.

Sinai. Reference is made in Exodus 24:10 to "a paved work of a sapphire (*Sapir*) stone" under the feet of God that appeared as "the body of heaven in his clearness," a passage that figured into the Kabbalists' etymology of the word *Sefirah*, which was understood as referring to the heavens' "sapphirine splendor" (Psalms 19: 2).

In the Book of I Kings (22:19) and Isaiah (6:1–3) we find descriptions of the Lord sitting upon a heavenly throne, surrounded by his hosts. Further detailed descriptions of the heavenly throne, angelic hosts, and even the Lord Himself are found in Ezekiel (I: 4–28) and Daniel 7: 9–10. These prophetic descriptions became the bases for the "throne mysticism" of the early centuries of the common era, and also provided prooftexts for later kabbalistic speculations regarding the heavenly *Adam Kadmon* (Primordial Man), the faces of God (*Partzufim*), etc.

Verman has distinguished among four periods of early Jewish mysticism.[10] The first, which extended from the eighth to the sixth centuries B.C.E. was the era of visionary experience of the prophets Isaiah, Ezekiel, and Zechariah. The second period, which reached its height in the third and second centuries B.C.E., witnessed a growth in angelology, speculation on the origins of the universe and the creation of man, and talk about the "end of days" and the afterlife. These apocalyptic themes are present, for example, in the Book of Daniel and first book of Enoch.

The third period of Jewish mysticism, which originates in the middle of the first century C.E., is an apocalyptic literature that puts forth theories regarding angelic and demonic beings and the nature of the celestial realm, and which provides detailed descriptions of the heavenly "Throne" and "Chariot" (*Merkava*) that had first been described by the prophet Ezekiel. This third period of early Jewish mysticism is also embodied in the writings of the Christian Jews, Paul, and the revelation of St. John. According to Verman, the mystical ideas attributed to such mishnaic teachers as Johanan ben Zakkai, Eliezer ben Hyrkanos, Akiva ben Joseph, and Ishmael the High Priest, belong to the same period and environment of mystical speculation as those of the early Christians. While mystical themes were certainly entertained by the rabbis of this period, the compiler of the Mishnah, Rabbi Judah, made every effort to exclude them, and they are therefore far more apparent in the *Tosefta*, a second mishnaic collection from this same period. The rabbis of the mishnaic and talmudic periods were reluctant to discuss mystical

---

10. Verman, *The Books of Contemplation*, p. 8.

themes in public or commit them to writing. They held that there was a serious danger associated with mystical activity. In Tractate *Chagigah* 14b we find this famous warning:

> Our rabbis taught: For men entered the garden, namely Ben Azzai and Ben Zoma, Acher and R. Akiba. R. Akiba said to them: When you arrive at the stones of pure marble, say not: Water, water.[11] For it is said: He that speaketh falsehood shall not be established before mine eyes (Psalms 101: 7). Ben Azzai cast a look and died. Of him Scripture says: Precious in the eyes of the Lord is the death of His saints (Psalms 116:15). Ben Zoma looked and became demented. Of him Scripture says: Has thou found honey? Eat as much as is sufficient for thee, lest thou be filled therewith and vomit it (Proverbs 25:16). Acher mutilated the shoots [i.e., brought about heresy]. [Only] R. Akiba went up unhurt, and went down unhurt.

The Talmud is virtually silent on the nature of the mystic's visions of ascent. However, other texts from the second to eighth centuries C.E. provide detailed accounts of these matters. These texts illustrate the fourth period of early Jewish mysticism, what is generally known as the *Merkava* or *Hekhalot* (Palaces) mysticism. Among the most important works of this period are the third *Book of Enoch*, *Hekhalot Rabbati* (The Greater Palaces), *Hekhalot Zutari* (The Lesser Palaces), and *Merkaveh Rabbah* (The Great Chariot).[12] These texts are said to show the influence of Greek, Persian, and Gnostic thought. Like the biblical prophets they treat of the splendor, beauty, and transcendence of God, reposed on a celestial throne, attended by His heavenly hosts who sing His praise. These texts speak of the *yored Merkaveh*, the spiritual adept who ascends (literally and paradoxically "descends") on the chariot, through the celestial gates, past the gatekeeping angels who attempt to deter him with fantastic and terrifying illusions, to a vision of the throne and the countenance of God Himself. In the *Book of Enoch* we find a detailed angelic

---

11. This is a veiled reference to the trials that the mystical adept experiences in his approach to the heavenly throne. One is provided with an illusion that he is being bombarded by millions of waves of water when he is only witnessing the glittering marble of the heavenly palace. If the adept asks about the meaning of the "water" he is not deemed worthy of the ascent and he is struck and wounded with iron bars. See Scholem, *Major Trends*, pp. 52–53.

12. See Peter Schaefer, *The Hidden and Manifest God: Some Major Themes in Early Jewish Mysticism*, trans. Aubrey Pomerantz (Albany: State University of New York Press, 1992).

hierarchy, which includes seven angelic princes who are said to be in charge of the seven heavens, and the angel Metatron, who is viewed as the attendant to the throne and the intermediary between God and the world. Metatron receives a "crown" on which God, with a finger like a flaming stylus, engraves the letters of creation, an image that will reappear over a thousand years later in the Zohar. In *Hekhalot Zutari* we find, in anticipation of later kabbalistic themes, an emphasis on the theurgic and magical power of divine names. In these works we also find a description of divine robes or garments, the vision of which, according to *Hekhalot Rabbati*, is the goal of the mystical adept. Finally this literature develops the rabbinic theme that God is mystically dependent upon man's liturgical praise, an idea that anticipates the Zohar's dictum that man can be said to "create" God.

The notion of a Primordial Man, which has appeared in religious thought throughout the world over at least two millennia, makes its first explicit appearance in Jewish thought in the early literature of *Merkaveh* mysticism of the second and third centuries C.E.[13] A work entitled *Shi'ur Koma* (The Measure of [the Divine] Body) describes the ascent to the celestial throne and the vision of a gigantic supernal man imprinted with magical letters and names. This Primordial Man, who had been hinted at in the prophecies of Ezekiel and Daniel, becomes a pivotal symbol in the later, theosophical Kabbalah.

Scholem theorized that the *Merkaveh/Hekhalot* literature is a Jewish form of gnosticism, parallel to the second-century Christian and other Gnostics. According to Scholem, the early Jewish mystics' preoccupation with the ascent of the soul and its return to its divine home is a quintessentially gnostic theme.[14] The early Kabbalists established themselves on a foundation in this older "Jewish gnosticism" and borrowed many of its images and vocabulary, combining them with cosmological and theosophical views derived from Greek,[15] particularly Neoplatonic, thought.

The doctrines of the *Sefirot* and the *Otiyot Yesod* (the Foundational

---

13. On *Merkaveh* mysticism see Gershom Scholem, *Jewish Gnosticism, Merkabah Mysticism and Talmudic Tradition* (New York: Schocken, 1965).

14. Scholem, *Major Trends*, p. 49.

15. Philo of Alexandria (c. 15–10 B.C.E.–50 C.E.) was a Greek-speaking Jewish philosopher who made efforts to synthesize the revealed religion of the Bible with Greek, particularly Platonic, thought. Philo proclaimed the unknowability of the divine essence and spoke of the mystic identification of man with the divine. Though Philo was unlikely to have been read in Jewish mystical circles, he was an important

letters), which became central features of the Kabbalah, make their first appearance in what is sometimes referred to as a "proto-kabbalistic" work, *Sefer Yetzirah* (The Book of Formation). This work, the earliest surviving text of Hebrew speculative metaphysics, is thought by most contemporary scholars to have been written in Palestine in the third to sixth centuries C.E.[16]

The Kabbalah proper, while owing much to the speculations contained in *Sefer Yetzirah*, is rooted in earlier Jewish mysticism, and, according to many, a Jewish form of gnosticism.[17] It achieves its own unique expression in the anonymous *Sefer Ha-Bahir*, which appeared in Provence late in the twelfth century and which is generally regarded as the earliest extant kabbalistic text.[18] It is in this work that the theory of the ten *Sefirot*, the value archetypes (Will, Wisdom, Understanding, Kindness, Judgment, Beauty, Glory, Splendor, Foundation, and Kingship), which the Kabbalists held to be the essence of creation, begins to take distinctive form. From Provence, the Kabbalah spread rapidly to Gerona and then Spain. The works of these early Kabbalists are rich in theological speculation and imagery.

The *locus classicus*, however, for the majority of kabbalistic symbols is the Zohar, traditionally attributed to the rabbinic sage Shimon Bar Yohai, but thought by contemporary scholars to have originated in Spain some time in the thirteenth century.[19] The Zohar is written as a wide-ranging commentary on the Torah, and contains diverse speculations on such topics as the hidden nature of God; the processes of creation; the nature of good and evil; the masculine and feminine aspects of the divine; the nature of death, sleep, and dreams; and the essence of the human soul.[20] Many of the ideas of the

---

influence on Christian theology, and therefore a possible vehicle through which Platonic thought was indirectly transmitted to the Kabbalists.

16. Gershom Scholem, "Yezirah, Sefer," *Encyclopedia Judaica*, Vol. 16, pp. 782ff.

17. For Gershom Scholem's views on Jewish gnosticism see Scholem, *Jewish Gnosticism* and Scholem, *Major Trends*, pp. 40–80.

18. On *Sefer ha-Bahir* and the early Kabbalah in general see Scholem, *Origins of the Kabbalah*.

19. The main body of the Zohar translated into English appears in Harry Sperling, Maurice Simon, and Paul Levertoff, trans., *The Zohar* (London: Soncino Press, 1931–1934). A more accessible treatment, in which translated sections of the Zohar have been grouped topically and explained through extensive introductions and annotations by Isaiah Tishby is to be found in Tishby and Lachower, *The Wisdom of the Zohar*.

20. The main body of the Zohar is indeed a Torah commentary. Many other

Lurianic Kabbalah, which will provide the main structure and focus of the present work, are dynamic developments of concepts and symbols that first appear in the Zohar.

THE LURIANIC KABBALAH

The Lurianic Kabbalah, the most complex and sophisticated kabbalistic theosophy, is thus a relatively late development in the history of the Kabbalah. Isaac Luria developed a small but dedicated fellowship in sixteenth-century Safed (near the Galilee in present-day northern Israel), where he recounted to his disciples his interpretations of the Zohar, as well as his visions and speculations regarding the origins of creation and the nature of the upper worlds. Luria himself left precious few writings, but his ideas have come down to us through the writings of his disciples (notably Chayyim Vital), which have received renewed interest in our century through the work of Gershom Scholem and others, who have catalogued, compiled, described, and (now) translated[21] significant portions of the Lurianic material.

One can find many ancient Gnostic themes reappearing suddenly in the Lurianists, and the study of both Christian and Jewish gnostic sources is invaluable as a background to the ideas of the theosophical Kabbalah. Lurianic ideas are also prominent in the seventeenth-century messianic movement surrounding Sabbatei Zevi in Poland.[22] They are clearly articulated in the kabbalistic works of Moses Chayyim Luzzatto (1707–1747)[23] and are also to be found among the Hasidim, whose philosophical and

---

additional sections, however, that do not follow this outline are appended to or interspersed within the main commentary, some of which, such as *Tikkunei ha-Zohar* and *Raya Mehemna*, appear to anticipate certain Lurianic themes that are not present in the Zohar proper. On the various sections of the Zohar, see Tishby and Lachower, *The Wisdom of the Zohar*, Vol. 1, pp. 1–12.

21. See Menzi and Padeh, *The Tree of Life*. This is first translation into English of a portion of Vital's *Sefer Etz Chayyim*, and the first English translation of a major portion of a work stemming from one of Luria's direct disciples.

22. Gershom Scholem, *Sabbatai Sevi: The Mystical Messiah*, trans. R. J. Zwi Werblowski (Princeton, NJ: Princeton University Press, 1973), Chapter 1.

23. In English see Moses Luzzatto, *General Principles of the Kabbalah*, trans. Phillip Berg (Jerusalem: Research Centre of Kabbalah, 1970).

psychological interpretations of the Kabbalah are invaluable for our own contemporary understanding of this tradition.

Let us examine, if only in outline, the basic metaphors and symbols of the Lurianic Kabbalah. The gloss on the Lurianic symbols provided here will, of course, be preliminary in nature, but should serve to both orient the reader to the Lurianic theosophical system and provide sufficient background for comprehending the methodological issues introduced in this chapter.

Luria adopted the earlier kabbalistic term *Ein-Sof* to designate the primal, all-encompassing "Infinite God." This God, according to the Kabbalists, was both the totality of being and the abyss of complete "nothingness" (*Ayin*).[24] As such, it is the union of everything in the world and its opposite.[25] Luria, in contrast to previous Kabbalists who had put forth a Neoplatonic, "emanationist" view of creation, held that *Ein-Sof* created the universe through a negative act of divine concealment, contraction, and withdrawal. This act, known in the Lurianic Kabbalah as the *Tzimtzum*, was necessary in order to make room in the divine plenum for the world. In the act of *Tzimtzum*, the Infinite God withdraws himself from himself, leaving a void. This void, known as the *tehiru* or *chalal*, is a metaphysically empty circle or sphere that *Ein-Sof* surrounds equally on all sides. Once established, this void becomes the metaphysical "space" in which an infinite number of worlds will take form through a positive, emanative phase in the creative process. A thin line (the *kav*) of divine light (the *Or Ein-Sof*) penetrates the void but does not completely transverse it. From this line, as well as from a residue (*Reshimu*) of the divine light that had remained in the metaphysical void after the divine contraction, the first created being, Primordial Man (*Adam Kadmon*), is formed.

According to Luria's disciple, Chayyim Vital, it is *Adam Kadmon* who is responsible for emanating the *Sefirot*. Lights flashing from the ears, nose, mouth, and eyes of the Primordial Man create these ten value-dimensions or archetypes of creation. These lights are also conceptualized as the twenty-two elemental letters (*Otiyot Yesod*) that comprise the *Sefirot*. Each light beams

---

24. This dialectical idea is present even among the earliest Kabbalists, for example, Azriel of Gerona (early thirteenth century). See Scholem, *Origins of the Kabbalah*, p. 423. Indeed, for the Kabbalists *Ein-Sof* is so vast as to include both existence and nonexistence (on this conception see Nozick, *Philosophical Explanations*).

25. Again, this view is present in Azriel; see Joseph Dan, ed., *The Early Kabbalah*, texts trans. by Ronald C. Kieber (New York: Paulist Press, 1966), p. 94.

down into the void and then returns, leaving a residue of divine light from which the "vessel" for each *Sefirah* is formed. A second light is projected from the eyes of *Adam Kadmon* and then returns, leaving behind a second residue that fills the vessels; thereby completing the formation of each of the ten *Sefirot*. The ten *Sefirot*, in order of their emanation (and with their alternate appellations) are as follows: *Keter* (Crown) or *Ratzon* (Will), *Chochmah* (Wisdom), *Binah* (Understanding), *Chesed* (Loving-kindness), *Gevurah* (Strength) or *Din* (Judgment), *Tiferet* (Beauty) or *Rachamim* (Compassion), *Netzach* (Glory), *Hod* (Splendor), *Yesod* (Foundation), and *Malchut* (Kingship). The *Sefirot* are the ten archetypal elements of the world. Alternatively, the world is understood as being composed of the *Otiyot Yesod*, the twenty-two foundational letters that are the particles of language and thus the elements of all ideas.[26]

The *Sefirot* are themselves organized into the "body" of Primordial Man with *Keter*, *Chochmah*, and *Binah* forming the "crown" and "brains," *Chesed* and *Gevurah* the arms, *Tiferet* the torso, *Netzach* and *Hod* the legs, and *Malchut* the mouth, or in some accounts, the feminine counterpart to *Adam Kadmon*. The *Sefirot* are also organized into a series of five "Worlds" (the Worlds of Primordial Man, "Nearness," "Creation," "Formation," and "Making," the lowest of which, *Assiyah* or Making, provides the substance of our earth. The cosmos, as it was originally emanated via ten discrete *Sefirot*, is known as the "World of Points."

Luria is completely original in his description of the fate of the *Sefirot* and worlds after their emanation from *Adam Kadmon*. The *Sefirot* "closest" to *Adam Kadmon*, the so-called "psychical" *Sefirot*, are comprised of the most powerful vessels and they alone can withstand the impact of the second series of lights emanating from the eyes of the Primordial Man. However, all of the "vessels" from *Chesed* to *Yesod* shattered, causing displacement, exile, and discord to hold sway throughout the cosmos. This is known in the Lurianic Kabbalah as the "Breaking of the Vessels" (*Shevirat ha-Kelim*). As a result of this shattering, shards from the broken vessels tumble down through the void, entrapping sparks of divine light in "Husks" (the *Kellipot*) that form the lower worlds, and the *Sitra Achra*, "Other Side," a realm of evil, darkness and death. Chaos reaches the upper worlds as well, where the masculine and feminine aspects of the deity, the celestial "Mother" and "Father," repre-

---

26. In some accounts, e. g. *Sefer Yetzirah*, there are thirty-two foundational elements, the ten *Sefirot* and the twenty-two letters.

sented by the *Sefirot Chochmah* and *Binah*, are prompted to turn their backs on one another, thereby disrupting the flow of divine erotic energy in all the Worlds.

The broken vessels must be reassembled and restored. This *Tikkun* or "Restoration" is possible because not all of the divine light that fell from the broken vessels is entrapped in the *Kellipot*. Some of this light returns spontaneously to its source, commencing a repair and reconstruction of the cosmos. This process, spoken of as *Tikkun ha-Olam*, the Restoration of the World, involves the reorganization of the broken vessels into a series of *Partzufim*, "Visages" or personality structures of God, each of which is dominated by one or more of the original *Sefirot*. The *Partzufim*, by organizing within themselves all of the *Sefirot*, are hence stronger than any of the original *Sefirot* were in and of themselves. According to Scholem, the *Partzufim* actually represent the evolution of the Primordial Man (*Adam Kadmon*) as it evolves towards a restored and redeemed world.[27] The Lurianists indeed held that the various stages of *Tikkun* are brought about by means of lights streaming from the forehead of *Adam Kadmon*.

The *Partzufim* are understood to be partial personalities of the deity. The five major ones are (1) *Attika Kaddisha* (The Holy Ancient One) or *Arikh Anpin* (The Long-Suffering One), (2) *Abba* (The Father), (3) *Imma* (The Mother), (4) *Zeir Anpin* (the Impatient One) or *Ben* (The Son), and (5) *Nukvah* (The Female) or *Bot* (The Daughter).

The *Partzufim* engage in certain regular relationships or unifications. *Abba* and *Imma* are unified in an enduring relationship of mutual friendship and support; *Zeir Anpin* and *Nukva* are unified in a passionate romance that brings them alternately together and apart. The lower *Partzufim* (and *Sefirot*) are "born" in the womb of *Imma*, the Mother.

According to Luria the erotic relations (and ruptures) of the various *Partzufim* determine the fate of God, man, and the world. It is mankind's spiritual task to help raise the sparks of divine light that are entrapped by the evil Husks of the "Other Side," thereby liberating divine energy for the service of erotic unions among the various *Partzufim*, not only between the "Mother" and "Father" but between the Son and the Daughter and even between the "Old Holy Man" (*Attik Kaddisha*) and his mate. In raising these sparks, mankind is said to provide the "feminine waters" for the renewed divine activity. The result of these erotic recouplings, and the overall result of

---

27. Scholem, *Kabbalah*, p. 142.

the "World of *Tikkun*," is that the perfection of the restored cosmos is far greater than the original "World of Points," which was comprised of the *Sefirot* as they were emanated prior to the Breaking of the Vessels. By assisting in the process of *Tikkun ha-Olam*, humanity becomes a partner in the creation of the world. Humanity, however, cannot by its own efforts, reclaim all of the sparks that have fallen into the realm of the "Other Side." Only those that remain in the uppermost levels of this realm, in what the Kabbalists referred to as *Kellipah Nogah* (the Husk of Brightness), can normally be reclaimed by man's own individual efforts. Only through a "great love" (*ahavah rabbah*) and divine grace can the lowest levels of the "Other Side" be reclaimed and redeemed.

Table 1–2 provides a schematic outline of the Lurianic theosophical system. We will in later chapters come to see that the entire scheme is understood by the Lurianists to be an atemporal, unitary "picture" or definition of *Ein-Sof*, the infinite God.

Table 1–2:
The Lurianic System

Ein-Sof (The infinite Godhead), of which nothing can be said . . .
is the Union of being and nothingness, of "everything and its opposite."
Ein-Sof performs a *Tzimtzum*
(Divine Concealment, Contraction, Withdrawal) which
leads to a . . .
Metaphysical Void (*Tehiru*), a circle surrounded by *Ein-Sof* on all sides . . .
containing a residue (*Reshimu*) of divine light,
and into which is emanated . . .
the light of the infinite (*Or Ein-Sof*), a thin line (*kav*) through which . . .
Adam Kadmon (Primordial Man) spontaneously emerges.
Lights, also conceived as holy "letters," flashing and recoiling from
Adam Kadmon's eyes, nose, mouth, and ears form . . .
Vessels (*Kelim*) for containing further lights, thus forming the
"World of Points" comprised of . . .
the *Sefirot* (Archetypes of Value and Being; constituents of the body of
Adam Kadmon):
Keter (Crown, Will, Delight, the highest *Sefirah*)
Chochmah (Intellect, Wisdom, Paternal)   *Binah* (Understanding, Maternal)
Chesed (Loving-Kindness)   *Tiferet/Rachamim* (Beauty, Compassion)
Din/Gevurah (Judgment, Strength)
Netzach (Glory)   *Hod* (Splendor)

Yesod (Foundation)

Malchut/Shekhinah (Kingship/Feminine principle). . . .

The vessels are also composed of the **Otiyot Yesod**, the twenty-two letters of divine speech, and are organized into . . .

Worlds (*Olamot*):

Adam Kadmon (A'K, identified with *Ein-Sof* and *Keter*)

Atziluth (Nearness)

Beriah (Creation)

Yetzirah (Formation)

Assiyah (Making, the lowest world, includes our material earth).

The weakness and disunity of the *Sefirot* leads to their shattering and displacement, known as . . .

The Breaking of the Vessels (*Shevirat Hakelim*), which produces . . .

a rupture in the conjugal flow between Masculine and Feminine aspects of God, and . . .

Netzotzim (Sparks), which fall and become entrapped in . . .

Kellipot (Husks), which comprise the . . .

Sitra Achra (the "Other Side," a realm of darkness and evil).

Lights from the forehead of *Adam Kadmon*, also conceptualized as **mystical names**, reconstitute the broken *Sefirot*/vessels as:

Partzufim (Faces or Personalities of God):

Attika Kaddisha (The Holy Ancient One)/ *Keter*

Abba (The Father)/ *Chochmah*

Imma (The Mother)/ *Binah*

Zeir Anpin (The Impatient One) *Chesed-Yesod*

Nukvah (The Female) *Malchut/Shekhinah*. . . . This begins. . . .

Tikkun ha-Olam (The Restoration of the World), which is completed by man, who via the "raising of the sparks" brings about the Reunification of the *Partzufim*, the masculine and feminine principles of God

THE PROBLEM OF INTERPRETATION

The interpretation of the Lurianic symbols has always been regarded as problematic. From the time of their dissemination in manuscript form the true nature and significance of the Lurianic Kabbalah has been the subject of heated debate; some Kabbalists held the Lurianic symbols to be uninterpretable while others sought to place them within a philosophical framework. Luria's students, most notably Chayyim Vital (1542–1620), Moses Jonah, and Joseph Ibn Tabul,[28] committed versions of the Lurianic system to writing shortly after Luria's death in 1572. In addition, Israel Sarug, who had no personal acquaintance with Luria, published a version of Luria's system that diverged in many ways from his teachings according to Vital. The difficulties connected with these alternative versions, however, are small, when compared to the problems inherent in the texts themselves.

Idel points out that the meaning of the Lurianic Kabbalah was somewhat opaque even to the Kabbalists.[29] For example, according to Jacob Emden (1697–1776),[30] by committing the Lurianic Kabbalah to writing its true meaning was lost, and for this reason

> . . . all the teachings of R. Isaac Luria, may his memory be blessed, in Etz Hayyim and his other books on these matters, are true from one point of view, and not true from another. They are true as understood by R. Isaac Luria and others like him, but not true at all, in the way we understand them, since all that is stated in books and [other] works is the plain sense of the Kabbalah, which is not true, but the esoteric sense of the Kabbalah alone is true, and it cannot be written in any book.[31]

Others such as Emden's archrival, R. Yonathan Eibeschuetz (1690/95–1764), held that the publication of the Lurianic Kabbalah is actually dangerous, because of its anthropomorphic descriptions of God.

The difficulties and anthropomorphisms inherent in the Lurianic texts prompted some to attempt a philosophical interpretation. For example, the late-eighteenth-century Jewish philosopher Shelomo Maimon held:

> originally, the Kabbalah was nothing but psychology, physics, morals, politics, and such sciences represented by means of symbols and hiero-

---

28. Ibid., p. 424.

29. Idel writes: "For some of the more orthodox Kabbalists, the ultimate meaning of the Lurianic Kabbalah was to some extent elusive; there was a feeling that its real message had escaped them." Idel, *Hasidism*, p. 41.

30. Jacob Emden was a noted rabbi, authority on Jewish law, and Kabbalist who engaged in a variety of disputations, the most famous of which involved the accusation that the great Rabbi Jonathan Eybeschuetz was a secret "Shabbatean," i.e. devotee of the false messiah Shabbatai Sevi. Emden was also among the first to question the antiquity of the Zohar.

31. Quoted in Idel, *Hasidism*, p. 35. Idel indicates that the passage is quoted in Emden's name in R. Pinhas Hurwitz, *Sefer ha-Berit*, p. 292.

glyphics in fables and allegories, the occult meaning of which was disclosed only to those competent to understand it. By and by, however, perhaps as the result of many revolutions, this occult meaning was lost, and the signs were taken for the things signified.

For Maimon, philosophy is the key to deciphering the secrets of the Kabbalah, which are otherwise meaningless: "In fact the Kabbalah is nothing but an expanded Spinozoism, in which not only is the origin of the world explained by the limitation of the divine being, but also the origin of every kind of being and its relation to the rest, are derived from a separate attribute of God."[32]

A similar point of view was held by Maimon's contemporary, Moses Mendelssohn, who held that the Kabbalah had a "consequent meaning" that was obscured by its being cast in the form of oriental metaphors. According to Mendelssohn the lack of philosophical terminology in ancient Hebrew necessitated the use of metaphor and analogy, which obscured the Kabbalah's true meaning.[33]

While Maimon and Mendelssohn took philosophy to be the original meaning of the Kabbalah, others, according to modern scholarship, sought to provide the Kabbalah with a philosophical content. Rachel Elior has argued, for example, that in their unqualified rejection of any literal interpretation of the Lurianic symbols the Chabad Hasdim retain "the Lurianic terminological system, although emptying it of its original meaning and replacing it with a philosophical position."[34] Elior's position is far too radical and fails to recognize the significant continuity between Hasidic philosophy and the Lurianic Kabbalah.[35] In later chapters we will see that the Chabad Hasidim (who were contemporaries of the German Idealists) actually developed a conception of the Kabbalah that closely paralleled Hegelian philosophy.[36] However, this conception was, as I will argue, already implicit in the Lurianic symbols themselves.

---

32. Shelomo Maimon, *Shelomo Maimon, An Autobiography*, trans. Clark Murray (London, 1888), p. 105. Quoted in Idel, *Hasidism*, p. 40.

33. Idel, *Hasidism*, p. 41.

34. Rachel Elior, *The Paradoxical Ascent to God*, p. 85.

35. This issue will be clarified in relation to the Lurianic doctrine of *Tzimtzum* in Chapter Three.

36. This topic is explored in detail in my book, *Jewish Mystical Themes in Ancient and Modern Thought*

PUSHING THE BOUNDS OF SENSE

The difficulties inherent in providing a logical and coherent interpretation of the Lurianic Kabbalah are no less formidable today. The content of the Lurianic writings, for example Vital's *Sefer Etz Chayyim*, is extremely metaphorical and obscure. Moreover, the more one tries to provide a coherent interpretation of this work, to "map out the system," the more one is confronted with abrupt, seemingly impossible transitions, contradictory statements, and transformations in such fundamental dimensions as gender, temporal sequence, and logical priority that appear to violate not only the Kabbalist's definitions of his terms but the very rules of significant discourse. Sections and paragraphs often begin coherently but soon break down into a barrage of qualifications and asides that belie the reader's attempt to reconstruct an overall theory or narrative.[37]

A portion of the incomprehensibility of Vital's *Sefer Etz Chayyim* and

---

37. Here I will provide by way of an example, a summary of a passage in Vital's *Sefer Etz Chayyim*, which deals with some aspects of the symbol of the Breaking of the Vessels. According to Vital, the Breaking of the Vessels (which we have spoken about in general terms above) results in the death of "the seven kings" who, according to the book of Genesis, ruled and died in the land of Edom. However, with the advent of *Tikkun ha-Olam*, the restoration of the world, these same kings return to their original place, bringing with them seven lights that had also been displaced into a lower world when the vessels shattered. The result of this, Vital explains, is that lower lights are now brought on high to the place of *Binah*, the Celestial Mother. It is in the womb of *Binah* that the kings will be reborn. Vital sees this as particularly appropriate for their *Tikkun* (Restoration) since *Binah*, as the *Partzuf "Imma"* is "after all, the mother of children." The divine lights are thereby "reborn" in *Binah*'s womb. Vital informs us that these broken lights or *kelim* do not arise into the womb of *Binah* together all at once, but rather do so over a period of forty days, which, according to Talmudic tradition, is the period of the initial formation of a child. The lights from the broken *Sefirot Chesed* and *Netzach* are the first to enter *Binah*, followed in ten days by the lights from *Da'at* and *Tiferet*, then those from *Gevurah* and *Hod*, and finally the lights of *Yesod* and *Malchut*. Vital identifies these lights, which are raised into the womb of *Binah* over this forty-day period, with the *mayim nukvim*, or "feminine waters", which *Ein-Sof* raises to commence the process of *Tikkun* via the coupling of *Chochmah* and *Binah*, the Celestial Father and Mother. This entire process, and particularly the recoupling of *Chochmah* and *Binah*, occurs in the world of *Adam Kadmon* (the highest of the Kabbalists' five "worlds") and results in the restoration of all ten *Sefirot* from *Keter* to *Malchut* in the next lower world, the world of *Atzilut*. Vital explains that this renewed coupling and pregnancy restores the entire world of *Atzilut*, form the highest *Partzuf*, *Attik Yomim* (which is the *pnimi*

similar texts can be attributed to the author's own confusion regarding his subject matter, and other accidental features such as bad editing, poor redactions, etc. In some ways, however, the book's lack of normal coherence follows from the tenets of kabbalistic theory itself; the mutual completion and "truth" of opposites, the interchangability in gender, and the simultaneity of sequential events, are, as we shall see, examples of legitimate kabbalistic doctrine, which can perhaps only be expressed in language that comes close to violating the bounds of sense and coherence. As we will come to see, kabbalistic doctrine is essentially deconstructive of the very distinctions that make for (traditional) rationality and coherence, and it is through such deconstruction that the theosophical Kabbalah offers its unique vision.

It is further possible that the incomprehensibility of portions of major kabbalistic texts is by the author's (conscious or unconscious) design, either in an effort to maintain the esoteric status of the doctrine, limiting its full disclosure to a circle of intimate disciples, or for deeper, mystical reasons. Among such possibilities are 1) that the ambiguity, and confusing intricacy of the text itself has a mystical or meditative effect upon the reader, leading him

---

[the inner aspect] of the *Sefirah Keter*) down to the lowest *Sefirah, Malchut*. The coupling of *Chochmah* (*Abba*) and *Binah* (*Imma*) in the world of *Adam Kadmon* restores the *Partzuf* (divine "visage") *Attik Yomim* (the "Ancient of Days," frequently identified with the *Sefirah Keter*) in the world of *Atzilut* by causing it to engage in a coupling process itself. Couplings (*zivugim*) now proceed down the chain of being in the same direction (top down) as uncouplings had occurred after the Breaking of the Vessels. The *zivug* (coupling) in *Attik Yomim*, for example, brings about a *Tikkun* in the *Partzuf Arich Anpin* (the "Long-Faced One"), causing a coupling in that *Partzuf* as well. There are subsequent *zivugim* between the *Partzufim Abba* and *Imma* in the world of *Atzilut*, as well as between *Zeir Anpin* and *Nukvah*. Through this latter coupling, which is spoken of liturgically as the union between "the Holy One Blessed Be He" and His bride or *Shekhinah*, all of the worlds are restored. Vital informs us that the pregnancy resulting from the coupling of "ZuN" (Zeir Anpin and his bride, Nukvah) must be delayed twelve months in order to correct and restore all twelve of the aspects or *Partzufim* in the world of *Atzilut*.

In order to accommodate all of the nuptial activity necessary to restore the world after the Breaking of the Vessels, the number of *Partzufim* are themselves expanded to twelve: *Attik Yomim* and his *Nukvah*, *Arikh Anpin* and his *Nukvah*, "Upper" *Abba* and *Imma*, *Yisrael Sava* and *Tevunah* (to who, we were introduced in Vital's account of the *Shevirah*) *Zeir Anpin* and *Nuvkah*, and *Yaacov* and *Leah*. Vital explains that these six couplings take twelve months, but that he is unsure (because he cannot remember what Luria told him) whether they took two months each or if all twelve months are necessary for the first pairing involving *Attik Yomim*.

away from its sense to an experience of the words themselves and the images they evoke, 2) that the text is designed to engage the reader in filling in gaps and, hence, in providing his own personal interpretation and experience of it, 3) that the fragmentation of the text is designed to mirror the fragmented state of the human personality and reality, and, as such, in addition to telling us about this fragmentation, the text provides us with a fragmentation experience, and 4) that the alteration between mystery and clarity in the text is designed to mirror the contrast between the "hidden" and "revealed" in the life of the Godhead.[38]

The obscure aspects of the Kabbalah, however, should not provide us with an excuse for failing to interpret the Lurianic system at all. The Kabbalah, like any system of thought that trades in metaphor, is, to a certain extent, indeterminate in its significance, and this indeterminacy is precisely what provides it with richness and depth. It is the very nature of metaphor that it hints at truths that are not (or are not as yet) articulable in literal terms.[39] It may therefore be that the very process of attempting to provide rational interpretations to mystical ideas not only pushes up against the bounds of significance and truth but expands them as well.

Indeed, it is my view that by examining the various interpretive possibilities with respect to the Lurianic myths we will see that part of their very meaning and intent is an *expansion of interpretation*. The *Sefirot*, for example, were understood by the Kabbalists to be the elements of both God and creation precisely because they reflect innumerable points of view. Hence the *Sefirot* can only be expressed and understood through an indefinite series of changing metaphors. For this reason, any interpretation of the Kabbalah, if it is to remain in the spirit of the Kabbalists themselves, must expand interpretive possibilities rather than remain satisfied with a single point of view.

Given the open-ended nature of the Lurianic system, it is hardly surprising that a number of hermeneutic alternatives have emerged, which

---

38, For the above reasons there appears to me to be a partial miscommunication in a text like *Sefer Etz Chayyim*, one that assumes that while the reader comprehends the basic outlines of the Lurianic system he is unable to grasp the total theory in detailed and logical form. This miscommunication has the effect of prompting one to continually engage the Lurianic theosophy in its own terms.

39. See Richard Rorty, "Unfamiliar Noises: Hesse and Davidson on Metaphors," in his *Objectivism, Relativism and Truth: Philosophical Papers*, Vol. 1 (Cambridge: Cambridge University Press, 1991), pp. 162–172.

purport to uncover its meaning and significance. The Lurianic myths have been interpreted as (1) expressing or allegorizing historical and political themes (e.g., the Jews' plight of exile and their hope for redemption), (2) referring to psychological as opposed to theological events (the Hasidic approach, later formalized in the theories of Carl Jung), (3) expressing philosophical ideas in mythical form (the views of Maimon and Mendelssohn), (4) providing a discursive context for certain acts and performances that are of greater significance than the myths themselves.[40] They have also been seen as (5) primarily deconstructive in intent (leading the mind down one apparently promising but ultimately empty avenue of thought after another), or (6) meditational in intent and/or effect (providing the reader with images or thoughts that have a mystical/experiential as opposed to an intellective outcome). While each of these points of view have much to be said for them, this book emphasizes the philosophical and psychological ideas that lie implicitly behind the kabbalistic myths.

SCHOLEM, SYMBOL, AND ALLEGORY

The fact that a contemporary *philosophically minded* explication of the theosophical Kabbalah has yet to be achieved is due in part to the views of Gershom Scholem, the founder of modern Kabbalah scholarship. Scholem held that the kabbalistic symbols are impenetrable to the rational mind. He made a distinction between "allegory" and "symbolism" and held that whereas allegory represents "an expressible something by another expressible something . . . the mystical symbol is an expressible representation of something which lies beyond the sphere of expression and communication."[41] According to Scholem, the symbol has no cognitive or even semantic content; it "signifies nothing and communicates nothing, but makes something transparent which is beyond all expression." The mystical symbol is, in effect, a window onto a prelinguistic world. For Scholem, "a hidden and

---

40. Idel, for example, holds that "what characterizes Lurianic Kabbalah is the concentration of Jewish ritual around the mystical goal of restructuring reality and the Godhead in order to reconstitute the shattered unifying entity: *Adam Qadmon*." Idel, *Hasidism*, p. 52. For Idel, the complex Lurianic mythos and theosophy is simply a context provided to supply meaning to this *performative act*. It is neither the primary goal of the Kabbalah nor even an end in and of itself.

41. Scholem, *Major Trends*, pp. 26–27.

inexpressible reality finds its expression in the symbol." In contrast to allegory, there is no point in interpreting mystical symbols: "Where deeper insight into the structure of the allegory uncovers fresh layers of meaning, the symbol is intuitively understood all at once or not at all."[42]

Since the major vehicle of kabbalistic expression is, according to Scholem, the mystical symbol, there is simply no point in providing a philosophical interpretation of the Kabbalah. This view, which has gone largely unchallenged by Scholem's followers, has seriously handicapped Kabbalah studies and has, in my opinion, slowed the entrance of kabbalistic ideas into contemporary intellectual life.

THE BREAKING OF THE VESSELS

In order to illustrate the limitations of Scholem's point of view I will examine two alternative interpretations of one of the main symbols of the Lurianic Kabbalah: the Breaking of the Vessels. Scholem is generally averse to providing interpretations of the Kabbalah. However, when he does interpret kabbalistic symbols, he seems to be influenced by the view first set forth by Vico that myths and symbols are neither false narratives nor allegories, but rather express the collective mentality of an age. For example in his analysis of the Breaking of the Vessels, the cosmic catastrophe in which the archetypes of creation (the *Sefirot*) were displaced and shattered, Scholem affirms that one of its consequences is that: "Nothing remains in its proper place. Everything is somewhere else. But a being that is not in its proper place is in exile. Thus since that primordial act, all being has been in exile, in need of being led back and redeemed."[43] Scholem continues: "Before the judgment seat of rationalist theology such an idea may not have much to say for itself. But for the human experience of the Jews it was the most seductively powerful of symbols."[44]

According to Scholem, this symbol is so powerful and seductive precisely because "from a historical point of view, Luria's myth constitutes a response to the expulsion of the Jews from Spain."[45] The power of this myth results

---

42. Ibid., p. 27.

43. Gershom Scholem, *On The Kabbalah and Its Symbolism*, trans. Ralph Manheim (New York: Schocken, 1969), p. 112.

44. Scholem, *On The Kabbalah*, p. 113.

45. Ibid., p. 110.

from its having given meaning to that historical exile, and through that to the experience of Jewish exile throughout history. The latent content of this myth, in Scholem's view, is a particular historical event, and it is by linking the myth to this event (and not by taking the myth on its own terms) that we can interpret it rationally. To take the myth on its own terms as a statement about God and being would either be an inappropriate entry into the "realm of the silent," or akin to taking historical or psychological experience as actual philosophy or theology.

While Scholem hints at another possibility when he says that "the mighty symbols" of Jewish life can be taken as "an extreme case of human life pure and simple" he immediately goes on to say: "We can no longer fully perceive, I might say, 'live,' the symbols of the Kabbalah without a considerable effort if at all."[46] This is so because Scholem's entire thrust is to interpret the kabbalistic myths (following Vico) as manifest expressions of latent historical themes. While one cannot argue against the viability of such an approach, it is instructive to compare its fruit to that of another point of view: one that takes the myths seriously and conceptually and that reads them as an expression of what they claim to be, that is, about God, man, creation, and the very nature of being itself.[47] When we do this we see that the kabbalistic symbol of the broken vessels and the related myth of the exile of God from Himself[48] actually implies (among other things) that all being is alienation, and that all of reality is somehow broken, flawed, and incomplete. In recognizing this we may be in a position to gather under one heading, one

46. Scholem, *On The Kabbalah*, p. 117.

47. Actually, the Lurianists regarded their system as being applicable to both the exile of the Jewish people and metaphysical exile of God. Like other Lurianists, Moses Chayyim Luzzatto held that the Breaking of the Vessels and subsequent *Tikkun* had both metaphysical and temporal implications. He writes that as a result of *Tikkun* "the divine spirit will be cleared of dross." Further, "Israel will be separated from the barbarians; as the Divine Spirit will be divorced completely from the husks. Then the world will remain completely perfected as never before. Israel will be redeemed. The redemption will be so complete that there will never again be exile, for it is already known that the single purpose of all the periods of exile was to select the Sparks of the Holy Spirit from amidst the husks." Luzzatto, *General Principles of the Kabbalah*, pp. 147–148.

48. In fact the Kabbalists utilized a number of myths to symbolize this basic idea, including the "exile" of God's *Shekhinah* (his presence or feminine countenance) from earth, the diminishment of (the light) of the moon, the "death of the kings," etc. These will each be explored in Chapter Seven.

symbol, such widely disparate phenomena as the exile of man from man (existentialism), of man from himself (Freud), of man from the products of his creative labor (Marx), and to grasp in one act of thought the seemingly unbridgeable gaps between our concepts of freedom and necessity, appearance and reality, good and evil, universal and particular, theology and science, to name but a few of the perennial antinomies of philosophy that can be said to illustrate the basic "fault" in the cosmos.[49]

Indeed, to say that all being is in exile from itself appears to be a strikingly apt description, not only of the condition of contemporary man, but of the condition of the world itself, particularly as it is mediated (and thus alienated) through the categories of human thought. Indeed, it can be argued that the Lurianic Kabbalah is far from being a mere commentary on the historical experience of Jewish exile, but rather that the experience of historical exile itself is but one instance of a much broader phenomena of *ontological* exile, which is made transparent in the kabbalistic and, particularly, Lurianic symbols. Understood in this way we can "perceive" and "live" the kabbalistic symbol of the Breaking of the Vessels as deeply, if not more deeply, than any generation before our own: for when has the alienation of man from himself and society, and the antinimous nature of the world, been more manifest than in our own time? As Menzi and Padeh write in the introduction to their translation of Gate One of Vital's *Sefer Etz Chayyim*:

> In Lurianic Kabbalah, the unity of the unseen realms—the intermediate levels between our finite universe and the undivided Infinite—is broken, and this broken-ness is reflected in our experience of this world as out-of-joint, incomplete, fragmentary, and unbalanced. The imbalance and disharmony so often present between male and female; between parent and child; between the diverse cultures, classes, and races of humankind; between religions and between religious denominations; between humans and their environment; and even between the various aspects of our own personalities are evidence of this underlying lack of unity.[50]

We can conclude then that the kabbalistic symbols can be understood as having *a universal, philosophical significance.* I am inclined to think of the kabbalistic myths as a blend of vision and reason, of dream and interpretation, and to see their value, like the value of all myths, in their ability to touch upon

---

49. A fuller discussion of these antinomies is found in Chapter Seven.
50. Menzi and Padeh, *The Tree of Life,* p. xlvii.

some basic experience that expresses but also transcends the particular history and psychology of those who create them. The latent content of myth on this view is philosophy: not in the sense that myth is a mere allegory for philosophical ideas, but in the sense that the mythical imagination is one that responds to the same stirrings within the human soul, the same fundamental questions about human existence and the world as a whole that stir and prompt the philosopher.

Scholem considers the possibility of a conceptual or philosophical interpretation of the Kabbalah, and indeed tells us that such interpretation was more than frequently practiced by the Kabbalists themselves. Yet he sees such an enterprise as an "obvious failure."[51] Such failure is due, according to Scholem, to the fact that "inexhaustible symbolic images" are in no way abbreviations for conceptual ideas. He holds symbols and concepts to be completely incommensurable: any attempt at translating the former into the latter ends up hopelessly distorting and hence losing the value of the symbols themselves. We need not, however, hold that mystical symbols are either exhaustively interpretable or that they are abbreviations for concepts, to maintain, as the Kabbalists did themselves, that such symbols have conceptual implications and that genuine insight can be obtained into both the nature of these symbols and their presumed referents by projecting the symbolic into the plane of philosophical discourse.

WHAT CAN BE SAID: MYSTICISM, MYTH, AND PHILOSOPHY

As we have seen, central to Scholem's thesis that the Kabbalah is opaque to rational interpretation is his distinction between the expressible plane of reality represented by allegory and the inexpressible plane referred to by symbols.[52] This is an important distinction that will be worth pursuing in some detail.

That there are fundamental "truths" that cannot be spoken about is certainly one of the foundations of mysticism. In mysticism (as contrasted with myth and philosophy) "truth" is not accessible to linguistic discourse, but is rather embodied in a private, contemplative, or ecstatic experience,

---

51. Scholem, *On The Kabbalah*, p. 96.
52. Scholem, *Major Trends*, pp. 26–27.

which can be referred to but not transmitted by language. (This is what the Kabbalist Isaac the Blind referred to when he spoke of truths that cannot be known but that are nonetheless "visible to the heart."[53]) In myth, truth is accessible to language but only partially. Myth, in the broad sense of this term, operates through a poetic/metaphoric language, which, unlike mysticism, actually transmits the "truth" to the hearer or reader, but in a manner that stirs his psyche or soul so that he approaches that truth with his own being. Because myth is metaphorical, and relies upon the emotional or existential response of the hearer, the truth of myth is always subject to a myriad of new interpretations and understandings and unlike the truth of philosophy, is essentially experiential. Finally, philosophy as it is traditionally understood regards "truth" (or at least the truth with which it is concerned) to be completely accessible to language and articulable in a full and unequivocal manner.

There have certainly been philosophers who held there to be a realm that cannot be circumscribed by language. Wittgenstein, the philosopher who perhaps more than any other attempted to draw a boundary between the "sayable" and the "silent," held that the realm of the silent involves the very conditions of experience and language: the willing, experiencing subject; the link or connection between language and the world; the basic fact that words and signs have meaning; etc.[54] None of these conditions can be spoken about without their being assumed and serving as the basis for what is being said. As such, they cannot be articulated as part of the world but are rather boundaries to it and hence part of the realm of the silent. The mystic, in his silence, and precisely because of his silence, claims access to these boundary conditions, and hence to the "Absolute."

There can be little doubt that the symbols of the Kabbalah push up against this presumably silent realm. The Kabbalists themselves were conscious of this fact. "We have no real ability," Vital writes, "to talk about the things before the emanation of the ten *Sefirot*. To make (these things) comprehensible to human ears we have to talk in allegorical and symbolic language. Even if we talk about some image above, it is only to make it understandable for the ear."

---

53. Scholem, *Origins of the Kabbalah*, p. 280.

54. Wittgenstein's comments on the realm of the silent can be found in his *Tractatus Logico-Philosophicus*, trans. D. F. Pears and B. F. McGuinness (London: Routledge & Kegan Paul, 1961) (originally published in 1921) and in his *Notebooks* (Oxford: Basil Blackwell, 1961) (originally written in 1914–1916).

Many of the symbols and concepts of the Kabbalah, e.g., *Ein-Sof* (the ineffable infinite), *Tzimtzum* (the contraction/ concealment in the infinite that makes a "place" for the world), *Keter* (crown, the highest *Sefirah*, which is identified with "nothingness" and "will"), *Ayin* (the nothingness of both *Keter* and *Ein-Sof*), the *Malbush*[55] (God's garment in which the "letters" that ultimately comprise all significance are folded over in *potentia*) etc., make reference to the very boundary conditions of the world rather than to the world itself. The questions remain, however, whether all kabbalistic theosophical concepts and symbols fall into this presumably silent realm, and whether nothing of rational (or other) significance can be said about those that presumably do. Scholem, it seems, would answer both of these questions in the affirmative. For two reasons, I cannot concur.

The first of these reasons is that while the Kabbalah is at times avowedly mystical, at other times, as I have pointed out, it is clearly both abstract and philosophical. According to Verman "all of the kabbalistic works exhibit significant influence from philosophy."[56] To take a textual example, *Sefer ha-Bahir*, which is regarded by Scholem to be the earliest kabbalistic work (c. 1180), speaks of a "tree" that God has planted as the world, which is at the same time the source of the soul of man: "It is I who have planted this 'tree,'[57] that all the world may delight in it, and with it I have spanned the All and called it 'All' for on it depends the All, and from it emanates the All, all things need it, and look upon it, and yearn for it, and from it all souls go forth."[57] In another passage the *Bahir* continues: "All powers of God are [disposed] in layers and they are like a tree. Just as the tree produces its fruit through water, so God through water increases the powers of the 'tree.' And what is God's water? It is *hokhmah* [wisdom]."[58]

These passages, like many others throughout the kabbalistic corpus, speak in symbol and metaphor (the tree), but immediately proceed to

---

55. This concept/symbol is found in the writings of Israel Sarug (fl. 1590–1610). Sarug, who may have known Luria when the latter briefly sojourned in Egypt, claimed to be one of Luria's main disciples. His writings are tinged with philosophical ideas.

56. Verman, *The Books of Contemplation*, p. 24.

57. Scholem, *Origins of the Kabbalah*, p. 71. Cf. *Book Bahir*, trans. Joachim Neugroschel, in *The Secret Garden: An Anthology in the Kabbalah* ed. David Meltzer (Barrytown, NY: Stanton Hill, 1998), p. 55.

58. *Sefer ha-Bahir*, sec. 85, as translated by Scholem, *Origins of the Kabbalah*, p. 75. Cf. *Book Bahir*, Neugroschel trans., p. 73.

penetrate their own mythical language with philosophical vocabulary and ideas (God as the source, substance, and sustenance of all being, here identified with intellect or wisdom). As such the Kabbalah, which undoubtedly shows the influence of Platonic and Neoplatonic ideas, itself invites a philosophical interpretation, and it is thus all the more surprising that contemporary scholars have not seriously considered the Kabbalah in philosophical terms. While it is clearly the case, as Idel has stated, that the Kabbalists occasionally adapted philosophical (particularly Aristotelian) terms for their own use, and thereby divorced these terms from their original significances, they also made use of such Neoplatonic terms as will, thought, worlds, etc., in a manner that retained their philosophical meanings.[59] At any rate, it is incumbent upon us today to decipher the Kabbalists' use of philosophical vocabulary, and where appropriate, to provide the Kabbalah with a vocabulary that is more suitable to its philosophical ideas.

As Ricouer so succinctly states, "symbols invite thought,"[60] and the Kabbalists' symbols are hardly an exception. While it is clear that some of the kabbalistic symbols push up against the boundary of the sayable, it is hardly the case that they are therefore *purely* mystical and hence completely opaque to interpretation. We might say that the theosophical Kabbalah is rooted in mysticism, expressed in myth, and ascendant toward philosophy. Its power lies precisely in its breadth, and in the fact that its language never becomes so opaque as that of the mystic, nor so forcibly and artificially transparent as that of the philosopher. As such the Kabbalah occupies a territory between logic and poetry, locution and silence, which enables it to mirror the very spirit of man and the world.

It is possible, in my view, to provide a rational interpretation even for those kabbalistic ideas and symbols (such as *Ein-Sof, Tzimtzum*, Worlds) that clearly make reference to the realm of the silent, and are hence *mystical* in their very essence. This is because reason has, as one of its tools, the power of analogy, and the boundary conditions of the world as a whole have their analogues in the boundary conditions of phenomena that occupy only a portion of the cosmos. Thus it is possible, for example, to shed rational light on the creation of "Worlds," which the Kabbalists affirm are "everything" to the finite creatures within them, but illusion to the emanator above them, by analogizing to the phenomenon of dreams, which are entire worlds to those

---

59. Moshe Idel, *Kabbalah: New Perspectives*, pp. 2–3, 40, 182.
60. Quoted in ibid., p. 232.

"within" them but illusions to the "waking" dreamer. I will have occasion to explore such analogies, along with their limitations, in detail in subsequent chapters.[61] The point I wish to make here is that much can indeed be said about those kabbalistic symbols that Scholem would regard as making reference to an inexpressible layer of reality. On my view the "unsayable" is hardly a static realm through which reason may never pass, but is rather a limit that reason must constantly endeavor to push up against. Indeed it is the very nature of what one might call "rational mysticism" to dare to speak as clearly and coherently as possible about such things that are only hinted at in mysticism and myth or that some would say completely transcend the medium of language. It is only, for example, by pushing the Kabbalah as far as possible into the realm of reason and philosophy that we can comprehend the limits of what can be expressed in words and provide what remains with the true imprimatur of the "unsayable," and not simply the "unsaid." We should not allow our concept of the "unsayable" to provide us with an excuse for obscurantism, for a laziness of thought that simply fails to make clear what is subject to clarification. Idel has pointed out that the Kabbalist Abraham Abulafia eschewed theosophical symbols precisely because their ambiguity is "indicative not of the inexpressibility of the object but lack of clarity on the part of the thinking subject."[62] We should keep Abulafia's skepticism in mind in our own approach to the kabbalistic symbols and metaphors.

Our assumption of "expressability" is completely consistent with the Jewish tradition in general, and the Jewish mystical tradition in particular. Judaism has always had a very positive attitude toward language. In contrast to those traditions that have held that language only alienates and obscures, Judaism has affirmed that words, as embodied in scripture, are indeed, the ultimate expression of God's will. The Kabbalists themselves held that reality is not only perfectly reflected in language, but that it is actually composed of letters in the holy tongue. For this reason, all hermeneutical acts have mystical as well as cognitive significance, as interpretation itself has an impact on the very spiritual substance of the universe. I will explore the details of this "linguistic mysticism" in Chapter Five. Here it should suffice to point out that the very process of interpreting the kabbalistic symbols not only has the imprimatur of the Kabbalists, but of the entire Jewish tradition.

To say, as I have claimed earlier, that the Kabbalah is expressed in *myth*

---

61. See Chapter Three regarding *Tzimtzum* and Chapter Six regarding "Worlds."

62. Idel, *Kabbalah: New Perspectives*, p. 203.

deprives it neither of symbolic nor philosophical significance. While some scholars of Jewish mysticism, notably Tishby,[63] have taken a literalistic view of myth in which the mythical image and that which it denotes are one and the same, my own view is that, to a greater or lesser degree, myth is always symbolic. In some instances, as in the Kabbalah, this is quite obvious, while in others, as in Greek mythology, it is much less apparent; but even in such myths that are apparently meant to be taken literally, a symbolic interpretation is latent in their images and underscores their depth and appeal. This, of course, follows from what even the literalists must acknowledge, i.e., that myth, in Tishby's words, arises from "certain unconscious emotional and visionary drives, affecting the very depths of the human spirit."[64]

On the opposite pole from Tishby is a view of myth that takes it to be allegory for imperfectly understood and expressed philosophical ideas. This, of course, was the view of Hegel, who saw religion in general, and myth in particular, as a means for conveying profound philosophical truths to minds unschooled in abstract thinking. My own view is that while myths can frequently be understood philosophically, their meaning is not exhausted through such an interpretation. All language, and myth is certainly no exception, is multivalent: abstract *and* concrete, symbolic *and* literal, cognitive *and* emotional, descriptive *and* evocative. While one can attempt to make distinctions among genres of discourse, to draw hard and fast distinctions between language that is mythical, symbolical, allegorical, and philosophical, especially with respect to a body of work such as the Kabbalah, is highly artificial and, in the end, unenlightening. That the Kabbalah is mythical does not mean that is not also symbolical, psychological, and philosophical.

THE PHILOSOPHICAL INTERPRETATION
OF THE LURIANIC MYTHS

The *philosophical* interpretation of the Kabbalah is a double-edged sword, for while conceptual categories are helpful in clarifying the Kabbalists' symbols, these same categories are transformed and ultimately transcended in response to the kabbalistic ideas. This proposition will become clear throughout this book. I will attempt, however, in the course of the next several pages to provide its basic sense.

---

63. Tishby and Lachower, *The Wisdom of the Zohar*, Vol. 1, p. 286.
64. Ibid., p. 287.

The Kabbalah organizes reality on its own terms, through a series of symbols (such as *Tzimtzum, Sefirot, Shevirah, and Tikkun*) which are not always obviously philosophical in nature. However, in order to gain insight into these symbols, we must first comprehend them in relation to familiar ideas, *project* them, so to speak, onto what we take to be the rational order.

By "projecting" the Kabbalists' myths into the realm of reason and philosophy, two things occur. The first is that the principles of logic and reason begin to deconstruct in the face of the antinimous nature of the kabbalistic symbols. The second is that there is a moment where we are able to understand the myths for the first time in a perspicacious fashion, before the vehicle of this understanding (reason) itself begins to fall apart before our eyes. In venturing our projection we are, I suppose, like the deaf, who, wanting to understand the nature of music, arrange to have sound isomorphically transformed into a series of visual patterns, which come and go, brighten and dim, alternate colors, etc. In performing this projection the deaf are provided with a genuine insight into what they otherwise cannot experience, and even the hearing are treated to a new, and in some ways clarifying, comprehension of musical sounds. If done well, such a projection of sound into sight permits one to actually "see" the music, and, in effect, grasp it in a way that one has never grasped it before. One obtains insight into seeing as well, as the inconstancies of the projected music allow us to better understand the very components of seeing (color, brightness, saturation, contrast, etc.) that were "withdrawn" phenomena in the everyday visual world. We shall see that the philosophical interpretation of Kabbalah provides us not only with a new understanding of Kabbalah, but new insight into philosophy as well.

THE "ELEMENTALIST" INTERPRETATION OF THE *SEFIROT*

As an example, let us briefly examine how the projection of myth onto philosophy helps elucidate the doctrine of the *Sefirot*. The words *Sefirah* (singular) and *Sefirot* (plural) are related to a variety of Hebrew roots (including the words for counting, sapphire, and narration).[65] Whatever its

---

65. Scholem, *Major Trends*, p. 206; Scholem, *Kabbalah*, p. 100.

etymological origins, however, it is clear that the Kabbalah uses the word *Sefirah* to refer to aspects or traits of the deity, which are at once vessels (*kelim*) for containing the infinite's light and stages in the divine emanation of finite worlds. There is a tradition, most aptly represented by Moses Cordovero, that held that the *Sefirot* are not only the archetypes of all existence, but the very component elements of the world's substance. Each thing is what it is by virtue of the particular combination of *Sefirot* that comprise it. By providing a philosophical interpretation of this notion we are able to gain conceptual insight into what, in the context of the Kabbalah, is generally a purely mystical or mythological idea.

From a philosophical point of view Cordovero's theory that the *Sefirot* are the world's basic elements is a proposed ontology, a theory of Being, which answers the question: What kinds of entities exist in the universe? Although the Kabbalists never argue this explicitly, when we examine the nature of the *Sefirot* symbolism, it becomes clear that theirs is an idealist or phenomenologically derived ontology. For the Kabbalah, the world consists first and foremost of archetypal ideas and values, and not some material substance that the mind then categorizes conceptually. These archetypes, the *Sefirot* themselves, are intuited through human experience and are, in effect, the experiential components of the ideational, spiritual, aesthetic, and material objects in man's world. Each *Sefirah* represents an ideational (e.g., *Chochmah*—Wisdom), spiritual (e.g., *Chesed*—Loving-Kindness), aesthetic (e.g., *Toferet*—Beauty), or material (e.g., *Yesod*—Foundation) element or dimension in the world of experience. When in Chapter Four we come to examine closely what the Kabbalists say about each *Sefirah*, we will discover a very close correspondence between the order of the *Sefirot*, and what might be described as ten dimensions or "values" of phenomenological experience: an entity's position in time; the three dimensions of space; its aesthetic, moral, and spiritual value; its existential status (i.e., does it exist or is it imaginary); the ideas it instantiates or represents; and the "will" or purpose it serves. Indeed it can be argued that the world's entities and events can be better described and understood through the ten-dimensional sefirotic scheme than they can be "scientifically." Science, by failing to include ideas, volition, and values as elements of its world, is thus handicapped in its account of such things as human personalities, historical events, aesthetic objects, etc.; whereas the sefirotic scheme, because it is phenomenologically more complete, provides an ontology of much broader scope and application.

THE KABBALAH AND DECONSTRUCTION

Without going into the details of this "Sefirotic elementalism," it should by now be clear how an application of philosophical concepts and vocabulary can provide insight into a doctrine (the *Sefirot*) that in the Kabbalah is essentially mythical and symbolic. By "projecting" the myth of the *Sefirot* onto reason, the *Sefirot* are first understood as archetypes of value and then as elements of the created world. However, this process of regarding the *Sefirot* as elements, while illuminative of the *Sefirot*, is ultimately deconstructive of the concept of "element" itself. This is because elements are normally regarded as discrete, static, unchanging structures, and the *Sefirot* are changeable, multifaceted, dynamic forces, regarded alternately by the Kabbalists as personalities, colors, names, levels of the soul, garments of the Absolute, aspects of the self, and even questions. The *Sefirot* are the ultimate elements of the world, but, paradoxically, they are elements that change their very character depending upon our perspective upon them. As such, the very rational concepts, elements, and structures that we use in order to make the kabbalistic symbols comprehensible begin to lose their own normal sense in the process of being applied to the Kabbalah.

The symbol of the Breaking of the Vessels (*Shevirat ha-Kelim*) is important to consider in this context, for it implies that any of the constructions we place on any idea, including the kabbalistic symbols (and the Breaking of the Vessels itself) are only temporary expedients for the understanding. Examined philosophically, the *Shevirah* implies the inadequacy of all concepts to "contain" the phenomena to which they refer. This is evident from the fact that in the Lurianic myth the vessels (i.e., the *Sefirot*), which represent perfection in the realm of values and ideas (e.g., wisdom, kindness, judgment, beauty), shattered because they could not hold the portion of divine light (ultimate truth, reality) that they were presumably meant to contain.

Understood philosophically, the Kabbalah actually performs a radical deconstruction upon the very language through which it (and all philosophy, for that matter) must be expressed and understood. Symbolized in the Breaking of the Vessels, this deconstruction provides us with a caution against being too satisfied with any of the interpretations or constructions we place upon the Kabbalah specifically, or upon the world in general. Indeed it is only by constructing, deconstructing, and then reconstructing our perspectives upon God, the world, and ourselves that we can hope to achieve anything near the breadth of view necessary for a valuable interpretation.

As such, contemporary deconstructionism provides an important entrée into the Kabbalah as philosophy. "Deconstructionism" has come to signify an entire movement in literary criticism and contemporary philosophy most often associated with the names Jacques Derrida and Paul de Man.[66] It is a movement that defies categorization and description precisely because it holds that there are no definable relationships between words and the things they presumably represent. Language, for deconstructionism, is not grounded in any prelinguistic reality but is rather an ever-changing, "infinite play of signification" unto itself. Applied to traditional philosophical ideas, deconstructionism, as its name suggests, dismantles or, better, "breaks apart" the "truths" that philosophy has attempted to promulgate about the world. All so-called truths, essences, and structures break down once it is realized that words do not directly refer to anything and achieve their significance only by virtue of the system of differences among linguistic signs. The origin of meaning in differences assures that all concepts and ideas will have what they are not woven into what they are, and that all acts of speech will be infinitely interpretable. Indeed, for deconstructionism it is impossible for a person to mean *precisely what he says*, for what he says will be subject to an infinite play of significance transcending his or her own intentions and resulting from the infinite system of differences, of which his words are of necessity a part. The Lurianic Kabbalah, by pointing to the impurity of all of our concepts (e.g., good and evil, man and God, etc.), by recognizing that such concepts imply their opposites (as well as accidental properties that are attendant to their instantiations in a world), by holding that there is no real distinction between reality and language, and by insisting upon the possibility of an indefinite number of interpretations of any linguistic act, can be said to perform a "deconstruction" on traditional philosophical ideas.[67]

However, while the Kabbalah can be said to anticipate some of the

---

66. On "deconstructionism" see Jacques Derrida, *Margins of Philosophy* (Chicago: University of Chicago Press, 1982); Christina Howell, *Derrida from Phenomenology to Ethics* (Cambridge, U.K.: Polity Press, 1999); Jonathan Culler, *On Deconstruction Theory and Criticism After Structuralism* (Ithaca, NY: Cornell University Press, 1982); Henry Staten, *Wittgenstein and Derrida* (Lincoln: University of Nebraska Press, 1984).

67. As we shall see in Chapter Five, there is also a sense in which the Kabbalists held a highly essentialist view of the relationship between language and being. This does not, however (as we will see) prevent them from holding a deconstructionist view as well. The Kabbalists held that all things and all points of view imply their opposites in *coincidentia oppositorum*.

moves of contemporary deconstructionism, even to the point of holding that reality is itself composed of letters and words,[68] its goals are far from those of Derrida or de Man. The Lurianic Kabbalah, one might say, sees deconstruction (symbolized in the Breaking of the Vessels), as one (albeit critical) moment in the evolution from a naive essentialism (embodied in the *Sefirot*) to a human-based ethic in which essences, instead of existing *sub species aeternae* become the responsibility of man (*Tikkun*). For the Kabbalah, the result of a deconstruction of the world's original structure is the need for a new order, *reconstructed* through the language of man. It is this *reconstructed* human order that, on the Kabbalist's view, is the highest expression of God.

DIALECTICS

The Kabbalist, in his poetical/symbolic manner of speaking, actually wishes to say that on the deepest of levels, the level that accords best with the actual human and worldly predicament, the opposing categories of our rationalistic schemes, blend in with one another, are dependent on one another, and are ultimately, in spite of their surface structure as oppositions, simultaneously true. The truth of such contradictions cannot be explained away through a clarification of terms, for it is (to take but a few examples to be elaborated on in later chapters), "God," in His capacity of "creator" who is also "created" (by man),[69] evil, in its malevolence, which is also "good,"[70] and "being" in

---

68. The view that the world itself is comprised of the twenty-two divine letters makes its first appearance in *Sefer Yetzirah* and was elaborated upon by nearly all, including the Lurianic, Kabbalists. Such linguistic mysticism is particularly evident in Vital's *Sefer Etz Chayyim* and among the Hasidim, in Schneur Zalman's *Tanya*.

69. The Zohar, for example, affirms: "He who 'keeps' the precepts of the Law and 'walks' in God's ways, if one may say so, 'makes' Him who is above" (Zohar III, 113a; Sperling and Simon, *The Zohar*, Vol. 5, p. 153). Moshe Idel has pointed out that this idea was quite widespread among the Kabbalists. For example, we read in the kabbalistic text *Sefer ha-Yichud*: "each and every one [of the people of Israel] ought to write a scroll of Torah for himself, and the occult secret [of this matter] is that he made God Himself" (quoted in Idel, *Kabbalah: New Perspectives*, p. 188).

70. The Zohar (183b–184a) explains:

There is no light except that which issues from darkness, for when the "Other Side" (*Sitra Achra*) is subdued, the Holy One is exalted in glory. In fact, there can be no true worship except it issue from darkness, and no

its fullest reality, which is "nothingness."[71] This is the doctrine of *coinciden-tia oppositorum* that is so basic in the Kabbalah.

The dialectical nature of the kabbalistic ideas is readily apparent. Indeed, dialectical thinking, in which presumably contradictory concepts critique and blend with one another until new, higher-order concepts emerge, is charac-teristic of the mythical imagination in general. According to Levi-Strauss, myths seek to reconcile and overcome binary oppositions that are present in the very structure of society.[72] Their purpose is to make what would otherwise be experienced as incoherence and contradiction, socially and intellectually tolerable. From a psychoanalytic point of view symbols that emerge in myth, very much like those that abound in dreams, follow the laws of what Freud called primary process thinking, in which contradictory and antinomous ideas are encompassed by a single word, image, or symbol. The Lurianic metaphors of the Breaking of the Vessels, the evil Husks, and the Restoration of the World express the idea that both the human soul and the cosmos embody such antinomies, and that they evolve precisely through a process in which contradictions are brought together and new, higher-order resolutions emerge.

Indeed each of the main kabbalistic symbols express part of the dialectical process, as they each embody an important philosophical or experiential antinomy and, when fully understood, a movement toward that antinomy's resolution. For example, in the symbol of the *Sefirot* the Kabbalists articulate and seek to resolve the contradiction between the simple unity of the Absolute and the apparent multiplicity of the world (the classical problem of "the one" and "the many"); in the symbol of the *Kellipot* (Husks), the antinomy between good and evil; in *Tzimtzum*, the chasm between being and nothingness; in *Adam Kadmon* (Primordial Man), the distance between God and man; and in the symbol of *Tikkun ha-Olam* (the Restoration of the World), the antinomy between theism (God created man) and atheism (man created God). Indeed, each of the kabbalistic symbols can

---

true good except it proceed from evil. And when a man enters upon an evil way and then forsakes it the Holy One is exalted in His glory . . . [Sperling and Simon, *The Zohar*, Vol. 4, p. 125].

71. For example, the Kabbalist David ben Abraham ha-Lavan (end of thirteenth century) held that God has: "more being than any other being in the world, but since it is simple, and all other simple things are complex when compared with its simplicity, so in comparison it is called 'nothing'" (quoted in Scholem, *Kabbalah*, p. 95).

72. Claude Levi-Strauss, *Structural Anthropology*, trans. Claire Jacobson and Brooke Grundfest (New York: Basic Books, 1963).

be understood as emerging dialectically, as a higher-order synthesis of an opposition (or contradiction) between traditional philosophical ideas, and, hence, as a "resolution" to a traditional philosophical problem. The problem of theodicy (of reconciling evil with the existence of God) can no longer arise, for example, once we speak the language of the Lurianic Kabbalah, because anyone who truly understands these symbols sees that what we call "evil" is in fact woven into the very essence of both creation (*Tzimtzum*) and redemption (*Tikkun*), the ultimate "Goods." (Regarding *Tzimtzum*, the Lurianists held that God could not create a world without first concealing or withdrawing His infinite presence, thereby introducing negation and evil into the world. With respect to *Tikkun*, the Kabbalists held that the acts that bring about the restoration of the world depend upon the overcoming, and hence the existence, of evil.)

The Kabbalah, then, organizes experience for us in a new way, one that transcends the traditional categories of philosophy and, further, cuts across the disciplines (e.g., philosophy, psychology, theology, ethics, and hermeneutics) that have traditionally addressed themselves to the human condition. If one is to understand the Kabbalah, one must stop thinking in terms of the traditional distinctions altogether. For example, the process of *Tikkun ha-Olam*, in which mankind is enjoined to "raise the sparks" of divine light that inhere within both his own soul and the world, is at once a psychological, theological, ethical, political, and mystical act. However, these traditional categories, while they can be helpful in one's initial approach to the Kabbalah, are ultimately like the ladders, described by Wittgenstein, that fall away once their purpose has been served.[73]

ACTIVISM AND QUIETISM

The dialectical nature of kabbalistic thought enabled the Kabbalists and Hasidim to transcend a fundamental religious and theological dichotomy, the distinction between "activism" and "quietism." This distinction is both a cardinal assumption in the study of mysticism and continues to have much relevance for contemporary religious life.[74]

---

73. Wittgenstein, *Tractatus Logico-Philosophicus* 6.54, p. 151.

74. This is a distinction that sees its modern equivalent in the distinction between political and psychological man.

A tension certainly exists in the Kabbalah between the activist, "this-worldly" tradition of Judaism and the quietist "otherworldly" tendencies that are common to nearly all forms of mysticism. However, as we shall see, this is a tension that is dialectically resolved in the kabbalistic notion of *Tikkun ha-Olam*, the repair and restoration of the world, a notion that literally implies active worldly engagement but that also implies the world's nullification or transcendence. The Kabbalist's dialectic is embodied in the image of the "raising of the sparks" that the Lurianists regarded as the most important symbol for *Tikkun*. Originally a Gnostic image that referred to the liberation of a spark of the deity that had been imprisoned in this lowly world in the form of man's soul, the "raising of the sparks" makes an inexplicable reappearance in the Lurianic Kabbalah, where it is understood both as a vehicle for transcending this world and as a liberation of divine procreative energy for correcting the faults and disharmonies within it. One who engages in *Tikkun ha-Olam* strives to both transcend and redeem every aspect of the present world.[75]

Nowhere is this dialectic more evident than among the contemporary Chabad (Lubavitch) Hasidim, whose efforts on behalf of numerous worldly causes are unremitting, but who regard these very efforts as completely in the service of bringing about the world to come.[76] Indeed, the founder of Chabad, Schneur Zalman of Lyadi, spoke of a twofold divine service. The

---

75. As we shall see the Kabbalists at times adopted a Gnostic formula of transcendence and escape, a tendency that led to the Lurianist's ascetic withdrawal from the world as well as to quietistic tendencies among the Hasidim. The tension between activism and escape from this world is a recurrent theme in the Kabbalah, one that was not completely resolved either within the Kabbalah or Hasidism. It is a tension that also, I might add, persists, in at least one contemporary secular heir to certain Kabbalistic and Hasidic traditions, psychoanalysis. As Philip Rieff has so eloquently argued, psychoanalysis has led to a "triumph of the therapeutic" in which the problems that were once thought to be correctable within the world are abandoned for conflicts that are now thought to be repairable only within the self (Phillip Rieff, *The Triumph of the Therapeutic* [Chicago: University of Chicago Press, 1966]). How to retain the insights and depth of mysticism and psychoanalysis without abandoning the world is a major issue for our own time. As we proceed, it will become evident how the Kabbalah provides us with some direction toward a solution.

76. As Idel points out, for Hasidism "extreme mystical experiences were often coupled with ritual acts performed for the sake of the community." In Hasidism there is a type of cultural *coincidentia oppositorum* in which the extremes of spiritualism and materialism are brought together and fused. "Hasidic masters would in most cases consider the mystical experience as a stage on the way toward another goal, namely

first entails a gnosticlike annihilation of both this world and the personal ego, and their eventual absorption within the Godhead; while the second involves an infusion of divine energy into the material world through mankind's religious service and worship: "Just as one annihilates oneself from Being to Nothingness, so too (divine light) is drawn down from above from Nothingness to Being, so that the light of the infinite may emanate truly below as it does above."[77]

KABBALAH AND PSYCHOANALYSIS

Several other contemporary modes of thought can shed interpretive light upon kabbalistic theosophy. In addition to deconstruction and dialectics, psychoanalysis, Jungian psychology, and studies in comparative religion and mysticism can provide important frameworks for the understanding, and further development, of kabbalistic symbols and ideas.

The relationship between Kabbalah and psychoanalysis has been a matter of interest since David Bakan's *Sigmund Freud and the Jewish Mystical Tradition* was published in 1958.[78] Unfortunately, Bakan lacked knowledge of even the most basic of kabbalistic symbols and ideas, and was completely unfamiliar with the Lurianic Kabbalah, the Kabbalah which is most readily comparable to psychoanalysis. Bakan's thesis that Freud was a crypto-Sabbatean, i.e., a follower of the kabbalistically inspired false messiah, Sabbatai Sevi, who arose in Poland in the sixteenth century,[79] was without any substantial warrant and did nothing to establish a genuine relationship between Kabbalah and psychoanalysis. Nevertheless, there are many fruitful parallels to be drawn between the Kabbalah and psychoanalytic ideas, and much to be gained by bringing a psychoanalytic perspective to the kabbalistic symbols. While a kabbalistic influence upon Freud has yet to be firmly

---

the return of the enriched mystic who becomes even more powerful and active in and for the group for which he is responsible." Indeed the theosophical Kabbalah has always held the welfare of the group to be more important than the mystical experience of any single individual. Idel, *Hasidism*, pp. 209–210.

77. Schneur Zalman, *Torah Or*, p. 58; quoted in Rachel Elior, *The Paradoxical Ascent to God: The Kabbalistic Theosophy of Habad Hasidism*, trans. J. M. Green (Albany: State University of New York Press 1993), p. 150.

78. David Bakan, *Sigmund Freud and the Jewish Mystical Tradition* (Boston: Beacon Press, 1971). Originally published in 1958.

79. On Sabbatai Sevi, see Scholem, *Sabbatai Sevi: The Mystical Messiah*.

established, the possibility of such influence through Freud's father, who was raised in a Hasidic environment, is certainly not to be discounted, as the Hasidim had transformed the Lurianic Kabbalah into a psychological theory that had application to the common man.[80]

If one examines the basic myth of the Lurianic Kabbalah from a psychoanalytic point of view, it becomes clear that the Kabbalah performs on the cosmic level much of what psychoanalytic theory posits for the individual man. Since the Kabbalists held that the microcosm (man) is a mirror of the macrocosm (God) the parallels between Luria and Freud were readily embodied in psychological form in the writings of the Hasidim; for example, those of the first Lubavitcher rebbe, Schneur Zalman of Lyadi.

As we have seen, according to Luria and his disciples, the source of all being whatsoever is the Infinite (*Ein-Sof*) whose energy or light (Or *Ein-Sof*) originally fills a unitary and undifferentiated universe. In order to create, and ultimately recognize itself through an "other" (i.e., a world), the infinite God must contract in upon itself (*Tzimtzum*), thereby opening a metaphysical space within which an "other" can subsist. Having done this, the Infinite proceeds to emanate structures of thought, feeling, and value (the *Sefirot*), which are, however, too weak and poorly integrated to hold the light or divine energy that they were meant to contain. This lack of integration also creates an instability in the erotic union of the masculine and feminine aspects of God. As a result of their own weakness and instability the sefirotic structures are shattered (*Shevirat ha-Kelim*); the feminine and the masculine are divided, and the shards resulting from the "Breaking of the Vessels" entrap sparks (*netzotzim*) of divine energy, alienating this energy from its source as it falls into the depths of the metaphysical void. These combinations of shards and sparks together form the "Husks" (*Kelippot*) that are the substance of the *Sitra Achra* or "Other Side," a nether realm that is the source of malcontent and evil, but that is completely parasitic upon the sparks of alienated divine energy that it contains. It is, according to the Lurianic scheme, man's divinely appointed task to extract (*birur*) the divine light entrapped both within the world and his own soul, and through the process of *Tikkun* (restoration) return these sparks to their source in the infinite God, where they can restore the unity between "male and female" and participate in the divine purpose and plan.

Especially when one considers that the Kabbalists, and particularly the

---

80. I discuss the issue of Freud's relationship to Kabbalah and Hasidism at length in my book *Kabbalistic Metaphors*.

Hasidim, held that the cosmic process I have just described is reenacted within the soul and life of man, the parallels with psychoanalysis become startlingly clear. Like the Lurianic Kabbalah, psychoanalysis posits a source of sexual/erotic energy, the libido, as the foundation of all human thought, action, value, and being. It too holds that the source of this energy, the human psyche, must withdraw or contract (via "repression") to create a (representational) world of images, fantasies, dreams, and ideas. Such images and ideas are regarded as modifications of the libido itself, and originally form systems or structures (e.g., the ego and superego) meant to contain the libidinous energy. These structures, however, are too poorly integrated to contain the energy and permit its uninterrupted flow, and consequently they break down, with the result that portions of the individual's libido are cut off from their source and are no longer available to serve his or her ends. This alienated libido not only creates an interruption in man's erotic activity, but is itself, as it were, entrapped in neurotic complexes (akin to the Kabbalist's *Kelippot*), and thereby comes to exist in the nether realm of the individual's unconscious, which is analogous to the *Sitra Achra*. For Freud, these unconscious complexes are the source of neurotic misery and maladaptive behavior, yet they are completely parasitic upon the quantums of libidinous energy that they, through an act of repression, entrap and contain, just as the *Kellipot* are parasitic on the entrapped sparks of God. Psychoanalytic therapy enjoins the individual to undo the repressions that maintain his or her neurosis, to thereby liberate the individual's entrapped libido and, as it were, return this libido to its source in "desire" so it can again serve the individual's consciously chosen ends. This act is akin to the Lurianic conception of Tikkun, as the "extraction" and "raising" of the holy sparks.

While the form of this brief presentation may obscure some important differences between the Lurianic Kabbalah and psychoanalysis, the parallels are immediately striking. It is hard to understand how Gershom Scholem, whose scholarly career emerged amidst the *Weltanschauung* of psychoanalysis, and who was undoubtedly more than familiar with Freudian ideas, should make no study or even comment on these parallels, either in his writings on the Lurianic Kabbalah, nor (even more remarkably) in his monumental study of Sabbatai Sevi, the psychologically disturbed false messiah who emerged from within a Lurianic milieu in sixteenth-century Poland.[81]

---

81. For example, Scholem, in his work *Sabbatai Sevi: The Mystical Messiah*, relates that "the sources suggest with almost absolute certainty that Sabbatai suffered

Scholem does, however, correctly acknowledge that the Kabbalah itself embodies a dynamic, living reality, which is likely to reassert itself in those times when the spontaneous, emotional, and the symbolical are suppressed in favor of the purely intellectual: "The more the philosophers and theologians strove to formulate a unity which negates and eliminates all symbols, the greater became the danger of a counter-attack in favor of the living God, who, like all living forces, speaks in symbols."[82] Yet Scholem fails to acknowledge the obvious psychoanalytic implications of even his own view, which put quite simply, understands the Kabbalah itself as a return of the repressed, i.e., as a symbolic representation of repressed emotion, spirituality, or libido, whose energy he sought to liberate (or kabbalistically, whose spark he sought to raise) for a new generation. The identification of the Kabbalah itself with the "repressed libido of Judaism" is given further support when we consider the Kabbalists' attitude toward human (and divine) sexuality. For example, in the Zohar we find the views that the conjugal relationship between man and woman is itself holy, because it reflects the relations between God and the *Shekhinah* (his feminine aspect); that man and woman are only "half a body" until they are united in conjugal bliss; that all souls, before they descend into the physical world, are essentially bisexual; that a couple should attempt to coordinate their intercourse with the precise time of intercourse in the "upper world"; and that kissing with the mouth is a union of a couple's souls prior to their physical union in sexual intercourse.[83]

---

from a manic-depressive psychosis," and provides several pages of discussion on this. However, there is no mention of Freud or psychoanalysis anywhere in this work. Nor is there any discussion of psychoanalysis in Scholem's *Major Trends, On the Kabbalah, The Kabbalah,* or *On the Mystical Shape of the Godhead,* trans. Joachim Neugroschel (New York: Schocken, 1991). Scholem is said to have dismissed psychoanalysis on the grounds that he knew several psychological myths, each of which were far more interesting than Freud's. Scholem seemed to show some more affinity to Jung. Nevertheless he felt:

> In treating the history and world of the Kabbalah, using the conceptual terminology of psychoanalysis—either the Freudian or Jungian version—did not seem fruitful to me. Even though I should have had a strong affinity to Jung's concepts, which were close to religious concepts, I refrained from using them. [Quoted in David Biale, *Gershom Scholem,* p. 69]

82. Scholem, *On the Kabbalah,* p. 89.
83. See Tishby and Lachower, *The Wisdom of the Zohar* III, Part VI, Sect. II. (Conjugal Life), pp. 1355–1406.

In Luria we find the view that in performing acts of *Tikkun ha-Olam* humanity provides the "feminine waters" for restoring the unity between the masculine and feminine aspects of God.

Like the relationship between Kabbalah and contemporary philosophy, the connection between the Kabbalah and psychoanalysis has simply never been carefully examined. When one considers that an authority no less formidable than Carl Jung held that a full understanding of psychoanalysis "would carry us . . . into the subterranean workings of Hasidism . . . and then into the intricacies of the Kabbalah which still remain unexplored psychologically,"[84] we can hardly ignore the points of contact between these apparently diverse disciplines. Apart from the remarkable theoretical coincidence between the Kabbalah and psychoanalysis, I will argue that many of the concepts of the Kabbalah can be best understood by the contemporary reader through a comparison with the basic metaphors of psychoanalysis (e.g., the unconscious, libido, the repressed) or with the peculiar phenomena (neurosis, dreams) with which psychoanalysis deals. Further, since the Kabbalah is never reluctant to draw metaphysical, axiological, and ontological conclusions from what are essentially psychoanalytic ideas, psychoanalysts who study the Kabbalah are in a position to comprehend a view of the entire cosmos that is highly compatible with their own understanding of man.

PSYCHOLOGICAL HERMENEUTICS IN THE KABBALAH

It is important to note in this context that a psychological perspective is to be found among the Kabbalists and Hasidim themselves, who held the human mind to be a mirror and, in some respects, the very origin of the theosophical realm.[85]

For example, one of the earliest Kabbalists, Azriel of Gerona (early thirteenth century), held that the energy of the human soul derives from the heavenly *Sefirot*, the ten archetypes through which God expresses himself in creation, and he equated each *Sefirah* with a psychological power or physical

---

84. Letter: Carl Jung to Edith Schroder, April 1957. In Carl Jung, *Letters*, Vol. 2, ed. Gerhard Adler (Princeton, NJ: Princeton University Press 1975), pp. 358–359. This comment was made at a stage in Jung's career when he had achieved a clearly positive view of Judaism and, in particular, Jewish mysticism.

85. See Idel, *Kabbalah: New Perspectives*, pp. 146–153, and Idel, "Psychologization of Theosophy in Kabbalah and Hasidism," in Idel, *Hasidism*, pp. 227–238.

organ in man.[86] An even more radical viewpoint was advocated by R. Meir ibn Gabbay (1480–1540), who interpreted an ancient Midrash to mean that God's anthropomorphic structure was itself copied from a human original![87] Even among the Lurianists, with their emphasis upon the theosophical structure of the Godhead and divine worlds, we find the doctrine that the *Sefirot* are mirrored in man's body and soul.

The notion that the divine macrocosm is mirrored in the mind of man was actually emphasized by the founders of the Hasidic movement, who can be said to have "psychologized" the Lurianic Kabbalah for their numerous disciples. For example, R. Jacob Joseph of Polonnoye (1704–1794) stated in the name of the Baal Shem Tov (1700–1760), the founder of Hasidism, that the ten *Sefirot* appear in man as a result of a divine contraction, whereby the deity progressively instantiates himself in a series of personal structures until, upon reaching man, he (and man himself) is called Microcosmos (*Olam Katan*).[88] Rabbi Dov Baer, the Maggid of Mezrich (1704–1772), who succeeded the Baal Shem Tov as the leader of the early Hasidic movement, taught "that everything written in (Vital's) *Sefer Etz Chayyim* (the major exposition of the Lurianic Kabbalah) also exists in the world and in man."[89] The Maggid went so far as to hold that the very significance of divine thought is contingent upon this thought making its appearance in the mind of man. Like Jung, who was later to expound a similar view regarding the "collective unconscious," the Maggid held that the Godhead has a hidden life within the mind of man.[90]

JUNG'S APPROACH

It is important, however, to both compare and distinguish the Hasidic point of view from that of Jung, who took a lively interest in the Kabbalah, and

86. Scholem, *Origins of the Kabbalah*, p. 95.

87. Ibid., p. 176.

88. Rabbi Jacob Joseph of Polonnoye, *Toldot Ya'akov Yoseph*, fol. 86a, quoted and translated in Idel, *Kabbalah: New Perspectives*, p. 150 (see also p. 352, note 366).

89. Maggid, Dov Baer of Mezrich, *Or ha-Emet* (Light of Truth), fol. 36 c–d. Quoted and translated in Idel, *Kabbalah: New Perspectives*, p. 15.

90. Rifka Schatz-Uffenheimer, *Hasidism As Mysticism: Quietistic Elements In Eighteenth-Century Hasidic Thought* (Jerusalem: Hebrew University, 1993), p. 207. Also see Rabbi Schneur Zalman's commentary in *Likutei Amarim-Tanya*, Chapter 36, p. 163.

regarded it as one of a series of expressions of man's "collective unconscious." Jung focused the greatest part of his attention on Gnosticism and alchemy, each of which he understood to be mythological or metaphysical expressions of man's quest to regain awareness and unity with an alienated, unconscious self.[91] The alchemists, in their material efforts to extract gold from base metals, and the Gnostics who earlier engaged in metaphysical efforts to release the divine spark contained within each human soul, were predecessors, on Jung's view, to contemporary depth psychologists who assist patients in their quest to regain awareness of the "spark" or "gold" of their unconscious minds.[92] Kabbalah, as I have intimated, performs an analogous task with respect to the *Kelippot*, which bind the human soul; and it is presumably an awareness of Freud's own Jewish/Hasidic background that led Jung to remark that Freud's discovery would find its origins in a Jewish version of the archetypal depth-psychology myth.[93]

My own view is that Jung is largely correct, and that moreover, had he focused greater attention on the Kabbalah, he would have indeed found a far more congenial predecessor to depth psychology than Gnosticism.[94] Gnosticism, while clearly sharing many of the Kabbalah's symbols and ideas, is decidedly dualistic and otherworldly. The Gnostics' "raising of the sparks" (unlike the analogous process in the Lurianic Kabbalah) is an effort to escape from an evil world of matter and history, which for Gnosticism is completely irredeemable. The Kabbalah, on the other hand, seeks a restoration of this world, much as depth psychology pursues a therapy for *this* life; and it interprets its symbols, for example, its raising of the sparks, in a manner that

---

91. Jung's writing on Gnosticism are conveniently collected with commentary in Robert A. Segal, ed., *The Gnostic Jung* (Princeton, NJ: Princeton University Press, 1992). His views on alchemy are found in a number of his works, including *Aion* (1951), *Psychology and Alchemy* (1944), *Alchemical Studies* (1929–1945), and *Mysterium Coniunctionis* (1955–1956), which constitute Volumes 9 (Part II), 12, 13, and 14 of *The Collected Works of C. G. Jung* (Princeton, NJ: Bollingen Series, Princeton University Press, 1953–1964). See References for complete citations.

92. Carl Jung, "Gnostic Symbols of the Self," in *Aion: Researches Into the Phenomenology of the Self, The Collected Works of C. G. Jung*, Vol. 9. Part II, trans. R. F. C. Hull (Princeton, NJ: Princeton University Press, 1969), pp. 184–221. Reprinted in Segal, *The Gnostic Jung*, 55–91.

93. Carl Gustav Jung, *Letters*, Vol. 2, pp. 358–359.

94. See my "Jung and the Kabbalah," in *History of Psychology* 2:2 (May 1999), pp. 102–118.

brings holiness into this world rather than prompting man to escape. Moreover, in Hasidism, we have a phenomenon in which the psychologization of the metaphysical symbols of the Kabbalah has already occurred. There is no such analogous process with respect to Gnosticism (or alchemy, for that matter) and Jung is forced to produce one himself.

It is in the interpretation of this psychologization process where I (as would the Hasidim) part from the Jungian approach. For Jung, when the Gnostics talk, for example, about God, they are *really*, though *not knowingly*, talking about the unconscious, and when they relate their myths of creation, they are *really*, though *not knowingly*, describing the development of the human psyche or "Self." Although Jung himself denies that there are any metaphysical implications to his work,[95] the thrust of his basic approach to Gnosticism is to reduce Gnostic theology to psychology. A Jungian approach to the Kabbalah would, of course, perform a similar reduction; a reduction that follows from Jung's theory of the psychological development of mankind. According to Jung, man has proceeded through four stages of development, the primitive, ancient, modern and contemporary, each stage marking a step toward the evolution of a fully independent ego. While primitives completely identify themselves with their environment, and ancients (whose egos are somewhat sturdier) project their unconscious onto the gods, moderns reject their unconscious altogether, attempting to live their entire lives on the plain of consciousness and reason.[96] Recognizing the

---

95. Jung's denials are sprinkled throughout his works and letters. For example, in his introduction to *Mysterium Coniunctionis*, 1955, p. vii, he states:

> I do not go in for either metaphysics or theology, but am concerned with psychological facts as the borderline of the knowable. So if I make use of certain expressions that are reminiscent of the language of theology, this is done solely to the poverty of language and not because I am of the opinion that the subject matter of theology is the same as that of psychology. Psychology is very definitely not a theology; it is a natural science that seeks to describe experienceable psychic phenomena . . . But as empirical science it has neither the capacity nor the competence to describe any truth or value, this being the prerogative of theology. [Carl Gustav Jung, *Mysterium Coniunctionis. The Collected Works of C. G. Jung*, Vol. 14, trans. R. F. C. Hull (Princeton, NJ: Princeton University Press, 1963).]

96. See Segal, *The Gnostic Jung*, pp. 11, 19. Also, Erich Neumann, *The Origins and History of Consciousness*, trans. R. F. C. Hull (Princeton, NJ: Princeton University Press, 1970).

emptiness and futility of the modern project of denying the unconscious, certain "contemporaries" (of Jung's) seek to reintegrate into their psyches what the ancients projected and the moderns denied. Jung's psychological analysis is extremely insightful, yet his metaphysical prejudices are clear: while the ancients are, in effect, "superior" to moderns in their recognition (through myths and religion) of the importance of the unconscious, they are misplaced in projecting the archetypes of the collective unconscious onto the gods and world. From a Jungian point of view the myths of Gnosticism and (by extension) Kabbalah have psychological but no ontological significance: they are not about the world but are rather about the psyche of man.

The Kabbalists and Hasidim are clear in their rejection of the Jungian reduction. While they themselves recognized the psychological implications of their theosophical concepts they maintained that these implication were a function of the mutual reciprocity or mirroring of the microcosm and macrocosm. Unlike the Gnostics who understood their myths in cosmological terms, and unlike Jung who understood them psychologically, the Kabbalists refused to give priority to either cosmos or mind. Like the philosophers of India, of Sankhya, Yoga, and Vedanta, the Kabbalists held that cosmos and psyche, divinity and soul are essentially one. The workings of man's mind give us as much insight into the nature of the world, as man's myths about the world provide insight into the nature of his mind. Although I have great respect for the Jungian point of view, and believe that the entire Lurianic dialectic can be understood in archetypal psychological terms, my position in this work is to take the Kabbalists at their word; when they speak about the deity I assume that, at least on one level, it is the deity to which they refer.

COMPARATIVE STUDIES

There is one contribution of the Jungian approach to the study of religion that, if it has not been completely ignored, has been underutilized in the study of the Kabbalah: the comparative study of divergent mystical traditions. One of Jung's core assumptions, expressed in the concept of the "collective unconscious," is that common themes and archetypes underlie religious phenomena separated widely in both space and time. As such Jungians seek out symbolic and thematic similarities even among those religions in which there is little or no reason to suppose any historical connection. This point of view, however, has been implicitly rejected by the vast majority of Kabbalah scholars, who do so out of either a religious conviction in the uniqueness of Jewish revelation; or, following the lead of Scholem, out of a commitment to detailed textual analysis and historical research. As such, the study of the Kabbalah has been somewhat myopic: the fascinating parallels between Jewish and Indian mysticism and theosophy, for example, have been for the most part ignored. One need not follow Jung in his hypotheses of a collective unconscious and archetypes to recognize the value of such comparative studies in our own contemporary quest for insight into Jewish mysticism. Here I simply wish to provide a brief example of how such comparative studies can provide us with insight into the Kabbalah itself.

A remarkable parallel is to be found between the kabbalistic symbol of *Kelippot* (Husks) and the concept of *karma*, found in Jainism and in virtually all the other spiritual traditions of India. The parallel is to be found in the fact that each of these notions involve the symbol of a spark or crystal of divine light, which is understood to be the individual's true or Godly self and which is enclosed by layers of darkness (*Kelippot* in Kabbalah, *lesyas* (colors) in Jainism) that weigh down and otherwise prevent the self from achieving its divine fulfillment. It is, of course, an intriguing if highly speculative possibility that the concepts under discussion were mediated from India to Judaism via a chain that included Gnosticism, but this is not the point I wish to pursue here.

What is interesting in this context is the *differing* accounts of the origin of *Kelippot* and *karma* respectively in the Kabbalah and Jainism. As we have seen, for the Kabbalists the *Kelippot* have their origin in a cosmic catastrophe, the Breaking of the Vessels, in which the value archetypes that originally constituted creation shatter, and the resulting shards fall through the metaphysical void, carrying with them sparks of divine light. The theory of karma, on the other hand, posits that the darkness (*lesyas*) that shrouds and encumbers one's inner self is a product of the individual's own behavior. A man, in performing any action, but most particularly an act like killing, which violates the actor's moral code, obscures and darkens his own life monad, making the possibility of his redemption more difficult and remote.

Upon first learning of the similarity between *karma* and *Kelippot* one might be inclined to the conclusion that the divergent accounts of their respective origins (one cosmic, the other psychological) renders the connection between these concepts superficial. However, upon closer examination we discover, for example, that the Kabbalists and Hasidism regard each individual as personally responsible for the *birur* or extraction of his spark from the Husks; and that a man's actions either serve to aid in this redemptive process or increase the power, darkness, and grip of the "Other Side." As put by the eighteenth-century Kabbalist, Moses Chayyim Luzzatto, "when man sins he gives the husk the power to seize the Upper Degrees, and he is himself punished by it. Conversely, when man expels the husk from himself he is rewarded."[97] Looked at more closely, the doctrine of *Kelippot* shines with a new discernible "*karmic* light." This *karmic* or psychological understanding of the *Kelippot* is strengthened by our knowledge that in the Kabbalah (as in Indian philosophy) the microcosm (man) is said to perfectly mirror the macrocosm (the divine) and the shattering of value archetypes that produce the *Kelippot* on the cosmic level is repeated in each individual psyche or soul. It is, indeed, when we shatter our values by immoral and unethical conduct that our true self becomes obscured and our divine spark dimmed.

Other examples of the philosophical usefulness of comparative study of the Kabbalah are to be found in the comparisons between the Kabbalah and Gnosticism, Platonism, and the philosophy of Hegel. Indeed, it is my view that the Kabbalah, whose symbolism is, for the uninitiated, somewhat remote and obscure, can best be understood by the modern reader precisely through the comparative studies that are notable for their absence in this field.[98]

THE NATURE OF MYTH AND THE KABBALISTIC SYMBOLS

We are now in a better position to make some general remarks about kabbalistic symbolism. In doing so an attempt will be made to strike a balance between dynamic and philosophical interpretations of the mystical metaphors.

We have seen that an important characteristic of Jewish mysticism is what Idel has called its *dynamic character*. According to Idel, whose views on this matter are set in apparently deliberate opposition to those (previously quoted) of Ricouer, "A kabbalistic symbol invited one to act rather than to think." This, Idel argues, is implicit in the very nature of the kabbalistic theosophy: the *Sefirot*, for example, were not seen as existing in "frozen perfection within the deity," but rather "as living human activity." For Idel,

---

97. Luzzatto, *General Principles of the Kabbalah*, p. 59.

98. Such comparative studies serve as the implicit, and at times explicit, background of this work. Readers interested in more detailed comparative studies are referred to my book, *Kabbalistic Metaphors.*

the dynamism of theosophical symbols is far more important than their "disclosure of a hidden realm of existence."[99] It is this dynamism that gives the kabbalistic myths their passion and life.

Idel's viewpoint echoes a more general viewpoint on "myth," which sees it as having a function that is completely other than that of philosophy. According to Alasdair MacIntyre:

> The subject matter of mythological narratives is no different from that of later philosophy and science; what differentiates myth from these is not merely its narrative form or its use of personification. It is rather that a myth is living or dead, not true or false. You cannot refute a myth because as soon as you treat it as refutable, you do not treat it as a myth but as hypothesis or history.[100]

For both MacIntyre and Idel the value of a myth is that it tallies, resonates, or awakens something that is alive in our psyche or soul. It does this irrespective of its "truth value" in terms of objective logic or science. We should note, however, that to the extent that a myth does resonate in our soul, or move us to change our lives, we are inclined to say that it expresses an essential "truth." Indeed, it can be said, for example, that a psychoanalytic or psychotherapeutic metaphor works in a similar fashion. An interpretation is either "alive" or "dead" for the patient at any given point in the treatment, and hence serves as a "myth" in the context of his personal life narrative. However, both analyst and patient are clearly inclined to describe such a valuable interpretation as a form of "truth."

The word "truth" is a term of *value*, one that the philosopher, the poet, the scientist, and the mystic each wish to claim as his own. To define "truth" in such a way that the mythical and mystical are excluded from its domain is perhaps enlightening at first, but is ultimately pernicious, for it removes from the mystic, the poet, and the mythologist any possibility of making knowledge claims for the results of their inquiry.[101] The Kabbalist wants, in fact, to

---

99. Idel, *Kabbalah: New Perspectives*, pp. 223–225.

100. Alasdair MacIntyre, "Myth," *The Encyclopedia of Philosophy*, Vol. 5, ed. Paul Edwards (New York: Macmillan, 1967), p. 435.

101. A point made eminently clear by Mary Hesse in "The Cognitive Claims of Metaphor" (in *Metaphor and Religion*, ed. J. P. Van Noppen (Brussels: n.p. 1984). Hesse holds that metaphor, of which myth is one important example, should be included within the categories of meaning, knowledge, and truth. The failure to do

say that his inquiry reveals a truth, a knowledge that, albeit different from that of the scientist or logician, is in some sense "deeper" and more valuable. Indeed, part of his claim is that his truth is superior precisely because it is "alive" in the sense we have just described.

"Truth," in its deepest sense, must encompass life; that is, it must stir man's soul and perhaps even transform him in the process. Man is not a purely cognitive being. Indeed, his very cognitions are determined by the passions that move him to think and act along certain "routes of interest." A myth is a narrative structure that enters into and evokes passion, action, and interest. It is not content to travel along the paths of intellect and cognition, which are the reinvested products of such interest. A myth is essentially *the dream, and the dream's interpretation*, and not simply the interpretation alone. It embraces both ego and id, conscious and unconscious, heart and mind. Dialectically, we might go so far to say that the Kabbalah, as myth, makes no truth claims as history in the sense described by MacIntyre; but that it is, by virtue of its dynamic character, a discipline that nonetheless reveals "truth" to those who participate in it.

Kabbalah, however, as we have already seen, is more than simply "mythology." It is myth and speculation, poetry and philosophy, metaphor and reason, woven into a discipline that invites passion, action, and idea. It is of course, a discipline that dare not become too articulated and final; if so, it would cut off the very wellspring of symbolic possibilities that gives myth, metaphor, (and language itself) its very life and meaning. Indeed, it is this very reinterpretability that, according to Idel, gives the Kabbalah its unique character. For Idel:

---

so leads to the distorted elevation of science over all other avenues of human inquiry. In a critique of Hesse's position, Richard Rorty ("Hesse and Davidson on Metaphor") follows the views of Donald Davidson and counters that metaphors have no meaning other than their literal one and their power lies not in their capacity to open up new vistas of truth or meaning but rather in the fact that they cause us to change our actions, beliefs and desires. For Rorty, a metaphor "dies" when its meaning is articulated, i.e., when it becomes a vehicle of knowledge. The Davidson-Rorty view of metaphor is, one might observe, the philosophical foundation for Idel's view that the Kabbalistic symbols invite action rather than represent truths and ideas. My own view, as I believe is evident in these pages, is that metaphor is both a call to (or cause of) action and a source of wisdom or gnosos, and that a dialectical relationship exists between these two modes (the ethical and the epistemological) in the Kabbalah as it does everywhere else. Each is prior to and foundational for the other. Practice is both prior to and dependent upon truth and knowledge.

the main aspect of the sefirotic realm is not its "indescribability" or "inexpressibility" as Scholem conceives it, but rather it dynamism. . . . Symbols are necessary precisely because several aspects of the ever-changing system need to be expressed, not because the revealed aspect of divinity is beyond expression in conceptual terms owing to its transcendence.[102]

So Idel, in his polemic with Scholem, comes full circle. Kabbalah is dynamic, and neither ineffable nor philosophical, but its dynamism itself leads to a form of epistemic revelation: "like a magic ball that remains always the same although reflecting varied moving lights, so the text of the Torah or Zohar enables us to perceive an ever-changing reality."[103] The symbols of the Kabbalah are akin to what the philosopher J. N. Findlay once spoke of as "iridescent concepts," showing us changing and sometimes contrasting images, depending upon the perspective we take upon them. That these symbols are iridescent should not deter us from treating them as instruments of knowledge. Rather than place the Kabbalah outside the sphere of truth, perhaps we need to understand "truth" in such a manner that the magic ball is the very vehicle of its expression.

The problem of providing a general definition of kabbalistic symbolism is essentially coextensive with the question of defining the Kabbalah itself, a question that, owing to the very nature of the subject matter, is impossible. For the Kabbalah objects of theosophical or philosophical interest cannot be defined a *priori*, but must be understood as evolving along with our own understanding of them. This is especially true for the definition of kabbalistic symbols, for the mystical symbol is the very vehicle for understanding the relationship among God, world, and man, a relationship that is itself always in flux and always incomplete. It is this difficulty of defining the mystical symbol that, I suppose, may have moved Scholem to affirm that "the mystical symbol is an expressible representation of something which lies beyond the sphere of expression and communication."[104] However, we have already seen how this view fails precisely because it cuts short all rational inquiry into the Kabbalah and makes kabbalistic knowledge a contradiction in terms.

Idel fares somewhat better than Scholem. He rejects the notion that symbols lack cognitive significance and that they simply provide an experi-

---

102. Idel, *Kabbalah: New Perspectives*, p. 231.
103. Ibid., p. 232.
104. Scholem, *Major Trends*, p. 27.

ential window into the inexpressible. However, like Scholem, Idel plays down the mythical symbol's epistemic potential. For Idel, kabbalistic symbols "strove to induce an active mood or approach to reality rather than invoke contemplation." While rejecting the notion that there can be a single view on the nature of kabbalistic symbolism, Idel adopts the following general definition of "symbol" from Erwin Goodenough: "an object or a pattern, which, whatever the reason may be, operates upon men, and causes effects in them, beyond mere recognition of what is literally presented in the given term."[105] Such a definition is extremely broad and not very informative, as its terms (e.g., "operates," "effects") are themselves vague and appear to conflate the concept of symbol with "connotative meaning." On this definition, everything meaningful, all objects, patterns, and words, would be symbolic. While I have no quarrel with this implication, I believe more can be said about the nature of symbols in general and kabbalistic symbols in particular than either the Scholem or Goodenough/Idel definitions would allow.

A symbol, as we normally understand one, is neither a thing, a word, an image, a feeling, nor a concept. It is, we might say, a vehicle through which we relate to ourselves and the world; one that is indefinitely wide in its range of applications and that connects itself to a range of ideas, affect, images, and words. This is why it is possible for many symbols to be expressed in art, molded into icons, articulated in poetry, and felt deeply in one's heart. While many symbols are intrinsically connected to a single image (e.g., the scales of justice, the American eagle), and others are elaborations upon the natural or social world ("the sun," "the king"), other symbols, including most of those that are of interest in the Kabbalah, have a more limited connection with specific images (e.g., "the raising of the sparks") or are more closely associated with feelings and/or ideas (the *Sefirot*). Nevertheless, symbols have a tendency to reach into all aspects of human endeavor, and naturally invoke expression in art, articulation in thought, and realization in action. A symbol is, one might say, a "pivot" around which the world is organized in its intellective, connative, and volitional dimensions.

How are symbols created? Ernst Cassirer, in his *Philosophy of Symbolic Forms*, argues that man, by his very nature, is a symbolic creature.[106] This is true enough, but perhaps it fails to go to the very heart of the matter.

---

105. Idel, *Kabbalah: New Perspectives*, p. 233.
106. Ernst Cassirer, *The Philosophy of Symbolic Forms*, Vols. 1–3, trans. Ralph

Symbols, it seems, are equiprimordial with both man and his world; indeed they reflect the archetypical relationship of man to the natural world (e.g., the symbols of the sun, moon, water, fire, etc.) or of man to man (the king, the fool, the "golden maiden") or man to the world of the spirit (angels and devils, crosses, mandalas, and stars, etc.). Indeed, we might go so far as to say that symbols are, in effect, the way in which *being-in-itself* is mediated for human consciousness. In this sense, they are the very structure of reality. It is even almost misleading to say that symbols are created by man; they evolve with him and are the very meaning structures in which man finds himself. To the extent that man creates them, they arise spontaneously from his partly unconscious relationship with "the world" (which is itself also a symbol) as condensations of vast plenums of significance. Since they are the very "world" within which he exists, symbols are the closest man comes to experiencing divine creation.

Symbols are like *food* for the human psyche. They are food in the sense that making sense of things is satisfying. Indeed, we might call symbols the ultimate consumable, as they are what the human psyche or soul needs to be a psyche at all. Unlike the terms of science, symbols organize reality in a manner that is commensurate with our psychological being. It is through symbols that man comes to know both himself and his world. And it is through reflecting upon symbols and attempting to explicate their meaning from a range of *perspectives* (which was, as we shall see, the essential practice of the theosophical Kabbalists) that we can hope to develop a satisfactory and comprehensive worldview.

BASIC METAPHORS

Among all the wealth and variety of symbolic forms there exists a class of symbols that I would call "basic" or "fundamental."[107] A basic symbol or

---

Mannheim (New Haven: Yale University Press, 1953, 1955, 1957). Originally published in Berlin, 1923, 1925, 1929.

107. Philosophers have long argued about the possibility of arriving at a single unique "basic metaphor." Derrida, for example, has argued that the "dream of philosophy" is to reduce all metaphors to "one 'central,' 'fundamental,' 'principal' metaphor" through which all metaphors would come to an end through "the assured legibility of the proper." (Derrida, *Margins of Philosophy*, p. 268.) This, of course, was the project of Hegel, who persuasively argued that his dialectical view of history and

metaphor is "basic" in the sense that it encompasses within itself the totality of being, and explains all things. A basic metaphor organizes everything around itself. The symbols of the Kabbalah are basic in this sense. Unlike natural symbols such as "fire," or manmade symbols such as "the automobile," the symbolic system represented in the Kabbalah, and particularly in the Lurianic myths, provides us with a metaphor that grants insight into everything whatsoever; the creation of the world, the role of man in the cosmos, the significance of our daily tasks of living. The symbols of the *Sefirot*, the "broken vessels," the "raising of the sparks," etc., are part of a mythical system which addresses itself not only to the core of reality, but to the very nature of thought itself.

There are other basic metaphors; Heraclitus' "flux" is one, the Gnostics' war between two cosmic powers is another. The danger of most basic metaphors, however, is that they tend to be so general that they cease to inform. The fascination of the Kabbalah and, particularly, the Lurianic myth, is that this myth is completely general and yet very specific at the same time. It organizes everything around itself, but not in an obvious manner, and as such it tells us something new about both ourselves and the world. It is incumbent upon us to decipher its message in a manner that is comprehensible in our own place and time.

---

philosophy (one that as we shall see is remarkably similar to that of the Kabbalists) was a basic metaphor in this sense. I make no such absolutist claim here for the Kabbalah, and am content to treat the Lurianic metaphor as one basic metaphor among others, and to allow it to rest upon its own intrinsic persuasiveness or appeal.

2

Ein-Sof[1]: The Dialectic of the Infinite

saac Luria, whose ideas are reported to us in the writings of his disciples, was once asked why it was that he himself never recorded his teachings in writing. "It is impossible," he is said to have replied, "because all things are related; I can hardly open my mouth to speak without feeling as though the sea burst and its dams had overflowed."[2] Anyone attempting to explain the kabbalistic deity, particularly as it is understood by the Lurianists, cannot help but identify with Luria's own reluctance, for the Kabbalists' God embodies a vast array of aspects, each of which (e.g., *Ein-Sof* (The Infinite), *Tzimtzum* (divine concealment, contraction), *ha-Olomot* (Worlds), *Sitra Achra* (the "Other Side"), etc.) are comprehensible only in reference to the others. Further, the God of the Kabbalah only achieves His identity through a dialectical evolution, part of which involves His comprehension and completion by mankind. A full understanding of this God requires, in effect, a thorough knowledge of (and participation in) each of the kabbalistic symbols, as well as a commitment to the very restorative acts (*Tikkunim*) through which humanity is said to complete both God and creation.

This chapter, which paints a portrait of the kabbalistic deity in broad strokes, must ultimately be placed within the context of a fuller knowledge of

---

1. Literally "without end."
2. Scholem, *Major Trends*, p. 254.

each of the major kabbalistic symbols (which will be presented in subsequent chapters). Here, however, I will focus in some detail upon certain more conceptual or philosophical aspects of kabbalistic theosophy. My discussion is centered upon the Kabbalah of Luria, but will also make reference to the Zohar and the earlier theosophical Kabbalists who preceded Luria, as well as to the Hasidim who are his heirs.

As we proceed with our discussion it will become apparent that for the Kabbalists *Ein-Sof* has no static, definable form. Instead, the deity is conceived of as evolving through, and thus embodying, a number of distinct stages and aspects, with later stages opposing but at the same time encompassing earlier ones. The Kabbalists' God is both perfectly simple and infinitely complex, nothing and everything, hidden and revealed, reality and illusion, creator of man and created by man, etc. As *Ein-Sof* evolves it is progressively revealed as "nothing whatsoever" (*Ayin*), the totality of being, the Infinite Will (*Ratzon*), Thought and Wisdom, the embodiment of all value and significance (the *Sefirot*), the wedding of male and female, and ultimately, the union of all contradictions. As we shall see, *Ein-Sof* is both the totality of this dialectic and each of the points along the way. *Ein-Sof* must be constantly redefined, as by its very nature, it is in a constant process of self-creation and redefinition. This self-creation is actually embodied and perfected in the creativity of humanity, which through its practical, ethical, intellectual, and spiritual activities strives to redeem and perfect an antinimous and imperfect world.

Insofar as is possible my exposition is designed to mirror the evolution of the deity itself; for like Hegel, centuries later, the Kabbalists held that the dialectic of thought is paralleled in a dialectic of God and the world. It should be remembered, however, that the development of *Ein-Sof* is not strictly an evolution in time. It has both temporal and atemporal aspects and is repeated *ad infinitum* throughout creation.[3]

---

3. According to Vital, *Ein-Sof* is timeless but its manifestations are temporal. *Adam Kadmon* and the worlds were created in time. "All of the worlds were created, expanded, and developed, with one coming along after the other at different times, each one later than the other, until it came to the time for this world to be created." *Sefer Etz Chayyim* 1:1, p. 21; Menzi and Padeh, *The Tree of Life*, p. 7. Nevertheless, such metaphysical events as the *Tzimtzim* and the Breaking of the Vessels are embodied in all things and all times. This issue is provided further discussion later in this chapter in the section "God Is Dialectically Evolving."

THE HIDDEN, UNKNOWABLE, AND INEFFABLE GOD

According to Scholem, *Ein-Sof* is a term and concept that originates with the early Kabbalists in Provence and Spain. It is a term that treats the adverbial relation "without end" as a noun, and was transformed into a technical term for the infinite, completely unknowable God. Scholem refers to a number of other terms equivalent to *Ein-Sof* that appear in various kabbalistic writings. Among these are the appellations "superfluity" (*Yitron*, a translation of the Neoplatonic "hyperousia"), "indistinguishable unity" or the "complete indistinguishability of opposites" (*ha-achdut ha-shavah*), and "the essence" (*ha-mahut*).[4]

The Kabbalists used a variety of negative epistemological terms to make reference to the hidden God: "the concealment of secrecy," "the concealed light," "that which thought cannot contain," etc.,[5] each of which signifies that this God is somehow beyond human knowledge and comprehension. However, there are other terms, e.g., "Root of all roots," "Indifferent Unity," "Great Reality,"[6] "Creator," "Cause of Causes," and "Prime Mover"[7] (as well as the term *Ein-Sof*, "without end"), which are ontological rather than epistemological and affirmative rather than negative; for example, signifying that God is the *origin* of the world, the *reality* of the world, or the *totality* of all things. Yet in spite of the positive connotations, even those Kabbalists who utilized such terms held that they referred to a God who is completely unknowable and concealed.[8] Of this God, the proto-kabbalistic work *Sefer Yetzirah* had earlier said, "restrain your mouth from speaking and your heart from thinking, and if your heart runs let it return to its place."[9]

---

4. Gershom Scholem, *Kabbalah*, p. 88.

5. Ibid., p. 89.

6. Scholem, *Major Trends*, p. 12.

7. Moses Cordovero, *Or Ne'erav* VI: 1; Ira Robinson, *Moses Cordovero's Introduction to Kabbalah: An Annotated Translation of His* Or Ne'erav (Hoboken, NJ: Ktav, 1994), p. 111.

8. For example, Cordovero, who has many positive things to say about the nature of *Ein-Sof*, says that it is "improper to investigate the hidden force which created all that exists." Interestingly, Cordovero follows this by stating that it is the essence of *Ein-Sof* that "His will and wisdom and understanding are one." Moses Cordovero, *Or Ne'erav* VI: 2, 37b; Robinson, *Moses Cordovero's Introduction to Kabbalah*, p. 125.

9. *Sefer Yetzirah* I: 8, as translated in Tishby and Lachower, *The Wisdom of the Zohar*, Vol. 1, p. 234. See also Aryeh Kaplan, *Sefer Yetzirah: The Book of Creation*, rev.

According to the Kabbalist R. Azriel of Gerona (early thirteenth century), it is *Ein-Sof*'s very infinitude that makes it incomprehensible: "*Ein-Sof* cannot be an object of thought, let alone of speech, even though there is an indication of it in everything, for there is nothing beyond it. Consequently, there is no letter, no name, no writing, and no word that can comprise it."[10] God is unknowable, according to Azriel, precisely because He is "without end," and hence there is no outside point of view from which He can be circumscribed and made into an object.

There is something inherently paradoxical in the Kabbalists' most fundamental axiom of theology; that God in and of Himself is completely hidden and unknowable to man. While the Kabbalists all seem to agree on this axiom, many of them present a theosophy that purports to set forth the inner nature of the Godhead. There is thus a dialectical tension in kabbalistic thought between God's hiddenness and ineffability on the one hand, and His knowability, appearance and revelation on the other.[11]

While the Kabbalists marshal biblical prooftexts in support of the unfathomability of *Ein-Sof*[12] (e.g., Psalms 145: 3, "His greatness can never be fathomed," Isaiah 40: 28, "There is no searching of his Understanding"), nearly all agree that the personal, creator God of the Bible (the God who is revealed to humanity) is at least one step removed from the unknowable

---

ed. (York Beach, ME: Samuel Weiser, 1997), p. 66. Later Kabbalists held, at least in theory, that one ought not inquire about *Ein-Sof* or even its highest manifestations. Vital, for example, states that one is not permitted to ask questions about the inner nature of the Primordial Man, or the highest two *Sefirot*. In support he quotes the ancient apocryphal text, *The Wisdom of Ben Sirach*: "Seek not what is too wonderful for you and do not search for what is hidden from you. You have no business with the hidden things; meditate in what is permitted to you." *Sefer Etz Chayyim* 1:1, p. 27; Menzi and Padeh, *The Tree of Life*, p. 58.

10. Tishby and Lachower, *The Wisdom of the Zohar*, Vol. 1, p. 234.

11. On the dialectic between *Ein-Sof*'s ineffability and knowability, see Steven T. Katz, "Utterance and Ineffability in Jewish Neoplatonism," in *Neoplatonism in Jewish Thought*, ed. Lenn E. Goodman (Albany: State University of New York Press, 1992), pp. 279–298. According to Katz, the kabbalistic theses that (1) the *Sefirot* are emanations within the Godhead, and (2) the *Sefirot* are clearly known to man in their manifestation on earth, yields the conclusion that "by knowing and naming (the *Sefirot*) we know and name '*Eyn sof*', obliquely but authentically" (p. 291). In fact, kabbalistic theosophy makes this very assumption.

12. See, for example, Schneur Zalman, *Likutei Amarim—Tanya*, p. 15. Schneur Zalman also quotes Job 11:7, "Canst thou by searching find God" and Isaiah 55: 8, "For my thought are not your thoughts."

Ein-Sof. Ein-Sof, according to the majority of Kabbalists (Azriel is an exception[13]), is an impersonal "that" rather than a personal "thou" or "who." According to the Kabbalists, *Ein-Sof* serves as the ontological and metaphysical ground for the revealed God, but *Ein-Sof* does not itself appear anywhere in the Bible. According to one anonymous Kabbalist: "*Ein-Sof* is not even alluded to in the Torah or in the prophets, or in the hagiographers or in the words of the sages; only the mystics received a small indication of it."[14] According to Isaac the Blind, *Ein-Sof,* in contrast to the biblical God to whom we may direct our praise and our prayers, is "not [even] conceivable by thinking." In contrast to the biblical God, it is impossible to attribute to *Ein-Sof* will, desire, thought, speech, deed or intentions for to do so would imply its limitation, inasmuch as it would be said to have willed or spoken one thing and not another.[15] According to the Zohar, "there are no ends, no wills, no lights, no luminaries in *Ein-Sof*" for to say anything at all about *Ein-Sof,* to posit any differentiation within it, as Tishby has put it, "blemishes its unparalleled and unknowable perfection."[16] In *Tikkunei* Zohar we read: "High above all heights and hidden beyond all concealments, no thought can grasp you at all . . . You have no known Name for You fill all Names and You are the perfection of them all."[17] The Lurianic Kabbalists affirmed the total unknowability of *Ein Sof.* Vital informs us that this term "indicates that there is absolutely no way to comprehend Him, either by thought or by contemplation, because He is completely inconceivable and far removed from any kind of thought."[18]

The first Lubavitcher rebbe, Schneur Zalman of Lyadi, makes it clear that the unknowability of *Ein-Sof* is not a function of the depth or difficulty of the concepts involved: "But it is not at all proper to say concerning the Holy One, blessed be He, who transcends intellect and wisdom, that it is

---

13. Scholem, *Origins of the Kabbalah,* p. 431. Scholem describes how for Azriel *Ein-Sof* is the "leader of the world and the master of creation."

14. Scholem, *Origins of the Kabbalah,* p. 443. Cf. Scholem, *Kabbalah,* p. 88. An early Kabbalist, the author of *Ma'arkhelut ha-Elohut* went so far as to say that *Ein-Sof* cannot be identified with God or serve as an object of religious thought.

15. Scholem, *Major Trends,* p. 12.

16. Tishby and Lachower, *The Wisdom of the Zohar,* Vol. 1, p. 235.

17. *Tikkunei* Zohar, Introduction: 17a–b, cited and translated in Immanuel Schochet, "Mystical Concepts in Hasidism," appendix to Schneur Zalman, *Likutei Amarim-Tanya* (Brooklyn, NY: Kehot, 1981), p. 827.

18. *Sefer Etz Chayyim* 1:1, p. 21; Menzi and Padeh, *The Tree of Life,* p. 6.

impossible to apprehend Him because of the depth of the concept, for He is not within the realm of comprehension at all."[19] According to Schneur Zalman, to say that one cannot comprehend *Ein-Sof* is akin to saying that one cannot literally touch an idea, "for the sense of touch refers and applies only to physical objects which may be grasped by the hands."[20] *Ein-Sof*'s wisdom is an order above thought, just as our thought is an order above the matter we apply it to; and just as inert matter cannot grasp our thoughts, we cannot fathom *Ein-Sof*'s wisdom.

We shall see that the Kabbalists (paradoxically) have much to say even about that which they regard as unsayable. Yet there is a strong tendency in the Kabbalah to simply define *Ein-Sof* as the "unknowable" and to hold that anything of which an attribution or statement can be made is, *by definition*, a lower manifestation of the Godhead. On some views, in fact, the term *Ein-Sof* is said to refer to *Keter*, the divine will, with no term being applicable to the divine essence.[21] The Zohar speaks of the "Supernal Will," the "Secret of All Secrets," and the "Primal Nothing" but denies that even these exalted ascriptions apply to *Ein-Sof* itself, instead attributing them to the highest *Sefirah* or emanation.[22] In its purest form we might simply speak of *Ein-Sof* as "the realm of the silent," that which can perhaps be referred to but not described. Like the German romantic philosopher Friedrich Schlegel, the Kabbalists held that one cannot speak about the "Absolute" or the "Totality" in the way one speaks about particular things and their relations to other finite entities. The Totality can be referred to, but it cannot itself be described, for to do so would be to contrast it with other things, and thereby limit it and rob it of its infinite character. Put in another way, *Ein-Sof* can be referred to, but it has no significance or meaning. Indeed, for *Ein-Sof* to have significance there would have to be something outside or beyond it for it to be contrasted *with*, or *have significance* for. Again, if this were the case, *Ein-Sof* would lose its very character as the infinite totality. I believe that Gershom Scholem expresses a similar line of thought when he says: "Totali-

---

19. Schneur Zalman, *Likutei Amarim — Tanya*, p. 327.

20. Ibid.

21. E.g., Moses Cordovero, *Pardes Rimonim* III: 1, referred to in Schochet, "Mystical Concepts," p. 830, note 11. Schochet notes that Schneur Zalman takes the intermediate view that *Ein-Sof* refers to a plane above the divine will but below the divine essence.

22. Tishby and Lachower, *The Wisdom of the Zohar*, Vol. 1, p. 257.

ties can be communicated only in occult fashion. The name of God can be pronounced but cannot be expressed, for only that which is fragmentary makes language expressible."[23] We will have occasion to pursue the significance of "referring to *Ein-Sof*" later in this chapter.

THE LIMIT OF DIVINE KNOWLEDGE

The Kabbalists went so far as to imply that *Ein-Sof* is hidden and ineffable even for itself. The Zohar, for example, refers to *Keter*, the highest *Sefirah*, occasionally identified with *Ein-Sof* itself, as "that which knows but does not know, and explains that the *Sefirot* are not themselves in a position to perceive *Ein-Sof*."[24] How can this paradoxical reference be understood?

An analogy may be helpful here: one that places *Ein-Sof* in the same relation to the finite universe as a dreamer is to the world conjured up in his dreams. It certainly could be said of the dreamer that "he knows but does not know." He "knows" in the sense that his awareness is the screen upon which all of the action, so to speak, takes place: it is his "knowledge" that is the sum and substance of the entire dream world. Yet the dreamer does "not know," because he is, in effect, completely unaware of the entire dream process. He is unaware precisely because (like *Ein-Sof*) he is (in the dream context) the totality; his awareness is the entire plenum of the dream reality. To become self-reflectively aware, to "know" in this sense, the dreamer would have to circumscribe the dream world; that is, get outside of this plenum. Now this is certainly possible for a (waking) dreamer, but only at the expense of a total collapse of the dream world.

Ein-Sof, by analogy, is the screen of *all*, and there is no getting outside of its Totality. *Ein-Sof* cannot make itself an object of contemplation, for this would mean that there is some vantage point beyond the Infinite All from which it could gain self-knowledge. Because this is logically impossible, *Ein-Sof* can be nothing more than the boundary, the screen, the knowledge/ consciousness on/in which All takes place. There is no metaperspective from which *Ein-Sof* can "know" in the second, reflective, sense, in which a dreamer

---

23. David Biale, "Gershom Scholem's Ten Unhistorical Aphorisms on Kabbalah: Text and Commentary," *Modern Judaism* 5 (1985): 86–87.

24. Zohar II, 239a (Tishby and Lachower, *The Wisdom of the Zohar*, Vol. 1, p. 257; see also p. 233).

knows that he has dreamed. And since *Ein-Sof* is the All, there is no possibility of its reflectively gaining perspective upon itself by looking at itself, as it were, through the eyes of another. To be precise, according to the Kabbalists, there is no possibility of this, *except* through *Ein-Sof*'s estrangement from itself through the creation of man. Man is the "other" through which God comes to know Himself. Creation, the Kabbalists tell us, is for the purpose of revealing God's glory.[25] But such revelation can occur to no one other than (an aspect of) God Himself, for God is the one true reality. Although in the kabbalistic tradition, creation is conceptualized as a free act of God, we here see that it is also a necessary consequence of God's own omniscience, for it is only through creation that God can perform the otherwise impossible task of achieving self-knowledge.

GOD AND NOTHINGNESS

The Kabbalists' identification of *Ein-Sof* with "Nothingness" is perhaps the most surprising of their doctrines concerning God.[26] Strictly speaking it is not *Ein-Sof* itself (which is beyond all predication—see below), but *Keter*, the first *Sefirah*, and *Ein-Sof*'s primal manifestation, which is identified with nothingness.[27] However, the Kabbalists often speak in a manner that suggests the predication of "nothingness" to the essence of the deity itself.

That God, who is identified as the creator and foundation of all being whatsoever, and who is otherwise identified as the Infinite All, should be referred to as "nothingness" is not only highly paradoxical, but, it would seem, blatantly heretical. The Kabbalists were not unaware of the heterodoxy of this view, but the dialectical nature of their thought led them to posit a negation at the very heart of the deity. As a comprehension of the doctrine of *Ayin* (Nothingness) is critical to our understanding of the kabbalistic view of God, I will, in the next several sections, explore in detail the reasons for the Kabbalists identification of *Ein-Sof* with the absolute "nought."

---

25. See, for example, Chayyim Vital, *Sefer Etz Chayyim* 1:1, p. 21; Menzi and Padeh, *The Tree of Life*, p. 4.

26. As discussed in my *Kabbalistic Metaphors*, the identification of the deity with "nothingness" is common to a number of mystical traditions.

27. Indeed, in *Sefer Yetzirah* the attribution "nothingness" (*beli-mah*, "without anything") is made with regard to all of the *Sefirot*.

A GOD BEYOND ALL PREDICATION

First, we should note that for the Kabbalists the *nothingness* of *Ein-Sof* follows from the deity's unknowability. If *Ein-Sof* is in its essence "eternally unknowable,"[28] then its ontological character is that of *the essentially unknown*, which the Kabbalists equated with "nothingness." Since for the Kabbalists thought or, more precisely, language, is central to being, that which cannot be conceived or spoken of, is "*nothing.*" Because *Ein-Sof* cannot be spoken of, neither "being" nor "existence" can be predicated of it, and as such, *Ein-Sof* has no being and does not exist.

However, this in itself does not quite enable the Kabbalists to equate *Ein-Sof* with *Ayin* (Nothing). The mere fact that "being" and "existence" cannot be predicated of *Ein-Sof* does not entitle one to call it "Nothing." If *Ein-Sof* lies outside of language, it lies outside of all predication, "nothing" included. In this sense, we might speak of *Ein-Sof* as transcending the very distinction between being and nothingness, or as including all possibilities of both being and nothingness within itself.

This is the perspective upon *Ein-Sof* that is suggested by the contemporary philosopher Robert Nozick. Nozick asks us to contrast an infinite that includes everything that exists with one that also includes all possibility:

> Suppose someone merged with or became the whole universe, and so came to include everything that exists. Even then, he would not be unlimited— he still would be that particular universe. We must imagine something that somehow includes all possibilities, all possible universes, and excludes nothing. This something not only is not limited to some portion of actuality while excluding the rest, it is also not limited to that one portion of possibility which is (all of) actuality.[29]

Nozick adopts the kabbalistic term *Ein-Sof* to denote this absolutely unlimited entity. While he does so without making any explicit claim regarding the Kabbalah, his conception of "*Ein-Sof*" can, I believe, help illuminate the kabbalistic idea.

Nozick explores the possibility that since existence implies limitation, i.e., something rather than nothing, then *Ein-Sof*, as he has defined it, strictly speaking *does not exist*. However, Nozick points out, *Ein-Sof* is not "nothing"

---

28. Scholem, *Major Trends*, p. 12.
29. Nozick, *Philosophical Explanations*, p. 600.

in the ordinary sense of the term. For Nozick, *Ein-Sof transcends the entire existence–non-existence distinction*, an idea, which by the thirteenth century began to play an important role in the Kabbalah.[30]

The Kabbalists, in referring to *Ein-Sof*, are speaking about an entity so vast, so all-inclusive, as to include *and be* both everything *and* nothing. God, for the Kabbalah, is not only both everything and nothing; He is completely identifiable both with every void and every finite thing as well. If God were simply the "totality of all things" and not also nothingness and each finite thing as well, there would be some things that are excluded from God's essence, or which, although they are included in God as parts, would be distinguishable from Him. On this view *Ein-Sof* is nothing but is also all other things as well.

The Kabbalist David Ben Abraham ha-Lavan proffered another reason for identifying *Ein-Sof* with *Ayin* or Nothingness. According to this thirteenth-century Kabbalist, *Ein-Sof* is a completely simple totality, beyond distinction or categorization and as such *Ein-Sof* cannot be identified as any thing in particular.

Ein-Sof has "more being than any other being in the world, but since it is simple, and all other simple things are complex when compared with its simplicity, so in comparison it is called 'nothing.' "[31] We can perhaps gain some insight into this view when we consider that a concrete illustration of our concept of an *infinite, undifferentiated unity* is an infinitely extending, empty void. Such an infinitely extending void is also what we must think of in order to represent absolute nothingness. Our conception of God's infinity is in this sense identical to our conception of "nothing at all."

CREATION *EX NIHILO*

By identifying *Ein-Sof* with "Nothingness" the Kabbalists were able to attack the ultimate problem of origins (Why is there anything at all?) from a perspective that does not already assume the existence of that which it purports to explain. In short, by identifying *Ein-Sof* with Nothingness, the Kabbalists could speak of a *deity who weaves his existence out of the depths of his*

---

30. Moshe Idel, "Jewish Kabbalah and Platonism in the Middle Ages and Renaissance," in *Neoplatonism and Jewish Thought* p. 344. See Sarah Heller-Wilinsky, "Isaac ibn Latif—Philosopher or Kabbalist," in *Jewish Medieval and Renaissance Studies* ed. Alexander Altmann (Cambridge, MA: Harvard University Press, 1967).

31. See Scholem, *Kabbalah*, p. 95.

own nothingness, as opposed to an already existent God for whom the question "whence?" could itself be proposed.[32]

For the Kabbalists, the entire creative process is understood as an oscillation between nothingness and being, with nothingness, as it were, the activating force. This is evident, for example, in the Lurianic doctrine of *Tzimtzum* (concealment, contraction), which understands God as *negating* Himself, withdrawing Himself from a point in His own totality, to make room for, and create, a finite universe. The world is not only created out of "nothing," but for the Kabbalists "nothing" is the very power that brings it into existence.

Nozick asks us to consider the possibility that nothingness itself is a nugatory force, which "sucks things into non-existence or keeps them there." Nozick speculates: "If this force acts upon itself, it sucks nothingness into nothingness, producing something or, perhaps everything, every possibility."[33] Nozick speaks here of "nothingness" having "nothinged" itself, an apparent allusion to Hegel's "negation of the negation." Here I should point out that if *Ein-Sof* is conceived as *Ayin* (nothing) then the negation (contraction, concealment) involved in the act of *Tzimtzum*, which the Lurianists posited as the principle of creation, can be understood in Nozick's sense as such a *negation of nothingness,* leading to a world.

NOTHING AS THE SOURCE OF ALL MEANING AND SIGNIFICANCE

According to the Zohar, when *Ein-Sof* removes Himself from His connection with creation, "He has no name of His own at all."[34] At the same time, the Zohar holds that the nameless God who, as such, is "nothingness" and *without significance,* is "the cause of all causes,"[35] and the source of all

---

32. Some of the early Kabbalists emphasized the fact that God creates Himself. For example, the author of the Fountain of Wisdom writes: "Know that the Holy One blessed be he, was the first existent being. Only that which *generates itself* is called an existent being." (Italics added.) Verman, *The Books of Contemplation,* p. 55.

33. Nozick, *Philosophical Explanations,* p. 122.

34. Zohar III, 225a, *Raya Mehemma;* Tishby and Lachower, *The Wisdom of the Zohar,* Vol. 1, p.259.

35. Zohar I, 22b, *Tikkunei ha-*Zohar, as quoted in Tishby and Lachower, *The Wisdom of the Zohar,* Vol. 1, p. 258.

meaning and significance whatsoever. The reason that nothingness is the source of all being and significance is that it is only via the introduction of a void or *negation* that things can be differentiated into various categories, ideas, and significances. To say that something is an X is *ipso facto* to say that it *is not* a Y, and indeed to create an X is to introduce an element of boundary, determination, or negation (what the Kabbalists referred to as judgment or *din*) between it and everything else. It is for this reason that according to the Kabbalist R. Joseph Ben Scholem of Barcelona [c. 1300] there is no change, alteration, or transformation, in short no creative act at all, in which the abyss of nothingness is not crossed and for "a fleeting mystical moment becomes visible."[36] God, in order to be the creator, must have an element of negation or nothingness as part of His very essence, and it is just this nothingness that the deity calls upon in creating the world *ex nihilo*. There is a "nothingness" implicit in all things, and this nothingness is that thing's participation in *Ein-Sof*.[37]

THE EXISTENTIAL POWER OF THE NOUGHT

God's unknowability, the limits to knowledge that appear when we confront the question of the origins of the universe, has an *existential* quality that ordinary "unknowns" don't seem to possess. It might well be misleading and superfluous to hypostasize an "unknown" or a nothingness to correspond to every lack of human knowledge (e.g., my lack of knowledge of today's temperature, or even the meteorologist's inability to predict tomorrow's weather) but it seems only natural to do so in response to the "abyss" of the world's origins that confronts us when we ask the ultimate philosophical question, "How is it that there is anything at all?"

The Kabbalists, it seems, were quite aware of the existential nothingness that confronts the individual who contemplates the seeming contingency of his own, and all, existence. And like some later existentialists, a few Kabbalists even held that contact with this nothingness was the *ultimate* religious experience. According to Azriel: "He who prays must cast off everything that obstructs him, and must lead the world back to its origin—literally to its

---

36. Scholem, *Major Trends*, p. 217.

37. This concept will become clear when we consider the concept of *Tzimtzum* in Chapter Three.

Nought." And this contact with one's origins in nothingness provides the self with the "power for its own existence."[38] "Nothingness" for the Kabbalists is the activator of the finite world in general, and of human existence in particular. Nothingness, as modern existential thought has affirmed, is the finitude, the "death," which circumscribes man as an historical individual and thus provides the very meaning to his life. The unknowability of man's and the world's origins has an ontological dimension to it which other unknowns don't seem to possess. The Kabbalah identifies this unknown with the nothingness of *Ein-Sof*.

THE INTERDEPENDENCE OF BEING
AND NOTHINGNESS

There is in the Kabbalah a dialectical interdependence between being and nothingness; they are, as it were, welded together as a circle is to its own boundary. This interdependence is spoken of directly in the following passage from Azriel's work on the *Sefirot*:

> He who brings forth Being from Nought is thereby lacking nothing, for the Being is in the Nought after the manner of the Nought, and the Nought is in the Being after the manner [according to the modality] of the Being. And the author of the Book of *Yetzirah* said: He made his Nought into his Being, and did not say: He made the Being from the Nought. This teaches us that the Nought is the Being and Being is the Nought.[39]

For Azriel, the deeper we penetrate into the mystery of being the more we arrive at nothingness and vice versa. And like everything else in the world (e.g., night/day, beginning/end, male/female) being and nothingness have their opposites woven into their very essences. Indeed, from this perspective, *Ein-Sof* can be understood as the negation that originates oppositions, antinomies, and dialectics in general, the very dialectics through which the world is created, evolves, and is maintained.[40]

For the Kabbalah, the dialectical interdependence of being and noth-

---

38. Scholem, *Origins of the Kabbalah*, p. 416.
39. Ibid., p. 423.
40. See Tishby and Lachower, *The Wisdom of the Zohar*, Vol. 1, pp. 229–55.

ingness expresses itself concretely in an interdependence between God and the world. God, for the Kabbalist, is a mere empty abstraction without a finite world as his implement and expression. This is because the values that God represents (and which are embodied) in the instruments of creation, the *Sefirot* (e.g., love, justice, beauty, etc.), have no reality or significance until they are actualized in the arena of a finite world. Hence God, who is the origin of, and whose ultimate nature is to be, these values, is an empty *nothingness* without a world in which these values can be brought to fruition and made real. Conversely, the world has no *value* or significance unless it is united with this "nothingness" (i.e., these "empty abstractions").[41] Hence Ibn Ezra can declare that the very "good" of creation (Genesis 1: 31) is the communion of all things with *Ayin* (nothingness). The world, according to the Kabbalists, is constantly renewed through its contact with God's goodness, which is the Nought.[42]

THE INFINITE WILL

The Kabbalists associated God's nothingness with His nature as the Supernal Will. The identification of will with nothingness has fascinated twentieth-century philosophers such as Sartre, for whom the willing subject is that which introduces a negation (and hence significant distinctions) into being, and the early Wittgenstein, who held that the will is "nothing" inasmuch as it is not a part of the world but a boundary to it. Neither idea is foreign to the Kabbalists, who held that God's will completely transcends the phenomenal world and yet introduces the very negation which enables that world to subsist. According to the Kabbalist Joseph Gikatila, the relationship between nothingness and "will" is expressed linguistically in the Hebrew words meaning "nothingness" and "I." *Ayin* (nothing) is composed of the same consonants as *Ani* (I), and Gikatila (and the Zohar) conceives of *Ayin*, nothingness, as passing through a dialectical transformation in becoming *Ani*, the primordial "I" or will.[43] The Zohar, in a passage we have in part

---

41. Elior has pointed out that the interdependence of God and world is a fundamental axiom of Chabad Hasidism. She writes that for Chabad "just as one cannot speak of the existence of the world without God, so too one cannot speak of the existence of God without the world." (Elior, *Paradoxical Ascent to God*, p. 62.)

42. Scholem, *Origins of the Kabbalah*, p. 422.

43. Scholem, *Major Trends*, p. 218.

already considered, identifies the nothingness of *Ein-Sof* with the Supernal Will: "that which knows but does not know (i.e., *Ein-Sof*) is none but the Supernal Will, the secret of all secrets. *Ayin* (nothing)."[44] While The Zohar denies that even "will" can be attributed to *Ein-Sof*,[45] our passage here seems to affirm that *Ein-Sof*, in its first emanation as *Keter*, is the *Supernal Will*. "Will" probably comes closest to specifying the nature of what the Zohar refers to in places as "the root of all roots" or the "cause of all causes."[46] The Will of *Keter* is described by the Zohar as being co-eternal with *Ein-Sof*. This is an apparent recognition that neither a deity without "will" nor a "will" arising from something more fundamental than itself can even be conceived. "Will" it seems, is a truly foundational concept in the Kabbalah.

Scholem points out that the early Kabbalists of Gerona understood God as acting through a "Primal Will" that is encompassed by and even united with *Ein-Sof*. Within at least one significant strand in the Kabbalah the Infinite Will (*ha Ratzon ad Ein-Sof*) is the highest level within the Godhead that thought can penetrate. In the writings of the Gerona Kabbalists and the Zohar, *Ein-Sof* is regarded as, in effect, united with its own volition. Many Kabbalists continued to regard *Keter*, understood as *Ratzon* (Will, Desire), as indistinguishable from *Ein-Sof* itself. For example, we read in *Tikkunei* Zohar: "It is called *Ein-Sof* internally and *Keter* externally."[47] The unity of *Ein-Sof* with its own Will is referred to in the Zohar as the *Partzuf Attika Kaddisha*, the Holy Ancient One, and this is the source of the later Lurianic identification of the divine Will with the highest of the *Partzufim*, or "visages" of God.

If we analyze the meaning of "will" we discover that on the simplest level "will" is that aspect of conscious life which chooses among alternatives and hence *lends* preference, interest, and ultimately significance to things. Without will or interest, things would have no importance or significance whatsoever. Hence *Ein-Sof*, which in an earlier moment in the Kabbalists' dialectic is devoid of significance, here becomes the ultimate signifier, the primal conveyer of meaning.

---

44. Zohar, 239a; Tishby and Lachower, *The Wisdom of the Zohar*, Vol. 1, p. 257.

45. "But there are no ends, no will, no lights, no luminaries in *Ein-Sof*." Ibid., p. 257.

46. Scholem, *Kabbalah*, p. 89.

47. Quoted in Scholem, *Kabbalah*, p. 91.

THOUGHT AND WISDOM

There are passages in the Zohar that instead of identifying the highest manifestation of *Ein-Sof* with will, identify this manifestation, or even *Ein-Sof* itself, with intellect or thought. For example:

> What is within the Thought no one can conceive, much less can one know *Ein-Sof*, of which no trace can be found and to which thought cannot reach by any means. But from the midst of the impenetrable mystery, from the first descent of the *Ein-Sof* there glimmers a faint indiscernible light like the point of a needle, the hidden recess of thought, which even yet is not knowable until there extends from it a light in which there is some imprint of letters, and from which they all issue. First of all is *Aleph*, the beginning and end of all grades, that in which all grades are imprinted and which yet is always called "one," to show that although the Godhead contains many forms it is still only one . . . The top point of the *Aleph* symbolizes the hidden supernal thought.[48]

Equally noteworthy for its identification of *Ein-Sof* with Thought is a passage in the Zohar in which Rabbi Simon relates that all the "lights which proceed from the mystic supreme thought are called *Ein-Sof*," and which holds that *Ein-Sof* both proceeds from the "mystic supreme thought" and is the "nine lights of thought" that emanate from a certain fragment of the "unknown."[49]

In general, the earlier Kabbalists, such as the author of *Sefer ha-Bahir* and Isaac the Blind, had granted a privileged status to "thought" as the essence of the divine. An important example of this is the early kabbalistic text *Sefer ha-Iyyun* (The Book of Contemplation), which holds that the Holy One is united with and created all things through the power of Primordial Wisdom (*Chochmah Kedumah*).[50] Later Kabbalists, beginning with the Zohar (the above passages notwithstanding) placed a primary emphasis upon "will."[51] Scholem has pointed out that the whole history of the Kabbalah involves a struggle between views that see the creative process as an intellectual versus a volitional act.

---

48. Zohar I, 21a; Sperling and Simon, *The Zohar*, Vol. 1. p. 89.
49. Zohar I, 65a; Sperling and Simon, *The Zohar*, p. 213.
50. Verman, *The Books of Contemplation*, pp. 41–42.
51. Interestingly, Moses De Leon, who is purported to be the author of at least portions of the Zohar, states elsewhere: "It is by means of thought that all things, above and below, come into being, the mystery of the creative thought being identical

It will be worth our while to reflect for a moment on the dialectic between thought and will as it appears in the overall context of kabbalistic thought. Perhaps the opposition between these two points of view can ultimately be resolved through the mediation of a "third term."

Thought, it might be said, both reaches a state of *impoverishment* and, paradoxically, achieves its *actualization* and fulfillment when it is embodied in material form. The idea of man, for example, is both infinitely wider than, and completely impoverished in relation to, an actual corporeal man. No man can hope to encompass anything but a fraction of the knowledge, skill, and value attributable to "man" in the abstract; yet without actual, living, breathing men and women, the idea of man is but an empty, dead abstraction. The world, as it were, "breathes life" into ideas, just as ideas provide a form or essence to the things of the world. Thought, as Hegel was to later claim, must, as part of its very nature, move to actualize and fulfill itself in material form, if it is to become all that, as "idea," it potentially is. This movement of thought, toward its actualization in creation, is totally interior to thought itself, yet it is (paradoxically) equivalent to a Primal Will.

Similarly, "will," as part of its very nature, must have an object: one cannot "will" in general, but must will some specific thing or state of affairs. It is for this reason that "will" logically passes over into "thought." This passage is illustrated in the Kabbalah by the fact that "Thought" (*Chochmah*) follows immediately upon "Will" (*Keter/Ratzon*) in the order of the emanation of *Sefirot*, and, further, by the fact that what is "willed" by *Ein-Sof*, i.e., the entire order of the *Sefirot*, is a series of values or ideas. According to the Zohar: "Desire, which is Thought, is the beginning of all things . . ."[52]

"Creation," then, becomes the "third term" uniting thought and will, expressing the idea that "will" (in the sense of the actualization of a thought) is part of the very notion of thought itself, and that "thought" (in the sense of the object of will) is part of the very nature of will. Creation, represented in the Kabbalah by the *Sefirot*, binds thought and will together, and shows them to be mutually determining terms or moments of being.[53]

---

with that of the hidden 'point.' " R. Moses De Leon, (From) *The Doctrine of the Ether*, selections trans. by George Margoliouth, in Meltzer *The Secret Garden* 1998, p. 157.

52. Zohar 200a; Sperling and Simon, *The Zohar*, Vol. 2, p. 259.

53. The preceding "dialectic," in which aspects of a given notion (or in kabbalistic terms, *Sefirah*), are said to imply, or pass over into, presumably unrelated or even opposite notions, is stated in doctrinaire terms by the Kabbalist Moses Cordovero, in his theory of the *behinnot*, the infinite number of aspects contained

EIN-SOF AND "THE ULTIMATE QUESTIONS"

I would like to propose that the views of *Ein-Sof* as "Thought" and "Will" can be understood as responses to two basic philosophical questions that have been asked since the dawn of reflective thought. The first of these questions is "Why is there anything at all?" and the second is "What is the meaning of existence?" The view that the Absolute or *Ein-Sof* is "Thought" follows from a consideration of the first of these questions, and the view that *Ein-Sof* is "Will" follows from a consideration of the second.

With regard to the ultimate question, "Why is there anything rather than nothing?", Nozick tells us that it is too late in this question's history for us to continue avoiding it or, as some philosophers are wont to do, *asking it insistently* as if the very asking is of philosophical moment and depth. I agree, but I believe that instead of rushing in to propose answers, we should focus for a moment on the *question* itself. In this way, the solution, or at least a possible solution, may be revealed.

In asking for an *explanation* of the world's existence we are, in effect, demanding a *reason* for its existence, or, at the very least, requesting that the cosmos be placed in a framework that makes rational sense. After all, we would hardly accept an irrational, i.e., illogical or absurd answer to our query.

It follows then that "reason" itself is a condition that is presupposed by our very question. If our question is to have any philosophical sense, indeed, if it is to be asked at all, then we must live in a world in which "reason" (i.e., intelligent, rational thought) is assumed. Perhaps "reason," i.e., the very idea that something, anything, should make rational sense, lies at the foundation of the world, of being and nonbeing, actuality and possibility, the finite and the "all"? Perhaps Reason itself, with a "capital R" is the Absolute.

This, of course, was the solution to the ultimate question provided by Hegel. For Hegel, the ultimate explanation of things could never be a causal explanation, for any presumed "first cause" would itself beg for an explanation and so on *ad infinitum*. According to Hegel, the first principle of the world must be a reason of which the world is a consequent, and he set out to

---

within a given *Sefirah*. As will be seen when we explore this doctrine in more detail in Chapter Four, Cordovero held that each *Sefirah* contains an aspect or *behinah* that allows it to receive "light" from the *Sefirah* above it or pass light to the *Sefirah* below it. For this reason such *Sefirot* as *Keter* (Will) and *Chochmah* (Thought) can be seen to contain aspects of the other implicit in themselves, a view that shows the Kabbalah to have anticipated the philosophy of Hegel. On Cordovero's *behinnot*, see *Pardes Rimonim* 5: 5, as quoted in Scholem, *Kabbalah*, p. 114ff.

prove that the only reason from which the world itself follows is *Reason itself.*
In short, Hegel argued that Reason must be the first principle of the cosmos
because it is the only self-explanatory principle. If we ask "What is the reason
of reason?" we can only respond rationally and, in effect, answer "reason
itself." The only possible answer, for example, as to why we should be logical
and rational in our quest to understand the origin of being, or anything else
for that matter, must itself involve reason. Reason is at the very core of what
it means to provide an explanation. Put another way, only rationality itself
requires no further reason, for it is sufficient reason for itself. One way of
understanding the Hegelian project in philosophy is, in effect, to deduce the
world from the very fact that we query about it at all. In Chapter Four, we
will see that for the Kabbalists, "Questions" reveal the very structure of the
cosmos.

When we ask the question "Why is there anything whatsoever?" we are,
in certain respects, like the man who asks "why should I be reasonable?" and
who, in asking this question, commits himself to the order of reason and
hence must accept the simple answer "Because it is only the reasonable thing
to do." When we ask the ultimate question we commit ourselves to the
possibility of an explanation that is, as we have just seen, tantamount to
committing ourselves to the existence of reason in the world. As such the
question "Why is there something rather than nothing?" is a question that
implies its own answer. The fact that we even ask it presupposes the existence
of something: i.e., "reason," and as such we conclude that Reason itself is an
ultimate, an "Absolute," a definition of *Ein-Sof.*

This is precisely the Hegelian (and, in effect, Aristotelian) solution to the
problem of ultimate origins that is implicit in the kabbalistic tradition that
identifies *Ein-Sof* with *Machshavah* (thought) or *Chochmah* (wisdom). If
Ein-Sof, in the very recesses of its own being, or, as the Kabbalists sometimes
like to put it, "in its first manifestation to itself," is the supernal thought or
wisdom than there is, perhaps, no better solution to the ultimate question
(i.e., the reason of the cosmos) than to say that the world exists as the fullest
possible expression of reason itself. *Ein-Sof* then becomes identifiable with a
universal mind: the Aristotelian "thought thinking itself."

THE MEANING OF *EIN-SOF*

But is this the only possible solution to our ultimate question regarding the
origin of the world? To answer this we must first ask whether the question of
the *origins of being* is the only possible ultimate question? And the answer

here is, no, it is not. Just as the Kabbalists maintained a second tradition to the effect that the ultimate essence of *Ein-Sof* is "will" or "desire" as opposed to thought, we may ask a second ultimate question (which, as we shall see, relates directly to this tradition), the proverbial "What is the meaning of existence?"

This question, like our earlier question that demanded an explanation for the world's existence, is itself predicated on an assumption. This time, however, instead of assuming a reasonable answer, our question assumes a "significant" one. Our question assumes a response that is valuable and good, something that one can *will*. For this reason, our second ultimate question, regarding the meaning of existence, points to a second ultimate, an ultimate of significance, value, and will. This ultimate is embodied in a second Kabblaistic tradition, one that identifies *Ein-Sof* with will and desire (*Ratzon*) rather than Thought and Wisdom (*Chochmah*).

The idea that *Ein-Sof* is the ultimate source of meaning and value is something that follows quite naturally from the Kabbalists' cosmology. *Ein-Sof* is said to have emanated ten *Sefirot* which serve as the archetypes for, or molecular components of, everything in the world. The very names of the *Sefirot* (e.g., Love, Justice, Beauty, Splendor, Glory, etc.) reveal them to be values (as opposed to material elements) and lend support to the view that *Ein-Sof* is essentially the origin of all value and meaning.

Ein-Sof as the ultimate source of meaning can be understood from two points of view. The first sees *Ein-Sof* as achieving significance only in relation to an "other" (i.e., humankind). The second point of view suggests that *Ein-Sof* is the ultimate source of meaning in and of itself.

Nozick, who perhaps more than any other contemporary philosopher, explores his questions from a kabbalistic point of view, raises the question of the "meaning of *Ein-Sof*." He considers the possibility that the question of the meaning of *Ein-Sof* cannot be answered because to ask about the meaning of x is to ask how x connects with *other* things. Since there is no "other" to *Ein-Sof*, the question about its meaning cannot even arise.

Considerations such as this prompted the Kabbalists to arrive at the view that God created the world, and particularly mankind, in order to achieve his own full significance in relation to an "other" for which he can be wise, merciful, beneficent, compassionate, etc., as well as serve as "king." Vital tells us;

> When it arose in His will to emanate the emanations and to create the creations it was for a reason that we know—so that He could be called

"merciful and gracious, etc."—for if there was no one in the world who could receive this mercy, how could He be called merciful? The same can be said for all the rest of his attributes.[54]

It is similar with regard to his lordship. Calling Him Lord means that He has servants and that He is a lord over them. But if he had not created them it would not have been possible to call him by the name Lord (*'adon*).[55]

On this view, divinity can only achieve significance in relation to humankind. Such relatedness is basic to the very essence of *Ein-Sof* itself.

But what of the possibility that *Ein-Sof* is its own meaning, without any reference to an "other"? Perhaps, Nozick suggests, the unlimited can "stand in a certain relation to itself that no limited thing can stand to itself: being its own meaning." Nozick provides several logical considerations in support of this possibility; for example, that only an infinite being could fully specify its own details, or that only an infinite being can be mapped onto a proper subset of itself or include itself as a part.[56] However, his main point in support of the view that *Ein-Sof* can be its own meaning is that in questioning or challenging the meaning of something, for example the meaning of our lives, we always look to a wider rather than a narrower context (e.g., "humanity as a whole," "the universe," etc.). While we can make such a challenge with respect to the actual universe, asking what meaning it has against the wider context of "all possible worlds," we cannot do so with respect to *Ein-Sof*, for any wider context we imagined for it would ipso facto be included within it. Hence, if the infinite is to be meaningful, it must be so simply *in and of itself*. The conclusion here is that *Ein-Sof* just is significant, for it alone is able to block all further contexts and questions about its own meaning. We might go a bit further than Nozick and say that in this respect *Ein-Sof* becomes the *source of all meaning* whatsoever, for it is the final context against which all meaning is measured.

In raising the question of "meaning" as a second "ultimate question" alongside the question "Why is there anything at all?", Nozick underscores the potential for at least two (if not multiple) approaches to the Absolute. The first, which proceeds from the question of "being," leads quite naturally to the identification of the Absolute (and *Ein-Sof*) with Reason or Thought.

---

54. *Sefer Etz Chayyim* 1: 1, p. 24, Menzi and Padeh, *The Tree of Life*, p. 24
55. *Sefer Etz Chayyim* 1: 1, p. 21; Menzi and Padeh, *The Tree of Life*, p. 4.
56. Nozick, *Philosophical Explanations*, p. 603.

The second, which proceeds from the question of "meaning," leads more readily to the identification of the Absolute with the basic archetypes of value and significance. This latter view is important for it leaves room for values other than reason, specifically for the irrationality, sexuality, eroticism, and "faith" that are so prominent in the Kabbalah.

"FAITH" AND THE ORIGINS OF THE WORLD

As will become clearer as we proceed, the Kabbalists refused to make the sharp distinction between epistemology and metaphysics that is traditional in Western thought. For traditional philosophy, the way we come to know the world has no bearing whatsoever on the question of how the world came into being. However, for the Kabbalists there is no essential distinction between the human mind and the world it comes to know, and for this reason the order of knowledge and belief is likely to tell us much regarding the order of things. Such a view is illustrated, as I am about to explain, by the Kabbalist Azriel's dictum that "faith" is the point of transition between nothingness and being.

The Kabbalists frequently speculated regarding the "primordial point" of being that arose when *Ein-Sof* thought or willed the world into existence. They equated this point with the "beginning," which is spoken of in the first word of in Genesis. According to the Zohar, in the beginning "there shone forth a supernal and mysterious point."

> Beyond that point there is no knowable, and therefore it is called *Reshith* (beginning), the creative utterance which is the starting-point of all.[57]

In the Zohar and other kabbalistic writings this point is identified as Divine Wisdom (*Chochmah*) or the "mystical seed of creation."[58] An unusual, but deeply profound interpretation is provided by Azriel, in his continuation of a passage we have already quoted in connection with the mutual interdependence of nothingness and being:

> . . . the place at which the Being is linked to the point where, from the Nought, it begins to have existence is called "faith" (*emunah*). For faith is

---

57. Zohar I, 15a; Sperling and Simon, *The Zohar*, Vol. 1 p. 63. See also Scholem, *Major Trends*, p. 219.
58. Scholem, *Major Trends*, p. 219.

not related to a visible and apprehensible Being, nor to the invisible and unknowable Nought, but precisely to the place where the Nought is connected to Being.[59]

"Faith," which is generally thought of as a psychological or epistemological concept, is here given an ontological status.[60] The "primordial" point itself is designated "faith." This view implies that God created the world out of his own nothingness through an act that is analogous to the *faith* that man has in God's existence! More radically, we might suppose that Azriel is here teaching that God's creation of the world is the same act as man's faith in God's existence. How can this be understood?

In faith, one has a wholehearted and steadfast belief, one which, unlike a scientific or empirical belief, is unalterable by any set of mere facts or circumstances. In faith, one believes that "it just is." Faith is a kind of belief that is "rock bottom" and stands with us, it seems, *as does the very foundation of the world*. It is because faith is so completely foundational that Azriel can claim that being itself exists as it were by an act of faith. There is a point at which the chain of inquiry, or, conversely, the chain of antecedent causes, must come to an end. This point, in which our belief in an Absolute Being, and its very existence converge, Azriel calls "faith" (*emunah*).

The concept of "faith" has, of course, been the subject of innumerable theological treatments, both within and outside the Jewish tradition. Interestingly, however, it has recently been examined by those who, working in the psychoanalytic tradition, see it is an epistemic act that gives birth to the individual's psychic reality. According to these authors, "faith" is the openness to what is most basic and authentic in human psychic experience. It is, according to Michael Eigen, an experience that one has "with all one's soul and all one's might."[61] Wilfred Bion holds that faith requires a suspension of all constructive cognitive activity, a suspension of memory, will, understanding, and expectation, which leaves one absolutely *nothing* to hold on to. By suspending our attachments, by genuinely opening ourselves to the "Unknown," an authentic psychic reality is able to emerge and evolve. Such a state of pure receptiveness, in which one tolerates chaos, fragmentation,

---

59. Scholem. *Origins of the Kabbalah*, p. 423.

60. A similar status is given to "faith" in *Sefer ha-Iyyun*, which was likely influenced by Azriel. See Verman, *The Books of Contemplation*, p. 40.

61. See Michael Eigen, "The Area of Faith in Winnicott, Lacan and Bion," *International Journal of Psychoanalysis*, 62 (1981): 413–433.

blankness, fragments of meaning, and meaninglessness, is, according to Bion, *the* condition for creativity and genuine psychological birth, growth, and change.[62] On the kabbalistic principle that the microcosm reflects the macrocosm, we might say that such a state of empty (nothing) receptiveness to an Unknown is the hidden supernal point of creation itself.

THE UNITY OF OPPOSITES

From its very inception, the Kabbalah maintained that the Godhead as well as the *Sefirot* and the lower worlds could be characterized as a unity of opposites, a *coincidentia oppositorum*. Indeed, *Sefer ha-Bahir*, which contemporary scholarship regards to be the earliest kabbalistic source, begins with a dialectic in which the apparent opposites of darkness and light are interpreted to be identical:

> Rabbi Nekhuna ben Hakhana said: A verse of Scripture says (Job 37: 21): "Men see not the light which shines in the skies" and another verse of scripture says (Psalms 18: 11): "He made darkness his covering" and likewise we read (Psalms 97: 2): "Clouds and darkness are round him." A contradiction! [However then] comes a third verse and strikes a balance (Psalms 139: 12): "Yea, darkness is not dark before thee, but the night shineth as the day, darkness as day."[63]

Azriel, in discussing the nature of *Ein-Sof*, tells us that "it is the principle in which everything hidden and visible meet, and as such it is the common root of both faith *and unbelief*" (my italics).[64] It is indeed, very typical of Azriel, and of the Kabbalah in general, to make a thesis about *Ein-Sof*, and then immediately to hold that the opposite of this thesis is true as well, on the principle that *Ein-Sof*, in its infinity, is the union of all opposites and contradictions. According to Azriel, even the nature of the *Sefirot* involves

---

62. Ibid.

63. *Sefer ha-Bahir*, sec. 1; *Book Bahir*, Neugroschel trans., p. 50. Aryeh Kaplan, in *The Bahir Illumination* (York Beach, ME: Samuel Weiser, 1989), translates the final line as "Even darkness is not dark to You. Night shines like day—light and darkness are the same" (p. 1).

64. Scholem, *Origins of the Kabbalah*, pp. 441–442.

the union of "everything and its opposite."[65] Indeed, as early as *Sefer Yetzirah*, the *Sefirot* were spoken of as being comprised of five pairs of opposites: "A depth of beginning, a depth of end. A depth of good, a depth of evil. A depth of above, a depth of below. A depth of east, a depth of west. A depth of north, a depth of south." Yet they were also thought of as being united in their opposition, inasmuch as a "singular master . . . dominates over them all . . ."[66] Similarly the early kabbalistic "Source of Wisdom" speaks of the Name of God as being comprised of thirteen pairs of opposites, and the Primordial Ether (*Avir Kadmon*) as a creative medium in which these oppositions are formed and fused.[67]

Because the Kabbalah recognizes a coincidence of opposites on the deepest ontological and theological levels it is, as Azriel's aphorism might suggest, the one Jewish perspective that is actually able to accommodate atheism as well as theism. Nothingness and being, unbelief and faith, hiddenness and revelation, ignorance and wisdom, reason and irrationality are all at the core of the Kabbalists' conception of *Ein-Sof*. Indeed, the Kabbalah is startlingly premonitory of Hegel in its view that *Ein-Sof* is the root and union of all contradictions. For both the Kabbalists and Hegel, reality itself is fundamentally contradictory, and those who speak the truth must say contradictory things about it. Indeed, by placing the principle of negation at the heart of *Ein-Sof*, the Kabbalists determined that their theosophy would be one that proceeds through a logic of opposition and antinomy. For negation is the very principle that gives rise to contradiction.

The "contradictoriness" of *Ein-Sof* is expressed in the Zohar with such terms as "the head that is not a head."[68] More formally, the notion that *Ein-Sof* is ontologically an indistinct unity of opposites is given (by Azriel and others) the Hebrew term *ha-achdut hashawah*, which denotes a *coincidentia oppositorum*, an equivalence of the divine substance in all aspects of the cosmos including those that are opposed to or contradict one another.[69] This concept is present in the Lurianic Kabbalah.[70] For example, Vital writes: "Know that before the emanation of the emanated and the creation of all that

---

65. Dan, *The Early Kabbalah*, p. 94.
66. *Sefer Yetzirah* 1: 5, Kaplan, *Sefer Yetzirah*, p. 44.
67. Scholem, *Origins of the Kabbalah*, pp. 332–333.
68. See Tishby and Lachower, *The Wisdom of the Zohar*, p. 245.
69. Elior, "Chabad: The Contemplative Ascent to God," p. 164.
70. The Lurianic theosophy actually involves a dialectical play of opposites: Emanation and contraction, revelation and concealment, breaking of the vessels and

was created, the simple Upper Light filled all of reality . . . but everything was one simple light, equal in one hashvaah, which is called the Light of the Infinite."[71]

The concept of "equalization," which relates to a state prior to emanation in Vital, achieves its fullest expression in the writings of the Chabad Hasidim, where it is understood to be characteristic of all things and all time. Chabad developed a dialectical view of reality in which both the divine substance, and hence all things, involve a unity or coincidence of opposites. This idea, which, according to Scholem made its way into the Kabbalah via Neoplatonism,[72] reaches an advanced stage of development among the Chabad Hasidim. As Rachel Elior puts it, for Chabad, "divinity is conceived as a dialectical process comprising an entity and its opposite simultaneously."[73] Among these opposites are emanation (*shefa ve-atsilut*) and contraction (*Tzimtzum*), and ascent (*ratso*) and descent (*vashov*), as well as revelation and concealment, annihiliation and embodiment, unity and plurality, structure and chaos, spirit and matter, the divine and the human points of view, and "being" (*yesh*) and "nothingness" (*ayin*).[74] The Chabad view is dialectical because each pole of any given opposition is said to condition its opposite.

For example, according to Schneur Zalman God descends into an earthly abode in order that the material world may ascend and become one with the divine.[75] God's twofold movement conditions man's twofold obligation both to annihilate his own and the world's being in favor of inclusion within the Godhead (*bittul ha-Yesh*) and to draw down the divine influx in order to spiritualize the material world (*Hamshakha el ha-Yesh*).[76] The former obligation is called the "upper unification" (*yihud ha-elyon*), and the latter, the lower unification (*yihud ha-tahton*). The purpose of these unifications is that each realm, the divine and the corporeal, will be revealed

---

restoration. As will become clear in Chapters Three and Seven, these opposites are understood to be mutually dependent ideas.

71. Quoted in Elior, *The Paradoxical Ascent to God*, p. 68.

72. See Scholem, *Origins of the Kabbalah*, p. 440.

73. Rachel Elior, *The Paradoxical Ascent to God*, p. 25.

74. Ibid. According to Elior, these *coincidentia* appear in the Lurianic Kabbalah, but presumably apply only to the heavenly realms. In Chabad they apply to the earthly and human realms as well (ibid., p. 26).

75. Ibid., p. 27.

76. Ibid.

in their opposites. Spirit is only fully revealed when it is embodied in matter, and matter only fully realized when it is raised to the level of spirit. The divine longs to be both being and nothingness, as well as immanent and transcendent simultaneously. The practical implication of these dual movements is that Chabad is both quietist and activist: man must both annihilate his ego and desire before God, and bring spirituality into each of his desires and mundane affairs. Further, according to Chabad, the world must be revealed and differentiated into all of its material particulars, and spiritually unified in the divine "One."

The notion of *coincidentia oppositorum* is provided dramatic expression in the writings of Schneur Zalman's pupil, R. Aaron Ha-Levi:

> the revelation of anything is actually through its opposite.[77]

> All created things in the world are hidden within His essence, be He blessed, in one potential, in *coincidentia oppositorum* . . .[78]

According to Schneur Zalman's son, Rabbi Dov Baer: "within everything is its opposite and also it is truly revealed as its opposite."[79] Indeed, for the Chabad Hasidim, the unity of opposites on earth provides for the *shelemut* or completeness of God on high: "For the principal point of divine completeness is that . . . in every thing is its opposite, and . . . that all its power truly comes from the opposing power, and, according to the strength of the opposing power, thus the power of its opposite will be found truly."[80] In their state of *Hashawah* within *Ein-Sof*, opposites become united in a single subject and their differences are, in effect, nullified. Again, according to R. Aaron: "He is the perfection of all, for the essence of perfection is that even those opposites which are opposed to one another be made one."[81]

We will have occasion to deepen our understanding of the kabbalistic principle of *coincidentia oppositorum* when we consider the reciprocity between God and man later in this chapter. There we will see that for the Kabbalists the propositions that God creates man and Man creates God are complementary rather than mutually exclusive ideas.

---

77. Quoted in ibid., p. 64.

78. Quoted in Elior, "Chabad," p. 163.

79. Rabbi Dov Baer, *Ner Mitzvah ve-Torah Or* II, fol. 6a. Quoted in Elior, *The Paradoxical Ascent to God*, p. 64.

80. Rabbi Dov Baer, *Ner Mitzvah ve-Torah Or* II, fol. 6a. Quoted in ibid., p. 64.

81. 'Avodat ha-Levi, Va-Yehi, 74, quoted in Elior, "Chabad," p. 166.

GOD AS THE DIALECTICAL LIMIT

How can we understand the unification of contradictory and opposing principles, which is said to take place within the divine perfection? I would suggest that insight can be obtained into this question by considering *Ein-Sof* as a sort of "dialectical limit" upon all of our concepts and notions. The idea here is that as soon as we begin to inquire very deeply into the meaning and significance of our ordinary notions of "good," "evil," "reality," "material object," etc., we discover that these notions imply their opposites, or, better, have their opposites built into their very essences. As we try to define the notion of "material object," for example, we find ourselves invoking a host of "ideas" (e.g., spatiality, weight, density, etc.) that leads us to conclude that matter cannot be understood except via its opposite, "mind." As will become clear in Chapter Three, when we push the notion of "good" to its logical conclusion we discover that our common understanding of "good" as "benefit to the world" is also "evil" (as the world is an estrangement from the ultimate good which is God). As we will see, the same can be said for "reality" and "illusion," "freedom" and "necessity," the "universal" and the "particular," and any of a number of other of apparent contraries or contradictions that we have as part of our philosophical and theological vocabularies. Concepts swing over into their opposites as we attempt to understand them more definitively. The point at which this dialectical "swing" occurs is the point of unity or interpenetration of opposites. This is the "dialectical limit," *Ein-Sof*, or what Azriel and the anonymous kabbalistic "Source of Wisdom" regarded as *ha-achdut hashawah*, the indistinguishable unity of the opposites.[82] *Ein-Sof* is thus the limit at which all concepts deconstruct and swing over into their negations. Examples of these deconstructions are provided throughout this book.[83] Here it will suffice to spell out one example in some detail. Our example derives from the kabbalistic doctrine of the relationship between the "divine unified substance" and the "finite material world."

According to kabbalistic metaphysics, the infinite divine perfection is the one true substance, and the material, finite world is an illusion that is predicated upon the contraction and concealment (*Tzimtzum*) of the divine essence. On this view the world of individual material things exists only in the

---

82. Scholem, *Origins of the Kabbalah*, pp. 313, 332.
83. See especially Chapters Seven and Eight.

minds of those who, owing to the imperfection of their intellect, are unable to comprehend the true unity of things in the infinite All, in much the same way as a multiplicity of superfluous mathematical terms (e.g., different expressions of the number 7) exists only in the finite intellect of one who cannot comprehend them instantaneously as equivalents of a single idea. For example, according to the Kabbalists, a single act of human kindness is what it is only by virtue of its participation in the divine trait (the *Sefirah Chesed*) that embodies "kindness" per se. On this view, finite things exist only insofar as they participate in the divine essence. It is this essence that is real. The finite is an illusion.

However, when the Kabbalists push this concept of "reality and illusion" to its limits they encounter a sudden reversal in which the divine is discovered to be an illusion and only the finite is understood as "real." This is because in order for the infinite divine perfection to be just what it is, it must manifest itself in finite, material things. For example, the divine perfection, in order to be a divine perfection, must embody the values that in the Kabbalah are defined as the *Sefirot*: yet these values are *empty abstractions* unless they are actualized in a finite world of matter and death. What, we might ask, is wisdom, justice, or compassion in the abstract? It is only among actual men and women living in a world of potential happiness (but also of potential sorrow and pain) that wisdom, justice, and compassion can be actualized as real. On this view the divine essence is, as we have previously discussed, an abstract nothingness, only the finite and material is real. The Zohar tells us: "Just as the Supernal Wisdom is a starting point of the whole, so is the lower world also a manifestation of Wisdom, and a starting point of the whole."[84] Rabbi Schneur Zalman of Lyadi, the first Lubavitcher rebbe, characterizes this dual view of being and nothingness as follows:

(Looking) upwards from below, as it appears to eyes of flesh, the tangible world seems to be Yesh and a thing, while spirituality, which is above, is an aspect of Ayin (nothingness). (But looking) downwards from above the world is an aspect of Ayin, and everything which is linked downwards and descends lower and lower is more and more Ayin and is considered as naught truly as nothing and null.[85]

---

84. Zohar 1, 153a; Sperling and Simon, *The Zohar*, Vol. 2, pp. 89–90.
85. Likutei Torah, *Devarim*, fol. 83a; translated and quoted in Elior, *The Paradoxical Ascent to God*, p. 137–138.

Figure 2–1

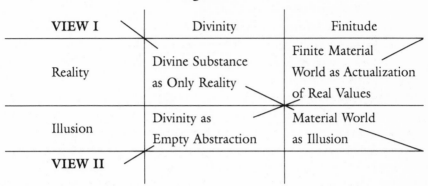

VIEW I	Divinity	Finitude
Reality	Divine Substance as Only Reality	Finite Material World as Actualization of Real Values
Illusion	Divinity as Empty Abstraction	Material World as Illusion
VIEW II		

The two views of "reality" and "illusion" are schematized in Fig. 2–1. What is reality? What is illusion? We might say that within the kabbalistic system of thought reality and illusion are each constantly exchanging places, jumping between two poles, as in those electromagnets whose positive and negative polarities are constantly shifting positions

One need not enter into the complexities of kabbalistic metaphysics, however, in order to understand the reversal of polarities that occurs at the dialectical limits of our concepts. Without reference to the deity, divine perfection, or substance, the above dialectic is reduced simply to the problem of universals and particulars that Hegel analyzed as an example of *coincidentia oppositorum*. The particular, e.g., a particular instance of a "red sensation," is only known as such, can only be "red," insofar as it *participates* in the abstract idea of "redness." Unless it is understood as an instance of an abstract concept, the concrete sensation (or concrete, finite, material anything for that matter) disappears into an inexpressible nothingness. On the other hand the concept of "red" when pushed to its limits is itself devoid of sense unless it is *actualized* in a concrete sensation or thing. Universal and particular, seeming opposites, pass over into one another, have each other embedded within their respective essences, and are bound together, as it were, to use a kabbalistic metaphor, as the sun is to its own light. Kabbalistic metaphysics, as expressed in the notion of *Hashawah*, the coincidence of opposites, suggests the same analysis for a great variety of seemingly opposite terms: creation and destruction, freedom and necessity, good and evil, God and man, etc. The point in which the opposites are joined and, as it were, become transformed into one another is the deconstructive or dialectical limit: and this limit is identified with *Ein-Sof*.

GOD IS DIALECTICALLY EVOLVING

It should by now be readily apparent that the God of the Kabbalah is no static, clearly definable entity, but is rather conceived of as a totality that evolves dialectically as an expression of its very nature and essence. The concept of dialectic is itself notoriously difficult to define. As I will treat of the relationship between the Kabbalah and dialectics in some detail in Chapter Seven, here it will suffice to say that a dialectic is a pattern of thought in which the implications of apparently simple concepts are spelled out in such a manner as to reveal that these concepts imply wider, more complex ideas, and, eventually their very opposites or contradictions. The mutual interdependence of these contradictions leads to new, higher-order integrative concepts that further imply wider, more complex ideas, etc. As Hegel uses it, the dialectic of thought is mirrored perfectly in the world, such that there is a natural, logical evolution in reality that mirrors such developments by implication that are evident in thought. Such an evolution is to be found in the kabbalistic concept of God, and according to kabbalistic theosophy in the development of the deity itself.

The Kabbalists realized that the proposition that *Ein-Sof* is evolving, is a startling one, one that would seem to imply a flaw or lack in the deity, an imperfection that necessitates redress through change. The Kabbalists, who tended to equate change with imperfection, were at pains to deny change in the deity, and while they recognized the dialectical evolution within God they insisted that this evolution was purely metaphorical[86] and only from "the point of view" of man. At any rate, in spite of the Lurianic (and general Jewish) view that the world was created in time, the "evolution" of *Ein-Sof*, i.e., the emanation and vicissitudes of the *Sefirot*, must be conceptualized in atemporal terms. According to Vital: "In Him there was no time or beginning to start, for He always existed and is everlasting and in Him there is no beginning (rosh) or end at all."[87]

While Vital tells us that *Adam Kadmon* and the worlds were created in a temporal sequence,[88] the transition, for example, from the unknown, to nothingness, to Will and Wisdom, to the God of the *Sefirot* is really a logical

---

86. On the metaphorical nature of kabbalistic descriptions see, for example, *Sefer Etz Chayyim* 1: 1, p. 28; Menzi and Padeh, *The Tree of Life*, p. 53–54, and Luzzatto, *General Principles of the Kabbalah*, p. 52.

87. *Sefer Etz Chayyim* 1: 1, p. 21; Menzi and Padeh, *The Tree of Life*, p. 6.

88. *Sefer Etz Chayyim* 1: 1, p. 21; Menzi and Padeh, *The Tree of Life*, p. 7.

or conceptual development rather than a historical one. It is part of the very logic of the deity that it should embody itself, for example, in nothingness, being, will, wisdom (and as we shall see), destruction and restoration, etc., and that each phase of this embodiment is equiprimordial and atemporal. Moses Cordovero preferred to speak of the deity as progressing through "non-temporal time,"[89] presumably a form of time in which one can logically differentiate a sequence but where there is as yet no past, present, and future.

In general, one can comprehend the entire kabbalistic system, including the emanation of the *Sefirot*, the creation of a finite world, the "Breaking of the Vessels," and their restoration by man via *Tikkun* as a *perfect, divine, atemporal totality*. It is only from the perspective of a finite, human mind, which sees things in temporal sequence, that God appears to be developing from a lower to a higher state of being, and that creation and man appear as Elior has put it, to be "stages in the process of becoming God."[90]

On the other hand, the Kabbalist's notion of God actually puts into doubt the very assumption that change implies imperfection. Why should we assume that on the scale of perfection "static" is superior to "dynamic"? For the Kabbalists *Ein-Sof*'s perfection is a dynamic process. On their view, in order for the Infinite is to be itself, it must "contract" itself and involve the finite, and, in effect, become ignorant. For the Kabbalists this moment of ignorance is necessary for the achievement of ultimate knowledge, in the same way that limitation and differentiation (within *Ein-Sof*) is necessary for it to become "all things." As Nozick finally concludes with respect to his own modern conception of *Ein-Sof*: "the process undergone is part of the perfection, not a means to it."[91]

THE THREE MOMENTS OF NEGATION

The dialectical development of the deity is conditioned by the presence of the attribute of nothingness at the core of *Ein-Sof* (*hamiddat ha-ayin*). It is through this attribute that all other elements within the Godhead evolve and pass into their opposites. As such, *Ayin* (nothingness) or negation is the power that fuels the development of *Ein-Sof*.

---

89. Scholem, *Kabbalah*, p. 103.
90. Elior, *The Paradoxical Ascent to God*, p. 167.
91. Nozick, *Philosophical Explanations*, p. 607.

While "negation" is apparent in varying degrees within different expressions of the Kabbalah, I believe we can discover three basic moments of negation within the most mature and philosophically interesting of the kabbalistic systems: that of Isaac Luria. In the thought of Luria (and the Hasidim who later adapted his point of view) the three moments of negation, are (1) the original *Ayin*, or primal nothingness out of which *Ein-Sof* creates itself as the hidden All, (2) the *Tzimtzum*, or contraction and concealment, which provides a metaphysical void or place for the existence of the *Sefirot* and a finite, created world, and (3) the *Shevirat ha-Kelim*, the Breaking of the Vessels, which brings chaos and disharmony into the finite world, paving the way for the restorative and redemptive activity of man. In short, these negations are nothingness per se (*Ayin*), distinction and limitation (*Tzimtzum*), and destruction and death (the *Shevirah*). They are the pivots around which the entire Lurianic system turns, the key moments in the evolution of God and the world. I have discussed the first of these (*Ayin*) in detail earlier in this chapter, and the latter two will be examined in detail in Chapters Three and Seven.

Here I will discuss each of these negations in general terms, in order to show that, for the Kabbalists, a rhythm or oscillation between negation and affirmation, constriction and emanation, and destruction and reparation pervades the cosmos. It is important to understand that each of the three moments of negation conditions a critical positive moment in the development of God. The first (*Ayin*) conditions being per se (*Ein-Sof*), the second (*Tzimtzum*) the creation of significance and value (the *Sefirot*) and the third (the *Shevirah*) the restoration and redemption of God, man, and the world (*Tikkun*). Table 2–1 outlines these three moments of negation, their metaphysical manifestations, and the positive moments that they condition in the development of God.

It will be well worth our while to articulate some of the implications of this scheme for the Kabbalists' conception of the deity. In our earlier discussion, we saw that, according to the majority of Kabbalists, *Ein-Sof* is not to be identified with the God of the Bible. One cannot direct one's prayers to it[92] and indeed, according to Isaac the Blind, *Ein-Sof* is not even mentioned in the Torah and Talmud. While *Ein-Sof* is the metaphysical ground for, and (the Kabbalists insist) ontologically identical with, the personal God of Israel, it must go through a dialectical transformation in

---

92. See Chapters Three and Seven.

Table 2–1

Negation	Symbol	Manifestation	Affirmation
The Primal Negation: Nothingness per se	*Ayin* (The Nought)	Abyss of World's Origins	The Primal Affirmation: *Ein-Sof*, Being per se.
The Secondary Negation: Distinctions	*Tzimtzum* (Contraction, Limitation, Concealment)	Metaphysical Void: Differences among finite things.	The Secondary Affirmation: Firmament of Values, The *Sefirot*.
The Tertiary Negation: Destruction	*Shevirat ha-Kelim* (The Breaking of the Vessels)	Chaos, antinomy, destruction, and death in a material world.	The Tertiary Affirmation: *Tikkun ha-Olam* (Restoration of the World).

order to become that God. This transformation occurs in two stages: in the first *Ein-Sof* is removed from the veil of hiddenness and becomes revealed; in the second it is transformed from an abstract principle or set of values, and becomes personal and concrete.

Before discussing this scheme (and particularly the emergence of a personal God) in more detail, it is important to point out that this developmental process is not a contingent evolution but rather proceeds with the force of logical necessity. Indeed, when we provide a full analysis of the kabbalistic symbols, we realize that the entire development of the deity, the world, and man is already prefigured in the very stroke where *Ein-Sof* refers to itself and begins to weave itself out of its own nothingness. As *Sefer Yetzirah*, and numerous Kabbalists since, have affirmed: "Their end is imbedded in their beginning and their beginning in their end."[93] The Lurianic Kabbalists took this idea to mean that the very origin of the cosmos, *Ein-Sof*, is dependent upon the so-called endpoint of the deity's development in *Tikkun ha-Olam*, and conversely that *Ein-Sof* contains within its original ineffability the entire progression from *Tzimtzum* to *Sefirot*, to the Breaking of the Vessels, etc., which leads to that endpoint in *Tikkun ha-Olam* (the Redemption of the World).

THE ORIGIN OF *EIN-SOF* IN LANGUAGE

The origin and development of *Ein-Sof* and the creation of the world can best be approached through a consideration of the kabbalistic metaphysics of language. As we have seen, the Kabbalists hold that the deity, indeed the cosmos itself, is, in its original essence, *Ayin*, absolute nothingness. Such nothingness would be the condition for a nameless, timeless, meaningless, eternity, but for the fact that a scintilla of significance, what the Zohar refers to as the "primordial point," emerges out of the vast, empty abyss as "being" pure and simple.

We have also already seen how the Kabbalist Azriel interpreted this primal point as equivalent to the act of "faith" that man has in God's existence. By opening himself to the possibility of a meaningful world, man, through his "faith" actually embodies the very process by which such a world comes into being. This is because the world, as it is conceived of in the

---

93. *Sefer Yetzirah* 1: 7; Kaplan, *Sefer Yetzirah*, p. 57.

Kabbalah, is not a vast assemblage of matter and energy, but rather a plenum of values and significances; and it is only through the *signifying acts of humanity* that such a world, the world of the *Sefirot* (a world of Will, Wisdom, Understanding, Kindness, Justice, Compassion, etc.) can arise.

That the world is a plenum of significance leads quite naturally to another important kabbalistic idea: that the world itself has the structure of a language, in particular, the language of Hebrew, the "holy tongue." This doctrine will be spelled out in full detail in Chapter Five. Here I would like to point out that for the Kabbalists there is an essential connection between the order of language and the order of the world. This is because they are each, on the Kabbalists' view, *bearers of significance*. The biblical tradition, of course, had affirmed that the world was created through an act of speech, and the Kabbalists went one step further in holding that the cosmos and even God himself is structured by language. It is for this reason that they were able to hold the view that the very language they utilized in speaking about the deity actually reflects the dynamics of *Ein-Sof* itself. For the Kabbalists, there is a sense in which the development of both God and the world follows directly from the language we utilize in speaking about this development.

By examining the language we utilize in speaking about the emergence of being from the primal Nothing we can actually gain insight into the process of creation *ex nihilo* and even the origin of *Ein-Sof* itself! One observation about language, made prominent in recent discussions of semantic theory and the philosophy of language, is that linguistic significance only exists as an interconnected system of meanings and differences among words. There cannot be a single meaningful term, for the meaning of any term is given by its location in an entire linguistic matrix. A word's meaning is determined by its *differences* with a whole host of other terms in the language and an implicit theory of the world, which the distinctions made in the specific language imply. To use or understand a single term is, in effect, to understand an entire language. This property of language provide us with a clue as to the transition from *Ein-Sof* as the primal Nothing to the infinitely diverse world of creation.

Recall the Kabbalists' claim that *Ein-Sof* is completely ineffable and beyond all description. Indeed, the early proto-kabbalistic work, *Sefer Yetzirah*, had declared in reference to *Ein-Sof*: "bridle your mouth from speaking and your heart from thinking."[94] Nevertheless, the Kabbalists do

---

94. *Sefer Yetzirah* 1: 8, Kaplan, *Sefer Yetzirah*, p. 66.

speak of *Ein-Sof*, and this very act of speech, even if it refers to *Ein-Sof* as a completely ineffable, unknowable "nothing," places *Ein-Sof* within a language, wherein it must be contrasted with an indefinite, perhaps infinite, array of other terms and expressions. The simple act of naming *Ein-Sof*, of referring to it, calling it "nothing," places it in the language and contrasts it with all other "somethings," and, in effect, brings out the possibility of an entire (significant) world.

The "primordial point," the scintilla of significance that emerges out of the abyss of nonbeing and that gives rise to the cosmos, is nothing other than the Kabbalists' reference to *Ein-Sof* itself. This is another meaning that can be given to Azriel's doctrine that the place where being emerges from the nought is called "faith." *The very act of speaking a language marks a faith in significance that gives rise to a meaningful world.*

Looked at kabbalistically, the doctrine that the Kabbalist's own reference to or faith in *Ein-Sof* gives rise to the world is actually equivalent to the traditional view that God creates the world *ex nihilo*. This is because, the Kabbalists, indeed all individuals, are (on the Kabbalist's view) a manifestation of *Ein-Sof*, and humanity's reference to or faith in *Ein-Sof* is actually a self-reference of *Ein-Sof* to himself. (The Christian mystic, Meister Eckhardt, whose worldview is very similar to the Kabbalists, summed up this view succinctly when he said, "The eye with which I see God is the same eye with which God sees me.") It is because of the identity of God and man that in a single act of self-reference God creates himself, man creates God, and the world is brought into being.

THE METAPHYSICAL BIG BANG

The process by which *Ein-Sof* creates itself from its own nothingness is thus metaphysically parallel (or even identical) to an act of human linguistic reference. In becoming itself, the deity performs a linguistic act in which it affirms itself *as a primal, undifferentiated totality*, which is contrasted with the primal Nought. We might say that *Ein-Sof*, in its first manifestation, is the "primal affirmation," the primal "yes" that stands out in relief against the background of an ageless "no." (This is what the Kabbalists refer to in their distinction between *Yesh* (Being or "Yes") and *Ayin* (nonbeing, or "No"). This "yes," this scintilla of significance, is sufficient, on the Kabbalists' view, to set into motion a virtual explosion of significations, a "big bang" in the realm of meaning: for implicit in this "yes" of this infinite being are all the "yeses," all the affirmations that could have, should have, or would have been. In short, just as a single significant word implies the existence of an entire language, or a single mathematical truth implies the existence of an entire mathematical system, an entire firmament of meanings and, more specifically, values, is entailed by the drawing out of *Ein-Sof* from the abyss of its own nothingness.[95]

The reason for this virtually infinite expansion of possibilities does not simply rest upon the specifically infinite character of *Ein-Sof*, for a whole cosmos of meaning and significance would also be implicit if the first referent, the first thing, were finite as well. If the first thing, for example, were Sherlock Holmes, John Kennedy, or some other finite fictional or nonfictional character, these could not exist (or be significant) without there being pulled out of the void a whole cosmos of significance to go with them. The point is simply that there simply can't be just one significant thing, or even one referred-to thing. The "big bang" of language and significance is inevitable. In and of itself, *Ein-Sof* is metaphysically unstable. Its very existence implies a world of values and possibilities. We might express this "big bang" schematically as follows:

(implies)

reference to or being x and *not* the nought ------> affirmation ----->
value/significance ----> matrix of value/significance ------> all possible
values---> value firmament -----> (the *Sefirot*)

The "primal yes" cannot be contained. God, in affirming *"Ehyeh asher Ehyeh"* (I will be that I will be), or in inscribing Himself as the primal letter, *Aleph*, must, in the process, say every possibility of language, thought, and existence.

---

95. Some Kabbalists, Schneur Zalman of Lyadi among them, hold that what we are here calling the "primal affirmation" is the *Or Ein-Sof* (the light of the infinite) rather than *Ein-Sof* itself (or "himself"). Perhaps, on this view, the term *Ein-Sof* would be reserved for the primal negation, *Ayin*, "that which the mind cannot comprehend nor the mouth speak," or for an even earlier essence that transcends both being and nothingness. Schneur Zalman speaks of a revelation or manifestation prior to the *Tzimtzum*, in which *Ein-Sof*, in a manner that is crudely analagous to a man revealing something to himself in thought, produces his "light." (See Schochet, "Mystical Concepts," p. 830, note 13.) The difficulty with this point of view is that it has God engaging in a "private revelation" and thus defeats one of his main motives for creating a world, i.e., to know himself through his manifestation to an "other."

This blossoming of meanings, values, and possibilities is, according to the Kabbalists, achieved via *a second negation,* an act of divine concealment and contraction that is referred to as the *Tzimtzum.* It is only by limiting itself (and thereby contrasting itself with an *other*) that *Ein-Sof* can bring into existence an infinite set of *distinct possibilities.* As a result of the *Tzimtzum* all possibilities other than *Ein-Sof* stand out in contrast against the background of *Ein-Sof*'s now-withdrawn presence.[96] If *Ein-Sof* had not withdrawn and concealed itself, than all possibilities other than itself would be nullified in its infinitude. By withdrawing and concealing itself, by negating the primal, infinite "yes" and introducing a second negation, *Ein-Sof* (via *Tzimtzum*) creates a distinction between itself and all other possibilities, and thereby "makes room" for creation.

The array of possibilities is represented in the Kabbalah by a secondary affirmation, the *Sefirot.* Unlike *Ein-Sof* itself, the *Sefirot* are not limited to a simple unitary "Yes," but rather affirm a whole variety of values and meanings. The *Sefirot,* which are ten in number (yet which combine into a plethora of combinations), represent the primal values (Will, Wisdom, Understanding, Loving-Kindness, Judgment, Mercy, etc.) that must prevail in a finite world. The *Sefirot,* in effect, rush out to fill the void of *Ein-Sof*'s withdrawn presence. They are, the Kabbalists affirm, the values that must exist in order to sustain a finite world.

Having flowered, so to speak, into what we have called a firmament of infinite possibilities, of values and significance (represented in the secondary affirmation or *Sefirot*), the primal affirmation, *Ein-Sof,* seeks to fulfill its essence as an infinite being that is contrasted with the primal Nought. But "to be" means something more than to expand into an array of *possibilia.* Being means "actual being," and demands that the value possibilities abstractly represented by the *Sefirot* be fully actualized. Yet, as we have already suggested, values can only be actualized in a finite world, where the reality of failure, destruction, and death puts these values (of kindness, justice, heroism, self-sacrifice, etc.) into play in an arena where they actually *matter.* The English word "matter" actually aids our understanding here: for the arena we are speaking of is the *material* world. Indeed, as Adin Steinsaltz has argued, the actualization of God's *being demands precisely the existence of a material world that is on the brink of despair,* for it is only in such a world (our own) that the values we speak of can be actualized most fully and

---

96. See Chapter Three.

completely. Our world, Steinsaltz says, is "the worst of all possible worlds in which there is yet hope"—for such a world, paradoxically (from the standpoint of the fulfillment of the possibilities within God) is the best world of all.[97]

And so, the primal "Yes" demands a "third negation," a negation of destruction and death, the tearing asunder that is referred to by the Kabbalists as *Shevirat ha-Kelim*, the Breaking of the Vessels. With the Breaking of the Vessels the once-pristine *Sefirot*, possibilities of value and significance, are torn asunder and fall into a dark, dangerous, and evil realm from which they must be extracted and restored to their proper place. This extraction and restoration constitutes for the Kabbalists a third and final affirmation, *Tikkun ha-Olam*. With *Tikkun ha-Olam* a personal God acts in concert with humankind to redeem a broken world through the very acts of Will, Wisdom, Kindness, Compassion, etc., which were broken when the *Sefirot* were shattered and displaced. In the end, the Kabbalists hold that a broken but redeemed world is far more perfect, far more valuable than an initially pristine one.[98] The kabbalistic scheme continues:

(implies)
Firmament of Value Possibilities ------> instantiation ------> failure, death and destruction (Breaking of the Vessels) -----> World on the brink of despair -----> Restoration and Redemption (*Tikkun ha-Olam*).

In the end, *Ein-Sof* sees its fulfillment and (we can now understand) its very origin and being (as value and significance) in the redemptive acts of mankind. Its beginning is truly "wedged in its end" and its "end in its beginning."

MAN MAKING DEITY:
TRANSITION TO A PERSONAL GOD

It is this process of redeeming a fallen world that transforms *Ein-Sof* from a hidden and abstract being into a personal God, from an "it" to a "thou," and

---

97. "The Mystic As Philosopher: An Interview with Rabbi Adin Steinsaltz,' *Jewish Review* 3: 4 (March 1990): 14–17.
98. Elior, "Chabad," p. 167.

ultimately to an "I."[99] This development, which is God's most immanent, revealed expression, is also God's highest ascent, for it is the process through which God ultimately becomes Himself. It is through his creation, humanity, that *Ein-Sof* becomes actualized as God. The Zohar even goes so far as to say that man, in effect, has the opportunity to make his creator. Adapting the wording of a rabbinic text,[100] the Zohar affirms: "He who 'keeps' the precepts of the Law and 'walks' in God's ways, if one may say so, 'makes' Him who is above."[101] Moshe Idel has pointed out that this idea was quite widespread amongst the Kabbalists.[102] For example, we read in the kabbalistic text *Sefer ha-Yichud*: "each and every one [of the people of Israel] ought to write a scroll of Torah for himself, and the occult secret [of this matter] is that he made God Himself."[103]

In such rather bold and surprising declarations the Kabbalists underscore the notion that there is a *reciprocal relationship between God and man*. God is indeed man's creator, but since man is the one being who can actualize the values that are only "ideas" in God, man can be said to complete, actualize, and even "create" God. Indeed, the human tendency to see "God" in the garb of the prophet, saint, *tzaddik*, or rebbe expresses the truth that it is in these figures that godliness finds its most fully realized expression. God, according to the Kabbalah, incarnates Himself in man, not just in one prophet or messiah but in each and every human deed that fulfills His ethical and spiritual potential. This is the inner meaning of the kabbalistic aphorism that "An arousal from above comes only in response to an arousal from below."[104] The atheistic claim that man has invented God is paradoxically placed into a context in which the Kabbalists, without abandoning theism, can affirm it. God both creates and is created by man: "Just as the Supernal Wisdom is the start of the whole, so is the lower world . . . also a start of the whole."[105]

It is actually mankind's activities that transform *Ein-Sof* into the personal

---

99. Scholem, *Major Trends*, p. 215.

100. Midrash *Leviticus Rabbah*, 35: 6.

101. Zohar III, 113a. Sperling and Simon, *The Zohar*, Vol. 5, p. 153. Idel translates this passage as follows: "Whoever performs the commandments of the Torah and walks in its ways is regarded as if he made the one above." Idel, *Kabbalah: New Perspectives*, p. 187.

102. Idel, *Kabbalah: New Perspectives*, p. 188.

103. Ibid.

104. Zalman, *Igeret Ha Kodesh*, Chapter 4. In *Likutei Amarim-Tanya*, p. 405.

105. Zohar 1, 153a. Sperling and Simon, *The Zohar*, Vol. 2, pp. 89–90.

God of Judaism. By forming a relationship with the Absolute through deeds and prayer, mankind constitutes God as a personal Being and (in another sense) further enables God to become Himself. Indeed, the Hasidim saw in the "nothingness" of *Ein-Sof* an infinite potential to be shaped by man. According to R. Livi Yitzhak:

> The Nought is the most general category of all the wisdoms because it is a potential power that may receive [every] form. And when man wants to cause the descent of wisdom from there, as well as anything else, it depends only on the will of man, because if he wants to worship God he can draw down [Him] upon himself.[106]

Idel points out that "the attachment to the Nought is, therefore, the encounter with the unshaped prime-energy, the pure potentiality, while worship by means of the commandments signifies the actualization of the divine potential by drawing the divine into the mundane world . . ."[107] On this view it is man's worship that will transform the indeterminate nought, a pure potentiality, into a positive divine being. If man does not actually *create* God through his worship, he provides the Infinite with a positive, recognizable form.

In the actions of the *Tzaddik* (the saintly man or woman), of the *Baal Teshuvah* (one who repents before his creator) and, most immediately, in man's pouring his heart out in prayer, we actually witness the transformation of *Ein-Sof* into a personal deity. This very thought is expressed by the Indian poet Tulsidas (d. 1623): "There is no difference between the Personal and the Impersonal . . . He who is Impersonal, without form and unborn becomes Personal for love of his devotees."[108] Such a view could well have been expressed by any of a number of kabbalistic and Hasidic thinkers.

THE DIALECTICAL DEDUCTION OF THE WORLD

It should by now be quite clear that the interpretation I have provided *Ein-Sof*, of being and nothingness per se, is such that the emergence of the

---

106. R. Levi Yitzhak, *Kedushat Levi*, fol. 6a–6b, quoted in Idel, *Hasidism*, p. 141.

107. Ibid.

108. Quoted in Louis Renou, ed., *Hinduism* (New York: Braziller, 1962), p. 220.

Sefirot, the consequent Breaking of the Vessels, and the development of the *Partzufim* through *Tikkun ha-Olam* proceeds with something of the force of logical necessity. That is to say, the entire dialectic (what I earlier referred to as the Kabbalist's "basic metaphor") is implicit in the very concept or essence of *Ein-Sof*, and can be derived solely from a meditation of the human intellect on what it is to have meaning or "to be." In sum, the world as we know it, as it is understood in the Kabbalah, is a necessary manifestation of *Ein-Sof*, or rather a necessary manifestation per se, derivable from that first scintilla of significance that shows itself against the background of *Ayin*, the primal Nought. The world conforms to what the Kabbalists tell us there must be if there is to be anything at all.

There is, however, another point of view (represented most clearly by the Kabbalist Moses Cordovero) that merits consideration. Indeed, according to Scholem this was by far the dominant view voiced by the Kabbalists themselves.[109] According to Cordovero, the process by which *Ein-Sof* emerges from concealment to revelation is an act of *free decision* that is an impenetrable mystery and is not in any way reducible to a necessary consequence of the essence of *Ein-Sof*.[110] According to Cordovero:

> Before the formation of the universe [*Ein-Sof*] had no need of emanation.[111]

> All of them [the *Sefirot*] need *Ein-Sof*, while He has need of none of them.[112]

I will discuss Cordovero's conception below. However, in order to properly do so we first must deepen our understanding of (and the objections to) the view that the development of *Ein-Sof* and the word proceeds with the force of logical necessary.

Scholem holds that while such Kabbalists as Vital spoke of God's desire or need to reveal or express his goodness to a world, or to actualize Himself as "King" by having subjects, such explanations of *Ein-Sof*'s activity were "mere expedients" that never developed into theory. Nonetheless Vital

---

109. Scholem, *Kabbalah*, p. 91.

110. Ibid.

111. Moses Cordovero, *Or Ne'erav* VI: 1, 34b; Robinson, *Moses Cordovero's Introduction to Kabbalah*, p. 114.

112. Moses Cordovero, *Or Ne'erav* VI: 2, 35a; ibid., p. 119.

certainly suggests that creation was an event that is necessitated by God's very being:

> The purpose for the creation was that the Blessed One had to be complete in all of His deeds and His powers, and all of His names of greatness, perfection and honor. If he had not brought forth His deeds and His powers, He could not have been called complete, so to speak, either in His actions or in His names or in His attributes.[113]

> If the worlds had not been created, along with all that is in them, the true manifestation of His blessed, eternal existence—past, present, and future—could not have been seen, for He would not have been called by the Name, HVYH.[114]

> When the worlds were created, however, the Blessed One's actions and powers came forth so that he could be called complete in all types of his actions and powers, and complete in all the names and attributes.[115]

Vital quotes Zohar Pinchas 257b: "For if there were no creatures in the world, how could He be called merciful and just? He was called this on behalf of the creatures that were to be created."[116]

I think it is a fair reading of the Lurianic system as a whole (a reading that is at least implied in Vital) that creation is, in a very important sense, a *necessary* event, necessary in order to complete and perfect God. The necessity of creation is also part of the philosophical meaning of the Zohar's pronouncements that man, in performing good acts, is actually the maker of God. Such necessity is implicit in the Lurianic view that the restored World of *Tikkun* is completed by the deeds of man on earth, and brings the cosmos (and by extension, the Godhead) to a greater level of perfection than when it was originally created. If *Tikkun* is necessary for God's perfection, then can creation be optional?

There are several possible objections to our "dialectical deduction of the world." One objection to our procedure stems from the *symbolical and*

---

113. *Sefer Etz Chayyim* 1: 1, p. 21; Menzi and Padeh, *The Tree of Life*, p. 3.

114. *Sefer Etz Chayyim* 1: 1, p. 21; Menzi and Padeh, *The Tree of Life*, p. 4. The term HVYH represents a rearrangement of the letters in God's holiest name, the tetragrammaton, YHVH, and has the meaning "existence." Vital implies that God's existence is dependent upon creation.

115. *Sefer Etz Chayyim* 1: 1, p. 21; ibid., p. 4.

116. *Sefer Etz Chayyim* 1: 1, p. 21; ibid., pp. 4–5.

poetical nature of the ideas involved. The kabbalistic symbols, it is said, are not ideas of sufficient precision to permit a logical, even a dialectical logical, deduction. The Kabbalah, it is said, provides a mythological vision of the world, not a rational one, and to place this view in a logical matrix violates its very nature and essence. A second objection argues, with S. I. Goldman, that it is always a mistake to assume that "the order and connection of ideas is the same as the order and connection of things,"[117] and on that assumption to attribute "ontological significance" to logical necessity. A third objection holds that to say that the world proceeds from *Ein-Sof* with "logical force" places an unwarranted limitation on the freedom and will of God.

With regard to the first objection, I have dealt with the question of the rational, philosophical content of the Kabbalah some length in Chapter One. Here I wish only to point out that the distinction between poetry and logic is hardly as sharp as is sometimes maintained. Indeed, poetical and mytho- logical "truths" seem to occupy a space somewhere between fact and logic, in a manner that encompasses them both. For example, the mythological "truth" that "man has been cast out from Eden" not only tallies with our intuition of the "facts" (though not in a strictly empirical or scientific sense) but also appears to be an essential (or necessary) part of the human condition. Could man be *man*, we might ask, if he had remained in paradise? Poetical and mythological truths appear then to be truths of such generality that they are woven into the very concepts to which they make reference; often, however, in ways that are not readily apparent in the concepts themselves, and most often in ways, as Levi-Strauss has pointed out, which reconcile an antinomy or relieve a tension that these concepts engender.[118] As such, mythological and poetical symbols, which on the surface may appear to be the antitheses of philosophical concepts, are actually readily projected into the philosophical arena, and hence quite amenable to logical and particularly dialectical logical inference. (The actual working out of this "projection" in this book is the best argument for its possibility.)

As for the other two objections to our dialectical deduction—i.e., that such a deduction confuses the order of things with the order of ideas, and fails to acknowledge that God's creation is a free and not necessary act—I would argue that each of these rest upon an Aristotelian, predialectical view of the world: one in which so-called opposites (things and ideas and freedom

---

117. S. I. Goldman, "On the Interpretation of Symbols and the Christian Origins of Modern Science," *Journal of Religion* 62: 1 (1982). Quoted in Handel- man, *Fragments of Redemption*, p. 112.

118. See Claude Levi-Strauss, *Structural Anthropology*.

and necessity) are held to be completely exclusive of one another. Dialectically (and I would argue kabbalistically) when fully analyzed, "freedom" implies an element of rational necessity: for we call precisely those acts "free" which are neither random nor caused by material forces but which rather correspond to some rational scheme, which motivates one to choose a particular act: and "thinghood" implies an element of idea, for we call X a "something" only to the extent that it is classifiable according to some general concept or idea. If the creation of the world did not correspond to some rational scheme we could hardly call it an act of divine will, and if the order of things did not in some way correspond to the order of ideas there would be no talking about "things" at all!

Now, I am certainly not under the illusion that my brief argument will dispel all questions regarding God's freedom. There will still be those who will ask about the original act (what the Kabbalists referred to by the term *dilug*) that prompted *Ein-Sof* to emerge from the primordial silence, or who will query whether once having emerged, *Ein-Sof* must will the presumably necessary consequences of its own essence. My own view is that such questions belong to the "realm of the silent": once they are asked the inquirer commits himself to the scintilla of significance (in *Ein-Sof*) and *ipso facto* to the kind of world that we have said follows from there being any significance, any meaning at all.

MIRRORED IN MAN

It is a fundamental kabbalistic principle that the dynamic evolution of the Godhead is mirrored quite precisely in the development of man. Basing themselves on the biblical concept of *Tzelem Elokim* (man is created in God's image), the Kabbalists (and particularly the Hasidim who followed them) adopted a psychology in which the basic transitions in the development of the Godhead (*Tzimtzum, Shevirah, Tikkun*, etc.) occur also in the life of man. Indeed from the very beginning the Kabbalah affirmed that the *Sefirot*, the archetypical components of the revealed God, are reflected and actually contained in the physical body and spiritual soul of man. In the symbol of *Adam Kadmon* (Primordial Man), the first creature to emerge after the *Tzimtzum*, the Kabbalists expressed the idea that the whole of creation is concentrated in humanity.[119] From this it was not a far leap to the assertion

---

119. Idel, *Kabbalah: New Perspectives*, p. 139.

that man, in coming to know himself, also comes to know God, and further that man's own psychological development has the "theurgic" implications of setting off a parallel development in the Godhead.[120] Psychology, for the Kabbalah, merges with theology. Kabbalah is not only, in effect, a "psycho-analysis of God," but a complete psychoanalysis of man is at the same time a kabbalistic inquiry into the deity.

A complete "psychoanalysis" of man would include what Schneur Zalman refers to as man's Godly (as well as his animal) soul, and what the Kabbalists spoke of as a man's *Tzelem* (image) or *astral body*. The *Tzelem*, is, according to kabbalistic tradition, both the unique determinative essence of each individual, and a sort of celestial counterpart to man's persona, a "personal angel" who wells up from the depths of his innermost being. It is just this personal angel or counterpart who is revealed to the prophet and who is also available as a spiritual guide to those initiated in the ways of kabbalistic meditation.[121]

It is the *Tzelem* that is the representation of the deity in the individual human soul. In the Lurianic Kabbalah it is referred to as the "spark" of divine light at the core of a man's being, which the individual must "raise" and "reunite" with *Ein-Sof*, via the process of *Tikkun*. It is the *Tzelem* that is the concrete expression of the creation of man in God's image (*b'tzalmo*, Genesis 1: 26). It is thus both a hypostatization of a biblical idea and a representation of a profound mystical experience, in which the mystic or prophet, in coming to know the depths of his own soul, encounters the depths of the cosmos as well. In such an act there is a fusion of the knower, the known, and the act of knowledge itself.

EIN-SOF AND THE UNCONSCIOUS

The notion that the dynamics of the Godhead are mirrored in the psyche of man suggests a parallel to *Ein-Sof* in the human unconscious. If on the cosmic

---

120. Here it must be said, however, that for the Kabbalah man's self-knowledge or self-discovery is also a confrontation with the unknown, a losing of oneself and a giving of oneself over to chaos. Just as in the depths of *Ein-Sof* lies an abyss of negation (the unknown), man himself has negation, otherness, and unknowability at his very core. It is primarily in recognizing this unknown core that man gains the self-knowledge we speak of here.

121. See Gershom Scholem, "The Concept of the Astral Body," in *On the Mystical Shape of the Godhead*, pp. 251–273.

level, *Ein-Sof* (the infinite) is "the concealment of secrecy," "the concealed light," "that which thought cannot contain," etc.,[122] it readily follows that in man *Ein-Sof* represents the primal unconscious, which remains mysterious and virtually unknown to the human subject. The Zohar describes *Ein-Sof* as "the limit of inquiry . . . since it is too deeply hidden and recondite to be comprehended."[123] It is descriptions such as these that led Jung[124] and others to equate the infinite Godhead with the essentially unknown, unconscious foundation of human subjectivity. Indeed, the opposite yet complementary inference has been made by several contemporary psychoanalysts, i.e., that a glimpse into the human unconscious affords an entrée into an unknown Absolute. For example, the psychoanalyst Wilfred Bion makes use of the sign "O" to designate both "ultimate reality," the "absolute truth," the unknowable, infinite Godhead, and the "emotional truth" of the psychoanalytic session. For Bion the attitude that enables us to reach out to "O," to our own unconscious, is one of no knowledge, memory, or desire.[125] Such an attitude is indeed quite similar to the mystic's approach to *Ein-Sof*.

"THERE IS NO WORLD"

True to the kabbalistic principle of *haachdut hashawah*, the unity of opposites, certain Kabbalists and Hasidim held a view that is in complete contradiction to the notion that man is the creator of God: the idea that man does not even exist. The Chabad Hasidim, for example, held that implicit within the Kabbalist's conception of *Ein-Sof* is the doctrine of "acosmism," or the notion that since God is everything, the world, including man, strictly speaking, does not exist, at least, not as a substance independent from the deity. As the philosopher J. N. Findlay has pointed out, any genuine notion of an infinite absolute must, by definition, leave room for nothing other than itself; and indeed a God who lay completely outside of a created world could not represent absolute value, for there would of necessity, in such a case, be

122. Scholem, *Kabbalah*, p. 89.

123. Zohar 1, 30a; Sperling and Simon, *The Zohar*, Vol. 1, p. 114.

124. Carl Gustav Jung, *Mysterium Coniunctionis, The Collected Works of C. G. Jung*, Vol. 14., trans. R. F. C. Hull (Princeton, NJ: Princeton University Press, 1963), p. 414.

125. Eigen, "The Area of Faith," p. 425.

many valuable things outside itself.[126] The Kabbalists themselves were clearly aware of these issues and several, such as Azriel of Gerona, early on adopted the Neoplatonic formula that "all comes from the One and all returns to the One."[127]

While some Kabbalists (Azriel, Meir ibn Gabbai, the Zohar[128]) appeared to embrace the pantheistic or, at least, *panentheistic*[129] implications of their theories, most were vague or ambivalent regarding the notion that God's substance goes forth into the world.[130] For example, Joseph Gikatilla denied that the world partakes of God's substance, but still could not prevent himself from declaring, "He fills all and is in all." At times, Moses Cordovero adopted what appears to be a fully pantheistic view of the divine: "He is found in all things, and all things are found in Him, and there is nothing devoid of His divinity, heaven forfend. Everything is in Him, and He is in everything and beyond everything, and there is nothing beside Him."[131] However, at other times Cordovero adopted a panentheistic position in which the substance of the *Sefirot* approaches unity with *Ein-Sof* asymptotically without ever becoming its equivalent.[132]

The Lurianists were highly ambivalent on this issue. For example, Vital holds both that *Adam Kadmon* includes all of the worlds,[133] and that the essence of *Adam Kadmon*'s light does not "reveal itself in his 'clothing,'" and thus the lower Worlds are called "created, formed, and made" and "have no

126. J. N. Findlay, *The Transcendence of the Cave* (London: Allen & Unwin, 1966), p. 182.

127. Scholem, *Kabbalah*, p. 90.

128. Ibid., p. 144.

129. In pantheism the toatality of the world is God; in panentheism God includes the world as part but not the whole of His being and substance. The relationship among Kabbalah, pantheism, and panentheism is discussed by Scholem in *Kabbalah*, pp. 144–152.

130. The biblical tradition generally affirms the idea of a completely transcendent God, and most Kabbalists were reluctant to contradict or reinterpret this idea.

131. Moses Cordovero, *Eilima Rabati*, fol. 25a; as cited in Rachel Elior, *The Paradoxical Ascent to God*, p. 50. Compare Cordovero, *Or Ne'erav* 33b: "the Creator, may He be blessed, [is found] in all things in actuality, while all things are [found] in Him in potential." Robinson, *Moses Cordovero's Introduction to Kabbalah*, p, 111.

132. Scholem, *Kabbalah*, p. 149.

133. *Sefer Etz Chayyim* 1: 1, p. 24; Menzi and Padeh, *The Tree of Life*, p. 27.

aspect of divinity."[134] Still, the Lurianic view of creation as an alteration between *Tzimtzum* and Emanation leaves little room for holding that anything exists apart from the absence or presence of the divine light and substance.

The Chabad Hasidim drew out the full implications of the Lurianic view in holding that *Ein-Sof* is the one true substance and the world is a mere epiphenomena or illusion. For example, according to R. Aaron Ha-Levi:

> For there exists in the world no entity other than Him . . . for there is no true substance other than Him. For if because of the vessels and conceal-ments, other entities appear to be substantial, in reality they are not substantial at all, for He, may He be blessed, is the substance of all substances, and there exists in reality, no other substance but Him.[135]

While the Lurianists were at times willing to grant that finite things participate peripherally in the substance of *Ein-Sof* (i.e., that "all the worlds share a single mode of being as garments of *Ein-Sof*"[136]), the Chabad Hasidim carried the Lurianic position to its logical conclusion: denying any substantiality to the created world. While they occasionally made a distinction between substance (*yeshut*) and existence (*qiyyum*), arguing that finite things have "existence" but no "substance," at other times they were more radical in denying even existence to the created world:

> Even though it appears to us that the worlds exist, this is a total lie.[137]

> Everything is absolutely as nothing and nought.[138]

> He is One Alone and there is no reality whatsoever apart from Him.[139]

It is easy to see why this radical "acosmic" position is the logical conclusion of the Lurianic system itself. The reason for this (as I will explain in detail in Chapter Three) is that, according to Luria, finite, material things appear only as a result of a contraction or concealment of the one true substance, which

---

134. *Sefer Etz Chayyim* 1: 1, p. 33; ibid., p. 110.
135. Elior, "Chabad," p. 160.
136. Scholem, *Kabbalah*, p. 149.
137. Elior, "Chabad," p. 80.
138. Schneur Zalman, *Igeret Ha Kodesh*, Ch. 6; *Likutei-Amarim Tanya*, p. 421.
139. Zalman, *Likutei-Amarim Tanya*, Chapter 35, p. 159.

is the *Or Ein-Sof* or divine light. Like images that have been, as it were, "carved" into a plenum of white light by selectively concealing (and hence darkening) aspects of that plenum, what we know as the world results from a concealment or diminishment of substance rather than its presence. If the full, substantial divine light were permitted to shine, the world (like the images projected on a movie screen) would be obliterated, i.e., dissolved in the totality of *Ein-Sof* itself.

God, on this view, is both nowhere in the world and everywhere in it. On the one hand, the world appears only because of God's absence (or concealment), but even in this absence enough of the deity remains to sustain the world. The world, we might say, has as much "reality" in comparison to God (to continue our earlier analogy) as a picture presented on a screen has in comparison to its source of light in the projector. Without the source the image would instantaneously disappear; the image has no more "substance" than (and is indeed a diminishment of) its source, and yet it is not completely identical with it. Transform that picture into moving, "living" images and we have an analogue to the kabbalistic view of an illusory but nonetheless seemingly independent world.

"FROM THE POINT OF VIEW OF MAN"

Paradoxically, the "independence" of the world is as important for the Kabbalists as its illusoriness and total cosubstantiality with God. The significance of this independence is explained by R. Schneur Zalman when he insists that creation: "is an entity distinct from Divinity so that the blessed Emanator can be a king over all separate entities by their fulfilling the commandments which he enjoins upon them."[140] What meaning could be given to God's *malchut*, his kingship, if his world and his subjects were truly an illusion?

The Kabbalists attempted to overcome this difficulty by invoking the Neoplatonic formula that the world exists only from "the point of view of the recipient."[141] There is, according to Schneur Zalman, no differentiation within the Godhead, and no emanated or created reality whatsoever, except

---

140. Schneur Zalman, *Igeret Ha Kodesh*, Chapter 20; *Likutei-Amarim Tanya*, p. 505.

141. See Idel, *Kabbalah: New Perspectives*, p. 138.

from the point of view of created things. From the point of view of God, there is no differentiation, no separate finite existence at all.

It will be worthwhile for us to examine this oft-quoted doctrine, in an effort to determine its precise meaning. In doing so we shall see that this doctrine, which seems to require that we attribute "consciousness," i.e., a point of view to an illusion, is perhaps the most difficult to resolve of all the kabbalistic paradoxes.

If created beings, including man, are *really illusory* how is it possible for them to *appear* real to themselves? If we project an image of some people onto a movie screen, how is it possible to attribute consciousness or a point of view to *them*? What would it even mean for a projected image, an illusion, to have consciousness or a point of view? Would it have an illusory consciousness? Yet, how can *consciousness* be an illusion? The Cartesian "*Cogito ergo sum*" (I think therefore I am) asserts that while anything presented to consciousness can be or not be an illusion, consciousness itself must be real: for if I am under the illusion that I have consciousness, then at the very least I am "under an illusion" which is itself a species of conscious-ness. On this view it is self-contradictory to assert that x is under the illusion that he has consciousness because having *an illusion is itself sufficient for x to be conscious.* If man exists only from his own *point of view* then this is sufficient to say he exists *sub specie aeternae* as well.

Further, as Schneur Zalman himself avows, God wills that there be a separate and distinct finite world in order that He may reign over it as king. Yet who is God fooling? Can He actually reign over an illusion? It would seem that if the world is real from *any* point of view it must be real from the point of view of God.

Perhaps, the solution to this puzzle can be modeled along the lines of an analogy with "dreams" and multiple personalities. When a man dreams, we might want to say that the figures in his dreams (particularly the figure with whom the dreamer identifies) have the "illusion" that they are conscious and have a "point of view." But is this an accurate way of speaking? Is it not better to say that it is the dreamer who has the illusion, i.e., that he is embodied in a particular "dream body," resides in a particular "dream world," and sees that world from a particular point of view? Does the dream image have any genuine point of view itself? If I dream that I am Napoleon, does the figure in my dream, the "Napoleon," have any experiences, any point of view on the world? Is *he* under the illusion that he is a finite intelligence, separable from his creator (me)?

Now the answer to this question I suppose is "Yes" and "No," interestingly the same "Yes" and "No" that answers the kabbalistic question of man's separate existence from *Ein-Sof*. For the Kabbalist wishes to assert that everything, including the existence of man's separate consciousness or soul is an illusion, like a dream, and all is in the mind of God. God, however, through an act of *Tzimtzum*—contraction, concealment or, in this context, "forgetting"—actually subjects Himself to this illusion. In doing so, God is like a man who suffers from a Dissociative Identity (Multiple Personality) disorder in which a variety of psyches or selves, each of which is "borrowed" from the same "mind" or "brain" (and hence identical with each other in "substance"), come to believe that they are separate and distinct personalities. Any one of the personalities of a "multiple" could coherently say "I don't really exist" or "I am under the illusion that I exist" or "It is only from my perspective that I have a separate existence." Indeed we could imagine circumstances in which a man might truly utter one of these strange propositions. For example, a woman falls in love with one of the "alternate" personalities of a "multiple" whose "main" personality is already married. As the "alternate" begins to merge with the main personality he might say to his lover with more than a degree of truth: "I don't exist. My existence is an illusion. I existed only from my perspective. I believed I existed but I really don't." The same, we might say, is true of man's relation to God. Like a multiple personality whose task it is to "heal the splitting" and come to realize the unity of his various personas, man himself must overcome the split between himself and his fellow man, and ultimately between himself and God and realize that his separate existence is itself an illusion. Only in doing so can man overcome the "trauma" (symbolized in the "Breaking of the Vessels"), which is responsible for the illusion of his separate existence.[142]

However, the illusion of separate existence is, as we have already seen, both *necessary* to the one true reality (*Ein-Sof*) and, from a certain perspective (in *coincidentia oppositorum*), indeed very real. True enough, it is only from man's perspective that the events of the created world have real (and indeed limitless) significance. To the cosmos as a whole the events in one man's lifetime, for example, are minuscule indeed. But since man himself is in *reality*[143] an aspect of God, the values and significance that he engenders have meaning for the deity Himself. "From the perspective of man" is

---

142. This is one more aspect in which we are all like a "multiple personality"—for the multiple is himself born of the trauma of a malevolent early environment.

143. See the discussion of "reality" in Chapter 1 and earlier in the present chapter.

therefore reduced to one more "perspective of God" and man's reality to himself thereby guarantees his ontological status *subspecies aeternae*. That God should be alienated from Himself, and thereby come to realize and know Himself through the point of view of man, fulfills His very essence. Indeed it has been said that the Absolute can only be conscious of itself as Absolute by providing, as it were, a "temporary seasonal independence" to finite beings.[144] This "independence" is created through the crises of *Tzimtzum* and *Shevirah*, what we have spoken of as the "second" and "third" negations within *Ein-Sof*. These traumas or crises in the Godhead are both acts of God's will and logically necessary events;[145] the function of which is to splinter the cosmos into an infinite array of independent fragments that must ultimately be reunited through the process of *Tikkun*.[146] According to Rabbi Aaron Ha-Levi, all of the various levels and details of reality must be revealed as separate essences that are nevertheless "joined in their value."[147] The fullest expression of divinity requires that *Ein-Sof* enter into a circular dynamic in which it becomes finite and particular only to have this finitude and particularity reunited with its infinite source.[148]

If we are to avoid what would amount to a fundamental misunderstanding, it is important to realize that for the Kabbalah, the entire system of the upper and lower worlds is all ultimately a part of God Himself. Kabbalistic theosophy is about the vicissitudes of *Ein-Sof*, the infinite Godhead, for there

---

144. Findlay, *The Transcendence of the Cave*, p. 186.

145. For *Ein-Sof* the "logically necessary" and the "willed" correspond in *coincidentia oppositorum*, in a way that is somewhat analogous to the manner that "I," if I wish to continue as myself, must *will* my own existence. God necessarily wills his own essence, which for him amounts to a "willing" of all things. We might say that were *Ein-Sof* not to will creation, this would amount to a failure to will his own being.

146. Elior, "Chabad," p. 165.

147. Ibid., p. 167.

148. The kabbalistic notion of reciprocity between the finite and the infinite is remarkably close to Hegel's later formulations regarding the self-alienation of Absolute Spirit, which, according to Hegel, must estrange itself from itself in finitude only to return to itself in a higher level of perfection. As we have seen, for the Kabbalists (as for Hegel), this self-estrangement has at least three functions. The first is that it enables the Infinite to come to know itself through the confrontation with and gaze of an "other." The second is that it enables the Infinite to actualize the full potential of its own perfection in the proliferation of an infinite array of finite particulars. The third, is that through its incarnation in man, the Infinite is faced with the material, intellectual, spiritual, and moral adversity that enables it to fully actualize the values that are at its very core.

is, strictly speaking, nothing else beside Him. When we speak about God needing man, and God creating man to complete Himself, we are speaking in terms of a metaphor; and unless we realize this we are in danger of adopting the point of view that God is (or was originally) a wholly transcendent Being who created an earth that is independent, which He then incorporates into Himself as His own completion. It cannot, however, be overemphasized that, according to the Kabbalah, everything (including all of the actions of man) are a part of the divine plenum, a part of God Himself. The kabbalistic metaphors then, are less an *explanation* of why God chose to create the world than they are a description of the inner workings of an all-encompassing divine reality.

COINCIDENTIA OPPOSITORUM

There remains something highly paradoxical, even contradictory, in the dual kabbalistic claims that the world as we know it is a concealment or negation, an illusion resulting from the withdrawal of God's omnipresence, *and* that nonetheless the higher, more "real" worlds, and even God Himself, are themselves dependent upon this very illusion. It stretches our philosophical credulity when we are asked to accept that our world is *both* an illusion or negation and that which is most fully actual and real!

Here we once again are faced with the kabbalistic doctrine of *coincidentia oppositorum*. The paradox expressed in the kabbalistic idea of the reciprocity between God and man points to a series of otherwise ineffable truths that are in accord with our most fundamental human experience, i.e., that we are both thrown into a life and world hardly of our choosing and yet at the same time we are the authors of our own existence; that we experience an awe and reverence for the moral order of the world, yet feel completely responsible for sustaining that order in our own actions; that we sense in our most spiritual moments the existence of a creator of both ourselves and the vast universe within which we reside, and yet feel that such a creator is nothing but the projection of our own human spirit.

The physicist Neils Bohr once made a distinction between what he called "superficial" truths and "deep" truths. The former, he asserted, were truths whose opposites or contradictories were false; the latter, the *deep* truths of science and philosophy, were truths whose contradictories are also true. It is such "deep" or "dialectical" truths that the Kabbalists are attempting to express in their view of the reciprocal dependence of God and man. They are attempting to find a place in their system of thought for each pole of human experience. One might even go so far as to say that because of its dialectical view of reality, the Kabbalah is the one "theism" that can embrace within itself the skepticism and "atheism" of the modern age. This is because for the Kabbalah, as we have seen, the atheistic view that man created God is not simply a denial of its opposite (that God creates man) but is instead its very completion. Both God and Heaven are in a sense created, or in the least, *completed* by the acts of mankind.

THEOSOPHICAL MAPS

We can perhaps gain a certain insight into the notion of *coincidentia oppositorum* that "the opposite is the completion" by considering an analogy with map making. Theosophy, after all, is itself a sort of a map of the spiritual universe.

It is a well-known principle of cartography that there is no perfect way to represent a sphere such as the earth's globe on a two-dimensional surface. Each cartographic projection (for example, the Mercator projection that represents global latitude and longitude through a series of equidistant parallel lines) will accurately represent some features of the globe while inevitably distorting others. (The Mercator projection achieves its parallelism at the cost of vastly distorting the size of land masses such as Greenland and Antarctica, which are located at or near the poles.) Philosophy itself, it seems is in the same predicament. Any given metaphysical (or antimetaphysical) system of thought will by its very nature be true to some aspects of reality while hopelessly distorting others. The only opportunity for a complete picture occurs when we entertain several projections, in the hope that they will be mutually correcting. In this context we can understand the kabbalistic views on the complementarity of form and instance, and of God and man, as analogous to two polar projections of the earth's sphere: the first centered about the north pole (and thereby hopelessly distorting everything south of the equator) and the second centered about the south pole (and thereby hopelessly distorting everything in the northern hemisphere). Only by taking these opposite views together can we hope to gain anything like a complete view of the earth's sphere. Similarly, the Kabbalists seem to affirm, it is only by combining opposite metaphysical perspectives that we can gain any genuine insight into the totality of God, man, and the nature of reality.

It is reported in *Pirke Avot* (The *Sayings of the Father*), in the name of

Rabbi Jacob: "One hour spent in repentance and good deeds in this world is better than the whole life of the world to come; yet one hour of a peaceful spirit in the world to come is better than a whole life in this world."[149] Here, in a mishnaic text, we find an affirmation of the kabbalistic paradox. Both this world and the world to come are each infinitely "better" than the other, and the text makes clear the way in which this paradox is to be understood. This world, which the kabbalists call, *Assiyah*, is the world of *creation* or *making*, is the only world where man can perform those activities that actualize his (and God's) moral worth. The world to come, on the other hand provides the context that makes these same actions valuable and meaningful, for it is only by virtue of their participation in values that transcend a particular self, place, and time that our actions can be truly said to be worthwhile, and provide us with any real satisfaction and fulfillment.

It is a dialectic of form and instance, of universal and particular, of God and man, which runs through kabbalistic thought and provides the foundation for the reciprocity of the upper and lower worlds. From this perspective we might even say the upper and lower worlds provide each other with their very sense or meaning. Virtue is meaningful on earth because it participates in the "peace" of a higher world where such virtue is success and reward; yet virtue is only meaningful in heaven because in the lower world it can be exercised in an arena in which it "counts."

GNOSOS VS. ACTION

Recently, Moshe Idel and others have questioned the entire approach of interpreting the Kabbalah in metaphysical or theosophical terms. According to Idel, the purpose of the kabbalistic symbols, as they were understood by the Kabbalists themselves, was not so much to bring knowledge or insight into the nature of the divine realm, but rather to implore the individual to ethical action.[150] Susan Handelman, following Idel's lead, has argued that the Kabbalah was distorted by its mediation through Neoplatonism, Hermeticism, and the Christian Kabbalah, which focused almost exclusively on its speculative and theosophical structure, thus detaching the Kabbalah from

---

149. *Pirke Avot* (The Sayings of the Fathers), 4: 22.
150. Idel, *Kabbalah: New Perspectives*, p. 233.

its connection with Jewish ethics, law, and ritual.[151] Indeed, both the German Idealists (who were, through Schelling, influenced by kabbalistic ideas) and subsequent scholars of the Kabbalah (notably Scholem) who then viewed the Kabbalah through the prism of German philosophy, have, on this view, distorted the Kabbalah, by interpreting it in mainly theosophical terms.

There is much, I believe, that can be said in favor of this point of view; one that places axiology (values) before ontology (being), and sees the Kabbalah more as "an inducement to action" rather than a "contemplation of static being."[152] This follows from the doctrines of the Kabbalists themselves, particularly the Lurianic Kabbalists, who, as we have seen, held that God truly becomes God only through the ethical actions of man. According to Luria, (and in this he is completely consistent with the Zohar) one cannot know God through simply an act of contemplation, because God Himself does not fully exist except through the ethical activity of humankind. One encounters God through one's *mitzvot*, one's *acts*, and not through one's *philosophy*. The encounter with God is, at the same time, in effect His creation! On this view, the "ultimate" questions that we spoke of earlier should be reversed in their order: value and meaning (particularly as they are embodied in action) are prior to reason and wisdom.

There are, indeed, other considerations, internal to the Kabbalah, which help to substantiate the claim that action is prior to being, and that God, as He is understood by the Kabbalah, cannot be an object of theoretical knowledge. The first of these is that, according to the Kabbalists, the Kabbalah itself is in constant flux along with the cosmos, and cannot be subject to a definitive interpretation. Idel quotes from Vital's *Sefer Etz Chayyim*: "The worlds change each and every hour, and there is no hour which is similar to another . . . and in accordance with these changes are the aspects of the sayings of the book of the Zohar changing, and all are the words of the living God."[153] Idel interprets this passage to imply that "even theoretically, the possibility of attaining its (the Zohar's) ultimate significance is nil: each moment brings its own novel understanding."[154] According to Handelman, "the supernal worlds are no static essences but are constantly in flux and in reciprocal relation with human activity."[155] As such, it is

---

151. Handelman, *Fragments of Redemption*, p. 96.
152. Ibid., p. 111.
153. Quoted by Idel in *Kabbalah: New Perspectives*, p. 248.
154. Ibid.
155. Handelman, *Fragments of Redemption*, p. 97.

impossible to have *fixed knowledge*, either of these "worlds" or of the Kabbalah itself. For Idel, the kabbalistic symbols invite "action rather than thought"[156] precisely because they are dynamic, changeable, and imperfect and are *themselves* in need of repair through the activities of man.

This view, which I have already examined in some detail in Chapter One, reflects a general trend in contemporary philosophy, rooted in pragmatism and the thought of the later Wittgenstein,[157] which emphasizes the performative over the referential function of language. Indeed, for Wittgenstein and those who followed him, the referential function of language is dependent upon its performative function: it is only by virtue of the fact that individuals respond to words in a certain way (i.e., that words induce certain actions) that they can be *used* to refer at all. Indeed, I myself, in a Wittgenstenian mood, have argued that this is particularly true for the use of the word "God."[158]

Without again entering into the general philosophical debate regarding the nature of linguistic signs, I believe it is possible to point out that for the Kabbalah, action and being, like everything else, exist in *coincidentia oppositorum*; in reciprocal interdependence. To argue that the Kabbalists' theosophical descriptions were regarded by them (or should be regarded by us) simply as inducements to action is to render senseless much of what they had to say. Idel is correct in arguing that the kabbalistic symbols do not have a single, static referent, and that they express "several aspects of an ever-changing reality." But this hardly leads to the conclusion that these symbols have only a performative function and no ontological significance. Indeed the very motive the Kabbalist has for performing *Tikkun*, for doing ethical deeds, is that such deeds have an impact upon the destiny of the world, that they have metaphysical implications. The value of the kabbalistic symbols is that in the very process of making the world transparent they also implore us to change it. Their reference is certainly ever-changing and dynamic, but it is a reference nonetheless. If kabbalistic theosophy teaches us anything it is that there is a reciprocal relationship between being and action, and as such an interdependence between God and Man. It is precisely this interdependence that is the subject of the kabbalistic knowledge. God,

---

156. Idel. *Kabbalah: New Perspectives*, p. 223.

157. Ludwig Wittgenstein, *Philosophical Investigations*, trans. G. E. M. Anscombe, (New York: Macmillan, 1953).

158. Sanford Drob, "Judaism as a Form of Life," *Tradition* 23:4 (Summer 1988): 78–89.

according to the Kabbalists, is most fully revealed in the redemptive activities of mankind. One such redemptive activity, according to kabbalistic tradition, is the study and practice of Kabbalah itself, what amounts to an intellectual and ecstatic contemplation of the nature of God, the purpose of creation, and the place of humanity in the world.

3

Tzimtzum[1]: A Kabbalistic Theory of Creation

T he concept of *Tzimtzum*[1] is a unique contribution of the Lurianic Kabbalah to the history of ideas. It is a conception that gives both content and meaning to the notion of creation *ex nihilo*, while at the same time providing the basis for a profound personal and social ethic. To the uninitiated, however, *Tzimtzum* is a strange, difficult, and perhaps even disturbing doctrine. It is a doctrine that gives expression to a series of paradoxical ideas, among which is the notion that the universe as we know it is the result of a *cosmic negation*. The world, according to Lurianic Kabbalah, is not so much a something that has been created from nothing; but rather a genre of nothingness resulting from a contraction or concealment of the only true reality, which is God. It is also part of the notion of *Tzimtzum* that the very unfathomability and unknowability of God and His ways is the *sine qua non* of creation itself. Creation, the doctrine of *Tzimtzum* implies, is, in its very essence, "that which does not know." God's contraction, concealment, and ultimate unknowability are thus the greatest blessings He could bestow on the world and mankind.

In this chapter I offer a philosophical and psychological exposition, commentary, and in some respects, elaboration of the concept of *Tzimtzum* as it appears in the kabbalistic system of Rabbi Isaac Luria (1534–1572) and

---

1. Contraction/concealment.

his disciples such as Rabbi Chayyim Vital (1542–1620) and, later, Rabbi Schneur Zalman of Lyadi (1745–1813). In addition, I offer an idealist and rationalist philosophical context in which these ideas can, I believe, be best understood.

The word *Tzimtzum* has at least two meanings. The first is an ontological meaning connoting "contraction," "withdrawal," or "condensation." The second is an epistemological meaning that connotes "concealment" or "occultation." We will see that both the ontological and epistemological senses of the term are necessary to a full understanding of the Lurianic theory of creation.

My plan in this chapter is to first describe and explain the notion of *Tzimtzum* in its philosophical (theosophical and cosmological) aspects, and then to explore the psychological and ethical implications of this symbol, as they were conceived by both the Kabbalists and such Hasidim as the Maggid of Mezrich and Nachman of Breslov.

ORIGIN OF THE DOCTRINE

While the concept of *Tzimtzum* is not fully articulated prior to Luria, there are clear precursors to this symbol in earlier kabbalistic sources. *Tzimtzum* is even hinted at in an early Midrash where we learn that when God descended to inhabit the holy *mishkan* or tabernacle, he "restricted his Shekhinah [the divine 'presence'] to the square of an ell."[2] While in this Midrash God contracts himself in order to occupy a particular place, we here have the germ of the idea that a *Tzimtzum*, or contraction, is necessary in order for God to be *manifest* in the world. The Kabbalists, who held that the world itself was a manifestation of the infinite God, reinterpreted this Midrasic notion and elevated it to the principle of creation itself.

Such an interpretation is evident, for example, in a very early source from Iyyun, which is quoted by the fourteenth-century Kabbalist Shemtov ben Shemtov:

> How did He produce and Create His World? Like a man who holds his breath and contracts (*mezamzem*) himself in order that the little may contain the many. So He contracted His light into a hand's breadth,

2. Midrash *Shemoth Rabbah* 34: 1.

according to His own measure, and the world was left in darkness, and in that darkness He cut boulders and hewed rocks.[3]

The Ramban (Rabbi Moses Ben Nachman, Nachmanides; 1194–1270) held that the beginning of creation involved the emergence of divine wisdom (*Chochmah*) as a result of a *Tzimtzum* or limitation of the divine light or will in the uppermost *Sefirah*. This limitation is said to have produced a region of darkness within which the clear light of *Chochmah* (Wisdom) could flow.[4] The Ramban's view is also significant inasmuch as it anticipates the later Hasidic view that a contraction of the self or will is also a prerequisite for human wisdom.[5]

The original light of Genesis 1: 3 ("let there be light . . .") is referred to in the Zohar as the "hidden light" on the theory that "had it not been concealed from everything, the world could not have endured for a single moment."[6] The Zohar informs us that this light was only manifest on the first day of creation. Since that time it has been concealed. In this passage the Zohar or "Book of Illumination" regards the light of *Ein-Sof* as *manifest only when it is concealed.*[7]

The Zohar refers to the first *Sefirah* as "the light that does not exist in light" and the last *Sefirah*, *Malchut*, as "a light that does not shine." Further, it holds that the *Sefirot* are themselves emanated through the *bozina di-kardinuta*, the "spark of blackness," graphically illustrating the dialectical tension between light and darkness, revelation and concealment, and being and nothingness, which is so prevalent in the Kabbalah[8] and which serves as the background for the Lurianic notion of *Tzimtzum*.

Moses Cordovero (b. 1522), an older contemporary and teacher of Isaac Luria, expanded upon these Zoharic notions and developed a dialectical view

---

3. See Scholem, *Origins of the Kabbalah*, p. 449, and *Kabbalah*, p.129.

4. Scholem, *Origins of the Kabbalah*, pp. 449–50.

5. See below, "*Tzimtzum*: Psychological Aspects."

6. Zohar II, 148b. The Zohar describes how the world is sustained by this concealed light: "And not a day passes without something emerging from it (the concealed light) into the world." Tishby and Lachower, *The Wisdom of the Zohar*, Vol. 1, p. 441. Also Zohar I, 140a where the numerical equivalence of *Or* (light) and *Raz* (mystery) is interpreted along these lines.

7. We learn that this light "was concealed and sown, like the seed that produces offspring, seeds, and fruit."

8. Zohar I, 15a, b; Tishby and Lachower, *The Wisdom of the Zohar*, p. 309, cf. p. 271.

of the world's creation that anticipates the full significance of *Tzimtzum*. According to Cordovero, the creation of the *Sefirot* involves the concealment of the infinite God. Indeed, for Cordovero, creation is simply another perspective on this concealment. Cordovero provides an example of the kabbalistic coincidence of opposites when he declares, "revealing is the cause of concealment and concealment is the cause of revealing."[9]

TZIMTZUM IN LURIA AND VITAL

While *Tzimtzum* is clearly anticipated in these earlier sources, it was Isaac Luria and his disciples (most notably Joseph Ibn Tabul and Chayyim Vital) who made *Tzimtzum* a central focus in their cosmology. Two theological problems, the first created by God's presumed omnipresence and the second by His presumed unchangeability, prompted Luria to introduce "contraction" and "concealment" as the basis for the creation of a finite world. The first of these problems arises because God is assumed to be infinite and omnipresent. As such, He originally fills the whole of Being and without an act of contraction or self-limitation there would simply be no "place" for a world to exist. *Tzimtzum* thus, as it were, "makes room" for a world.[10] The second problem arises because God is thought of as complete, self-sufficient, and unchangeable. He, therefore, cannot be said to create a world that in any way adds to or alters His essential being. While most previous Kabbalists seemed either unaware of or unable to address the first of these problems (the problem of finding a "place" for creation) they had sought to resolve the latter problem (God's unalterability) by analogizing creation either to the lighting of one candle from another (which in no way alters or diminishes the first candle) or to the "replanting" of already living plants, or the uncovering of pre-existent roots (as a result of which nothing really changes).[11]

The notion of *Tzimtzum*, which has the dual meaning of "contraction" and "concealment," was introduced by Luria to resolve each of these theological dilemmas. As we have seen, *Tzimtzum* entails that God *contracts* to provide a "place" for the world. Further, according to this doctrine, the very existence the world is predicated not on a metaphysical addition to, or

---

9. See Scholem, *Kabbalah*, p. 402.
10. Luzzatto, *General Principles of the Kabbalah*, pp. 42, 51.
11. Tishby and Lachower, *The Wisdom of the Zohar*, p. 272.

alteration in, an infinite God, but upon a *concealment* of God's "light" or manifestation. As the sun is not changed or diminished by a concealment of its light, the infinite God is unchanged as a result of creation.

In his comprehensive account of the Lurianic Kabblah, *Sefer Etz Chayyim*, Vital declares:

> know that before the emanated things were emanated and the created things were created there was a supernal light that was simple, without composition or external relations, and it filled the whole of existence. There was no empty place, ether, or void. Everything was filled with the infinite light. There was neither beginning nor end. All was one simple light in perfect equanimity. This was called *Or Ein Sof* (the Light of the Infinite God). When it arose in His simple will to create the world and emanate the emanations, and to bring to light the perfection of His acts and names, then He contracted Himself into the central point that was in the middle of His light. He contracted Himself into this point and then retreated to the sides encircling this point. Then there remained an empty space or ether, an empty hollow (or void).[12]

It is this *Tzimtzum*, the withdrawal of *Ein-Sof* from a central metaphysical (not spatial) void or hollow, which provides, according to the Lurianic scheme, the foundation for all God's creation.

It is interesting to note that, according to Vital, the first act of creation is the contraction or concentration of divine energy into a central cosmic point. It is only after *Ein-Sof* concentrates all of its energy into a central point that it can withdraw and conceal itself from that point. I will have reason to comment on this later when I discuss the psychological ramifications of *Tzimtzum*.

A further point of interest in Vital's account is his emphasis on the *Tzimtzum* as a perfectly even process, resulting in the hollow taking on circular form.[13] Vital explains that the reason for this is that *Ein-Sof* is equal in all of its qualities and dimensions, and further, that the *Sefirot*, which were

---

12. Chayyim Vital, *Sefer Etz Chayyim*, 1: 1, p. 22. This passage in Vital is discussed and translated somewhat differently by David Ariel, in his book *The Mystic Quest* (Northvale, NJ: Jason Aronson, 1988), p.106ff. See also Menzi and Padeh, *The Tree of Life*, p. 1. (I am indebted to Rabbi Joel Kenney for his assistance in translating this and other passages in *Sefer Etz Chayyim*.)

13. It is unclear to me from the text in *Sefer Etz Chayyim* whether the *iggulim* (circles) of the *Sefirot* are to be understood three-dimensionally as spheres. The

to be emanated into this hollow, would themselves also be perfectly circular as well.

A question, which gave rise to considerable controversy among the Kabbalists, is whether the *Tzimtzum* involved *Ein-Sof* itself or just its light. Luria and Vital held that *Ein-Sof* itself is concealed or withdrawn, while other Kabbalists suggested that even prior to the *Tzimtzum*, *Ein-Sof* accomplished an act of (self) revelation through this light; and that it was this light, the *Or Ein-Sof*, which withdrew from the metaphysical hollow or void (*chalal*).[14]

THE "CATHARSIS OF *DIN*"

The Lurianists place *Tzimtzum* within the context of their bold speculation regarding events that transpired within *Ein-Sof* itself prior to the creation of the world. They explain that the fundamental reason for the *Tzimtzum* is to expose the "roots of judgment" (*Din*) within *Ein-Sof*, in order to purge limitation from the deity and introduce it into the cosmos. According to Luria and Ibn Tabul the original *Tzimtzum* results from a differentiation or "gathering" of forces within the Godhead, specifically the forces of judgment (*din*).[15] "Prior" to this gathering, all the divine forces or traits exist perfectly commingled within God. Thus the original divine act is one in which God's attributes (*middot*) become distinguished from each other. The limiting factor of judgment (*din*) is separated from mercy (*rachamim*). This internal

---

question may be irrelevant, because in either case the geometric imagery is to be regarded as nonspatial and metaphoric.

14. Among those Kabbalists holding the latter view are Israel Sarug (Scholem, *Kabbalah*, p. 133) and Schneur Zalman of Lyadi. On Schneur Zalman's view there is a (self) revelation of light, in a manner that is akin to an individual speaking or thinking to himself, which precedes the creation of the world. This revelation, the *Or Ein-Sof*, is what undergoes the *Tzimtzum*. Schneur Zalman even goes so far as to say that the contraction of the *Or Ein-Sof* is itself relative to creation and does not occur from the perspective of the deity (see Schochet, *Mystical Concepts*, p. 831, note 18). In *Torah Or*, Miketz (39a), Schneur Zalman states: "It was in this Light that the entire *Tzimtzum* mentioned in *Etz Chayyim* took place. A Constriction took place in this Light, forming a vacuum and a Vacated Space. All this took place in the Light of the Infinite—in the Light, and not in the Infinite Being Himself, heaven forfend." (Trans. and quoted in Aryeh Kaplan, *Chasidic Masters* [New York: Maznaim, 1984], p. 101.)

15. See Scholem, *Kabbalah*, p. 130.

separation of the limiting factor, judgment, within *Ein-Sof* paves the way for a "catharsis" of this factor through the *Tzimtzum*, which is itself an act of judgment and limitation. The act of *Tzimtzum* is the instrument and archetype of finitude, and thus the very principle or essence of a created world. Vital tells us that as a result of the *Tzimtzum* "there was now a place for emanations, creations, formations and actions"; in short a place for the creation of the "worlds."[16]

According to Luria, the deity holds a somewhat ambivalent attitude toward the finite. On the one hand the finite is contained within *Ein-Sof* and is an essential part of God's perfection. This view had been clearly stated centuries before Luria by the Kabbalist Azriel of Gerona: "*Ein-Sof* is perfection without any imperfection. If you propose that He has unlimited power and does not have finite power, then you ascribe an imperfection to his perfection."[17] However for Luria, this necessary presence of finitude results in a certain discomfort or instability within the Godhead, as it entails that God contains, as part of his essence, limitation, and thus the negativity and evil that limitation implies. The act of *Tzimtzum*, and the very process of creation, then becomes a means for *Ein-Sof* to purge itself of finitude and evil. This occurs through a *catharsis of Din*, a purgation of the limiting, judgmental factor within the Godhead, resulting in the creation of a finite world.[18] As we will see, the divine catharsis results in a world that becomes the repository of evil.

ISRAEL SARUG

An early expositor of the Lurianic system (though not one of his actual disciples), Israel Sarug engaged in even more daring speculation regarding the events internal to *Ein-Sof* prior to the *Tzimtzum* and creation of the void. As summarized by Scholem, Sarug held that God's pleasure in his own self-sufficiency produced a "shaking" of *Ein-Sof* within itself.[19] This shaking aroused the roots of Judgment, *Din*, and caused "points" to be engraved in

---

16. Vital, *Sefer Etz Chayyim* 1: 1.

17. Dan, *The Early Kabbalah*, p. 90.

18. See Scholem, *Kabbalah*, p. 129. Scholem explains that this (cathartic) aspect of the theory of *Tzimtzum* is clear in Luria's own literary remains, and in the account of Joseph Ibn Tabul, but obscured in Vital.

19. Scholem, *Kabbalah*, p. 132.

Din, such engravings forming the contours of the metaphysical void. The light of *Ein-Sof*, acted upon these engravings in such a manner as to create a Primordial Torah, which serves as a garment (*malbush*) for *Ein-Sof*, woven out of the very fabric of his being and barely distinguishable from him. The structure of this garment is composed of the 231 two-letter combinations of the twenty-two Hebrew letters (the so-called 231 "Gates" of *Sefer Yetzirah*). The *Tzimtzum*, according to Sarug, is a folding of this garment that leads it to occupy only half its original space, creating a rectangular void within which emerges the finite world.

Like many of the Kabbalists' cosmological speculations, Sarug's account is fascinating from a psychoanalytic point of view, as it appears to internalize within the Godhead a very human dynamic involving narcissism, pleasure, judgment, language, and shame (here symbolized by the garment woven from judgment). Centuries later Freud would, of course, describe a similar dynamic as occurring within the psyche of man.

EMANATION

It is only subsequent to the original *Tzimtzum* or concealment that a positive act of creation, an emanation of divine "light" into the place resulting from God's withdrawal, can occur. An emanation prior to the *Tzimtzum* would be impossible, as such "uncondensed" light would cause the disappearance of worlds[20] as soon as they were created. *Ein-Sof* thus emanates light into the void or hollow (*chalal* or *tehiru*) that remained after the initial divine contraction. However, because even a void cannot subsist independently from God, the *tehiru* contains within itself some residue (*reshimu*) of the original divine ominpresence that serves as a vessel (*keli*) or container for subsequent emanations. The void is also a container for the expelled "roots of *Din*," which had been eliminated from the Godhead via the very act of *Tzimtzum* that had brought the void into existence.

For Luria, creation is a dialectical process in which a series of negations or concealments alternate with a complementary series of positive acts, emanations, or divine revelations.[21] Frequently, the negative and positive acts are complementary descriptions of the same event. This is the case with the

---

20. Luzzatto, *General Principles of the Kabbalah*, p. 42.
21. Typically contraction is associated with the divine attribute of judgment

Tzimtzum, which is both a contraction or negation of *Ein-Sof* and an excretion or emanation of the limiting, negative factor of *Din* into the void. From a broader perspective, *Tzimtzum* is both a negation of God and the positing of the vessels (the *kelim*), which ultimately serve as the structures of the world. To make a mathematical analogy, the limitation of *Ein-Sof* through the negation of the limiting factor within it is like the subtraction of a negative number, which always has a positive result. In the case of *Ein-Sof*, this positive result is the creation of the world.[22]

The dialectical nature of creation is also illustrated in the fact that the Lurianists occasionally spoke of the emanations giving rise to the *Sefirot* as a *hitnotzetnut*, or "flaring up" of the primordial point after God's light had been withdrawn. It is as if the nothingness of the metaphysical void itself flares up, i.e., rushes out from itself, and carves contours and details in the residue of divine light remaining after the *Tzimtzum*. This concept appears to have its source in the Zohar, which speaks of the *kav ha-middah*, the standard of measure that gives rise to and fixes the dimensions of the *Sefirot*. This *Kav* or ray originates in the *bozina di-kardinuta*, the "spark of blackness," a concealed flash of negative divine light, which lay hidden within but which ultimately emerges from *Keter*, the divine will.[23]

According to Vital, the whole of creation, everything that can possibly be known or conceived, exists in the central metaphysical point or hollow created by *Ein-Sof*'s withdrawal. Logically (but not temporally) subsequent to the *Tzimtzum*, a line or ray (*kav*) of divine light enters the hollow, circles along its external perimeter, and creates the first *Sefirah* (dimension or archetype of creation). According to Luria, the ray, which is sometimes conceived of as a divine letter, a Hebrew *yud*, creates the *Sefirot* by ordering the inchoate mixture which remained in the void after the initial *Tzimtzum*.[24] After the emanation of the *Sefirah Keter* the remaining nine *Sefirot* are created in turn as the ray spirals closer and closer to the center of the void. The final *Sefirah*, *Malchut*, channels what remains of the infinite light into the very center of the hollow, creating our world, at the farthest remove from *Ein-Sof*, which surrounds it from all sides.

(*Din*) and emanation with the attribute of *Chesed*. See Luzzatto, *General Principles of the Kabbalah*, p. 102.

22. See the discussion of Nozick's theory that creation is the result of nothing being "nothinged" in Chapter Two.

23. Zohar I 15a, b; Tishby and Lachower, *The Wisdom of the Zohar*, Vol. 1, pp. 271–272.

24. Scholem, *Kabbalah*, p. 130.

The ray, Vital informs us, is very narrow, and except by means of it the *Sefirot* are neither connected with the surrounding divine light, nor with each other. An element of void, indeed an element of the *Tzimtzum* itself, must remain between the light of *Ein-Sof* and the first, outermost *Sefirah*, for if the latter "were connected (to the light) it would return to its original state and be nullified."[25] The *Tzimtzum* thus fulfills its role of bringing actual limitation into the cosmos, for by creating a place that is void of the divine presence, it sets up the possibilities of distinction within that presence, which are fully realized when the positive, emanative act of creation begins.

THE "VESSELS"

Vital, following Luria, refers to these "possibilities of distinction" as *kelim*, or vessels. He introduces a distinction between *atzmut* (essence) and *kelim* (vessels) to distinguish the light that comprises the *Sefirot* from the empty or negative boundaries that limit or "contain" them. Vital is very clear in his view that the vessels were created through the negative act of God's contraction/concealment. "The process of removing light," he tells us, "revealed a vessel."[26] Indeed Vital asserts that the entire purpose of the divine contraction is the creation of such vessels: "Now we can understand the reason for the *Tzimtzum*, that *Ein-Sof* contracts itself in the middle of its light to leave the hollow place. Why? The idea is to make vessels (*kelim*)."[27] However, the status of these vessels, i.e., whether they have an independent existence, is somewhat unclear. Vital informs us that the *kelim* are not really vessels but are called vessels only in relation to the light that exists between them. This seems to imply a view of relationship between vessel and essence that is similar to Aristotle's view regarding the relationship between "form" and "substance." On such a view the *kelim* (vessels) and *atzmut* (essence) exist only in a state of mutual interdependence, defining each other in the same way that a circle defines the area it contains and vice versa. The problem with this view that the kelim have only a relative existence stems from the fact that the Lurianists hold that some of the vessels (in a "later" development, metaphysically speaking) are *shattered* in the process of being overfilled with

---

25. Vital, *Sefer Etz Chayyim* 1: 1.
26. Vital, *Sefer Etz Chayyim*, 1: 1.
27. Vital, *Sefer Etz Chayyim*, p. 26.

divine light, breaking into numerous shards, which then entrap sparks (*netzotzim*) of the divine light that they had hitherto contained.[28] While it is clear, on the view of most Kabbalists, that this description is to be taken metaphorically, it nevertheless attests to a measure of independence of the vessels from the light they contain.[29]

A second reason for holding that the *kelim* have a quasi-independent "negative existence" stems from the fact that Vital holds that they could not have been created in the same act that created the light that they contain. Vital considers and rejects the possibility that *Ein-Sof* could have created a finite world of limited light all at once, simply by having left some energy (the *kav*) in the hollow and removing all the other light.[30] He concludes that the only way to obtain the structure necessary to form *kelim* is by removing the light completely (and then to make *Sefirot* by returning the light to fill vessels in a measured way).

Regardless of what position is taken regarding the vessels' independence, for Luria and Vital, the world's structure is clearly the result of a negation, and the vessels have a negative ontological status resulting from the *Tzimtzum*. The vessels are likened to curtains that conceal the divine light in varying degrees. Cordovero had compared them to a series of colored glasses that change the appearance of water that is poured into them but that do not change the water itself.[31] A more contemporary analogy would be to a photographic slide that casts a differentiated and detailed image onto a screen, not by adding anything to the screen, but by selectively concealing or occulting portions of what would otherwise be a pure, unitary white light. This, indeed, is a good way to understand the *Tzimtzum* itself, as a process that creates finite plurality through a partial occultation of that which is infinite and whole.

In thinking about the vessels one may also imagine an ocean that has completely withdrawn from the beach at low tide, and which leaves lines in the sand representing its progressive retreat. In *Tzimtzum*, the marks of *Ein-Sof* having once been in the void remain, and these marks provide the

---

28. Vital, *Sefer Etz Chayyim* II: 2, p. 79ff.

29. This is because if a circle were to suddenly "explode" its geometric boundary, i.e., its perimeter, could not be said to fragment and later entrap portions of the circle itself.

30. Vital, *Sefer Etz Chayyim* 1: 1.

31. Moses Cordovero, *Pardes Rimonim* IV: 4, as discussed by Schochet in "Mystical Concepts," p. 868.

structure or vessels for a created world. Even in its emptiness and negativity this world retains a trace of the divine. At first, according to Luria, the vessels take on the form of a "primordial ether" (*avir kadmon*) but later they take on the more definite form of Primordial Man (*Adam Kadmon*).[32] The vessels, however, only achieve their true essence (*atzmut*) through their being filled with the light of *Ein-Sof* by means of the raising and lowering of the ray in the metaphysical void.[33]

WORLDS, *SEFIROT, ADAM KADMON*

Vital informs us that the *Tzimtzum* occurs in a myriad of grades, corresponding to the myriad of worlds, some quite translucent and others dark and opaque, which comprise the cosmos. Each of these worlds is filled with a *kav* (ray) of ten *Sefirot* and each exists in the single hollow that arose from the original *Tzimtzum*. The first world is spoken of as *Adam Kadmon* (often abbreviated as '*AK*), and it is so translucent and exalted that it is barely distinguishable from the *kav* itself.[34] In subsequent worlds, the occultations of divine light become progressively darker, and the *kav*, which brings the light into these worlds, itself goes through a series of contractions and concealments. As we have seen, the alteration between *Tzimtzum* and emanation is a recurrent theme throughout all facets of the creative process. The alternating movement between *histalkut* (regression) and *hitpashut* (emanation),[35] akin to the ebb and flow of the tides, ultimately results in the creation of our own world, *Assiyah*, the world of "action" or "making." It is only quite late in this creative process that the material world as we know it comes into being.

The specific details and order of creation are important topics that Vital details extensively in *Sefer Etz Chayyim*.[36] Here, however, it will suffice to remind ourselves that creation has two original aspects: the formation of an archetypical or Primordial Man (*Adam Kadmon*) and the formation of a

---

32. Scholem, *Kabbalah*, p. 130.
33. Scholem, *Kabbalah*, p. 130.
34. This topic is discussed more fully in Chapter Six.
35. Scholem, *Kabbalah*, p. 131.
36. Vital, *Sefer Etz Chayyim*, 1: 2. These details are discussed more fully in Chapters Four and Six.

series of realms or dimensions, the *Sefirot. Adam Kadmon* is indeed the first being to emerge after the original *Tzimtzum*. This Primordial Man serves as a created, albeit very abstract and ethereal, representation of the divine *middot*, values or traits that are ultimately reflected in humanity. Similarly, the *Sefirot*, which are ten in number, correspond to the divine attributes of *chochmah* (wisdom), *binah* (understanding), *da'at* (knowledge), *chesed* (kindness, grace, benevolence), *gevurah* or *din* (power, prevalence, or judgment), *tiferet* (beauty), *netzach* (endurance, victory), *hod* (splender, majesty), *yesod* (foundation), and *malchut* (sovereignty or kingship). The *Sefirot*, as we have seen, are understood as themselves emerging from Primordial Man.[37]

The concepts of *Adam Kadmon* and the *Sefirot* give expression to the view that the *Tzimtzum* results in the creation of essentially human intellectual, spiritual, and ethical values. The universe, according to the Kabbalists, is not essentially material, but is rather conceptual, spiritual, and axiological at its core. It will be important to recall this observation when we examine the concept of *Tzimtzum* from a more philosophical point of view.

MYSTICAL METAPHORS

We must remember that the discussion of *Tzimtzum* in terms of a physical or spatial contraction, as well as the notion of a concealment of God's "light," is, on the view of most Kabbalists, purely metaphorical in nature. Although a controversy raged for some time between those Kabbalists who interpreted *Tzimtzum* naturalistically and their opponents,[38] a physical interpretation of the "contraction" involved in *Tzimtzum* is really impossible. This is because the kabbalistic tradition is clear that God or "*Ein-Sof*" does not originally exist within space and time. Indeed, as will shortly become clear, it is only through the original *Tzimtzum* that space, time, matter, and light come into being at all. The *Tzimtzum* itself cannot, therefore, occur in a spatiotemporal frame. It is most simply a self-limitation within the plenum of Absolute Being. The purpose of *Tzimtzum* is thus to create an ontological

---

37. The relationship between the *Sefirot* and *Adam Kadmon* is quite complicated and intricate, as detailed in *Sefer Etz Chayyim* 1: 1, 1: 2 and 1: 4. See Chapter Four re: *Iggulim* and *Yosher*.

38. Scholem, *Kabbalah*, pp. 133–135.

region in which finite beings are able to exist without being dissolved in God.[39]

CONTRACTION INTO LANGUAGE

In his *Shaar Ha Yichud Veemmunah*, the founder of the Chabad Hasidic movement, Schneur Zalman of Lyadi, describes how in the act of *Tzimtzum* God contracts the life force and invests it in the combinations of letters that comprise the so-called "ten utterances of creation."[40] These utterances are phrases in the book of Genesis in which the world is referred to as being created by divine speech (e.g., "And God *said* 'Let there be light' and there was light"). The world, according to Schneur Zalman, is created in all its multitude through these letters; "combinations of combinations, by substitutions and transpositions of the letters themselves and their numerical values and equivalents."[41] The idea expressed here is that there is a linguistic chain, stretching from "the ten utterances" leading to the creation of all worlds and things. This chain involves the recombination of words and letters of the ten utterances, and the numerical equivalents of these words and utterances via *Gematria*,[42] resulting in the *names* of all things in this world, and by extension the very existence of the things thereby named.

Schneur Zalman regards the very act of God revealing himself in letters and words as an act of *Tzimtzum*, a radical contraction of the divine essence. Each substitution and transposition of words and letters indicates a further contraction of the divine light and life, degree by degree. The vessels, which, a moment ago, we saw as the products of the *Tzimtzum*, are regarded by Schneur Zalman as "letters" whose "roots" are the five letters in Hebrew that always terminate a word, and which no letter can follow.[43] Letters, by structuring and limiting divine thought, serve to carry out the function of the

---

39. Schochet, "Mystical Concepts," p. 828.
40. Zalman, *Likutei Amarim-Tanya*, p. 319 (*Shaar ha Yichud VehaEmunah* 7).
41. Ibid.
42. *Gematria* is a hermeneutic method whereby the meaning of a word or scriptural passage is derived (and hence altered) by considering the numerical value of the Hebrew letters in that word or passage and then either interpreting that number or finding other linguistic expressions that have the same numerical value and substituting them for the word or passage in question.
43. Zalman, *Likutei Amarim-Tanya*, p. 299 (*Shaar ha Yichud VehaEmunah* 5).

divine contraction and are thereby held to be equivalent to the sefirotic vessels.

Implicit in Schneur Zalman's interpretation of language are a number of important ideas not only about creation, but about human nature as well.[44] With regard to our present theme, Schneur Zalman holds that *Ein-Sof* constricts Himself into language, because language is paradigmatic for both concealment and revelation. The vessels are like letters precisely because language, for which "letters" are the constituent parts, *reveals*, but at the same time *limits* and *conceals*, thought and expression. Here we have another example of the *coincidentia oppositorum* that is basic to kabbalistic thought. Pushed to its limit, the notion of language as divine concealment leads to the conclusion that there is a sense in which the very words of revelation in scripture are themselves the results of *an emptying or concealment* of divine significance. Looked at kabbalistically scripture itself is both "original revelation" and the "primal concealment."

TZIMTZUM AND THE PROBLEM OF EVIL

The fact that *Tzimtzum* implies both creation and negation suggests a connection with both good and *evil*, and an inherent relationship between evil and the created world. We have already seen that, for Luria, the *Tzimtzum* involves a divine catharsis of the negative element (Judgment) within the Godhead. God's contraction or concealment creates a region of being alienated from the divine goodness, and hence a region of being that contains God's negative, evil potentialities. For Luria, the very act of contracting or concealing God, who is the infinite good, necessarily entails the production of evil. As Schneur Zalman puts it: "Indeed so great and powerful are the contractions and concealment of the (divine) countenance that even unclean things, the *Kelippot* [the "Evil Husks"] and the *Sitra Achra* [the "Other Side"] can come into being."[45] These unclean things, and evil in general, are, according to the Lurianists, a necessary byproduct of *Tzimtzum*, and hence, part of the logical structure of creation itself.

It is for this reason that Jewish theologians have appealed to *Tzimtzum* in order to explain the existence of evil in the face of their faith in an all

---

44. I will explore Schneur Zalman's "linguistic mysticism" in detail in Chapter Five.

45. Zalman, *Likutei Amarim-Tanya*, p. 91.

knowing, beneficent God. Thinkers as varied as Martin Buber,[46] Joseph Soloveitchik,[47] Adin Steinsaltz,[48] and Eliezer Berkowitz[49] have turned to Tzimtzum (and the thematically related but earlier concept of hester panim, the hiding of the divine countenance) in order to explain both moral and natural evil from a theological point of view.[50] If indeed it is part of the very logical structure of creation that, in the words of Moses Chayyim Luzzatto, "God should hold back His light and hide His presence,"[51] then evil itself becomes a necessary byproduct of what God, in Genesis, declared to be good. Indeed, one implication of the doctrine of Tzimtzum is that evil is ontologically and metaphysically (though not axiologically) identical to the good.

Recently, David Birnbaum has made creative use of Tzimtzum in arguing (along the lines we have been discussing) that in creating man, whose destiny it is to maximize his own freedom, independence, and creative potential, God must of necessity conceal Himself and retreat further and further into "eclipse." Humanity's destiny, Birnbaum argues in kabbalistic fashion, is to become God's partner in the fulfillment and completion of creation, and it is only by granting man increasing measures of independence,

---

46. See Martin Buber, "God and the World's Evil," in Contemporary Jewish Thought (New York: B'nai B'rith, Department of Adult Jewish Education 1963), vol. 4, p. 256.

47. See Joseph Soloveitchik, Halakhic Man, trans. Lawrence Kaplan (Philadelphia: Jewish Publication Society, 1983), p. 108; also compare Joseph Soloveitchik, "The Lonely Man of Faith," Tradition 7: 2 (Summer 1965): 31.

48. Adin Steinsaltz, The Thirteen-Petalled Rose, trans. Yehuda Hanegbi (New York: Basic Books, 1980), p. 37.

49. Eliezer Berkowitz, God, Man, and History (Middle Village, NY: Johnathan David, 1959), p. 145–146.

50. For a discussion of this problem see, David Birnbaum, God and Evil, pp. 122–135. It is of interest to note that Schneur Zalman, in Tanya, relates the two notions of Tzimtzum and hester panim. He writes: "These tzimtzumim are all in the nature of a "veiling of the countenance" (hester panim), to obscure and conceal the light and life-force . . . so that it shall not manifest itself in a greater radiance than the lower worlds are capable of receiving" (Tanya I, C. 48, as cited by Schochet, "Mystical Concepts," p. 829). The concept of hester panim had been used in earlier rabbinic literature as a metaphor for certain specific periods where God chooses to withdraw a portion of his providence from the world. By connecting hester panim to Tzimtzum, Schneur Zalman is relating it to a pervasive ontological principle.

51. Moses Chayyim Luzzatto, Derech Hashem (The Way of God), trans. Aryeh Kaplan (Jerusalem and New York: Feldheim, 1977), p. 123.

and thereby exposing him to the potential and choice of evil, that this destiny can be fulfilled.[52]

PHILOSOPHICAL PERSPECTIVES

The ideas I have outlined regarding *Tzimtzum* can, I believe, be best understood against the background of philosophical *idealism* and *rationalism*. Contemporary scholarship has indeed discovered an affinity between Lurianic Kabbalah and the thought of modern idealist philosophers such as Schelling, Hegel, and Whitehead. This should come as no surprise, for a number of Kabbalists themselves realized that the basic notions of Jewish mysticism paralleled Platonic, Neoplatonic and other ancient idealistic systems of thought.[53]

In order to gain philosophical insight into the Kabbalah, it will be useful to contrast the basic idealist and rationalist assumptions implicit in such notions as *Tzimtzum*, the *Sefirot*, and *Adam Kadmon*, with the materialism and naturalism that has come to be taken as common ("scientific") sense in our day. We shall see that in every instance the kabbalistic notions are the inverse of corresponding materialist ideas. Once this is clear, it will be important to indicate how our own pre-theological experience provides a justification for the idealist/rationalist point of view, for only then will we be in a position to attain genuine philosophical insight into the *Tzimtzum* idea.

The universe, thought of naturalistically, is a vast assemblage of material forces and objects within a vast plenum of space and time. Space, time, matter, and energy are thought of as the primordial givens, and it is only through a slow *causal* process that matter evolves to the point that a biological creature, man, introduces concepts and values into the world. Values, on this view, far from being the constituent core of reality, are actually rather late additions to it, or more to the point, ways in which reality is viewed or colored by humanity.

Kabbalistic thought completely reverses this order in the chain of being. For the Kabbalah, the supreme reality, "being as such," is not an undifferentiated mass of matter and energy, but rather an ineffable perfection that unifies within itself all spiritual, intellectual, aesthetic, and moral values. The

---

52. David Birnbaum, *God and Evil* (see also Sanford Drob, "Foreword," in the fourth and subsequent editions of Birnbaum's work). Zalman, *Likutei Amarim-Tanya*, p. 293.

53. A notable example is the Spanish Kabbalist Abraham Cohen Herrera.

material world is regarded as a secondary development, which arises as a result of an intellective process through which the divine perfection comes to instantiate particular concepts and values in the objects of a finite world. It is only on the lowest of levels, at the end of a logical series, that the most highly differentiated ideas are imperfectly represented in material form.

Kabbalah is thus an idealistic (as opposed to materialistic) system of thought because for it the most fundamental reality is mind, value, or idea. It is also a rationalistic system of thought because within it the main impetus to development, progression, and creation is intellectual or logical as opposed to natural or causal.

What reason do we have to believe that the world is essentially comprised of idea and value as opposed to objects and matter? The most fundamental warrant for this belief is the very general observation that no thing or material object can be perceived, described, or even said to exist except under the aegis of some general concept or idea. Even the notion of "material object" is itself an idea, a concept, and our experience of such objects is completely determined by the existence of this idea-category. We cannot help but see or conceive of each thing we encounter as an instance of some concept or type. What we see before us at any given time is immediately categorized as a table, a pen, a mountain, a cloud, a bird, the sky, etc. This is no accident of our human predicament, but is rather a logical truth about reality itself; things are inconceivable except as instances of some concept or kind. Furthermore, things constantly appear as good or poor examples of what they are, as if (or rather because) there were some ideal type of "round," "red," "gold," "person," "act of kindness," etc., which the things of experience only approximate.

The world is, as it were, shot through and through with concepts and values. Value and idea, far from supervening upon reality, are actually logically embedded within it. It is easy to see how the conception arises that the original, most fundamental, nature of the universe is purely undifferentiated thought and value as such. This, of course, is close to the kabbalistic understanding of the *Sefirot* and God.

COMPUTERS AND CREATION

The case for rationalism and idealism can perhaps be made clearer through an analogy with the world of computers. The function of any computer is dependent upon two major components: a software package or program, which instructs the hardware or actual machine on how to produce the desired analysis or results. The software package can be understood as a set of ideas and logical relations, expressed in a (computer) language and designed to serve some interest or end. The hardware can be understood as a set of material components and causal connections that instantiate the computer program (the software) and enable it to run. It takes but little reflection to realize that the software package is the essence of the computer operation. The hardware is, in fact, a purely accidental, exchangeable aspect of the system (the same software can be run on any compatible machine). An individual with the software controlling the operations of a particular structure or organization has in his hands the essence of that organization; not the individual who happens to possess the organization's computer. And so it is with the world. The software package can be understood as the ideas, logic, values, and language which idealist philosophy (and Kabbalah) regards as the world's essential structure. The hardware, with its purely mechanical operations, is equivalent to the material, natural world, a world that functions only on the direction of a program from outside itself. It is interesting to note that from within a computer's electronic hardware, it would appear that the computer's operation is purely material and causal in nature. It is only from our broader perspective that we realize that the casually connected electronic events are occurring according to a rational pattern.

We are now in a position to deepen our understanding of the kabbalistic metaphors. *Adam Kadmon* and the *Sefirot*, representing what appear to be gross anthropomorphisms, can now be understood as expressing the higher truth that the entire universe is garbed in meaning and value. Values are reflected in the human soul, but also form the most fundamental core of reality as well.

While we have thus far come to see creation as a conceptual, valuational act, we are still far from having uncovered its inner logic, a logic that is embodied in the dynamics of *Tzimtzum*. Explicating precisely what *Tzimtzum* is and does is our task in the following sections.

CREATION AS EPISTEMIC LIMITATION (LIMITATION IN KNOWLEDGE)

As we have seen, one of the problems the Kabbalists faced was the question of how God could limit Himself, withdraw His presence from a point in the plenum of Being, give rise to creation and yet remain perfect and unchanged.

The Kabbalists attempted to solve this problem though an analogy with the sun's rays, which can be obscured in certain areas of the world without in any way diminishing the light of the sun itself. We can deepen our understanding of this metaphor, and at the same time increase our understanding of *Tzimtzum* itself, by explicating the metaphor in purely epistemological terms, i.e., in terms of God's and man's knowledge.

According to Schneur Zalman (who follows Maimonides), God's knowledge is perfect knowledge. For God, unlike for man, there is no distinction between the knower and the known. God is, to play on the Aristotelian metaphor, *the perfection of all virtues knowing itself.* This self-knowledge, unlike human knowledge, is complete and instantaneous. In God, and, to a lesser extent, in mystical states of knowledge in which man approaches God, there is the immediate apprehension that all which appears as a plurality is indeed One.

Our understanding of this idea can be clarified through an analogy from the world of mathematics. An infinite perfect mind sees immediately that the arithmetical expressions $21/3$, $126/18$, $6.72 + .28$, etc., are all equivalents of the number 7: it is only from the point of view of a limited intellect that these expressions appear to represent different mathematical ideas. Indeed, as the mathematical philosophers Russell and Whitehead painstakingly demonstrated, all of mathematics is predicated on a very small number of logical principles, and an infinite mind would in an instant intuit the entire world of higher mathematics as an elaboration of the simplest of ideas. So it is with the world. From the point of view of God, the whole world is subsumable under the simplest concept of *the One*; it is only from our limited point of view that there appears to be a plurality of virtues, concepts, and instantial things. Creation does not involve a limitation in the divine being, which remains completely intact, but rather a limitation in knowledge of the Divine: an estrangement of certain points within the "world" from the knowledge that all is One. God does not change in His being, it is rather that His presence is obscured. He is not completely known in a certain region of Being, and that region of Being becomes our world.

As Schneur Zalman put it: "The reason that all things created and activated appear to us as existing and tangible is that we do not comprehend nor see with our physical eyes the power of God and the 'Breath of His Mouth' which is in the created thing."[54] The "Alter Rebbe" continues that

---

54. Zalman, *Likutei Amarim-Tanya*, p. 293 (*Shaar HaYichud VehaEmunah* 4).

if we were ever permitted to see this *power* or *breath* of God in created things, "then the materiality, grossness, and tangibility of the creature would not be seen by our eyes at all, for it is completely nullified in relation to the life force and the spirituality which is within it; since without the spirituality, it would be nought and absolute nothingness, exactly as before the Six Days of Creation."[55]

ILLUSION AND REVELATION

While, according to Schneur Zalman, "it is not within the scope of the intellect of any creature to comprehend the essential nature of the *Tzim-tzum*,[56] one can go as far as to say that the essence of *Tzimtzum*, the essence of creation itself, is a partial concealment of the divine unity that brings about an illusion of individuality, plurality, materiality, and freedom. This explains why it is that God is not completely manifest in the world. It is essential to the concept of creation, to the existence of the world itself that He be partially hidden. If God were completely manifest, it would be as if an infinite array of mathematical equivalents were to collapse in an instantaneous apprehension of their utter unity: the world itself would collapse into the perfect unity of *Ein-Sof*. This, we might say, is why even the greatest of God's prophets, Moses, could only fathom the "back" of God; for according to the Torah (Exodus 33: 20) no man can see God's full countenance and yet live. With respect to the concept of human freedom, Rabbi Nachman of Breslov declared that "Free will can only exist as long as the intellect is not great enough to resolve the paradox of omniscience and free will."[57] According to Rabbi Nachman a full understanding of this paradox would mean a loss of finite mortality and raise man to the level of the angels, who understand but are not free.

We can now repeat with understanding what seemed so enigmatic when we began: God's unfathomability is the *sine qua non* of a finite created world. While from a certain point of view creation is an *illusion* of plurality, this illusion is necessary in order to spell out, in all of its particular details, the perfection of intellect and value that is the essence of the Divine Being. To

---

55. Ibid.

56. Ibid.

57. Nachman of Breslov, *Likutei Moharan* 21: 4, 5. Trans. by Kaplan, *Chasidic Masters*, p. 118.

make a human analogy: we may understand instantaneously and completely that a certain man is utterly righteous or brilliant, but it is, nonetheless, a wonderful revelation to hear or read of the details of each of his righteous words and deeds. The "spelling out" of the divine essence is thus the positive or emanative complement to *Tzimtzum*.

THE ORIGIN OF SPACE, TIME, AND MATTER

Space, time, and matter as well as individual personal existence can now be understood as the logical consequence of *Tzimtzum* as concealment or epistemic limitation, for each of these "categories" serve as a vehicle through which conceptual knowledge is limited. That which is remote in space or time, that which is concealed in or by material objects, and that which belongs to another person or self, is in principle unknown or only partially known. As philosophers since Kant have understood so well, the concept of a world requires the existence of the categories or principles of space, time, matter, and personal identity to provide the means for differentiating finite experienced things. Similarly, the concept of concealment or limitation in knowledge can have no meaning without such categories: space, time, matter, and personality are the logical prerequisites for creation, the very principles through which an undifferentiated divine "All" is concealed and hence, paradoxically, manifest as finite, particular things. This interpretation of space, time, matter, and individual existence helps explain how it can be that a knowledge of the world's particular aspects (scientific knowledge) does not guarantee an awareness of truth as a whole (ontological knowledge). This is because particular things are in essence a concealment of the unified "One." It follows that unless a science of particular things is guided by a mystical-philosophical vision, it remains simply an inquiry into the devices of divine self-concealment.

As I have emphasized, *Tzimtzum* is essentially an epistemological category, a concealment or limitation in knowledge. By understanding *Tzimtzum* in this way, we can avoid all the problems inherent in understanding *Tzimtzum* as a contraction within an already pre-existing space and time. While *Tzimtzum* does carry the additional connotation of contraction, this is to be understood metaphysically as opposed to physically. For the Kabbalists, who maintain a metaphysics of "ideas," such contraction (in the realm of ideas) is equivalent to a limitation in knowledge. On the deepest level, as we have begun to see, for the Kabbalists the distinction between knowledge and reality completely breaks down. For them, the basic category of knowledge (idea) is the basic category of metaphysics (reality) as well.

Still, we may be troubled by the apparent leap from a world of ideas and concepts to a world of matter and things. We are troubled by this transition if only because it seems an unalterable principle of human experience that ideas do not become realized as material objects except through the agency of other material events. Our question, in short, is how it is that the Kabbalist-rationalist accounts for the existence of physical bodies. It is in response to this question that the Kabbalist is most tempted to posit a leap (*dilug*), a radical act of divine will that brings matter into the universe. While we cannot, as Schneur Zalman warns us, completely circumvent the necessity for such a leap, we can provide a hint of how it is that as knowledge is progressively limited, ideas ultimately coalesce into a material form.

Again, a mathematical analogy will be useful. As we have seen, all of mathematics can be understood as being implicit in one or several principles of logic. A perfect mind sees this at once. A less perfect mind, for whom mathematical knowledge is not self-knowledge, must see and understand the truth of each mathematical operation one by one. An even less perfect mind, the mind of a child for example, can only understand numbers as they are instantiated in things (five fingers, six apples, etc.). For such a limited mind, the abstract concept of number as such makes no sense. As mind dissolves to a vanishing point, the concept of number can have no reality whatsoever except as it is manifest and ultimately exists in concrete things. Without a perceiving mind, there are still, for example, six trees in the forest, but that is all, no abstract notion of six and no sense of six as part of greater unity. Thus we can see in mathematics that as mind is limited, as knowledge is concealed, concepts progressively take on instantial, material form. Conversely, as mind is expanded and knowledge progresses, concepts are freed from their material instants and become objects of pure thought.

The same is true for the ideas and values that comprise the material world. A material object is, almost by definition, a concept that is imperfectly manifest or known. A material object is what it is by virtue of the fact that it shows only some of its aspects at any given time (its surface as opposed to its depths, one or at most two of its sides, its shape, but not its weight), etc. If it were known perfectly and instantly, it would become a pure conception and hence cease to exist in its material forms. A material object is thus always an imperfectly known idea.

TZIMTZUM IN LURIA AND SCHNEUR ZALMAN

The philosophical interpretation of *Tzimtzum* that I have provided above rests, in part, upon the view of this doctrine that appears in the writings of Schneur Zalman of Lyadi. As I indicated in Chapter One, Rachel Elior has argued that the Chabad interpretation of the Lurianic doctrines retains kabbalistic terminology only by introducing completely new meanings for the Lurianic terms. Here, as promised, I will take up this issue in some detail. It is my view that the Chabad philosophical interpretation uncovers a new layer of meaning for the Lurianic symbols, and does not simply negate or reverse their original intent.

We can begin by noting that the Hasidim interpreted *Tzimtzum* in such a manner as to comply with their view that *Ein-Sof* remains the immanent substance in all things. Schneur Zalman inisisted upon a nonliteral interpretation of this doctrine, holding that a literal interpretation of *Tzimtzum* entails that God removes His essence from the world and only guides the world "from above." A literal interpretation of *Tzimtzum* also risks the conclusion that God's contraction is itself a corporeal event.[58] According to Schneur Zalman, the change resulting from *Tzimtzum* is not a metaphysical alteration in the Godhead, but an epistemological limitation in man's awareness of *Ein-Sof*. For Chabad, *Tzimtzum* only has reality from the point of view of man, who receives God's light through the veil "of many 'garments' which obscure His blessed light."[59]

Elior argues that the Chabad interpretation of *Tzimtzum* "represents an effort to retain the Lurianic terminological system, although emptying it of its original meaning and replacing it with a philosophical position."[60] Elior, however, fails to take into account the fact that Vital[61] and other Lurianists[62]

---

58. Elior, *The Paradoxical Ascent to God*, pp. 79–82.
59. Schneur Zalman, *Likutei Amarim-Tanya*, Ch. 36, p. 163.
60. Elior, *The Paradoxical Ascent to God*, p. 85.
61. *Sefer Etz Chayyim* 1: 1, p. 28; Menzi and Padeh, *The Tree of Life*, p. 53–54. Vital writes that higher spiritual things cannot be grasped by our understanding and so corporeal metaphors are used to "appease the ear." However, there is absolutely nothing corporeal about the higher realms.
62. The eighteenth-century Lurianist, R. Shalom Buzalgo, quotes the first phrases of *Kanfey Yonah*, a contemporary account of Isaac Luria's teaching by Moses Jonah: "Know that in order to help one understand, permission was granted to utilize the limbs of the body as a simile . . . Yet you in your wisdom purify your thoughts

insisted that all of the kabbalistic symbols are to be taken metaphorically, that any attribution of corporeality to *Ein-Sof* is a grave error, and that creation does not result in a fundamental change in the Godhead. Interpreting *Tzimtzum* philosophically does not "empty it of its original meaning"; rather, it provides additional insight into a doctrine that hitherto had not been clearly articulated or understood. By understanding *Tzimtzum* in epistemological terms, Schneur Zalman is able to explain how *Tzimtzum* can occur in a non-corporeal medium and how *Ein-Sof* can remain both concealed and fully immanent in the world. According to Schneur Zalman, the finite world results from a concealment of God's light which is equivalent to a failure of man to see the full divine presence. Like the details of a photographic projection that are revealed only through the film's partial obstruction of the projector's light, the existence of independent, finite entities is a function of garments, or *tzimtzumim*, that obscure the divine emanation. Yet just as the film image remains completely dependent upon the (partially obscured) light that reaches the screen, finite entities obtain their only substance through the contracted divine light that reaches the lower worlds. As such, finite entities result from both the concealment and immanence of the Or *Ein-Sof*, the light of the Infinite God.

Elior points out that Chabad rejects the Lurianic view that the process of *Tzimtzum* originally took place *within the Godhead* prior to creation.[63] It is true that later Kabbalists and Chasidim took pains to reinterpret this notion to accord with their view of *Tzimtzum* as a purely relational event, and to avoid any hint of change in the Godhead in and of itself. However, it does not follow, as Elior argues (and in spite of Schneur Zalman's protestations), that for Chabad *Tzimtzum* is a completely extra-divine occurrence. Indeed, Schneur Zalman regards even the world and man to be an epiphenomenon or illusion, and strictly speaking everything, *Tzimtzum* included, occurs atemporally within the Godhead and not, as Elior suggests, outside *Ein-Sof* at the time of creation.

---

to know that in the above there is nothing physical" (Buzalgo, *Mikdash Melech*, Schachter trans., p. 164). According to Jonah it is only from the *Sefirot* downward that we have permission to talk in metaphor; regarding everything above the emanation of the *Sefirot* in the world of *Atzilut*, "we have no permission to deal with, or to compare it with anything that has form and likeness." Interestingly, Jonah omits all discussion of *Tzimtzum* from his account of the Lurianic system (Scholem, *Kabbalah*, p. 424).

63. Elior, *The Paradoxical Ascent to God*, p. 87.

Nor does it follow from Schneur Zalman's doctrine of *Tzimtzum* that between Chabad and Luria "there is no common ideological ground, but only an overlap in terminology."[64] Elior is correct that for Schneur Zalman, creation is a relational event. In the course of his discussion of *Tzimtzum*, Schneur Zalman quotes Exodus 33: 20: "For no man shall see me and live," and it is in this context that we can understand God's original contraction as the *primal* relational event. In order for there to be a man for God to relate to, *Ein-Sof* first had to diminish the overwhelming intensity of his infinite radiance. Indeed the Hasidim took this as a lesson for human relations as well; before we can relate to another we must diminish our own egos and, in effect, contract ourselves so an other can emerge in his or her own right.[65] This view of *Tzimtzum* as a bridge between God and man is not altogether foreign to the Lurianists, for, as we have seen, Vital himself held that a prime purpose of creation was to set up a relationship between God and man in order that God could reign properly as "King."

THE MYSTICAL ASCENT

We have seen that as *Ein-Sof* conceals Himself or limits knowledge of His indivisible and complete Unity, this concealment proceeds in stages ultimately leading to a material world. First there is a division of the One into a series of differentiated values, and then into a series of differentiated concepts exhibiting those values, and finally into a series of material objects imperfectly and incompletely instantiating these concepts, as schematized below:

The One
Kindness, Judgment, Beauty, Splendor
Concept of kind, beautiful, splendorous things
Instantial, material objects

If we reverse the process of *Tzimtzum*, if we reverse the process of creation via God's concealment, it can readily be seen that the ascent to God is one in which the material universe is transcended in favor of more conceptual, supernal realms; and ultimately, in meditation or prophecy, to a kind of thought in which there are no distinct concepts at all. This, it can now

---

64. Ibid., p. 87.
65. See below, "The Ethics of *Tzimtzum*."

be understood, is why the kabbalistic mystic, through a concentration on sheer "nothingness,"[66] is able to transcend the world of material objects, wants, and desires and approach a most glorious sense of union with the Absolute, *Ein-Sof* or the infinite God.

TZIMTZUM: PSYCHOLOGICAL ASPECTS

Scholem has observed that the Hasidim provided the theosophical concepts of the Kabbalah with a psychological interpretation.[67] In truth, this psychologization process had begun already with the Kabbalists themselves. Azriel of Gerona, for example, held that the energy of the human soul derives from the *Sefirot*, and he equated each *Sefirah* with a psychological power or physical organ in man.[68] Moshe Idel has shown how the *ecstatic* Kabbalah, with its focus on the *experience* of the initiate, regarded the *Sefirot* as human spiritual and psychical processes.[69] For example, Abraham Abulafia understood the names of the ten *Sefirot* (Thought, Wisdom, Understanding, etc.) as referring to processes taking place in the mind and body of man. Abulafia held that it is possible for man to elicit these attributes through proper meditation.[70] While the psychological understanding of the Kabbalah was somewhat obscured by the Lurianic emphasis upon the theosophical structure of the Godhead, Luria and Vital held that the *Sefirot* are mirrored in man's body and soul.[71]

The Hasidim emphasized the notion that the divine macrocosm is mirrored in man. For example, R. Jacob Joseph of Polonnoye (1704–1794) stated in the name of the Baal Shem Tov (the founder of Hasidism) that the

---

66. By concentrating on *nothing* the mystic is able to achieve a glimpse of the absolute "All," a condition in which "no thing," in the sense of differentiated finite objects of experience, exists. See Aryeh Kaplan, *Jewish Meditation* (New York: Schocken, 1985), pp. 83–91. On meditations derived from Lurianic Kabbalah in general see Aryeh Kaplan, *Meditation and Kabbalah* (York Beach, ME: Samuel Weiser, 1982), pp. 199–260.

67. Gershom Scholem, "The Unconscious and the Pre-Existence of the Intellect in Hasidic Literature" (Hebrew, 1944), cited in Rifka Schatz-Uffenheimer, *Hasidism as Mysticism*, p. 179.

68. Dan, *The Early Kabbalah*, p. 95.

69. Idel, *Kabbalah: New Perspectives*, p. 146.

70. Ibid, p. 147.

71. Vital, *Sefer Etz Chayyim*, 1: 2.

ten *Sefirot* appear in man as a result of the *Tzimtzum*. According to Jacob Joseph, God progressively contracts himself into a series of visages (*Partzufim*) until he (and man) is called Microcosmos (*Olam Katan*).[72] Rabbi Levi Yitzchak of Berdichov (1740–1809) held that "Man is a counterpart of the Attributes on high," and he provided a one-to-one correspondence between these attributes and parts of the human body.[73] Similarly, the Apter Rebbe, Rabbi Yehoshua Heschel (1745–1825), held:

> Man is a microcosm, a miniature universe, and his body therefore constitutes a complete structure. All universes, both spiritual and physical, have a similar structure. Entire universes therefore parallel the various parts of the human body. Some universes correspond to the head, others to the brain, nose, eyes, ears, hands and feet, this being true of all parts of the body. Each of these universes contains thousands upon thousands of worlds.[74]

Rabbi Schneur Zalman of Lyadi viewed the ten *Sefirot* in man's soul as the origins of all human thought and emotion.[75] Interestingly, he used the occasion of his discussion of the sefirotic attributes to provide a lesson in the rearing of children, one in which he advocates a balance between "contracting" and asserting oneself in relation to one's child.

The successor of the Baal Shem Tov, Rabbi Dov Baer, the Maggid of Mezrich (1704–1772) taught "that everything written in (Vital's) *Sefer Etz Chayyim* also exists in the world and in man."[76] The Maggid made the radical claim that the significance of divine thought is dependent upon this thought making its appearance in the mind of man. *Tzimtzum*, according to the Maggid, is the process by which divine thought is condensed into the human intellect, and it is through this appearance in the human psyche that divine thought becomes actual and real. The Godhead himself is the foundation and

---

72. Rabbi Jacob Joseph of Polonnoye, *Toldot Ya'akov Yoseph*, fol. 86a, quoted and translated in Idel, *Kabbalah: New Perspectives*, p. 150 (see also p. 352, note 366).

73. Rabbi Levi Yitzchak of Berdichov, *Kedushat Levi*, Bo, p. 108 (trans. by Kaplan, *Chasidic Masters*, p. 78).

74. Rabbi Yehoshua Heschel, *Ohev Yisrael*, Va Yetze 15b (trans. by Kaplan, *Chasidic Masters*, p. 150.)

75. Schneur Zalman, *Tanya, Igeret HaKodesh*, Ch. 15. Zalman, *Likutei Amarim-Tanya*, pp. 467–69. See also Kaplan, *Chasidic Masters*, p. 97.

76. Maggid, Dov Baer of Mezrich, *Or ha-Emet* (Light of Truth), fol. 36 c–d. (quoted and translated in Idel, *Kabbalah: New Perspectives*, p. 15).

source of thought, but actual thinking can only occur within the framework of the human mind.[77] Thus, for the Maggid, the psychologization process is one that is necessary for the completion and fulfillment of God himself. As we have repeatedly seen, for the Kabbalists there is a reciprocal relationship between God and man. God is the ultimate source of the human attributes of thought and emotion, but the psyche of man is the realization of what is only potentiality within God. As with Carl Jung who was to expound a similar view two centuries later, for the Maggid the Godhead has a hidden life within the mind of man.[78]

The Maggid held that the act of *Tzimtzum*, through which God becomes condensed into the human soul, is mirrored in the life of individual men and women. Accordingly, man must strive for a state of *bittul ha'ani*, self-designification, whereby an individual achieves full relatedness with God by performing his own personal act of *Tzimtzum*. "When he (man)," says the Maggid, "considers himself as nothing and makes himself small, God also contracts himself . . . and then he will certainly acquire wisdom."[79] In this light, it is worth noting that the Hasidim referred to their saintly *tzaddikim* as *Ayin*, "nothing," expressing the view that the *tzaddik* has contracted himself to a state that approaches the "nothingness" of God.

Mordecai Rotenberg has pointed out that the self-contraction advocated in Hasidism contrasts sharply with the self-nullification that is commonly advocated in both Western and Eastern mysticism.[80] This is because the mystical self-nullification is typically associated with a negative view of the temporal/material world. By way of contrast the Hasid's efforts at self-contraction (and even self-nullification) are part of an active effort to improve the world. This is evident in a passage from the writings of Rabbi Levi Yitzchak of Berdichov (1740–1809): "A person must fear God so much that his ego is totally nullified. Only then can he attach himself to Nothingness. Sustenance, filled with everything good, then flows to all universes . . ."[81]

---

77. Schatz-Uffenheimer, *Hasidism As Mysticism*, p. 207.

78. Ibid. See Schneur Zalman's commentary *Likutei Amarim-Tanya*, p. 163.

79. Maggid, Dov Baer of Mezrich, *Maggid Devarav Yaacov*, 86. Quoted in Mordecai Rotenberg, *Dialogue with Deviance* (Lanham, MD: University Press of America, 1993), p. 73.

80. Rotenberg, *Dialogue with Deviance*, p. 72.

81. Levi Yitzhak of Berdichov, *Kedushat Levi, Bereshit*, p. 5. Translated by Kaplan, *Chasidic Masters*, p. 73.

THE ETHICS OF *TZIMTZUM*

The Hasidim applied their psychological conception of *Tzimtzum* to the relations between man and man, as well as between man and God, comparing, for example, God's *Tzimtzum* to the contraction performed by a father in relation to his son, or a teacher in relation to his pupils. Rabbi Dov Baer tells us:

> Through your actions and humbleness you should cause the Almighty also to contract himself and reveal himself to you in smallness. As in the case of the father who sees his son playing with nuts, and then due to his love plays with him, although for the father this seems a childish act of "smallness," nonetheless out of love for his son and so that he should receive pleasure from his son, he contracts his mind and remains in "smallness" so that the little one will be able to bear him, for if he would have been unable to bear his father, then the father would not have derived pleasure from him.[82]

In another place the Maggid compares the divine *Tzimtzum* to "a father who has a small child": "The child wants to ride on a stick and make believe that it is a horse. But there is an important difference between the stick and a horse, since the horse propels its rider, while the child is actually propelling his stick. Still, the child has pleasure from this, and the father helps by providing a stick with which he can play."[83] Implicit in this simple parable is the idea that both the father and the son perform a psychological contraction in order to bring about a game of make believe. The father contracts himself to the level of the child in supplying him with materials for his game, and the child contracts his own knowledge regarding the "true" nature of this material, using his imagination to "create" a fantasy world in the psychological space where he has concealed or suspended this knowledge. Like *Ein-Sof* who constricts his being and knowledge to create a universe, the father and the child suspend their knowledge to create a world of play.

The Maggid also speaks of a *Tzimtzum* in the relationship between a student and teacher:

---

82. Maggid, Dov Baer of Mezrich, *Maggid Devarav Yaacov*, p. 63. Quoted by Rotenberg, *Dialogue with Deviance*, p. 82.

83. Maggid, Dov Baer of Mezrich, *Maggid Devarav Yaacov*, 9. Trans. by Kaplan, *Chasidic Masters*, pp. 39–40.

When the Rabbi wants his student to understand his broad mind, and the student cannot apprehend it then the Rabbi-teacher contracts his mind in talk and letters. For example, when a person wants to pour from one container to another and he is afraid to spill, then he takes an instrument called a funnel, and by this the liquid is contracted . . . and he will not spill. So it is when the Rabbi's mind is contracted in talk and letters which he says to the student, and through this the student can apprehend the teacher's broad mind.[84]

I have quoted the Maggid on the human dimensions of *Tzimtzum* at some length to illustrate how there is an ethic of *Tzimtzum* implicit in Hasidic thought. The human acts that the Maggid describes are not only meant as analogues to God's creativity, but, because they are such analogues, are meant to be prescriptive for the conduct of human affairs. Rotenberg, in commenting on this ethic, contrasts the Maggid's model of a beneficent contracting father with the Freudian "Prussian-Oedipal" model, within which the father does not constrict himself to provide a place for the son, but where the son, after striving completely on his own to find such a place, must surrender to the father.[85]

The Hasidic ethic, it would seem, implies an admonition that in relating to others, in particular to our children, we must first emulate the Infinite God and perform an act of *Tzimtzum* whereby our own thoughts and desires are contracted and concealed so that the other may emerge in his or her own individuality. Only later is an act of self-assertion possible. Rotenberg argues that mutual *I–Thou* relationships and communal institutions must be based upon mutual contraction rather than the assertiveness that is taught by contemporary psychology.[86]

Martin Buber, in his work on the Hasidim, has described the act of *Tzimtzum* as follows: "God Contracted Himself into the world because He who was the unity free from all duality and relations willed to let relations emerge."[87] On Buber's view, *Tzimtzum* is the very act that brings relatedness into the cosmos. When the self contracts, the other emerges, in much the same way as the Lurianic Kabbalists held that the Primordial Man emerges

---

84. Maggid, Dov Baer of Mezrich, *Maggid Devarav Yaacov*, p. 47. Quoted by Rotenberg, *Dialogue with Deviance*, p. 83.

85. Rotenberg, *Dialogue with Deviance*, pp. 81–88.

86. Ibid., pp. 89–96.

87. Martin Buber, *Hasidism* (New York: Philosophical Library, 1948), p. 64.

with the contraction of God. For Buber, the lesson of *Tzimtzum* is that there is no relationship until the ego has contracted and made room for an other.

I have already alluded to the psychological significance of Vital's notion that before God could contract himself away from a point he first had to concentrate all of his energies upon it. This notion suggests that the human process of *Tzimtzum* in relation to an other is not one of simple withdrawal, but rather involves an intense interest and focus upon him, and only then a retreat or restraint, allowing the other to fully emerge in the face of our interest and attachment.[88]

Perhaps another Hasidic parable, one told by Rabbi Nachman of Breslov (1772–1810), can be instructive in this regard:

> A royal prince once became insane and thought he was a turkey. He felt compelled to sit naked under the table, pecking at bones and pieces of bread like a turkey. The physicians all gave up trying to cure him of this madness, and the king suffered great anguish.
>
> A sage came along and said, "I will undertake to cure him." He undressed and sat naked under the table next to the royal prince, and also picked crumbs and bones. The prince asked, "Who are you and what are you doing here?" He answered, "And you, what are you doing here?" The prince replied, "I am a turkey," to which the sage responded, "I too am a turkey."
>
> In this manner they sat together for some time, until they became friends. The sage then signaled the king's servants, and they threw him a shirt. He said to the prince, "Do you think that a turkey cannot wear a shirt? One can wear a shirt and still be a turkey!" The two of them then put on shirts.[89]

In this way the sage slowly convinced the prince to wear pants, eat regular food, and sit at the table until such point that the prince was completely cured. The parable perfectly illustrates the ethic of *Tzimtzum* in action.

Rabbi Nachman's story also illustrates the maxim that in addition to contraction there is certainly a place for assertion, wisdom, and knowledge in human relationships. The Lurianists recognized that the negative act of *Tzimtzum* must be followed by a positive act of *hitpashut* or emanation, and that the relationship between God and the world, or between man and man,

---

88. Rotenberg, *Dialogue with Deviance*, p. 73.

89. Rabbi Nachman of Breslov, *Maasiot U'Mashalim* (in *Kokhevey Or*), p. 26. Trans. by Kaplan in *Chasidic Masters*, p. 120.

involves an alteration between contraction and expansion, withdrawal and assertion, retreat and encounter. In discussing the concept of *chutzpah*, which has been much maligned in America as an inappropriate expression of nerve and gall, Rotenberg has pointed to its original Talmudic meaning as a perfectly legitimate challenge to authority. Abraham exercised *chutzpah* in arguing with God about the destruction of Sodom and Gomorrah. Yet Abraham's assertiveness was only possible with a God who had contracted Himself and was willing to listen to a finite creature, one who, we know, had earlier made himself small before God.[90]

TZIMTZUM AND DREAMS

The Kabbalah (like the Vedanta) can be understood to regard the whole of creation as akin to a dream in the infinite mind of the Absolute. In withdrawing himself from himself and (what amounts to the same thing) by concealing himself from his own reality, the dreamer performs an act that is very similar to an act of *Tzimtzum* whereby the infinite God creates an illusion of finitude and multiplicity that is our world.

We each perform an act of *Tzimtzum* and, in effect, play God to dream worlds of our own creation each night. In dreaming we perform an act of contraction whereby we withdraw or remove our interest (in Freudian terms, cathexis) from the world and substitute a new world or reality in the dream. And just as the world is said to complete God, our dreams can be said to complete ourselves; for, according to Freud and those who follow him, it is only through our dreams and fantasies that we can achieve a perspicacious notion of who we really are. Jung, who was more theologically inclined than Freud, viewed the dream as our portal into "heaven," holding that in dreams we gain access to the archetypes that are the psychological foundation for "the gods."

TZIMTZUM AND HUMAN CHARACTER

As I have already mentioned, the word *Tzimtzum* has a connotation of concealment as well as contraction, and it is this connotation that is of

---

90. Rotenberg, *Dialogue with Deviance*, p. 14.

particular relevance to human character. We might say that an act of *Tzimtzum* or concealment lies at the very core of our character, for it is only through concealment and its variants, i.e., denial, repression, symbolization, displacement, condensation, etc., that a division is set up between the conscious and the unconscious mind and our personalities are born. An important inference from psychoanalytic theory is that it is the unconscious mind that adds depth and flavor to life, and is essential to the formation of an individual's character. Just as God, according to the Kabbalists, creates a world through an act of concealment (if you will a cosmic repression), man creates his own character, and, as Freud understood it, his culture, through an earthly concealment: the repressions of everyday life. We can see a dialectic at work on both the theological and psychological levels, for in both instances we find that reality gives rise to illusions, which are in turn productive of the very realities that brought them about. The "illusion" of a finite world is theologically the perfection and completion of God, and the "illusion" of a world of fantasies and dreams is the ground and the depths of the *reality* of man. This, by the way, is yet another example of the kabbalistic doctrine of *coincidentia oppositorum*, the principle that profound opposites complement and complete each other.

TZIMTZUM AND THE "WORLD SOUL"

A final psychological theme that emerges from a consideration of *Tzimtzum* involves a human contraction that makes room for an external world. Since the time of Copernicus man has become decentered within the physical universe while at the same time becoming far more central spiritually. Indeed, man has become spiritually central to such a degree that he himself has become completely coextensive with "soul."[91] The world itself has lost its soul and the hermeneutic disciplines that once found spiritual meaning in nature have now been limited to the study of man. In effect, the soul has been taken out of the world and confined to the individual man. The neo-Jungian psychologist James Hillman has spent the past thirty years bemoaning this occurrence, urging us to regard the world itself as well as our own

---

91. James Hillman, "Anima Mundi: The Return of the Soul to the World," Spring (1982): 71–93. Reprinted in part in Thomas Moore, ed., *A Blue Fire: Selected Writings of James Hillman* (New York: Harper & Row, 1989), pp. 99–102.

productions in art, language, and science as filled with soul and spirit.[92] We have boxed ourselves into such a corner that the psyche is confined to ourselves and our relationships, and we are no longer capable, as were previous generations, of sensing the great depth and soul of the world at large. Indeed, our generation is one in which to be "deep" means to turn inward toward the self. Involvement in such matters as politics, science, or the natural world are deemed psychologically and spiritually uninteresting. Many of the most creative minds of our own generation have spent the better part of their lives in self-reflection and analysis with little regard for the soul of the world. Such individuals are in a position that is in some ways analogous to that which according to Sarug was the position of God before creation: we are narcissistically preoccupied and thereby remain incapable of encountering an ensouled world. Perhaps a new *human* act of contraction or *Tzimtzum* is necessary at this stage to recognize that there is as much soul and depth in that world as there is within our own souls.

When individuals take a genuinely deep and abiding interest in the world around them and turn away from the machinations of their personal souls, this is a humanly and theologically hopeful sign. While such an interest can, on occasion, be a sign of an avoidance of the conflicts within one's psyche, it is very frequently a sign that the individual has contracted himself; that he has moved himself out of the way and permitted a world to emerge outside the confines of his own mind. Such a *Tzimtzum* is a wonderful example of *imitatio dei*, and when it occurs, it provides warrant for the assertion that man was created *b'tzelmo*, in the image of God.

92. See James Hillman, *Re-visioning Psychology* (New York: Harper & Row, 1976), and Moore, *A Blue Fire*. Hillman, a neo-Jungian, perhaps comes closer than any living psychologist to developing a psychology compatible with the kabbalistic worldview.

4

Sefirot: Foundations for a Ten-Dimensional Universe

In recent years the imaginations of both the scientific community and the public have been stimulated by a controversial idea in contemporary physics: "super-string theory," which implies that the universe contains ten dimensions. Impressed by its sheer mathematical elegance and its ability to explain all known physical forces, but unable to account for an additional six dimensions in a universe they thought to contain only four, advocates of the theory suggest that at the very beginning of time, when our present universe came into existence as a result of a cosmic "big bang," six dimensions *contracted* in on themselves to a point smaller than the smallest subatomic particle. While some physicists have rejected this theory on the grounds that its assumptions stretch beyond the bounds of the scientific imagination, others, including Edward Witten of Princeton's Institute for Advanced Studies, suggest that the theory (ten dimensions, cosmic contraction and all) is a piece of twenty-first-century physics that had fallen, by a sort of intellectual happenstance, into the twentieth century.

One remarkable thing about super-string theory is that it seems, in some manner, to have been presaged in the conceptual system of Lurianic Kabbalah. Even the *New York Times* took the opportunity to note in an early article on super-string theory that in Isaac Luria's system of Kabbalah the universe is understood as a function of ten *Sefirot* (roughly boundaries or realms), which express the inner life of God. In addition, as we have seen, the

Lurianic system conceives of these ten *Sefirot* as having been created through an initial act of *Tzimtzum* or contraction within the Godhead, seemingly analogous to the contraction posited by the super-string interpretation of the "big bang."

The similarities in metaphor between an ancient mystical tradition and an advanced theory in contemporary physics, while certainly remarkable, are, at least at this point, little more than suggestive.[1] Still, the intense excitement generated by super-string theory and its startling resemblance to the Lurianic conception of *Tzimtzum* and the ten *Sefirot* should at the very least encourage us to take a close and perhaps fresh look at these kabbalistic ideas.

One goal of this chapter will therefore be to consider the *Sefirot* as a model for understanding a ten-dimensional universe. In the process we will see that the Kabbalists had good reason to move beyond a naturalistic concept of the universe, limited to the dimensions of space and time.[2] A second goal is to understand the kabbalistic view that the *Sefirot* are the elements not only of the world but also of the human mind. As we have seen, the Kabbalists held the human mind to be a mirror of the cosmos, and that the *Sefirot* are thus the elements of human character.

A UNIVERSE OF TEN DIMENSIONS

What is the nature of the ten *Sefirot* that allows them to serve both as the building blocks of creation and the constituents of the human mind? To answer this question we must, at least for the moment, set aside our "scientific" assumptions about what constitutes reality and take what can be called a pretheoretical or *phenomenological* attitude toward the world. If we do so we will see that a presumably "objective," materialistic framework is seriously limited in its capacity to account for the *phenomena of human experience.* Philosophers have long noted that a whole variety of intangible objects: consciousness, will, freedom, fictional and imagined entities, pure

---

1. An interesting possibility, one that deserves more serious consideration, is that theories of mysticism and science each reflect certain archetypal routes, or basic metaphors of the human psyche.

2. It is an intriguing possibility that physics itself may need to include within its purview dimensions that are decidedly nonphysical, i.e., values and experience, in order to provide a complete account of the physical world.

numbers, concepts, and ideas, as well as spiritual, ethical, and aesthetic values, are recognized in everyday experience as lying outside the four-dimensional world. Each of these intangible objects is present to us every day, forming an essential part of our world, yet none can be located in a purely physical universe of space and time. As Edmund Husserl, the founder of the phenomenological movement brought to our attention, it is only the prejudice of a scientific *Weltanschauung* that denies reality to these intangibles and insists they are merely subjective qualities brought to the world by individual minds.[3] Husserl held that we must bracket our naturalistic and scientific assumptions about the world in order for the full measure of human experience to emerge.

It is the *phenomenological* point of view, which allows for the reality of *volitional, conceptual, axiological,* and other intangible entities, that is the starting point of all kabbalistic theology. Without stating so explicitly, the Kabbalists, in their doctrine of the *Sefirot,* have provided us with a phenomenology of human experience. Each *Sefirah* represents a fundamental psycho-emotive category that is fundamental to human psychology as well as to the phenomenological construction of the world as it presents itself in experience. In addition, each of the *Sefirot* provides us with an important lesson and opportunity for the development of human character and the actualization of the human soul. However, the Kabbalists ultimately went beyond phenomenology to speculate, in the tradition of Plato and in anticipation of the German Idealists, that their phenomenological categories of Will, Wisdom, Understanding, Love, Judgment, Compassion, etc., actually stand closer to the *source of being* than the material objects of everyday life. In their *idealist* system of thought, the scientific view of things is reversed: ideas and values, far from being an abstraction imposed on the world by the mind, are the basic reality for which material, finite things are mere instantiations.[4] For the

---

3. For a discussion of Husserl and the phenomenological movement in philosophy see Herbert Spiegelberg, *The Phenomenological Movement.* (The Hague: Martinus Nijhoff, 1971), especially Part V, Ch. XIV, "The Essentials of the Phenomenological Method." See also Edmund Husserl, *The Crisis In European Philosophy and Transcendental Phenomenology,* trans. Davis Carr (Evanston, IL: Northwestern University Press; 1970), Part I.

4. The Platonic influences upon the Kabbalah, and the notion that the *Sefirot* are in essence "Platonic Forms," is discussed in Moshe Idel, "Jewish Kabbalah and Platonism in the Middle Ages and Renaissance," in Goodman, *Neoplatonism in Jewish Thought,* pp. 319–351.

Kabbalists, the structures of the mind are said to be equivalent to the elements of the world itself.

The experiential, phenomenological, *and idealist* basis of kabbalistic thought is not always obvious; frequently, as with the *Sefirot*, it requires textual interpretation in order to be clearly understood. In order to comprehend the *Sefirot* both as structures of the human mind and as archetypes for the world as it is phenomenologically constructed, we must understand each *Sefirah* hermeneutically in its role within the complex dialectic of kabbalistic theosophy. Only then can we uncover the kernels of human experience to which the *Sefirot* refer and the aspects of human character that they inform.

Here, however, we can begin by noting that in the first known reference to the *Sefirot*, in *Sefer Yetzirah*, they are described as *Beli-mah*, "without anything."[5] Kaplan has pointed out that this term can also be used to mean "closed, abstract, absolute or ineffable," and as such indicates that the *Sefirot* "are purely ideal concepts without any substance whatever."[6] That the *Sefirot* name the general concepts through which the world is constructed and experienced will be brought out in detail as we proceed.

THE *SEFIROT*: THEIR ORIGIN AND NATURE

In its earliest form the doctrine of the *Sefirot* gave expression to the view that they are the instruments or building blocks of creation. The earliest reference to the *Sefirot* is in the proto-kabbalistic source, *Sefer Yetzirah* (*The Book of Formation*), which speaks of "thirty-two wondrous paths of wisdom" through which God "engraved and created the world."[7] These paths consist of ten primordial numbers and twenty-two letters of the Hebrew alphabet.[8] The ten primordial numbers are called *Sefirot*. The word *Sefirah* has the

---

5. *Sefer Yetzirah* 1: 2; Kaplan, *Sefer Yetzirah*, p. 22.

6. Ibid., p. 25.

7. *Sefer Yetzirah* 1:1; Kaplan, *Sefer Yetzirah*, p. 5. Cf. Scholem, *Origins of the Kabbalah*, p. 26. Kaplan's Hebrew/English edition is helpful for its translations of several manuscript versions. His commentary, while interesting from a traditional point of view, is misleading from a historical perspective, as Kaplan anachronistically attributes much later kabbalistic doctrine to this early work.

8. Scholem, *Origins of the Kabbalah*, pp. 26–27, referring to *Sefer Yetzirah*, Chs. 1 and 2. The "twenty-two letters" will be the subject of Chapter Five.

literal meaning of "counting." *Sefer Yetzirah* itself suggests several other etymological connections, including *sephar* (number), *sepher* (text), *sepharim* (books), and *sippur* (communication), which considerably broaden the term's connotative significance.[9] According to Scholem, since the term is derived from the Hebrew *sapar* (to count) it has no relation at least at this early stage to the Greek *sphaira* (sphere). However, the word *Sefirah* is introduced in place of *mispar* to indicate that the author of *Yetzirah* wished to speak not of ordinary numbers, but of metaphysical principles or *stages* in God's creation.[10] According to *Sefer Yetzirah*, the *Sefirot* are the "Breath of the living God."[11] They are living numerical beings and the hidden "depth" and "dimension" to all things.[12]

Commentators on *Sefer Yetzirah* interpreted the theme of ten divine powers in philosophical terms. For example, in the tenth century Saadiah Gaon equated the ten *Sefirot* from *Sefer Yetzirah* with the ten categories of Aristotelean philosophy, and Pseudo-Bahaya Ibn Pakuda spoke of ten levels of created being: the *Shekhinah* (God's presence or Active Intellect), universal soul, nature, hyle, the sphere, planets, fire, air, water, and earth.[13]

---

9. Among the Kabbalists the word *Sefirah* has been variously interpreted as derived from or related to a variety of Hebrew roots including *mispar* (number), *sapar* (to number), *sefer* (book), *sipor* (to tell, relate), *sapir* (sapphire, brilliance, luminary), *separ* (boundary), and *safra* (scribe). Kaplan (*Sefer Yetzirah*, p. 19) points out that the English word "cipher" (to count) is derived from the same Hebrew root as *Sefirah*. Each of the derivations can provide us with some insight into the nature of these iridescent entities, whose ability to reflect the nature of both man and the cosmos is a function of the breadth and depth of their metaphoric range. Their vast range of symbolism defines the *Sefirot*'s fundamental character as aspects of God and man that are simultaneously the essential elements of the world. It should be noted that a variety of synonyms for the *Sefirot* are used in the kabbalistic literature, including *ma'amarot* (sayings), *shemot* (names), *orot* (lights), *ketarim* (crowns), *middot* (qualities), *madregot* (levels or stages), *levushim* (garments), and the term most frequently found in the Zohar, *sitrin* (aspects); see Scholem, *Kabbalah*, p. 100.

10. Scholem, *Origins of the Kabbalah*, p. 26. *Sefer Yetzirah* 1:7; Kaplan, *Sefer Yetzirah*, p. 57; see also Zohar III, 70a. Later Kabbalists, including Vital, came to link the *Sefirot* with the heavenly spheres of classical cosmology.

11. *Sefer Yetzirah* 1:14; Kaplan, *Sefer Yetzirah*, p. 88.

12. This idea corresponds to the view attributed to Plato (by Aristotle) that the Forms, which in Greek thought are the "ideas" behind creation, are indeed numbers.

13. Verman, *The Books of Contemplation*, pp. 127–8. According to Verman, such ideas were synthesized by the Sufi theoretician Suhrawadi Maqtul (d. 1191), who, combining them with Oriental concepts, may have been the first to equate the

By the time of the earliest kabbalistic work, *Sefer ha-Bahir* (late twelfth century), the *Sefirot* are understood as *aeons, logoi,* or attributes (*middoth*), which serve as the instruments of creation.[14] The *Bahir* speaks of "ten *Sefirot* that seal heaven and earth," which are equivalent to the "ten words" with which the world was created.[15] The *Bahir's* description of the individual *Sefirot* at times leans on the symbols of *Merkaveh* mysticism (e.g., the sixth is described as "the throne of splendor").[16] However, in identifying the *Sefirot* with *ma'amoroth* (the ten words or sayings by which the world was created,[17] and with such *middoth* (God's attributes or traits) as "Wisdom," the author of the *Bahir* also forges a link between the *Sefirot* doctrine and certain *aggadic* and talmudic ideas. For example, in the Midrash *Aboth de Rabbi Nathan* we find the aphorism: "Seven *middoth* serve before the throne of Glory: they are Wisdom, Justice and the Law, Grace and Mercy, Truth and Peace."[18] The Midrash follows with a comment that serves as a precursor to the kabbalistic view that the *Sefirot* are themselves reflected and embodied in the soul, particularly in ethical acts: "Everyone who has these qualities as *middoth,* obtains the knowledge of God." Further, we read in the Talmud: "By ten things was the world created, by wisdom and by understanding, and by reason and by strength (*Gevurah*), by rebuke and by might, by righteousness and by judgment, by loving kindness and compassion" (Talmud, Tractate *Hagiga,* 12a). The connection with the *Sefirot* doctrine is so strong as to suggest that the *Sefirot* are in reality a hypostatization of these *aggadic* and talmudic ideas. Indeed the talmudic view that God has essentially two basic traits—*chesed* (loving-kindness) and *din* (strict judgment)—is adopted

---

ten divine powers with divine illumination; he thereby produced an early metaphysics of light, which was to become so important in the Kabbalah. Verman holds that Arabic Neoplatonic writings may have influenced the early Kabbalists.

14. See Scholem, *Origins of the Kabbalah,* p. 82.

15. *Sefer ha-Bahir,* sec 87. *Book Bahir,* Neugroschel trans., p. 74.

16. Other early kabbalistic texts speak of God's "powers" in a manner that is even more closely related to the earlier *Merkaveh* mysticism. For example, in *Sefer ha-Iyyun* (The Book of Contemplation) we find the following order of God's creative powers (which, however, are not spoken of as *Sefirot*): Primordial Wisdom, Marvelous Light, *Hashmal* (Electrum), *Arafel* (Darkness), Throne of Light, Wheel of Greatness, Cherub, Wheels of the Chariot, Encompassing Ether, Celestial Curtain. See Verman, *The Books of Contemplation,* pp. 42–48.

17. As found in the talmudic tractate *Pirke Avoth* 5:1. Philip Blackman, trans., *Tractate Avoth: The Ethics of the Fathers,* (Gateshead, England: Judaica Press, 1985).

18. Scholem, *Origins of the Kabbalah,* p. 82.

by the *Bahir* and subsequent Kabbalists in the view that these *Sefirot* are the two most essential for the creation of the world.

Sefer ha-Bahir connects the concept of the *Sefirot* with God's light. It is the *Sefirot* that are referred to when the *Bahir* reinterprets the Psalm (19: 2), "The heavens declare the glory of God," as "the heavens are radiant in the sapphire radiance of the glory of God."[19] Here the Hebrew *sipor* (to tell) is reinterpreted as *sappir* (sapphire).[20]

The doctrine of the *Sefirot* receives further development in the work of Isaac the Blind,[21] the first Kabbalist to consistently use the word "*Sefirot*" and relate them to the biblical enumeration of God's traits in Chronicles 29: 11. There, reference is made to God's greatness, power, beauty, victory, majesty, and sovereignty. Each of these was eventually adopted (by at least some Kabbalists) in the ordering of the lowest seven *Sefirot*.

Azriel of Gerona (early thirteenth century) offers a rather developed philosophical conception of the *Sefirot*, according to which they are the finite manifestations or powers of *Ein-Sof*, the infinite Godhead. As such, they are a necessary part of God's totality and perfection, providing God with finite power to complement his infinite divine power.[22] The *Sefirot*, according to Azriel, embody the order of generation and decay in the finite world; they are "the force behind every existent being in the realm of plurality."[23] They are ten in number because they are bounded by such categories as substance, place, length, width, and depth, which according to Azriel add up to ten, and which presumably correspond in some rough manner to Aristotle's ten categories of being. The *Sefirot* are one with *Ein-Sof*, in the sense that the flame, the sparks, and the aura are one with the fire.[24] Some of the *Sefirot* are

---

19. *Sefer ha-Bahir*, sec. 87. *Book Bahir*, Neugroschel trans., p. 75.

20. In Exodus 24: 10 we find the earliest reference to the sapphirine nature of the heavens: "And they saw the God of Israel: and there was under his feet as it were a paved work of a sapphire (*Sapir*) stone, and as it were the body of heaven in his clearness."

21. Dan, *The Early Kabbalah*, p. 94.

22. Ibid., p. 90.

23. Ibid., p. 91.

24. Ibid, p. 92. According to Nachmanides God acts through the *Sefirot* in roughly the same way that individuals act through their bodies. Understood in this way, the *Sefirot* are not outside the deity. While they are sometimes spoken of as God's garments, they are certainly not the kinds of garments that anyone or anything could remove. Perhaps they are better understood simply as God's *mode of expression*; an expression that, according to the Lurianists, is also God's *completion*. It is only in

pre-existent in *Ein-Sof* prior to the emanation; and like *Ein-Sof* itself, "the nature of *Sefirah* is the synthesis of everything and its opposite."[25] This synthesis, according to Azriel, is the source of all energy in everything whatsoever; and like the soul, which is the synthesis of all our desires and thoughts, the *Sefirot* are likened to the absolute "Will." Indeed, even the energy and will of the human soul is drawn from the *Sefirot*.[26]

The Zohar provides a classic description of the "identity in difference" that obtains between God and *Sefirot*, which are here referred to as God's "Crowns": "The Holy One, blessed is He, emits ten crowns, supernal holy crowns. With these He crowns Himself and in these He vests Himself. He is they and they are He, just as a flame is bound up in the coal, and there is no division there."[27] The Zohar does not commonly use the term *Sefirot* but instead uses a multiplicity of terms,[28] which suggest that its author conceptualized the *Sefirot* as dimensions of the cosmos, archetypes for nondivine existence, spiritual forces within the world, activities within the Godhead, gates or doors to the divine world, aspects of God, or ways in which God is perceived. Indeed, the Zohar, in utilizing a wide range of terms (and thereby extending the boundaries) of the *Sefirot* doctrine, gives expression to a unity among the knower, the known (the cosmos), and the act of knowing that is common in mystical, but unusual in philosophical or speculative, thought. For the Kabbalah, God, the cosmos, the human soul, and the act of knowledge are all a single, unified essence or substance. It is in the light of this higher-order unity that the multiplicity of symbols (that the Kabbalah uses as windows into, or metaphors for, the *Sefirot*) can be best understood.

---

relation to created, seemingly independent things (i.e., the *Sefirot*) that God can become differentiated and distinctly manifest wisdom, kindness, beauty, sovereignty, etc. Creation, as the derivations of *Sefirot* from *sipor* (to relate), *sifra* (scribe), and *sefer* (book) indicate, is thus God's *self-expression*. Without creation the Holy One could not express the characteristics that make God divine.

25. Dan, *The Early Kabbalah*, p. 94.

26. Ibid., p. 95.

27. Zohar III, 70a; Sperling and Simon, *The Zohar*, Vol. 5, p. 66.

28. Among these terms are "levels," "powers," "sides," "areas," "firmaments," "worlds," "pillars," "lights," "colors," "dates," "gates," "streams," "garments," and "crowns." See Tishby and Lachower, *The Wisdom of the Zohar*, Vol. 1, p. 269. Other terms used by the Kabbalists for the *Sefirot* are "mirrors," "names," "shoots," "qualities," "sources," "aspects" (*sitrin*), "supernal days," and "inner faces of God." See Scholem, *Kabbalah*, p. 21.

Joseph Gikatilla's *Sha'are Orah* (Gates of Light),[29] which was written at the end of the thirteenth century, shortly after the Zohar was first distributed by Moses de Leon in Spain, provides a detailed exposition of the *Sefirot*, connecting each *Sefirah* with a biblical name of God, and exploring their value dimensions through detailed exegesis of hidden references in scripture. Gikatilla's work reveals the *Sefirot* to encompass a heavenly firmament of Jewish values.

Moses Cordovero developed a philosophically sophisticated conception of the *Sefirot*. According to Cordovero: "*Ein-Sof* caused and emanated His *Sefirot*, and his actions are [performed] through them. They constitute the ten 'sayings' through which he acts. They serve him as vessels for the actions which derive from Him in the World of Separation below."[30] According to Cordovero, prior to their emanation the sefirotic qualities were utterly hidden within Him in the greatest possible unity,"[31] but even subsequent to their emanation they "have no [physical] location."[32] Cordovero developed the notion that each *Sefirah* is "contained" in each of the others, and held that as a result "the *Sefirot* have the power to perform opposite actions," for example, "at times [partaking of] Judgement, and at times [partaking] of Mercy."[33] He enumerated the major channels through which they interact, noting that there are actually an infinite number of interactional combinations.[34]

Cordovero detailed a commonly accepted order for the *Sefirot* and described their traditional alignment in three basic triads, which also form three basic columns. The central *Sefirah* in each triad acts as a dialectical mediator between the two other opposing *Sefirot* (e.g., *Tiferet* mediates between *Gevurah* and *Chesed*), and *Sefirot* in the same column share significant commonalties (e.g., *Binah*, *Gevurah*, and *Hod* share in the qualities of the left: stern judgment and evil).[35] *Malchut*, which channels the powers of the other nine *Sefirot*, is a member of none of the triads, but is part of the central column.

---

29. Joseph Gikatilla, *Sha'are Orah* (*Gates of Light*), trans. Avi Weinstein (San Francisco: HarperCollins, 1994).

30. Cordovero, *Or Ne'erav* VI: 1, 33b–335a; Robinson, *Moses Cordovero's Introduction to Kabbalah*, p. 115.

31. Cordovero, *Or Ne'erav* VI: 1, 35b; ibid., p. 116.

32. Ibid., VI: 2, 35a; ibid., p. 120.

33. Ibid. VI: 2, 36b; ibid., p. 121.

34. Ibid., VI: 2, 36b; ibid., pp. 120–121.

35. Ibid., VI: 2, 35a, 39b; ibid., pp. 119, 130.

Keter

Binah   *Chochmah*

Gevurah (Din)   *Chesed*

Tiferet

Hod   *Netzach*

Yesod

Malchut

The doctrine of the *Sefirot* took a further turn in the Kabbalah of Isaac Luria, through whom we can gain insight into the seeming distinction (but actual unity) among God, the *Sefirot*, and the world. As we have seen, according to the Lurianic Kabbalah, the creation of a finite world is predicated on God's self-limitation. Without this self-limitation, expressed in the act of *Tzimtzum* (concealment or contraction), God would fill the entire universe with infinite light and nothing whatsoever could be distinguished from God. In creating a finite world, therefore, God must *contract* or *conceal* an aspect of the divine to "make room," as it were, for finite, independent things. The initial results, however, of this concealment or contraction occur, in most interpretations, totally within God and result in a differentiation of divine *middot* or traits, which ultimately become the archetypes for the elements of the created universe.[36] It is the progressive differentiation of these divine traits that gives rise to the ten *Sefirot*, which become the receptacles (*Kelim*) for the divine light emanated into the lower worlds.

According to Luria the *Sefirot*, as they were originally created, were unstable, disunified structures, which were unable to hold the energy that they were meant to contain. As a result, the upper three *Sefirot* were displaced and the lower seven shattered, causing a fundamental flaw in creation, a flaw that is humankind's divinely appointed task to correct. Shards from the shattered vessels attached themselves to sparks of divine light and were scattered throughout the cosmos. These kernels of entrapped divine energy are to be found everywhere and especially within the human soul. According

---

36. Though a number of Kabbalists, including the first Lubavitcher rebbe, Schneur Zalman of Lyadi, held that all of these changes occur in the *Or Ein-Sof* (the divine light) and not within *Ein-Sof* himself.

to Luria, each man and woman is enjoined to "complete creation" by liberating and raising the sparks within his or her own soul and environment and reconstructing the *Sefirot* into a new, more complete, and stable form that reflects the image of both God and humanity.

THE ORDER OF THE *SEFIROT*

According to Tishby, the names of the *Sefirot* were originally selected for exegetical as opposed to conceptual reasons.[37] As we have seen, Isaac the Blind named six of the *Sefirot* directly for the praises of God enumerated in Chronicles 29:11: "Yours, O Lord, is the greatness (*gedullah*), power (*Gevurah*), the beauty (*tiferet*), the victory (*netzach*), the majesty (*hod*) . . . yours is the kingdom (*malchut*)." The Kabbalists, however, recognized that the scheme would be much more useful if, for example, *Greatness* were to be renamed *Love*, *Power* renamed *Judgment*, and *Beauty* renamed *Compassion*. The result of these and other renamings is a system in which there are often several names for each *Sefirah*. *Keter* (Crown), for example, is also referred to as *Ayin* (Nothingness), *Ratzon* (Will), *Atika Kaddisha* (the Holy Ancient One), and *Ehyeh* ("I will be").

It will be useful, however, to orient ourselves around a basic appellative scheme. One that was fairly uniformly adopted in the later Kabbalah is according to the order of the *Sefirot* as given by Moses Cordovero.[38] This scheme (along with the most common alternative appellations) is outlined in Table 4–1.

The scheme is frequently altered, however, in the Lurianic Kabbalah, which eliminates *Keter*, and interposes the *Sefirah Da'at* (Knowledge) between *Binah* and *Chesed*.[39]

---

37. Tishby and Lachower, *The Wisdom of the Zohar*, Vol. 1, p. 270.

38. This scheme is found in Cordovero's *Pardes Rimonim* (3:1ff.).

39. Chayyim Vital regards *Keter* as virtually indistinguishable from *Ein-Sof* and thus holds that *Chochmah* is the highest *Sefirah*. He inserts the *Sefirah Da'at* (attachment, union, knowledge) between *Binah* and *Chesed* (see *Sefer Etz Chayyim* 23: 1, 2, 5, 8; 25: 6; 42: 1). In the Lurianic scheme *Da'at* is regarded as a derivative of *Keter* (the "Supernal Will," see below), and is sometimes referred to as the "external aspect of *Keter*" (Scholem, *Kabbalah*, 107). This is the scheme that is generally followed by Schneur Zalman of Lyadi, and, indeed, the characterization of his (the Lubavitcher) Hasidim as *ChaBaD* derives from an acronym of the names of

Table 4-1

Order of the *Sefirot*

1. *Keter Elyon* (Supreme Crown)   or *Ratzon* (Will)

2. *Chochmah* (Wisdom)

3. *Binah* (Intelligence)

4. *Chesed* (Love)   or *Gedulah* (Greatness)

5. *Gevurah* (Power)   or *Din* (Judgment)

6. *Tiferet* (Beauty)   or *Rachamim* (Compassion)

7. *Netzach* (Lasting Endurance)

8. *Hod* (Majesty)

9. *Yesod Olam* (Foundation of the World)   or *Tzaddik* (Righteous One)

10. *Malchut* (Kingdom)   or *Atarah* (Diadem), or *Shekhinah* (Feminine divine presence)

A complete understanding of the *Sefirot* requires not only an inquiry into the individual significance of each *Sefirah* but also an awareness of the interrelationships among the *Sefirot*, their participation in each of the five "Worlds" postulated in the kabbalistic scheme, their reorganization as a result of the "Breaking of the Vessels," and the various symbolisms through which the Kabbalists understood the entire system. In the pages to follow I will describe a number of divisions and models utilized by the kabbalists in their descriptions of the *Sefirot*.

---

the first three *Sefirot* according to this scheme, *Chochmah*, *Binah*, and *Da'at*. (The first three *Sefirot* are given the appellation ChaBaD, the next three ChaGaT, (*Chesed, Gevurah, Tiferet*), and the third triad NeHY (*Netzach, Hod, Yesod*). However, even the Lurianists (including Vital and Schneur Zalman) regard the first scheme (in which *Keter* is included) as correct with regard to the *Sefirot* in their "essential" aspects, and only eliminate *Keter* and insert *Da'at* after *Binah* when considering the *Sefirot* from a "general" or "external" (*chitzoniyut*) point of view. We will therefore feel justified in basing our phenomenological interpretation of the *Sefirot* (which, at any rate follows Cordovero) on the "*Keter*" scheme.

THE CREATION OF THE *SEFIROT*: CIRCULAR AND LINEAR MODELS

In his systematic work on the Lurianic Kabbalah, *Sefer Etz Chayyim*, Chayyim Vital describes how previous Kabbalists have been divided on the question of the precise organization of the *Sefirot* at the time of their emanation. Some Kabbalists held that the *Sefirot* were emanated as a series of concentric circles or spheres, while others held that that they were emanated in linear form "consisting of ten linear *Sefirot* in three lines, in the form of a human being (*'adam*) with a head, arms, thighs, body, and feet . . ."[40]

According to the first model (*Iggulim* or "Circles"), the primordial void was irradiated with divine light moving in a spiral fashion parallel to the hollow's perimeter and gradually approaching the center. In moving in this circular fashion, this *kav*, or ray of divine light, forms each of the *Sefirot*, first creating *Keter*, the highest and most exalted *Sefirah*, closest to the hollow's perimeter. Progressively this ray revolves and produces the other nine *Sefirot*, culminating with the formation of *Malchut* at the center of the hollow, where we find the origin of our own lowly world. Each *Sefirah*, in this scheme, is a self-contained sphere, and each from *Keter* to *Malchut* is progressively closer to the center of the hollow, and therefore, progressively further from the light of the infinite God.

In the second model (*Yosher* or "Lines") the *Sefirot* are said to be emanated in a manner that organizes them into an organic, living unity. The term *Yosher* (straightness, upright) is derived from the verse in Ecclesiastes 7: 24 "God made man *yasher* (upright)."[41] According to this model, the *Sefirot* are emanated in a sequence of three lines that ultimately takes on the form of *Adam Kadmon*, the Primordial Man. The *Sefirot* are here conceived as corresponding to the organs of the human body, as implied in the following passage in the Zohar:

> For there is not a member in the human body but has its counterpart in the world as a whole. For as a man's body consists of members and parts of various ranks all acting and reacting upon each other so as to form one organism, so does the world at large consist of a hierarchy of created things,

---

40. *Sefer Etz Chayyim* 1: 1, p. 22; Menzi and Padeh, *The Tree of Life*, p. 11.
41. Vital, *Sefer Etz Chayyim* 8: 1.

which when they properly act and react upon each other together form literally one organic body.[42]

The *Sefirah Chochmah*, for example, was conceived by the Kabbalists as corresponding to the brain, *Binah* to the heart, *Gevurah* to the right arm, *Chesed* to the left arm, etc.[43]

Vital tells us that both schemes, the circular and the linear, are "the word of the living God," and that each are different perspectives on the same metaphysical events. The circular (*Iggulim*) view, according to Vital, has the advantage of emphasizing the cosmic aspects of the creative process, those aspects that link the Kabbalah to the (Aristotelian) system of heavenly spheres. Indeed, as Scholem points out, the scheme of *Iggulim*, in which the *Sefirot* are depicted as concentric circles surrounding a central emanative point, is the closest the Kabbalists came to equating the *Sefirot* with the ancient and medieval cosmological picture of a world composed of ten spheres; the sun, the moon, seven planets, and the sphere of the fixed stars. The *Sefirot*, according this view, are the most perfect and well-balanced of geometric figures, reflecting the sublime harmony and balance of the original divine act (*Tzimtzum*) that brought them into being.

The second view, involving the emanation of the *Sefirot* in linear fashion, and ultimately into the form of *Adam Kadmon* (Primordial Man), has the advantage of representing the cosmos as an organic unity, reflecting the physical and spiritual qualities of man. The linear scheme, which is predominant in the Zohar, is called "the image of God," alluding to the verse in Genesis that speaks of God creating man in His own image.

We should note that the dual metaphors of "circle" and "line" can be traced back to the pre-Socratic philosophers Parmenides and Heraclitus. Parmenides held that the Universe was "one" and (like a circle, which always returns to each of its points) not susceptible to genuine development or

---

42. Zohar I, 134a; Sperling and Simon, *The Zohar*, Vol. 2, p. 36.

43. In addition to the corporeal figure of Primordial Man, the scheme of *Yosher* organizes the *Sefirot* according to three lines or triads: *Chochmah-Chesed-Netzach* on the right, *Binah-Gevurah-Hod* on the left, and *Keter-Tiferet (Rachamim)-Yesod-Malchut* in the center. This arrangement underscores the dynamic relationship among the *Sefirot*; for example, the mediating or harmonizing functions of the middle group, in which *Tiferet* or *Rachamim* is said to harmonize the bounty of *Chesed* (Kindness) with the severity of *Din* (Judgment), and where *Malchut* is said the channel or mediate all of the other sefirotic powers.

change. Heraclitus, on the other hand, regarded change and development as the essence of the cosmos, and therefore likened the world to a line, which never returns to the same point twice. Like Hegel,[44] several centuries later, the Lurianists were satisfied with neither view alone, preferring to hold them in a dialectical relationship, whereby the One (the circle) can only become itself through a process of linear change and development, and (what amounts to the same thing) God can only become Himself through man.

What is of interest in Vital's discussion of the circular and linear models is not simply the fact that Vital believes that two seemingly contradictory views on the origin of the *Sefirot* can be reconciled, but rather that these views complement one another precisely because they are, symbolically speaking, each other's inverse or contradiction; for as we discover in *Sefer Etz Chayyim*, what is "outside" for one is "inside" for the other. Here we have yet another illustration of the kabbalistic principle of *coincidentia oppositorum*. Further, according to Vital: "Each world, and every single detail of each world, has these two aspects—circular and linear."[45]

The circular model conceptualizes the *Sefirot* as emanating from the heavens, while the linear model understands them as centered in the mind of man.[46] With respect to the circular model Vital states that the *Sefirot* resemble "the encircling firmaments, the heavenly spheres"[47] This is because in the circular model it is the outermost *Sefirah* that is the most spiritual and

---

44. See Cyril O'Regan, *The Heterodox Hegel* (Albany: State University of New York Press, 1994), pp. 297–298.

45. *Sefer Etz Chayyim* 1: 1, p. 25; Menzi and Padeh, *The Tree of Life*, p. 33.

46. Vital is not completely consistent or clear in this characterization of the linear and circular models. In one place he says that "from our perspective the Infinite is in the inside of all the emanations" (*Sefer Etz Chayyim* 1: 2, p. 23; Menzi and Padeh, *The Tree of Life*, p. 22), implying that the "linear model" is from the perspective of humanity. Elsewhere, however, he explicitly states that the circular model is from the perspective of man. This is because divinity is outside and transcendent, whereas the linear model is "from the perspective of the Infinite," and from this point of view our world is on the outside as a shell that covers the divine essence (*Sefer Etz Chayyim* 1: 2, p. 27; Menzi and Padeh, *The Tree of Life*, p. 51). His view can be clarified as follows: in the circular model, divinity is on the outside, and man searches the heavens for God. In the linear model, divinity is on the inside and man must search for divinity within himself. The latter point of view is both humanistic and Godly: humanistic because it involves an immanent, human identification with the divine; Godly because, unlike the circular model, it is centered on *Ein-Sof*, the Infinite God.

47. *Sefer Etz Chayyim* 1: 2, p. 29; Menzi and Padeh, *The Tree of Life*, p. 73.

exalted, the one most closely associated with *Ein-Sof*. From this perspective, *Ein-Sof*, by the act of *Tzimtzum*, removes Himself from a circular hollow, and subsequently emanates a series of *Sefirot* and worlds into that hollow from the *outside in*. His light diminishes by degrees as it approaches the center, in such a manner that the innermost point of the hollow, our world, is the least exalted finite entity, distant and alienated from its source in God.

The opposite, however, is the case from the perspective of *Yosher*, the linear model, in which the *Sefirot* are said to be emanated in the image of the Primordial Man. On this model, in which *Ein-Sof* is said to contract Himself into a central point, it is the innermost *Sefirah* that is the most exalted and sublime. This is because each *Sefirah* is a "brain" or mind to the one that surrounds it, in such a manner that *Ein-Sof* is the "inner brain to them all." Indeed the Zohar itself declares:

> The whole world is constructed on this principal, upper and lower, from the first mystic point up to the furthest removed of all the stages they are all coverings one to another, brain within brain and spirit within spirit, so that one is a shell to another. The primal point is the innermost light of a translucency, tenuity, and purity surpassing comprehension.[48]

Although at first a vestment, each stage (each *Sefirah*) becomes a brain to the next outer stage.

It would seem that from the linear perspective we must look inward, toward an inner core of mind, to discover the essence of divinity. In the first model *Ein-Sof* is a cosmic creator, *on the outside of the world looking in*; in the second model he is an inner brain or mind, *on the inside of the mind looking out*.

From a contemporary point of view, we might say that Vital, in his description of *Iggulim* and *Yosher*, is contrasting two models of the cosmos: one centered in a transcendent cosmic deity, the other centered in the divinity within man. The first can be equated with the transcendent perspective of traditional theology, or (Aristotelian) science; the second with the immanent perspective of history and the humanities. In the first, man is a lowly creature, alien and distant from what is truly exalted and significant in the cosmos; in the second he is the most exalted of all creatures, who, by turning inward toward his own soul, discovers divinity itself. These dual perspectives, of transcendence and immanence, permanence and change, cosmos and man, or

---

48. Zohar I, 19b; Sperling and Simon, *The Zohar*, Vol. 1, p. 83.

(in a contemporary idiom) science and the humanities, complement one another in *coincidentia oppositorum*, in such a manner as to suggest that the world's outside is wedged in its inside and vice versa. *Ein-Sof* is both the most transcendent of beings, actually lying outside the cosmos, and the most immanent, to be discovered within the innermost "brain" of man.

These metaphors can provide us with a template for understanding many other oppositions, between God and man, reality and illusion, good and evil, etc.[49] When we reach the center of the Chinese Box, the innermost box changes positions with the outer one and we must start anew. Carl Jung, for example, (working, we might say, in the model of *Yosher*), thought he could understand the gods immanently, through an awareness of man's collective unconscious. But perhaps, if we take Vital's metaphors to heart, such an understanding must itself lead out to the transcendent gods once more, like water that has been poured into one of those paradoxical bottles whose opening leading inside ultimately leads out again, and then in, *ad infinitum*.

THE WORLDS OF POINTS, STRIPES, CHAOS, AND RESTORATION

Closely related to the metaphor of Circles and Lines are two other distinctions made by the Lurianists; the first between the "World of Points" (*Nekudim*) and the "World of Stripes" (*Berudim*), and the second between the worlds of Chaos (*Tohu*) and Restoration (*Tikkun*). Although Vital introduces the circular and linear schemes as contemporaneous manifestations of, or alternate perspectives upon, the *Sefirot*, the circular scheme, which corresponds to the World of Points and Chaos, is logically (if *not* temporally) prior to the linear scheme, which corresponds the World of Stripes and Restoration. These correspondences are indicated in Table 4–2.

Table 4–2

Basic Worlds

Circles (Iggulim)-------World of Points (Nekudim)------------World of Chaos (Breaking of the Vessels, Tohu)

Lines (Yosher)----------World of Stripes (Berudim)------------World of Restoration (Tikkun)

---

49. As discussed in Chapter Two.

According to Vital, the circular scheme leads to the ontologically primitive state of the World of Points, in which each *Sefirah* is an independent point within the cosmos, unrelated to any other. In this world, the *Sefirah* of Kindness (*Chesed*), for example, is unrelated to and unmitigated by the *Sefirah* of Judgment (*Din*) and vice versa, and none of the *Sefirot* are integrated with *Chochmah*, the *Sefirah* of Wisdom. As a result of their radical independence, the *Sefirot* in the World of Points were unable to contain the full emanation of divine light, and shattered. This event, known as the Breaking of the Vessels (*Shevirat ha-Kelim*), is a major turning point in the history of God and the universe, dividing the Worlds of Points and Chaos from the ontologically more developed worlds of Stripes and Restoration. Indeed, it is because of the initial chaos of the circular scheme and World of Points and their inevitable end in the Breaking of the Vessels, that this stage in the development of the *Sefirot* is spoken of as the *tohu* and *bohu*, "chaos and void" of the first chapter in the Book of Genesis. By way of contrast, the *Sefirot* arranged in the form of a man, are organically interrelated, and come under the guidance of intellect (*sachel*). They are therefore spoken of as the World of Stripes, as they are connected linearly, like reeds that have been brought together for their combined strength. This is the condition of the *Sefirot* after they have been restored. In this state they are therefore spoken of as the World of Restoration or *Tikkun*.

"INNER" AND "OUTER"

According to Vital, each *Sefirah* has an "inner" and an "outer" aspect. The inner aspect, known as the essence (*atzmut*) or inwardness (*pnimiyut*) of the *Sefirah*, is closest to the *Sefirah*'s divine light. The outer aspect of the *Sefirot*, the *chitzonuyut* (externalites), are nonessential, peripheral, and frequently negative and maleficent in character.[50] The inner and the outer were originally a single light. However, because the vessels were unable to hold the original divine emanation, the light was severed into two aspects. That part of the light that is received and held by the vessels is the "inner" light, and that which overflows is the "outer" light.[51] Vital compares the

---

50. *Sefer Etz Chayyim* 1: 2, 3.

51. *Sefer Etz Chayyim* 1: 2, p. 31, Menzi and Padeh; *The Tree of Life*, p. 83. At other times the Kabbalists held that the outer or surrounding light (the *or makiv*) is

"inner light" to the soul that animates the human body: "The light that shines into the vessels of the ten *Sefirot* and keeps them alive, is enclothed within the vessel in the same way that the soul enters into the body, enclothed within human limbs, giving them life and illuminating them from the inside. This is called the inner light."[52] Vital tells us that the "inner light even though it is smaller than the surrounding light, is more highly concentrated and compressed within the vessel, so it illuminates the inside of the vessel strongly and completely."[53] On the other hand the surrounding light, while it is a greater light, overflows the vessels because they lack the strength to limit or contain it within themselves. Those aspects of divine energy that cannot be structured and contained by humanity are a source of negativity and evil.

THE UNFOLDING OF INTELLECT AND EMOTION

The *Sefirot* are conceived of in the Kabbalah as moments in the unfolding of God's creative process, which the Kabbalists compared to the development of thought, emotion, and action in man. We will have occasion to make reference to some of these comparisons when we speak of each *Sefirah* individually. However, in general, the scheme can be described as follows: *Keter*, the supreme crown, highest of the *Sefirot*, is compared to the initial, most general creative urge of the will, prior to the articulation of any specific thought or intention. *Chochmah* is the first intuition of an intention or idea, an idea that is spelled out and elucidated in *Binah*, and which (through the mediation of *Da'at*—see below) comes to be enacted as emotional dispositions via the *Sefirot* from *Chesed* to *Yesod*, and as action in the world via *Malchut*.[54] This sequence, which involves a temporal development in man, is completely atemporal in God; and, according to the Kabbalists, implies no actual distinction between God's will and its development and execution in thought, emotion, and action.

---

the light that connects each *Sefirah* to the *Sefirah* above it; and in the case of the outermost, highest, *Sefirah*, *Keter* of A'K, actually makes contact with *Ein-Sof.*

52. *Sefer Etz Chayyim* 1: 2, p. 31; Menzi and Padeh, *The Tree of Life*, pp. 82–83.

53. *Sefer Etz Chayyim* 1: 2, p. 31; ibid., p. 85.

54. Schochet, "Mystical Concepts," p. 835.

COSMIC STRUCTURES

The lower seven *Sefirot* are occasionally conceptualized in terms of cosmic structures and powers. In one arrangement *Tiferet* is equated with heaven and *Malchut* with the earth, the latter being thought of as a feminine force, receiving "male waters" in much the same manner as the earth is fructified by heavenly rain.[55] A similar arrangement equates *Tiferet* with the sun and *Malchut* with the moon. In yet another image, *Chesed*, *Gevurah* (*Din*), and *Tiferet* (*Rachamim*) are conceived of as light, darkness, and the firmament where light and darkness are blended in the hours of twilight. This symbolizes the blending of loving-kindness and judgment in compassion and mercy. In other schemes several of the *Sefirot* are equated with points on the compass (*Chesed* with south because of its light, *Din* with the north because of its darkness) or the seven lower *Sefirot* are equated with the seven days of creation.[56]

INTELLECTUAL, PSYCHICAL, AND NATURAL *SEFIROT*

From a philosophical perspective the *Sefirot* were often ordered into discrete groups. One distinction, reflecting Neoplatonic ideas, was made by the Kabbalist Azriel among three categories of *Sefirot*; the intellectual (*ha-Muskal*), the psychical (*ha-Murgash*), and the natural (*ha-Mutba*).[57] As can be seen in Table 4–3, three *Sefirot* were assigned to each of these categories. In this scheme the tenth *Sefirah*, *Malchut* was regarded as an actualizing principle that brings the other nine *Sefirot* into a created world.

Another division was traditionally made between the higher *Sefirot*, which were regarded as *hidden*, and the lower *Sefirot*, which were regarded as *revealed*. Sometimes the hidden and revealed *Sefirot* were divided evenly (with five hidden and five revealed). At other times only the first three *Sefirot* were regarded as hidden, while each of the seven "moral" *Sefirot* were spoken of as revealed.

A third set of schemes, based on mathematics, came close to interpreting the *Sefirot* as *dimensions* of the physical world. In one such scheme, which

---

55. Tishby and Lachower, *The Wisdom of the Zohar*, Vol. 1, p. 282.
56. Ibid., p. 283.
57. Scholem, *Kabbalah*, p. 107.

Table 4-3

Threefold Division of the *Sefirot*

Intellectual *Sefirot*	Psychical *Sefirot*	Natural *Sefirot*	Actualizing Principle
(*ha-muskal*)	(*ha-murgash*)	(*ha-mutba*)	
Keter	*Chesed/Gedullah*	*Netzach*	*Malchut/Diadem*
Chochmah	*Gevurah/Din*	*Hod*	
Binah	*Tiferet/Rachamim*	*Yesod Olam*	

combines geometrical and natural metaphors, the first *Sefirah, Keter*, is understood as *Ayin* or nothingness and the second is understood as the primordial central point or *hathalat ha-yeshut*, the "beginning of being." This central point expands into a circle that becomes the third *Sefirah*, which is substantial being itself. Subsequent *Sefirot* are understood as structures emanating from the primal point[58] or as the tributaries of a river that empties into the final *Sefirah, Malchut*, which is metaphorically understood as the "great sea."[59] Another geometrical scheme, put forth in *Sefer Yetzirah*, sees the fourth through ninth *Sefirot* as the "six sides of space."

THE *BEHINNOT*

Within kabbalistic thought there developed what was to become the generally accepted doctrine of the *interpenetration* of the *Sefirot*. In brief, this doctrine holds that each *Sefirah* contains within itself an element of each of the others,[60] so that *Chesed* for example, is composed of the *Chesed of Chesed* (i.e., pure Chesed), the *Gevurah of Chesed*, the *Tiferet of Chesed*, the *Netzach of Chesed*, etc. Theologically the doctrine of interpenetration meant that God's *middot* or traits were all integrally related. From a moral point of view it meant that the development of character in man must consist of work on

---

58. Tishby and Lachower, *The Wisdom of the Zohar*, Vol. 1, p. 282.

59. Scholem, *Kabbalah*, p. 112.

60. Moses Cordovero, *Or Ne'erav* VI: 2, 35a; Robinson, *Moses Cordovero's Introduction to Kabbalah*, p. 119. Cordovero tells us "each of the [*Sefirot*] is made up of [all] ten" (ibid., p. 120).

all forty-nine possible combinations of the seven moral *Sefirot* (*Chesed* through *Malchut*).

Cordovero's ideas regarding the interpenetration of the *Sefirot* are formulated in his doctrine of the *behinnot*, the infinite number of aspects contained within a given *Sefirah*.[61] According to Cordovero, these "aspects" are dependent upon the perspective of one who would discover them. As such his theory anticipates contemporary notions that regard reality itself to be a function of the constructions placed upon experience.[62]

In order to make this doctrine more transparent it will be helpful to consider how an indefinite number of aspects, dependent upon the perspective of the individual who would discover them, can be discerned within a particular *Sefirah*, I will take as an example the fourth *Sefirah*, *Chesed*, "loving-kindness."

We can immediately observe that implicit within the notion of loving-kindness is an act of volition or will, the value ascribed to the first *Sefirah*, *Keter*. One who performs such an act does so not by virtue of the act itself but by virtue of the good, loving *intentions* that enter into it. It is no act of kindness if the wind blows the money of a miserly scrooge into the hands of a pauper; or rather the kindness is credited to the "wind," or to "the hand of God" through whose providence the act was willed, and certainly not to the miser who had no will in regard to the matter whatsoever. In this example, we discover the "will" implicit in kindness. In kabbalistic terms we have discovered the "*Keter*" of "*Chesed*."

That *thought*, the value associated with the second *Sefirah*, *Chochmah* (Wisdom), is equally an aspect of loving-kindness is apparent in the colloquial phrase "it's the thought that counts" (which also implicitly assumes a relationship between thought and will). That acts of kindness must be rendered "thoughtfully," and informed with a certain wisdom regarding their consequences, further establishes an aspect of *Chochmah* in *Chesed*.

The relationship between *Chesed* and the next *Sefirah*, Judgment (*Din*),

---

61. Scholem, *Kabbalah*, p. 114, referring to Cordovero, *Pardes Rimonim* 5: 5.

62. There are, according to Cordovero, six main *behinnot*, and these involve aspects that are both hidden and manifest within any given *Sefirah*, as well as properties that are both "essential" and "relational." Of particular significance are those *behinnot* that enable a given *Sefirah* to receive "light" from the *Sefirah* above it, and those that enable it to pass light onto the *Sefirah* below. Scholem is correct in pointing out that in this aspect of the *behinnot* doctrine Cordovero is close to a dialectical mode of thinking within a kabbalistic framework.

is subject to lengthy treatment by the Kabbalists themselves, one that I will discuss in detail later in this chapter. For now we can observe that the Kabbalists held that kindness unrestrained by a *judgment* regarding the merit and capacities of the recipient is no kindness but rather an arbitrary and even harmful discharge of action and emotion. Hence we have the *Din* (Judgement) of *Chesed* (Kindness), i.e., the aspect of kindness that involves judgment of merit, capacity, etc.[63]

The same procedure can be applied to all of the *Sefirot* in relation to *Chesed*. Not only does the notion of kindness contain hidden within itself aspects that can be described as will, thought, and judgment, but also aspects of understanding (*Binah*), knowledge (*Da'at*), compassion (*Rachamim*) or beauty (*Tiferet*), endurance (*Netzach*), majesty (*Hod*), foundation (*Yesod*), and kingship (*Malchut*). While the derivations of each of these relationships may be more obvious in some cases than in others, Cordovero assures us that by adopting an appropriate perspective it is possible to see not only the sefirotic notions essential to "kindness" but a vast array of subsidiary notions or aspects as well, so that *Chesed* indeed has within itself an indefinite if not infinite number of *behinnot* or aspects. Consider, for example, the role of "action," "creation," "expectation," "greatness," "wholeness," "peace," "truth," "strength," "weakness" or "vulnerability," "genuineness," "fairness," "courage," "concentration," "attention," etc., in the value we call "loving-kindness." Indeed, it would appear that almost any "axiological" or even "psychological" notion has a role in the notion, or place in the *Sefirah*, of *Chesed*. To take one example at random: What would *Chesed* be if the supposed giver fled from his benevolence and did not have the *courage* to bestow his gift of kindness in the face of potential hardship, ridicule, etc.

What's more, not only "loving-kindness" but any of the *Sefirot*, and, again, any axiological or psychological notion whatever, can be shown to contain within itself virtually all of the others, in a vast network of relationships that binds everything to everything else in a comprehensive unity of all values and ideas. This, of course, is perfectly consistent with kabbalistic theory, which indeed posits such a unity behind the diversity of

---

63. If one were here to object that what I have just described as the "judgment of kindness" is also or better conceived of as the "thought of kindness" then we would say that he was getting the *behinnot* idea, for there is also the *Chochmah* of *Din*, the "thought of judgment." The dialectical thinking involved in the doctrine of the *behinnot* is designed to break down barriers between concepts and values one initially thought to be separate and distinct.

our concepts and ideas. Our reading of Cordovero's theory of the *behinnot* explains, dialectically, the unity of the "one" and the "many" within the *Sefirot* doctrine.[64]

THE DOCTRINE OF THE FIVE WORLDS

The Kabbalists generally posited two stages in the emanative process. In addition to the emanation of the ten *Sefirot* themselves, God is said to have progressively structured the *Sefirot* into a series of *Olamot* or "worlds."[65] The Lurianists spoke of "thousands upon thousands and myriads upon myriads" of worlds,[66] and made numerous distinctions between levels of reality that were only implicit in the earlier Kabbalah. Traditionally, however, the Kabbalah speaks of four or five major *Olamot*: the worlds of *Adam Kadmon* (Primordial Man), *Atzilut* ("Nearness" or Emanation), *Beriah* (Creation), *Yetzirah* (Formation), and *Assiyah* ("Making" or Action). Sometimes *Adam*

---

64. The philosopher Ludwig Wittgenstein, having himself recognized such a boundless proliferation of relationships within the orbit of our mental life, argued that the apparent essential relations between the so-called referents of our mentalistic vocabulary say nothing about the order of "things," but are actually part of the order of "words"; it being part of the conventional definition of our terms that "reading" requires so-called "mental acts" of thinking, intention, concentration, attention, expectation, memory, insight, comprehension, perception, recognition, interpretation, integration, etc., and, by extension, simply part of the linguistic system that kindness involves acts of will, thought, truth, fairness, judgment, and all of the other acts and values the Kabbalists thought were contained within it. To hold that these discoveries about the connections in our linguistic system are actually discoveries about the nature of values, mind, and the world is one of the results of the "bewitchment of our intelligence by means of language," which Wittgenstein held to be one of the main diseases of metaphysics.

I have considered the entire Wittgensteinian critique of metaphysics elsewhere at some length (Sanford Drob, *Are Mental Acts Myths?*, Doctoral Dissertation, Boston University, 1981). Suffice it to say that having once been held under its sway I have been moved in the direction of the metaphysics one finds in the Kabbalah precisely because I can find no reasonable basis for distinguishing between discourse about the word "world" and discourse about the world. I don't know what it means to say, for example, that the word "kindness" has a linguistic relationship to the word "fairness" if this does not mean that part of kindness is to be fair.

65. See Schochet, "Mystical Concepts," pp. 860–866.

66. *Sefer Etz Chayyim* 1: 1, p. 23; Menzi and Padeh, *The Tree of Life*, p. 19.

Kadmon is identified with *Ein-Sof* and is eliminated from the scheme, and *Atzilut* is regarded as the highest of the worlds.

The term *olam* is etymologically related to and, in Hebrew, occasionally even spelled the same as the word *alam*, meaning "hidden" or "concealed." Consistent with the kabbalistic doctrine that the act of creation or *Tzimtzum* was essentially a concealment of the divine presence, each of the five main worlds was seen as being progressively more remote from God's infinite light (*Or Ein-Sof*).[67] Like the *Sefirot*, the "worlds" were regarded as allegorical concepts that have reality relative to man but no reality relative to God (who in truth encompasses all things within Himself). From man's point of view, however, it can be said that the higher worlds receive a divine radiance or revelation free from the interposition of many "screens" or "garments," whereas the lower worlds receive little if any divine revelation or light.[68] At the lowest level, there is a crystallization of only corporeal, completely lifeless things. Our physical world therefore is understood as the most hidden from God's light, and according to the Zohar this is why the prophet refers to God Himself as "The Most Hidden of All Hidden."[69]

While all of the *Sefirot* are considered to be operative in each of the worlds, particular *Sefirot* are dominant in each particular world,[70] a consideration that will be of significance in our interpretation of the nature of the *Sefirot* themselves. Table 4–4 provides an outline of the five worlds along with their dominant *Sefirot*.

The doctrine of "worlds" will be explored more fully in Chapter Six.

PARTZUFIM

The Lurianists held that the *Sefirot*, in all worlds but the World of Points, are organized into *Partzufim*, "visages" or personal aspects of *Adam Kadmon*. Moses Luzzatto describes the distinction between *Sefirot* and *Partzufim* as follows:

> Each of these *Sefirot* is constructed of ten Lights, each of which in turn is composed of an equal number of Lights and so on *ad infinitum*. When, in

---

67. See Zalman, *Likutei Amarim-Tanya*, p. 197ff.
68. Ibid.
69. See *Tikkunei Zohar*, Intro., 17a.
70. Zalman, *Likutei Amarim-Tanya*, p. 187ff.

Table 4-4

The Five Worlds

World	Dominant *Sefirah*
1. *Adam Kadmon* (Primordial Man)	*Keter* (Crown)
2. *Atzilut* (Emanation)	*Chochmah* (Wisdom)
3. *Beriah* (Creation)	*Binah* (Intelligence)
4. *Yetzirah* (Formation)	*Chesed, Gevurah, Tiferet* (Love, Power, Beauty)
	Netzach, Hod, Yesod (Endurance, Majesty, Foundation)
5. *Assiyah* (Action or Making)	*Malchut* (Kingdom)

one of these vessels only a single light is illuminated it is called a *Sefira*. When all ten Lights in a vessel is illumined then it is defined as a *Parezuf* (Person). In order that it may be called a complete and perfect *Parezuf*, every division within must shine with all its Lights so that the number of lights will total six hundred and thirteen—the number of parts in a man's body. Only then is it considered complete.

According to Chayyim Vital, a *Partzuf* is an aspect or "face" of the divinity, structured like a person with "248 limbs" and arranged in a pattern encompassing all ten *Sefirot*. The first *Sefirah*, *Keter*, is the skull of the *Partzuf*. The next three *Sefirot*, *Chochmah*, *Binah*, and *Da'at* (Wisdom, Understanding, and Knowledge) are the "three brains" that are figuratively contained inside the head. *Chesed* and *Gevurah* (Kindness and Judgment) are the right and left arms, while *Tiferet* (Beauty, Compassion) is the torso. *Netzach* and *Hod* are the two thighs and *Yesod* the phallus. Significantly, Vital describes *Malchut* (which is often identified with the feminine *Shekhinah*) as the *Partzuf's* "female," reflecting the ancient and biblical notion that originally male and female were joined together in a single "complete" person.

Although each *Partzuf* contains all ten *Sefirot*, specific *Sefirot* are identified with particular *Partzufim*. The six major *Partzufim*, into which the *Sefirot* are reorganized, are *Attika Kaddisha* or *Arich Anpin* (The Holy Ancient One or Long-Suffering One), which is identified with the *Sefirah Keter*, *Abba* (the Supernal Father) corresponding to *Chochmah*; *Imma* (the Supernal Mother) corresponding to *Binah*; *Ze'ir Anipin* (The Short-Faced One) or *Ben* (the Son) corresponding to the *Sefirot* from *Chesed* to *Yesod*; and *Bat* (the Daughter) or *Nukvah* (the Female) (corresponding to *Malchut*).[71] Vital informs us that in the feminine *Partzufim*, the *Sefirah Yesod*, which is the phallus in the male, is the womb and female genitalia.

Sometimes *Atika Kadisha* is spoken of as a separate *Partzuf* above *Arich Anpin*, bringing the total number of *Partzufim* to six.[72] There are also six secondary *Partzufim*: Jacob and Israel, which are aspects of *Ze'ir Anpin*; Rachel and Leah, which are aspects of *Nukvah*; and *Israel Sava* and *Tevunah*, which personify the *Malchut* of *Abba* and *Imma*.[73]

As we have seen, according to Luria, the *Sefirot* were radically transformed as a result of the Breaking of the Vessels.[74] Prior to this event the *Sefirot* in the World of Points were completely independent and self-contained vessels (*Kelim*), which were to be filled by the "light" of the Infinite God. As a result of their disunity the final seven *Sefirot* in the World of Points were unable to contain the light of the Infinite God and "shattered." These *Sefirot* disintegrated into a multitude of shards, which fell throughout the lower worlds, some of them trapping "sparks" (*netzotzim*) of divine light as they fell. This broken world was now in need of reorganization into a restored cosmos, the World of *Tikkun*. Only with the broken shards' reorganization as *Partzufim* could the *Sefirot* interpenetrate and support one another,[75] and the process of *Tikkun ha-Olam* (the Restoration of the World) begin. However this process can only be completed through the spiritual and ethical conduct of mankind. In the meantime, the shards that remain from

---

71. *Sefer Etz Chayyim* 1: 1, p. 28; Menzi and Padeh, *The Tree of Life*, p. 56.
72. *Sefer Etz Chayyim* 1: 1, p. 26; ibid., p. 44.
73. Menzi and Padeh, *The Tree of Life*, p. 44, note.
74. The *Shevirah* is discussed in Chapter 7. We should here note that although the *Partzufim* only arise "after" the Breaking of the Vessels, the Lurianists often speak of them in contexts that appear to be temporally "earlier." We should recall, however, that the events described in the Lurianic theosophy are only *metaphorically* ordered in time and that each of the stages described actually exist in all things at all times.
75. *Sefer Etz Chayyim*, 11: 7. See Schochet, "Mystical Concepts," Ch. 8, pp. 880–883, and Scholem, *On the Kabbalah and Its Symbolism*, pp. 114ff.

the Breaking of the Vessels are the source of both crude matter and evil in the world.[76]

The *Partzufim* engage in regular sexual and procreative relations that have implications for the restoration and repair of the worlds. For example, *Abba* and *Imma*, the Celestial Mother and Father are mates, who alternately engage in "face-to-face" interaction or turn their backs upon one another. The state of their relatedness, which is at least in part dependent upon the worship and ethical deeds of humankind, has a major impact on the flow of divine energy throughout all the worlds. *Abba* and *Imma* are also said to produce *Ze'ir Anpin*, who is said to develop in the womb of the Celestial Mother.[77] As we will see in Chapter Nine, this procreation also contributes to *Tikkun ha-Olam*. The reorganization of the *Sefirot* into *Partzufim* places them into a dialectical and procreative frame in which the creation and renewal of the world is a function of the union of God's masculine and feminine aspects.

THE *SEFIROT* AS STRUCTURAL ELEMENTS OF THE WORLD

The Kabbalists, most notably Moses Cordovero, held that the *Sefirot* were not only divine traits or emanations, but were also the very structural elements of the created world. According to Cordovero, the nature of any created thing depends upon the manner in which the various *Sefirot* have been combined in its formation.[78] A sefirotic elementalism is also present in the Lurianic Kabbalah. Vital suggests that the entire world, in all of its manifestations and changes, is a function of the various permutations and

---

76. Their existence, for example, assures that the fifth of the five worlds, *Assiyah*, which was originally meant to be spiritual, is a material world. As we will see in Chapters Seven through Nine, these shards introduce evil and negativity into the world because they contain within themselves sparks (*netzotzim*) of divine light, which have been *exiled* from their source in God and remain trapped in what are referred to metaphorically as the "Husks" (*Kelippot*). The process of *Tikkun ha-Olam* will restore these sparks to their proper source and bring about the perfection and complete respiritualization of the world.

77. These matters are discussed below in the section entitled "Sexuality and the Family Romance," and are also considered again in Chapters Seven and Nine.

78. Scholem, *Kabbalah*, p. 115.

positions of the *Partzufim* (which are themselves comprised of *Sefirot*). These combinations are akin to the permutations that obtain through the successive combination of the various letters in the alphabet. In the following passage Vital likens the *Partzufim* both to the letters and in a rather dramatic image, to the constellations in the night sky:

> The eye cannot encompass them all because they look like the constella-
> tions of the zodiac—the "scroll of the skies"—with part of the limb of one
> *partzuf* connecting to a limb of the *partzuf* that is next to it. Sometimes an
> eye will meet a nose or an ear will meet a heel. It goes on like this endlessly,
> somewhat like the practice of combining the twenty-two letters of the
> alphabet: *'alef* with all the rest of them and all the rest with *'alef*, and so on
> with each of the letters. They are the cause of all change, so that no one day
> is like the next, no righteous person is like his neighbor, and no creature
> resembles any other.[79]

At various points in the Lurianic writings the *Sefirot*, the *Partzufim*, and *Otiyot Yesod* (Foundational Letters) are all held to be the structural elements of the universe. I will have occasion to provide a philosophical interpretation of the sefirotic elementalism when I consider the *Sefirot* as representing the dimensions of the experience of a finite world (see below). The *Otiyot Yesod* will be discussed in Chapter Five.

THE DYNAMICS OF THE *SEFIROT*:
THE KABBALAH AND ASTROLOGY

The *Sefirot*, according to Vital, are in a constant state of flux, changing as a result of various natural occurrences,[80] and historical events (e.g., the creation and sin of Adam, the exodus from Egypt, the destruction of the temple, etc.). In addition, the *Sefirot* are said to correspond to different days of the year (e.g., *Malchut* with the Sabbath, *Binah* with the festivals) and are in this way influenced by the calendar. The Kabbalists (Vital in particular) regarded the procession of the stars to be one influence on the status of the *Sefirot*, and, hence, an influence on the events of our own lowly world.

---

79. *Sefer Etz Chayyim* 1: 2, p. 31; Menzi and Padeh, *The Tree of Life*, pp. 101–102.

80. E.g., the "diminishment" of the moon; see Talmud, Tractate *Hullin* 60b.

However, they held that the astrologers were mistaken in regarding the stars as the only significant influence upon the cosmic order. Indeed, for Vital the number of the cosmic influences are so great as to transcend man's understanding. We learn in *Sefer Etz Chayyim*:

> At every hour of the day the worlds change, and each hour is not the same as the next. If you consider the movements of the constellations and the shifts in their position, how in one moment they are different, and how someone born at a certain time will experience different things than someone born slightly beforehand (you will see) the upper worlds are unlimited in number. You have to come to some kind of intellectual middle ground because a human mind cannot understand it all.[81]

Apart from the clear reference to astrology, this passage is noteworthy for Vital's frank admission that the human mind is not capable of assimilating all the cosmic events that have an impact on the lower worlds. Vital goes on to say that the multiplicity of changes in the upper worlds have an impact upon the theoretical structure of the Kabbalah as well. After quoting *Tikkunei Zohar*[82] to the effect that "the clothes He (God) wears in the daytime are not the same as they are at night" Vital tells us: "With this you'll understand how the worlds change (with) the garments of *Ein-Sof*, and, according to these changes, the statements in *Sefer haZohar* change."[83] The Zohar is, according to Vital, written from different places at different times and (even if it is the hand of a single author) it is full of apparent inconsistencies and even contradictions. But under the principle of the "changing garment" all are "words of the living God" with "different passages corresponding to different divine moments."

One should therefore not be disappointed if we discover apparent inconsistencies in the Zohar, or *Sefer Etz Chayyim* for that matter, for such inconsistencies accurately reflect the dynamic, changing character of the worlds themselves. Vital actually makes the claim that the nature and structure of kabbalistic writing reflects the essential structure of its subject matter, which, as a result of the flux of the worlds, is ever changing, and, as a result of the Breaking of the Vessels, highly fragmented. One should, therefore, not expect a coherent logical system from the Kabbalists but rather

---

81. *Sefer Etz Chayyim*, p. 29a.
82. *Tikkunei* Zohar 22: 65.
83. *Sefer Etz Chayyim*, p. 29a.

one where partial incoherence and fragmentation is a suitable mirror for a fragmented world.

SEFIROT: THE BASIC SYMBOLS

For the Kabbalists, the *Sefirot* promised to provide insight into the totality of both divine and created reality. Given the magnitude and breadth of this claim, it is no wonder that the *Sefirot* were understood through a variety of symbolic schemes, each of which is thought to reflect an aspect of the infinite cosmos. For the Kabbalists, no one point of view could be said to adequately comprehend the "all," and as such, a whole array of metaphors developed to shed light on the *Sefirot* doctrine. I will discuss the most important of these in turn.

THE COSMIC TREE

As early as *Sefer ha-Bahir* we find the notion that God's powers are arranged in the form of a cosmic, primordial tree:

> It is I who planted this "tree" so that all the world might delight in it, and I vaulted the universe with it and named its name "Universe," for the universe hangs on it and the universe goes forth from it, and they look upon it and yearn for it, and from there the souls go forth.[84]

> And what is [this] "tree" of which you have spoken? He said to them. All the powers of God are stratified, and they are like a tree. Just as the tree brings forth its fruits with the aid of water, so does God multiply the powers of the "tree" with the aid of water. And what is God's water? It is "chochmah" [wisdom].[85]

Scholem points out that the tree in the *Bahir* is watered by *Chochmah* or wisdom, and actually begins with the *Sefirah Binah*. This reflects this early kabbalistic work's identification of *Ein-Sof* with Intellect as opposed to Will.

Beginning in the fourteenth century the *Sefirot* were depicted in

---

84. *Sefer ha-Bahir*, sec. 14c; *Book Bahir*, Neugroschel trans., p. 55.
85. *Sefer ha-Bahir*, sec. 85; ibid., p. 73.

diagrammatic form as a tree growing downward from its roots. The roots represent the "highest" *Sefirah*, *Keter*, and the tree spreads through a trunk, branches, and crown representing the remaining *Sefirot*. The notion that the *Sefirot* comprise the trunk and branches of a "cosmic tree" reflects the kabbalistic notion that the inner life of God is reflected in (a) the living natural order (the biblical "tree of life"), (b) the realm of knowledge (the "tree of knowledge"), and (c) the Torah (which is itself spoken of as *Etz Chayyim*, a tree of life).[86]

Carl Jung, whose archetypal psychology was influenced greatly by the metaphors of the Kabbalah, took a lively interest in the sefirotic tree. Jung held that the ancient mind projected the archetypes of the unconscious onto the heavens, and he took the fact that the Kabbalists depicted their tree with its roots in the air as a metaphor for the conjunction between the depths of the psyche and the spiritual worlds.

THE PRIMORDIAL MAN (*ADAM KADMON*)

The symbol of Primordial Man, the first being to emerge with the creation of the cosmos, is common to a number of religious and philosophical traditions. The Upanishads describe a primal man composed of the elements that were to become the world.[87] According to the Upanishads this "gigantic divine being" is both infinitely far and deposited near the innermost recesses of the human heart.[88] Indeed, in the Hindu tradition, the Primordial Man is identified both with the entire Universe and the soul or essence of all things.

Interestingly, a similar image is found in Plutarch, who relates that the entirety of the heavens is arranged in the form of a *macroanthropos*, a colossal human being who is conceived as a model for the human world.[89] For Plutarch, the sun is at the heart of this being and the moon, the sun's androgynous messenger, is located in between the heart and belly.

---

86. For a discussion of the Cosmic Tree see Scholem, *Kabbalah*, p. 106.

87. R. C. Zaehner, ed., *Hindu Scriptures* (Rutland, VT: Charles E. Tuttle, 1966), p. 208 (Mundaka Upanishad II, 4).

88. Heinrich Zimmer, *Philiosophies of India* (Princeton, NJ: Princeton University Press, 1971), pp. 366–367 (Mundaka Upanishad III, 1, 7; cf. Zaehner, *Hindu Scriptures*, p. 212).

89. Giovanni Filoramo, *A History of Gnosticism*, trans. Anthony Alcock (Cambridge: Basil Blackwell, 1990), p. 51.

The Primordial Man is also an important symbol in Gnosticism. The Gnostics inferred from the verse in Genesis, "Let us make man in our own image," that the first earthly man was created on the model of a cosmic Adam on high.[90] In the Nag Hammadi text, the *Apocryphon of John*, we learn that this anthropos is the first creation of "knowledge and Perfect Intellect" and the first luminary of the heavens.[91] This Anthropos becomes the heavenly model through which the demiurge forges an earthly Adam. Other Gnostic sources relate how the "archons" (conceived of as female demigods corresponding to each of the seven planets) formed an earthly Adam to fulfill their sexual desire for the heavenly anthropos who was beyond their spiritual reach. Among the Mandeans (a Gnostic sect that today survives in Iraq) the Primordial Adam is coextensive with the cosmos, his body is the body of the world, and his soul the soul of all souls.[92] In an image that would later reappear in the Kabbalah, the Gnostics held that individual human beings are descended from the cosmic anthropos as a result of the fragmentation of the Primordial Man.

The notion of a Primordial Man makes its first appearance in Jewish thought in the early literature of *Merkaveh* mysticism of the second and third centuries C.E.[93] As we have seen, the clearest example of this is found in a work entitled *Shi'ur Koma* (The Measure of [the Divine] Body), dating from no later than the sixth century, where the author seeks a vision of one "who sits upon the throne," a gigantic supernal man who is imprinted with magical letters and names.

It is said that he who knows this mystery, is assured of his portion in the world to come . . .

Rabbi Ishmael said: What is the measure of the Holy One, Blessed be He, who is hidden from all creatures? The sole of his foot fills the whole world, as it is said (Isaiah 66:1) "The heaven is my throne, and the earth my

---

90. Gershom Scholem, "Adam Kadmon," *Encyclopedia Judaica*, 2: 248.

91. Filoramo, *A History of Gnosticism*, p. 65.

92. Kurt Rudolph, *Gnosis: The Nature and History of Gnosticism*, trans. R. M. Wilson (San Francisco: Harper & Row, 1987) (first published in German 1977, revised and expanded 1980), p. 109.

93. On *Merkaveh* mysticism see Gershom Scholem, *Jewish Gnosticism, Merkabah Mysticism and Talmudic Tradition*.

foot-stool." The height of each sole is three ten thousand thousands of parasangs. The sole of His right foot is called: PRSYMYA, ATRQTT.[94]

Although its defenders held that its doctrines were not to be taken literally, many Jewish authorities, including Maimonides, believed that *Shi'ur Koma* was heretical and should be burned. Scholem held that these early "Jewish gnostics" were actually elaborating upon an old *tannaitic* teaching that did not imply that God himself has a body, but held that a bodily form could be attributed to God's "glory" or the divine presence (*Shekhinah*).[95]

The kabbalistic scheme in which the *Sefirot* are depicted as the bodily organs and appendages of a primal man was subject to numerous variations beginning with *Sefer ha-Bahir*, where it is written:

> . . . God has seven holy forms. And they all have their correspondence in man, as it is written (Gen. 1: 27): "God created man in his likeness" . . . And they are as follows: the right and the left leg, the right and the left hand, the trunk and the place of procreation, and the head. Those are six . . . and they are seven with his wife, of whom it is written (Gen. 2: 24) "And they form one flesh."[96]

According to the earlier Kabbalists, the *Sefirot* are embodied in the supernal, archetypal man, of which the earthly man is but a mere reflection. While the kabbalistic tree is envisioned with its top down, the sefirotic man stands perfectly erect.[97] *Tikkunei* Zohar, for example, places the *Sefirah Keter* at the man's "crown of royalty," *Chochmah* (Wisdom) in his brain, and *Binah* (Understanding) in his heart. *Chesed* (Kindness) is identified with the right arm and *Gevurah* (Strength) with the left, *Tiferet* (Beauty) with the man's torso, *Netzach* (Endurance) and *Hod* (Majesty) with the two legs, and *Yesod* (Foundation) with the phallus. *Malchut* (Kingship), which is sometimes understood as the feminine completion of Primordial Man, is here depicted

---

94. *Shi'ur Koma*, secs. 2 and 5. Translated as "Shiur Qoma" in Meltzer *The Secret Garden*, pp. 21–37.

95. Scholem, *Kabbalah*, p. 17.

96. *Sefer ha-Bahir*, sec. 116; cf. 55, 115. *Book Bahir*, Neugroschel trans., p. 86; cf. pp. 65–66, 85. As Scholem (*Origins of the Kabbalah*, p. 139) points out, while the concept of a Primordial Man is not explicitly stated in *Sefer ha-Bahir* it is present in nascent form.

97. Scholem, *Kabbalah*, p. 106.

as the organ of vocal expression, the mouth.[98] The Zohar is replete with other organic imagery equating the various *Sefirot* and *Partzufim* with different bodily organs and appendages. Sometimes the lower seven *Sefirot* are spoken of as a distinct personality (*Zeir Anpin*, the "Impatient One") and are equated with the entire image of man, and the upper three *Sefirot* are depicted as a single head or three heads.[99] In other parts of the Zohar (*Raya Mehemna, Tikkunei ha-Zohar*) each *Sefirah* is depicted as a complete man formed in the likeness of the *Sefirah* immediately above it.[100] In one passage three images of man, the first corresponding to the *Sefirot Keter* and *Tiferet*, the second to *Chochmah* and *Yesod*, and the third to *Malchut*, are described respectively as the men of "Creation," "Formation," and "Making."[101] These images are said to correspond to the tripartite division in man's soul among the *neshamah, ruach,* and *nefesh,* traditionally thought of as the intellectual, emotional, and animated spirits in man.[102]

In the Lurianic Kabbalah, the Primordial Man is known as *Adam Kadmon,* a term that was first used in the anonymous Provencal kabbalistic text the "Source of Wisdom,"[103] where it was understood as an embodiment of the supreme divine powers. In Luria *Adam Kadmon* becomes a pivotal notion linking God, Man, and the World. We read in Vital's *Sefer Etz Chayyim*: "Then there came forth from the Infinite the great light that we call '*Adam Kadmon*'—Primordial Human—the precursor of everything."[104] *Adam Kadmon,* as the first being to emerge from the infinite Godhead *Ein-Sof,* is essentially indistinguishable from the deity, yet at the same time his body is said to both emanate and constitute the *Sefirot.* Man, having been created in God's image, is said by the Kabbalists to be comprised of the very same *Sefirot,* which comprise the "body" of *Adam Kadmon.*

According to Luria, *Adam Kadmon* is an all-encompassing world comprised of the highest, most powerful lights and *Sefirot.* Vital tells us: "This Adam Kadmon extends from one end to the other, from the highest to

---

98. See Tishby and Lachower, *The Wisdom of the Zohar*, Vol. 1, p. 260. *Tikkunei Zohar*, 2nd Preface, 7 a, b.

99. Tishby and Lachower, *The Wisdom of the Zohar*, Vol. 1, p. 297.

100. Ibid.

101. These man-images are not to be confused with the Worlds bearing these names.

102. Tishby and Lachower, *The Wisdom of the Zohar*, Vol. 1, p. 297.

103. Scholem, *Origins of the Kabbalah*, p. 339.

104. *Sefer Etz Chayyim* 1: 1, p. 21; Menzi and Padeh, *The Tree of Life*, p. 6.

the lowest extremities of the whole empty space of the emanation . . . Included within this Adam are all of the worlds."[105] Vital further specifies that the essence of *Adam Kadmon* is the "five levels of the soul"; his body is the World of Emanation and his clothing, the three worlds of Creation, Formation, and Action.[106]

Vital is careful to indicate that description of a divine primordial human is purely metaphorical in nature:

> It should be clear that there is no body, or the faculties of a body, in the higher realm, God forbid! As for all the images and pictures that we use, it is not because it is actually so, God forbid, but only to appease the ear so that one can understand the higher spiritual things that cannot be grasped or comprehended at all by the understanding . . . [107]

> Certainly if the Torah itself speaks in this way, we too are able to use this language even though it is clear that there is nothing up above except pure light, utterly spiritual, which cannot be grasped at all.[108]

The various metaphors equating the cosmic *Sefirot* with the human image can be understood as giving expression to various ideas, including (a) that the cosmos itself has both a soul and body very much like that of man, (b) that the universe is garbed in the very sorts of interests, values, and activities that are attendant to man, (c) that the world is in effect the instrument and expression of the divine spirit and character, just as the body is the expression of man's personality and soul, and (d) that man, being created in the likeness of God, is himself comprised of the very elements that form the essential traits of the divinity.

---

105. Ibid., 1: 1, p. 24; Menzi and Padeh, *The Tree of Life*, p. 27.
106. Ibid., 1: 1, p. 33; ibid., p. 109.
107. Ibid., 1: 1, p. 28; ibid., p. 53–54.
108. Ibid., 1: 1, p. 28; ibid., p. 54. Other Kabbalists held that even the use of the term "light" should be used with caution. For example the eighteenth-century Moroccan Kabbalist Shalom Buzalgo held: "this is all total spirituality and has nothing to do with physical light . . . The reason we are permitted to use the word "light" in speaking of the divine and the spiritual is because it is the most subtle of all of the senses, the most precious." Buzalgo, *Mikdash Melech*, trans. Zalman Schachter, in Meltzer, *The Secret Garden*, p. 166.

THE GATES OF THE EYES, EARS, NOSE, AND MOUTH

The Primordial Man lies at the foundation of several other symbolic schemes that the Kabbalists used in conceptualizing the world and the human soul. Vital informs us that the Primordial Man is the first being to emerge after the *Tzimtzum*, and that it is he who emanated the lights that were to become the *Sefirot* through four of his bodily organs, the eyes, the ears, the nose, and the mouth:

> [It] is because the light of the Infinite is so very great that it can only be received if it is transmitted through the filter of *Adam Kadmon*. And even this light from *Adam Kadmon* could not have been received until after it had emerged from his openings and apertures, which are the ears, the nose, the mouth, and the eyes.[109]

The lights emanated by *Adam Kadmon* correspond to the senses of vision, hearing, smell, and speech (*Reiah, Shmecha, Re'cha,* and *Dibor*). The orifices of the Primordial Man (and the skull that encompasses them) each correspond to one of the four letters of the divine name (YHVH) and also to various levels of "soul," four divine personas (the *Partzufim*), specific *Sefirot*, and Worlds. These orifices also correspond to a variety of divine names constructed on the basis of the numerical values (*Gematria*) of the letters that comprise different ways to spell out the pronunciation of God's name.[110] In somewhat simplified form these equivalencies are detailed in Table 4–5:

---

109. *Sefer Etz Chayyim* 1: 1, pp. 25–26; Menzi and Padeh, *The Tree of Life*, p. 40.

110. This is achieved as follows. The pronunciation of the four letters in God's name, YHVH, can be "spelled" out in one of four ways using Hebrew letters. The first of these, known as the *millui de yudin*, the filling out of the "Name" with the Hebrew letter *yud* (Y), is spelled out in Hebrew as follows: YVD, HY, VYV HY, where the *Gematria* or numerical equivalent of all these letters adds up to 72. The second name is spelled out using a combination of *yuds* (Ys) and *alephs* (As) YVD HY VAV HY, and adds up numerically to 63. A third spelling, using only *alephs* (As) YVD, HA, VAV, HA adds up to 45, and a fourth, using *hehs* (Hs), YVD HH VV HH, adds up to 52. These "names" are known by the letters that most economically express their numerical values. Hence, name 72 is known as *Ayin Bet* or *'aB*, because the Hebrew letter *ayin* has a numerical value of 70, and the letter *bet* a value of 2. Similarly, the 72 name is called *SaG*, the 63 name is called *MaH*, and the 52 name is called BeN. As with the *Sefirot* these four names are thought of as being compounded of one another so that it is possible to speak of SAG of *'Ab* the MaH of BeN, etc. See Louis Jacobs,

The scheme outlined in Table 4–5 provides a substantial (but by no means complete) overview of the metaphors used by the Lurianists in their description of the Primordial Man and the emanations proceeding from him. While the Lurianic system has sometimes been called fragmented and needlessly repetitious, even a cursory review of the table reveals that the Lurianists, in their conception of Primordial Man, have attempted to integrate an array of perspectives that are often fragmented in more philosophical and naturalistic views of the world. These perspectives are outlined in Table 4–6.

On this basis we can see how the Kabbalists developed a theosophical system in which the corporeal, phenomenological, psychical, personal, metaphysical, linguistic, and theological aspects of the cosmos are understood as different perspectives upon or metaphors for a single underlying reality. This reality is expressed in the image of Primordial Man and mirrored in the human soul. Each of these perspectives or metaphors opens up its own series of dimensions or points of view, thereby creating a vast "three-dimensional" structure of "perspectives" (rather than entities) constituting a kabbalistic ontology.

The Kabbalists of Safed became open to a seemingly infinite series of perspectives on reality, a reality that they understood to be in continual flux. The result is a system of thought that is remarkably open, multidimensional, and, more importantly, both spiritually and intellectually "alive."

The various components of the Primordial Man can also be understood as a *phenomenology of the self*. Jung, who encountered the symbol of *Adam Kadmon* in alchemy as well as in the Christian Kabbalah, was explicit in his identification of *Adam Kadmon* with the self archetype, which he held was essentially indistinguishable from God. Each of the symbols of *Adam Kadmon* can be understood as providing a definition of the self, and the foundation for a distinct psychological point of view. For example, the metaphor of bodily orifices and organs defines the self in terms of its physical being and sensual relations; the *Sefirot* metaphor defines the self through its

---

"The Uplifting of the Sparks," in Green, *Jewish Spirituality*, p. 105. Also in the same volume, Lawrence Fine, "The Contemplative Practice of Yihudim in Lurianic Kabbalah," p. 85.

As can be seen in Table 4–5, each of these names of God corresponds to particular *Sefirot*, worlds, and soul levels. These "names" play an important role in the restoration of the cosmos after the Breaking of the Vessels. The Lurianic doctrine of divine names will be discussed in greater detail in Chapter Five.

Table 4-5

Orifice of Adam Kadmon	Sefirah	Level of Soul	Partzuf	World	Letter of YHVH	Names of God
			Attik Yomin	Adam Kadmon	Tittle of Y	*Arikh Anpin*
Skull	Keter	Yechidah				
Eye (Vision)	Chochmah	Neshamah of Neshamah	Abba (Chaya)	Atziluth	Yud	'aB 72
Ear (Hearing)	Binah	Neshamah	Imma (Tevunah)	Beriah	Heh(1)	SaG 63
Nose (Smell)	Tifereth -Yesod	Ruach	Zeir Anpin	Yetzirah	Vav	Mah 45
Mouth (Speech)	Malchut	Nefesh	Nukvah	Assiyah	Heh(2)	BoN 52

Table 4-6

Lurianic Metaphor	Epistemological Perspective
orifices	sensual, corporeal
Sefirot	phenomenological/axiological
level of soul	psychical
Partzufim	personal/developmental
worlds	metaphysical
letters of tetragrammaton	linguistic
Names of God	theological

values; in the metaphor of the *Partzufim* the self is defined through its "personas" or developing character; the metaphor of "worlds" defines the self through the environments that it inhabits; and the "names of God" define it through narrative and language.

THE INDIVIDUATION OF GOD

Carl Jung interpreted the symbolism of the Kabbalah, and related symbolical systems such as Gnosticism and Alchemy, as a projected awareness of the development and individuation of the (human) self. On Jung's interpretation the Kabbalists, for example, projected their own psyches onto God and the heavens, and their concept of the development of God is a thinly veiled theory of the development of the human self. For Jung, this "self" develops out of a primal, undifferentiated unconscious (represented by *Ein-Sof*) into a series of highly differentiated axiological and psychological structures (the *Sefirot*).

The Kabbalists were themselves fascinated with the development of God's "I." Scholem has pointed out that nearly all of the Kabbalists of the thirteenth century adopted a theory wherein the *Sefirot* progressively reveal the identity of God,[111] as it is esoterically described in the first words of the

---

111. Scholem, *Kabbalah*, p. 110.

book of Genesis: *Bereshit bara Elohim* (In the beginning God created . . .). According to the Kabbalists these words mystically refer to God's creation of Himself and His transformation from the nothingness (*Ayin*) of the first *Sefirah, Keter,* to the individuated selfhood (Ani, or "I") of the final *Sefirah, Malchut.* The explanation of this is detailed as follows:

It is a property of the Hebrew language that the subject of a verb (I, You, He) is most often hidden (and as such is simply "understood") in the conjugation of the verb itself. In the opening passage of Genesis the verb form *bara* (he created) contains the subject "he" (here equivalent to "God") in a "hidden," nonexplicit manner. The Kabbalists equated this hidden "he" in the verb *bara* with the first *Sefirah, Keter,* which as the hidden Primal Will does not yet explicitly involve a differentiated divine "he" or self. The Kabbalists typically equate the second *Sefirah, Chochmah* with *reshit,* the "beginning" or primal point of creation; and the third *Sefirah, Binah,* is equated with *Elohim,* one of the names of God. In the kabbalistic reading of the first words of Genesis, *Bereshit bara Elohim* becomes a complete sentence with *Elohim* as its object. *Bereshit* ("through reshit"—the second *Sefirah*) *bara* (he—the first *Sefirah*—created) *Elohim* (God, the third *Sefirah*).

With the creation of this third *Sefirah,* God has begun to become an individuated being (*Elohim*), but He is still not the "Thou" whom man addresses in prayer. This, according to the Kabbalists, does not occur until the advent of the sixth *Sefirah, Tiferet,* which, in harmonizing God's kindness and judgment, is equated with the most exalted name of God, the tetragrammaton, YHVH. Still, even this "thou" is not the full achievement of God's selfhood. This does not occur until the emanation of the final *Sefirah, Malchut,* which the Kabbalists equated with the divine "I," according to the formula "Nothingness changes into I." The highest *Sefirah, Keter,* is equated by the Kabbalists with *Ayin,* "nothing" (in Hebrew spelled AYN). They affirm that through the emanation of the *Sefirot,* the hidden "he" of *bara* (the *Sefirah Keter*) is transformed into the manifest "I" of *Malchut.* All of this occurs via a transformation of the letters within AYN (nothing), which when rearranged as ANY, form the personal pronoun, I. The creation of the world is the manifestation of God's selfhood, the emergence of an "I" or self out of a primal nothingness or will. This individuation process is mediated through "relatedness," symbolized by the "thou" of Tiferet/YHVH. As we have seen in Chapter Two, *Ein-Sof* becomes a personal God through his relationship with humankind.

BIBLICAL PERSONALITIES

Each of the *Sefirot* is connected with biblical personalities who are said to embody the characteristics or traits symbolized in their corresponding *Sefirah*. For example, Abraham, who was known for his deeds of loving-kindness, is linked to *Chesed* (Kindness) and David, who is the paradigm of Jewish royalty, is paired with *Malchut* (Kingship).[112] A scriptural exegesis is provided for each equivalence, and while the effect of this scheme was at times the mythical apotheosis of the biblical figures into quasi-deities,[113] its intent was rather to engender the idea that a spark of divinity inhabits the souls and *deeds* of all saintly individuals, and that the key to understanding the structure of the world is to be found in comprehending the acts and traits of the righteous.

Cordovero provides the following equivalencies between biblical figures and the *Sefirot*:[114]

Chochmah	Adam
Binah	Noah
Da'at	Shem
Chesed	Abraham
Gevurah (*Pachad*)	Isaac
Tiferet	Jacob
Netzach	Moses
Hod	Aaron
Yesod	Pinchas
Malchut	David

THE LETTERS OF DIVINE SPEECH

The idea of an equivalence between the *Sefirot* and the letters of divine speech originated, as we have seen, in *Sefer Yetzirah*. In that work, the world is

---

112. Moses Cordovero, *Or Ne'erav* VI: 6, 44a; Robinson, *Moses Cordovero's Introduction to Kabbalah*, p. 146.

113. Tishby and Lachower, *The Wisdom of the Zohar*, Vol. 1, p. 288.

114. Moses Cordovero, *Or Ne'erav* VI: 6, 44b; Robinson, *Moses Cordovero's Introduction to Kabbalah*, pp. 146–147.

alternately seen as being created through the ten *Sefirot* and the twenty-two divine letters, which together comprise the thirty-two paths of wisdom. Further, *Sefer Yetzirah* implies that the *Sefirot* themselves are to be understood in linguistic terms, likening them to books (*Sepharim*), text (*Sepher*), number (*Sephar*), and communication (*Sippur*).[115]

Later Kabbalists held that one could achieve insight into God's creative process by comparing it to the expansion of thought into speech. *Keter*, the highest *Sefirah*, represents the will or desire, and *Chochmah*, the concealed representation or thought of that desire. *Binah* is the internal, inaudible voice, the breath expelled from the throat. It is only at *Tiferet* that audible speech breaks through:[116] "If you examine the levels (*Sefirot*) [you will see] that it is Thought, Understanding, Voice, and Speech, and all is one, and Thought is the beginning of all . . . actual thought connected with *Ayin* (*Keter*, will)."[117] The Jewish mystics from *Sefer Yetzirah* to Schneur Zalman of Lyadi have theorized that language is the very vehicle of creation. The Zohar regards the words and letters of the Torah as the "blueprint" for creation, and Schneur Zalman held that the *kelim*, which serve as vessels for the *Sefirot*, are each letters of the holy tongue into which *Ein-Sof* has been contracted and concealed.[118]

In his *Sefer Etz Chayyim*, Vital explains that there are two basic metaphors that can be used to describe celestial events, the form of the human body and the shape of written letters. He states: "There is yet another way to describe by analogy, which is to depict these higher things through the shape of written letters, for every single letter points to a specific supernal light."[119] According to Vital, everything that can be described in terms of *Adam Kadmon* and the *Sefirot* can also be described in terms of the shapes of the Hebrew letters that comprise the divine name, YHVH. Vital states: "All ten *Sefirot*, including each and every single world, when considered as a whole, are like an aspect of a single Divine Name, YHVH."[120] Vital explains

115. *Sefer Yetzirah* 1: 1; Kaplan, *Sefer Yetzirah*, p. 5.

116. Tishby and Lachower, *The Wisdom of the Zohar*, Vol. 1, p. 292.

117. Zohar I, 246b. Tishby and Lachower, *The Wisdom of the Zohar*, Vol. 1, p. 326. Compare Sperling and Simon, *The Zohar*, Vol. 2, p. 382.

118. As discussed in Chapter Three.

119. *Sefer Etz Chayyim* 1: 1, p. 28. Also see, Menzi and Padeh, *The Tree of Life*, p. 54.

120. *Sefer Etz Chayyim* 1: 1, p. 28; Menzi and Padeh, *The Tree of Life*, p. 59.

an old kabbalistic tradition[121] that *Sefirah Keter* is the tip of the letter *yud* in YHVH, *Chochmah* is the letter *yud* itself, the first letter *heh* is *Binah*, *vav* is *Tiferet* and the six *Sefirot* of *Ze'ir Anpin*, from *Tiferet* to *Yesod*, and the final *heh* is *Malchut*.[122] Further, each *Partzuf* is understood as being comprised of the divine name, with the tip of the *yud* corresponding to the cranium, the letter *yud* and the first *heh* corresponding to the right and left parts of the brain, the *vav* making up the main part of the body, and the final *heh* making up the feminine counterpart to that *Partzuf*.[123]

The significance of the *Otiyot Yesod*, the "foundational letters," will be discussed in detail in Chapter Five. There we will see that the Kabbalists developed a comprehensive linguistic mysticism that fully paralleled their sefirotic metaphysics.

THE NAMES OF GOD

The bible contains numerous terms and names that represent the one God of the Jewish faith. An age-old midrashic tradition links each of these names with a trait or *middah* of God (e.g., *Elohim* with God's justice, *Yahweh* with his mercy).[124] Following this tradition, the Kabbalists linked each of the *Sefirot* with a particular name of God. The Zohar provides a wide variety of correspondences between the *Sefirot* and divine names, and this theme is provided an even more comprehensive treatment in Joseph Gikatilla's *Sha'are Orah* (Gates of Light).[125] For example, Gikatilla and later Kabbalists equate *Keter* with the divine name *Ehye*, *Chochmah* with *Yah*, *Binah* with YHVH, etc. In doing so they elaborate on the values that each of the *Sefirot* and divine names embody and illustrate. Cordovero explains, for example, that

---

121. These identifications are present, for example, in Joseph Gikatilla, *Sha'are Orah*; see Gikatilla, *Gates of Light*, p. 319.

122. *Sefer Etz Chayyim* 1: 1, p. 28; Menzi and Padeh, *The Tree of Life*, pp. 59–60.

123. *Sefer Etz Chayyim* 1: 1, p. 28; Menzi and Padeh, *The Tree of Life*, pp. 60–61.

124. The Kabbalists held that the Torah is both a blueprint for the cosmos (i.e., the *Sefirot*) and a single name of God. Indeed, it is not far to the proposition that the whole of language is a single, all-encompassing, divine appellation (i.e., we name God whenever we speak). See Chapter Five.

125. Joseph Gikatilla, *Sha'are Orah*, (Gates of Light).

the divine name of *Keter*, *Ehyeh* ("I will be") "indicates the sublimity of *Keter*, which is to be revealed in the future but which is not [yet] revealed at all."[126]

As we have seen, according to the Lurianists, the various orifices of *Adam Kadmon* are associated both with different *Partzufim* and with different letters of the divine name YHVH. In addition these orifices of *Adam Kadmon* correspond to four basic forms of the tetragrammaton, the four-letter name of God. These four basic forms of the divine name are referred to by the different numerical equivalents (72, 63, 45, 52) of the *millui*, or "spelling out" of the letters that comprise them. As Lawrence Fine has described, the various "organs" of *Adam Kadmon* are understood as divine lights, which combine to form divine names that represent different aspects of the divine structure.[127]

THE LEVELS OF THE SOUL

The Lurianists related the structure of the *Sefirot* to the "five lights" or levels that are said to exist within man's soul. These five levels of soul, derived from the verses of a talmudic benediction (*Baruchy Nafshy*), are the *nefesh*, or bodily soul; the *ruach*, which corresponds to the heart and emotions; the *neshamah*, corresponding to the brain; the *chaya* or "living soul," and the *yechida*, meaning "united," referring to the Godly soul that is united with man. Vital informs us, for example, that the *Sefirot*, as they are emanated according to the scheme of *Iggulim* (Circles), correspond to the lowest level of the soul or *nefesh*. The *Sefirot* that are emanated according to the scheme of *Yosher* (Line) correspond to the next higher level of the soul, the level of *ruach*.[128]

According to Vital, both the levels of *Iggulim/nefesh* and *Yosher/ruach* exist in each world, and simultaneously inform every detail or fact within the

---

126. Moses Cordovero, *Or Ne'erav* VI: 5, 44a; Robinson, *Moses Cordovero's Introduction to Kabbalah*, p. 143.

127. The derivation of these names will be discussed further in Chapter Five. Lawrence Fine, "The Contemplative Practice of *Yihudim* in Lurianic Kabbalah," in Green, *Jewish Spirituality*, pp. 64–98.

128. *Sefer Etz Chayyim* 1: 1, p. 24; Menzi and Padeh, *The Tree of Life*, pp. 29–30.

cosmos. This is an interesting proposition in view of the relationship that Vital posits between *Iggulim* (Circles) and Chaos and between *Yosher* (Line) and *Tikkun* (Repair and Restoration). The first of these relationships implies that each entity or "fact" within the world is in chaos; the second implies that they are each ordered and repaired. It would seem that everything within the world is simultaneously both chaotic or in need of restoration, and also already fully restored. Like a book that simultaneously contains within itself the history of an entire man or nation, each entity within the world contains within itself the entire history of the cosmos, beginning with the original chaos and ending with *Tikkun ha-Olam*, the Restoration of the World.

THE METAPHOR OF LIGHT

The metaphor of light is as pervasive in the Kabbalah as it is in other mystical traditions. For example, Hai Gaon (early thirteenth century) is reported by later Kabbalists to have held that above all emanated things there are three lights, existing in "the root of all roots" as "its name and essence . . . beyond the grasp of thought." These three splendors or *tzachtzachot* are referred to as the roots of the ten *Sefirot*.[129] Cordovero adopted the view that above the *Sefirot*, in *Keter*, there are "ten brightnesses" that exist in *Keter* and are "designated primordial light, the burnished light, the clear light."[130]

One kabbalistic metaphor comprehends the *Sefirot* themselves as a series of lights and another likens them to ten colored translucent spheres, which modify the transmission of the *Or Ein-Sof*, God's infinite light. The Zohar regards *Ein-Sof* itself as the "light that does not exist in light"[131] and regards the highest *Sefirah*, *Keter*, as the innermost, "concealed" light. The seven lowest *Sefirot* are comprised of four lights, only the last of which, *Malchut*, is revealed:

> Come and see. There are four lights. Three of them are sealed and one is revealed: a light that shines; a light of splendor that shines like the splendor of the heavens in its purity; a light of purple that receives all the lights; a

---

129. Scholem, *Kabbalah*, p. 95.

130. Moses Cordovero, *Or Ne'erav* VI: 4, 40b; Robinson, *Moses Cordovero's Introduction to Kabbalah*, p. 134.

131. Tishby and Lachower, *The Wisdom of the Zohar*, Vol. 1, p. 290.

light that does not shine but gazes at these and receives them, and these lights appear in it as a crystal ball against the sun.[132]

As in other mystical and mythological traditions, light for the Kabbalists symbolizes revelation, the good, consciousness, will, life, and the spirit. Light is the knowledge, goodness, and being of creation, contrasted with the darkness of ignorance, evil, and the void. That *Ein-Sof* is referred to as "the light that does not exist in light," and the *Sefirot* spoken of as lights that are concealed, or, as in the Zohar, as the "light of blackness" (*bozina di kardinuta*) suggests that both *Ein-Sof* and the *Sefirot* participate in being and nonbeing, revelation and concealment, and that both knowledge and ignorance are basic "constituents" of all things.

COLORS

The Kabbalists frequently assigned specific colors to the various *Sefirot*. For example, *Chesed, Gevurah* and *Tiferet* are assigned white, red, and yellow respectively. According to Cordovero, *Chesed* is white because of its "virtue," and *Gevurah* red because of the "heat of fire" involved in severe judgment and the arousal of love. *Tiferet* is the color of an egg yolk because it is a medium or mixture of the other two.[133] It also possesses the color purple. *Chochmah* is the color blue, "which is the beginning of the development of color from blackness (of *Ein-Sof* and *Keter*)." *Binah* is green.[134] *Malchut*, which has no light of its own but channels the light of all the other *Sefirot*, "contains all the colors."[135]

As we have seen, Cordovero also compared the *Sefirot* to a series of colored glass filters that selectively transmit various aspects of the light of *Ein-Sof*. Another color metaphor, found in the Zohar, is based upon the variety of colors that dance together in the depths of a burning flame. The interplay of these colors, their appearance, disappearance, and reappearance,

---

132. Zohar II, 23a–23b. Tishby and Lachower, *The Wisdom of the Zohar*, Vol. 1, p. 323.

133. Moses Cordovero, *Or Ne'erav* VI: 3, 38b; Robinson, *Moses Cordovero's Introduction to Kabbalah*, p. 127. Cf. Tishby and Lachower, *The Wisdom of the Zohar*, Vol. 1, 292.

134. Moses Cordovero, *Or Ne'erav* VI: 4, 40b; Robinson, *Moses Cordovero's Introduction to Kabbalah*, p. 132.

135. Moses Cordovero, *Or Ne'erav* VI: 4, 41a; ibid., p. 133.

is said to characterize the condition of the final *Sefirah, Malchut,* which exists only by virtue of reflected light, and which transmits the lights of the upper *Sefirot* to the lower worlds. Just as the various colors alternate in their prominence within an open flame, *Malchut* alternates in its reflection of the powers of Judgment, Mercy, etc., to our realm.

Such alteration in the transmission of sefirotic "colors" is expressed in another metaphor, that of *Malchut* holding a "crystal ball against the sun."[136] Like the astrological imagery later utilized by Vital,[137] the dance of sefirotic colors expresses the dynamic nature of the cosmos, the essence of which is not delimited structure but iridescent variation. Attempting to comprehend the universe, like the attempt to understand the human soul, can never proceed from a single, definitive point of view, but can only advance through a panoply or "dance" of readings, which themselves change according to the object of contemplation and the ever-changing position of the subject.

The color black is of particular importance in the Zohar, representing both the primordial darkness of *Keter,*[138] the blackness of the *bozina di kardinuta* (the black light of creation), the obscuring blackness of judgment (*Din*), and the darkness of *Malchut,* the only *Sefirah* to have no light of its own.[139] Cordovero associates black with the "Emanator" himself.[140] Black is also an apt symbol of *Gevurah/Din* (for the darkness that obscures the light of mercy). The entire *Sitra Achra,* the "Other Side," is conceived of as a dark realm, which is nonetheless essential to the proper function of the cosmos. The Kabbalah is here premonitory of Jung in its view that the shadow realm of evil is integrally related to the essence of the light and good, a topic that will command our attention in Chapter Eight.

GARMENTS (*LEVUSHIM*)

The Kabbalists frequently referred to the *Sefirot* as *levushim* or "garments," holding that the *Sefirot,* as garments of *Ein-Sof,* are, like the shell of a snail,

---

136. Zohar II, 23a–23b. Tishby and Lachower, *The Wisdom of the Zohar,* Vol. 1, p. 323.

137. As discussed below.

138. Tishby and Lachower, *The Wisdom of the Zohar,* Vol. 1, p. 292.

139. Ibid., p. 291.

140. Moses Cordovero, *Or Ne'erav* VI: 4, 40b; Robinson, *Moses Cordovero's Introduction to Kabbalah,* p. 132.

woven out of the fabric of his own being and hence indistinguishable from him. The notion of "garments," however, also plays off the concepts of interchangeability and superfluity, as clothing can always be changed or discarded. In equating the *Sefirot* with garments the Kabbalists express the dialectical notion that the *Sefirot* are both "essential" and "accidental" properties of *Ein-Sof*.

SEXUALITY AND THE FAMILY ROMANCE

A fascinating series of symbols, related in certain respects to the symbolism of *Adam Kadmon*, express the idea that the *Sefirot* represent the process by which divine procreative energy flows and is received in the world of emanation.[141] On this view the creation of the world is the consummation of a divine sexual act.

We have already seen that in the context of Primordial Man (*Adam Kadmon*), the *Sefirah Yesod* is frequently spoken of as the male genitalia. The final *Sefirah*, *Malchut*, which is often understood as the mouth of *Adam Kadmon* himself, is more frequently, however, referred to as the image of the female (the *Shekhinah*). This image is understood as the perfection and completion of *Adam Kadmon*. Man, it is thought, can only be whole through a harmonious partnership between man and woman. Man without woman is defective, a mere "half body."[142] Sometimes the female, which completes "man," is understood as an actual woman; but at other times it is conceived of as a female "image," which arises within a man's soul and is viewed as his spiritual counterpart or completion. The Zohar speaks of such a counterpart accompanying a man, and making him "male and female," when, for example, he is on a journey away from his wife and home.[143] The Zohar clearly anticipates the psychoanalytic view that all individuals are essentially bisexual, and, particularly, the Jungian view that each person's psyche is a juxtaposition and blend of *anima* and *animus*. There is indeed an old Jewish tradition, which is traceable to the biblical story of Eve being born from "Adam's rib" (and which may have also found its way into rabbinic sources through Platonic influence), which holds that all souls, prior to their descent into the physical world, are both male and female.

---

141. Tishby and Lachower, *The Wisdom of the Zohar*, Vol, 1, p. 288.
142. Ibid., p. 298.
143. Zohar I, 49b–50a; Sperling and Simon, *The Zohar*, Vol. 1, p. 158.

The relations between man and woman are represented in each of the *Sefirot*. Each *Sefirah* is conceived bisexually, as male to the *Sefirah* below it and female to the *Sefirah* above it. The entire sefirotic scheme announces the idea that sexual and romantic union in man is a reflection of basic cosmological dynamics. For example, the *Sefirah Chochmah* (Wisdom) is frequently equated with the Celestial Father (*Abba*), while *Binah* is understood as the Celestial Mother (*Imma*), with the lower *Sefirot* being formed in *Binah*'s womb. The union of *Tiferet* with *Malchut* (*Shekhinah*) is said to give rise to the lower worlds. Here the understanding of the *Sefirot* in sexual terms subtly passes over into a symbolism of birth and human development, and ultimately into a symbolism of the family.

The two pairs of *Sefirot* we have just discussed, *Chochmah* and *Binah*, (the Celestial Father and Mother), and *Tiferet* and *Malchut* (Son and Daughter), play an important role in what can only be described as a *family romance*. The Zohar describes how the father, *Chochmah*, has a particular fondness for his daughter (the *Shekhinah/Malchut*), which stirs the jealousy of *Binah*, the Celestial Mother.

> The father's continual desire is solely for the daughter, because she is the only daughter among six sons, and he has shared out portions, gifts and presents to the six sons, but to her he has apportioned nothing, and she has no inheritance at all. But despite this he watches over her with more love and longing than over anyone else. In his love he calls her "daughter"; this is not enough for him and he calls her "sister"; this is not enough for him, and he calls her "mother" . . . Therefore, the supernal world [mother] says to her [to the daughter]: "Is it a small matter that you have taken away my husband? [Gen. 30:15] for all his love is centered on you."[144]

Conversely the "mother" is said to favor the son over her husband,[145] thus completing a sort of cosmic Oedipal triangle: a vision of the cosmos in which "the world" is conditioned by archetypal interest and desire, the very desire that contemporary psychoanalysts have found reflected in the psyche of man, and at the foundation of human society.

The Zohar distinguishes between two forms of *desire* in its account of

---

144. Zohar I, 156b (*Sitrei Torah*) as quoted in Tishby and Lachower, *The Wisdom of the Zohar*, Vol. 1, p. 299.

145. Zohar II, 145b; III, 100b; 258a. Cited in Tishby and Lachower, *The Wisdom of the Zohar*, Vol. 1, p. 299.

creation. The first, which is symbolized in the union of *Chochmah* and *Binah*, is "familial" and gives rise to the upper worlds (those that are akin to the Platonic Forms). These *Sefirot* are called "friends." The second form of desire, symbolized in the intermittent union of *Tiferet* and *Malchut*, is passionate and gives rise to the lower world: that of corporeal creation.[146] These lower *Sefirot* are called "lovers."[147] Both kinds of union are necessary on both the cosmic and human levels.

The Zohar involves itself in detailed speculations regarding sexual behavior in the sefirotic realms. For example, in *Tikkunei ha*-Zohar we learn that amongst the *Sefirot* incest is not forbidden: "In the world above there is no 'nakedness,' division, separation or disunion. Therefore in the world above there is union of brother and sister, son and daughter."[148] It is only as a result of man's imperfect state, caused by our world having fallen into the realm of the *Sitra Achra*, that such relations are forbidden to man. Indeed, the Kabbalah interpreted the story of Adam's fall as an indication that through eating from the tree of knowledge man was forbidden from enjoying sexual relations on the model of those on high.

The act of intercourse and the emotions associated with it are described in the Zohar as paradigmatic for all creation. For example, creation is said to commence with the movement of the Primal Man's left arm, leading to the embrace of sexual intercourse. This left arm represents the *Sefirah Gevurah/ Din* (Strength/Judgment), and is said by the Zohar to embody the evil inclination.[149]

The Zohar borrows images from the biblical Songs of Songs and describes the development of the *Sefirot* in metaphors of intercourse and love.[150] The Zohar even goes so far as to claim that the harmony of all the worlds is dependent upon the origin of the arousal in celestial love:

> If she first makes approaches to Him and draws him towards her in the strength of her love and desire, then she is replenished from the side of the right (kindness) and multitudes from the side of the right are found in all

146. Tishby and Lachower, *The Wisdom of the Zohar*, Vol. 1, pp. 299–300.

147. Zohar II, 7b; Tishby and Lachower, *The Wisdom of the Zohar*, Vol. 1, pp. 288, 299. For the full context of this passage see Sperling and Simon, *The Zohar*, Vol. 4, pp. 330–331.

148. Tishby and Lachower, *The Wisdom of the Zohar*, Vol. 3, p. 1369.

149. Tishby and Lachower, *The Wisdom of the Zohar*, Vol. 1, p. 300.

150. Zohar III, 61b–62a. Sperling and Simon, *The Zohar*, Vol. 5, p. 48.

worlds. But if the Holy One, blessed be He, is the first to make advances and she only rouses herself afterwards, then all is on the side of the female and many multitudes arise on the side of the left (severe judgment) in all worlds.[151]

The eroticization of the cosmos is a theme that also appears in the Lurianic Kabbalah. "The whole universe," Vital tells us, "functions according to the principium of the masculine and the feminine."[152] As I will explain in detail in Chapter Seven, Vital conceptualizes the *Sefirot* in terms of a series of conjugal relationships. The *Sefirot Chochmah* and *Binah*, for example, are understood as the celestial "Father" and "Mother" who are maintained in their "face-to-face" *coniunctio* by the "upward flow" of "feminine waters" emanating from the body of *Binah*. The vicissitudes of the *Sefirot*, including their shattering as a result of the "Breaking of the Vessels," as well as their restoration in *Tikkun*, are understood as so many ruptures and reunifications in the conjugal life of these and the other *Sefirot*, which are reconceptualized as *Partzufim*, personalities, or personal "faces" of *Ein-Sof*.

According to Cordovero, the erotic couplings of the *Sefirot* are "imagined as the union of male and female, [but actually signify] something the human mind cannot comprehend."[153] I have dwelt at length upon these sexual metaphors because I believe them to be a unique and vivid illustration of a dynamic metaphysics in which presumably subjective emotions and values (those aroused by human desire) are regarded as supremely objective and cosmically *real*. These metaphors show the Kabbalah, in certain of its aspects, to be tantamount to what might be called a "psychoanalysis of God." The Kabbalah suggests in its anthropomorphic and sexual symbolism that the very nature of the cosmos can only be understood through man's turning inward and comprehending his own inner nature.

QUESTIONS

Intriguingly, the Zohar equates certain of the *Sefirot* with "questions" that are presumed to provide an indication of the *Sefirah*'s nature and level. For

---

151. Zohar II, 45a–45b. Ibid., Vol. 1, p. 300.

152. Vital, *Sefer Etz Chayyim* 11: 6: cited and translated in Schochet, "Mystical Concepts," p. 824, note 6.

153. Moses Cordovero, *Or Ne'erav* VI: 2, 37b; Robinson, *Moses Cordovero's Introduction to Kabbalah*, p. 124.

example, *Binah*, which is the *Sefirah* connected with the "beginning" of creation, is referred to with the question "Who?" (*Mi?* in Hebrew). *Malchut*, which is at the end of the emanative process, and which can therefore prompt a contemplation of the cosmos as a whole, is called "What?" (*Mah?*). The Zohar informs us that this "What?" pertains to "these" (*eleh*) *Sefirot*, and when the letters comprising the Hebrew terms for "What are these?" (*Mah Eleh*) are rearranged we arrive at "Elohim," the revealed God of the bible.[154] In short, without their ever having been answered, a set of questions leads us to the creator God.

The whole notion of naming the presumed structures of the universe with questions reveals much about the Kabbalists' attitude toward the cosmos, which, in spite of their elaborate theosophy, remains essentially *unknown*, reflecting the very awe and wonder with which man confronts creation. In spite of their status as "unknowns," the *Sefirot* are such that they can be addressed and queried. Indeed, the very act of questioning may reveal more about the ultimate nature of things than any speculative attempt to answer the questions posed.

THE *SEFIROT* AS DIMENSIONAL PARADIGMS

We have noted a number of characteristics that pertain to the *Sefirot* in general and that are relevant to any attempt to understand them in their particular nature. After an admittedly selective review of the vast literature on the *Sefirot*, I will now consider each of them individually. As we have seen, the Kabbalists, on the principle that the microcosm perfectly mirrors the macrocosm, held that the *Sefirot* are not only the elements or dimensions of the universe, but also the constituent elements of the human mind.[155]

---

154. See Zohar I, 2a; Sperling and Simon, *The Zohar*, Vol. 1, p. 6, and discussion in Tishby and Lachower, *The Wisdom of the Zohar*, Vol. 1, p. 294–295.

155. The psychological interpretation of the *Sefirot* doctrine has a long and venerable history that has been briefly reviewed in Chapter One. For example, one of the earliest Kabbalists Azriel of Gerona (early thirteenth century) held that the energy of the human soul derives from the heavenly *Sefirot*, and he equated each *Sefirah* with a psychological power or physical organ in man (Scholem, *Origins of the Kabbalah*, p. 95). This view was prominent throughout the Kabbalah and later became a basic tenet of Hasidism.

The *Sefirot*, as the archetypes of all creation, are far more complex than any theory about them can hope to grasp. They constitute an infinitely rich firmament of values, and each *Sefirah* is irradiant with innumerable facets. Like Leibnizian monads, each of the *Sefirot* mirrors each of the others in their resplendent multiplicity. However, in order to make sense of the Kabbalists' claim that the *Sefirot* are the elements of creation or the "dimensions" of the world, we must simplify our interpretation, focusing upon key elements in each *Sefirah*; and, at least momentarily, excluding both other aspects, as well as the interpenetration of each of the *Sefirot* into each of the others. In comprehending a simplified scheme, we can perhaps catch a glimpse into the the *Sefirot* as elements in their richness and multiplicity.

We should not expect the *Sefirot* to have a precise one-to-one correspondence with the phenomenological elements of either our finite universe or the human psyche. After all, the *Sefirot* themselves are conceived within the Kabbalah as stages in the creative process, and hence reflect aspects of God's inner life or creativity rather than fixed entities in an already created world. My main purpose in this section is to interpret the *Sefirot* so as to show how each provides an underlying qualitative basis for the phenomena of human experience, and hence for the structural elements of both humanity and the world.

ETHICAL AND PSYCHOLOGICAL ASPECTS OF THE *SEFIROT* SYMBOLISM

However, I also have a second, more practical goal, and that is to uncover the psychological or psychotherapeutic principle or lesson inherent in each of the *Sefirot*. The psychological significance of the *Sefirot* doctrine is actually written into the calendar of Jewish ritual observance. The forty-nine days between Passover and Shavuot are known in Jewish tradition as the *sefirat ha-Omer*, the "counting of the Omer." While this "counting" literally refers to an offering of grain that was brought to the temple in Jerusalem on Shavuot, tradition holds that during this seven-week period, men, women, and children must prepare themselves emotionally and spiritually for the reception of the Torah at Mount Sinai, which took place on the fiftieth day after the exodus from Egypt. Playing upon the word *Sefirah* (one meaning of which is "counting"), the Jewish mystics have handed down the tradition that on each of these days a person must concentrate upon developing within him or herself an aspect of each of the seven emotional *Sefirot*. In dwelling upon the cosmic characteristics represented in each *Sefirah* (e.g., love, strength, compassion, etc.), the individual is said to channel divine energies through his own psyche and in the process perfect his/her character in anticipation of a renewed commitment to the Torah.

The ethical aspects of the *Sefirot* are elaborated in Moses Cordovero's *Tomer Debhorah* (The Palm Tree of Deborah)[156] in which detailed instructions are provided on how the individual can attain the qualities inherent in each of the *Sefirot*. According to Cordovero, it is incumbent upon man to imitate his creator both in form and deed, "so that the crown of the *Shekhinah* never departs from his head."[157] My own interpretations of the psychological aspects of the *Sefirot* differ from, and on my view complement those of Cordovero, and reflect my work as a psychologist and psychotherapist. I should point out that these interpretations are in no way meant to be exclusive. As Vital tells us: "in every single hour the worlds are changing, so that no hour is like any other . . . And just as every hour and every minute is different, so too the various aspects (i.e., interpretations) of the passages in the Zohar differ from one another."[158]

KETER ELYON (THE SUPREME CROWN)

The highest of the *Sefirot*, *Keter Elyon*, qualitatively distinct from all of the others and barely separable from *Ein-Sof*, the Infinite God, is so sublime and concealed that, according to the Kabbalists, nothing at all can be predicated of it.[159] Just as a "crown" is separable and distinct from one who wears it, *Keter* is separate and distinct from the *Sefirot*, which comprise the body of the

---

156. Moses Cordovero, *Tomer Debhorah* (The Palm Tree of Deborah), trans., Louis Jacobs (New York: Hermon Press, 1974).

157. Ibid., p. 126.

158. *Sefer Etz Chayyim* 1: 1, p. 29; Menzi and Padeh, *The Tree of Life*, pp. 63–64.

159. Zohar II, 42b; Sperling and Simon, *The Zohar*, Vol. 2, p. 131. In relation to *Keter*, the Zohar applies the formula: "Search not the things that are too hard for thee, and seek not the thing which is hidden from thee" (Ben Sira 320–324, cf. Talmud, *Chagigah* 13a). See discussion in Schochet, "Mystical Concepts," pp. 836–837.

Primordial Man,[160] who is the living archetype for the creation of the world. Unlike the other *Sefirot*, which are each assigned a holy letter, no linguistic sign can represent *Keter*; instead, it is equated simply with the thorn or point of the letter *yud* in God's name. The proximity and even identity of *Keter* with *Ein-Sof* is underscored by its sometimes being referred to as the Holy Ancient One, a term that is otherwise reserved for *Ein-Sof*.[161] As such, *Keter* is said to reflect the divine essence and to anticipate the "image of God" in created human form.

At times *Keter* is referred to as the *will of all wills*.[162] It is frequently called *Ratzon* (Will) by the Kabbalists themselves.[163] In the Zohar, *Keter* is called *Ehyeh* ("I will be"), which recalls the biblical expression of God's "absolute will" in His declaration to Moses, "*Ehyeh asher ehyeh*," "I will be who (or *that* which) I will be."[164] The appellation *Ehyeh* indicates *Keter*'s limitless potential and its willful movement toward the future.

The Lurianists occasionally spoke of two aspects of *Keter*: its face (*pnimi*) or inner aspect, referred to as *Tinug* (delight), and an outer (*chitzonit*) aspect referred to as *Ratzon* (desire or will). Such "delight" is present, according to Luria's disciple, Israel Sarug, in the first stirrings of *Ein-Sof*, even prior to the *Tzimtzum*. That delight is even above the Primal Will accords well with the psychoanalytic view, which explains volition and action via the "pleasure principle." In identifying *Keter*, the uppermost *Sefirah* and first manifestation of *Ein-Sof*, with delight and desire, the Lurianists place themselves in a tradition that elevates emotion above intellect and desire above wisdom. As Immanuel Schochet explains, while the Kabbalists understood the cosmos in terms of the progression of Reason (*Chochmah, Sachel*) toward a certain goal, this higher aim is "a deep-seated, innermost desire or will."[165] As Schneur Zalman, the first Lubavitcher rebbe,

---

160. *Sefer Etz Chayyim* 25: 5, 42: 1, and *Tikkunei* Zohar, 2d Preface, 17a–b, cited in Schochet, "Mystical Concepts," p. 837.

161. Schochet, "Mystical Concepts," p. 852, note 34.

162. Zohar III, 129a, 288b. See discussion in Tishby and Lachower, *The Wisdom of the Zohar*, Vol. 1, p. 270 and p. 302, note 4. See also Schochet, "Mystical Concepts," p. 837.

163. Tishby and Lachower, *The Wisdom of the Zohar*, p. 270.

164. Exodus 3:14. Tishby and Lachower, *The Wisdom of the Zohar*, Vol. 1, p. 270. Zohar III, 65a–b; Tishby and Lachower, *The Wisdom of The Zohar*, Vol. 1, p. 345.

165. Schochet, "Mystical Concepts," p. 853, note 41.

writes: "The Torah derives from *Chochmah* (Wisdom, Reason), but its source and root surpasses exceedingly the rank of *Chochmah* and is called the Supreme Will."[166] *Keter* is spoken of in the Zohar as *Ayin*, nothingness, a "darkness" that is at the same time the source of all light.[167] Such nothingness is both the epistemological and ontological gulf between *Ein-Sof* and creation. According to Cordovero, "*Keter* is called *Ayin* (Nothingness) on account of its great transparency and closeness to its source."[168]

In the view of Moses De Leon, *Keter* is beyond the limit of perception; according the Kabbalists of Gerona, it is "the cessation of thought."[169] Like a metaphysical "black hole" from which no light can escape, it is a darkness or annihilation that both extinguishes the lights of the *Sefirot* as they strive to return to their origin in *Ein-Sof* and conceals the light of *Ein-Sof* as it spreads downward into creation. According to Abraham Ben David this "annihilative" property of *Keter* figures in all change in the life and substance of things.[170] A "negation" figures in all transitions. It is "the cessation from which comes the emanation of all beings."[171] *Keter*'s very negativity is what brings all of the succeeding *Sefirot* into being. This negativity is, in fact, the essential manifestation of the primal will.

The relationship between negation and will is known from both logic and psychology. Logically, "will," in its most fundamental sense, is a setting of limits, an imposition of a negation. It was Otto Rank who first observed that the primary assertion of "will" on the part of a child is always in the form of a negation, a saying "no" to the breast. According to Rank, it is only through a nurturance of this "negative will" that the child's positive volition can arise.[172] The affirmation of the status quo requires only passive acquiescence; negation, however, brings will into the world, and will reveals negation. In the primal act of will, "Let there be light . . .", God paradoxically but necessarily opens up the gaping abyss of nothingness. We can now

---

166. Zalman, *Igeret HaKodesh*, sec. I, as cited in Schochet, "Mystical Concepts," ibid.

167. Tishby and Lachower, *The Wisdom of the Zohar*, Vol. 1, p. 280.

168. Cordovero, *Or Ne'erav* VI: 1, 34b; Robinson, *Moses Cordovero's Introduction to Kabbalah*, p. 114.

169. Tishby and Lachower, *The Wisdom of the Zohar*, Vol. 1, p. 280.

170. Ibid.

171. Ibid., p. 281.

172. Such negative will is also observable in other behavior.

understand why the light that emerges from *Keter* is known as the *bozina di kardinuta*, a "spark of blackness."[173]

Each of the above considerations points to the view that *Keter* is best understood as pure *will* or desire without any reference to a world outside. This "will" is *Keter*'s light, darkness, negation, and simplicity; and in these capacities *Keter* gives rise to the entire system of the *Sefirot*. In humans, *Keter* can be regarded as a primary source of psychic energy or volition, and in view of the fact that the Kabbalists understood it as initiating a series of sexual relations among the *Sefirot*,[174] *Keter* is not far from the Freudian libido. But unlike Freud, for the Kabbalists this libido is not only the foundation of the human psyche but of the cosmos as a whole.

Keter suggests that the supreme psychological task is an awareness of one's own desire and will. *Keter*'s hiddeness reflects the elusiveness of such desire. Most often we speak and act out the desires of others—without the slightest awareness of our own. In conversing with others, we find ourselves saying what we think they want to hear rather than what we want to say. One lesson of *Keter* is that we must listen quietly for our own desire, for like *Keter*, our desire is hidden and dark, occupying the recesses of our unconscious, a "nothing" that is nevertheless the undiscovered origin of our psychic life.

In *The Palm Tree of Deborah*, Cordovero associates the *Sefirah Keter* (Crown) with the divine trait of "humility," and states that in order to achieve this trait one should value oneself as "naught," flee honor, and seek repentance for one's sins. He indicates that "Crown" signifies the head, and proceeds to state that like the *Sefirah Keter* "that is ashamed to gaze at its source (*Ein-Sof*)" and therefore "looks downward" toward creation, "man should be ashamed to gaze proudly upwards, but he should ever look downwards in order to abase himself as much as possible."[175] Cordovero analyzes the spiritual traits associated with *Keter* according to several different aspects of the human head and face. With respects to the "thoughts" in one's mind he says that one should refrain from judgment and negativity. One's "forehead" should never be hardened, and one should show good will to all, even to those who provoke one to anger. One's "ears" should avoid hearing an evil or ugly report about others. The "nose," which is associated with the emotion of rage, should refrain from anger and one should seek to fulfill

---

173. Ibid., p. 220.

174. The sexual unions of the various *Sefirot* are dwelt on by Chayyim Vital in his *Sefer Etz Chayyim* See especially 2: 3a.

175. Cordovero, *Palm Tree of Deborah*, p. 70.

other's needs and desires. One's "face" should "shine constantly, so to welcome all men."[176] Finally one's "mouth" should strive to produce a good word at all times. Cordovero recognizes that one cannot always conduct oneself in accord with each of these qualities, as there are others that at times may conflict with them. Yet he holds that these traits, which can all be subsumed under the banner of humility (holding one's head "low" rather than "high"), bring one closest to the "highest sources."

At first glance, Cordovero's approach appears to be in complete opposition to the view of *Keter* as *Ratzon* or desire that I have discussed above. However, on closer examination these two approaches, like so much else in the Kabbalah, are actually complementary rather than contradictory. For it is only in finding one's true desire, a desire that is as much spiritual as it is corporeal, that one can finally surrender the eternal quest of the ego, an ego that is otherwise never satisfied and is constantly demanding *more*. In this way finding one's "desire" becomes not only the complement to but the requisite for the kind of humility that Cordovero sees embodied not only in *Keter* but throughout the *Sefirot*.

CHOCHMAH (WISDOM)

Chochmah is regarded as the first creative act of *Ein-Sof*, and, as such, is frequently referred to as *reishit* (beginning). *Keter Elyon*, God's will, is first channeled through *Chochmah*.[177] The emergence of wisdom or intellect from will also accords well with Freud's later claim that intellect (cognition) emerges as a superstructure built upon desire. Yet for the Kabbalists, intellect is, in effect, a new beginning both for the human psyche and the world. Rabbi Moses De Leon declared that "the beginning of existence is the mystery of the hidden point which is called *Chochmah* . . . and from a single point you can draw out all things."[178] Although this primal point of wisdom can be understood ontologically, it is, I believe, best to first understand it as an initial axiom or idea from which all other conceptions can be derived: "When the most secret of secrets (*Keter*) sought to be revealed, He made, first of all, a single point, and this became thought. He made all the

176. Ibid., p. 74.
177. See Zalman, *Likutei Amarim-Tanya*, Ch. 35, p. 155ff.
178. Tishby and Lachower, *The Wisdom of the Zohar*, Vol. 1, p. 281.

designs there. He made all the engravings there."[179] The Zohar here teaches that all of the "forms" were condensed within this single point of wisdom. *Chochmah*, above all, expresses the notion (which was later boldly spelled out by Hegel) that the entire world can be derived from a single, simple idea, which in the Kabbalah is equated with a dialectical system expressing the interdependence of *Ein-Sof* and *Sefirot*, subject and object, God and the world.

While *Chochmah*, according to the Kabbalists, cannot be seen or apprehended in and of itself, it is inherent in and "animates" everything. *Chochmah* is variously described as the "seed of all creation" and "the potentiality of what is."[180] As a moment in the intellectual process it is compared to "the original idea" or "inner thought." In the Zohar, *Chochmah* is referred to as *Machshavah Setumah* (hidden thought) and is considered to be void of all individuality, instantiation, and separateness. It is "existent and non-existent, deep buried, unknowable by name."[181] According to Cordovero, *Chochmah* is called "being from nothingness" (*yesh me-ayin*). It is the "beginning of being and not being itself," requiring "a third point (*Binah*) for the revelation of existents."[182]

As it is manifest in our world, *Chochmah* is the *hyle*,[183] the most fundamental instrument for creation, and can be considered roughly equivalent to the Platonic "Forms" or "Ideas." Scripture relates that God has created the world *be-Chochmah* (with wisdom, Psalms 104: 24, Proverbs 3:19), which the Kabbalists interpreted to mean "by *Chochmah*" (making *Chochmah* the instrument of creation) and "in *Chochmah*" (making it the potentiality of being in all things).[184] *Chochmah* is also referred to as the Garden of Eden, in all likelihood because the Kabbalists conceived of the primeval garden as an ideal world of forms. While *Chochmah* is clearly something (*yesh*) in relation to *Keter*, it is *nothing* in relation to the world, inasmuch as the ideas embodied within it have yet to be made actual and concrete. As such it, like *Keter*, is occasionally referred to as *Ayin*, nothing.

---

179. Ibid., p. 281, 331; Zohar I, 2a; Sperling and Simon, *The Zohar*, Vol. 1, p. 6.

180. Zohar III, 235b; *Tanya* II, Ch. 3.

181. Zohar I, 2a; Sperling and Simon, *The Zohar*, Vol. 1, p. 6.

182. Cordovero, *Or Ne'erav* VI:1, 35a; Robinson, *Moses Cordovero's Introduction to Kabbalah*, p. 116.

183. See Maimonides, *Moreh Nevuchim* II: 30. English translation by M. Friedlander, *The Guide For The Perplexed* (New York: Dover, 1956).

184. Schochet, "Mystical Concepts," p. 838.

The kabbalistic dialectic permeates the *Sefirot* in such a manner that none can be said to have a permanent structure or essence.

Cordovero's ethical analysis of *Chochmah* is rooted in the fact that *Chochmah* is a *Sefirah* of the "right pillar," and as such is connected with the attribute of loving-kindness. Cordovero indicates that the "lesson" of the *Sefirah Chochmah* is that one should think to improve the lot of others and, as "Wisdom is the father of all created things,"[185] show mercy and respect to all creatures, "neither destroying nor despising any of them."

Psychologically, *Chochmah*, as has already been intimated, refers to the cognitive dimension of the human psyche, a dimension that, according to Freud and his followers, lies at the foundation of the ego, and is instrumental in directing the libido or will. It is in *Chochmah*, the realm of ideas, that the relationship between the human psyche and the external world can be understood, for it is through our ideas that the world is experienced and, in effect, constructed. This is a powerful psychotherapeutic notion, for it frees us from regarding ourselves simply as victims of the world, and gives us both the opportunity and responsibility to forge our own experience. There is, indeed, *wisdom*, in recognizing that many of the forces that we believe impede our progress in the world are of our own making. Victor Frankl, in speaking of his experiences in the concentration camps, said that he learned the great lesson that while the Nazis could control his body they had no control over his mind, and, as such, his fate, in an important sense, remained within his own hands.[186] The wisdom of *Chochmah* is not, of course, to be complacent in the face of evil or to believe in the unlimited sovereignty of the human subject but rather to recognize how much control our own psyche affords us in relation to the major and minor calamaties that befall us, and to exercise control over the *interpretations* we place upon the events in our lives.

BINAH (UNDERSTANDING)

Binah is the third of the intellectual *Sefirot*. *Binah* is conceived as a "palace" erected around the point of *Chochmah*.[187] From a cognitive point of view *Binah* is the expansion or fulfillment of the concealed thought that comprises

---

185. Cordovero, *Palm Tree of Deborah*, p. 82.

186. Victor Frankl, *From Death Camp to Existentialism*, trans. Ilsa Lasch (Boston: Beacon Press, 1959).

187. Tishby and Lachower, *The Wisdom of the Zohar*, Vol. 1, p. 282.

Chochmah.[188] *Binah* is thus the spelling out of the details and implications of the original "inner thought" of wisdom. *Binah* is frequently equated in both rabbinic and kabbalistic sources with the process of reasoning itself.[189] We can gain some insight into *Binah* by observing that it is the dominant *Sefirah* in the World of *Beriah* (creation), which according to the Kabbalah is the world in which we first find the appearance of finite, distinct entities. *Binah* is also transformed into the *Partzuf Imma*, the Celestial Mother, a fact that underlies its creative role.[190] Indeed as the "Cosmic Mother" *Binah* is the womb in which all the lower *Sefirot* develop and eventually unfold in all their detail. These lower *Sefirot* are conceived as seven children emanating from *Binah*'s womb.[191] In the mathematical metaphor *Binah* is symbolized as a "circle" that represents the beginning of substantial existence. In contrast to *Chochmah*, which the Kabbalists symbolized with the nondimensional point of the Hebrew letter *yud*, *Binah* is symbolized by the letter "*heh*,"[192] which has dimensions of length and width[193] and which, according to the Kabbalists, represents the "dimensions" of explanation, understanding, and manifestation.[194] While we should not take this representation to connect *Binah* itself with space or physicality, we can regard *Binah* as the paradigm for the experience of all finite existence, whether manifest in the psychical or natural realms. According to the Zohar, it is in *Binah* that existence is first separated and differentiated.[195] It is in *Binah* that the sketches and engravings of *Chochmah* first take on a permanent, subsistent reality.[196]

Psychologically, *Binah* is said to perform a reconciliation between the "desire" of *Keter* and the intellect of *Chochmah*. Indeed, *Binah* is the first of

188. *Tikkunei* Zohar 22: 63b.

189. Schochet "Mystical Concepts," pp. 838, 853, note 59.

190. Zohar III, 290a ff.; *Pardes Rimonim* 8:17.

191. Tishby and Lachower, *The Wisdom of the Zohar*, Vol. 1, p. 282.

192. Zohar III, 17a, 258a. See Schochet "Mystical Concepts," p. 838, p. 852, n. 37.

193. Schochet, "Mystical Concepts," p. 838, 853, note 61, referring to Zalman, *Tanya* III: 4, *Igeret HaKodesh*, sec. 5, and Zohar II, 158a. Similarly, Zohar 1, 6a refers to *Chochmah* and *Binah* respectively as the "supernal point (*Chochmah*) which is situated in his palace (*Binah*)."

194. Zalman, *Likutei Amarim-Tanya*, p. 408 (*Igeret HaKodesh*, Ch. 5). See discussion in Schochet, "Mystical Concepts," p. 838.

195. Tishby and Lachower, *The Wisdom of the Zohar*, Vol. 1, p 270.

196. Zohar I, 90a, *Sitrei Torah*; Tishby and Lachower, *The Wisdom of the Zohar*, Vol. 2, p. 568; cf. discussion in Vol. 1, p. 270.

several *Sefirot* that are said by the Kabbalists to reconcile and harmonize opposing principles. Such reconciliation of opposites, or *coincidentia oppositorum*, is perhaps the hallmark of kabbalistic psychology. Here we see that it is neither will nor wisdom, emotion nor intellect, which defines the creativity and *understanding* of the human mind, but rather the dialectical blending of the two. It is only when the knowledge of *Chochmah* is informed by the desire of *Keter* that one can create something of *value* or be said to truly "understand." My understanding of my fellow human being only occurs when, via the process that Dilthey and others referred to as *verstehen*, I can actually stand in the other's shoes and cognize the world from the standpoint of his/her goals and desires.

A more general principle, however, is to be gleaned from *Binah*, and this is that the apparent contradictions within the human psyche are (as Jung later observed) mutually dependent relations, and that opposites need to complement and modify one another. Intellect is empty without interest and emotion, and emotion unfulfilled without thought. A person's goodness is interdependent with his or her potential for evil, love is not real without the potential for jealousy and hate, and a man's masculinity is impossible without a complementary femininity and vice versa. In Cordovero's ethical scheme *Binah* is associated with repentance, which he describes in terms of modifying the bitterness of both evil and judgment in order that a man can "repent and rectify every flaw."[197]

It is the acceptance and embodiment of opposing principles that connects *Binah* with motherhood and creation. The created, as opposed to the ideal, man or woman is riddled with conflict and contradiction and it is to the understanding archetypal "Mother" within ourselves that we must turn to accept, even embrace, the contradictions within our own souls. Those who do not achieve such an acceptance—who, for example, strive to be perfectly rational, good, and loving—inevitably bring about the opposites of these traits in their most unbridled, perverse forms.

DA'AT (KNOWLEDGE)

As I have indicated earlier, an alternative scheme for the ten *Sefirot* excludes *Keter*, on the grounds that it is essentially identical with *Ein-Sof*, and

---

197. Cordovero, *Palm Tree of Deborah*, p. 86.

interposes *Da'at* as the third *Sefirah*, after *Chochmah* and *Binah*.[198] Among certain Kabbalists *Da'at* appears between *Chochmah* and *Binah*, not as a separate *Sefirah* but as the "external" aspect of *Keter*.[199] The word *Da'at* derives from a root meaning "attachment" or "union," and this *Sefirah* is said to bring about a union or mediation between the two *Sefirah* above it, again establishing a pattern in which two opposing *Sefirot* are mediated and resolved by a "third."[200] Indeed, according to Vital, *Da'at* is actually necessary for the revelation of the upper *Sefirot*: "*Chochmah* and *Binah* are to no avail, for *Chochmah* and *Binah* are concealed and become manifest only by means of *Da'at*."[201] The significance of *Da'at* is emphasized by Cordovero, who regards *Da'at* to be a manifestation of *Keter* that rises like a soul and informs the body of each of the *Sefirot*.[202] Because it is the "soul" of each *Sefirah*, and does not have its own independent vessel, it cannot be counted among the ten *Sefirot*.[203] Cordovero also emphasizes that *Chochmah* and *Binah* "unite in the mystery of the primordial *Da'at*, which is the middle between 'Father' and 'Mother' . . . The result of this union is the existence and renewal of the *Sefirot*."[204]

In the metaphor of the *Partzufim*, *Chochmah* is equated with the Father, *Binah* with the Mother, and *Da'at* with the offspring or Son.[205] This is said to signify the fact that *Da'at* brings to fruition the intellectual process that was begun in *Chochmah* and developed in *Binah*. The concept, which is pure potential in *Chochmah*, is reasoned through and elaborated in *Binah*, and becomes unified and practical in *Da'at*.

The Kabbalists spoke of two aspects of *Da'at*, an "upper" aspect (*Da'at Elyon*), which is directly derived from *Keter* and serves as the force that brings about a dialectical union between *Chochmah* and *Binah*; and a lower aspect (*Da'at Tachton*), which is the vehicle through which the intellectual activity

---

198. Schochet "Mystical Concepts," pp. 839–40.

199. Scholem, *Kabbalah*, p. 107.

200. See Scholem, *Kabbalah*, p. 107. This dialectical pattern becomes even more significant in the mediation of *Chesed* and *Gevurah* by *Tiferet* (see below).

201. *Sefer Etz Chayyim* 22:1, as cited and translated by Schochet, "Mystical Concepts," p. 854, note 73.

202. Moses Cordovero, *Elimah Rabbatai* 2: 7.

203. Schochet, "Mystical Concepts," p. 854, note 76, citing Vital's *Sefer Etz Chayyim* 23: 5, 8.

204. Moses Cordovero, *Or Ne'erav* VI: 3, 38b–39a; Robinson, *Moses Cordovero's Introduction to Kabbalah*, p. 127.

205. Schochet, "Mystical Concepts," p. 840.

of the upper *Sefirot* is channeled into the lower seven emotional *Sefirot*, or *middot*. *Da'at Tachton* is, in fact, the essence of these lower *Sefirot* that serve to channel the divine will and intellect into feeling and, ultimately, action.

Psychologically, *Da'at* can also be conceived of as the principle that unites intellect and emotion (*Sechel* and *Middot*). This balance, according to the Kabbalists, is essential for both the world and the health of the human psyche.

CHESED (LOVE) OR *GEDULLAH* (GREATNESS)

Chesed is the first of seven lower *Sefirot*, which are conceived of in the Kabbalah as the moral *middot* (traits). It is also the first of the three *psychical Sefirot*. *Chesed*, which denotes boundless love or kindness, is the very principle through which God created and continuously renews the world.[206] Cordovero informs us that the function of *Chesed* is, as its name implies, "to help and succor man." According to Cordovero, "it also serves to nullify the power of the Outside Ones who accuse and vex man . . . Among its actions is love."[207]

Chesed reflects God's unlimited benevolence toward His creation and it is only natural that it develops after *Sefirah Binah* that represents the first inkling of a finite created world. It is the *middah* and *Sefirah* that is glimpsed by prophets and mystics in their experience of God's grace and love. As *Gedullah* (greatness) this *Sefirah* reflects God's awesome presence, what modern theologians have referred to as the *mysterium tremendum*.[208] In its purest form, *Chesed/Gedullah* would be overwhelming to mankind and hence this divine trait is generally experienced as it is moderated by the other *Sefirot*, particularly *Din* (judgment). *Chesed*, as it is manifest on earth, corresponds to the dimension of experience that can best be described as pure Godliness or *spirituality* and the various aspects of human love that reflect God's beneficence. As such it introduces *spiritual* values into the created world. Its negative side, created by the shattering of this *Sefirah*

---

206. Zohar II, 168b; Sperling and Simon, *The Zohar*, Vol. 4, p. 81. See Psalms 89: 3, "The world was built by *Chesed*."

207. Moses Cordovero, *Or Ne'erav* VI: 3, 37b; Robinson, *Moses Cordovero's Introduction to Kabbalah*, p. 124.

208. Rudolf Otto, *The Idea of the Holy* (London: Oxford University Press, 1970) (originally published in 1923).

during the "Breaking of the Vessels," is to be found in the negative expressions and purposes to which spirituality and love can be directed.

For Cordovero, the ethic of *Chesed* involves acts of loving-kindness toward both others and God. Visiting the sick, providing charity to the poor, welcoming guests, attending the deceased, and bringing the bride to the wedding canopy are all *mitzvot* that reflect the supernal trait of *Chesed*.[209] In addition, *Chesed* makes it incumbent upon one to accept his or her fate with equanimity, to remind oneself even in the face of misfortune of the saying *Gomzu le-Tova*, "This too will be for good."

Psychologically, *Chesed* is the primary ingredient in all human relationships. It is, for example, the vehicle through which parents transmit a basic sense of love and security to their children, the power that animates lovers, and the care that is a prerequisite for psychological healing. As Irwin Yalom and others have pointed out, in spite of the claims for the efficacy of various psychotherapeutic techniques, the single most important curative factor is the *regard* of the therapist for his or her patient.[210] This is indeed the *power* of *Chesed*, and through a consideration of this "power" we are led naturally to the next *Sefirah*, *Gevurah/Din*, power and judgment per se.

GEVURAH (POWER) OR *DIN* (JUDGMENT)

This *Sefirah* is understood as a principle of measure, limit, and restraint. The "power" of *Gevurah* is in the fact that it constrains God's boundless love (*Chesed*) and distributes it according to the capacity of the receiver and, more importantly, according to the receiver's *merit*.[211] Unrestrained, *Gevurah* is also the root of evil. Cordovero tells us that "among the actions of *Gevurah* are stern Judgment . . . It is a lash to punish man. From it stem all the Outside Forces which denounce and oppose man."[212]

Gevurah is a singularly important *middah* both because it reflects the very essence of creation itself (which is limitation and restraint) and because

209. Cordovero, *Palm Tree of Deborah*, pp. 90–91.

210. Irwin Yalom, *Existential Psychotherapy* (New York: Basic Books, 1983).

211. Whereas *Chesed* is distributed freely regardless of the receiver's merit (Zohar II, 168b; Sperling and Simon, *The Zohar*, Vol. 4, p. 82.

212. Moses Cordovero, *Or Ne'erav* VI: 3, 37b; Robinson, *Moses Cordovero's Introduction to Kabbalah*, p. 126.

it introduces a dimension of divine *justice* and *righteousness* into the world.[213] *Gevurah* is thus the *Sefirah* that is reflected in the experience of *ethical* values. Its negative aspect is *moral evil*.

We have already seen the significance of *Gevurah* or *Din* for the doctrine of *Tzimtzum*.[214] Indeed, *Gevurah* implies the very measured restraint that is the essence of *Tzimtzum* as contraction, withdrawal, and concealment. According to Vital, "Every limitation of emanation is from *Gevurah* and *Din* . . . Every *Tzimtzum* is (a notion of *Din*)."[215] *Chesed*, on Vital's view, represents a boundless extension that, if unchecked, would prevent the creation of a finite world.[216] *Gevurah*, which is on the one hand diametrically opposed to the principle of creation in *Chesed*, is on the other hand its very fulfillment; for it is only with the restraint of *Gevurah* that finite creatures can subsist without being reabsorbed into *Ein-Sof*. A full analysis reveals that neither *Chesed* nor *Gevurah* alone could sustain creation. Only as a result of their tension and complementarity does a world come into being at all. There is thus a true dialectical relationship between *Chesed* and *Gevurah*, whereby each can be derived from, and even be regarded as essential for, the other. Without *Gevurah* as limitation there could not be true *Chesed* (benevolence), yet without *Chesed* as emanation and revelation *Gevurah* would have nothing to judge, contract, or conceal. As *Sefirot*, both *Chesed* and *Gevurah* are, as we have seen, absolutely identical with the divine essence. This idea is expressed in the well-known Zoharic formula: "He is they and they are he, being linked together like a flame to the coal;"[217] hence, each contain implicit within themselves all aspects of the Absolute.

Cordovero takes a somewhat startling perspective on the ethics of *Gevurah* or power. According to Cordovero, a man should never exercise power and judgment for his own sake, because "this bestirs Power in Supernal Man and so destroys the world." One should only exercise power on behalf of his wife, for *Gevurah* is more appropriately contained by the

---

213. Zohar II, 175b; Sperling and Simon, *The Zohar*, Vol. 4, p. 108.

214. See Chapter Three.

215. Schochet, "Mystical Concepts," p. 855, citing C. Vital, *Mevoh She'arim* I: 1, 1.

216. Schochet, "Mystical Concepts," p. 841.

217. Zohar III, 70a; Sperling and Simon, *The Zohar*, Vol. 5, p. 66. Cf. Zohar 176a; Sperling and Simon, *The Zohar*, Vol. 4, p. 110: "So one quality emanates from another, each imbibes from each, and finally it is made manifest that all are One, and all depend on One, and the One is in the all."

female. A husband should, for example, provide his wife with such things as clothing, adornments, and a house, but should not exercise *Gevurah* in the aggrandizement of himself. Cordovero associates *Gevurah* with man's evil inclination, and this includes sexual desire, which "should be directed chiefly towards the benefit of the wife whom God has chosen to be a help meet for him."[218]

On a psychological level, the dialectic of kindness and judgment represents a critical balance that must obtain both in relationships with others and with oneself. Consider, for example, the balance between unconditional love on the one hand and discipline and restraint on the other, which must obtain in rearing children; or the balance between self-love and self-criticism, which is a prerequisite for personal growth. Psychotherapists often work to obtain a balance between positive regard and criticism, empathy and interpretation, open-mindedness and limit setting, etc. The blending of kindness and judgment becomes particularly clear, for example, in working with individuals who have committed a serious crime and who must achieve a balance between self-forgiveness (*Chesed*) and assuming responsibility (*Din*) with respect to their criminal acts. Such a balance must be achieved with respect to all human failings and transgressions.

TIFERET (BEAUTY) OR *RACHAMIM* (COMPASSION)

The dialectical relationship between *Chesed* and *Gevurah* is manifest and resolved in the *Sefirah Tiferet* (Beauty) or *Rachamim* (Compassion). This *Sefirah* is a harmonizing principle that tempers both the unboundlessness of God's love (*Chesed*) and the severity of His judgment (*Gevurah*). We read in the Zohar: "It is evident that there can be no perfection except that one aspect be joined to the other and a third hold them together to harmonize and complete them."[219] This balancing or harmony is also understood as the foundation for beauty.[220] We might say that beautiful things contain the spiritual (*Chesed*) in a way that is conditioned and limited through form (*Gevurah*). Perhaps this is why, for most individuals, spirituality is mediated by and experienced through natural beauty and the beauty of artistic objects.

---

218. Cordovero, *Palm Tree of Deborah*, p. 104.
219. Zohar II, 176a; Sperling and Simon, *The Zohar*, Vol. 4, p. 110.
220. *Tikkunei* Zohar 70:133b. See Schochet, "Mystical Concepts," p. 842.

Tiferet understood in this way introduces an *aesthetic* dimension to creation. Its negative aspect is aesthetic ugliness and indifference.

The relationship among the first three emotional *Sefirot*, *Chesed*, *Gevurah*, and *Tiferet*, abbreviated ChaGaT, is, like the relationship among *Chochmah*, *Binah*, and *Da'at*, paradigmatic for all the *Sefirot*. That opposites reciprocally determine, and in effect, create one another, is the central idea distinguishing "dialectical" from "linear" thought, and, perhaps, the central idea of the Kabbalah. This idea is embodied in the concept of *Tiferet*, and it is for this reason that the Kabbalists identified *Tiferet* with *Emet* or absolute Truth.[221] According to Cordovero, the quality of *Tiferet* (Beauty) is associated with "Truth" and is found in the study of Torah, which should be done in a humble and pleasant manner, with the thought of benefiting many students.[222]

Chesed and *Gevurah* are each "relative truths," for it is only from a limited point of view that *Chesed* is, for example, "the principle of creation," or *Gevurah*, as limitation, the principle of a finite world. The absolute truth of *Tiferet* is, however, understood in the idea that these *relative truths reciprocally determine one another*, and it is precisely this dynamic, reciprocal determination that is *Emet* in the ultimate sense. It is precisely because *Tiferet* is understood as harmonizing within itself the "truths" of the various *middot*, that it takes a central position in the sefirotic tree, and is identified with "The Holy One Blessed Be He."

From a psychological perspective, *Tiferet*, perhaps even more than *Binah*, represents the notion, propounded by modern thinkers as varied as Hegel and Jung, that the human mind is defined by its very capacity to tolerate and harmonize conflict and contradiction. That such tolerance of conflict is a central psychotherapeutic task is clear. Those who suffer from anxiety, depression, and other psychological disorders invariably reveal an intrapsychic conflict that they find intolerable—for example, an inability to reconcile their sexual preferences or desires with the teachings of their religion, their feelings of rage and even hatred for their parents or other loved ones with their feelings (and obligations) of love for them, their marriage to a single partner with their desire for many such partners—to name but a few of the perennial "contradictions" that patients bring to psychotherapy. That

---

221. Schochet, "Mystical Concepts," p. 855, note 103, citing Zohar *Chadash*, Toldot 26, Yitro 31b, *Sefer Etz Chayyim* 35: 3.
222. Cordovero, *Palm Tree of Deborah*, pp. 105–109.

Rachamim, compassion, is essential for psychological healing is clear, for it is only through such compassion that one can live with the contradictions within oneself and others, and ultimately, as the other name of this *Sefirah*, *Tiferet* (Beauty), implies, realize the harmonizing beauty of the human soul.

NETZACH (ENDURANCE), HOD (SPLENDOR), AND YESOD (FOUNDATION)

We now enter into the realm of what some Kabbalists (Azriel in particular) referred to as the "natural" *Sefirot*. Since God Himself is conceived of as being totally incorporeal we cannot possibly assert that these *Sefirot* are material or spatial in and of themselves. As *middot* of God they are still regarded as moral qualities. Still, the Kabbalists' descriptions of their inner nature provide hints that suggest that in creation they are archetypes for a spatial, corporeal world. *Netzach, Hod,* and *Yesod* are regarded as branches or channels for the higher *Sefirot* of *Chesed, Gevurah* and *Tiferet*, respectively.[223] They are considered *receptacles* for the upper *middot* and serve as tools or vessels for the factual application of kindness, justice, and compassion in the world.[224] However, unlike the upper *Sefirot*, which act through the stimulus of will and reason, these *Sefirot* act *mechanically*[225] and thus follow the causal order of the natural, spatio-temporal world.

In the anthropomorphic representation of the *Sefirot*, *Netzach* and *Hod* are referred to as the "kidneys that advise."[226] Their role is, in effect, to provide "advice" or measure to the distribution of *Chesed* and *Gevurah*, of divine benevolence and restraint. *Netzach* represents the "Endurance" of the divine benevolence and, as such, the continual outpouring of *Chesed*; whereas, *Hod* represents the preservation of the divine "Majesty and Splendor," in such a manner that it is not wantonly dissipated by *Chesed*. *Yesod*, which mediates between *Netzach* and *Hod*, represents the "Foundation" through which the world receives the appropriate mixture of emanations from the higher *Sefirot*.

It does not require much of an interpretive leap to see these *Sefirot* as the

---

223. Schochet, "Mystical Concepts," p. 843, citing *Tikkunei* Zohar 19: 45a, 22: 68b, 30: 74a; Zohar III, 236a.
224. Ibid.
225. Ibid.
226. Ibid., p. 844.

foundation for spatial, corporeal creation. Their characterization as the "natural" *Sefirot*, as the "receptacles" for the actualization of the upper *middot*, and as *Sefirot* that act "mechanistically," point to this conclusion. It is not altogether obvious, however, what aspects of material creation are to be derived from each of them. We know that *Netzach* and *Hod* are almost always paired together. The Zohar refers to them, in decidedly spatial terms, as "two halves of one body"[227] and also as the "supports of the upper *Sefirot*."[228] *Yesod*, on the other hand is thought of as the completion of *Netzach* and *Hod*, and as the *Sefirah* that serves as a *container* for the light of all the upper *Sefirot*. We might think of *Netzach* and *Hod* as the origin of two spatial dimensions, which are dependent on each other (as length is dependent on width) in the creation of form. This two-dimensional form is completed and becomes a "container" with the addition of a third spatial dimension (depth), which is derived from *Yesod*. As such one way of conceptualizing these *Sefirot* is that they are paradigmatic for the three spatial dimensions in our world. On this reading their negative aspects would involve all the alienating, debilitating, and destructive consequences that derive from proximity, distance, and corporeality.

From a psychological point of view we may regard Endurance, Splendor, and Foundation as the cultural fulfillment of earlier, more individualistic psychological principles. This follows from the very names of these *Sefirot*; for civilization and culture are the very aspects of the human psyche that are *splendorous* and *enduring*, and which serve as a *foundation* for human communal life. It is not sufficient that we as humans have individual desire, intellect, and emotion; we must also build something of enduring value. Such cultural pursuits—achievements in work, the arts, religion, the family, society, etc.—are the human equivalents to God's creation of the material world; for through them, as Hegel observed, the human spirit expresses itself and becomes concrete and real. Psychological (and psychotherapeutic) work does not begin and end with the harmonizing of conflict in one's own inner life; it must extend to the achievement of a wider expression and balance in one's work in the world, an achievement of something more enduring than the individual self. *Netzach*, *Hod*, and *Yesod* therefore repeat (and deepen) on the level of society and culture what *Chesed*, *Gevurah*, and *Tiferet* secured for the individual.

---

227. Zohar III, 236a. See Schochet, "Mystical Concepts," p. 843.

228. Zohar *Chadash*, Vayera 26d. Cited in Schochet, "Mystical Concepts," p. 844.

MALCHUT (KINGSHIP)

Malchut, the last of the ten *Sefirot*, can be understood as bringing to fruition the purpose of the entire sefirotic or emanative process. If the goal of creation is the actualization of what only exists potentially within *Ein-Sof*, if the divine purpose is to have subjects over whom a God can reign, and upon whom He can manifest His qualities of kindness, judgment, mercy, etc., then the *Sefirah Malchut* is the very fulfillment of the divine plan.[229] In *Malchut Ein-Sof* finally comes to know himself in an "other."

Cordovero refers to *Malchut* as the architect that brings about creation, and declares that nothing reaches the lower world except via its portals.[230] *Malchut*, which is frequently identified with God's feminine aspect (the *Shekhinah*), is referred to as the "Lower Mother" (*Imma Tataah*)[231] and is said to receive the embryo of the world, which was originally implanted and concealed in the womb of *Binah*. It is in *Malchut* that this "embryo" develops into a manifest reality. While *Binah* is the "Celestial Mother," *Malchut* is truly the mother of the earth.

Malchut is also spoken of in the Zohar as "the mouth of God"[232] and, as part of the metaphor that understands the *Sefirot* as reflective of the progression of divine thought, *Malchut* is the manifestation of thought through speech.[233] It is, according to Schneur Zalman, the equivalent of the divine speech, i.e., the ten divine utterances (*Pirke Avot* 5:1) through which the world was created.

A variety of considerations suggest a link between the *Sefirah Malchut* and the dimension of time. Unlike the other *Sefirot*, *Malchut* is a state of being and not an activity in and of itself. Just as a king has no reign without his subjects, the *Sefirah Malchut* has no existence apart from the activity of the other *Sefirot*.[234] The Zohar states that *Malchut* exerts no influence of its own. It is a passive *Sefirah* that is compared to the moon, which only shines

---

229. Schochet, "Mystical Concepts," p. 835, citing Zohar III, 69b, 237b; *Pardes Rimonim* 2 :6; *Sefer Etz Chayyim* 1:1.

230. Schochet, "Mystical Concepts," p. 846, citing Cordovero, *Pardes Rimmonim* 11: 2 and *Tikkunei* Zohar 19: 40b.

231. Zohar I, 50a; Sperling and Simon, *The Zohar*, Vol. 2, p. 160; II, 22a; ibid, Vol. 2, p. 74 ("two transcendent mothers").

232. *Tikkunei* Zohar, Intro., 17a, cited in Schochet, "Mystical Concepts," p. 846.

233. Schochet, "Mystical Concepts," pp. 846, 867, note 138.

234. Schneur Zalman discusses this and other issues in relation to the *Sefirah*

by reflected light.[235] The Kabbalist Vital states that *Malchut* "has nothing of its own except that which the other *Sefirot* pour into it."[236] These descriptions of *Malchut* are very reminiscent of Maimonides' view of time, which he does not consider to be an independent substance and which accordingly exists only by virtue of the motion of other things.

According to the Zohar there is a reciprocal relationship between *Malchut* and finite beings. It is only through *Malchut* that everything finite comes into Being,[237] but it is only through finite creatures that *Malchut* (sovereignty) itself becomes real.[238] Again the analogy to the dimension of time is quite striking: for although time, it seems, is the force that actualizes all finite creatures, time itself is dependent on the activity of these creatures for its own existence. One may also recall that the connection between *Malchut* or kingship and time is made quite clear in scripture, where we find that time itself is often reckoned in terms of years into the reign of a particular king.

The connection between the final *Sefirah* and time, is, indeed, made explicitly in *Sefer ha-Bahir* where the lowest of the divine powers is referred to as *nischono shel 'olam*, "the duration of the world."[239] *Malchut*'s temporality is further clarified in the Zohar where *Malchut* is referred to as "the tree of death" and where it is recorded that *Malchut* is "the destruction of all, the death of all."[240] Finally, Schneur Zalman explicitly states that *Malchut* is the origin of both time and space.[241]

Malchut at length in *Shaar Hayichud Vehaemunah* (*Tanya*, Part II), Chapter 7. Zalman, *Lukutel Amarim-Tanya*, p. 307ff.

235. Zohar II, 145b; Sperling and Simon, *The Zohar*, Vol. 4, p. 13, and as discussed metaphorically in Zohar I, 249b, 250a; Sperling and Simon, *The Zohar*, Vol. 2, pp. 389–390. In Zohar 23a we learn that the *Sefirot* are "lights upon lights, one more clear than another, each one dark in comparison to the one above it from which it receives its light." Sperling and Simon, *The Zohar*, Vol. 1, p. 94.

236. *Sefer Etz Chayyim* 6: 5, 8: 5, as cited in Schochet, "Mystical Concepts," p. 845. Compare Zohar II, 127a; Sperling and Simon, *The Zohar*, Vol. 3, p. 159.

237. *Shaar Hayichud*, Chapter 7, Zalman, *Likutei Amarim-Tanya*, p 309.

238. Ibid. This idea is also reflected in the hymn *Adon Olam*, which is recited daily in the prayer service.

239. Scholem, *Origins of the Kabbalah*, p. 160. Cf. *Sefer ha-Bahir*, sec. 115. *Book Bahir*, Neugroschel trans., p. 85.

240. Zohar I, 50b–51b; Tishby and Lachower, *The Wisdom of the Zohar*, Vol. 1, p. 320.

241. Schneur Zalman relates that it is "the attribute *Malchuth* from which space

That "time" is the element that transforms an ideal reality into an actually existent universe is apparent from the common identification of the ideal with the "timeless" and the concrete, actual world with the "temporal." It is in time, symbolized by the *Sefirah Malchut*, that God reveals himself to man; and that both God and man struggle to realize their values and actualize their very being.

Both the temporal and feminine aspects of *Malchut* are of interest from a psychological point of view. Time is indeed the very arena in which humanity can actualize its psychological potential. This is illustrated in the "counting of the Omer," the forty-nine day period wherein, as we have seen, each man and woman is enjoined to accomplish the task of perfecting the *Sefirot* within his or her own soul. The very act of noting the passage of each day through the recitation of an appropriate blessing is said, in and by itself, to accomplish part of this task. Here we should note that modern existential psychologists, following Heidegger, have held that the manner in which individuals relate to time, and, particularly, their own finitude and death, is the critical element in their self-actualization and relationships with others. The rabbis who prescribed the Omer counting must have had an intuitive grasp of this idea.

In this connection we should be reminded that the *Sefirah Malchut* also embodies the very notion of the "other," and thus the potential for relationship. As we have seen, *Malchut*, the final *Sefirah*, is often spoken of as the *Shekhinah*, the feminine counterpart to God. On the other hand, the ninth *Sefirah*, *Yesod*, is said to be the equivalent of the phallus; and it is through this phallus that all the potencies of the other *Sefirot* are channeled into a unity between masculine and feminine principles, which is also symbolically represented as a union between God and humanity.[242] The goal of both the cosmos and humanity is a union between self and other, psychologically between masculine and feminine principles, interpersonally between man and woman, and cosmically between God and humanity. Such an encounter and union between souls is, according to the Kabbalists, the goal of both cosmic and personal existence. Indeed, Cordovero, in his ethical

and time are derived and come into existence." *Shaar Hayichud*, Chapter 7, Zalman, *Likutei Amarim-Tanya*, p. 309.

242. For a discussion of *Yesod* in the context of divine sexuality see Elliot R. Wolfson, "Crossing Gender Boundaries in Kabbalistic Ritual and Myth," in his *Circle in the Square: Studies in the Use of Gender in Kabbalistic Symbolism* (Albany: State University of New York Press, 1995), pp. 79–122.

analysis of *Malchut/Shekhinah*, emphasizes the importance of the relationship between husband and wife.[243]

However, both the cosmos and the individual must each become fully individuated prior to being reunited with the creator. It is for this reason that the Jew must ascend through forty-nine levels of perfection prior to receiving the Torah. A man or woman must strive to perfect his/her character before he/she is prepared for a union with God.

By striving to perfect his or her nature as a finite creature, the individual completes him/herself as a being in time, and therefore fulfills the prerequisites for completing God's own eternal unification and perfection, which, according to the Kabbalists, can only occur when humanity has "received the Torah" and fulfilled each of the values (i.e., *Sefirot*) for which the world was created. This is the ultimate meaning of the final *Sefirah*, *Malchut* (sovereignty), for it completes God's *reign* on earth.

THE *SEFIROT* AS TEN DIMENSIONS OR ELEMENTS

I have now completed my explication of the individual *Sefirot* as well as my interpretation of them as divine traits that give rise to ten phenomenological dimensions in human experience and the created world. We have also seen how various "lessons" derived from these dimensions or archetypes contribute to the individual's ethical and spiritual development, thereby enabling one to participate in the reconstruction and restoration of these same *Sefirot* and the world as a whole.

At this point I would like to clarify how the ten *Sefirot* *might* be understood as the ten dimensions or elements through which all things are created and comprised. Table 4–2 provides a summary of my interpretation of the sefirotic "elements." We are now in a position to gain some insight into the phenomenological and logical validity of these dimensions and to use this dimensional scheme both as a vehicle for understanding human experience and for gaining further insight into the mysteries of kabbalistic thought. Before beginning it is important to repeat that this "dimensional" interpretation is not meant to be exclusive or absolute. It is a simplification that is offered as *one means* by which the notion of the *Sefirot* as the molecular components and structures of the world can be understood. To make an

---

243. Cordovero, *Palm Tree of Deborah*, pp. 118–119.

analogy, if we consider the *Sefirot* in their complexity as 'spheres' I have reduced them, as it were, to "points" in order to provide a means of grasping them as the interactive elements of creation.

Consider the ten-dimensional scheme outlined in Table 4–7.

Table 4–7

The *Sefirot* and The Ten-Dimensional World

Sefirah	Derived Dimension	Philosophical Discipline
1) *Keter Elyon* (Supreme Crown)	Will/ Consciousness	Philosophy of Mind
2) *Chochmah* (Wisdom)	Conception/ Idea/ Essence	Epistemology
3) *Binah* (Intelligence)	Existence/ Non-existence	Ontology
4) *Chesed/Gedullah* (Kindness/Greatness)	Spirituality	Philosophy of Religion
5) *Gevurah/Din* (Power/Judgment)	Ethics, Morality, and Values	Axiology
6) *Tiferet/Rachamim* (Beauty/Compassion)	Beauty	Aesthetics
7) *Netzach* (Endurance)	Length	Metaphysics, Philosophy of Natural Science
8) *Hod* (Majesty)	Breadth	
9) *Yesod Olam* (Foundation of the World)	Depth	
10) *Malchut* (Kingdom)	Time	

What reasons other than an apparent connection to kabbalistic philosophy do we have for positing *just these* ten dimensions? Such a scheme recommends itself for a variety of phenomenological, logical, and historical reasons that are independent of its connection to the doctrine of the *Sefirot*. I will summarize these reasons as briefly as possible.

1. The scheme is *phenomenologically* more valid and complete than a naturalistic model of the world. Unlike the four-dimensional scheme, which limits the universe to only those objects that have a spatio-temporal form, these ten dimensions can account for the entire range of human experiences. Any thought, object, or experience, whether referring to the material or the conceptual, to the existent or the nonexistent, to the sentient or the lifeless, to values or events, etc., can be described within this scheme. In addition, any conceivable object can be exhaustively described by appealing to predicates derived from one or more of the ten dimensions, in their positive or negative forms.

2. The dimensions are orthogonal to or independent of one another. This means that descriptions of objects from the point of view of one dimension do not logically dictate the descriptions of these objects from the point of view of any of the others. Just as the length of an object does not dictate anything about its depth or time, the ethical value of an object does not dictate anything about its aesthetic value or, for that matter, its existence. (Many good things are not beautiful and many more good things do not exist.) An examination of each of these dimensions will reveal that they are all essentially independent of each other in the sense I have just described. It is this indepen-dence or orthogonality that allows us to speak of each of them as dimensions in the same way as we speak of the dimensions of space and time.

3. The scheme essentially corresponds to the categories of traditional philosophy and the philosophical disciplines derived from these categories, as indicated in Table 4–7. This is an important consider-ation because it is almost a truism that the categories of traditional philosophy embody the basic structure or dimensions of historical human experience. That the *Sefirot* correspond to these categories suggests that they do indeed contain a reasonably valid phenomenol-ogy of the experiential world.

The derivation and validity of the ten dimensions I have outlined is a topic of immense proportions that could be debated at length. It is not, however, my purpose to defend this scheme in specific detail or to provide any more than an outline of its philosophical basis. My main purpose is to provide a rational context for the dimensional interpretation of the *Sefirot*, in order to show that it *makes sense* for Kabbalists like Cordovero to hold that the *Sefirot* are, in effect, the molecular components of the cosmos. This purpose can best be served by illustrating the application of the scheme to human experience through a consideration of a single, almost randomly chosen, object of experience, the fictional character "Sherlock Holmes."

There can be little doubt that Sherlock Holmes, in spite of his fictional status, has been experienced and continues to be experienced in our world. Within the ten-dimensional scheme we would discover that "Holmes" has (per dimensions seven through ten) certain spatial and temporal characteristics (his height, weight, physical features, location in nineteenthth-century London). He is a conscious, sentient, indeed strongly willed individual (dimension one) whose essence is that of a brilliant detective (dimension two). As a detective he embodies a series of ethical, aesthetic, and, perhaps, spiritual values (dimensions four through six), but as a fictional character he does not, has never, and presumably, will never exist (dimension three). One might imagine a huge ten-dimensional graph with axes for descriptors along each of the dimensions I have outlined and then *locate* Sherlock Holmes at a unique point on that graph. The same, indeed, could be done for *any other* object of human experience.

The above example illustrates how we might understand the *Sefirot*, in their capacity as dimensions, as the elements of the world. They are not elements in the sense in which atoms are the constituent elements of a material body,[245] but rather in the sense of aspects or qualities that when "assembled" together become the basis for all experience of anything whatsoever, including those things which, as the example I have chosen illustrates, do not *exist* and are hence "merely" imagined.

THE CIRCLE OF BEING

Theologically the *Sefirotic* system is a guide to both the inner nature and creative expression of the Godhead. Psychologically and ethically, the *Sefirot* provide us with a guide to the development of the human personality in its libidinal, cognitive, cultural, and interpersonal dimensions, which in turn, provides us with an understanding of the phenomenology of our world. There is a circular determinacy between God, humankind, and the world,

---

245. Scholem speaks of them as archetypes for every created thing (Scholem, *Kabbalah*, p. 105).

and the *Sefirot* are meant to serve as the dimensions or archetypes where the three meet. The Kabbalists held that the theological and the psychological are completely interdependent, and it is for this reason that pious Jews, in concentrating upon the various *Sefirot* and their combinations during the period between Passover and Shavuot, can be said not only to have an impact upon themselves but on the cosmos and deity as well.

DREAMS, PROPHESY, AND "HIGHER WORLDS"

The interpretation of the *Sefirot* as paradigms for dimensions in our world has a variety of implications for our understanding of a whole host of concepts and phenomena, including dreams, mystical experience, prophesy, and "higher worlds." To grasp how this is so we must place our phenomenological understanding of the *Sefirot* back into the context of the Kabbalist's hierarchical ordering of the *Sefirot* and the "five worlds."

One can readily see that the kabbalistic distinction between hidden and revealed *Sefirot* has its parallel in an experiential distinction between dimensions that are intangible and tangible in the every day world. As readily verified in experience, the higher dimensions, those corresponding to the "hidden" *Sefirot* (*Keter, Chochmah, Binah*, and perhaps *Chesed* and *Gevurah*) are essentially intangible, while the lower dimensions, those corresponding to the revealed *Sefirot*, are tangible. The length, width, depth, and time of an object are obviously things that can be grasped by the senses and measured. On the other hand, consciousness or will, ideas, spiritual, and ethical values (corresponding to the higher *Sefirot*) can neither be sensed directly nor measured by science. Indeed, the distinction between the tangible and the intangible is what has classically divided the sphere of the natural sciences from art, religion, and the humanities.

There is, however, no logical necessity that the tangible aspects of a given world be the *spatio-temporal* dimensions, while the intangible aspects are those dimensions that embody will, consciousness, and values. That there indeed are other, "higher" worlds, in which what is hidden (intangible) in our world is revealed (tangible) is at the heart of kabbalistic philosophy. While our world is dominated by the *Sefirah Malchut* (time), there are indeed higher worlds that are dominated by those *Sefirot* that represent values, ideas, consciousness, and will. Indeed we are provided with a window into such worlds in the phenomenon of dreams, which the *Midrash* speaks of as a variety of prophesy.[246] As I will discuss more fully in Chapter Six, the very strangeness of dreams derives from the fact that within them tangibility and intangibility are reversed. Space and time are extremely fluid in dreams and, as psychoanalysis affirms, merely illustrative of unconscious motives, values, emotions, and ideas. The dreamer and more significantly (because this occurs when he or she is fully conscious), the mystic and the prophet, experience the willful, the ethical, and the spiritual as if they were as tangible and as "real" as the furniture in one's room. For the mystic, life and death itself are transcended and to the prophet what is future is revealed. This is because the world in which these elevated souls dwell is not a world that is dominated by time. They are privy to a higher universe which, while composed of the same *Sefirot* or ten dimensions as our own, is more brightly illuminated by the light of the Infinite God.

THE DEPTH OF THE *SEFIROT* SYMBOLISM

We can now see how, for the Kabbalists, the *Sefirot* are not only the elements of creation, but the basic constituents of the human psyche and the bases for human character. We have also seen how the *Sefirot* provide us with insight into worlds that are organized according to principles that differ, in many ways, from our own.

It would, however, be misleading to understand these sefirotic dimensions in static, structural terms, for as we have seen in our discussion of the symbolism of the tree, Primordial Man, sexuality, and family romance, the Kabbalists conceived of the *Sefirot* in living dynamic relation with one another. The *Sefirot*, as dimensions, are continuously interacting with one another (uniting, competing, blending, breaking apart, reforming) within both the cosmos and man, and it is such a *dynamic* that lends significance and "life" to the sefirotic scheme. As we have seen, according to *Tikkunei ha Zohar*, "the garments He (*Ein Sof*) wears in the daytime are not the same ones he wears at night,"[247] and this, Vital explains, reflects the astrological and metaphysical truth that "the world's change at every hour, and one hour

---

246. R. Hanina B. Isaac in *Genesis Rabbah*, 17:5.
247. See the discussion of this theme in Idel, *Kabbalah New Perspectives*, pp. 248–249.

is not the same as the next."[248] I have provided an interpretation of the *Sefirot* doctrine that in this "hour" seems useful and valid. I hope that my approach to the *Sefirot* encourages some readers to engage these archetypes themselves and uncover other meanings latent within them; meanings that will not simply yield yet another theological scheme, but rather an integration of the *Sefirot* into the fabric of one's life and relationship with the divine.

---

248. Vital, *Sefer Ez Chayyim* 1:2, as cited and discussed in Idel, *Kabbalah New Perspectives*, pp. 248–249. I have discussed this passage from a somewhat different point of view in Chapter Two.

5

Otiyot Yesod:[1] The Linguistic Mysticism of the Kabbalah

P hilosophy in the twentieth century, if it can be summed up in a single phrase, can be characterized by what Richard Rorty has called "the linguistic turn."[2] Philosophers as varied as Heidegger and Wittgenstein, Derrida and Gadamer, have proposed philosophical theories that, whatever their differences, are more concerned with the *language* of philosophical discourse than with the *reality* to which this discourse presumably refers. Some twentieth-century philosophers (the logical positivists and the "Wittgensteinians" among them) focused on language in the belief that the problems of philosophy result from linguistic confusion and could therefore be eliminated through a proper analysis of words. Others, the so-called "hermeneuticists," focused on language in the belief that reality itself is analogous to a "text" and that insight into this text/reality can only be achieved through a proper understanding of the language through which we speak of it. Each of these approaches, by way of introducing into philosophy a new self-consciousness about language, is thought to have broken radically with much, if not all, of the philosophy that preceded it.

However, as with many revolutions in philosophical thinking, the years

---

1. Elemental letters.
2. Richard Rorty, *The Linguistic Turn: Recent Essays in Philosophical Method* (Chicago: University of Chicago Press, 1967).

after the rebellion bring with them a sobering account of how the "revolution" was presaged in a different area of inquiry or in works seemingly unrelated to the problems at hand. It is therefore hardly surprising to discover a resurgence of interest in those aspects of the Jewish and Christian hermeneutical traditions that, owing to their focus upon the nature of revelation and authority in religious texts, developed a remarkable degree of sophistication in their theories that the language of scripture represents both the inner dynamic of God and the ultimate nature of the world. Among scholars of the Kabbalah this resurgent interest has manifest itself in, for example, David Biale's discussion of linguistic mysticism in the Kabbalah[3] and in Moshe Idel's study of hermeneutics in the writings of the Kabbalists, particularly Abraham Abulafia.[4]

While these and other authors have contributed considerably to our understanding of what might be called the kabbalistic philosophy of language, none, as far as I can tell, have attempted to explain and critique this aspect of kabbalistic thought in a contemporary philosophical framework. Indeed there are many kabbalistic and Hasidic doctrines about language (particularly those regarding the relationship among God, Torah, language, and the world) that cry out for such explication in a modern idiom. Among these are the doctrines that the world is created and sustained by divine speech, that the world's substance is composed of letters in the holy tongue, that the name of an object is its soul, and that the entire Torah is the name of God. On first hearing, these are strange notions indeed, and it will be our task in the following pages to make these ideas comprehensible and perhaps even convincing.

In order to achieve these goals I will have occasion to conduct a dialogue with the linguistic and hermeneutic theories embodied in writings of certain of the Kabbalists and Hasidim and, particularly, Schneur Zalman of Lyadi[5] (the first Lubavitcher rebbe) whose writings are particularly illuminating in this regard. My purpose is not so much to show that these thinkers anticipated many of the basic concepts of the "linguistic turn" (which they did) but rather to demonstrate, through a dialogue with the Jewish mystics,

---

3. David Biale, *Gershom Scholem, Kabbalah and Counter-History*.

4. Moshe Idel, *Language, Torah and Hermeneutics in Abraham Abulafia*, trans. Menahem Kallus (Albany: State University of New York Press, 1989). See also Idel, *Kabbalah: New Perspectives*.

5. Translations from the works of Schneur Zalman of Lyadi are from *Likutei Amarim-Tanya*, bilingual edition (Brooklyn, NY: Kehot, 1981).

that their linguistic approach to God and the world is of profound philosophical relevance and interest to us in our own day.

THE WORLD IS CREATED AND SUSTAINED BY DIVINE SPEECH

A linguistic theory of creation is present in the earliest proto-kabbalistic work, *Sefer Yetzirah* (The Book of Formation). In this work we find, alongside the notion that the world is composed of ten *Sefirot*, an additional and at times parallel symbolism in which the entire cosmos is said to be created from the twenty-two consonant/letters of the Hebrew alphabet. The letters and the *Sefirot* together are spoken of as "the thirty wondrous paths of creation."[6] According to the author of *Sefer Yetzirah* it was through the *Otiyot Yesod*, the foundational letters, that God "formed substance out of chaos and made nonexistence into existence."[7] *Sefer Yetzirah* emphatically expresses the role of these in the creation of the world: "Twenty-two foundation letters: He engraved them, He carved them, He permuted them, He weighed them, He transformed them, And with them, He depicted all that was formed and all that would be formed."[8]

Linguistic mysticism is amply evident in the earliest kabbalistic source, *Sefer ha-Bahir*,[9] major portions of which are written as an exegetical inquiry into the mystical significance of the Hebrew alphabet. A linguistic theory of creation is also set forth in the anonymous early kabbalistic text, "Source of Wisdom," which held that the world came into being through the inscription of divine speech in the *Avir Kadmon* (Primordial Ether). According to this work, the letters *aleph* and *yud* have a special significance in generating both the divine name and the "thirteen oppositions" through which the world is created and governed.[10] This work was apparently studied carefully by the founder of Hasidism, the Baal Shem Tov.[11]

A mysticism of language, as we shall see, is echoed consistently among the subsequent Kabbalists and Hasidim. For example, in the Zohar we read:

---

6. *Sefer Yetzirah* 1:1; Kaplan, *Sefer Yetzirah*, p. 5.
7. *Sefer Yetzirah* 2: 6; ibid., p. 131.
8. *Sefer Yetzirah* 2: 2; ibid., p. 100.
9. See especially *Sefer ha-Bahir*, secs. 11a, 13, 18, 27, 48, and 54. *Book Bahir*, Neugroschel trans., pp. 53–65.
10. Scholem, *Kabbalah*, p. 332.
11. Ibid.

"For when the world was created it was the supernal letters that brought into being all the works of the lower world, literally after their own pattern."[12] The *Otiyot Yesod*, the foundational or supernal letters, provides an alternative and complementary symbolism to the *Sefirot*. According to Scholem, this dual symbolism of *Sefirot* and letters creates a parallel between creation and revelation. For the Kabbalists these two ideas merge into one another. Creation is revelation and vice versa. Such a view, of course, is implicit even in the biblical tradition, which held that the means of revelation (language) is precisely the vehicle through which God created the world.

That the Jewish tradition regards language as the very vehicle of creation is made eminently clear in the very first chapter of Genesis: "and God *said*, Let there by light and there *was* light." According to rabbinic exegesis of the early chapters of Genesis, the world was actually created by ten divine utterances and the view ultimately developed that the language of the Torah sustains creation as well.

The Midrash (Midrash *Tehillim* 90:12) had spoken of a "Primordial Torah," which serves as a blueprint for the creation of the world. According to the Zohar, this Torah is itself devoid of letters but serves as the impetus to the development of "spiritual letters," which are born in the womb of the celestial mother, *Binah*. These letters are used to construct the written Torah in *Tiferet*, the secrets of which are not revealed until the Oral Torah is produced in the full voice of *Malchut*.[13] Thus, according to the Zohar, the linguistic/theosophical process that produces the world is perfectly paralleled in the process of written and oral divine revelation.

The Talmud records the advice of Rabbi Ishmael to Rabbi Meir, a scribe: "be careful in your work for it is the work of God, if you omit a single letter, or write a letter too many you will destroy the whole world" (Talmud, Tractate *Eruvin*, 13a). According to the founder of the Hasidic movement, Israel Baal Shem Tov, the idea that the world is sustained by divine speech is hinted at in Isaiah 40: 8 where it is said, "The word of our God shall stand forever." According to the Baal Shem Tov this passage refers to God's very words and letters. Schneur Zalman of Lyadi, the first Lubavitcher Rebbe, comments on the Baal Shem Tov's view as follows:

> For if the letters (which comprise divine speech) were to depart [even] for an instant, God forbid, and return to their source, all the heavens would

---

12. Zohar 1, 159a; Sperling and Simon, *The Zohar*, Vol. 2, p. 111.
13. Tishby and Lachower, *The Wisdom of the Zohar*, Vol. 1, pp. 292–293.

become nought and absolute nothingness, and it would be as though they had never existed at all, exactly as before the utterance, "Let there be a firmament." And so it is with all created things, in all the upper and lower worlds, and even this physical earth, which is the [inanimate] "kingdom of the silent." If the letters of the Ten Utterances (*Avot* 5:1) by which the earth was created during the Six Days of Creation were to depart from it [but] an instant, God forbid, it would revert to nought and absolute nothingness, exactly as before the Six Days of Creation.[14]

What meaning, we might ask, can be provided to these startling doctrines? From a philosophical perspective we might say that the world is created and sustained by divine language because it is through such language that the very idea of creation and existence is brought into being. If God's "letters" were to return to their source it would be as if the heavens and earth and all creation never existed, because their very idea would be nonexistent. Ordinarily when we think of the "end of the world" we imagine the destruction or disappearance of the earth and the heavens and all existing things, but what Schneur Zalman is asking us to consider is the end, or rather the negation of *the very concept of existence itself.* Indeed it is this very concept that is so remarkable, i.e., that there should be a "state of affairs" in which there *is* the very possibility of *being* or *not-being.* God's words bring about the very possibility of existence and being as such. It is this that is truly creation *yesh min ayin,* (something from nothing).

Creation, for the Kabbalists, is *linguistic* because it is essentially *conceptual* rather than material. Language is the vehicle through which concepts are born; through which conceptual, ideational distinctions are made, or at least made available or "real." God did not create the world with an immense physical force because He is not primarily in the business of creating *instants,* finite, temporal beings that instantiate a given idea; rather, He creates with words because He is primarily a creator of possibilities, of forms, categories, and ideas. The Kabbalists clearly recognized this to be the case. In their doctrine of *Shevirat ha-Kelim,* the Breaking of the Vessels, they put forth the view that it was only as the result of an original *imperfection* in the created order, exemplified in the fall of Adam, that material beings came into existence at all. The world as originally created by God is a purely conceptual/spiritual realm.

---

14. Schneur Zalman, *Shaar Hayichud Vehaemunah,* Chapter 1; Zalman, *Likutei Amarim-Tanya,* p. 287.

When creation is understood in conceptual terms, it is easy to see how Schneur Zalman can say that with the withdrawal of divine language all would revert to "nought and nothingness" exactly as before the six days of creation. The reason for this is that concepts are essentially atemporal and that God and the conceptual world that He creates exists completely *outside of time*. The withdrawal of God's creating and sustaining force brings an end to a given thing in all of its manifestations, past, present, and future; for it brings an end to the very idea of the thing itself. Man can create and destroy a given object, one for example that is made of copper or gold; he may, as the alchemists dreamed, even be able to create and transform gold itself, but only God, through divine language, can bring the very *idea* of gold in and out of existence. It is this that the kabbalistic doctrine of creation by divine speech is attempting to convey.

THE WORLD'S SUBSTANCE IS COMPOSED OF LETTERS IN THE HOLY TONGUE

Perhaps even more startling than the doctrine of linguistic creation is the kabbalistic view that the world's substance is actually composed of letters in the holy language. Schneur Zalman articulates a doctrine, first described in *Sefer Yetzirah*, that those things not specifically named in the book of Genesis as being created directly by God (the so-called ten utterances of creation) were created as a result of the substitution, transposition, and rearrangement of the "letters" that comprise the ten sayings with which God created the world. According to *Sefer Yetzirah* there are 231 primary gates of creation, which refer to all the possible two-letter combinations of the twenty-two letters of the Hebrew alphabet. With combinations of greater than two letters the number of permutations becomes incalculable, indeed infinite, giving rise to a potentially infinite number of created beings.[15]

This theory of linguistic creation finds its parallel in a theory of Torah that originated in the early Kabbalah but that was most fully developed by the Kabbalists of Safed. According to Moses Cordovero, the language of the Torah we actually read (and the language that thereby ultimately comprises the world) is the result of transformations in a hidden, primordial language, which is the ultimate "deep structure" of our world. Cordovero, following

---

15. Ibid., pp. 287–289.

the Zohar, held that the Torah was originally comprised of spiritual letters of light, which took on material form and entered into various linguistic combinations only with the progressive materialization and differentiation of the world. Indeed, according to Cordovero, as the world "fell" toward its current state of corporeality and finitude, the letters of the Torah rearranged themselves in such a manner as was appropriate for each age. He provides a rather illuminating example of this in his analysis of the biblical prohibition of *Sha'atnez*, which forbids the mixture of wool and linen in fabric to be worn as clothing. According to Cordovero, the letters of the words of this prohibition, *sha'atnez tzemer u-fishtim* (*sha'atnez* of wool and linen) were originally, before the fall, combined in such a manner as to read *Satan'az metsar u-tofsim*, a warning that the insolent Satan will bring "fear and hell" to Adam if he exchanges his "garment of light" for the clothes of the serpent (i.e., corporeality). It is only after Adam's fall, after he does indeed exchange his "garment of light," that the material prohibition of *sha'atnez* became necessary and the actual letters of the Torah were rearranged.[16] Here Cordovero seems to hold a theory of linguistic/ontological parallelism in which the "being" of the world is determined by language and vice versa.

Scholem has pointed out that according to the school of Israel Sarug, the original Torah, in the supernal world of *Atziluth*, consisted of all possible combinations of the twenty-two consonants of the Hebrew language, an idea that suggests the possibility of an infinite number of "possible worlds," corresponding to the whole of *logical* or *linguistic* "space."[17] With their descent through the worlds of *Beriah*, *Yetzirah*, and *Assiyah*, the letters took on more distinct combinatory forms in a sequence of holy and then angelic "names," and finally in the Torah that we actually know and read. Each world, as it were, receives a linguistic structure, and hence a Torah, which is

---

16. Moses Cordovero, *Shi'ur Komah* 63b, as cited and summarized by Gershom Scholem in "The Meaning of the Torah in Jewish Mysticism," in Gershom Scholem, *On the Kabbalah and Its Symbolism*, trans. Ralph Manheim (New York: Schocken, 1969), p. 71.

17. The doctrine of "logical space," of which actual existing things are but a mere subset, originates with Ludwig Wittgenstein in the *Tractatus Logico-Philosophicus*. By analogy, "linguistic space" would consist of all possible utterances (or *all possible combinations of letters*), and "possible reality" being only those utterances or combinations of letters that make sense (i.e., say something). The "actual world" would be a subset of these.

appropriate to its nature. Indeed, each world is actually constructed out of the various ways in which the letters are combined.[18]

Other Kabbalists and Hasidim held that even each man's utterance of the Torah creates new powers and lights in the world.[19] Indeed, it follows from the kabbalistic view of language, that man, in his incessant recombination of the letters (or phonemes and morphemes), is constantly, as it were, weaving new worlds and continuing the creative process initiated by God.

The ideas we have been considering amount to what can be described as a form of *semantic atomism*: the view that the basic constituents of the universe are units of meaning rather than particles of matter. It is important to realize that in Hebrew, letters do not have a merely phonetic function as in English but also serve as bearers of numerical and other significance. For example, the Hebrew letters *aleph*, *bet*, and *gimmel*, which carry the numerical values of one, two, and three, are respectively symbolic of "unity," "creation" (or "understanding"), and "loving-kindness" as well as bearing a variety of other meanings.[20] Thus, when the Kabbalists speak of the world being composed of letters in the holy tongue, they are affirming the proposition that our world is primarily a world of meaning, value, and spirit rather than space, matter, and time.

In order to make full sense of the linguistic theory of the world's structure it is important to recall that for Schneur Zalman, as for others working in the tradition of the Lurianic Kabbalah, the world is created through a primal act of self-contraction or concealment (*Tzimtzum*) on the part of the infinite God (*Ein-Sof*). It is through this primal creative act that God, who is essentially an undifferentiated and all-encompassing spiritual Unity, reveals Himself in ten distinct aspects (the *Sefirot*) and ultimately in the manifold distinctions of a finite world. Creation is thus simultaneously a concealment (of God's infinite unity) and a revelation of his infinite particularity. Indeed, the former *must* be concealed for the latter to be revealed. At the heart of this concealment/creation process is an operation known as judgment or *Din*. The term *Din* generally refers to God's strict judgment concerning the moral value of man and the world, but in this

---

18. Scholem, "The Meaning of the Torah in Jewish Mysticism," p. 80.

19. Ibid., p. 76.

20. Talmud, Tractate *Yoma*, 83b. In later years while an authority as significant as the Rambam maintained a decidedly conventionalist view of language, the clear tendency among the Kabbalists was to hold an *essentialist* view of *loshon hakodesh*, the Hebrew language.

cosmological context it is understood as the principle of differentiation within the infinite God Himself. *Din* is the principle through which God's aspects come to be separated from one another, and it is thus the principle through which *Tzimtzum* operates, and through which distinct ideas, values, and concepts are brought into the world.

One can readily understand how the Kabbalists would regard *language* as the vehicle for this differentiation process, for it is only through language that we can articulate that something is indeed itself and *not* another thing. As we have seen in Chapter Three, Schneur Zalman regards language as the vehicle for *Tzimtzum*; God is said to create the world by contracting and thus revealing his essence in letters and words. Language, in this sense, is the vehicle of thought, the means by which an infinite unity is differentiated into a multitude of finite ideas. Since God's creation is primarily conceptual, it follows that divine language is the vehicle of creation itself. What's more, since the world is, as it were, woven out of God's very own substance, it is the words through which this is accomplished that constitute the world's own substance and essence.

This view, that the world is composed of concepts articulated by words, has much in common with the idealistic and rationalist traditions in Western thought. The view that the world is composed of letters, which also serve as signs of significance and number, is reminiscent of Plato himself, who, at least according to one tradition, viewed the *Eide* (the "forms") as being composed of numbers and numerical ratios.[21] The entire Jewish tradition of number mysticism (*Gematria*) can be understood as an elucidation of the theory that the essence and substance of a thing is to be found in the letters of its name, letters that are themselves numerical signs.

The various combinations of letters (to play on a notion from the early Wittgenstein) create a "linguistic space" for concepts and ideas. In a language (or world) in which ideas were limited to two combinations of two letters of the twenty-two consonants in the Hebrew alphabet, there would be a linguistic space comprising 231 or (counting letter reversals) 462 potential ideas. If each of these combinations named a concept or thing, this space would be "filled." In actual language, however, we have combinations of far greater than two letters, and the linguistic space for concepts in any natural language is infinite. The actual concepts which comprise our world

---

21. See J. N. Findlay, *Plato: The Written and Unwritten Doctrines* (London: Routledge & Kegan Paul, 1974).

consist of only a subset of that linguistic space (not every combination of Hebrew or English letters names an actual thing or idea) and our instantial, material world is comprised of an even smaller subset of these actual concepts, many of which (e.g., unicorns, false gods) name noninstantiated or nonexistent things. The linguistic atomism of the Kabbalah thus provides the basis for a rather sophisticated philosophical apparatus that can encompass such notions as the possible, the actual, the instantial, and the real within a quasi-idealistic philosophical framework. It is a system of thought that shows striking similarities to the ideas of the twentieth-century philosopher Ludwig Wittgenstein who in his *Tractatus Logico-Philosophicus* argued that the world consists of propositions and atomic facts that are mirrored in a linguistic world of sentences and *names*.[22]

To summarize, the linguistic atomism of the Kabbalah expresses the view that the world is essentially a world of ideas rather than things; that ideas are distinguished by language; and that language is composed, in its most basic sense, of letters in the holy tongue. Letters are not merely phonetic signs but are also the bearers of significance, and it is in their role as the fundamental units of meaning that they are the building blocks of the world.

THE NAME OF AN OBJECT IN THE "HOLY TONGUE" IS THE VESSEL FOR ITS LIFE FORCE OR SOUL

The Kabbalists held that there is an important parallel or equivalence between "language" and "life." The Kabbalists find scriptural justification for this view in the traditional Jewish doctrine that the Torah is a "tree of life," a living being, or even a "man."[23] According to the Kabbalist Azriel, the Torah, with each of its letters, verses, and diacritical markings, is comparable to a living organism, the continued life and function of which is dependent upon each of its organs functioning as an integrated whole.[24] This simile recalls the image of the *Sefirot* being ordered as the limbs and organs of a cosmic man. Indeed, the Zohar makes a comparison among the Torah, the human body, and the world as a whole, each of which form a single, organic body:

---

22. Wittgenstein, *Tractatus Logico-Philosophicus*, trans. D. F. Pears and B. F. Guiness (London: Routledge and Kegan Paul, 1961).

23. Scholem, "The Meaning of the Torah in Jewish Mysticism," p. 44ff.

24. Ibid., p. 45.

Whoever labors in the Torah upholds the world, and enables each part to perform its function. For there is not a member of the human body but has its counterpart in the worlds as a whole. For as man's body consists of members and parts of various ranks all acting and reacting upon each other so as to form one organism, so does the world consist of a hierarchy of created things, which when they properly act and react upon each other form literally one organic body. Thus the whole is organised on the scheme of the Torah, which also consists of sections and divisions which fit into one another and, when properly arranged together, form one organic body.[25]

In an important sense, the Kabbalists held that each of these "organic bodies," man, the world, and language (Torah), are aspects of a single cosmic structure.

According to Schneur Zalman of Lyadi, everything in the world, including inanimate objects such as stones, water, and earth, has a soul or spiritual life-force, which is to be found in the letters of divine speech from which they and their names are composed.[26] Paralleling a very early kabbalistic tradition that "the name of a thing is that thing itself,"[27] Schneur Zalman tells us that "The name by which (a thing) is called in the Holy Tongue is a vessel for the life force." This view, that all created things have a linguistic essence, can be traced at least as far back as the Talmud, where it is reported that Rabbi Meir could grasp the nature and character of an individual simply by knowing his name.[28]

Sometimes the essence of a given being is not immediately obvious from its name. It will, however, according to Schneur Zalman, be comprehensible by means of the rules of substitution and transposition of letters or *Gematria* (the numerical significance of the letters involved). For example, when all the numerical values of its component letters are summed, the name *Moshe Rabeinu*, "Moses our teacher," has the numerical value of 613, which refers to the 613 commandments transmitted by God through Moses at Sinai and taught to the Jewish people by Moses. The fact that the essence of an object or individual may be partially or wholly "concealed" in its name (for example,

---

25. Zohar I, 134b; Sperling and Simon, *The Zohar*, Vol. 2, p. 36. Cf. Tishby and Lachower, *The Wisdom of the Zohar*, Vol. 3, pp. 123–124.

26. Zalman, *Shaar Ha Yichud Vehaemunah*, Chapter 1; Zalman, *Likutei Amarim-Tanya*, p. 287, referring to Vital.

27. *Sefer ha-Bahir*, sec. 54. *Book Bahir*, Neugroschel trans., p. 65.

28. Talmud, Tractate *Yoma*, 83b.

via *Gematria*) stems, according to the Kabbalists, from the fact that the life force issuing directly from the Torah is generally too great for individual creatures to absorb; hence they must receive their soul only after it has descended and been progressively concealed and diminished through the transpositions of letters and terms.[29] Vital, for example, informs us that even the Zohar refers to the letters of language as hidden, because a person can hide them within himself. This view is related to the linguistic understanding of *Tzimtzum*, which was discussed in Chapter Three. It is part of the essence of both creation and language that neither is obvious on its face. Meanings are always partially concealed. This assumption gives rise to the science of *hermeneutics* (exegesis and interpretation) as the vehicle to authentic knowledge.

It is thus clear that Schneur Zalman holds an "essentialist" theory of language and meaning. The names that are given to objects in *Loshen Hakodesh* (the Holy Language) are not mere conventions but are essentially related to the nature or, in Schneur Zalman's terms, the "soul" of the object or person to which they refer. Objects, according the Kabbalists, have a deep structure or underlying essence, and it is language that points to, represents, and in a sense, provides that essence. As we have seen, according to the Kabbalists, created things are fundamentally instances of concepts, and concepts are identified with the names through which they are differentiated and expressed. It is for this reason that the essence or "soul" of an object is its name.

To see why this is so we can examine the way names function in our own everyday language and life. If we know "Reuven," for example, just hearing his name tells us more, much more, than any conceivable series of descriptions about him. Names do not simply "attach" to objects or persons as if we have numbered them. Nor do names simply refer to entities in time or space. Rather they connote a wealth of meaning, a meaning that is more complete than either any observation or description of an object or person can provide. "Chaim Weizmann" is not just another way of referring to the first president of the state of Israel, or simply a label for a once living breathing man. It is the *name* of a person, and captures the very essence of a unique individual. Names match the essence of that which they name, including those aspects of that essence which are not as yet revealed, either to ourselves or to the person

---

29. Zalman, *Shaar Ha Yichud Vehaemunah*, Chapter 1; Zalman, *Likutei Amarim-Tanya*, pp. 287–289.

named. "Reuven" signifies not only all that a given man has been, but all that he will be in the future, as well.

It is because names tell us more than an observation or description of the person, thing, or event that they denote, that we can say that to know the name of a thing is to know it better than if we had the thing itself before our eyes. This is why individuals who meet or speak with us without giving us their name, remain "anonymous," essentially unrevealed and unknown. It is also why we say upon seeing an exotic plant or animal, for example, that we have no idea what it could be, until such time as we learn its name. And if we are told that its name is one with which we are familiar ("Oh, of course, it's an 'alligator'") we feel that we now understand it completely.

This is why the naming of a child is so important in Judaism. There is a tradition that, like Adam (who was given the task of naming the animals in the garden of Eden), the parents of a newborn receive *ruach hakodesh* (a holy spirit) in the moment when they name their child, and the name with which the child is provided is thought of as matching its essence or soul.

This "essentialist" view of names and language can be contrasted with an empirical or conventionalist view in which "names" are thought of simply as labels for "percepts" or tangible objects in space and time. Rather than denoting a single discrete percept, sensation, object, or fact, a name, for the Kabbalists, connotes a whole world of meaning relevant to the concept or essence to which it applies. (Indeed it is only through specialized, technical, or scientific language that we can divide the world up into percepts, discreet material entities, or simple facts.) Names in our everyday languages refer to meaning plenums or essences, what the Kabbalists speak of as "souls."

Granted that names refer to such meaning plenums or essences, we might still query as to whether the names we have for these essences in any given language are anything more than arbitrary conventions. What difference does it make whether a certain essence or concept is represented by one combination of sounds or letters or another?

To answer this question we must, in the first place, recognize that it is a question that is purely hypothetical or abstract. In actual discourse we cannot *arbitrarily* alter the names of people or objects without losing the meaning or essence of the things so named. If asked the name of a person or object we can't, in *Alice In Wonderland* fashion, respond in any manner we so choose; and as Wittgenstein has so cogently argued, we can't even do this for ourselves, i.e., create our own "private language" of arbitrary names and symbols. This is because the words of any natural language are so interconnected with one another, and with the experience and way of life of a community of native speakers, as to make an arbitrary alteration in a word's meaning, or in the name of an object or idea, a virtual impossibility. In other words, to inquire into the name of a given object, person, or idea is not simply to inquire into the sound or symbol for a given discrete thing, but is rather an inquiry into the place of that "object" in an entire language, and ipso facto in an entire perspective upon the "world." The kabbalistic view that finite created beings are, in essence, part of a greater infinite unity in God, is reflected in the observation that the meaning of a given word (referring to created things) is dependent upon an entire language. To fully comprehend an object or idea is to know an entire world. Words can be translated from one natural language into another, but the effect of this is not to arbitrarily give a "rose," for example, *any* other name, but rather to provide an alternative expression for the rose's essence by placing it in the context of another *total* perspective on the entire world.

Recall, however, that for Schneur Zalman, as for the Kabbalists, it is only the name of the object in the "holy tongue" that serves as a vessel for its "life force" or "soul." While there may be a conventional element in other languages, there can be nothing (according to the Kabbalists) arbitrary in the language of the Torah, the language of God. This is because the "total perspective" on reality afforded by the Torah, is, according to the Kabbalists, the one true spiritual or Godly point of view; and the words or names of the holy tongue are in many ways untranslatable into alternative linguistic systems. (There is, of course, nothing to prevent an adherent of Islam, Hinduism or any other faith from making a similar claim about his/her own "holy tongue.")

Take, for example, the Hebrew term *tzaddik*, which is sometimes translated into English by the terms "righteous one" or "saint." While "righteous one" misses the godliness or piety implied by *tzaddik*, the word "saint" captures these aspects but embeds them within a decidedly Christian rather than Jewish associational context. We quickly come to see that the idea of a *tzaddik* cannot be adequately expressed at all except by way of the term *tzaddik* itself; and the same for a whole host of other Hebrew terms, particularly those that have spiritual, ethical, and specifically Jewish significances. Indeed, it is the very terms that refer to spiritual matters, philosophical ideas, and human qualities that are most difficult to translate from one language to another, and in the case of Hebrew, are unique to the language of Torah. (This is incidentally, I suspect, the reason why certain Hebrew terms were directly incorporated rather than translated into Yiddish.) It is these spiritual, ethical, and human terms, as opposed to those that refer to material entities (particularly as these are understood scientifically), which the Kabbalists would say have the strongest "life-force." In other words, they are most unique to *loshen hakodesh*, the holy tongue, and most pregnant with meaning. We might say that an electron by any other name would be an electron, but a *tzaddik*, a *baal chesed* (master of kindness) or *bitochin* (trust in the Lord), owing to their wealth of associations and their wide connotation, are unique expressions of Torah ideas. They cannot be translated without losing at least part of their life-force, without losing at least part of their "soul."

We might be inclined to ask whether a *tzaddik* could be called by another name *in Hebrew*. To answer this we must repeat that with *loshen hakodesh*, the "holy tongue," its wealth of associations, its roots, links to other worlds, *Gematria*, etc., we would have to dismantle much of if not the entire linguistic system in order to make such a change. Change *tzaddik* (the virtuous, just, pious man) and one would have to change *tzadak* (to be clear, pure, sincere), *tzedek* (righteousness, justice, equity), *tzedakah* (purity, liberality, charity, almsgiving), etc. One would also have to change the function of the letter *tzadeh*, which according to the Kabbalists, denotes righteousness in all words in which it appears (for example *mitzvah*, commandment). Even the shape of the letter *tzadeh*, which is crooked or bent, is spoken of as connoting the manner in which the *tzaddik* bends or humbles himself before God, and hence the humility that is a prerequisite for true righteousness. Words are not linked to their objects one at a time (and it is the fallacy of this view that leads to the belief that they must be arbitrary conventions) but rather they are linked to their objects; or as the Kabbalists would have it, construct their objects, within the context of an entire language, way of life, and world. It is for this reason that to know an object's *name* is to know its essence, the very vessel for its soul.

GOD IS IDENTICAL WITH HIS HOLY TORAH: THE TORAH IS THE NAME OF GOD

In the Zohar we find the statement that "The Torah and the Holy One, blessed be He are entirely one."[30] Schneur Zalman explains that unlike human speech, God's speech or language is not separated from His self: "for

---

30. Zohar II, 60a; Sperling and Simon, *The Zohar*, Vol. 3, p. 188.

there is nothing outside of Him and no place devoid of Him."[31] It follows from the identity of God and His Torah that the Torah expresses God's essence; and since, according to the Kabbalah, the essence of a thing is expressed in its name, that the Torah is the *name of God*. And indeed, we find this doctrine expressed in the Zohar where it is said, "The Torah is all one holy supernal name."[32] The older contemporary of Nachmanides, Ezra ben Solomon, held that the five books of the Torah are the Name of the Holy One, blessed be He; a view that, according to Scholem, was found in the writings of several other Kabbalists in the Catalonian city of Gerona.[33]

The meaning of this seemingly obscure doctrine follows from the view that names refer to souls, essences, or *concepts*. The Torah, with all of its descriptions of events in the history of God's revelation to mankind, and its expression of that revelation in *halakha* or Jewish law, is, in a fundamental sense, a single concept, a single seamless web of spiritual meaning, one that cannot, because of its all-encompassing nature, be adequately translated or described, but only studied or lived. It is because "Torah" names this single, unified, all-encompassing concept that the Jewish tradition includes in the Torah not just the Five Books of Moses but the entire corpus of Jewish literature, law, custom, and life, to the extent that these too are considered to be a part of God's teaching or way.

The idea underlying the notion that the whole of Torah is the name of God is that a given name, word, or phrase can be composed of a number of morphemes or units of meaning (e.g., *halakha l'Moshe m'Sinai*, a law from Moses from Sinai) and yet name a single concept or idea. The Torah itself (in the wide sense described above) is, of course, composed of a virtually infinite number of morphemes, but it too names a single, albeit infinitely rich being or concept: the all-encompassing, infinite God. The Torah as the Name of God connotes the fullest plenum of value and Jewish spiritual meaning imaginable, and it is in this sense that the Zohar can say, "the entire Torah is a single holy mystical name." In a more modern idiom one might be inclined to say that one implication of the linguistic atomism described above is that an entire language is the *name* of an entire world.

---

31. Zalman, *Likutei Amarim-Tanya*, Chapter 21, p. 87. Referring to *Tikkunei Zohar*, *Tikkun*, 57, p. 91b.

32. Zohar III, 36a; Sperling and Simon, *The Zohar*, Vol. 4, p. 395: see also Zohar III, 80b (ibid., Vol. 5, p. 92).

33. Scholem, "The Meaning of the Torah in Jewish Mysticism," p. 39.

LANGUAGE IS THE VEHICLE OF MYSTICAL REVELATION AND INSIGHT

If, as the Kabbalists supposed, creation is primarily conceptual rather than material, and language is the vehicle of concepts or thoughts, it follows that language is also the vehicle through which creation can be best understood. This is a view that certainly agrees with our common intuition. A child, we feel, does not have even the most basic understanding of reality until such time as he or she begins to understand speech. Similarly, as adults we ourselves feel that we do not really know a thing until we can name it or describe it in words and thereby bring it into a connection with our own linguistic/conceptual schemes. From a psychological point of view, it is a fundamental psychoanalytic truth that a person does not know himself until he can put his affects, his *desire*, into words. Language is the vehicle through which the unconscious becomes conscious, by which the unknown becomes understood. The fact that for Judaism revelation occurs in sacred texts underscores the notion that the most fundamental truths about the world are embodied in language. For the Kabbalists, the inner world and life of the Godhead is a world of linguistic expression. In contrast to other mystical views in which language is thought only to *obscure* reality, and in which the *real* is only understood when the mind is devoid of language and thought, the main kabbalistic view is that language is both constitutive and revelatory of the essential nature of the world. The deepest mystical truths can be expressed, experienced, and understood through language, if they can be expressed or understood at all.

This view is hinted at in a passage in the Talmud[34] where it is related that four men entered *Pardes* (the heavenly garden of esoteric or mystical thought); one saw and died, the second saw and lost his reason, the third laid waste to the young plants (became a heretic). Only the fourth, Rabbi Akiba, entered and left in peace. Later, medieval tradition interpreted the "Pardes" of this story to refer to four levels of Torah interpretation; *P'shat* (or literal meaning), *Remez* (allegorical meaning), *Derasha* (talmudic and *aggadic* interpretation), and *Sod* (mystical significance). One implication of this tradition is that it conceives of the "paradise" of mystical contemplation in linguistic, hermeneutical terms.

According to the Zohar, there are hidden, esoteric levels of meaning not

---

34. Talmud, Tractate *Hagiga*, 14b.

only in the Torah, but also for every conceivable aspect of existence, including God and all creation.[35] This idea, that reality itself can be profitably understood as a decipherable and interpretable text, anticipates several significant trends in contemporary secular thought, including the later Wittgenstein's and Derrida's denials that man has access to a pre-linguisticized reality and Gadamer's assertion that "Being that can be understood is language." Less radical, but equally significant modern parallels to kabbalistic hermeneutics are present in the psychoanalytic view that dreams, symptoms, and other psychological productions are symbolic, interpretable "texts," and the Heideggerian view that the most essential truths about "Being" (about reality or existence as such) are to be found encoded in the language of the earliest philosophers.

There arose in the twentieth century a historical/philological approach to the study of texts that held that it is the job of the historian/philologist to rediscover the essential truth, for example of scriptural texts, by uncovering their original significance from behind the accrual of conventional meanings that have obscured them.[36] The Kabbalists themselves, however, held a view (consonant with talmudic tradition) that the meanings attributed to the Torah by succeeding generations of rabbinical exegetes are indeed implicit as one of the "seventy facets" of the original Torah text.[37] Rather than see succeeding interpretations as obscuring the Torah's (or reality's) original meaning or intent, they understood them as expanding upon and thus deepening its essential core. The new, on this view, is always implicit in the old.

"DIVINE NAMES": LANGUAGE AND MUSIC IN THE THEOSOPHICAL KABBALAH

Having discussed the philosophical principles that underlie the Kabbalists' linguistic mysticism we are now in a position to comprehend aspects of the Lurianic theory of "divine names," which is one of the more difficult and complex aspects of the Lurianic system. We have already touched upon this

---

35. Zohar II, 230b; Sperling and Simon, *The Zohar*, Vol. 4, p. 285; Zohar III, 159a; ibid., Vol. 5, p. 226.

36. Walter Benjamin is the clearest Jewish representative of this point of view. See Biale, *Gershom Scholem, Kabbalah and Counter-History*, p. 138.

37. Midrash, *Numbers Rabbah*, XIII, 15.

doctrine in our discussion of the *Sefirot* in Chapter Four, where we learned that, according to Luria, each of the *Sefirot* are equivalent to linguistic structures that name God.

The doctrine that "The Torah and the Holy One, blessed be He are entirely one" reflects the kabbalistic notion that like the world, God himself is structured by language. This doctrine manifests itself in the theosophical Kabbalah through a proliferation of "holy names" that are said to represent different aspects of *Ein-Sof,* as it conceals, manifests, and restores the sefirotic system. The Zohar refers to the traditional distinction between YHVH, the name of God that is not pronounced, and ADNY, the name of God that is pronounced, as referring to the undisclosed and disclosed aspects of divinity.[38]

The Lurianists equated the *Sefirot* with a whole variety of divine names, and these names take on a symbolic, dynamic significance that parallels and in some ways rivals the *Sefirot* themselves. These parallels continue the tradition, first elaborated in *Sefer Yetzirah,* that understands the universe to be simultaneously composed of sefirotic and linguistic elements.

On one rather simple level the ten *Sefirot* are said to represent the divine name, YHVH. *Keter* and *Chochmah* together form the "thorn" and body of the first letter in God's name, the *Yud* (Y). *Binah* is the second letter, *Heh* (H), the *Sefirot* from *Chesed* to *Yesod* (and particularly the *Sefirah Tiferet*) represent the third letter, *Vav* (V), and *Malchut* represents the final *Heh* (H).

These representations become extremely complex, however, as a result of *Gematria,* the system of number mysticism employed in the Jewish, and particularly the kabbalistic, tradition. *Gematria* is based upon the linguistic convention that each letter in the Hebrew alphabet has a specific numerical value, e.g., Aleph = 1, Heh = 5, Vav = 6, Yud = 10.

The Kabbalists read a great deal of significance into the fact that the letters of the four-letter name of God (Yud Heh Vav Heh) could be *spelled out* in a variety of ways. For example, the letter H (*Heh*), which appears twice in the tetragrammaton, can itself be spelled out in Hebrew as Heh-Aleph (HA), Heh-Yud (HY), or Heh-Heh (HH). As a result, different manners of spelling out the letters of the divine name yield different numerical values. Based upon these different values, the Kabbalists derived several new "names" of God; for example, Name 72, Name 63, Name 42, Name 52, and Name 45, according to the numerical equivalents of the letters that comprise them.

---

38. Zohar II, 230b; Sperling and Simon, *The Zohar,* Vol. 4, p. 285.

Let's examine a specific example (the so-called *millui-de yudin*, the filling out of the "Name" with the Hebrew letter Yud [Y]). The letters of the tetragrammatton, YHVH, are, in Hebrew, pronounced Yud, Hay, Vav, Hay. One way in which this *pronounciation* of the tetragrammaton can be spelled out *in Hebrew* is as follows: YVD, HY, VYV, HY. The letters comprising this fully-spelled-out Holy Name have the following numerical values:

YVD	Y = 10	V = 6	D = 4
HY	H = 5	Y = 10	
VYV	V = 6	Y = 10	V = 6
HY	H = 5	Y = 10	

The sum total of the numerical values of all of these letters is 10 + 6 + 4, + 5 + 10, + 6 + 10 + 6, + 5 + 10 = 72. This, according to the Kabbalists, is a mystical name of God (Name 72) that is equivalent to the *Partzuf Abba* (the Celestial Father) and the *Sefirah Chochmah* (Wisdom). Since the number 72 is generally and most efficiently expressed using the Hebrew letters *Ayin* (= 70) and Bet (= 2), the Kabbalists referred to Name 72 as *Ayin-Bet*. Since the Hebrew letter *Ayin* is (like the Hebrew letter Aleph) pronounced like the English letter "a," and the Hebrew letter Bet is prounced like the English letter "v," the Kabbalists were able to refer to Name 72 as "av," which we will spell 'aB.[39]

The Lurianists derived three more Holy Names in the manner described above, by utilizing alternate means for spelling out the pronunciation of the tetragrammaton, YHVH. For example, by simply changing the spelling of the third letter in the tetragrammaton V from VYV to VAV, the numerical value of the fully-spelled-out tetragrammaton changes from 72 to 63. This is because this one change involves the replacement of a letter (Y) that has a numerical equivalent of 10, with a letter (A) with a numerical equivalent of 1. Further changes yield values of 45 and 52. These additional three names are spoken of in the Kabbalah as SaG (63), MaH (45), and BoN (52), and are regarded as equivalents to various other aspects of the Lurianic system as was detailed in Table 4–5.

These names have important theosophical significance in the Lurianic Kabblah; some of which will be explained below and others of which will be

---

39. Our convention will be to capitalize the spelling of all letters present in the original Hebrew. The letter Ayin will be spelled 'A, to distinguish it from the letter Aleph, which will be spelled A.

discussed in the context of *Tikkun ha-Olam* (the Restoration of the World) in Chapter 9. Here it will suffice to point out that the various names have equivalencies among the *Sefirot* and the worlds; e.g., Name 72 corresponds to the world of *Atzilut*, Name 63 to *Beriah*, and Name 42 to *Yetzirah*.

The Lurianists also held that each of these four divine names are equivalent to various notations utilized in writing a Torah scroll.[40] They represent the *Ta'amim*, the musical notation that indicates pitch in the recitation of the Torah; the *Nekudot*, the vowel sounds and corresponding notation; the *Tagin*, the ornamental strokes above certain letters; and the *Otiot*, the actual letters themselves.[41] Further, each one of these comprises all the other four[42] so that the *Ta'amim* are themselves comprised of the *Nekudot*, *Tagin*, and *Otiot*, etc.

According to Lurianists the Name 72 ('aB) (and the *Ta'amim*, the musical notations that comprise it) is so recondite that it cannot even be spoken of. This name is held to be concealed in the "cranium" of Primordial Man. It is interesting to note, however, that the highest expression of the deity is here conceptualized as a series of musical notes, suggesting that the first step of creation, in which the Primal Nothing (*Ayin*) takes scrutable form, is akin to a musical composition. One is here reminded of Newton's "Music of the Spheres." God is frequently depicted in abstract, pictorial, and especially, linguistic terms; but in spite of the fact that many would hold that music provides us with what is perhaps the most intimate and expressive experience of the divine, God is rarely thought of as *musical* in his very essence. In the Jewish tradition, music is integrally tied to prayer and the experience of the divine. The Torah itself, which the Kabbalists regarded as identical to God and a blueprint for creation, is *musical as well as linguistic* in its essence. The musical notes that comprise the Cranium of *Adam Kadmon* cannot be spoken of, but perhaps they can be heard. This would suggest that instead of formulating our "ultimate" questions in proposi-

---

40 Luzzatto, *General Principles of the Kabbalah*, p. 55.

41. The role of letters, vowel points, and musical notation in creation is already present in the Zohar, which informs that with the advent of creation there is "movement given by the accents and notes to the letters and vowel-points which pay obeisance to them and march after them like troops behind their kings. The letters being the body and the vowel-points the animating spirit, together they keep step with the notes and come to a halt with them." Zohar 1, 15b; Sperling and Simon, *The Zohar*, Vol. 1, p. 65.

42. Ibid., p. 57.

tional, linguistic terms, we might formulate them musically, and understand the history of music, along with the history of pictorial art and philosophy, as aspects of mankind's collective "answer."

THE INFINITE PLURALITY OF MEANINGS

A great deal has been made in the contemporary literature on the Kabbalah of the Kabbalists' belief in the infinite interpretability of scripture. Scholem, for example, speaks of the kabbalistic belief in the "unlimited mystical plasticity of the divine word," quoting from the Kabbalist Azulai to the effect that each time a man reads a given verse of Torah the combination of its linguistic elements change in response to the call of the moment, resulting in the creation of new Torah meanings.[43] More recently, Moshe Idel has shown that the exegetical methods of Abraham Abulafia involved the meditation upon rearranged letters of the Torah text and a form of free association to these letters, suggesting an interpretive latitude among the Kabbalists that is unheard of among traditional Torah scholars and exegetes.[44] Indeed, many Kabbalists, while not quite as extreme in their methods as Abulafia, held views suggestive of a radical deconstruction of the biblical text and its traditional meaning.

The kabbalistic emphasis on the near-infinite interpretability of both the world and scripture took an almost ecumenical turn in their adoption of the midrashic notion that every passage, phrase, and even letter of the Torah has seventy aspects or faces, corresponding to the seventy nations that were traditionally thought to inhabit the world.[45] In the Zohar, this number (70) stands for the inexhaustibility of divine meaning.

The Safedian Kabbalists held that there are 600,000 aspects of meaning to the Torah, corresponding to the number of Israelites present at the revelation at Sinai, and hence to the number of "primordial souls" present in each succeeding generation.[46] As we have seen, some Kabbalists even held that the Torah itself was originally given as an incoherent scramble of letters

---

43. Scholem, "On the Kabbalah and Its Symbolism," p. 76.

44. Moshe Idel, *Language, Torah and Hermeneutics in Abraham Abulafia.*

45. Midrash, Numbers Rabbah xiii,15; see Scholem "The Meaning of the Torah," p. 62.

46. Scholem, "On the Kabbalah," p. 65. Referring to *Sefer ha-kavvanoth* (Venice, 1620), p. 536.

and that these letters rearranged themselves in response to historical events. The Kabbalist Israel Sarug held that the Torah manifests itself in different ways in different levels of spiritual and material existence. At the highest level (the world of *Atziluth*) it exists as all possible combinations of Hebrew letters, thus adumbrating the set of all possible conceptual/linguistic worlds.[47] Similar views of the Torah's plasticity are attributed to the founder of the Hasidic movement, Israel Baal Shem Tov.[48]

If the meaning of the Torah is as subjective and plastic as these kabbalistic views seem to imply, the question arises as to whether scriptural exegesis is not an arbitrary function of the views of the interpreter. Are we not, as Biale implies, simply discovering our own thoughts in the words (or letters) of the text before us.[49] Is there anything of a *revealed* nature in scripture at all? Contemporary secular scholarship (Scholem, Idel, Biale) comes perilously close to asserting that the Kabbalists themselves, if they were consistent with their own belief and methods, would have to answer this last question in the negative. Indeed, this is certainly the position adopted by those contemporary philosophers, such as Davidson and Rorty, who argue that symbolic and metaphoric discourse simply serves as a stimulus to the interpreters' ideas and beliefs but has no cognitive content in and of itself.[50]

Can the view that Torah has an infinite plurality of "changeable" meanings be reconciled with the traditional belief in its absolute immutability? Is an indefinite series of subjective interpretations compatible with a text's having a definite objective sense? The tradition, of course, answered each of these questions in the affirmative, conceptualizing the Jewish hermeneutic method as one that creates a dialectical balance between the subjective and objective, between the Torah's interpretability and its immutability. It is a balance that, according to the tradition, was achieved, in part, through the permitting of wide latitude in one's freedom of thought, *while fostering a restriction in one's freedom of action and behavior.*

An obvious but sometimes overlooked fact is that the Kabbalists themselves, even those who believed in the infinite plasticity and interpretability of the Torah text, regarded the *halakhot* (Jewish laws) that the rabbinic tradition had derived from the Torah as completely binding on all Jews

---

47. Ibid., p. 75.
48. Ibid., p. 76.
49. Biale, *Gershom Scholem, Kabbalah and Counter-History*, p. 144.
50. See Richard Rorty, "Unfamiliar Noises: Hesse and Davidson on Metaphors."

regardless of their level of exegetical understanding. Even so radical a deconstructionist of the Torah text as Abulafia held that the commandments were completely binding upon and necessary for the mystic (even though they may not be specifically relevant in the moment that he achieves mystical union with the creator).[51] The Torah text may be open to 600,000 different subjective interpretations, but from the point of view of Jewish practice this same text is clear, immutable, and one.

The Torah's immutability is guaranteed by *practice* rather than exegesis, a view that, interestingly, is quite similar to certain concepts in contemporary philosophy of language. Wittgenstein, for example, in considering the infinite interpretability of virtually *any* linguistic symbol or sign, argued that there indeed must be some signs that, although they could be, *are not* further interpreted. Without the existence of some signs that we *could* interpret differently *but don't* there could, according to Wittgenstein, be no communicable significance at all. The ultimate support of meaning in language is to be found in *action*, or as Wittgenstein puts it, in the "form of life" of a community of language users. The orthodox Jewish community, as I have argued elsewhere, constitutes such a form of life,[52] one that sustains the significance of its basic "language" through its highly specific code of behavior embodied in the *halakha*.

It is thus the case that in an observant Jewish context the multiplicity of interpretations that can and have been placed upon the Torah text do not alter that text but rather, on the Kabbalists' own view, deepen our understanding of the text's very essence. Any interpretation that violates this essence, i.e., that calls upon one to violate the *halakha*, would be regarded as antinomian, and be excluded. The fact that Torah has infinite layers of meaning does not entail that it can be subject to any interpretation whatsoever. The Jewish form of life, embodied in Jewish law, creates a limit on the possibilities of interpretation. Those Kabbalists, for example, who were wont to interpret Torah through a recombination of its letters, for example, must, according to tradition, be completely versed in the revealed aspects of Torah to assure that their mystical exegesis does not violate the Torah's halakhic core.

That the essence of the Torah is to be found in the *mitzvot*, in Jewish law, is a fundamental assumption of the rabbinic tradition. The study of

---

51. Idel, *Language, Truth and Hermeneutics*, p. xiii.
52. Sanford Drob, "Judaism as a Form of Life."

Torah was considered to be equivalent to all the *mitzvot* (commandments)[53] because such study leads to their performance. Indeed Torah and *mitzvot* are the two complementary poles within which the whole of Judaism can be circumscribed. Each is essential for the fulfillment of the other. Thus while the rabbis can assert the superiority of Torah knowledge over the other *mitzvot*[54] they can equally affirm a principle that declared "not study, but practice is the main thing" in Jewish life.[55]

In the Kabbalah, as we have seen, we find the view that God's revelation is achieved via the language of Torah: it is only through Torah that God can be understood, and God is, in a sense, equiprimordial with his expression in the hermeneutic Torah tradition. Yet this hermeneutic tradition, as varied and multifaceted as it is, is (or at least *was*) nevertheless anchored and constrained by the *halakha*, the system of Jewish law. The validity, and hence the value (mystical or otherwise) of any Torah interpretation is, on this view, totally dependent on its being broadly in accord with such law. It is this interdependence of *halakha* and hermeneutics that leads Schneur Zalman to express the essence of the Torah's linguistic mysticism as follows:

> When a person [through the study of Torah] knows and comprehends with his intellect . . . in accordance with the law as it is set out in the *Mishnah*, *Gemara* or *Posekim* [codes], he has thus comprehended, grasped and encompassed with his intellect the will and wisdom of the Holy One, blessed be He, Whom no thought can grasp . . . except when they are clothed . . . in the laws that have been set out for us . . .
>
> This is a wonderful union, like which there is no other, and which has no parallel anywhere in the material world, whereby complete oneness and unity, from every side and angle, can be attained.[56]

A CRISIS IN CONTEMPORARY INTERPRETATION

If the boundaries of significance of any given linguistic sign, symbol, or metaphor are guaranteed, as we have just described, by practice rather than

---

53. Mishnah, Tractate *Peah*, 1:1.
54. Talmud, Tractate *Shabbat*, 127a.
55. Mishnah, Tractate *Avot* 1:17.
56. Zalman, *Likutei Amarim-Tanya*, Chapter 5, p. 19.

thought, what is the result if that practice breaks down, as the practice of the Jewish form of life has (for so many) broken down in the contemporary world? I believe it is no accident that the hermeneutical movement known as deconstructionism, with its assault on the objectivity of linguistic meaning, has arisen only with the massive breakdown of traditional values that has occurred in the twentieth century. When speakers of a given language are no longer held together by a given practice or tradition (as was true, for example, for most speakers of Hebrew and Yiddish prior to the century), they are left without an ultimate foundation for the interpretations of each other's discourse. In a world where one can do anything, one can also mean anything with one's words.

Language, for deconstructionism, is ungrounded. There is no prelinguistic reality that gives meaning to words; rather, language is an infinite play of signification that has nothing to answer to other than itself. For deconstructionists like Jacques Derrida[57] language achieves significance only by virtue of the system of differences between linguistic signs. An "apple" is what it is only by virtue of it being different from "pool," a "pear," and a "ppela" (which is presumably nonsense). In effect, deconstructionism subscribes to what we have spoken of as linguistic atomism, with the proviso that the system of differences that the linguistic atoms comprise is completely autonomous. No God, no thing-in-itself, no law, no set of behaviors guarantees or prescribes what anything whatsoever means. A further implication of the deconstructionist view of language is that all things, concepts, and ideas have what they are *not* written into their very essences, for what anything *is*, is *essentially* defined (in the system of differences) by what it is *not*. For the deconstructionist, a given symbol or phrase is indeed open to an infinite series of interpretations precisely because that phrase can be placed (and understood) in a virtually limitless series of contexts, none of which has any more legitimacy than any other!

The Kabbalah, can actually be said to have anticipated these very ideas both in its concept of the infinite interpretability of the Torah, and especially, in the symbol of the Breaking of the Vessels, a symbol that embodies the notion that both the world and our conception of it (which for the Kabbalah are one and the same) are essentially broken, flawed, and incomplete. The idea behind the Breaking of the Vessels is that no conception, of God, law, science, etc., is capable of holding the infinite plenum of meaning. All

_____

57. See Derrida, *Margins of Philosophy.*

concepts, practices, and languages ultimately break down in the face of the *Or Ein-Sof*, "the light of the Infinite God." According to the Kabbalah, this breakdown is written into the very essence of the cosmos, and is to be found repeatedly in nature, history, in the world, in man, and in language itself. I will have occasion to explore this doctrine further in Chapter Seven. Here however, it is important to note that through the concept of the *Shevirah* the Kabbalah can be said to perform a radical deconstruction upon all of the concepts that it treats, and that when turned in upon itself, can be said to anticipate the very deconstruction of normative Judaism that we are witness to in our own time.

From the point of view of language, the Lurianic Kabbalah would understand the *Shevirah* (and ipso facto, contemporary deconstructionism) as one critical moment in the evolution from a divine essentialism (embodied in the original *Sefirot*) to a human-based ethic, in which language, instead of referring to essences that exist *sub species aeternae*, becomes the responsibility of man. For the Kabbalah, the deconstruction of traditional categories, whether they be those of traditional Western philosophy or of normative Judaism, is not an end into itself, but rather a call for a new order, to be reconstituted through the language and action of man. As we shall see, this reconstructed humanistic order is precisely what, on the Kabbalists' view, is the highest expression of God. God's language, the very language that according to Schneur Zalman sustains the world, is in reciprocal relation with the language of mankind. It devolves upon man to reconstruct (and in effect redefine on a higher level) the divine speech through which the world was created and is sustained.[58]

---

58. How this can be achieved in the context of the contemporary, deconstructed Judaism is a question that lies beyond the scope of this present work. However, the problem and an outline of a proposed solution, was framed (in a completely different conceptual context than our own) by Mordecai Kaplan in the late 1920s, 1930s and 1940s. The movement he founded, Reconstructionism, seeks in effect to reconstruct a Judaism relevant to contemporary man through a humanistic encounter with the fragments of what Kaplan regarded to be the broken Jewish tradition. See Mordecai Kaplan, *Judaism as a Civilization* (New York: Macmillan, 1934).

6

Olamot: The Worlds of the Kabbalah

The notion of "higher worlds," in the sense of the abode of "The Lord and His hosts" is implicit throughout biblical and postbiblical literature. Jacob's dream of angels ascending and descending a heavenly ladder is but one early reference to an earthly portal into a higher realm (Genesis 28:12). However, a systematic treatment of the upper worlds is not found until much later times. The Zohar alludes to "three different worlds"[1] and *Tikkunei* Zohar speaks of the emanation of God's ten *Sefirot* into the realms of *Atzilut, Beriah, Yetzirah*, and *Assiyah* without explicitly calling the latter "worlds."[2] Later Kabbalists spoke of the three worlds of *Beriah* (Creation), *Yetzirah* (Formation), and *Assiyah* (Making), the names of which were derived from the phrase in Isaiah 43: 7: "Everything called by my name—for I have *created* it, have *formed* it, yea I have *made* it." The full doctrine of the four worlds, while implicit in the Zohar, is, according to Scholem, not found until the writings of Isaac of Acre and the anonymous *Massekhet Atzilut*, where four worlds are spoken of as corresponding to each of the four letters of the tetragrammaton, God's name.[3] To the three worlds

---

1. Zohar I, 62a, Sperling and Simon, *The Zohar*, Vol. 1, p. 203.
2. *Tikkunei* Zohar I, 22b, *Tikkun* 6, as cited in Gershom Scholem, "The Four Worlds," *Encyclopedia Judaica*, Vol. 16, p. 641.
3. Scholem, "Four Worlds," p. 642.

of traditional medieval philosophy, the worlds of angels, the heavens, and nature, these Kabbalists added a fourth world, *Atzilut* (Emanation) corresponding to the source of divine light in the Godhead. Later Kabbalists took the doctrine of the Four Worlds for granted; some added a fifth, the world of *Adam Kadmon* (Primordial Man) as a supernal realm most closely identified with the Infinite God, *Ein-Sof*. Others, including Luria and Vital, spoke of a nearly infinite number of worlds interspersed between our world and *Ein-Sof*.

THE BASIC DOCTRINE

A full comprehension of the mature kabbalistic doctrine of higher worlds requires an understanding of related kabbalistic concepts, particularly the doctrines of *Tzimtzum* and the *Sefirot*. As I have discussed these concepts extensively in previous chapters,[4] I will here provide only a brief review of these notions as they apply to the creation of the Four Worlds.

Creation, according to a view that is found in its most mature form in the Lurianic Kabbalah, involves an act of self-limitation on the part of an infinite God. As we have seen without this self-limitation, or *Tzimtzum*, God would be completely coextensive with all "being" and there would be neither conceptual nor metaphysical "space" for anything to be distinguished or exist apart from him. God must therefore *conceal* or *contract* his being in order to provide for the existence of independent finite entities, much as an extremely bright light must be dimmed in order for there to be differences in color, shading, and visual texture in the surrounding space.

The creation of the worlds, therefore, initially involves a contraction as opposed to an emanation, a concealment rather than a revelation, a subtraction as opposed to an addition. God, who contains the fully realized potential of all being and value within Himself, must limit himself in order to create entities whose potential is only incompletely realized. It is only after the divine contraction, and the consequent existence of a region of being that is relatively devoid of God's presence, that the positive "emanative" aspect of creation can begin. The doctrine of the *Sefirot* and "worlds" provides expression to this view of creation as a dialectic between divine contraction and emanation.

The *Sefirot*, which are ten in number, represent a progressive conceal-

---

4. *Tzimtzum* is discussed in Chapter 3; the *Sefirot* in Chapter 4.

ment or contraction of the infinite God. Using the metaphor of God's infinite light (or *Ein-Sof*) the Kabbalists likened the *Sefirot* to light that has been progressively dimmed as a result of passing through a series of colored glass filters. At other times they compared the *Sefirot* to vessels (*Kelim*) that serve as containers for the limited divine light that emanates into the void after God's *Tzimtzum* or contraction. All agreed that the *Sefirot* do not exist in any absolute sense but have only a relative existence from the point of view of finite beings i.e., man. Just as the light of the sun may appear to be distinct from the sun's orb but is in reality simply the sun as it appears on earth, the *Sefirot* appear to be distinct from God but are in reality completely bound up within him, "like a flame bound up in the coal."[5]

The *Sefirot* represent the instantiation and fulfillment of God's essential attributes. They are the archetypes through which God manifests and hence "make real" his traits of wisdom, understanding, knowledge, love, power, and compassion, to name (according to one kabbalistic scheme) the first six of the *Sefirot*. These attributes, or divine *middot*, exist only in potential in *Ein-Sof*. They become actualized (while at the same time remaining completely "within" God) with the emanation of the *Sefirot*, which embody them.

The *Sefirot* are said to completely interpenetrate one another, so that each one is made up of proportionate degrees of each of the others.[6] In addition, they are thought of as being the architectural elements, even the "molecules," of all creation, and, in particular, are said to be the constituent parts or aspects of the soul of man.[7]

The *Sefirot* are also thought of as providing the structural elements for each of the Kabbalist's "Worlds," which comprise a second stage in God's creative process.[8] In this second stage the *Sefirot* are organized into a series of four (and in some schemes five) basic "Worlds" (*Olamot*), which are thought of as being progressively distinct from God's primordial essence or light. Each of these worlds serves to conceal aspects of the divine presence. The very term *Olam* (world), being etymologically related to (and occasionally even spelled the same as) the word *alam* (meaning "hidden"), gives expression to the kabbalistic doctrine, first intimated in *Sefer ha-Bahir*, that

---

5. Zohar III, 70a; Sperling and Simon, *The Zohar*, Vol. 5, p. 66.
6. Adin Steinsaltz, "Worlds, Angels and Men," in his *The Strife of the Spirit* (Northvale, NJ: Jason Aronson, 1988).
7. Scholem, *Kabbalah*, pp. 115, 153.
8. Idel, *Kabbalah: New Perspectives*, p. 146.

the "Worlds" are like divine garments in which God clothes and hides Himself.[9] It is through the multiplication of such garments or screens that God ultimately creates the material world within which we live. Our physical world is the one most hidden from God's light. It receives only a fraction of the divine revelation, accounting for the prophet's reference to God as "the Most Hidden of All Hidden" (Isaiah 45:12). It is, as we have already seen, part of the logic of creation that God should remain essentially hidden from man.

The four worlds are distinguished from one another via their relative proximity to their source, but also via the relative "admixture" of the *Sefirot* contained within them. While each of the *Sefirot* are considered operative in each of the worlds, each world is dominated by a particular *Sefirah*, with *Atzilut* (Emanation), the highest of the four worlds being dominated by the *Sefirah Chochmah* (Wisdom); and *Assiyah* (Action or Making), the lowest of worlds, dominated by the lowest *Sefirah*, *Malchut* (Kingship).[10] In those schemes that regard *Adam Kadmon* as the highest world, this world is said to be dominated by the *Sefirah Keter*.

Worlds, like the *Sefirot* of which they are comprised, are regarded as metaphorical ideas that have reality relative to man, but no reality relative to God Himself. Numerous analogies were offered by the Kabbalists as vehicles to understand them. According to one such analogy the four worlds are likened to stages in the building of a house, i.e., (1) the initial desire, (2) the mental idea, (3) a detailed architectural design, and (4) the final construction.[11] This analogy embodies the idea that the upper worlds are undifferentiated and conceptual. It is only in the lowest worlds that we begin to see creation in a differentiated, material form.

DETAILS OF THE FOUR WORLDS DOCTRINE: HIGHER WORLDS, MYRIAD OF WORLDS

While the earlier Kabbalists most often speak of four worlds—*Atzilut*, *Beriah*, *Yetzirah*, and *Assiyah*—later Kabbalists, particularly the followers of

---

9. See *Sefer ha-Bahir*, sec. 8. *Book Bahir*, Neugroschel trans., p. 52. Cf. Schochet, "Mystical Concepts," p. 865, note 10.

10. See Zalman, *Tanya*, Chapter 39; *Likutei Amarim-Tanya*, pp. 188–189.

11. Nissan Mindel, *The Philosophy of Chabad*, Vol. II (Brooklyn, NY: Kehot, 1973), p. 82.

Isaac Luria made reference to many others. For example, in his *Sefer Etz Chayyim*, Chayyim Vital warns us against thinking that the *Sefirot* of *Atzilut* are higher than all the other emanations. He informs us that, in fact, many worlds came before *Atzilut*, but they are not mentioned in the Zohar because they are secret and hidden. Above *Atzilut*, in a realm so ethereal as to be almost completely identified with *Ein-Sof* itself, is the World of *Adam Kadmon*, abbreviated as *A'K*. However, not only this world but many others as well exist in a nearly infinite series between *Atzilut* and the World of *Adam Kadmon*. According to Vital, even the *Gaonim* (ninth- and tenth-century rabbinic sages) recognized the existence of ten proto-*Sefirot*, the so-called "ten glimmering things" or *Tzaatzahot* that transcend *Keter Elyon*. There is no end to the number of worlds that are emanated into the void. According to Vital:

> It is clear and obvious that many different kinds of worlds were emanated, created, formed, and made—thousands upon thousands and myriads upon myriads. Every single one of them is inside the empty space [the primordial void] that was described above, and nothing is outside of it. Every world has its own individual ten *Sefirot*, and every *Sefirah* that is within each world is also made up of ten individual *Sefirot*. All of them are in the form of concentric circles, with no end to their number. They are like the layers of an onion, with rings inside each other, the way circles are illustrated in geometry books.[12]

According to Vital, all of the worlds spread out from a single *prat*, detail or point. This point is none other than *the* Primordial Man, who is "the first of all firsts."

As we have seen in Chapter Four, an important distinction is made by the Lurianic Kabbalists between the so-called "World of Points" and the "World of Restoration (*Tikkun*)." According to Vital, the "World of Points" is one of the myriad worlds that exists in the space between the worlds of *Adam Kadmon* and *Atzilut*. The *Sefirot* in this world are completely independent and disunified and were thus subject to being shattered during the cosmic catastrophe known as the Breaking of the Vessels. It is only subsequent to the Breaking of the Vessels that these shattered *Sefirot* of the original World of Points are restored, united with one another, and thereby strengthened to form the World of Restoration.

---

12. *Sefer Etz Chayyim* 1: 1, p. 23; Menzi and Padeh, *The Tree of Life*, p. 19.

Vital tells us that it is only after the Breaking of the Vessels and the subsequent reconstruction of the sefirotic fragments from the World of Points that the four worlds of *Atzilut, Beriah, Yetzirah,* and *Assiyah* and the six *Partzufim* or divine personalities are fully formed and created. These *Partzufim,* which roughly correspond to the various *Sefirot* and worlds, are the Ancient of Days (*Attik Yomim*), the Long-Enduring One (*Arich Anpin*), the Father (Av), the Mother (*Em*), The Impulsive One (*Zeir Anpin*), and the Maiden (*Nekevah*).

WORLDS FROM *ADAM KADMON* TO *ASSIYAH*

The kabbalistic doctrines of the *Sefirot* and worlds were, as we have seen, invoked to explain how a perfect, unified, spiritual "One" came to differentiate itself into an imperfect, infinitely multiple, material universe. The Kabbalists had difficulty comprehending the initial act (*dilug,* leap) that set in motion the differentiation process within God Himself. As such, they were wont to posit higher and higher worlds closer to the initial creative act of *Tzimtzum.* The world of *Adam Kadmon* or A'K (Primordial Man) was posited at the apex of all the others. The Kabbalists derived the characteristics of this world from the biblical notion that Adam, the first man, was created *betzaltzel,* in God's "image." Based upon this, the Kabbalists declared that the first being to emerge after the original *Tzimtzum* was a very abstract and ethereal representation of the divine *middot* or traits that ultimately came to be reflected in man. As we have seen they termed this "reflection" Primordial Man and held that it was so closely bound up with the *Or Ein-Sof* (the Light of the Infinite God) as to be almost indistinguishable from God Himself. The Primordial Man is deemed to be equivalent to the world bearing its name. Its dominant *Sefirah* (*Keter,* crown) is, as we have seen, variously spoken of as *Ayin,*[13] nothingness, or the primordial "will of all wills,"[14] and just as *Keter* is eliminated from many kabbalistic schemes because it is too sublime and too close to the *Ayin* (nothingness) of the infinite God *Ein-Sof, Adam Kadmon* is frequently elevated above and hence eliminated from discussions regarding the other four worlds.

---

13. Zohar, 239a. Tishby and Lachower, *The Wisdom of the Zohar,* Vol. 1, p. 257, cf. p. 280.

14. Zohar III, 129a, 288b. Cf. Tishby and Lachower, *The Wisdom of the Zohar,* Vol. 1, p. 243.

Atzilut, the world of emanation, is thus also frequently spoken of as the highest of the four worlds, the one most closely identified with the Infinite God, *Ein-Sof*. The term *Atzilut* is derived from a biblical Hebrew term (see Numbers 11:17, Ecclesiastes 2:10) that has the connotation of being "near," "by the side of," or "with," suggesting this world's proximity to God. It is in *Atzilut* that the *Sefirot*, which are perfectly unified and commingled within the Godhead, begin to take on more distinct form.[15] *Chochmah* (Wisdom) is the dominant *Sefirah* in this world, suggesting that *Atzilut* is a world of pure thought or conception. *Atzilut* is variously spoken of as a "garment of light to the source of all Being"[16] or as a realm in which "the king, his real self and his life" are one,[17] i.e., a realm in which God's transcendence and immanence have yet to become distinguished.

Below *Atzilut* lies the world of *Beriah* (creation). In *Beriah* we find the first appearance of distinct, finite creatures, though in this world they retain a purely spiritual form. In *Beriah* the *Sefirot* are garbed[18] and hence begin to be limited in their radiance. While the souls of the righteous and the *molochim* (angels) are said to appear in this world, *Beriah* is nonetheless still closely identified with God Himself and is spoken of as "the throne of God and the seven surrounding palaces."[19] It is, according to one tradition, the world that pertains to the study of the "divine chariot," *maaseh merkaveh* (others place this study in the next lower world—*Yetzirah*) and was accessible to Ezekiel as well as to the other prophets. Steinsaltz refers to *Beriah* as the "matrix through which passes all the divine plenty that descends to the lower worlds."[20] *Beriah*, which is dominated by the *Sefirah Binah* (intelligence), is the first realm of creation in which the effects of the *Tzimtzum* become noticeable and, at least relatively speaking, real.

The world of *Yetzirah* (Formation) is dominated both by what the Kabbalist Azriel referred to as the three "Psychical" *Sefirot* (*Chesed, Gevurah, Tiferet*: Kindness, Strength, Beauty) and the three "natural" *Sefirot* (*Netzach,*

---

15. Cordovero, *Or Ne'erav* VI: 4, 42b; Robinson, *Moses Cordovero's Introduction to Kabbalah*, p. 138.

16. Scholem, "Four Worlds," p. 642.

17. Ibid.

18. Cordovero, *Or Ne'erav* VI: 4, 42b; Robinson, *Moses Cordovero's Introduction to Kabbalah*, p. 138.

19. Scholem, "Four Worlds," p. 642.

20. Steinsaltz, "Worlds, Angels and Man," p. 47.

Hod, Yesod: Endurance, Majesty, Foundation),[21] suggesting that the *middot* or divine traits that these *Sefirot* represent and that serve as the archetypes or basic categories of the "sublunar" realm, first take independent form in this world. *Yetzirah* can thus be regarded as an architectural plan for our world, and might be thought of as akin to the realm of Platonic "forms." *Yetzirah* is, by some accounts, dominated by the Angel Metatron and his ten ranks of *molochim* (angels).[22] It is, on some views, the realm of the *merkaveh* (chariot) seen in Ezekiel's vision; as well as the world referred to in Jewish liturgy, in the *kedusha* (sanctification) of the angels recited daily in the introductory *berahkot* (blessings) to the *Shema*, a declaration in which a Jew affirms the absolute oneness and unity of God. *Yetzirah* is a world of both intellect and emotion, and is the repository of those spiritual entities (lower angels) that man creates through the *kavannot* (intentions of mind and heart), which accompany the performance of the divine commandments (*mitzvot*).

The world *Assiyah* (action, making, enactment) is, by most accounts, the world of physical, corporeal being.[23] It is dominated by the *Sefirah Malchut* (Kingship), clearly suggesting that it is the world (our world) over which God reigns as king. It is also the world that sees within itself the origin of time. Some Kabbalists divide the world of *Assiyah* into two realms, the spiritual and the material *Assiyah*; the former being the realm of consciousness, the latter being the realm of physical and biological nature, with man existing in between. *Assiyah* is also the world of the Husks (*Kelippot*), the realm of evil.[24] According to Luria and his followers, *Assiyah* was originally a completely spiritual world[25] until such time that the *Shevirah* or "Breaking of the Vessels" caused the *Sefirot* from *Chesed* to *Malchut* to shatter and give rise to shards (*Kelippot*), which ultimately produced matter and evil, alienated from the light of the Infinite God. *Assiyah* became enmeshed in these shards, accounting for the "mixed" nature of our world, a world of spirit and matter, of good and evil.

Assiyah, the lowest of the worlds is, of course, considered the furthest from God, and the most removed from ultimate truth. Happenings in the higher worlds, particularly *Beriah* and above, are essentially hidden from

---

21. Scholem, *Kabbalah*, p. 107.
22. Scholem, "Four Worlds," p. 642. Cf. Cordovero, *Or Ne'erav* VI: 4, 42b; Robinson, *Moses Cordovero's Introduction to Kabbalah*, p. 138.
23. Cordovero, *Or Ne'erav* VI: 4, 42b; ibid., p. 138.
24. Steinsaltz, "Worlds, Angels and Man," p. 43.
25. Scholem, "Four Worlds," p. 642.

man's view; and to use the Platonic analogy, are like mere shadows in the cave of human experience. Yet even *Assiyah* is completely sustained by divine activity. According to Vital, *Assiyah,* "the globe that we are standing on, is the very center point of all the worlds, like the pit of a date." This pit, while coarse and inedible, is surrounded by "food" on all sides. Vital here makes reference to the view that *Ein-Sof* surrounds the void left by its contraction and radiates its light from the outside in, in such a manner that the center of the void contains the world that is most distant from God.[26]

THE WORLDS ARE REVEALED TO MAN

According to Vital it is a necessary part of the development of God and the cosmos that the world within which mankind dwells should include elements from each of the upper worlds. Vital informs us that the Four Worlds or levels of existence are brought together in man himself, specifically in the people of Israel, who were chosen by God to be of particular assistance in *Tikkun ha-Olam.* Elements of the upper worlds were in fact communicated to Adam when he ate from the *Etz Ha Daas,* the tree of knowledge. Adam's transgression was, according to the Lurianists, responsible for the Breaking of the Vessels, and the subsequent condition in which divine sparks, *netzotzim,* from each of the four worlds have descended into our world and have become entrapped both in the world and in men's souls. It is man's divinely appointed task to perform a *birur* (extraction) of these sparks leading to the restoration (*Tikkun*) of our own world.

"OTHERWORLDLY GEOGRAPHY"[27]

While the Kabbalists differed with respect to their description of the specific nature of each of the four worlds (e.g., whether prophecy reaches into *Atziluth* and *Beriah* or only *Yetzirah:* whether *Assiyah* is to be identified with our material universe; whether there are not actually five worlds, etc.), a consistent pattern emerges regarding the inner logic of the higher worlds in general, a logic that we might refer to as their "geography."

---

26. However, as we have seen in our discussion of the *Sefirot,* from another perspective our world is the most external, the most removed from God, like the external skin of an onion, separated from the divine core by many layers, many worlds.

27. I borrow this phrase from Findlay (*Transcendence of the Cave,* p. 118).

The geography of the higher worlds follows logically from the nature of *Tzimtzum* (divine contraction or concealment) in both its metaphysical and epistemological aspects. As we have already seen, God is originally completely coextensive with the totality of being and nonbeing. He contains within himself, in a perfectly integrated manner, all possible concepts and values. He is, as David Birnbaum has argued, "potentiality as such."[28] The *Tzimtzum*, by (metaphysically) contracting God's being, and (epistemologically) concealing the full nature and breadth of his absolute unity, leads to the (apparent) existence of finite values and ideas, and ultimately to the existence of individual souls and material objects. The progressive contraction and concealment of divine light creates a "descent" from those highest worlds, closest to the divine light, to our world within which that light is almost completely obscured. This descent, as we have seen in Chapter Four, moves from those higher realms that are conceptual and universal to those lower ones that are material and particular.

That this descent provides a progressive diminution of "living," divine light and a progressive increase in dark, "dead" matter provides a rationale for the Kabbalists' view that the higher worlds are undifferentiated and nonmaterial and the lower ones are highly differentiated but paradoxically less "real." It also helps us understand a series of other propositions with respect to the worlds' logic or geography. These propositions, as Adin Steinsaltz has elaborated, are (1) that the four worlds interpenetrate and interact with one another, (2) that each is a replication or transformation of the world immediately above it, (3) that all of the worlds are "projected" into the world of everyday experience, (4) that each of the worlds participates in the dimensions of existence referred to as "world," "year," and "soul" (but that these dimensions are highly attenuated in the highest realms),[29] and (5) that consciousness of the individual self increases with the concealment of and distance from God.[30] I will explore each of the propositions briefly in some detail.

That each of the higher worlds *interpenetrate and interact* with one another follows logically from the idea that the lower worlds are a concealment or differentiation of the higher realms. The truth, for example, of any "reality" in *Yetzirah* is completely dependent upon its being penetrated by

---

28. David Birnbaum, *God and Evil*, p. 54ff.
29. Steinsaltz, "Worlds, Angels and Man," p. 41.
30. Ibid., p. 49.

the truth or reality of *Beriah*. For example, the "goodness" of *Chesed* (Kindness or Love), which is one of the dominant *Sefirot* in *Yetzirah*, is "good" only by virtue of its participation in the higher, more unified "Good" represented in *Beriah*; and ultimately in the absolute Good, which is approached as we proceed up the ladder of Being to *Atzilut, Adam Kadmon*, and ultimately to the infinite God, *Ein-Sof* itself. This is the kabbalistic way of saying that love is good because, and only because, it participates in or reflects the absolute goodness of the love in God.

Put another way the divine light received by any given world is a dimmer, obscured (and in many ways prismatic) representation of the light transmitted to it from the world just above it, just as the "red," "indigo," and "violet" of the spectrum that emerges on the near side of the prism is completely dependent upon the "white" light that enters into the prism from the far side. This is the kind of idea that the Kabbalists are attempting to express when they say that each world receives its life-force or essence from the world above it. Without the higher worlds the lower worlds could have no existence at all.

Our prism analogy enables us to understand how it is possible for there to be an interpenetration of the worlds from the "bottom up" as well as from the "top down." For the lower worlds are a differentiation (or component parts) of the reality that is unified in the higher realms. Indeed the whole of creation can be understood as a manifestation in all of its potential detail of the divine glory. In later sections we will reexamine the idea that God, in order to be fully realized, for example, as God-the-King, is as dependent upon creation as creation is upon him. We will then be able to see how the interpenetration of the higher and lower worlds is truly a reciprocal one.

There is yet a third way in which the interpenetration and interdependence of the four worlds can be understood, and this is the interpenetration that a "form" can be said to have with its "instance." The lower worlds are each an instantiation of the forms represented in the world immediately above them. For example, goodness is itself an instantiation of *Ein-Sof* and *Chesed* (Kindness) an instantiation of goodness, with specific acts of kindness an instantiation of *Chesed*.

This analogy of form and instance grants us insight into our next two propositions; that *each world is a replication or transformation of the world immediately above it*, and that *all of the worlds are "projected" into the world of everyday experience*. The concrete goodness in this world is an instance of and hence a transformation of the idea of goodness in a more abstract, "higher" world. Furthermore, it is our own concrete, material world that provides us with a window into the higher worlds. It is only, for example, through an individual's physical behavior that we gain knowledge of or access to his mind or "soul," and it is only through earthly love and compassion that, as Martin Buber explains, we can catch a glimpse of Godly love in the "eternal thou." The higher worlds are indeed projected into the world of everyday experience, and further, as will become increasingly clear, our world would not make sense without them. However, as a result of the *Tzimtzum*, (the concealment/contraction that gives rise to finite being) this projection is not always clear. God is, we might say, in partial "eclipse" and in a certain mood our world appears opaque, a function of purely physical forces, devoid of value, mind, and spirit.

Our fourth proposition is that *each of the worlds participates in three dimensions of existence; world, year, and soul.* According to Adin Steinsaltz, these dimensions or "mansions" are manifest in our own world of *Assiyah* in the realms of "space," "time," and "being." Since all of the *olamot*, all of the worlds, participate in these three traditional dimensions of existence, the worlds above ours (while nonmaterial) have as part of their "geography" analogies to the "space," "time," and "matter" of everyday experience. For example, in spite of the fact that higher worlds exist beyond space and time they nevertheless do consist of substantial elements that are related one to another and sequenced according to a definite scheme.

It is helpful to understand the nature of higher and lower worlds in terms of the principles on which experience is organized within them. We might, for example, suppose with the philosopher J. N. Findlay that in the worlds just above our own that experience is organized in such a manner that physical objects serve simply to illustrate or enact the purposes of minds, providing individuals with common frames of reference and vehicles of differentiation but "without oppressively forcing on them in and out of season what they do not care to see and know."[31] Such worlds are, we may suppose, experienced by those individuals, such as writers and artists, who become completely absorbed in their ideas and become masters of the material and/or linguistic mediums they utilize to express themselves. In yet higher worlds, closer to the infinite divine light, completely non-material persons, concepts, moods, and feelings—in short, "spiritual beings"—are ordered solely by their essential affinity with one another. Such worlds are

---

31. Findlay, *Transcendence of the Cave*, p. 127.

experienced on earth when two thinkers or artists sense they are very "close" to one another in spite of the fact that they reside in different continents (or even eras!) and have certainly never even met. In the highest of the worlds we might assume that the distinctions between individual souls are absorbed by their most characteristic "types" or *Sefirot* (for example, the biblical patriarch Abraham is subsumed under *Chesed* (Kindness), Isaac under *Gevurah* (Strength), etc.), and that these *Sefirot* are ordered in a purely conceptual manner in "logical space." In the world of *Atzilut* and beyond, even these matrices break down and objects, notions and ideas have the Plotinian quality of being in all places (logical or otherwise) at once,[32] in a manner that is perhaps hinted at in our world by the observation that opposites are fully present in the things they oppose as a necessary background or *counterpoint* to the latter's very existence.

As for the dimensions of "year," manifest in our world as "time," we might posit the existence of a logical as opposed to temporal ordering in the higher realms; in much the same way as "unity" is logically (but not temporally) prior to "duality." For example, the *Sefirot Chesed* (Kindness) and *Gevurah* (Strength) are logically but not temporally prior to the *Sefirah Rachamim* (Compassion), which is itself a blending of these "earlier" traits. One might expect to see the complete chronological unfolding or development of a human soul, from birth to death, laid out, as it were, "at once" in the world of *Yetzirah* without, however, a distortion of the logical sequence of this development; much as a mathematical proof or the complete story of a famous person's life is ordered, *yet there at once*, in the pages of a book. We might even suppose the existence of an attenuated species of time, analogous to the attenuated matter and space (spoken of earlier) within which sentient beings, occupying those upper Worlds nearest our own, can move forward and backward at will in much the same manner as we are able to do with respect to our audio and video recordings. Indeed, such a control over time has always been at least partially available to those with powerful memories or profound historical imaginations.

The nature of the dimension of "soul" provides us with our best clue as to the nature or being of those worlds that are beyond our own. Wittgenstein once observed that the soul or subject is not a part of this world but is rather a boundary or limit to it.[33] We might say that "consciousness" is itself not

---

32. Ibid., p. 129.
33. Wittgenstein, *Tractatus Logico-Philosophicus*, 5.632, p. 117.

found in the world but is rather revealed as a boundary to or "warp" within our universe, which leads us, as it were, into another reality or dimension; in much the same way as a movie on a screen leads beyond itself to a film projector, which exists outside of the movie but is nonetheless necessary for the film's display.

The nature of the soul or consciousness is at once both very obvious and very mysterious. In philosophical moments one can be awestruck by the fact that the human "bodies" we encounter daily are themselves each a window into a "world within a world": each a Leibnizian monad, they are worlds complete unto themselves. We know of these "worlds" in our most intimate acquaintances with others, yet even in such encounters our knowledge of other minds is apparently only by way of inference, via the effects that these other minds or worlds, mediated through human bodies, have upon our own.

Such "worlds," the worlds of human souls, are, as it were, the "tips of icebergs"; each iceberg, however, is so large that it threatens, as we know from our own case, to swallow up the whole of reality in a mood of solipsism where it seems that the entire world exists only inasmuch as *"I" experience it.* However, we might suppose that in the higher worlds we are able to understand and hence navigate these icebergs (other minds) in the same way as we are, in this world, able to paddle the waters between their tips. Upon entering such worlds, the unity that we thereby achieve with other minds offers us as perspicacious a view of *their* souls as we now have of our own.

According to the Kabbalah there is an element or dimension of consciousness or "soul" in all beings, and it is this dimension that becomes the true substance of all things as they are manifest in the higher realms. Higher worlds, far from being composed of a series of disembodied, disensouled, abstract concepts, or ideas, are indeed realms in which consciousness (which is only a warp or a boundary phenomena in the world of *Assiyah*) is the most substantial of all things. We might well understand the *Or Ein-Sof*, the infinite Godly light, as "will" or "consciousness" pure and simple. This light or consciousness is hidden and obscured by matter on earth, but is revealed as the basic "substance" of the higher realms. Such consciousness is not only manifest in individual souls (who bridge the lower and upper worlds in earthly life and who reside in the upper worlds in death) but also in those entities that "cut across" individual persons, and that are, as it were, the common property, not only for mankind, but all sentient beings whatsoever. Such entities, which include ideas, feelings, character traits, ways of looking at things, etc., are, according to the Kabbalah, instantiated as angels and other celestial beings (e.g., angels of truth, peace, death, etc.).

When we speak of higher worlds as worlds of concepts and ideas, we should therefore avoid the tendency to think of them in terms of statue-like templates or forms, or as purely abstract entities that exist, as it were, only for our minds; rather they are living, spiritual realms, which receive their consciousness, their souls, from the source of all consciousness whatsoever: *Ein-Sof* itself. Accordingly, our own souls, our own consciousness, are but single rays of the Infinite's light penetrating the veil of the world of *Assiyah*.

It follows from our geography of higher Worlds that among the four worlds ours is the lowest and hence the furthest from God. It is also the world that is most highly differentiated. A corollary of this principle is our fifth and final proposition that *consciousness of the individual self increases with the concealment from and distance from God,* and is hence greatest in our own world. Such a proposition accords well with those earthly mystical experiences in which a loss of individual consciousness is reported as a precondition or corollary of mystical ecstasy. Conversely, a plodding, encumbering, inescapable consciousness of self, of one's every feeling and thought, is reported to accompany those moods of depression and despair which can justly be called *negatively mystical*: moods that provide us with an intuition of even lower realms than our own. Hell, we must assume, is what it is precisely because its inhabitants can neither escape from themselves nor from an acute awareness of their past (evil) deeds. As Adin Steinsaltz puts it:

> As one descends in the system of worlds, there is more and more matter. Another way of stating this is that the beings of the lower worlds have a greater awareness of their independent, progressively separate selves, of their private "I." This consciousness of self obscures the divine light, and dims the true, unchanging "I" that exists within each individual being.[34]

---

34. Steinsaltz, "Worlds, Angels and Man," p. 48. While the lower worlds, as we have just seen, contain progressively more "matter," this is not to say that they are composed of an essentially different substance from the higher realms. Rather, the Kabbalists are clear in asserting that all the worlds are composed of the same substance or substances, i.e., the *Sefirot*; however in each world the *Sefirot* are simply ordered in a different manner. It is the ordering and dominance of particular *Sefirot* that gives our world its material character and the upper worlds a spiritual or ideal cast.

The true, pure, unchanging "I," which Schneur Zalman refers to as the individual's "Godly soul," is not only the aspect of the self that draws a man closer to God and the higher worlds; it is the aspect of the self that the individual has in common with his fellow man. By way of contrast, the individual's false self (in Schneur Zalman's terms, his "animal soul") is a function of material pursuits and desires, which are unique to the individual and which distinguishes him/her both from God and other people. Such a false self achieves its fullest expression, so to speak, in corporeal death, which is, in effect, the most individuating experience of all.

Lest we perpetuate a serious misunderstanding, it is also important to remember that the individual, empirical self (the so-called animal soul in Schneur Zalman's scheme), is, according to the Kabbalists (in spite of its status as a phenomenon of the lower worlds), an *absolutely necessary aspect of man, and an essential part of creation*. Man, according to the Kabbalah, is not enjoined to escape or simply transcend his empirical self in favor of a transcendental, Godly existence. Man's purpose, as will become evident, is rather to place his empirical self, his individual and unique talents, in the service of God and his fellow man, and in so doing elevate his uniqueness and thereby actualize his full spiritual potential. The story is told of the Chasidic Rabbi Zusya, who is reported to have said shortly before his death: "In the world to come they will not ask me, 'Why were you not Moses?' They will ask me, 'Why were you not Zusya?'"[35]

ROUTES TO THE HIGHER WORLDS

Having explored the nature or "geography" of the higher realms I will now ask how it is possible for us to arrive at the *conviction* that they do indeed exist, and are accessible in our own experience. In pursuing this task it will do us well to remember that the higher worlds as they are described in Jewish mystical literature, and as I have spoken of them here, in spite of the fact that they are composed of the same *Sefirot* as are own, are decidedly *not* realms of being that are similar to our own but for the fact that they exist in a distant space and time. The worlds of *Yetzirah, Beriah*, and *Atzilut* are of another logical order altogether, and stand to our world in a manner that is perhaps

---

35. Quoted in Francine Klagsbrun, *Voices of Wisdom* (New York: Pantheon, 1980), p. 6.

best thought of as being analogous to the way that the "world" of spherical geometry stands to the "world" of plane geometry or even to the way the "world of mathematics" stands to the world of empirical things. Yet in spite of the logical gap between our world of matter, space, and time and the higher worlds (which stand outside of the space–time continuum), the latter are not mere abstractions from earthly experience. They are, as I have emphasized, vital, living realms in which those things that in our world reside at the boundary or limit (values, and particularly consciousness or "soul") take center stage. They are realms in which experience is organized in a way that is different from the way it is organized in our everyday world of "Action." The journey into the higher worlds will not, therefore, be one that follows a continuous, purely logical (in the Aristotelian sense) progression, but will rather be one in which the traveler must push up against the boundary of this world (i.e., the very consciousness that is so necessary for this world's *presence* yet which is found nowhere within it) in such manner as to completely reverse the "within" with the "without"; much like those toys, which children find so fascinating, in which what appears to be one thing is transformed into something completely different by opening a zipper in the casing and pushing out material from the inside in such a manner that it expands and eventually envelops and encases the original toy itself.

Our journey into the higher worlds will involve us in essentially two distinct but parallel, and in many ways complementary, routes: the routes of experience and reason. The first route will involve us in a discussion of such phenomena as dreams and "mystical" experience; the second in a consideration of the conceptual antinomies and experiential absurdities that plague any attempt to understand "reality" apart from its connection to and dependence upon higher realms. The route of experience will provide us entrance into those regions in which the higher worlds interpenetrate our world: the route of reason will, as it were, show us how the existence of higher worlds provides us with solutions to what otherwise amount to "unsolvable equations" in our own earthly realm.

Before proceeding, it is important that we address one source of potential confusion. We have already remarked that the entire scheme of worlds is an "illusion" from the point of view of the Infinite God, *Ein-Sof*. This, I should point out, however, is even more true of our own world, the material realm of *Assiyah*, than it is of realms above our own. While the higher worlds are logically (as opposed to physically) distant from our own, for the Kabbalists they are bathed with a greater portion of divine light, and, in this sense, are more, rather than less, substantial than the world of everyday life and experience.

DREAMS

The phenomenon of dreams provides us with what is perhaps the most direct and easy access into the higher worlds. The Midrash regards dreams to be "a variety of prophecy"[36] and there are many instances in the Bible in which a dream is accorded the status of a portal into a higher realm.[37] Dreams are also mentioned among the techniques of mystical ascent described in the Zohar.[38]

Indeed dreams seem to be all but tailor-made as aids to the understanding not only of higher worlds but of kabbalistic thought in general. This is in part because in dreams our experience is organized in a manner that differs radically from the way it is organized in waking life. In dreams what is outside is "in" and what is inside is "out." This is because in dreams, consciousness or "mind," which, as we have said, is but an ephemeral boundary in our (wakeful) world, takes first, center, and, in a sense, only, stage. On the other hand, matter, which is apparently the bedrock substance of wakeful "reality," is but a mere boundary phenomena in dreams both in the sense that matter in dreams is (simply speaking) an illusion and in the sense that while dreams are dependent upon the physiological functions of a living human brain, this brain is in no sense present within the dream itself.

Dreams, like higher worlds, are dominated (as psychoanalysis has consistently brought to our attention) by wishes, emotions, and ideas. Material objects appear in our dreams only, and precisely, to the extent that they are needed to symbolize or express thoughts and emotions. Rather than the obstacles and foils to mental life that they so often seem to be in our wakeful states, material objects (or their dream world surrogates) are completely subservient, in dreams, to the dreamer's own desires and forms of mental representation. Indeed, dreams exist, as it were, outside the space–time continuum. Freud called the world of the unconscious and dreams

---

36. Midrash, Genesis Rabbah 17: 5.
37. E.g., Genesis 20: 3, 6; 31: 10–11.
38. Zohar I, 83a; Sperling and Simon, *The Zohar*, Vol. 1, p. 277. On dreams in the Zohar, see Tishby and Lachower, *The Wisdom of the Zohar*, pp. 815–830. On Jewish/Kabbalistic dream interpretation see Joel Covits, *Visions of the Night* (Boston: Shambhala, 1990).

"timeless." In dreams individuals are able to travel through time, be themselves as children and adults simultaneously, and traverse apparent eons in less than a night. In dreams one cannot only meet the dead and the not-yet-living but one can experience such things as "the past being born out of the future" without being troubled by such violations of wakeful logic.

Dreams also provide us with an experiential analogue to the problem of "higher worlds." This occurs when the dreamer experiences his dream world as somehow "queer" and hinting at the possibility of its own transcendence in wakeful life. Upon awakening the dream world is indeed turned "outside in," and is in fact transcended in favor of what is, from one point of view, a "higher world." There is, as I have mentioned, a sense in which the dream world itself is a portal into a higher reality, as one is often able to comprehend, with the aid of an "interpretation," the light that the seemingly opaque and bizarre images of a dream sheds upon wakeful life. This is analogous to the manner in which "higher worlds" promise to provide us with some "backstage" insight into the apparently absurd and opaque machinations of our everyday, empirical world.

If nothing else, the analogy with dreams provides us with some insight into the radical transformations needed for a journey into higher worlds. One can imagine the insuperable difficulties encountered by characters "locked" in one of our dreams who attempted to surmise that their very existence was dependent upon activities in our brain and further that their behavior was dependent upon our own earlier, waking interactions with persons and objects in the material world! Indeed any dream character obtaining such profound insight would (as our own dream life affirms) completely self-destruct, as occurs when a dreamer attains the realization that his "torture" or "bliss" is *nothing but a dream.*[39] In such instances one's dream world evaporates and immediately merges with one's wakeful self, in much the same way that a mystic achieving too perspicacious a vision of the Infinite would dissolve in sheer unity with an all-encompassing God.

As I have indicated in Chapter Three, it would not be pressing our analogy too far to argue that from a kabbalistic viewpoint, in our dreams we each play God to worlds of our own making.[40] There we noted the analogy

---

39. So-called "lucid" dreams are an interesting exception to this generalization.

40. In Hindu thought we find this view of dreaming stated explicitly. The Upanishads, for example, give special importance to the state of dreaming, for in dreaming the self "takes with him (all) the materials of this all-embracing world." There in the dream state he destroys this world and then builds it back up again, and

between dreams and the kabbalistic principle of creation, i.e., *Tzimtzum* (concealment, contraction). In order for an individual to form a dream he must, as it were, perform his own act of *Tzimtzum*; withdrawing his consciousness from the world at large (in Freudian terms contracting or "decathecting" his "libido") and concealing (again from himself) both the fact that he is dreaming and the meaning of his dream creation. Freud himself placed great emphasis on this latter point in his view that dreams, being the guardian of sleep, must work to assure their own continued existence by concealing from the dreamer their true meaning and nature, a meaning that, if it were known, would be so disturbing as to be incompatible with continued sleep. This concealment occurs, according to Freud, via the principles of displacement, condensation, symbolization, etc., the very hermeneutic/linguistic principles that the Kabbalists assume are utilized by God in concealing His presence in the material world.

The psychoanalytic theory of dreams can provide insight not only into the *Tzimtzum* but into the kabbalistic symbols of the Breaking of the Vessels and *Tikkun ha-Olam* as well. The process by which a dream's latent content is *broken up* and reorganized by the "dream work" into a latent dream image and then via an act of interpretation, is *restored* to its original form (but in a superior manner that integrates that latent dream content with the dreamer's life and personality) is a psychoanalytic analogy to the processes of *Shevirat ha-Kelim* (the Breaking of the Vessels) and *Tikkun* (Restoration), which, according to the Lurianic Kabbalists, are the further ramifications of God's ultimate plan for this world.[41]

It is a well-known principle of contemporary dream interpretation that each of the characters or personalities within a dream are versions of the dreamer himself; and indeed, how could it be otherwise, when the only life

---

dreams up a world lighted by his own brilliance, bringing forth "chariots, spans, and paths," "joys, pleasures, and delights," "tanks, lotus-pools, and rivers," from himself (Brihadaranyaka Upanishad IV, iii, 9, 10; Zaehner, *Hindu Scriptures*, p. 74). Interestingly, the Upanishad relates that the man who dreams that he is being called, overpowered, or dared by an elephant, is "only imagining in ignorance the horrors he sees when he is awake." "But when, like a god or king, he thinks, 'I surely am this [whole universe: I am] whole,' that is his highest state of being" (IV, iii, 20; ibid. p. 75). In such a state of being, which is akin to but beyond the dream state, he is beyond desire, and free from all fears and evil.

41. The practice of psychoanalysis itself can be understood as a specific instance of *Tikkun ha-Olam*. See my discussion in Chapter 9 and my book *Kabbalistic Metaphors: Jewish Mystical Themes in Ancient and Modern Thought*.

or consciousness informing the dreamworld is that which issues forth from the dreamer's own mind. Here we have a final analogy with Jewish mystical thought, for according to the Kabbalists the only true consciousness, the only real "mind" informing each of the worlds from *Atzilut* down to *Assiyah*, is the mind of God. Indeed, according to the Kabbalah, our world is itself like a dream in the mind of God, for although it is real from our own finite perspective, it is purely an illusion from the infinite perspective of the deity. Ours is a world woven completely out of the fabric of God's desire, and just as our own dreams are the illusory product of our wishes; we, in a sense, are the illusory products of God's *ratzon*, his infinite desire or will. Our consciousness, our self, is completely dependent upon God's infinite mind. If He were, according to the Kabbalists, to turn His sustaining thoughts away from us even for a moment, we would (like the figures that populate our dream worlds) vanish without a trace, as if we had never existed at all.[42]

Yet as apt and telling as is the analogy between dreams and higher worlds, it is an analogy that is ultimately unsatisfying and incomplete, as incomplete as is any comparison between God's creativity and man's. The worlds created and sustained by our dreams are the merest ephemera as compared to the vast cosmic edifice resulting from God's *Tzimtzum*. Our dreams, while they occasionally provide a window into a higher reality, are perhaps more frequently portals into even lower worlds than our own, worlds in which the thoughts, actions, and desires of the personalities we conjure up spin themselves into oblivion after serving in a psychodrama reflecting our personal conflicts; only to be conjured up again on a subsequent night as actors on a new stage. To be a character in the dreams of man is (like certain elementary particles in physics) to go in and out of existence, literally, with the wink of an eye. Still, in spite of these limitations, the transition from wakefulness to dreaming and vice versa yields what is perhaps the best insight into the vast chasm that exists between our world and the "realm above," and provides us with an important experiential signpost pointing in the direction of a higher reality.

MYSTICAL EXPERIENCE

There are other experiences, apart from dreams, that provide insight into higher worlds. The most dramatic of these are the visions of higher worlds

---

42. Schneur Zalman, *Shaar Ha Yichud Vehaemunah*, Chapter 1; Zalman, *Likutei Amarim-Tanya*, p. 287.

that were accorded the biblical prophets and that, according to the Kabbalists, are, to a greater or lesser extent, vouchsafed for the initiates among the pious of each generation. The talmudic term *Maaseh Merkaveh*, the "working of the Chariot," refers to the visions not only of the prophet Ezekiel but to those of later mystics who attempted to replicate his supernal ascent. In such visions the prophet or mystic is said to create the conditions within his own soul, i.e., set up a *merkaveh* or chariot, which enable him to reach an awareness of supernal realms. The term *merkaveh* is derived from the root *rakhav* (to ride) and refers to God Himself leaving his natural state, in which he is completely unknowable, and allowing himself to be "seen" by those who experience a *merkaveh* vision.[43] According to the Talmud, Rabbi Yochanan ben Zakkai was himself in possession of the technique for achieving *Maaseh Merkaveh* and had provided lessons in this technique to a select few of his disciples.[44] The Talmud warns of the dangers of expounding such techniques, stating that when Rabbi Eleazar ben Ayakh repeated his master's lesson, "Fire came down and surrounded all the trees of the field . . ."

We have already alluded to the talmudic story of "Four who entered the Orchard (*pardes*)," which according to Rashi refers to their "ascending to heaven by means of a [Divine] Name."[45] Again, the dangers of such mystical "meditations" are brought out by the fact that of the four only Rabbi Akiva emerged from the vision unscathed. Of the others it is said that "Ben Azzai gazed and died," "Ben Zoma gazed and was stricken" (lost his mind), and Elisha ben Abuya "cut his plantings" (became a heretic). Yet in spite of the dangers associated with such mystical experience, there developed an elaborate tradition of kabbalistic meditation designed in part to provide the initiate with a direct experiential route to the higher worlds. Such techniques involved, among other things, the silent repetition of holy words and phrases ("mantra" meditation), visualization of the tetragrammaton (the letters of the divine name), meditation upon colors associated with each of the *Sefirot*, and the recitation and recombination of sounds and letters.[46]

---

43. For a discussion of *Merkaveh* mysticism see Gershom Scholem, *Jewish Gnosticism, Merkava Mysticism and Talmudic Tradition*; Scholem, *Major Trends*, pp. 40–79; and Naomi Janowitz, *The Poetics of Ascent* (Albany: State University of New York Press, 1989).

44. Talmud, Tractate *Chagiga*, 14b.

45. Ibid.

46. For a discussion of kabbalistic meditation, see Aryeh Kaplan, *Jewish Meditation*, and Aryeh Kaplan, *Meditation and Kabbalah*.

According to the Safedian Kabbalist Moses Cordovero (1522–1570), while philosophers can only speculate about what exists in the higher realms, the mystic can actually see them.[47] Indeed, Chayyim Vital held that the prophets and later mystics utilized techniques that enabled them to have direct visions of higher worlds.[48]

While there is some debate among the Kabbalists as to which worlds were vouchsafed to whom, there is a clear tradition that the various meditational techniques afforded both the prophets and mystics access to at least a portion of the heavenly order. What is not clear, however, is the precise manner through which the various mystical techniques grant the devotee access into these higher worlds. While this question is beyond the scope of the present study we might mention in passing that for the mystics, increased levels of concentration, self-mastery, and openness to immediate experience can be thought of as placing the initiate in contact with higher realms in at least three ways: by granting him a more perspicacious vision of external reality itself, by providing him with deeper insights into the meaning of the language of scripture (which is itself said to be a reflection of the higher worlds), and/or by granting him insights into the depths of this own soul (which reproduces within itself a microcosm of the higher worlds and *Sefirot*), and, most importantly, by organizing his experience in a manner that accords with one or more of the "higher orders" I have discussed earlier in this chapter. A meditational technique, for example, that enables one to experience a deep affinity with nature or fellow human beings, would, ipso facto, provide one with access to a "higher world."

Mystical experiences, and the metaphysical claims that are sometimes based upon them are, of course, open to the skepticism that is appropriate with reference to all philosophical claims based on so-called "religious experience." Either one has such an experience or one does not. The same, of course, can be said of dreams or any other experiential route to the divine. Any metaphysical claim based upon them will be of very limited *philosophical* value.

VALUES

What of ordinary, nonmystical, even *nonreligious* experience? Are there experiences that are unmediated through the categories of religion that can

---

47. Quoted in Kaplan, *Meditation and Kabbalah*, p. 170.
48. Ibid., pp. 187–198.

provide us with an intuition of the divine and serve as a signpost pointing in the direction of the higher worlds?

It should be acknowledged straight away that there is a sense in which ordinary experience is decidedly of this world, decidedly *mundane*. Indeed it is the very uninspiring nature of so much that goes under the rubric of "day-to-day existence" that prompts the artist, the mystic, and the visionary to penetrate beyond the "mundane" (from the Latin *mundi*, world) in an effort to commune with a higher realm. That ordinary experience is most often cold, hard, neutral or, as the existentialists would have it, "absurd," accords well with the kabbalistic view that our immediate world is separated by many "curtains and garments" from the source of all meaning and value. Nevertheless, the higher worlds are, as we have seen, presumably projected into and interpenetrate the world of experience and we should, by properly directing our attention, be able to detect their presence even in the most ordinary of our affairs.

It is I believe, through a consideration of "meaning" and "value" that the presence of higher worlds is revealed in everyday life. As I have pointed out in Chapter Three, the Kabbalah, as an *idealistic* (as opposed to materialistic) system of thought, reverses our ordinary way of looking at things and regards "value" or "idea" as the most basic reality. Such a perspective becomes credible when we realize that *material objects*, which are presumably the very substance of our universe, can neither be conceived of nor described except under the aegis of a general concept or idea. We cannot, as it were, look at the world (as materialistic philosophy claims) as "it really is" and see things apart from their participation in categories or "kinds." The objects of experience constantly appear to us as good or poor examples of the type or kind that they are, as if they were imperfect instances of the ideal forms of "roundness," "redness," "truth," "kindness," etc. Further, they only appear as objects insofar as they are related to our practical, moral, aesthetic, and other interests and values. The world as we experience it is inseparable from values and ideas, and it is this fact, as Plato was perhaps the first to articulate, that offers us a glimpse into a world "behind the appearances."

There are, of course, those who agree with the proposition that things are never experienced except insofar as they are examples of concepts that reflect some aesthetic, moral, or practical concern, but who insist that such concerns (and therefore all values) are, in effect, created and thus imposed on a neutral reality by man. The "value ladenness" of reality, instead of pointing to some higher realm or moral order, which infuses the world with meaning, actually points us, according to this view, toward the constitutive function of the human mind.

It is, however, just this constitutive function that the Kabbalists held to be a reflection of the divine *Sefirot*. That values are a function of mind does not imply that they are arbitrary and subjective. Indeed, for the Kabbalists it is values that are most objective and real. They would likely point out that, in spite of our disagreements on *what* is valuable and good, the *beauty, goodness, righteousness*, etc., of a given person or object is itself experienced by us in completely *objective* terms. We do not, in any way, for example, experience ourselves as constituting the beauty of a sunset, but rather experience that beauty as being *there* as much as the sunset itself. More significantly while we may indeed disagree as to the goodness or beauty of a given, particular thing, we do not disagree on the values themselves: there are clearly such things as beauty, kindness, love, truth, etc., and only the most perverse of outlooks can sway us from affirming them. We simply disagree, at times, as to precisely which *objects* represent the values we all intuit and avow; and it is the values themselves, and not the objects that may or may not instantiate them, which for the Kabbalists provide access to a higher reality.

RATIONAL MYSTICISM

Having explored the "experiential" routes to higher worlds, it remains for us to examine the purely rational or intellectual considerations that can lead us to acknowledge another realm as a complement to our own. Adin Steinsaltz was once asked what it was that led him to form such a firm belief in God. His answer was that as a young student of mathematics he was intrigued by a problem in plane (two-dimensional) geometry that could not be solved unless one violated the assumptions of a two-dimensional world and posited a single point in a third dimension. So it must also be the case, he concluded, with our own phenomenal world.[49] There are *insoluble conundrums and antinomies* in our world that can only be resolved by positing the existence of another dimension, a "higher world" and a focal point of that "world," the Infinite, *Ein-Sof,* or God. This is just the kind of solution to philosophical dilemmas sought by Kant, especially in his *Critique of Judgment*. Kant observed a contradiction or "antimony" between the fundamental axiom of

---

49. Steinsaltz, "The Mystic as Philosopher," pp. 14–17.

scientific thought that every event in the phenomenal world has an anteced-ent material cause, and what he held to be the fundamental principle of moral life, that there exists freedom from material causation. Kant's solution to this antinomy was to acknowledge universal causation in the *phenomenal world* but to posit the existence of a *"noumenal"* reality (which the Neo-Kantians interpreted as a *higher realm*) in which freedom from such necessity is assured. Steinsaltz extends this species of reasoning to include the totality of philosophical and ethical dilemmas that plague the human mind and spirit, arguing that the very sense of our experiential world is dependent upon our recognition of another reality, which serves as its essential background. To take one simple example, Steinsaltz argues that the very notion that serves as a foundation for democracy, the supposedly self-evident truth "that all men are created equal," is anything but self-evident from the perspective of the phenomenal/ experiential world. Individuals are indeed decidedly *unequal* with respect to any and all of their natural endowments, and it is futile to appeal to such endowments as a foundation for their equal rights in a democratic society. According to Steinsaltz, it is only by positing the existence of a "soul," created by God, which exists *behind* each individual's "natural self," that we can justify our belief that all men, in some fundamental sense, are equal, and that they must be afforded equal treatment in politics and law.[50]

This species of argument, has been put to remarkable effect by the philosopher J. N. Findlay in his profound but little-known Neoplatonic work, *The Transcendence of the Cave*,[51] a work in which he argues, in the same spirit as Steinsaltz, that higher worlds provide the missing parts of the puzzle of life in our own realm. We will have occasion to examine some of these arguments in a bit more detail and place them within the context of the Lurianic metaphor of *Shevirat ha-Kelim* (the Breaking of the Vessels) when we consider the latter concept in Chapter Seven. For now it should suffice to say that according to Findlay (as well as for Steinsaltz) the philosophical and spiritual conundrums of our own world, including but not limited to antinomies with respect to space and time, freedom and necessity, random-ness and teleology, inner experience and the external world, "other minds," and the problem of evil, are the result of our world being one in which matter

---

50. Ibid.

51. Findlay, *Transcendence of the Cave*. See also J. N. Findlay, *The Discipline of the Cave* (London: Allen Unwin, 1966).

is alienated from spirit and idea. These antinomies are only resolved when we consider the possibility of a purely spiritual and "unified" world existing as a complement to our own.

Here I will provide a single but, I believe, telling example. Philosophers have long been troubled by the question of how it is that we know that individuals other than ourselves possess minds. It is argued that while we *know* our own minds directly through introspection, we can only *infer* the existence of others' minds on the basis of their physical behavior. It is readily apparent that this entire problem would not arise in a world in which all consciousness was effectively one; or, less dramatically, in a (slightly lower) world in which there was direct communication between separate minds, unmediated by behavior or other material events. Indeed, we might, in the spirit of Steinsaltz, posit the existence of a higher, unitary world in order to solve the problem of other minds in our own. We might also recognize that such a world, in which experience is organized quite differently than in our own, is actually accessible to some individuals in our own world, and, to all of us, at least on occasion. In those experiences in which the mystic, for example, recognizes the unity of all souls, or in those interpersonal encounters in which one immediately understands another's thoughts and feelings and experiences them as if they were one's own, we are, as it were, in contact with one of the Kabbalists' higher realities. When we conceptualize higher worlds simply as (radically) different ways of organizing experiences, the great mystery about higher worlds and their penetration into our own disappears, and what at first appears as a distant, alien concept becomes familiar and relevant to daily life.

WORLDS AND THE PSYCHE OF MAN

Drawing on the biblical notion that man was created in God's own image, the Kabbalists arrived at the idea that all of the worlds of creation are somehow embodied in the soul of man. The Kabbalist Moses Baal Shem Tov de Leon, for example, quotes from the presumably ancient kabbalistic treatise known simply as the *Yerushalmi* that man's soul "is from the world of creation, and from the world of formation, and its completion (or perfection) is nowhere but in the world of action which is this our world."[52] According

---

52. Quoted by Scholem, "Four Worlds," p. 641.

to R. Moses Cordovero, "man comprises in his composition all the creatures, from the first point until the very end of [the world of] Creation (*Beriah*), [the world of] Formation (*Yetzirah*), [the world of] Making (*Assiyah*), as it is written: 'I have created him, formed him and even made Him.'"[53]

As we have seen, Vital in his *Sefer Etz Chayyim* holds that "in [primordial] man all of the worlds are concentrated,"[54] a view that was apparently taught by Isaac Luria himself and that became one justification for the psychologization of the Kabbalah in Hasidic thought. Indeed, the founder of Chabad Hasidism, Rabbi Schneur Zalman of Lyadi, bases his major work, *The Tanya*, on the notion that the heavenly *Sefirot* and "Worlds" are mirrored in the workings of the soul of man. While Schneur Zalman did not go so far as to argue that the *only* significance of the doctrine of the *Olamot* is insofar as they refer to aspects of man's soul, it is clear that in Hasidism we find a shift from a primarily theosophical to a primarily psychological and ethical interpretation of the "Worlds" symbolism. There is, according to Schneur Zalman (and in this he is following the tradition of the Zohar), a common structure to God, the heavens, and man's soul. Therefore, if we wish to understand either God or the upper worlds we must understand the roots of our own psyche.

CREATION AND EVOLUTION

The kabbalistic doctrine of worlds can provide us with a framework through which we can understand the claims of scripture and reconcile them with apparently contradictory claims made in the name of science. It is indeed common nowadays for "enlightened believers" to hold that scripture and science are each *true in their own realms*, or that each is referring to *a different level* of being or analysis. Indeed, we often speak of the "world of science," contrasting it with the "world of religion" as a sort of offhand metaphor for the view that religion and science are not in direct competition. This is because they operate on the basis of such radically different assumptions as to place each in its own realm or cognitive sphere. The

---

53. Moses Cordovero, *Pardes Rimmonim* (quoting Isaiah 43). Quoted by Idel in *Kabbalah: New Perspectives*, p. 119.

54. Vital, *Sefer Etz Chayyim*. Quoted in Idel, *Kabbalah: New Perspectives*, p. 119.

Kabbalah, with its distinctions among the four worlds, provides a metaphysical basis for this intuitive (but often poorly articulated) point of view.

For example, the apparent contradiction between the scientific/evolutionary and the biblical accounts of creation can be reconciled on the assumption that the scientific account refers to the material world of *Assiyah* (action or making) whereas the biblical account makes primary reference to a higher archetypical world, *Beriah*, the world of "creation." When we consider the fact that, according to the Lurianic Kabbalah, the material world is itself a function of the Breaking of the Vessels and that this event is frequently identified with the fall of Adam, we realize that the entire biblical story of creation right up until Adam's fall refers to a purely spiritual/conceptual or "*archetypical*" realm, which had "yet" to realize its material and temporal nature. Indeed the great biblical and talmudic commentator, Rashi, in his explication of the first chapter of Genesis, holds that the biblical account is an *atemporal* description from which "no before or after" can be inferred. Following Rashi we can argue that it is only after Adam and Eve's fall that they become mortal, finite, temporal beings. In kabbalistic terms, it is only "after" the Breaking of the Vessels that space, time, and matter as we know it were introduced, and that the curtain fell on an idyllic, archetypal, spiritual world. At such "time" (really the beginning of all time) the cosmos was reorganized into a realm in which Adam's partaking of the fruit can even be regarded as an historical event, which either did or did not occur in time.

"Prior" to Adam's fall (and metaphysically prior to the Breaking of the Vessels), there was no history, no time as we know it. By choosing to eat from the tree of knowledge of good and evil, Adam became a being incarnate, capable of freely altering his own life course and participating in a historical world. This is indeed the metaphysical meaning of Adam's becoming both free and mortal after eating from the tree of knowledge.

It is worth noting the apparent coincidence that human historical consciousness is itself only approximately 5,700 years old, the very age that the biblical account would give to the "world." If the Torah account of creation, as I have argued, refers to a spiritual/conceptual world, that world, when translated into spatio-temporal history with Adam's fall, might indeed be equivalent to the epoch of human historical self-consciousness, or approximately 5,760 years.

I am not of the view that with the fall of Adam 5,760 years ago that God *first* created a biological and material history for man and his world. My point is *not* that of the nineteenth-century biblical apologists, who, when confronted with the evidence of million-year-old fossils, argued that such fossils were created to appear millions of years old by God only several thousand years ago. Such a response confines God's activity to our own historical world. God Himself exists and creates *outside of time*. I am here suggesting with Rashi that the six "days" of creation, the eating of the forbidden fruit, and the Breaking of the Vessels all occurred outside of time as we know it, and that "Adam and Eve" were only, as it were merged with time, with the advent of their "sin." The "time" they merged into is, obviously enough, the very time we have come to know and understand as history.

It is as if, as a result of the *Shevirah*, Adam and Eve, who had existed in one plane (the plane of spirit and mind) were tilted along with that plane so as to coincide with another plane of being, the plane of space, time, and corporeality. According to the Kabbalists, it was only with the *Shevirah* that spirit became enmeshed with matter and the two planes of being merged in our world.

Perhaps we can gain some insight into the notion of an atemporal process merging with a temporal one by again considering the phenomena of dreams, particularly the transition from a dream state to wakefulness. Dreams, as I have already pointed out, involve an atemporal series of images and events. On those occasions in which a dream seems to follow a temporal sequence, days, weeks, months, and even years can apparently transpire in "dream time," in what dream-researchers assure us is a matter of seconds or minutes of R.E.M. (rapid eye movement) sleep. Upon awakening, of course, one's dream would collapse into the "real" world and a dream that apparently spanned years of personal history, or eons of world history, is said to have occurred, for example, "last Thursday night."

I have already discussed how the transition from a dreaming to a waking state provides an analogy to the transition among the kabbalistic four worlds. Here we see that the analogy can also be useful in understanding how the "time" of one world can be totally incommensurable with the "time" of another, until such point when these worlds merge and the temporality (including the entire history) of one world is projected into and subsumed by the temporality of the second. This, I have argued, is precisely how we might understand the fall of Adam and Eve; the entire history of their world of *Beriah* (creation) merged, as it were, with our spatio-temporal material universe (the world of *Assiyah*) and became, from our perspective, an event, corresponding perhaps to the rise of historical consciousness among men, some 5,760 years in the past! Just as there were, from a wakeful perspective, events prior to an individual's dream about the creation of the world last Thursday night, there can be events, from the perspective of the world of *Assiyah,* prior to the actual creation of the world in *Beriah,* 5,760 years ago.[55]

---

55. This is in fact the very account suggested by Rashi in his gloss on Genesis 1:1. There Rashi explains that scripture does not teach us anything about the "earlier or later acts of creation." One cannot, for example, infer that the heavens and the earth were created first because (among other *grammatical* reasons) scripture later tells us "that the earth was unformed and void and God hovered over the face of the waters," which seems to imply that water was created before the earth. In addition, Rashi points out that heaven, *shamayim,* is a combination of *aish* (fire) and *mayim* (water), suggesting that these elements were created before the heavens. In short we can, according to Rashi, make no inference about the order of creation from the words of scripture, and we might infer that the reason for this is that the events described in the beginning of Genesis actually occurred in a spiritual realm outside of time. Confirmation of this is indeed forthcoming when Rashi tells us that the words "In the beginning God [Elohim]" do teach us that originally God thought to create a world of strict justice (this is inferred from the word *Elohim* itself, which is said to refer to God's attribute of justice or *Din*) and only later gave precedence to His attribute of mercy (Genesis 2: 4). From this we can infer that creation as described in Genesis is a function not of material causation but rather of God's *middot* or traits of *Din* and *rachamim,* the very traits that came to be embodied in the *Sefirot,* the kabbalistic archetypes of divine spirituality. The world as it was originally created was therefore a spiritual world.

There are indications that the Kabbalists and Hasidim themselves interpreted Rashi (and scripture) in the manner described above. There is, for example, a tradition that according to the Baal Shem Tov:

> Wherever Rashi uses (the phrase), "the plain meaning of the verse," he intends (to say) that, when you shall divest yourself of your corporeality and be stripped of any material issue, you will (surely) apprehend the plain meaning of the verse, stripped of any idea (referring) to the hidden secrets. [Quoted and translated in Idel, *Kabbalah: New Perspectives,* p. 239]

We thus learn that according to the Baal Shem Tov, Rashi held that a mystical attitude is needed as a prerequisite even for understanding the plain meaning of a biblical verse; one must strip oneself of corporeality, i.e., think in purely spiritual terms, if one is to understand the Bible's literal, plain meaning. That this is so with respect to the "plain meaning" (as Rashi puts it) of the biblical story of creation is quite apparent. To think otherwise is to further enmesh two distinct worlds that for the purpose of understanding scripture ought best to remain separate and apart.

7

Shevirat ha-Kelim:
The Breaking of the Vessels

One of the most captivating images in Jewish mystical literature is to be found in the Lurianic symbol of the "Breaking of the Vessels" (*Shevirat ha-Kelim*). In this symbol, a series of cosmic structures, metaphorically spoken of as vessels of colored glass, are instantaneously filled with and then shattered by the infinite light of God. This shattering causes a rupture between the masculine and feminine aspects of the cosmos, and the shards of these broken vessels fall through primordial space, each shard capturing a portion of divine light. With the aid of humankind, the vessels are ultimately reassembled into new configurations that bear the image of God.

The Breaking of the Vessels introduces a dynamic element into the heart of the Lurianic Kabbalah, one that was only implicit in earlier Jewish mysticism. The notion that God's original creation must be radically altered and even destroyed is, of course, recorded in the biblical stories of the Fall of Adam and the flood.[1] However, the Lurianic symbol of the Breaking of the Vessels introduces this "crisis in creation" into all things, divine and human, great and small, into the very "molecular" structure of the cosmos itself. This crisis, as symbolized in the dynamic of *Shevirah* (Breaking or Destruction)

---

1. According to the Lurianists the Breaking of the Vessels is implicit in the conditions that prevailed at the time of creation: Genesis 1, 2: "the earth was empty and void." See Luzzatto, *General Principles of the Kabbalah*, p. 69.

and *Tikkun* (Restoration or Repair) is, according to Luria and his followers, the basic vehicle for change and progress in the world. The logic of *Shevirah* and *Tikkun*, as we shall see, is dialectical, and it operates in all spheres: in reason, spirit, and emotion; in history and the immediate moment; in the life of nations and the development of the individual. The Breaking of the Vessels is individual and relational, material and psychological, intellectual and erotic. As such it is a symbol that is capable of uniting the most diverse genres of human experience under a single, powerful, dynamic idea.

If we explore the historical background of the Breaking of the Vessels we discover that on the one hand it can be regarded as a metaphor that expresses in cosmic terms the historical Jewish experience of "exile" (*galut*) and the consequent hope for "redemption" (*ge'ulah*).[2] The broken shards fall into a nether realm known as the *Sitra Achra* (the "Other Side") and are as Scholem has pointed out cut off from their source in God, much as the Jewish people, dispersed throughout the world, were cut off from their spiritual source in the land of Israel. The gathering and reassembling of these shards, and the sparks of divine light that they contain, is, according to Scholem and others, symbolic of the ingathering of the Jewish people and their ultimate restoration to their spiritual home. While this analysis is certainly a powerful one, it reduces the Breaking of the Vessels to a symptom of a particular historical experience and robs it of its claim to philosophical significance. In this chapter, I will attempt to show that the metaphor of *Shevirat ha-Kelim* indeed has deep metaphysical significance and that it represents a dynamic aspect of both the human psyche and the structure of the Godhead. Indeed, the Kabbalists held that the Breaking of the Vessels expressed, in symbolic terms, certain metaphysical truths about the origins of the material world, the nature of good and evil, and the ultimate purpose of mankind. It devolves on us, in our own age of analytic and critical thought, to express these truths in philosophical terms and to examine their validity from a rational as well as a mystical point of view.

---

2. According to Idel, Scholem's analysis of both *Tzimtzum* and *Shevirat ha-Kelim* in terms of the historical themes of exile and redemption is purely speculative and is not in any way supported by the Lurianic texts. However, this interesting interpretation has been hardened into "fact" by some of Scholem's followers. See Moshe Idel, *Messianic Myths* (New Haven: Yale University Press, 1998), pp. 179–80.

THE VESSELS

If we meditate for a moment on the concept of "vessel," we realize that vessels can be understood as core constituents of both the human and natural orders. Vessels, in their functions as "containers," are the very structures that make civilization possible. They are, for example, essential, for the activities of storage, transportation, and measurement, upon which all commerce is based. They are the structures that enable us to separate inside from outside (as in the vessels that serve as our homes), essence from waste (as in our toilet and sewage systems), and even good from evil (as the containers that serve as our jails and prisons). While we rarely reflect upon the matter, vessels are completely ubiquitous. One can look virtually anywhere in the human world to witness a plethora of vessels and containers: homes, rooms, kitchen utensils, sinks, bathtubs, pens that hold ink, wires that hold electricity, drawers and files, bags and briefcases, furniture to contain the human form, cars, boats, planes, trains, etc. An introduction to man is, from one perspective, an introduction to his vessels. And now with the so-called information explosion, we have computers and compact disks, in addition to the papers, magazines, books, phonographs, and magnetic tapes that serve as *vessels to contain information*. Indeed, one could argue, contra Aristotle, that the defining property of man is not so much his capacity for reason (which itself is often doubtful) but rather his nearly infinite capacity to *vesselize*, to contain.

Vesselization, of course, is not confined to human reality, but is a core constituent of the natural order as well. This, of course, is affirmed in the kabbalistic doctrine of the *Sefirot*, which envisions God as creating the world through a series of *kelim* or vessels. From the point of view of contemporary physics, one might say that a vessel is a limited and temporary locale of *negative entropy*, that is, a place within the universe in which the tendency of the cosmos to "wind down" into states of increasing entropy, disorganization, or chaos is (temporarily) reversed or contained, and a certain organization or structure prevails. It is in this sense that all of the structures of the universe, from galaxies to stars, planets, elements, molecules, and atoms, to living things and the human body, are each *vessels* that structure the energy of the cosmos in such a manner as to reverse its natural tendency to revert to random chaos; much in the manner that a ceramic vessel structures water that would otherwise, randomly and chaotically, spill onto the floor. Although contemporary physical theory (and, as we shall see, Lurianic theosophy) holds that the universe is gradually and inexorably progressing toward a completely entropic (chaotic) state, its history is replete with the creation and destruction of negative entropic structures and the reorganization of their constituent parts into new structures, and information. Information is in essence simply another perspective on structure; a completely entropic, structureless, universe would contain virtually no information at all.

Enter the Kabbalists' conception of the vessels and their destruction. Having comprehended the full extent to which *kelim* (vessels) pervade the human and natural world, we can understand the full implication of their shattering. According to Luria, the ten vessels that were originally meant to contain the emanation of God's light were unable to contain that light and were hence either displaced or shattered. It is significant that for the Kabbalists, only six of the ten *Sefirot* (from *Chesed* to *Yesod*) were fully shattered (*Malchut*, the final vessel was partially broken). Had all of the vessels, *Keter*, *Chochmah*, and *Binah*, been shattered, the universe would have been thrown back into the state of complete and utter chaos, the *toho* and *bohu* prior to creation. As it is, the three highest *Sefirot*, which as we have seen represent Will, Wisdom, and Understanding, remained intact; only the six *Sefirot* representing the spiritual, moral, aesthetic, and material values were broken, and are, hence, in need of restoration or repair (*Tikkun*). Nevertheless, the Breaking of the Vessels is a truly cataclysmic event. Will, Wisdom, and Understanding remain, but all other *values*, particularly those embodied in the cultural and symbolic order of mankind, have been shattered. Further, while certain forms (may) remain, their embodiment in matter is chaotic and confused. The Breaking of the Vessels is, according to the Lurianic Kabbalah, a clearing of the decks, a fresh start, and a challenge to the structures that we equate with our own civilized life. It is, in short, an eruption of chaos into the heart of our spiritual, conceptual, moral, and psychological structures.

There is also a decided sexual aspect to the Breaking of the Vessels. The vessels, as described by Luria's most important disciple, Chayyim Vital, are envisioned as being located in the womb of the feminine *Partzuf*, the Cosmic Mother, an expression of the age-old symbol of the feminine as "vessel," "receptacle," and "container." Further, the shattering of these vessels brings about a state of affairs in which the masculine and feminine aspects of the cosmos, which had hitherto been in a "face-to-face" sexual conjunction, turn their backs upon one another and become completely disjoined. The "chaos" brought about by the *Shevirah* leads to an erotic alienation, a condition that can only be remedied through a rejoining of opposites via a renewed *coniunctio* of the sexes. At the same time, like the water that breaks signaling the birth of a new human life, the Breaking of the Vessels also heralds a new birth, that of a new personal and world order to be completed by man in the process of *Tikkun*.

As we explore the vessel imagery in the Lurianic Kabbalah we will discover that the Breaking of the Vessels is, in a remarkable way, premonitory of a number of contemporary ideas in psychology, psychoanalysis, and philosophy. By understanding the relationship of the Lurianic system to these contemporary ideas we will better be able to comprehend the metaphysical notions of which the Kabbalists of Safed first spoke over 400 years ago.

THE COSMIC CATASTROPHE: THE BASIC DOCTRINE

Along with the doctrine of "*Tzimtzum*" (concealment and contraction), the "Breaking of the Vessels" (*Shevirat ha-Kelim*) distinguishes Lurianism from the previous Kabbalah. Indeed, it is the dynamic treatment of the *Sefirot*, through their breaking asunder, which separates the system of Luria and his disciples from prior kabbalistic schemes. However, as we saw in the case of *Tzimtzum*, a number of developments in the Kabbalah prior to Luria anticipate the *Shevirah* idea. For example, the Zohar takes a profound interest in the midrashic notion of earlier worlds that had been created and then destroyed prior to the creation of the earth (Genesis Rabbah 3: 9) According to the Zohar, these worlds were primal emanations of the Holy Ancient One (*Atika Kaddisha*, or *Keter*). These emanations, the Zohar tells us, are the lights from the *bozina di kardinuta* ("spark of blackness"), which, like sparks from a blacksmith's hammer and anvil, "flared, shone, and then went out immediately."[3] They are, according to the Zohar, ephemeral worlds that were emanated prior to the emanation of the *Sefirot*, and are called "kings." These kings are equated with the "kings of Edom," referred to in Genesis 36: 31, who reigned and died before there reigned any king over Israel. According to the Zohar the "kings" of earlier worlds were destroyed because they issued forth from a measure of unrestrained judgment that had not yet been part of a perfectly balanced system of love, judgment, and mercy.[4] The Zohar also

---

3. Zohar III, 292b (*Idra Zuta*), Tishby and Lachower, *The Wisdom of the Zohar*, Vol. 1, pp. 276, 289.

4. Tishby and Lachower, *The Wisdom of the Zohar*, Vol. 1, p. 276.

relates that the world had not yet achieved a balance through the union of cosmic masculine and feminine elements, and, above all, that the earlier worlds had to be destroyed "because Man had not yet been prepared."[5]

As will be evident shortly, many of the themes in the Zohar's discussion of the ephemeral worlds and kings are reiterated or transformed in the Lurianic symbol of the Breaking of the Vessels. Of particular interest is the Zohar's notion that only with the advent of man can the cosmic forces be sufficiently harmonized to sustain a world. We shall see, in Chapter Nine, that for Luria, it is precisely humanity that bears much of the burden of repairing and restoring the world (*Tikkun ha-Olam*) after the Breaking of the Vessels.

Moses Cordovero, whose approach to the Kabbalah is generally philosophical, reinterpreted the Zohar's account of the ephemeral worlds in purely conceptual terms. According to Cordovero, these "worlds" refer to possibilities within the divine mind that remained unrealized because of their inherent illogicality or unworkability.[6] We will have occasion to provide a conceptual understanding of the *Shevirah* later in this chapter. Here, however, it should be pointed out that for Luria and his followers, the Breaking of the Vessels was meant to refer to each and every department of existence, from the physical to the conceptual, from the psychological to the historical.

In order to appreciate the breadth and depth of the doctrine of the Breaking of the Vessels, it will be useful to provide a brief review of the place of this doctrine within the Lurianic system as a whole.

We recall, that according to Luria, the creation of the world is predicated on an act of self-limitation or concealment (*Tzimtzum*) on the part of the Infinite God (*Ein-Sof*, literally "without end"). God, who is completely coterminous with Being itself, "makes room," as it were, for finite creatures by contracting or concealing Himself. This concealment gives rise to a metaphysical void (*tehiru* or *chalal*). This void has none of the characteristics of physical space but is rather conceived in epistemological terms as a point or aspect of Absolute Being within which the divine presence is relatively obscured or unknown. Into this void the "light of the Infinite" (*Or Ein-Sof*) emanates or manifests itself as "Primordial Man" (*Adam Kadmon*), a

---

5. Zohar III, 135a–135b, *Idra Rabba*, Tishby and Lachower, *The Wisdom of the Zohar*, Vol. 1, pp. 332–333.

6. Tishby and Lachower, *The Wisdom of the Zohar*, Vol. 1, pp. 289, 305, note 83.

nonmaterial representation of the characteristics (*middot*) of God, which ultimately come to be reflected in mankind. "Lights" from the eyes of Primordial Man emanate further into the void and create a series of luminaries or spheres (the *Sefirot*), which serve as vessels (*kelim*) for containing and structuring the light of the infinite God. These vessels, which are an extension of God's own substance, are distinct from God only from the perspective of man. They are likened to a series of curtains or colored glass containers, which alter the perception of God's light from the point of view of an observer but which create no change whatsoever in the light itself.

The *Sefirot* are ten in number and represent a series of divine traits (*middot*) that, "prior" to the initial act of *Tzimtzum*, exist perfectly commingled and unified as part of the divine plenum. The *Sefirot* (usually labeled "Wisdom," "Understanding," "Knowledge," "Kindness," "Judgment," "Beauty," "Endurance," "Majesty," "Foundation," and "Kingship") are understood to be the archetypes that combine with one another to form the structural elements of the "upper" and "lower" worlds (*olamot*). In themselves, the *Sefirot* are said to each represent a progressively greater concealment of the infinite light. However, their presence in each of the four worlds from *Atzilut* to *Assiyah* also represents a diminishment, so that, for example the "*Tiferet of Atzilut*" is on a much higher or more divine level than the "*Tiferet of Beriah*," and so on. The *Sefirot* are also tentatively organized into a series of *Partzufim* or "divine visages." These *Partzufim* will become more stable and prominent with the advent of *Tikkun* (the restoration) but even (logically) prior to the *Shevirah*, the *Sefirot* are organized into such visages and they are frequently referred to (e.g., in *Sefer Etz Chayyim*) by the names of their corresponding *Partzufim*. As such, the *Sefirot Chochmah* and *Binah* are spoken of as "*Abba*" (Father) and "*Imma*" (Mother), and the *Sefirot* from *Chesed* to *Yesod* are collectively spoken of as the *Partzuf Zeir Anpin* (the Short-Faced One), or simply by the abbreviation "*Z'A*." It should, however, be remembered that while each *Partzuf* and world is as it were "dominated" by a particular *Sefirah* (and vice versa), each of the *Sefirot* have a manifestation in each world and *Partzuf*, creating a huge system of multiple connections and names that is made even more complex by yet other designations referring to psychic and cosmic levels.[7] All of this language and imagery, particularly as it relates to the Worlds, *Sefirot*, and

---

7. As discussed in Chapter Four.

Partzufim becomes especially prominent in Vital's discussion of the *Shevirat ha-Kelim*.

As we have seen, the *Sefirot* were originally meant to be vessels or containers for the structuring of God's light in the created world. However, according to Luria and his disciples, what was meant, was not to be. The lights destined for the first three *Sefirot* were contained by their respective vessels, but the remaining vessels were neither large nor strong enough to contain the lights that were to fill them. As Vital put it, "the opposite act which created (the vessels) destroyed them." The vessels were created by the removal of divine light and destroyed by the light's emanation.[8] These *Sefirot* or vessels (*kelim*) were thus broken into a multitude of shards, which fell through the metaphysical void, each shard capturing within itself some of the divine light, which by now had been alienated from its source in God. The final *Sefirah* (Kingship) was also partly shattered and it too broke into a number of shards that also trapped divine light and fell through the void.

With the Breaking of the Vessels much of the light that was destined for the *Sefirot* rose to the upper worlds and was reorganized into a series of five configurations (*Partzufim*), each of which represents a visage or basic aspect of God as He is reflected in mankind (the Long-Faced or "Ancient One," the Supernal Father and Mother, the Son, and the Daughter). However, the shards that fell through the metaphysical space gave rise to the *Kelippot* (shells or *Husks*) that constitute the dark forces of *Sitra Achra* (the "Other Side"). These *Kelippot* are conceived of as the source of all evil. They are essentially lifeless waste and dross that are maintained in their power by the spark of divine light that they enclose. Because this light is separated from the light of the Infinite God, the *Kelippot* obtain a measure of independent existence and are the source of all that is not spiritual, i.e., material, in the created world.

If not for the Breaking of the Vessels the universe would be harmonious, purely spiritual, and devoid of both matter and evil. As a result of the cosmic catastrophe, however, the world must, according to Luria, be repaired or restored. This restoration process, known as *Tikkun ha-Olam* (the mending of the world) was begun as soon as the lights from the original *Sefirot* were partially reorganized and reconstituted as the five visages or *Partzufim*. However, the complete restoration and respiritualization of the universe must be completed by mankind. Indeed this restoration, according to the

---

8. Chayyim Vital, *Sefer Etz Chayyim*, p. 26.

Kabbalah, is the task of man on earth, and particularly the task of the Jewish people, who through their observance of Torah and *mitzvot* (the precepts of the Jewish religion) have the power to release the "sparks" (*netzotzim*) of divine light trapped in the multitude of *Kelippot*, and raise them to be reunited with the infinite light from which they came.

SOME DETAILS OF THE *SHEVIRAH* DOCTRINE

The above provides an account of the doctrine of the Breaking of the Vessels or *Shevirah* in bare outline, as understood, for example, by the Hasidim, and as it is commonly presented in popular expositions of the Kabbalah. However, Vital actually provides us with a far more detailed, almost obsessive account of the sefirotic events that constitute the Breaking of the Vessels.[9] While it will not serve us to follow him through the entirety of his baroque description of these metaphysical events, a review of some of the main details will provide us with insight not only into the incorporation of zoharic themes into the heart of the Lurianic Kabbalah but, more importantly, with a deeper understanding of the *Shevirah* itself. We will see, for example, that the Breaking of the Vessels is on a basic level a rupture in the sexual harmony that exists between male and female on the cosmic level.

   According to Vital, with the original emanation of the Worlds, the Celestial Father and Mother (the *Partzufim Abba* and *Imma*, which correspond to the *Sefirot Chochmah* and *Binah*) were in a state of *coniunctio*, existing "face to face." This state of affairs derives, Vital informs us, from the original divine unity, an aspect of which has been transferred to these *Partzufim/Sefirot* by virtue of their having emerged from the highest *Sefirah*, *Keter*. Male and female were, as it were, in a state of continuous, harmonious, union, and the facets of the ideal or intellective realm represented by the Celestial Father and Mother were unified as well. Vital describes how the face-to-face (*panim a panim*) status of the Father and Mother visages was maintained by "feminine waters" (*mayim nukvim*) emanating from the interior of the Mother. Strangely, he attributes the existence of these feminine waters to the presence of "seven kings," which had been inserted

---

9. See Vital, *Sefer Etz Chayyim* 2: 2, "The Breaking of the Vessels." In addition a detailed description of these events is presented in Luzzatto, *General Principles of the Kabbalah*.

into the Mother by the Father. For Vital no less than for the Zohar, these "kings" are a reference to the "seven kings" who reigned and died in Edom (Genesis 36: 31) and who are taken by the Zohar to represent the earlier worlds that, according to a Midrash, were created and destroyed prior to the creation of the earth. Vital has, with this image of the "kings," relocated an entire biblical, midrashic, and zoharic tradition in the viscera of the Celestial Mother.

Initially there is a reciprocal relationship between the seven kings and the Father and Mother. The seven kings inside the Mother raise up the feminine waters and cause the coupling of Father and Mother. This in turn results in divine lights of the *Sefirot Chesed* and *Gevurah* being drawn down to sustain the "brains" of the kings. Had the kings not died, they would have kept the father and mother face to face, and, in turn, would have been maintained in their own essence.

The kings, we learn, represent the seven lower *Sefirot* in the body of the Mother. It is these *Sefirot,* Vital informs us, which are the first to shatter, with repercussions for the entire cosmic structure. The death of the kings, or what amounts to the same thing, the Breaking of the Vessels, results in a cessation of the upward flow of feminine waters and, further, a loss of support in the bodies of both *Chochmah* and *Binah* (Father and Mother), with the result that these *Sefirot/Partzufim* can no longer maintain their face-to-face, *coniunctio* status.[10]

There is a logical progression in the *Shevirah,* beginning with the death of the first king, *Da'at,* and ending with the partial shattering of the last, *Malchut.* This progression proceeds broadly as follows. Each *Sefirah* consists of a *keli* or vessel that is meant to contain the divine light projected into it, initially from the eyes of *Adam Kadmon* but more immediately from the *Sefirah* above it in the chain.[11] The vessels closest to the origin of the divine light were large and strong enough to contain the lights projected into them. Even though *Chochmah,* for example, is slightly smaller and weaker than *Keter,* the vessel of *Chochmah* is able to contain all of the light transmitted to

---

10. As we have seen in Chapter Four, there is a disagreement among the Lurianists in their enumeration of the ten *Sefirot.* Vital, who normally excludes *Da'at* from the ten, here regards this *Sefirah* as the first "shattered king." He now, of course, has eleven *Sefirot* but he eliminates this problem by holding in this context that *Netzach* and *Hod,* which are often thought of as "supports" for the upper *Sefirot,* are to be regarded as a single *Sefirah.*

11. See Schochet, "Mystical Concepts," pp. 874–877.

it by *Keter* with the exception of a small excess, which becomes an *Or Makif*, or encompassing, external light around the *Sefirah Chochmah*. However, the light transmitted from *Binah* to the fourth *Sefirah*, *Da'at*, not only contained the light that was meant for this *Sefirah*, but also the light destined for all of the lower *Sefirot* as well. *Da'at* was simply unable to contain this light and it shattered, the shards of its broken vessel falling into the lower worlds (particularly the world of *Beriah*), and the light that it could not contain being transmitted to the next *Sefirah*, *Chesed*. In like manner Chesed shattered, the shards from its vessel falling into *Beriah*, and its light transmitted to *Gevurah*, and so on down the order of the *Sefirot* until the *Sefirah Yesod* that initially receives only the light destined for the last *Sefirah Malchut*. As a result of this interruption in the flow of light, *Yesod* remained temporarily intact, and thus was able to transmit an appropriate level of light to *Malchut*, the lower regions of which were thereby strengthened through this suffusion of divine energy. Ultimately, however, light remaining from the shattering of the upper *Sefirot* were transmitted to *Yesod*, and this vessel also shattered; but *Malchut*, having been strengthened in the manner just described, remained partially intact, shattering only in its higher, more subtle regions.[12]

Vital points out that the *Shevirah* has repercussions for the *Sefirot* above *Chesed*, which did not shatter. He tells us that the correct terminology with regard to the impact of the *Shevirah* on *Chochmah* and *Binah* is *bittul* (nullification) as opposed to *mita* (death), for death only applies to those entities that "fall out of their own world into another," as occurs with the lower vessels that shatter. *Keter*, the highest *Sefirah*, does not even suffer nullification: the term appropriate to it is *pagam*, "blemish." We thus have three levels of catastrophe: "death," "nullification," and "blemish." However, "death" does not even fully apply to the shattered *Sefirot*, the so-called "kings who died," for these "kings" are eventually restored to new life in the World of *Tikkun*.

The Breaking of the Vessels occurs initially among the *Sefirot* in the world of *Atzilut*, which is adjacent to the emanator, *Adam Kadmon*. However, the same events, in what amounts to a cosmic chain reaction, occur in all of the other worlds as well: the shards from the vessels of *Beriah* falling into the world of *Yetzirah*, those from *Yetzirah* into *Assiyah*, etc. As these shards fall they entrap sparks (*netzotzim*) of divine light that were originally

---

12. Schochet, "Mystical Concepts," p. 874–875.

meant to be contained in the vessels. Originally there were 288 sparks falling out of *Atzilut*, but these sparks subdivide into far greater numbers, each attaching to a shard, as they tumble through the metaphysical void. As the sparks descend they become more material and crude, their more subtle and ethereal aspects being absorbed by the upper worlds. The lowest, crudest sparks, which could not be reassimilated into the realm of the holy, become, in conjunction with the shards which enclose them, the *Kelippot* (Husks) that form the "Other Side" (*Sitra Achra*), the realm of impurity. Because the Husks contain a faint kernel of divine light and life they have the energy to be the origin and sustenance of all that is malevolent and evil.[13] Our world, as a result of the Breaking of the Vessels, is partially sunk into this impure realm, and, hence, both moral wickedness and natural evil abound on earth. The sparks contained within the Husks await release and restoration with the advent of *Tikkun*.

The Husks not only give rise to wickedness and evil, they are also, according to the Lurianists, the origin of matter and individual existence. As the broken shards tumble down through the worlds they become further and further estranged from their source in God, and, as such, more distinct in their independent existence. The Husks are the roots of the "four elements" that comprise the material world. Earlier we said that the *Sefirot* are the constituent elements of the world. We are now in a position to see that this is true of the worlds as they were originally conceived and emanated by *Ein-Sof*. However, *our actual world* is composed of the broken shards of the original sefirotic elements. Ours is a distorted, displaced, deformed existence that calls out for restoration and repair.

SEPARATION OF THE CELESTIAL FATHER AND MOTHER

A major consequence of the Breaking of the Vessels is, as we have seen, the separation of the Celestial Father (*Abba*) and Mother (*Imma*). This separation, or "turning," proceeds in an almost mechanical fashion, step by step with the death of each of the seven kings. One of the functions of the kings, particularly of the first king, *Da'at*, is to draw the light of Kindness (*Chesed*) and Strength (*Gevurah*) from the Primordial Adam into the "heads" of the

---

13. As will be discussed in detail in Chapter Eight.

Celestial Father and Mother. With the death of the first King, the Father and Mother lose the lights of both Kindness and Strength and thereby turn their gaze from one another. Though they are still connected "corporeally," the Father and Mother *Partzufim* have lost their spiritual connection with one another. We might say that one of the first results of the Breaking of the Vessels is a disruption in what Martin Buber has called the relationship of "I and thou." With the death of the subsequent kings there is a further rupture in the relationship between Father (*Abba*) and Mother (*Imma*). The first to completely turn its back on the other is the Father. Eventually both *Abba* and *Imma* completely turn their backs on one another, with the exception of *Yesod Abba*, the phallus of the father, which, according to Vital, has no "back" to turn. Indeed, we learn that the entire *Partzuf* of *Abba* descends before there is any damage to the "unity of *Yesod* in *Abba*." The disjunction between the Father and Mother does not cripple the Father's future procreative capacity. This capacity, of course, is critical for the reunification of the Mother and Father that will occur in *Tikkun*.[14]

The images we have been describing are celestial but their significance is very human. The very act of creation, according to the Kabbalists, has written into it the potential, even the necessity, of its own demise. Creation, here represented in its supreme form as the relationship between man and woman, is imperfect in its very essence (a conclusion that follows from the fact that "individuality" is, as we have seen, already an estrangement from God). The "ideal world," in which a celestial or earthly mother and father gaze happily and eternally into each other's eyes, and in which all ideas, values, and emotions are in their proper place, is an illusion. The Kabbalists were aware of this illusion, and they expressed their understanding of the confused, conflictual, antinomous, condition of human experience in the images and symbols we have just described.

---

14. Our picture is complicated by the fact that, according to Vital, the *Partzufim Abba* and *Imma* are associated with two other "subpartzufim," *Yisrael Sava* (Old Israel) and *Tevunah* (a diminutive form of *Binah* or Mother). While *Abba* and *Imma* are completely "descended" (turned back to back) by the time of the death of the fourth king, *Tiferet*, these lower *Partzufim* do not descend until all seven *Sefirot* have been shattered. The whole scheme calls to mind a mechanical "pinball" type device in which machinations among the seven shattering Vessels or Kings automatically cause further machinations among lights and images representing two caricatured male/female relationships.

THE *SHEVIRAH* AS A NECESSARY COSMIC OCCURRENCE

The confusion and chaos that resulted from the Breaking of the Vessels was, for the Kabbalists, an inevitable result of the infinite becoming finite, of the divine unity giving itself over to individuality and freedom. Indeed, the Kabbalists imply that the price we pay for the supreme values of freedom and individuality is confusion, conflict, and disharmony in the arena of *all other values*. For them, the Breaking of the Vessels was a necessary (if, in some ways, unfortunate) byproduct of creation itself.[15] The Kabbalists held that the disharmony and conflict resulting from the Breaking of the Vessels was ultimately necessary for the establishment of the very values that were shattered and for the ultimate perfection of God himself.[16] This idea is articulated quite clearly in Chabad, where it is held that God's revelation must proceed through destruction and restoration. For example, according to Rabbi Aharon Halevi Horowitz: "So that His blessed divinity could be revealed, there had to be a *breaking* and a *restoration* so that the aspect of

---

15. According to Luzzatto the Breaking of the Vessels "was no accident . . . for it was the intention of the Supreme Thought to effect what actually took place at the time of the shattering." Luzzatto, *General Principles of the Kabbalah*, p. 198.

16. This disharmony, as we have seen, is conceived by Vital as an erotic separation between the Celestial Father (*Abba*) and Mother (*Imma*). It is of interest to note that according to Vital, *Abba* and *Imma* originally needed no arousal to achieve their *coniunctio* status. God's will to emanate them this way, Vital relates, was all that was needed for them to remain "face to face." For reasons that are not fully explained by Vital, but that are connected with the inevitable fate of finite creatures to separate and then seek unity, *Chochmah* was compelled to introduce the seven kings into *Binah*, with the result that their continued relationship would now be completely dependent upon their own sexuality. It is only subsequent to this primal sexual act that the conjunction of *Abba* and *Imma* becomes dependent upon the flow of *mayim nukvim*, the feminine waters. Once the erotic element is introduced into the cosmos, it, and not God's original unity, becomes the force that maintains the world's cohesion. We can surmise that sexuality, by introducing an attractive force between finite creatures, paradoxically both contributes to these creatures' separateness, while, at the same time, holding out the basic possibility for their being joined together. As we shall see in Chapter Nine, *Tikkun ha-Olam*, the repair and restoration of the world, is, for Vital, a rejoining of the broken erotic bonds between man and woman.

Yesh would be revealed as a separate aspect and through the 'restoration' Divinity would be manifest in the aspect of the Yesh."[17]

LINGUISTIC ASPECTS OF THE *SHEVIRAH* DOCTRINE

As with each of the other aspects of the Lurianic system, the Breaking of the Vessels is also elaborated in linguistic terms. According to Luzzatto

> all the stages of extended Light are also represented by combination of letters. These are the functioning lights from which everything comes into being. Since they were unable to endure the abundance of Light, the combination of letters became disarranged and were severed from each other. They were thus rendered powerless to act and to govern. This is what is meant by their "shattering."[18]

On this view the Breaking of the Vessels, like a cosmic Tower of Babel, is a disruption in linguistic coherence and meaning. As we will see in Chapter 9, the reversal of this process, *Tikkun ha-Olam*, the Restoration of the World, involves a re-creation of meaning and significance, and thus a respiritualization of the cosmos.

THE *SHEVIRAH* IN HISTORY

Luria and his disciples understood the Breaking of the Vessels as a process that permeates the entirety of creation. As Luzzatto puts it: "It is necessary to bear in mind the principle that all things existing in the world exemplify that which occurred in those 'Kings.'"[19] In particular, the Breaking of the Vessels is reflected and reenacted in the history of mankind, and in the history of the Jewish people in particular. For example, according to Luria, when the biblical Adam was created, *Tikkun ha-Olam*, the restoration of the world, was almost complete. Adam's task was to complete the *Tikkun* and hence restore all things to their divinely appointed place, an event that could occur only

---

17. Rabbi Aharon Halevi, *Sha'arei ha-'Avodah* II, Chapter 7 as cited in Elior, *The Paradoxical Ascent to God*, p. 74.
18. Luzzatto, *General Principles of the Kabbalah*, p. 64.
19. Ibid., p. 90.

through Adam's exercise of free choice and decision. Had Adam obeyed the one commandment he was provided, had he made a choice for good, the Husks would have been cut off from the divine light and evil rendered null and void. However by "separating the fruit from the tree" Adam failed in his *Tikkun* and thus, as it were, reenacted the Breaking of the Vessels in the human psychic realm. Originally, Adam was himself meant to be an eternal, purely spiritual being, but his failure to follow the command of God made him temporal and mortal[20] and caused his and our world (the world of *Assiyah*) to sink to the level of the Husks, thereby mixing good with evil and giving birth to corporeality and human finitude. Adam and Eve's banishment from Eden, the first in a long series of biblical *exiles*, is reflected on the cosmic level by the exile of the *Shekhinah*, the alienation of God's presence on earth from God Himself. This alienation is in turn symbolized by the severed divine sparks that are trapped in the "Other Side," the realm of the *Kelippot*.

There have been other times in human history, the Sinaitic revelation being one, where *Tikkun ha-Olam* and cosmic redemption were nearly at hand. However, on each of these occasions the Jewish people failed in their mission, freely choosing to align themselves with the forces of the "Other Side" (e.g., in the incident of the Golden Calf) and thereby reenacting the Breaking of the Vessels and strengthening, rather than destroying, the Husks.

PSYCHIC ASPECTS OF THE *SHEVIRAT HA-KELIM*

There is a psychic aspect to *Tikkun ha-Olam* that is relevant to each and every individual. According to Luria, it is not only the divine presence that is imprisoned in the shards of the broken vessels, but the sparks (*netzotzim*) of human souls as well. Most of these "souls" and "soul roots" are trapped in the realm of the Husks where they give rise to an unholy anti-Adam in the "Other Side." An aspect of each individual's soul is also entrapped in the Husks of the "Other Side" and it is incumbent upon each man and woman to free his or her own sparks from that realm. Thus the "raising of the sparks" expresses both the meaning of Jewish (and human) history and the signifi-

---

20 Indeed the very act of disobedience was, in effect, the first temporal act, and in performing it Adam is already placed in time and surrenders his immortality (see Chapter Six).

cance of the individuals' task in life as well. The Kabbalist Moses Zacuto expressed the mystical task of the individual in the following succinct fashion: "It behooves every man to inquire diligently and to know the root of his soul as to be able to perfect it and restore it to its origin, which is the essence of its being. The more a man perfects himself, the closer he comes to his self."[21]

Another psychic manifestation of the *Shevirah* is experienced in the course of a man's lifetime. The *structures* a man or woman builds from birth, the vessels that contain his energy, his passions, his ideas, and his pain, are subject to the same shattering and consequent possibility for renewal that pervades the world as a whole. Indeed such a shattering is virtually inevitable. According to the Kabbalists, the *Sefirot* shattered because they were disunited and thereby unable to contain the overflowing abundance of God's divine light. On another interpretation, the original *Sefirot* were a premature crystallization of divine energy. As an individual matures, he or she too creates structures that serve to contain his psychic energy or libido. For many, however, the structures developed at age twenty (the ideas, values, economic and social arrangements, friendships, marriages, loves, etc.) are unable to contain one's passion, pain, and energy at age forty. For some a crisis results in the shattering of many of the old structures and an opportunity for personal and spiritual renewal. The Breaking of the Vessels thus raises a number of important questions. Among these are whether the "vessels" that society provides an individual to structure his lifetime are large and flexible enough to contain that individual throughout the life span? Or is the symbolic order of culture, like the divine *Sefirot*, inherently incapable of containing man's light? Further, the same questions may be asked with respect to Judaism and its structures. Do these, in kabbalistic terms, inevitably shatter as well?

One set of answers to these questions develops from the idea that with the fall of Adam, the *Shevirah* was introduced into the heart of every (now) mortal man. With the fall of Adam, not only did Adam's body become mortal and finite, but all of the structures within which he lived became finite as well. The fall was, as Scholem has pointed out, the origin of man's dialectical condition, in which life develops through conflict, rather than through the smooth evolution of incremental variation.

---

21. Moses Zacuto, commentary on Zohar I, 78a in Shalom B. Moses Busalgo, *Mikdash Melech* (Amsterdam, 1750), as quoted and translated by Scholem, *Sabbatai Sevi: The Mystical Messiah*, pp. 41–42.

THE *SHEVIRAH* AND DIVINE CATHARSIS

An important development within the Lurianic system is reflected in two fundamental questions that are raised and tentatively answered by the Kabbalists of Safed. These questions, *"Why was the process of Tzimtzum set in motion?"* and *"Why did the Breaking of the Vessels occur?"* are integrally related, and the answers provided can grant us further insight into the Lurianic worldview.

The Kabbalists offered several theories about the purpose of creation, most of which revolve around the premise that part of God's perfection is embodied in a "desire to give" and that God is hence incomplete without a complementary aspect which embodies the "desire to receive." Just as there can be no giver without a receiver, there can be no Godly king without a finite world to rule.[22] According to the Zohar, God could not become one with himself "until he created the world."[23] Thus creation, which is an essential complement to divinity, follows with the force of logical necessity: creation is, on this view, part of the very *idea* of God.

Among Luria and his followers, as we have already seen in Chapter Three, there arose the speculation that creation involved something akin to a "divine catharsis." God, for the Kabbalists, is originally coterminous with being and contains within Himself all the potential aspects of the universe in a unified or "homogenized" form. According to Luria, this is indeed one level of perfection. Yet this level of perfection somehow seeks a higher level in which the forces of *Din* (judgment), which embody the potential for negation and evil, are purged from the divine plenum. Creation begins when these forces are crystallized within the heart of (God's) Being. These crystallized forces provide the "negation" that brings about the original act of *Tzimtzum* and the creation of the *Sefirot*. The *Sefirot* themselves, which are meant to hold the infinite light, cannot do so because (as a result of their creation through *Din* [judgment, negation]) they are separate, disunified, and (in part) negative structures.

The Breaking of the Vessels, which according to some Kabbalists was an unfortunate accident, is seen, in this view, to be a continuation of the divine

---

22. Schneur Zalman writes, "It is known to all that the purpose of the creation of the world is for the sake of the revelation of His kingdom, may He be blessed, for 'There is no King without a nation.'" *Shaar Hayivhid Ve'Emunah*, Ch. 7; Zalman, *Likutei Amarim-Tanya*, p. 307.

23. Zohar 1, 29a; Sperling and Simon, *The Zohar*, Vol. 1, pp. 110–111.

catharsis and a vehicle for the ultimate elimination of the forces of *Din* or evil. In order to purge the absolute being of evil, evil must first be given a manifest as opposed to purely latent form. This is achieved through the Breaking of the Vessels, which brings about a crystallization of these negative forces in the form of the Husks that descend into the "Other Side."

The essential idea behind the cathartic theory is that since God as the whole of Being contains evil within Himself, historical, finite creatures must become the vehicle through which the divine plenum is purged of all that is not purely good. The *freedom of choice* granted man to decide between good and evil is God's means of purging evil from Himself. The world will have a greater perfection after *Tikkun* than it had before the Breaking of the Vessels and even before the original *Tzimtzum*. Again, as we have seen, the Lurianic Kabbalists entertained the notion that man's destiny is a part of the improvement or perfection of God Himself.[24]

THE CAUSES OF THE *SHEVIRAH*

The Kabbalists did not tire of speculating as to the causes of the Breaking of the Vessels. While one reason for the *Shevirah* could, as we have just seen, be traced to the gathering of the forces of judgment within the Godhead and the consequent necessity for a "divine catharsis," the Lurianists attributed the *Shevirah* more immediately to the imperfect structure of the *Sefirot* as they were originally emanated in "the World of Points." On one view the *Sefirot* in that world were too weak, atomized, isolated, and disorganized to contain the power of the divine light. Vital uses a common saying to express this idea: "if you take ten reeds separately they will easily break, but if you take just three together they will endure,"[25] On a second, related, view an imbalance was created by the completely circular nature of the original *Sefirot*. As we have discussed in Chapter Four, the *Sefirot* emanated according to the scheme of *Iggulim* (Circles) were completely disjoined.[26] Only when they are structured linearly, according to the scheme of *Yosher* (Lines) do they take the integrated, organic form of Primordial Man, and have the power to contain the full emanation of divine light. On a third view, the *Sefirot* were

---

24. Chapter Two.
25. Vital, *Etz Chayyim* 11: 5, 9: 2, 19: 1, as cited in Schochet, "Mystical Concepts," p. 875.
26. See Chapter Four.

held to be incomplete because they were composed only of "branches" of emanations, the "roots" remaining hidden within the emanator, *Adam Kadmon*. Scholem has referred to these explanations as "mythological," in contrast to the "theological" perspective embodied within the theory of "divine catharsis."

An interesting perspective on the *Shevirah* is provided by Israel Sarug, who, as recounted by Scholem, held that "the world of points was like a sown field where seeds could not bear fruit until they had first split open and rotted."[27] This metaphor is intriguing for its suggestion that destruction and degeneration is necessary to further creation. It suggests that only in an imperfect, "split open," even "rotted" world, can the values that make creation worthwhile (the world's "fruit") become actual. Indeed, this very suggestion is implicit in the writings of such Kabbalists as Cordovero[28] and Vital,[29] who held that evil serves the divine purpose of providing an arena in which man can exercise his free will and thereby be rewarded according to his righteousness. According to Schneur Zalman of Lyadi, God's very purpose in creating the lower worlds is that he might delight in man's subjugation of evil.[30] The reason for the cosmic catastrophe is the creation of a material world of infinite possibilities in which man can exercise his freedom to choose good over evil, and thereby actualize the Godly attributes of Kindness, Judgment, Compassion, etc.

This, in outline, is the doctrine of the Breaking of the Vessels and the related concepts in the Lurianic Kabbalah within which this doctrine is embedded. As has been my practice throughout this book, many of the details of the Lurianic system have, of course, been neglected, not only for the sake of brevity but also because with Luria's thought one runs the risk of being overwhelmed by the details and imagery, thus failing to see the profound philosophical concepts that underlie them. In the following sections we will explore some of the philosophical implications of the vessels theory and thereby gain an understanding of the power of the *Shevirah* metaphor to shed light on the philosophical and psychological dilemmas of our own time.

---

27. Scholem, *Kabbalah*, p. 140.
28. Moses Codovero, *Pardes Rimmonim* 25: 3. Cited in Schochet, "Mystical Concepts," p. 890.
29. Vital, *Etz Chayyim* 11: 6, 37: 2, 39: 1. Cited in Schochet, ibid.
30. Zalman, *Tanya*, Ch. 36. *Likutei Amarim-Tanya*, p. 163ff.

THE *SHEVIRAH*: EXILE AND ALIENATION

According to Gershom Scholem, Lurianic Kabbalah is marked by a dominance of mythological over speculative themes. Scholem held that the Lurianic system gained widespread acceptance because it couched the Jewish experience of exile (*galut*) and the wish for redemption (*ge'ulah*) in cosmic, mythological terms.[31] The individual Jew, by immersing himself in the Lurianic imagery, was made to feel that his own plight and the plight of his people had a metaphysical significance for the entire universe and for the inner life of God Himself. The Jewish people's own exile from their homeland in *Eretz Yisrael* was indeed paralleled by the exile of God's *Shekhinah* among the forces of the "Other Side." The wish for a Jewish Messiah was reinterpreted by Luria's disciples in such a manner as to link the return of the Jewish people to the land of Israel with the raising of the "divine sparks," the restoration of harmony in the universe, and hence, the perfection of God Himself.

Scholem's analysis has recently been challenged from a historical point of view.[32] More importantly, as I have discussed in the first chapter of this book, Scholem fails to consider the wider philosophical bases for each of the Lurianic claims. As we have seen, the Lurianic system is, on its own account, purely metaphorical in its cosmic descriptions. We are therefore entitled to ask what it is a metaphor for, and whether the ideas to which it points can be articulated and verified in the court of reason and experience.

Earlier, in Chapter One, I suggested an alternative reading of the *Shevirah* doctrine, one that understands the Breaking of the Vessels as symbolic of exile and alienation on an existential and ontological as well as on the historical level. There I argued that the Kabbalistic symbol of the broken vessels and the related myth of the exile of God from Himself implies that the world, as it is experienced by humankind, is indeed broken, flawed and incomplete. Modern thought, in declaring man's alienation from man (existentialism), from himself (Freud), and from the products of his creative labor (Marx), and in deconstructing what, had for centuries been the foundations of culture and religion, has articulated the significance of the *Shevirah* metaphor. To hold, as the Lurianists did, that all being is in exile from itself, is a strikingly apt description of the modern temper. From this

---

31. Scholem, *Kabbalah*, p. 168.
32. By Idel, Wolffson, and others. See Idel, *Messianic Mystics*, pp. 179–182.

perspective the Breaking of the Vessels is not simply a metaphor for Jewish exile, but is rather a symbol for the alienated, antinimous, and deconstructed nature of modern historical experience, which is itself, as I will discuss later in this chapter, a symptom of "ontological exile."

DIALECTICAL PROCESS IN KABBALISTIC THOUGHT

Our understanding of the Breaking of the Vessels can be further enhanced by considering it in relation to "dialectical" thought. Dialectical thinking, in which opposing concepts are mediated and reconciled by a third term, in which ideas are found to imply their contraries, and in which concepts and structures are found to be inadequate and "break down" in favor of new syntheses that transcend but include them is characteristic of the Kabbalah in general. Scholem notes in the Kabbalah "a most astonishing tendency to a mode of contemplative thought that can be called 'dialectic' in the strictest sense of the term used by Hegel."[33] For example, we read in the Zohar:

> In the work of creation there was an antagonism of the left against the right, and the division between them allowed the Gehinnom to emerge and fasten itself to the left. Then the Central Column, which is the third day, intervened and allayed the discord between the two sides, so that Gehinnom descended below, and the Left became absorbed in the Right and there was peace over all.[34]

Dialectical reasoning is also, as we have seen, at work in the Zohar's and Cordovero's theory of the "interpenetration of the *Sefirot*," whereby each of God's traits are said to imply and pass over into each of the others.[35] However, dialectical reasoning in the Kabbalah reaches its apex in Luria, and the symbol of the Breaking of the Vessels is the Lurianists' most powerful metaphor for the dialectical process.

The *Shevirah* can readily be understood as symbolizing a critical moment in the dialectic whereby old concepts and structures break down in favor of new structures and ideas. The Breaking of the Vessels embodies the idea that

---

33. Scholem, *Kabbalah*, p. 143.
34. Zohar 1, 17a; The Zohar, Vol. 1, p. 72.
35. As discussed in Chapter 4.

finite, singular concepts are always insufficient to encompass the subject matter to which they are applied and are consequently always breaking apart and passing over into other concepts, or developing into new ideas that they imply. What the Breaking of the Vessels signifies is that any finite progression of thought will ultimately come to a point where the concepts it generates prove inadequate and must be resynthesized anew in order to account for the subject matter or phenomena to which they are applied. This, in brief, is the essence of dialectical logic.

What evidence do we have to support the idea that the Kabbalists made use of such dialectical reasoning, let alone that one of their major symbols is a metaphor for this reasoning process? If we examine the manner in which the Kabbalists work with their symbols and concepts we soon discover that their logic is decidedly not the sort of Aristotelian reasoning in which nothing can obtain in a conclusion that is not explicitly entailed by the premises. Indeed Kabbalistic reasoning is remarkably similar to the logic of Hegel, in which concepts are said to break down through internal contradiction and then develop in the direction of new, opposing notions and ideas, and in which the results of one's reasoning are only indirectly implied by one's premises.[36]

The Kabbalists make use of such dialectical reasoning when they, for example, infer from the notion of *Tzimtzum* (which is a concealment of knowledge) the existence of structures (the *Sefirot*) and ultimately categories (space, time, and matter) that act to conceal; or when they infer that the *all-inclusive* perfection (*Ein-Sof*) must include within itself (as part of its "all-inclusiveness") certain aspects that would tend toward imperfection (the forces of *Din*) and hence that *Ein-Sof*'s original perfection implies a tendency toward improving itself by eliminating those (potentially) negative strains. It is dialectical reasoning that is at work in Cordovero's notion of the *behinnot*, i.e., that each of the *Sefirot* leads inexorably to each of the others and that each therefore has each of the others contained within itself as an aspect.

It is dialectical reasoning, or better put, a *dialectical* process that begins with an all-inclusive Godhead and results in the existence of *Orot* (Lights), *Kelim* (Vessels), *Partzufim* (Visages), and *Olamot* (Worlds). These entities are not, as one might suppose, speculative inventions of the kabbalistic

---

36. Such dialectical reasoning is the sort of reasoning used by Descartes when he argued from the premise that the world may or may not exist to the inference that there *are beliefs* or *doubts about its existence* and as this example shows, unlike the case of deductive logic, it is a form of reasoning through which we can be introduced to new entities and ideas (I am indebted to J. N. Findlay for this example).

thinkers, or intuitions encountered in states of mystical meditation (although they may be these things as well). Rather, as we have seen already in Chapter Two, the entities that fill the Lurianic universe are, according to the Kabbalists, implied by the very notion of "being" (or "God") itself. "Being," which is perfect, infinite, and One, dialectically tends toward the creation of that which is other, finite, and many. Such creation proceeds through stages in which the created becomes increasingly differentiated, finite, and spatial, and culminates in the existence of a fully instantiated, material world, only to return in the end to a restored, infinite unity. Each stage in the process is seen to be inadequate by its own criterion and as such dialectically evolves into the next stage, only to return back to the beginning in the infinite God. The point where a given notion (e.g., an unchanging, static, infinite God) is seen to be inadequate and begins to pass over into a new phase, is the logical moment of *Shevirat ha-Kelim*, the Breaking of the Vessels.

COGNITIVE AND SCIENTIFIC DEVELOPMENT

We can further clarify the logical significance of the Breaking of the Vessels by relating its dialectic to two seemingly disparate phenomena: the development of intellectual functioning in children and the formation of theories in science. Each of these shows a development that is remarkably analogous to the progression spoken of in the Lurianic "myth."

According to Piaget, intellectual development in children involves the formation of cognitive schemes or structures that, at a critical point in the child's development, "break apart" and are reorganized into new schemes that are more accommodating to the realities of the adult world.[37] Thus the young child, whose functioning is characterized by "concrete operations" maintains a concrete, self-centered view of physical motion in which the moon is thought to follow him as he walks down the street and in which a horse on the inside track of a circular raceway is thought to go "faster" than a horse on the outside track, simply because the "inside" horse is ahead of or "in front" of the outside one. Similarly a child in this stage of cognitive development believes a tall, thin glass to contain more water than a short, broad glass simply because the water level in the former glass is higher. At a

---

37. See Jean Piaget, *Genetic Epistemology* (New York: W. W. Norton, 1970) and Jean Piaget, *Psychology and Epistemology* (New York: Viking, 1971).

certain point in the child's development, as a result of an interaction between biological maturation and experience, the child's concrete structures are reorganized into the more abstract schemas of adult cognition. In the adult schemas, the apparent motion of the moon is understood as a function of its great distance from the earth; the concept of velocity is reorganized as a function of distance over time; and the volume of a cylinder is understood as a function of its height, width, and depth. It is as if the child's concrete structures develop to the point where they can no longer "contain" the world they were designed to mediate, and like the vessels in Luria's image they break down and are reorganized in a fashion that retains elements of the original scheme (the concepts of motion, velocity, and volume) understood in a completely new and more integrated light.

A similar dialectic occurs, according to recent views in the philosophy of science, in the development of scientific theories. According to Thomas Kuhn[38] and others, [39] progress in science occurs as the result of cognitive "revolutions" in which older structures of thought (e.g., the Ptolemaic earth-centered universe) are "shattered" and ultimately yield (through a reorganization of data and concepts) to new structures (e.g., the Copernican sun-centered universe) that replace them. Kuhn, in his now-classic work, *The Structure of Scientific Revolutions*, provides numerous examples that can be interpreted to show that progress in the sciences follows a dialectic that is very much akin to the Lurianic scheme. Another parallel can be seen in the fact that in science as in the kabbalistic concept of *Tikkun*, it is the activity of mankind that is the critical factor in the creation of new, superior structures and forms.

Our discussion of the dialectic implicit in the doctrine of the Breaking of the Vessels and its parallels to progress in individual cognitive development and science is obviously very abbreviated. What it does suggest, however, is that the developments of which Luria and his disciples spoke as occurring within the Godhead have parallels not only in the history of the Jewish people but in other spheres of human endeavor as well. In the following sections we will pursue these parallels in two areas of modern thought: contemporary philosophy and psychoanalysis.

---

38. Thomas S. Kuhn, *The Structure of Scientific Revolutions* (Chicago: University of Chicago Press, 1970).

39. E.g., Paul Feyerabend, *Against Method* (London: NLB, 1975).

CLASSICISM AND ROMANTICISM

The concepts implicit in the symbol of *Shevirat ha-Kelim* are subject to an interesting discussion by the contemporary philosopher Robert Nozick.[40] Nozick, though he shows himself to be familiar with certain kabbalistic concepts (e.g., *Ein-Sof*), does not mention the Breaking of the Vessels by name, but his consideration of what he describes as the role of structure and destruction in classicism and romanticism is wholly relevant to the symbols of *Shevirah* and *Tikkun*. Nozick's discussion raises the question of whether the value of the *Shevirah* is only insofar as it clears the way for a new and better structure via *Tikkun*, or if the destruction wrought by the Breaking of the Vessels might have value in and of itself.

Nozick comments that on "one view, change, novelty and the breaking of the bonds of the previous order," when worthwhile, is so precisely because it opens the way for higher synthesis and unity. Such a pattern of destruction paving the way for a higher synthesis is "exhibited in the arts and sciences as well as in an individual's life."[41] His explanation of this pattern of thought amounts to a conceptual account of the Breaking of the Vessels:

> The pattern involves four stages. (1) Diverse materials are organized in an order, structure, theory, style, hierarchy, unity. (2) The content of this order is extended, new material is introduced (while some old material may be rejected or ignored); *the older modes of organization are broken apart, either under pressure of the new material which they only inadequately could organize*, or through criticism of features intrinsic to that order. (3) A new organization of material is introduced, with new modes of patterning and unification; the new material and much (most?) of the old is combined in a new unity. (4) This unity is then disrupted by the introduction of further new material and the saliency of the fact that it does not perfectly unify the old material. And so on. [italics added][42]

Nozick points out that in the usual view it is the odd-numbered steps, the unifications, that are regarded as valuable. The "breakings asunder" are transition points only to new, better organic unities.

An alternative view, however, sees the goal "in the destruction of the

---

40. Nozick, *Philosophical Explanations*, pp. 613–616.
41. Ibid.
42. Ibid., pp. 613–614.

unities rather than their creation, the breaking asunder of patterns and forms, thereby showing reality or the self or whatever is too protean to be encompassed."[43] On this second view, transcendence, not unity, is the goal to which to aspire. Nozick calls the first view broadly "classical" and the second "romantic." For romanticism, the purpose of unifications is simply to heighten the challenge of the "bursting through." According to Nozick, modernism in art, by using, for example, broken-apart nonartistic objects to *make art*, is an example of the romantic vision. Nozick further illustrates the difference between the first and second views of destruction and unification by contrasting comedy (which he understands as an art form that breaks apart old restrictions in the service of a new unity) and satire, which breaks down without seeking renewed unification.

Finally, Nozick introduces a third alternative, i.e., that the ongoing process, the alteration between destruction and unity is the highest value. He states:

> The process is valuable because, in addition to containing valuable unities as its stages, it itself constitutes a pattern which unifies the widest diversity of human activity. Into this patterned process fall our hopes and activities, our desires to attain and to transcend, our search for value and meaning. Processes as well as resulting end states, becoming as well as being, can have value and can provide the context in which meaning is embedded.[44]

Such a view, of course, accords well with Fichte's and Hegel's notion that the dialectics of this world provide the arena for the development of the human spirit, and Steinsaltz's "Jewish optimism," which holds that the "best of all possible worlds" is "the worst of all possible worlds in which there is yet hope."[45] The very potential for the demise of our efforts, along with the further potential to transcend such demise, is, according to Steinsaltz, the condition for man becoming most fully man, and, hence, for God to become most fully God.

---

43. Ibid., p. 614.
44. Ibid., p. 616.
45. See Steinsaltz, "The Mystic as Philosopher: An Interview with Rabbi Adin Steinsaltz." These views are discussed in detail in Chapter 8.

"PATHOLOGIZING" AND "FALLING APART"

The contemporary psychologist James Hillman provides an interesting extension of the romantic notion of "bursting through." According to Hillman, psychology universally understands psychopathology and the consequent experience of "falling apart" as an ill to be cured, or at best a phase leading to the reorganization of the self or ego. Hillman, however, argues that pathology lies at the core of our very being and has an intimate connection with our uniqueness and individuality. The psyche, according to Hillman, does not exist at all without its own inner sense of "deconstruction."[46] He cites Freud to the effect that we can only "catch" the unconscious in pathological material, and argues that it is precisely through our major and minor life crises, through our confrontation with death, and in our uncanny sense of "crazy" differentness that we achieve our psychic identity.

According to Hillman, the soul produces crazed patterns of sickness, perversion, and degeneration; in dreams and behavior, in art, thought, politics, religion, and war. It does so because pathologizing is a basic archetype of the soul, a fundamental psychic activity per se. Indeed, from a certain perspective, the seemingly uncontrollable fragmentation embodied in the Lurianic notion of the Breaking of the Vessels, and expressed in what is to some a perverse proliferation of fragmentary images in Vital's *Etz Chayyim*, is an example of the soul's pathologizing. Hillman's dictum that such activity must be respected and understood recalls the Zohar's maxim that man must give his due to the "Other Side." According to Hillman, the multiplicity of mythical images embodied in a system of thought such as polytheistic religion, or, in our own context, Vital's *Etz Chayyim*, "provides archetypal containers for differentiating our fragmentation."[47] His discussion of such Greek myths as Bellerophon falling from his crazed white horse, Icarus falling into the sea for flying too close to the sun, and Phaeton's sun chariot hurtling into flames provide graphic analogues to the Kabbalists' Breaking of the Vessels. Each of these myths expresses the view that a sense of humanity is, paradoxically, to be gained through the shattering of man's ego and his consequent fall from the "heavens." Kabbalistically, it is only when the "vessels break" that man can become truly human.[48]

---

46. Hillman, *Revisioning Psychology*, p. 70.
47. Ibid., p. 26.
48. Interestingly, Hillman argues that man is both fragmentary and multiple,

THE *SHEVIRAH* AND PSYCHOANALYSIS

As we have seen, the anthropomorphic metaphors of Lurianic Kabbalah underscore the philosophical point that the universe as a manifestation of God is a personal living Being whose inner dynamic is most clearly reflected in man. It should, therefore come as no surprise that the dialectic described in the Lurianic doctrine of *Shevirat ha-Kelim* should be mirrored in the workings of the individual mind. For this reason it is surprising that so little has been made of a remarkable set of parallels that are to be found between Luria's dialectical descriptions of the cosmos and Freud's dialectic of the human psyche.[49] It is my view that nearly every key concept in the Lurianic system is echoed by an equivalent conception in psychoanalysis. These parallels can only be hinted at below and are discussed more fully in my book, *Kabbalistic Metaphors.*

In psychoanalysis the decidedly Jewish theme of *galut* and *ge'ulah* (exile and redemption), which, according to Scholem and others, plays such a significant role in Luria's cosmology, is, as it were, reconceptualized on the level of the individual. According to Freud, the development of the individual originally involves the formation of the structures id, ego, and superego, which are in essence receptacles designed to channel and modulate the individual's libido, his procreative energy: much as the *Sefirot* for Luria serve as vessels for structuring and modulating the light of God's creative energy or will. For reasons to be discussed momentarily, which are related to Luria's notion of a "divine catharsis," the psychological structures posited by Freud are not consistently able to contain and modulate the libidinous energy in ways that are most adaptive to the individual. There is, one might say, a shattering of these structures and a splitting off (exile) of ideas and emotions from the main fabric of the individual's personality, just as in Luria's system, as a result of the Breaking of the Vessels, divine sparks are separated from the main infinite light of God. This "splitting off" occurs, for example, when an

and that the Jungian goal of restoration to a unified self is an illusion. He would, I believe, welcome the kabbalistic notion that the *Tikkun* or restoration of the cosmos results in the creation of multiple *Partzufim*, "partial personalities" within the Godhead.

49. See Bakan, *Sigmund Freud and the Jewish Mystical Tradition*, where Lurianic Kabbalah is barely even discussed. I have treated this problem in Chapter One.

individual becomes aware of an impulse, thought, or desire that his conscious self finds repugnant or unacceptable. The impulse or idea is cut off and *repressed* (in much the same way as *Ein-Sof* separates out the forces of evil or *Din*) and subsequently exists in a nether psychological realm spoken of as the "unconscious," which is quite analogous to Luria's *Sitra Achra* or "Other Side." Once in the unconscious these "complexes" of thought and affect, which are very much akin to the kabbalistic *Kelippot*, are inaccessible to the individual. They become "exiled," and are the source of all manner and variety of psychological mischief that the individual experiences as depression or other neurotic symptoms, in the same way as the *Kelippot* are the source of negativity and evil on the cosmic level. The job of the psychotherapist is to make these unconscious thoughts and emotions conscious, and more importantly, to free the libidinous energy attached to them so that this energy can be made available to the individual for his own life goals, just as in Luria's system the sparks entrapped by the *Kelippot* must be freed to rejoin the Infinite light and thereby be put in the service of God's ultimate plan.

Thus the Freudian dialectic is itself a form of *Tikkun* (restoration), which brings an end to a *galut* ("exiled" aspects of the individual's personality) and ushers in a *ge'ulah* or psychological redemption. It is also important to note that as the result of psychoanalysis there is a restoration and reorganization of psychological structures in which the harsh, negative aspects of the superego (which embodies "judgment") are eliminated and its function resumed by a realistic but less judgmental ego. This restructuring is quite analogous to Luria's reorganization of the *Sefirot* into *Partzufim*, which subsequent to the Breaking of the Vessels and *Tikkun* are no longer dominated by the negative *trait* of judgment (*Din*) but rather by the positive value of compassion (*Rachamim*).

Of equal significance from a psychoanalytic perspective is the fact that in the Lurianic Kabbalah the Breaking of the Vessels and the resultant splitting off of the "cosmic libido" from the main fabric of the divine personality causes the cosmic Mother and Father to turn their backs on one another, and all sexual and erotic activity to cease. For the Lurianists, as for Freud, psychic exile is essentially a disruption of sexuality, and "cure" amounts to a restoration of erotic love.

It is very tempting, of course, to speculate how the themes of *galut* and *ge'ulah*, and so much of the machinery of Lurianic Kabbalah, should make its way into a theory so seemingly remote from Jewish mysticism as is psychoanalysis. Perhaps Freud was consciously or unconsciously influenced by kabbalistic or Hasidic ideas;[50] perhaps the theme of exile and redemption is a part of the Jewish "collective unconscious," destined to appear and reappear whenever Jews think deeply about the human predicament, or perhaps as the Kabbalists themselves believed, and as I have argued, the themes of exile and redemption, the significance of sexuality, and the dialectic set forth in the doctrine of *Shevirat ha-Kelim* is written into the very fabric of creation and can be seen by all who look intently upon the ways of humanity and the world.

THE PROBLEMS OF PHILOSOPHY

As we have seen, according to Luria, a principal effect of the Breaking of the Vessels was the inauguration of a state of affairs in which divine spiritual forces are exiled into a material realm. This exile manifests itself not only through the existence of gross matter and evil, but also in the human experience that somehow *things are out of place, are not as they should be.* It is as if the universe itself has been subject to a cosmic "dissociative reaction" in which aspects of the world (or "cosmic self") that should operate together have been split off, repressed, and otherwise kept apart. What philosophical sense can be given to this aspect of Lurianic thought, to the notion that things in our world are out of place and not as they should be?

If we reflect for a moment, I believe we can see that much of the *impetus to philosophy* grows out of a similar set of "alienating" experiences or convictions. This is because a philosophical view of experience reveals the world to be filled with what can only be described as a series of *antinomies*, puzzling contradictions at the heart of, and between, many of our most fundamental concepts and ideas.[51] Among these antinomies are the classic philosophical paradoxes regarding space and time and the seemingly unbridgeable gaps that exist between our concepts of teleology and causality, freedom and necessity, human knowledge and its objects, appearance and reality, and the requirements of ethics and the reality of evil.

We can elaborate briefly on just a few of these antinomies: (1) *the*

---

50. For a detailed discussion of Freud and Hasidism see my book, *Kabbalistic Metaphors: Jewish Mystical Themes in Ancient and Modern Thought.*

51. The concept of a philosophical antinomy was specified in Immanuel Kant's *Critique of Pure Reason*, trans. Norman Kemp Smith (New York: St. Martin's, 1965) but the sorts of puzzles that this term refers to were known in ancient times.

antimony of space and time, whereby it seems as though these categories should be the superstructure, if not the very substance of the universe, while we know that both space and time are relative to, and in a sense created by, the very objects and events contained within them; (2) *the antimony of randomness and teleology* whereby it seems that the same occurrences are both randomly determined by past events and rationally determined by future ends and goals; (3) *the antinomy of freedom and necessity* whereby it both seems that human actions proceed from an exercise of *free will*, and that they are *causally determined* by antecedent events and conditions; (4) *the antinomy of knowledge* where it seems as though all we can really know is the data of our own senses and yet we feel certain of the existence of an objective, external world; (5) *the antinomy of "other minds"* whereby we know that we only have direct awareness of our own minds but nevertheless feel certain of the existence of the minds and inner experiences of others,[52] and (6) *the antinomy of "universals"* whereas it seems that all we can truly know are particular objects while at the same time we realize that we can have no knowledge of such particulars except through concepts of a general or universal kind.

Each of these antinomies (and there are many others) contribute to the philosophical impression that somehow things are not right, are out of place, in this world.

For the Kabbalists, the dialectical condition represented by the Breaking of the Vessels, as we have already pointed out, is a necessary stage in the development of God and man. This is because a broken, antinomous state of affairs is precisely the environment within which man can best exercise those virtues of spirit, endeavor, morality, and intellect that will enable him to instantiate the *values* that make man a reflection of God. Indeed, for the Kabbalists, it is only through man's efforts in a broken, alienated, and antinomous world that God most fully becomes God. Paradoxically, it is only by virtue of their shattering and destruction that the *Sefirot* (which each represent a specific value) come to be real: for it is only by virtue of the *Sefirot*'s reconstruction in *Tikkun* that mankind performs the acts of kindness, justice, harmony, glory, endurance, etc., which instantiate the *Sefirot* ideas. In effect, the *Sefirot must be shattered to be what they are.*

Each of the antinomies of this world is, in effect, a call to human endeavor. The antinomies of space and time for example challenge us to

---

52. As I have discussed in Chapter Six.

become the technological masters of the physical universe, the antimony of "other minds" calls upon us to use our scientific and human resources in the service of knowing and better understanding our fellow man, and the antinomies of teleology and freedom require us to master the environment in a manner that is as fully as possible consonant with the highest human and divine ideals.

It is thus clear that the Breaking of the Vessels and the antinomous state of affairs that it engenders is necessary to provide an arena in which man can complete the work of *Tikkun ha-Olam*, and thus truly be a partner with God in the world's creation. There is, however, a second significance of the *Shevirah*, one that points as much to a transcendence of this world as it does to its immanent repair.

ANTINOMIES AND HIGHER WORLDS

Philosophers have long been inspired to posit the existence of an underlying reality, or "different world" (Plato's ideal forms, Kant's "noumenal" reality, Hegel's "absolute spirit," the linguistic philosopher's "ideal language") in which the antinomies and philosophical conundrums of our own world are presumably resolved. Just as one might posit the existence of an "afterworld" to explain the moral antinomy manifest in the "suffering of the righteous," one might also posit the existence of a "higher" reality in order to solve other enigmatic and disturbing philosophical problems.[53] This is precisely what, on my view, the Kabbalists of Safed have done in describing the dialectic of *Shevirah* and the mystical ascent to higher worlds.

Indeed, when we reflect upon the kind of world that would resolve *our* philosophical dilemmas, we begin to recognize it as very much akin to the world (or worlds) that the Lurianic Kabbalah posits as existing in a metaphysical region between our world and *Ein-Sof* and that as we have suggested serves as the complement or completion of our own world. This is because such a higher world is a *unified*, purely spiritual and conceptual world that exists outside the vexing realm of space and time. It is a world that follows a purely *rational* order in which there is no place for randomly caused

---

53. In making this suggestion I am following J. N. Findlay (*The Discipline of the Cave*) whose "Neoplatonism" attempts to uncover the rational basis of mysticism in general.

events. It is a world in which "acts of will" need not proceed through the medium of matter and hence involve themselves in the problems of material necessity. It is a world in which we are in direct communion with both the (purely ideational or spiritual) objects of experience and the thoughts of other minds, and hence a world within which the philosophical problems of "knowledge and its objects" and the "existence of other minds" cannot conceivably arise. It is a world without gross matter, and hence it is a world in which the distinction between a concept and its instance cannot be maintained and thus where to know an instance is ipso facto to know its universal and vice versa. Finally, it is a world in which there is neither material harm nor gain and, hence, where virtue and righteousness exist as their own and only reward.

We cannot, of course, infer that Luria and his disciples created their system in order to solve *our* philosophical problems. The perception or intuition of philosophical antinomies seems to a certain extent to be relative to one's historical point of view. It is therefore all the more remarkable that the vision of the world which the Kabbalists symbolized in their concept of *Tzimtzum*, *Shevirat ha-Kelim*, and *Tikkun* and which they posited in order to resolve their own theological problems[54] are relevant to the philosophical conundrums of our own age.

The value of Lurianic Kabbalah in resolving our philosophical dilemmas stems from the kabbalistic view that as a result of the Breaking of the Vessels, confusion results when "ideas" become enmeshed in "matter." To take several philosophical examples of how this confusion occurs: Teleology is problematic because it is manifest in a world of random, *material* events; freedom becomes philosophically perplexing because it is exercised in a world of *material* necessity; knowledge is problematic because of the apparently unbridgeable gulf between *matter* and mind; empathic understanding of others is indirect and uncertain because others' minds are "enclosed" in seemingly opaque *bodies*; and the problem of universals arises because of the existence of *corporeal* individual entities. From a Lurianic perspective we might say that each of our philosophical notions (teleology, freedom, knowledge, good, evil, etc.) are incapable of "containing" the material phenomena to which they are applied. They become problematic, are

---

54. For example, the problems engendered by the doctrine of creation *ex nihilo* and the difficulty of conceiving of creation at all by an omnipresent and (already) perfect deity.

"shattered," and hence point to their own reorganization into a new set of concepts that refer to a higher realm.

We can now see that there are two related but distinct aspects of the *Tikkun* process. The first is the repair and restoration of the *Shevirah* through human acts that bring divine/human values into our world. The second is the meditational or mystical/rational act that enables the kabbalistic devotee to transcend the *Shevirah*, as it were, and intuit a divine reality, i.e., become a witness to "higher worlds."[55] At times those two aspects of *Tikkun* are combined and the Kabbalist is deemed, by virtue of his proper intention or *kavannah*, to be capable of healing separations within the upper worlds as well.

It is in the concept of *Tikkun* that the confluence of inner (spiritual) and outer (worldly) acts that is the hallmark of the Jewish religion, finds its fullest kabbalistic expression. The reason for this is that just as the higher worlds resolve the antinomies that exist in our own, *our world was created to resolve the antinomies of the higher, more Godly realms.* This is because it is only in our material world that the values that are abstractions in the higher worlds become instantiated and real. As we have said, the vessels *must* break, spirit *must* become enmeshed in matter, if the *Sefirot* (and God Himself) are to be fully actualized and real. The Kabbalah, like the philosophies and traditions of the East, posits a transcendence of this material world as a means for relieving the puzzles, contradictions, and sufferings of our own. The Kabbalah is, however, unique in positing a transcendence in the other direction as well. In creating our material world God, as it were, transcends Himself and thereby completes Himself as God. Our world is, in a sense, a heaven for the angels. Indeed it is these dual trends in which the corporeal yearns to transcend the wheel of life and death and the spiritual yearns to become actual, which explains both man's love for this world and his simultaneous desire to escape it. It is only in the process of restoration and reunification of two realms that are complementary realities (and illusions) that the purpose of creation is ultimately realized and fulfilled.

---

55. See Chapter One, "Activism and Quietism."

8

Kelippot and *Sitra Achra*:
The Kabbalistic Doctrine of Evil

The Kabbalists were clearly aware of the problem of evil and offered their own unique solutions to it. Their interest in evil did not stop with an attempt to justify its existence in the face of a presumably all-powerful and beneficent God. The Kabbalists were interested in a more fundamental pursuit, that of coming to understand evil on its own terms, penetrating to its heart and confronting it in its own realm, the world they called the *Sitra Achra*, the "Other Side."

Having reviewed the kabbalistic symbols of *Ein-Sof*, *Tzimtzum*, *Sefirot*, Worlds, and the Breaking of the Vessels, we are now in a good position to understand the Kabbalists' theories of evil, and in the process, I hope, gain some insight into the vexing philosophical problems that both moral and natural evil pose for contemporary theology.

On the most general level, we will discover that for the Kabbalists *evil issues forth from God Himself, and is a logically necessary consequent of creation*. Evil is to creation, and the individual finite existence that is creation's very essence, as the outside of a container is to the space it contains. Evil is written into the very idea of creation and is woven into the fabric of the human soul. The "Other Side" exists within our own hearts and, indeed, it could not be otherwise, for without *evil* we could have no hearts, no freedom, and indeed no individual existence whatsoever. Evil, according to the Kabbalists, cannot simply be dismissed as an illusion; neither can it be transcended or ignored. Rather, it must be taken very seriously, and given its due so to speak, both in our philosophies and our lives; if not, like the return of the Freudian repressed, it will take its due on its own terms.

The Kabbalists spoke of evil on a variety of levels. Their language is at once conceptual and metaphoric, philosophical and mythological. In what follows I attempt to organize kabbalistic thought on evil according to a variety of conceptual and symbolic themes. Each theme is integrally related to each of the others, and the total picture can only emerge through a consideration of them all.

EVIL IS ROOTED IN GOD

Evil, according to Jewish tradition, is firmly rooted in the very essence of God. As it is written in Isaiah (45. 7): "I make peace and create evil." Unlike the Greeks who sought to deny the ultimate reality of evil by designating it as a "privation" or lack, or the Gnostics who acknowledged evil but conceived of it as a "second power" completely independent from and opposed to God, Judaism has fully acknowledged evil's reality, placing it within the context of God's goodness and His ultimate plan for the world and mankind. The Kabbalists were led by a commitment to monism to maintain that evil is somehow inherent in God's essence and they made this idea a cornerstone of their theodicy, placing evil at the very core of the sefirotic system. As stated rather succinctly by Luzzatto: "from the very beginning then, all the *Sefirot* in the world of the points possessed the capacity to issue evil, so that the source of evil is high indeed, issuing as it does from these exalted degrees."[1]

There are, to be sure, places in the kabbalistic corpus, particularly some notable passages in the Zohar, in which evil is spoken about from what appears to be a Gnostic or dualistic perspective, and is seen as a separate realm, or as a powerful demonic force opposed to God. For example, the Zohar relates that: "there are two grades, 'blessed' and 'cursed,' each ranged on its own side. From one side issues all blessings . . . beneficence, all light, all deliverance, all redemption; whilst the other is the source of all curses, all wars and bloodshed, all desolation and evil, and all defilement."[2] In a

---

1. Luzzatto, *General Principles of the Kabbalah*, p. 207.
2. Zohar, 184b; Sperling and Simon, *The Zohar*, Vol. 2, p. 204. Elsewhere the

passage, part of which we have already considered in Chapter Four, the Zohar is somewhat ambiguous regarding the connection between The Holy One and the "crowns of evil," which serve as the foundation for the *Sitra Achra*, the "Other Side":

> The Holy One, blessed is He, emits ten crowns, supernal holy crowns. With these He crowns Himself and in these He vests Himself. He is they and they are He, just as a flame is bound up in the coal, and there is no division there. Corresponding to these are ten crowns beneath, which are not holy, and which cling to the uncleanness of the nails of a certain Crown called Wisdom, wherefore they are called "wisdoms."[3]

As Tishby points out, the very idea of the *Sitra Achra* or "Other Side" creates the impression of an independent power, an idea that runs contrary to the entire Jewish tradition. In holding, as did Isaac the Blind, that "there is a positive root to evil and death,"[4] the Kabbalists could solve the problem of "a separate power" but were at the same time confronted with the potential embarrassment of asserting, as did the Gnostics, that God himself was evil.[5]

The Kabbalists attempted to avoid this problem by alleging that it was not evil but evil's "roots" that lay embedded within the mystery of *Ein-Sof*, the Infinite God, and that these roots, when commingled with other roots within the divine essence, were not evil at all. According to Moses Cordovero: "The origin of Judgement (*Din*, evil) is on high in the will of the Emantor. However, it is hidden, as all of the qualities were hidden in *Keter* and *Ein-Sof* and were united there . . . Thus the action of Judgement . . . did not appear there until its place of revelation in (the *Sefirah*) *Gevurah*."[6]

Zohar speaks of a "nether realm" that "consists of two sections, one enveloped in light, the other in darkness, and there are two chiefs, one ruling over the light, the other over the darkness. These two chiefs were at perpetual war with each other, until the time of Cain's arrival (to this nether world), when they joined together and made peace; and therefore they are now one body with two heads. These two chiefs were named '*Afrira* and *Kastimon*.'" Zohar 1, 9b; Sperling and Simon, *The Zohar*, Vol. 1, p. 39. Cf. Tishby and Lachower, *The Wisdom of the Zohar*, Vol. 2, p. 449.

3. Zohar III, 70a; Sperling and Simon, *The Zohar*, Vol. 5, p. 66.

4. Scholem, *Kabbalah*, p. 123.

5. For the Gnostics, the God of the "Old Testament" is equated with a demiurge who is himself ignorant of his origins in the infinite divine principle.

6. Moses Cordovero, *Or Ne'erav* VI: 2, 37a; Robinson, *Moses Cordovero's Introduction to Kabbalah*, p. 122.

According to the Kabbalists, evil only comes into full potentiality when the roots are expelled in the act of creation, and its *actuality* awaits the free choice of man. But even here the Kabbalists were not always clear. In *Sefer ha-Bahir* we read, "The Blessed Holy One has an attribute trait that is called Evil."[7] This trait, according to the *Bahir*, is the *Sefirah Din* (Judgment), and is spoken of in that work as Satan.

THE SYMBOLS OF EVIL

The Kabbalists identified evil with a series of symbols and ideas that made it clear that the evil implicit in God is rooted in His very perfection and goodness, particularly in His beneficence as the creator of the universe. Each of these symbols of "creative evil" are related to the Kabbalist's identification of *Ein-Sof* with *Ayin* (Nothingness).

As we have seen in Chapter Two, the Kabbalists, who generally spoke of God as the "Infinite All," also held the dialectical opposite, that God Himself, without creation, is a species of nothingness. They thereby elevated nothingness to the most basic category of the Absolute. If God is "nothing" in His very essence, then this essence contains Evil, for what could be more evil than total nothingness? If God's essence is nothingness "prior" to creation, then He contains within Himself the most fundamental root of Evil, nonbeing. Such nonbeing, according to the Kabbalists, is present in three aspects of *Ein-Sof*: Judgment (*Din*), Contraction (*Tzimtzum*), and Breakage (*Shevirah*).

The first of these aspects or symbols is the divine trait of Judgment (*Din*). According to the Kabbalists, Judgment (not only in the sense of distinguishing good from evil, but in the sense of making any distinction whatsoever) contains within itself the roots of finitude, death, and evil. This is because in judgment one introduces a fundamental negation: *Something is x and not y.* God, in His perfection, must Himself embody the possibility of judgment/negation in order to create a world that is *not* Him, but this very possibility introduces evil into the world.

The second symbol is *Tzimtzum*, the divine contraction or withdrawal that makes possible the existence of a created world. In *Tzimtzum* God must

---

7. Scholem, *Origins of the Kabbalah*, pp. 149–150 (*Sefer ha-Bahir*, sec. 109). Cf. *Sefer ha-Bahir*, sec. 109. *Book Bahir*, Neugroschel trans., p. 82.

limit Himself, and therefore limit His goodness in order to create the world. If as a result of *Din*, the world is filled with *distinctions* between good and evil, as a result of *Tzimtzum* the world is *alienated* from the ultimate source of goodness and therefore must embody evil as a sort of "privation."

The third symbol, *Shevirat ha-Kelim*, the Breaking of the Vessels, gives rise to a group of symbols and ideas that constitute the most unique and original kabbalistic contribution to the theory of evil. Evil, according to Luria and his disciples, results from a necessary and inevitable shattering of the *Sefirot*, the value archetypes through which God structured the world. This shattering, or "*Shevirah*," results in the many contradictions and failings of worldly life that are embodied in the symbol of the *Kelippot* or "Husks." These Husks result from the intermingling of divine sparks with the dead shards of the once pristine but now shattered *Sefirot*. The Husks constitute the *Sitra Achra*, the dark realm of unholiness and evil. It is mankind's task to gather the sparks (*netzotzim*) of divine light, extract (*birur*) them from the *kelippot*, and restore them to their place in a newly perfected God and world. This process, known as *Tikkun ha-Olam* (the Restoration of the World) reveals that the full purpose and significance of evil in God's plan is to provide the context for man's and the world's redemption.

Each of these symbols of evil will be analyzed in some detail in the following pages. As the discussion proceeds we will also have occasion to analyze several other concepts that the Kabbalists held to be intimately connected with evil: freedom, individuality, and knowledge. We will see that for the Kabbalists, each of these ideas is equivalent to evil; yet each, paradoxically, is necessary for the realization of the good, and for the restoration of the world.

EVIL, JUDGMENT, AND THE DIVINE CATHARSIS

The first, and historically the earliest, kabbalistic symbol of evil, judgment, or *din*, is significant for the role it plays in the remarkable theory of divine catharsis, which we have encountered in Chapters Three and Seven. According to kabbalistic tradition, evil originates in a cathartic act within the Godhead, one in which *Ein-Sof* seeks to purge itself of the very roots of *Din* or judgment that exist at its core. For example, in the Zohar, the origin of evil is understood as a process of excretion through which the divine organism maintains its pure essence as the good. The Zohar speaks of a fire within the Godhead that melts and refines the roots of evil, or *din*. The "dross" from this "smelting" process is externalized into the *Kelippot* ("Husks") that form the substance of the "Other Side." In this way God's severe judgment is externalized and gives rise to a counterworld, which parallels the world of holiness and is ruled by Satan.[8] In one passage in the Zohar, the Godhead is said to be purged of the forces of uncleanness through the cutting of the hairs containing sparks from the *bozina di kardinuta* (Lamp of Darkness) on the head of the Primordial Man.[9] In other passages the separation of evil is seen as an organic process comparable to the letting of evil blood to cleanse the body, or to a metallurgical refinement in which dross is separated from gold.[10] Luria proposes a similar analogy, and one of his followers, Ibn Tabul, held that subsequent to the original divine emanation, lights in the primordial void rearranged themselves in such a manner that *Ein-Sof* could eject the latent evil within itself.[11]

While the Kabbalists asserted that God needed to refine Himself through a catharsis of "harsh judgment," they paradoxically also held that the restrictive and limiting elements of evil are originally canceled out and rendered impotent in the totality of the divine essence. Like heavy elements that exist but are rendered virtually indistinguishable within the atomic furnace of the sun, *Din* exists within God, but only attains a measure of individuation when precipitated out in the divine catharsis. It is difficult to understand why *Ein-Sof* felt called upon to expel the neutralized evil inherent within it. An even more vexing problem concerns how it is possible for *Ein-Sof* to "excrete" part of its essence, i.e., expel a part of its own definition! The Kabbalists, it would seem, have God performing an act akin to the number 15 excreting or expelling from itself its divisibility by five!

All of this, of course, is only possible in a system of thought whose logic is dialectical and whose mode of expression is mythological. As Scholem has pointed out: "Genuine evil, the evil that can be experienced, imposes itself upon us in mythical images."[12] Hence, if the all good deity discovers within itself the roots of evil, it is only natural, in mythological terms, (which reflect

---

8. Gershom Scholem, "Sitra Ahra: Good and Evil in the Kabbalah," in Gershom Scholem, *The Mystical Shape of the Godhead* (New York: Schocken, 1991), p. 63.

9. Zohar III, 48b–49a; Sperling and Simon, *The Zohar*, Vol. 5, pp. 16–17. See Tishby and Lachower, *The Wisdom of the Zohar*, Vol. 1, p. 290.

10. Tishby and Lachower, *The Wisdom of the Zohar*, Vol. 2, p. 460.

11. For a discussion of the cathartic theory see Scholem, *Kabbalah*, p. 130.

12. Scholem, "Sitra Achra," p. 73.

the psychology of man) that these roots be expelled. This is true even if these "roots" are themselves logically connected to and required by the very good that their expulsion is meant to preserve. The logic here is purely dialectical and produces another example of a kabbalistic coincidence of opposites: it is part of the essence of evil to be both logically required by and to be expelled by the good. Later, we will see that the converse is true as well: evil is itself completely parasitic upon, and yet seeks to destroy, holiness. The Kabbalists were quite enamored of turning such (dialectical) logical relationships into mythological dramas.

We shall see that evil, for the Kabbalists, is the very essence, definition, or equivalent of creation, inasmuch as both evil and creation are the restriction, delimitation, differentiation, and negation of the fullness of the Absolute God. It is for this reason that the Kabbalists could hold that at the same time God creates a world He purges himself of *Din*, and death. Thus the act of creation is one in which God excretes, as it were, His evil into a world. Yet, as we have seen, creation is also magnificent good, for it is the vehicle through which God can bestow His holiness and beneficence, however delimited, upon one other than Himself. Evil, in the sense of delimitation, restriction, and death, is necessary to maintain this "good" creation, for otherwise the world would automatically flow back into the infinite God.

JUDGMENT AND COMPASSION

The equivalence of evil and judgment is nowhere more graphically illustrated than in the kabbalistic interpretation of the midrashic tale of earlier worlds that were created and destroyed prior to the emergence of earth.[13] These earlier worlds consisted, according to the Zohar, of the dross or refuse of the original divine catharsis. They were destroyed precisely because they consisted of harsh, untempered judgments that had been purged from the divine plenum. Their existence is known to us, according to the Kabbalists, indirectly through veiled biblical references[14] and directly through the presence of evil in our world; for fragments of those destroyed worlds,

---

13. Genesis Rabbah, 3: 7 and 9: 2.

14. I.e., to the "four kings who died" in Genesis 36: 31 ff.; see also Chronicles 1: 43ff.

shrouded in darkness, remain, as Scholem has put it, "floating about our universe like debris from extinct volcanoes."[15] These fragments exist as the *Kelippot* or "Husks," which ultimately comprise a counterworld of unholiness: the *Sitra Achra* (the "Other Side"), which opposes itself to the divine realm of the *Sefirot*.

By way of contrast, our world, according to this myth, was emanated subsequent to the initial purge of *Din*, and hence was created only after the roots of evil had been purged from the Godhead. As such the restriction and limitation which was necessary to create our world was modified: *Din* (Judgment) was tempered by *Chesed* (Kindness), resulting in a world in which *Din* and *Chesed* are blended in the *middah* or trait of *Rachamim* (compassion). In our world, an initial restriction or negation was followed by a positive emanation, and a blending of good and evil.

This myth has important psychological as well as axiological implications. In purging itself of the roots of evil, the Godhead gives rise to a dark realm, which in many ways resembles the Freudian repressed or Jungian "shadow." For both God and man, the effort to purge the unacceptable has a malevolent result. For God, the result of such efforts is the growth of the "Other Side," while for man the result is the appearance of the unconscious or "shadow." In neither case is evil eliminated. The attempt to purge evil from one's midst simply relocates it to another part of the cosmos or psyche, and results in what is tantamount to a repression as opposed to an expulsion. God's "catharsis of *din*" can actually be likened to a *cosmic repression*. This is because *Ein-Sof*, in attempting to rid itself of the unacceptable aspects of its own essence (negativity, destruction, limitation), actually crystallizes these aspects into a region of being that remains a part of itself. The result is the growth of the "Other Side," a negative region within *Ein-Sof*, which shadows and ultimately fills our world with evil, negativity, ambiguity, and death. God's catharsis of *Din* gives rise to a metaphysical parallel to the dark forces of the repressed unconscious. On both a psychological and cosmic level, evil for the Kabbalists can be understood as a "return" of these repressed forces.

TZIMTZUM: EVIL AND CREATION

A fuller understanding of the origin of evil and the relationship between evil and creation can be gained through a consideration of *Tzimtzum*, the second

---

15. Scholem, "Sitra Achra," p. 62.

of the symbols of negation that the Kabbalists identified with the base and corrupt. As we have seen, *Tzimtzum* is the theory of creation advanced by R. Isaac Luria and his followers in late sixteenth-century Safed. Luria's great innovation was to introduce the notion that creation, far from being a positive addition to the cosmos, is itself actually an act of constriction, concealment, and negation. I have discussed this doctrine at length in Chapter Three and will here only enter into such of its details as they have a direct bearing on the nature of evil.

The doctrine of *Tzimtzum*, in its simplest form, holds that creation is a limitation upon the utter fullness of God, who, if not for a constriction or concealment, would fill the entire cosmos with his own unitary Being. It is only because God, as it were, removes or conceals himself from a "point" or "region" within his own Being, that a seemingly independent cosmos, which includes individual finite souls, can arise. An "illusion" of independent, finite entities is created by this *Tzimtzum* or concealment, much as an illusion of difference and distinction is created in the mind of one who does not realize, e.g., that a thousand different arithmetical expressions of the number 7 are all equivalent. For this reason, finite, independent existence, i.e., creation, exists only from the point of view of the finite intellect (i.e., man) from whom God is concealed, but not from the point of view of God Himself. In *Tzimtzum* God, as it were, conceals Himself from Himself. In doing so *Ein-Sof* actually conceals one aspect of Himself (God) from another aspect of himself (man). In this manner he furthers and deepens the act of divine repression.[16]

Several startling propositions follow from the doctrine of *Tzimtzum*: *evil is necessary for creation, creation is evil, evil is necessary for good, and evil is good.* The meaning of these seemingly paradoxical propositions should become quite clear as we proceed.

That *evil is necessary for creation* follows from the notion that creation is a limitation upon God, a limitation upon the ultimate Good. As Scholem has

---

16. If *Tzimtzum* is akin to a cosmic repression, it also shares repression's positive and negative aspects. In *Tzimtzum*, we might say, God hides from Himself to create a world; in repression man hides from himself to produce character and culture. Just as without *Tzimtzum*, the world would be absorbed in a transparent union with the Absolute, without repression, character, culture, and the sublimations upon which they are founded would dissolve in a perpetual fulfillment of immediate desire. Repression implies "no" on the level of the individual, just as *Tzimtzum* implies "negation" on the level of the cosmos. Without *Tzimtzum* there could be no creation. Without repression there could be no personality.

pointed out, a perfect world could not be a created world, for such a world would of necessity be identical with God Himself. It is only by making distinctions within God, within being itself, that individual, finite, things can be created. Further, these distinctions can only be made by placing a limitation on God's infinite goodness.

It is clear that for the Kabbalists the very notion of creation involves negation, distinction, limitation, and death.[17] As we have seen in our discussion of *Tzimtzum* in Chapter Three, creation means the limitation of the infinite through the limitations of space, time, and evil.

The Kabbalists held that the act of *Tzimtzum* occurs by gradations and degrees, in such a manner that a system of worlds is created, each world being characterized by its relative admixture of divine light and darkness. Our world is among the lowest of such gradations, and is characterized by individuation, separation, darkness, and only a small spark of holiness (which even the most evil of things must retain in order to subsist). It is because our world is near the end of the series of contractions that "all mundane affairs are severe and evil and wicked men prevail."[18] It is for this for this reason, and from this point of view, that *creation is evil.*

We have in this doctrine some elements of a Neoplatonic theodicy: Evil is the result of an estrangement, concealment, and diminution of divinity. Further, the very condition of human existence and desire, the material world, is the most illusory and the most wicked of all things. Our world is wicked because it is the most estranged from God. Yet, paradoxically, it is this very estrangement which is the condition of our individual existence. Again, God could not create a completely good world, for creation by its very nature is estrangement from God and hence is at least partially evil. At this stage in our understanding we can move from asserting that evil is necessary for

---

17. This, of course, is well known among contemporary European philosophers (e.g., existentialists like Heidegger and Sartre and deconstructionists like Derrida) who have explored in depth the dialectics between being and negation, and who see that the very possibility of logic, being, and discourse is predicated upon the possibility of negation, absence, darkness, and death. Indeed, for Derrida, the very act of my writing these words is a constriction of my intellect and implies the possibility of my communicating with one who is absent, who understands only partially or differently, who may not exist, etc. See Harry Staten, *Wittgenstein and Derrida*, p. 120. Every act of human creation is itself a *Tzimtzum* in miniature, and contains within it the roots of evil.

18. Zalman, *Likutei Amarim-Tanya*, Ch. 6, p. 23, referring to Chayyim Vital, *Etz Chayyim*, p. 42.

creation to the propositions that creation itself is evil, and further that both creation and evil (as concealments and contractions of the one real being) are each, as it were, the same "illusion."

No sooner have we uttered these propositions than we are confronted by their seeming opposition to the entire Jewish tradition, a tradition that has placed a value on existence in this flesh-and-blood world, and moreover, that has based its ethic on the divine declaration about each element of creation: "And God said it was good." The solution to this paradox, or better, the next stage in its development, comes from the realization that even in the basest, most estranged, and differentiated of created things, there exists a spark of holiness, without which that thing would revert to utter nonbeing. God, as it were, has created an evil world, but has also, by design and necessity, placed sparks or *loci* of holiness within that world, by virtue of which that world can be redeemed. As we shall later see in greater detail, it is mankind's task to redeem these sparks of holiness, separate them from matter, and, as it were, complete the process that turns creation from an evil illusion, to the most fully actualized of "goods." What's more, it is only by creating an estranged, and "evil" world that God can fully actualize his own potential for good. We thus arrive at the third of our paradoxical proposals: *Evil is necessary for good*. In discussing this very problem the Zohar recites: "For this reason it says 'And behold it was very good' (Genesis: 13). This (refers to) the angel of death. He should not be banished from this world. The world needs him . . . It is all necessary, good and evil."[19]

The value of the "Other Side," the necessity for evil, is that it brings into the world the possibility for sin, and hence also (by way of choice and contrast) the possibility for virtue. Without the possibility of evil there could indeed be no value to this world. It is in this sense that *evil is good*, for it is the condition for good's realization. As the Zohar states: "There is no true worship except it issue forth from darkness, and no true good except it proceed from evil."[20] This does not, however, sanction the doing of evil (as was proclaimed by the Sabbateans—heretical Kabbalists who praised a God who "commanded us to perform the forbidden") but rather the very opposite: we are commanded to do good in the face of evil. There is no value to the world when sin itself becomes actual. Rather it is when man turns away

19. Zohar II, 63a–63b, *Raya Mehemna*. Tishby and Lachower, *The Wisdom of the Zohar*, Vol. 2, pp. 510, 523.

20. Zohar II, 184a; Sperling and Simon, *The Zohar*, Vol. 4, p. 125.

from sin that God becomes real: "when man enters upon an evil way, and then forsakes it, the Holy One is exalted in His glory . . ."[21]

PROOF IN THE UTMOST CASE

These ideas were made clear to me in a dialogue in which I was privileged to engage with the contemporary Kabbalist and sage, Adin Steinsaltz. According to Steinsaltz, far from living in a Leibnizian "best of possible worlds," we live in "the worst of all possible worlds in which there is yet hope." "Creation," he continues, "would have been pointless unless it was creation under precisely these difficult circumstances . . . The worst of all possible worlds is the only world in which creation makes sense." "Creation," Steinsaltz affirms, is "an experiment in existence, an experiment of what I might call conquering the utmost case." He tells us that "existence in any other world would not be proof, for proof in the utmost case occurs only when you can do things under the worst of circumstances."[22] Steinsaltz's words echo those of the novelist Thomas Mann: "With the generation of life from the inorganic, it was man who was ultimately intended. With him a great experiment is initiated, the failure of which could be the failure of creation itself."[23] Steinsaltz analogizes to a road test of a new automobile, which can only be performed under the worst of all possible conditions in which the car could still be expected to perform. One doesn't test a new car by driving it off a cliff, but neither does one test it on a straight, flat, perfectly paved highway on a beautiful spring afternoon. If one is going to provide a real test, the car must be put under precisely those difficult conditions that will elicit the limits of its performance capabilities.

And so it is with our world. It is only in our finite, evil world where death, destruction, and evil are constant possibilities, that man's greatest intellectual, aesthetic, moral, and spiritual virtues can be elicited. It is only under these "not quite hopeless" conditions that man can actualize the very values that are the potential essence of God. By living in an evil world man completes God. As Steinsaltz puts it:

---

21. Zohar II, 184a. Ibid.

22. Steinsaltz, "The Mystic as Philosopher: An Interview with Rabbi Adin Steinsaltz."

23. Quoted in Yalom, *Existential Psychotherapy*, p. 425.

Placed at the end of the series of contractions, together with the gross matter and the evil impulse, man is also the purpose of it all. Having been granted a Divine soul in a material body, man stands between light and darkness, between good and evil; and in choosing the light and the good, he raises himself to holiness. By doing so he justifies the emanation of all the worlds; he gives the creative process a meaning.[24]

The notion here is quite Hegelian in spirit. Hegel posited that the world was evolving toward the *Absolute*, through mankind's intellectual, ethical, aesthetic, and spiritual efforts to transcend the dilemmas posed by historical existence. The same idea is present in the Kabbalah: God, in the sense of the Absolute Good, is both the origin of finite, historical existence and its endpoint. God creates an evil, material world, and it is only through historical worldly events (the deeds of man) that God can become finally actualized as God. To borrow another Hegelian term, *Entfremdung*, or estrangement: God must estrange himself from himself (through *Tzimtzum*) in order to become Himself. The whole of creation, including the very existence of evil, becomes a logically necessary stage in the development of the Godhead and the actualization of the Absolute Good. A similar notion of "descent for the purpose of ascent" is expressed in *The Tanya* of R. Schneur Zalman: "Why then, has God done such a thing, to cause a portion of his blessed light . . . to descend and be clothed in a 'serpent's skin' and in a fetid drop? It cannot be otherwise than that descent is for the purpose of an ascent . . . The ascent . . . is the ultimate purpose of the creation of the world."[25]

According to Schneur Zalman, the goodness that emerges from an evil world is even superior to the pure goodness, issuing forth from higher worlds closer to the infinite God Himself:

> The ultimate purpose [of creation] is this lowest world, for such was His blessed will that He shall have satisfaction when the *Sitra Achra* is subdued and the darkness is turned to light, so that the divine light of the blessed *Ein-Sof* shall shine forth in the place of the darkness and *Sitra Achra* throughout the world, all the more strongly and intensely with the

---

24. Adin Steinsaltz, *The Long Shorter Way: Discourses on Chasidic Thought* (Northvale, NJ: Jason Aronson, 1988). Chapter 49, "Man as the Purpose of Creation," p. 329.
25. Zalman, *Likutei-Amarim-Tanya*, Chapter 21, p. 143.

excellence of light emerging from darkness than its effulgence in the higher worlds.[26]

THE DESTRUCTION AND RESTORATION OF THE WORLD

The idea of man actualizing values and thereby completing creation is given its ultimate kabbalistic expression in a third set of symbols, the Lurianic doctrines of the Breaking of the Vessels (*Shevirat ha-Kelim*) and the restoration of the world (*Tikkun ha-Olam*). As with the doctrine of *Tzimtzum*, I deal with these concepts elsewhere in this book,[27] and will focus upon them here only insofar as they provide us with further insight into the nature and structure of evil.

The concept of the Breaking of the Vessels gives a fuller symbolic expression to the reference in the early midrashic literature concerning evil worlds that were created and destroyed by God prior to the emergence of our own world.[28] The Zohar implies that the evil in our universe has its origins in the remnants of the previous worlds that were destroyed. Fragments of these worlds remain, as Tishby puts it, "mutilated and covered in darkness outside the divine system."[29] From these fragments the system of the *Sitra Achra* was constructed.

It is somewhat difficult to reconcile this account of evil with the earlier account of evil as intrinsic to the *Tzimtzum*, contraction/concealment. Yet the two accounts sit side by side, as it were, in the Kabbalah of Luria and his followers. As Joseph Dan has pointed out, evil elements are responsible for both the *Tzimtzum* (the withdrawal of God's Being from a part of the universe) and the *Shevirah* (the destruction of God's first attempt to emanate *Sefirot* into the metaphysical void).[30] Yet, we might ask, if *Tzimtzum*, a purely negative act, is sufficient to account for both evil and creation, why is it that the Kabbalists must invoke an emanative or positive divine act, and then a further act of destruction, to account for what appears to be the same thing: a created, mainly evil, world?

---

26. Zalman, *Likutei-Amarim-Tanya*, Chapter 36, p. 165.
27. In Chapters 7 and 9.
28. Midrash Genesis Rabbah, 9: 2. Compare Ecclesiastes Rabbah, 3: 11.
29. Tishby and Lachower, *The Wisdom of the Zohar*, Vol. 2, p. 458.
30. Joseph Dan, *Gershom Scholem and the Mystical Dimension of Jewish History* (New York: New York University Press, 1987).

The answer to this question lies in the Kabbalists' faith in the possibility of redemption. A second destructive act is invoked to pave the way for the world's restoration and repair. With the Breaking of the Vessels, sparks of divine light penetrate our material world and shine through this "veil of tears," particularly in the soul of man. Creation involves a dialectical movement through *Tzimtzum*, emanation, and the Breaking of the Vessels because these sparks of divine light are needed in this world to provide the impetus for evil's redemption. This divine light is encapsulated in the lifeless shards of the broken vessels that fell through the worlds and, in the form of the "Husks" (*Kelippot*) comprise the substance of the *Sitra Achra* or "Other Side." The world of the *Kelippot* mixes with our world in such a manner that the evil that is estranged from God now intermingles with the evil that is flawed and shattered.

However, immediately after the Breaking of the Vessels, a process of healing or reconstruction begins. Restorative lights shine forth from the forehead of *Adam Kadmon*. Thus begins the process of *Tikkun ha-Olam*, the repair and restoration of the world, a process that is to be carried out in full by mankind. According to the Lurianic Kabbalah, it is the purpose of each individual man and woman to discover his or her own personal *Tikkun*, his or her own role in the restoration and reconstruction of the self and world. *Tikkun* is conceived of as a liberation of the divine sparks of light entrapped by the *Kelippot* and the return of this light to its source in God. Divine sparks (*netzotzim*) exist throughout the material world, but are found particularly in the human soul. Individuals must liberate the sparks within their own souls, and those sparks that their destiny leads them to encounter in the path of life. The manner in which this is achieved is through leading a spiritual/ethical life in accordance with God's will and law, and through the process of *teshuvah*, sincere repentance for one's transgressions.

THE *KELIPPOT*

The symbol of the *Kelippot* (Husks) is already present in the Zohar, which speaks of all the worlds of emanation as consisting of *layers of kernel and shell*. Each layer of creation is a husk or shell to that which is above it and kernel to that which is below it. Elaborating upon the analogy of a fruit or nut, the Kabbalists conceived the husk or shell as relatively lifeless but containing (and protecting) a living, edible fruit or kernel. A similar idea is expressed using the biblical image of the snake: "The Holy One set about the inmost chamber of His presence a serpent, the 'Other Side.'"[31] At times the Zohar refers to a "membrane" surrounding an inner brain or spirit: "The whole world is constructed on this principle, upper and lower, from the first mystic point up to the furthest removed of all the stages. They are all coverings one to another, brain within brain and spirit within spirit, so that one is shell to another."[32]

It is for the good of mankind that the universe is constructed on the model of the *Kelippot*.[33] According to the Zohar, the *Kelippot* consist of four husks or shells, which are presumably named in Ezekiel's vision of a "stormy wind, a great cloud, a flashing fire, and a brightness (or *electrum*)" (Ezekiel 1: 4). They are arranged around the spark or kernel of holiness like the layers of an onion. The innermost shell is known as *nogah* (electrum or brightness). It is the thinnest shell, the one closest to the realm of holiness, and it is translucent, allowing some of the light of the holy spark to penetrate into the realm of darkness. The Zohar refers to this realm when it speaks of the "Other Side" as having a brightness around it, connecting it to the side of the holiness and faith.[34] Accordingly: "there is no sphere of the 'Other Side' that entirely lacks some streak of light from the side of holiness."[35]

There is thus, a spark of goodness at the very heart of evil, and man should approach the *Kelippot*, approach what appear to be the carriers of evil, with the thought of extracting the good, disencumbering (*birur*) the kernel of holiness, and raising the sparks of light, that exists within them. According to Schneur Zalman the righteous "convert evil and make it ascend to holiness," and in the Zohar we learn of a heavenly voice that states to Rabbi Chaya: "Who among you have labored to turn darkness into light and bitter into sweet before you entered here?"[36] However, not all *Kelippot* can be disencumbered by every man. There are some *Kelippot* that man must avoid altogether. There are three *Kelippot* that are shrouded in the darkness of the shells beyond electrum (*nogah*). These constitute the forbidden evils and no

31. Zohar II, 172a; Sperling and Simon, *The Zohar*, Vol. 4, p. 99; cf. Tishby and Lachower, *The Wisdom of the Zohar*, p. 519. For a discussion of snake symbolism in the Zohar, see Tishby and Lachower, *The Wisdom of the Zohar*, Vol. 2, p. 467ff.

32. Zohar 1, 19b; Sperling and Simon, *The Zohar*, Vol. 1, p. 84. Cf. Tishby and Lachower, *The Wisdom of the Zohar*, Vol. 2, p. 495.

33. Zohar 1, 19b; Sperling and Simon, *The Zohar*, Vol. 1, p. 84.

34. Zohar II, 203b; Sperling and Simon, *The Zohar*, Vol. 4, p. 189.

35. Zohar II, 69a–69b; ibid. Vol. 3, p. 216.

36. Zohar I, 4a; ibid., Vol. 1, p. 16.

man may approach them and expect to have anything but evil as his reward. Only under very special circumstances, through the greatest love and repentance that places the penitent even above the wholly righteous, can the three "unclean" *Kelippot* be redeemed. Otherwise these *Kelippot* will remain embedded within the *Sitra Achra*, until "death is swallowed up forever."[37]

As a symbol of the relationship between good and evil the *Kelippot* are, of course, subject to a multiplicity of interpretations. One is, however, struck by the image of evil as a force or energy that is essentially good, but which becomes malevolent by virtue of its being encapsulated and estranged from its source. A psychological, moreover, psychoanalytic parallel, readily comes to mind, for it is precisely estranged and encapsulated energy, in the form of repressed sexuality, rage, etc., which in the psychoanalytic scheme is the source of depression, negativity, and neurotic symptomatology for the individual. As we have seen in Chapter Seven, for psychoanalysis there is an estrangement and subsequent encapsulation of psychic energy (what Freud refers to as libido) from the main fabric of the individual's personality, in much the same way as in the Lurianic Kabbalah there is an estrangement (and encapsulation) of sparks of energy from the infinite God. In the psychoanalytic scheme, this occurs, for example, when an individual becomes aware of a thought or emotion that is unacceptable to his conscious self. The thought, with its associated affect, is repressed and subsequently exists in a nether realm known as the "unconscious," which, as we have seen, is quite akin to Luria's *Sitra Achra* or "Other Side." To carry the analogy a step further, the restorative work of psychoanalysis is to make the unconscious conscious and moreover to free the libidinous energy and make it available for the individual's life endeavors, in much the same way as (in the view of the Kabbalah) the divine energy or sparks trapped in the *Kelippot* must be liberated and made available for the service of God.

The evil of this world (at least the human evil), as represented in the symbol of the *Kelippot*, is a repressed, estranged, encapsulated, and ultimately distorted form of the good. The child, for example, whose quest for love and independence, and whose healthy expressions of sexuality and aggression are suppressed and stifled by those who raise him, may ultimately repress his own "true self" and pervert his own life-serving energies into instruments of negativity and destruction. Yet the *Kelippot*, in spite of their status as bearers

---

37. Zalman, *Likutei-Amarim-Tanya*, Ch. 7, p. 29.

of evil, have, as we have seen, a purpose in the ultimate destiny of the world. This purpose can also be understood through a psychological comparison. Freud proclaimed that the entire glory of culture and civilization is the product of repressed, rerouted, and sublimated libido and that civilization itself is the source of the repression we find in neurosis.[38] Whereas for Freud, neurosis and its concomitant wickedness is the price of civilization and culture, for the Kabbalists, the *Kellipot* and evil are the price of creation.

Much more can be said on the subject of the *Kelippot* from a contemporary point of view. The artist Jan Menses, for example, has devoted ten years to a series of hundreds of paintings on the subject, paintings that explore the dark forces that contain within themselves the potential for their own undoing.[39] The image of these vessels, formed out of the broken shards of the world's highest values, is a captivating one for an era that senses that its own values and ideals have been shattered and are in dire need of restoration and repair.

Part of the power of the *Kelippot* image is derived from the fact that the *Kelippot* are formed from the shards of a firmament of shattered values. As we have seen, the Kabbalists held that the universe is comprised of ten value archetypes known as the *Sefirot*. As we have proposed in Chapter Four, it is hardly an extension of their metaphor to propose that in God's original plan for the world each entity, including man himself, was to be composed of a particular combination of *Sefirot*, that is a particular proportion of *Chochmah* (Wisdom), *Binah* (Understanding), *Chesed* (Kindness), *Din* (Judgment), *Tiferet* (Beauty), etc. However, with the Breaking of the Vessels, most of these elementary particles were themselves torn asunder, estranged from the source of their vital energy in God, and transformed from life to death and from good to evil, obtaining a new vitality only by capturing and attaching themselves to sparks of divine light. The result of these events is that things in our own world are both material and evil, yet they are composed of the broken shards of what were once pristine values.

The *Kelippot* comprise the *Sitra Achra*, which is also conceptualized as a world of "impurity" that fully parallels the ten *Sefirot* of holiness. Thus we read in the Zohar: "The summation of all: Just as there are ten crowns of faith

---

38. Sigmund Freud, *Civilization and Its Discontents. The Standard Edition of the Complete Works of Sigmund Freud*, ed. James Strachey (London: Hogarth Press, 1955–1967), Vol. 21.

39. See Sanford Drob, "The Kabbalistic Art of Jan Menses," *Jewish Review*, Vol. 2.

above, so there are ten crowns of sorcery and uncleanness below; and whatever exists on earth is attached partly on this side [of holiness] and partly on the 'Other Side.' "[40]This mixture of holiness and uncleaness is represented in the *Kelippot*, which in a post-*Shevirah* world are the elements of reality itself. It follows from the kabbalistic doctrine of the Husks that evil has no life of its own but is completely parasitic upon the Good, both because it is comprised of the Good's shattered substance and because it is dependent upon the energy of God for its life and vitality. The *Kelippot* are themselves dross, waste matter, completely infertile with no independent existence: "The 'other God' (the principle of evil) is emasculated and has no desire to procreate, and does not multiply or bear fruit."[41]

According to Schneur Zalman, the "chambers of the *Sitra Achra* derive their vitality from the *Sefirot* of *nogah*," the translucent shell closest to the spark of divine light that the *Kelippot* have captured and contained.[42] The essence of this divine light, according to kabbalistic tradition, derives from the "288 sparks from the fire of *Din* or judgment," the hardest and heaviest of which fell through the metaphysical void and mingled with the fragments of the broken vessels. Evil is then parasitic on the divine traits of judgment or *din*. In the order of the *Sefirot*, *Din* is the second of the lowest seven, after *Chesed* (kindness), and before *Tiferet* (beauty). This *Sefirah* is called *Din* (severe Judgment) or *Gevurah* (strength or power) and is identified with that aspect of the infinite God that is powerful, severe, judgmental, and potentially destructive. It is also, as we will see, identified with "knowledge" (see below).

The symbol of the *Kelippot* reveals that evil is parasitic on the divine traits of judgment and power. The quest for power and the insistence upon severe judgment are hence the "roots of all evil." But even these traits, the Kabbalists tell us, are essentially "good." Their goodness, however, can only be established when they are mitigated by the *Sefirah Chesed* (Kindness) and dialectically blended with that *Sefirah* into a third *Sefirah*, variously known as *Tiferet* (beauty) or *Rachamim* (mercy). We will see that this blending of Judgment with Kindness is a major aspect of *Tikkun*, the restoration of the world.[43]

According to the Kabbalist Isaac the Blind, the origins of good and evil

---

40. Tishby and Lachower, *The Wisdom of the Zohar*, Vol. 2, p. 499.
41. Zohar II, 103a; Sperling and Simon, *The Zohar*, Vol. 3, p. 314.
42. Zalman, *Likutei-Amarim-Tanya*, *Igeret Hateshuvah*, Chapter 6, p. 365.
43. In Chapter Nine.

in the world are to be traced to the attributes of *Chesed* and *Din/Gevurah* in the Godhead.[44] That the world is governed by two opposing yet potentially harmonious forces each having their origin in the infinite God, invites comparison with the Freudian notion that man is driven by two opposing (yet potentially harmonious) urges that have their origins in human nature. *Chesed* (loving-kindness) and *Din/Gevurah* (severe judgment) have more than a superficial resemblance to the Freudian opposition of Eros and Thanatos (the drives of "Love/Life" and "Death").[45] The Kabbalists also adopted the talmudic view of man being driven by both a good (*Yetzer ha Tov*) and evil (*Yetzer ha Ra*) impulse, and held that each man has both a Godly and an animal soul; one stemming from *electrum* (or *Kelippot nogah*) and the other from dark forces that, as we have seen, have their origins in a perversion of Din. In making his distinction between Eros and Thanatos, Freud echoes an age-old myth of a battle between the forces of light and dark. The Kabbalah echoes this Avestian or Gnostic view as well, but insists that the entire battle has its origins and purpose in a single beneficent source.

The *Kelippot*, which are composed of the shattered value archetypes, symbolize the experience of a world that is broken, flawed, and incomplete. As we have seen in the previous chapter, one result of the *Shevirah* is that the world is replete with antinomies, insuperable puzzles, and contradictions concerning our most fundamental experiences, concepts, and ideas. Such antinomies are not only to be found in the deepest questions of philosophy, science, and religion (e.g., the seeming contradiction between ethics, which requires that man is free, and science, which requires that his behaviors are determined) but in the everyday experience of the human heart and soul.[46] As Adin Steinsaltz has put it: "The world contains enough contradictions,

---

44. Tishby and Lachower, *The Wisdom of the Zohar*, Vol. 2, p. 449.

45. However, the relationship between the Kabbalists' evil (*Din*, severity, destructiveness, knowledge) and the Freudian concept of Thanatos is complex. Freud describes his death instinct as seeking the obliteration of all individual existence (a return to a tension-free state of maximum entropy), whereas for the Kabbalists evil tends to increase individuality (see below) and therefore move the soul further from its primal unity with God. Interestingly, in the Kabbalah it is "life," while in Freud it is "death," which propels man to achieve a unity with all being. This is one reason why we can speak of psychoanalysis as a "negative mysticism." Yet on each view, evil or Thanatos can only be tempered by its unity and subservience to the life principle: *Chesed* or Eros.

46. See Sanford Drob, "Antinomies of the Soul," *Jewish Review*, Vol. 3, p. 2.

enough destructive elements as to eliminate any possibility of a solution."[47] Each of these contradictions is, according to Steinsaltz, a "vicious *Kelippah*" and while it may be impossible for mankind to resolve them all, it is our task or *Tikkun* to struggle to untie the knots of the *Kelippot* that bind our own souls. Man, according to Schneur Zalman, is created for conflict and: "no person should feel depressed, nor should his heart be troubled, even though he be engaged all his days in this, for perhaps because of this was he created and this is his service, constantly to subjugate the *Sitra Achra*."[48]

"Evil," from this perspective, is the conflict, antinomy, and contradiction that lies at the heart of our world and souls, and that constitutes a broken, flawed, and incomplete reality. Things are out of place; they are, somehow, not as they should be. Yet it is only by exercising his passion, intellect, and intuition in an antinomous world that man will actualize the values that can potentially set that world aright.

EVIL AS EXILE

The symbol of the *Kelippot* is connected both conceptually and historically with the Jewish preoccupation with "exile and redemption." Exile and redemption, perhaps the key dialectic in Jewish history, thus makes a prominent appearance in the Jewish concept of evil. Early on, a metaphysical exile of an aspect of the deity was seen as reflecting the historical exile of the Jewish people. For example, we find in the Talmud: "When they [the Israelites] were exiled in Eden the *Shekhinah* [God's feminine aspect and presence on earth] went with them."[49] Later exile was understood as the basic metaphysical process that has given rise to our current evil, antinomous state of affairs. For example, the Zohar speaks of evil resulting from the "banishment of the queen"; here speaking of the exile of the *Shekhinah* as a theosophical event in which the masculine and feminine principles within God have been separated as the result of human sin.[50]

The concept of evil as exile is reflected in the Kabbalist's interpretation of Genesis. Adam's sin is said to have exiled the *Shekhinah* and caused a cleavage between the masculine and the feminine, between the trees of life

---

47. Steinsaltz, "The Mystic as Philosopher," p. 14.
48. Zalman, *Likutei-Amarim-Tanya*, Chapter 27, p. 117.
49. Talmud, Tractate *Megillah*, 29a.
50. See Idel, *Kabbalah: New Perspectives*, p. 108.

and knowledge, and thereby between life and death. The exile of the *Shekhinah* is such an important symbol for evil that many *siddurim* (Jewish prayer books) to this day preface a variety of benedictions with a meditation that states that such prayers are "for the sake of the reunion of God and His *Shekhinah*."

Evil, for the Kabbalah, is a separation of those things that should remain united; it is, in psychological terms, a "splitting" of two aspects of an emotion, value, or idea. As we have seen, evil results when the feminine is alienated from the masculine, when kindness (*chesed*) is splitoff from judgment (*din*), when life is separated from knowledge, and death is exiled from life. Each of these alienations has both a metaphysical and psychological aspect, and each is embodied in the concept of evil as exile. The Zohar understands the "splitting," resulting from the exile of the *Shekhinah*, as a blockage of cosmic libidinous energy. Accordingly, redemption will see the masculine and the feminine "carried back to their original unity, and in this uninterrupted union of the two, powers of generation will once again flow unimpeded through all the worlds."[51] According to the Zohar evil is either something that has been alienated from its natural unity or, conversely, something that enters into a unity for which it was not created. As the Kabbalist Joseph Gikatilla had affirmed: "every act of God, when it is in the place accorded to it at creation is good; but if it turns and leaves its place, it is evil."[52] For example, according to the Zohar, the attribute of *din*, when in its proper place, serves the divine purpose of measuring the flow of reward and punishment according to the dictates of justice.[53] However when *din* is separated from its prescribed unity with *chesed* (loving-kindness), and the natural "balance of opposites" is broken, *din* becomes the destructive foundation for evil.

Later Kabbalists expanded upon the theme of evil as exile via the notions of *Tzimtzum* and the Breaking of the Vessels. *Tzimtzum* is itself a primordial exile, or self-banishment, for in *Tzimtzum* the deity's powers of *Din* or stern judgment are concentrated in a primordial point from which God withdraws. Further, in *Tzimtzum*, God must of necessity conceal or "exile" his full countenance from the world in order that the world can maintain its separate

---

51. Ibid.
52. Scholem, *Kabbalah*, p. 126.
53. See Tishby and Lachower, *The Wisdom of the Zohar*, Vol. 2, p. 459.

existence. God's exile or his "eclipse," as Martin Buber has termed it,[54] is an important element in many contemporary theodicies. Birnbaum, for example, has argued that *hester panim*, the "hiding of God's face," while resulting in the potential for evil, is also a metaphysical prerequisite for man's own spiritual and moral progress.[55]

With their conception of the *Shevirah*, Isaac Luria and his followers introduced a higher and more dynamic conception of evil as exile and alienation. Subsequent to the *Shevirah*, God's own light is "exiled" in matter (the *Kelippot*), and the *Sefirot* are broken and dispersed throughout the cosmos. Nothing is in its proper place. All being is in a state of exile.[56] The prophetic promise of the ingathering of an exiled Jewish people is reinterpreted in metaphysical terms. As phrased by Luria's disciple Chayyim Vital: "the ingathering of the exiles itself means the gathering of all the sparks (*netzotzim*) that were in exile."[57] With this ingathering God is returned to himself and *Tikkun ha-Olam* (the restoration of the world) is complete.

The concept of evil as exile certainly accords well with the experience of contemporary man. The idea that man is somehow alienated or exiled from his true self has echoed through the modern psyche. Far from being a simple reflection of the Jews' experience of exile from his native land,[58] the Kabbalists' conception of evil as exile seems to penetrate to the very heart of the human spiritual malaise.

EVIL AS THE CONDITION FOR FREEDOM

The doctrines of the *Shevirah*, *Kelippot*, and *Tikkun* entail that each individual man and woman has a crucial role to play in actualizing the Good, which is the goal of creation. This role, which is expressed in such symbols as "the raising of the sparks," is placed within the context of man's freedom to choose between good and evil. Evil thus becomes a condition for free choice, and, as such, a condition for the realization of the Good on earth.

---

54. Martin Buber, *The Eclipse of God: Studies in the Relation between Religion and Philosophy* (New York: Harper & Brothers), 1952.
55. David Birnbaum, *God and Evil*.
56. Idel, *Kabbalah: New Perspectives*, p. 112.
57. Scholem, *Kabbalah*, p. 167, quoting Vital, *Etz Chayyim* 42:4.
58. As argued by Scholem. See my discussion in Chapter One.

Man's freedom derives from the fact that his highest soul originates in *Kelippah Nogah*, the innermost layer between the sparks and husks, which contains a blending of good and evil; as such he is given the ability to exercise free choice between the two.[59] Because the *Sefirot*, through which God reveals himself, are found in man's soul, and even in his physical being, man, in exercising his free choice, is able to exert influence upon the upper worlds and ultimately upon God Himself.[60] In other words, the entire value firmament is mirrored or, better, concentrated in man's soul, and as such the fate of good and evil lies in his hands.

The Zohar relates a parable of a king who has his son tempted by a whore but who secretly wishes for him to resist the temptation and prove his worthiness as a prince.[61] Evil, in effect, is the temptation that permits man to exercise and prove his own value. All evil originates in God's goodness and will. The cosmic battle between good and evil is, as Tishby puts it, "a mere theatrical play to put man to the test."[62] Man is refined as if in a crucible, by descending into and being tempted by the "Other Side."[63]

Evil, according to the Kabbalah, is equiprimordial with freedom. God could not create evil without creating freedom (in man), nor could he create freedom without providing a choice for evil. Man's choices in essence bring evil into the world. On the other hand man's choice itself makes no sense unless there are possibilities (including bad ones) to choose among. Freedom and evil are thus really two aspects of the same concept.

That man's choice brings evil into the world is symbolized in the story of Adam, and the tree of knowledge of good and evil. According to the Kabbalists, it was only when Adam was seduced into disobeying God and eating from the tree of knowledge that the Breaking of the Vessels occurred. Up until that point in cosmic history, Adam was simply an archetypical, nonmaterial being. By partaking of the apple, Adam caused the vessels to shatter, and indeed prompted the creation of a material, finite world. Freedom breaks the world into a thousand broken fragments and brings conflict, contradiction, and evil in its wake.

An emphasis upon man's freedom is found in the Hasidic interpretation

---

59. Scholem, "Sitra Achra," p. 78.
60. Scholem, *Kabbalah*, pp. 153–154.
61. Zohar II 163a, b; Sperling and Simon, *The Zohar*, Vol. 4, pp. 62–63. Cf. Tishby and Lachower, *The Wisdom of the Zohar*, Vol. 2, p. 806.
62. Tishby and Lachower, *The Wisdom of the Zohar*, Vol. 2, p. 457.
63. Ibid.

of the Kabbalah. "Free will" is written all over the pages of *Tanya*, whose author, Schneur Zalman, interestingly enough, was a contemporary of Kant:

> The choice, ability and freedom are given to every man that he may act, speak and think even what is contrary to the desire of his heart and diametrically opposed to it. Even when the heart craves and desires a material pleasure, whether permitted or, God forbid, prohibited, he can steel himself and divert his attention from it altogether, declaring to himself, "I will not be wicked even for a moment."[64]

For Schneur Zalman, as for Kant, freedom resides in the individual's ability to transcend his or her natural impulses and act in accordance with a moral principle or law. A free act is not one that proceeds "freely" and "naturally" from the character of the agent (as Hume had argued), but rather, one that goes *contrary* to the individual's impulses. Perhaps God could create a man who always "chose" the right thing (and according to Schneur Zalman there are indeed such saints or *tzaddikim*) but there is, in the order of things, a higher value given to the man who turns away from his evil urges, or who repents from his sins, for it is only in this way that evil is truly overcome. When a man turns away from evil: "Then all the *Kelippot* are made null and void, and they vanish, as though they had never been in the presence of the Lord."[65] For this reason it is said that the penitent stands on ground that is higher than that of the perfect *tzaddik* or saint. If evil is created by freedom, it is also only through freedom by which it can be overcome.

EVIL AND INDIVIDUALITY

It is of interest in this context to note that while the *Sefirot* on the side of holiness are referred to as abstract ideas, spiritual forces, or emotional attributes, the *Sefirot* of the "Other Side" are, as Tishby has pointed out, "stamped with the seal of individuality."[66] For example, the Zohar sees the evil figures of Samael (worthless man) and Lilith (evil woman) as originating in the fiery judgment of *Din*. Samael is regarded as the "shadow" and Lilith as "death," and when they are joined together they are called "the shadow of

---

64. Zalman, *Likutei Amarim-Tanya*, Chapter 14, p. 59.
65. Ibid., Chapter 19, p. 81.
66. Tishby and Lachower, *The Wisdom of the Zohar*, Vol. 2, p. 464.

death." Their intercourse brings evil into the world. As a result of man's sins, Samael and Lilith have intercourse with the divine *Sefirot*, which even in reference to this act are, again, spoken of only as abstractions (*Tiferet*, the supernal male and *Malchut* or *Shekhinah*, the supernal female).[67]

Goodness can be an abstract idea, but evil, it seems, must be personified as an individual. Our images of the devil are far more individualized than those of the deity, and we conceive of Satan, Lucifer, or Beelzebub as not only possessing a name but as possessing, in extreme form, those traits of avarice, greed, and destructiveness that so often characterize individual men. Goodness, it seems, can exist in and of itself but evil requires the free choice and responsibility that can only be attributed to an individual.

In the course of his discussion of the problem of freedom and evil Schneur Zalman tells us: "angels are called *chayyot* (beasts) and *behemot* (cattle) . . . for they have no freedom of choice, and their fear and love are their natural instincts . . ."[68] The angels are superior to us by virtue of their comprehension of the creator, but we are superior to them by virtue of our volition and individuality. Angels, being closer to God, are essentially archetypes that simply express God's will. Man, on the other hand, more distant from God, in possession of free will, and hence partly immersed in evil, is an individual. Indeed, human individuality is another expression of the potential for both freedom and evil within the soul. As we have seen, the *Tzimtzum*, God's contraction and concealment, is the process by which both evil and individuality come into being. According to the Kabbalist Azriel, Adam's fall, which further alienated man from the divine, is responsible for his individualized condition. Paradise would be a completely nonindividuated state.[69]

Cast out from Eden, man lives his life in an estranged condition in which he is knowledgeable and free, and yet burdened by guilt, responsibility, and isolation. Individuation, freedom, and evil are stations on the train to death. They are partial deaths, partial alienations from the All that is the source of life. We are free, quite simply, because we die, or more precisely because we already know death in the midst of our lives.

---

67. Zohar I, 148a–148b, *Sitrei Torah*. Samael and Lilith are said to originate in the flame of Isaac, who is equated with judgment or *din*.

68. Zalman, *Likutei Amarim-Tanya*, Chapter 31, p. 187.

69. Scholem, *Origins of the Kabbalah*, p. 454.

EVIL AND KNOWLEDGE

The identification of evil with knowledge is biblical in origin. Adam's fall, his expulsion from paradise, and consequent mortality are the result of his partaking of the *tree of knowledge*, and thereby learning to distinguish between good and evil. The Kabbalists equated knowledge with the *Sefirah Gevurah/Din* (Power/Judgment), for knowledge grants *power* by virtue of the ability to *judge* or distinguish among different values and alternatives. For this reason, knowledge is another capacity, along with freedom and individuality, that is equiprimordial with evil.

It is in the context of these ideas that the Kabbalists made a distinction between a primordial, spiritual Torah, which they equated with the "Tree of Life"; and the historical Torah, which they equated with the "Tree of Knowledge." The latter Torah represents the restrictive, limiting aspects of our present world of good and evil; the former Torah, the liberation of a world in which such knowledge, limitations, and distinctions simply do not apply.[70] According to the Kabbalists, it was only after the fall of Adam and his attainment of "knowledge" that an earthly Torah, proceeding from the divine trait of judgment (*din*), had to be created for the purpose of containing and binding evil.

However, the knowledge that results in evil is not the *ontological* knowledge of the Absolute, but rather the partial, limited, *ontic* knowledge of the distinctions among finite, "separated" things. The Kabbalists held that it is only a knowledge of particulars that fails to place things in a wider context of life and its values that is equated with evil. The Kabbalists used a variety of metaphors of separation ("chopping away the plantings," "separating the chutes," and "causing destruction") to symbolize an act of contemplation that separates knowledge from the ultimate values of God and life. Indeed, they held that the root of all evil stems from a separation of the natural conjunction between the trees of life and knowledge. As we read in an early work from the Spanish Kabbalah, *Etz ha Da'at* (The Tree of Knowledge):

So long as the Tree of Life, which comes from the side of the East and is the Good Urge, and the quality of peace [harmony], is connected with the Tree of Knowledge, which comes from the side of the North, from the side

---

70. Scholem, "The Meaning of the Torah," p. 69.

of Satan and evil, then Satan can do nothing . . . But the moment it [the Tree of Knowledge] is separated [from the Tree of Life] its strength is freed and Satan is able to act.[71]

When knowledge is separated from life, it becomes purely technical, and an end in and of itself. The inevitable result of such merely technical knowledge is evil. For the Kabbalists such knowledge is an act of contemplation that does not embrace the *Sefirot* in their totality, but that isolates an individual *Sefirah*, particularly the final one, *Malchut* or Kingship. Knowledge for the sake of "kingship," for the sake of power, enhances one's freedom and individuality, but ultimately leads to evil. When knowledge is disconnected from life, as in Adam's sin, the tree of knowledge becomes a tree of death.[72]

Knowledge, of course, can be separated from "life" in a variety of ways. One of these, for example, occurs when an individual suppresses the emotional correlates of his ideas, and his intellectual life continues in a manner that fails to take cognizance of his full, living self. Such a dynamic occurs very frequently in families (and cultures) that, for one reason or another, cannot tolerate the affective life of their members. In such cases the individual's intellect comes to govern his behavior without any real connection with values (which require feelings), or his repressed emotional self returns to direct his intellect and volition in demonic ways.

A question arises: If evil is integrally related to freedom, individuality, and knowledge of particular things, and the latter are "stations on the way to death," how is it that mankind in general and Judaism in particular has come to value the individual, his knowledge, and his freedom? The answer to this lies in a full understanding of what we have previously spoken of as the value of evil itself. Evil, freedom, individuality, and knowledge are necessary in order to provide for the possibility of the good. It is the individual who is responsible for obtaining that knowledge which will enable him or her to choose the good and act in a manner that "raises the sparks," overcomes evil, and completes creation. The individual's choice for good will ultimately, in effect, overcome his status as an individual and subjugate his freedom to the will of God. Man's freedom, individuality, and knowledge have value precisely in the possibility that they themselves can be overcome. They are, to borrow a metaphor that Wittgenstein once used in a different context, ladders that must be discarded once one's work has been completed. The

---

71. Scholem, "Sitra Achra," p. 76.
72. Ibid.

man who fails to discard the ladder but who turns his freedom, knowledge, and individuality into ends unto themselves is invariably led away from the source of life into sin and spiritual death. The Talmud says of the wicked, that even when alive they are dead.[73] Their egoism lowers their soul into the realm of the *Sitra Achra* where the finite and the "dead" have a virtually independent existence from God.

It is the identification of evil with individuality, freedom and knowledge, that provides evil with its great seductive power. According to Schneur Zalman, when a man looks inward he discovers within himself two souls: the Godly soul and the natural soul. It is the latter with which man as an individual identifies and which distinguishes his personality from that of all other men. This natural soul, as we have seen, is the fulcrum of creation itself, yet it is also the soul that brings evil into our world. It is for this reason that it can be said that human individuality is both absolutely necessary yet inherently evil.

The identification of evil with knowledge will certainly be unsettling to those who are familiar with traditions in both Western and Eastern thought that hold precisely the opposite view, i.e., that ignorance is the source of evil, and knowledge the font of its demise. The doctrine of *coincidentia oppositorum* permits the Kabbalists to accept both views. Evil is *knowledge* of particular finite things and *ignorance* of their relation to God. The doctrine of *Tzimtzum* is based upon the idea that the world, and particularly the "Other Side," results from a concealment or ignorance of the divine plenum. The Kabbalists understood "knowledge" under two different lights, one that unifies and one that divides; it is only the latter, *ontic* knowledge that the Kabbalists identify with evil; the former, *ontological* knowledge is indeed the essence of the Good.

EVIL AS INERTIA

An interesting view of evil is found in the writings of Nathan of Gaza, the prophet of the false Messiah, Sabbatai Sevi, who created a great stir both in Poland and the Holy Land during the sixteenth century.[74] Nathan's views are officially heretical but nonetheless instructive, as they provide us with a dialectical counterpoint to the notion of evil as creation.

---

73. Talmud, Tractate *Berakhot*, 18a–b.
74. See Scholem, *Sabbatai Zevi: The Mystical Messiah*.

Nathan conceives evil as an inertial force within the Godhead that is *indifferent to or resistant to creation*. Nathan spoke of this force as "the thoughtless light" as it is an energy or power that is resistant to the idea of creation. Opposing itself to the creative or "thoughtful light," the thoughtless light seeks to return everything into a formless, undifferentiated state of affairs, serving as a sort of metaphysical principle of disorganization or entropy. For Nathan, the Zohar's description of the "Other Side" refers to the "Other Side" of *Ein-Sof* itself, the "half" of God that resists differentiation, organization, and creation.[75]

One might, on first thought, be tempted to identify Nathan's inertial principle with the matter (or *hyla*) that is opposed to "form" in Greek thought. There are indeed kabbalistic texts that connect matter with evil,[76] and it is clear, in the Lurianic view, that pure, lifeless, matter is the end-stage of the process of *Tzimtzum*, in which God's light is contracted and concealed. But Nathan's doctrine of the inertial, "thoughtless light" is really quite opposite in its intent. For the Zohar, matter is evil because it is the very end-stage of creation, in which the process of individuation/differentiation has formed an entity (or illusion thereof) that is completely estranged from God. For Nathan, however, the "thoughtless light" is evil because it strives to maintain everything in an undifferentiated state within God and opposes the very concept of creation/individuation altogether. Evil, for Nathan, is not an estrangement from the divine; rather, it is the aspect of God that keeps all unto Himself, and refuses to create, or allow the continued existence of, a world. Nathan's view is actually close to the Freudian concept of Thanatos, which understands man's evil and aggression as rooted in an urge to undo the process of creation/individuation and return to a (biologically) unformed, entropic state.

From a philosophical standpoint, Nathan's view serves as a dialectical complement to the identification of creation as evil, and provides a metaphysical basis for the biblical (and commonsense) view that creation in itself is good. Indeed, with his doctrine of the "thoughtless light," Nathan makes explicit what has been implicit in the kabbalistic view of evil all along: that there are not one but *two* poles of evil, and not one but *two* poles of good.

On the one hand there is the view that creation, with its differentiation, individuation, materialization, and estrangement from God, is the source of evil. The good, on this view, is identified with an undifferentiated, all-

---

75. Ibid., pp. 301–302.
76. Scholem, *Origins of the Kabbalah*, p. 67.

knowing, spiritual state of union with the light of the infinite God. On the second view, made explicit by Nathan of Gaza, but, as we have seen, implicit in the Kabbalist's recognition of creation as God's completion, evil is identified with a formless, inertial, union with the Godhead: "the thoughtless light" that is indifferent or hostile to creation and individuation. On this view, individuality, materiality, and freedom are the essence of the good.

Figure 8–1

	Good	Evil
Unity with God	*Kabbalist's View*	*Nathan's View*
Finite/ Separate Creation	*Nathan's View*	*Kabbalist's View*

We might, of course, ask, "Which view is correct?" and in doing so become mired in a debate about the nature of "the good" that has been implicit in both Western and Eastern thought since the dawn of religious philosophy. Is the good life, one might ask, a life in which one actualizes his or her fullest potential as an individual, and through the exercise of free will makes a unique and distinctive mark in a historical world? Or rather is the good life one in which the individual transcends his "self," and his particular, historical circumstances, dissolving his ego in the service of a higher cause or unity with a higher being? We might identify these views respectively as Western/practical and Eastern/mystical, but they are each implicit as "poles" within even our most everyday conceptions of good and evil. The conflict between the individual and the community, between allegiance to self and others, is but one expression of this contrast. Within contemporary psychoanalysis, debate about "the good" mirrors this essential dialectic, with those who see the work of analysis as the strengthening of the ego and the creation of an individuated "self"; and others (for example, Lacan) who see all such pursuits as a chimera, and who understand the work of analysis as dissolving the ego and moving asymptotically toward a glimpse of the unconscious or unknown.

The kabbalistic concepts of good and evil are in constant motion. They move in conjunction with "being and nothingness," which, as we have seen in Chapter Two, are in constant motion themselves. On the one hand, the Kabbalists identified "being" and hence the "good" with the infinite unity of God, and identified "nothingness" and hence "evil" with the finite, individuated condition of creation. On the other hand, being (and the good) is conceived as creation, freedom, and individuation, and is contrasted with the nothingness of a perfectly undifferentiated God. Depending on one's perspective, both being and nothingness each participate in both good and evil. Indeed it can be said that they participate even in each other, ready to change places with a change in our point of view. As we have seen, for the Kabbalists, concepts are only complete when they reveal their opposites to be part of their very significance.

APPEASING THE "OTHER SIDE"

In the Zohar we find the doctrine that just as one must have faith and grant sacrifices to the side of holiness, one must do the same for evil in an effort to "appease" the *Sitra Achra*, the "Other Side." Several of the *mitzvot* (Torah commandments) are described in the Zohar as an appeasement or bribe; including the goat dispatched to "Azazel" (a ritual that the Cohanim performed on Yom Kippur when the Temple still stood in Jerusalem) and the inclusion of animal hair in the *tephillin* (phylacteries) that are donned by Jewish men during morning prayer. The "Other Side," which is here represented as man's animal instincts or impulses, cannot simply be defeated or overcome; it must be distracted and appeased, in effect "granted its portion."[77]

Here we have a powerful metaphor for the psychological truth that one's aggressive urges cannot simply be willed away. The Kabbalah has a healthy respect for man's baser, destructive instincts, and it recognizes the real power of destructiveness in the human heart. Indeed the Zohar criticizes the biblical personage Job for, in effect, believing himself to be so righteous and pure

---

77. Tishby and Lachower, *The Wisdom of the Zohar*, Vol. 2, p. 452.

that he failed to "give a portion" to the *Sitra Achra*.[78] By failing to take the evil impulse into consideration he actually increased the powers of uncleanness and destruction. Schneur Zalman tells us that it is an almost impossible task for an ordinary man to come to genuinely abhor and reject the evil in his heart. This can be done only through "a great and intense love for God, the kind of ecstatic love and Divine bliss which is akin to the world to come."[79] For all practical purposes evil is an inevitable part of the human spirit; one that can neither be completely transcended nor ignored.

The Zohar interpreted the entire sacrificial system of prerabbinic Judaism as, at least in part, a method for appeasing the "Other Side." The animal sacrifices, presumably by channeling man's aggressive/thanatic urges, provided the necessary appeasement to evil. Indeed the strength of man's thanatic urges, and the necessity for their sublimation and appeasement, is made clear in the biblical story of the *Akedah*, where Abraham, the great patriarch of the Jewish people, nearly sacrifices his own son Isaac in the name of faith and holiness. This act, which involves the willingness of Abraham to kill his own son in the name of God, serves as a somewhat unnerving paradigm for the faith of the Jewish people, and illustrates the Zoharic axiom that evil (here in the guise of a filicidal impulse) must be included in the worship of God.

Just as there must be *a descent for the purpose of ascent* on the cosmic level, just as the potential for evil is a necessary condition for the good, each individual man and woman must be prepared to descend into the realm of the Husks if he or she is to effect a personal *Tikkun*. The Zohar interprets Abraham's, and later Israel's, descent into Egypt as an earthbound representation of the theosophical "descent for ascent" principle. According to the Zohar, Adam and Noah each descended into and became entangled in the "realm of the Husks" but the patriarchs entered and emerged in peace. The Jews' 400 years in *Mitzrayim* (Egypt) and their *aliyah*, or ascent with Moses to the Promised Land, is the paradigmatic example of the "descent for ascent" principle operating in history. Though it is a dangerous undertaking from which he may not return, man, it is said, achieves his perfection by entering the domain of evil and refining himself there as in a crucible.

In our discussion of the *Kelippot* we learned that evil itself is parasitic upon and intrinsically connected to holiness. It is for this reason, the Zohar

---

78. Ibid., Vol. 2, p. 453.
79. Ibid., Vol. 2, p. 457.

tells us, that we must learn to accept the evil or thanatic urges within our own nature:

> Here we learn that even though this side (*Sitra Achra*) is nothing but the side of uncleanness, there is a brightness around it, and man does not have to drive it away. Why is this? Because there is a brightness around it; the side of holiness of faith exists there; and there is no need to treat it with disdain. Therefore one must give it a portion on the side of the holiness of faith.[80]

What is it to give "faith" to evil? As the psychoanalyst Michael Eigen has pointed out, "faith" is that which proceeds from our deepest levels of experience.[81] If faith exists at all it is conducted "with all one's might and all one's soul." One cannot, therefore, have "faith" unless one "gives a portion" to one's darker side, to the evil aspects of one's "might and soul." The faith that pretends to be "lily white" is a faith in name only and is bound to be haunted by a return of the repressed.

In keeping with the kabbalistic view that evil has a vital role in creation, the Zohar suggests that we must include the "Other Side" in our worship in order to assure its continued existence! With respect to the ritual of dispensing the goat to "Azazel" (Leviticus 16: 8), by throwing it off a cliff on the Day of Atonement, the Zohar comments:

> The proverb states: "throw the dog a bone, and he will lick the dust off your feet . . ." The World needs one as much as the other for this reason it says "And behold it was very good" [Genesis 1: 31]. This refers to the angel of death. He should not be banished from the world. The world needs him . . . It is all necessary, good and evil.[82]

How does man grant a portion to or appease the "Other Side" in contemporary life? Primarily, it might be said, by acknowledging and affectively experiencing the totality of one's urges, particularly those that are hateful and destructive, and further by acknowledging the great power of death over the very essence of life. To deny the existence of death and destruction is to permit those twin demons to propagate and grow on their own terms. By failing to grant them their portion we are inviting them to devour the whole.

---

80. Ibid., Vol. 2, p. 463.
81. Michael Eigen, "The Area of Faith in Winnicott, Lacan and Bion."
82. Zohar III, 63a–63b; Tishby and Lachower, *The Wisdom of the Zohar*, Vol. 2, pp. 510–523.

9

Tikkun ha-Olam:
The Restoration of the World

The kabbalistic concept of *Tikkun ha-Olam*, the repair or restoration of the world, has been reignited in the Jewish imagination in recent years. Jewish philosophers have adapted this concept for their own use[1] and a major Jewish periodical, *Tikkun*, has emerged, which identifies *Tikkun ha-Olam* with a liberal but family and religiously oriented political stance that its editor has referred to as "neo-compassionism."[2] The contemporary interest in *Tikkun ha-Olam* makes it all the more urgent that we understand this notion in its original, kabbalistic context. In so doing we may be able to gain some insight into the connection, if any, between the recent versions of *Tikkun* and the Jewish mystical tradition, and learn something of what this mystical symbol has to offer in our own time.

The concept of *Tikkun ha-Olam* has parallels in various religious and philosophical notions from ancient times down to the present day. For example, in ancient Iranian (Zoroastrian) thought we find the concept of

---

1. See, for example, Arthur Waskow, *These Holy Sparks: The Rebirth of the Jewish People* (San Francisco: Harper & Row, 1983).

2. Michael Lerner, "Tikkun: To Mend, Repair and Transform the World," *Tikkun*, (1986) Vol. 1, No. 1: 7–13; Michael Lerner, "Neo-Compassionism," *Tikkun*, Vol. 2, (1987) No. 5: 9–13.

the *kwhar*, or "talents," which have been entrusted to each individual at birth.[3] These talents, it is said, must be actualized in full, in a "continuous evolution of making excellent" in order to help realize the perfection of humanity and the world planned for by God. The key to understanding the notion of *kwhar*, and one of the keys to a full comprehension of *Tikkun ha-Olam*, is that these ideas refer to an inner, psychological realization that has the purpose of perfecting the (outer) world. It is this dialectic of "inner" and "outer" that is critical to Lurianic and Hasidic understanding of *Tikkun*.

The concept of *Tikkun ha-Olam* is implicit throughout the history of Jewish mysticism. Its origins are, in part, to be found in the biblical conviction that the paradise lost to mankind because of Adam's sin would be restored in a future age, and in part in the late biblical belief that an exiled Jewish people would be returned to the land of Israel. While the repair or restoration of the world is therefore a theme that is recurrent throughout Jewish history, the concept of *Tikkun ha-Olam* reaches its fullest development in sixteenth-century Safed in the Lurianic Kabbalah. Isaac Luria (1534–1572) and his disciples, most notably Chayyim Vital (1542–1620), dwelt upon *Tikkun* at great length, reinterpreting old kabbalistic ideas and providing a grand symbolic scheme within which the "repair of the universe" plays the most significant role. Indeed, the Kabbalists of Safed understood every event in the created universe, indeed the very act of creation itself as a mere introduction to or preparation for *Tikkun ha-Olam*.[4]

---

3. R. C. Zaehner, *The Dawn and Twilight of Zoroastrianism* (London: Weidenfeld and Nicolson, 1961), p. 268.

4. The Lurianic theory of *Tikkun* is the major preoccupation in the locus classicus of the Lurianic Kabbalah, Chayyim Vital's *Sefer Etz Chayyim*. More than half of this work is devoted to the intricate process through which the "kings" who had died, and the "divine configurations" (*Partzufim*) that were divided, as a result of the cosmic catastrophe, the Breaking of the Vessels, are reintegrated and reorganized into new configurations that fulfill the divine plan for creation and perfect the very nature of God. I will, in this chapter, explore Vital's account in some detail, an account that Scholem speculated is so complex as to be "a challenge to mystical contemplation" (Scholem, *Kabbalah*, p. 140). We will see that Vital places great significance on those metaphors that liken the *Tikkun* process to the human life cycle, specifically sexual union, birth, and the process of individual development.

SEPARATION AND UNIFICATION

Two metaphors dominate the Lurianic conception of *Tikkun ha-Olam*: the *separation* and extraction of divine light from the encumbering evil forces of the "Other Side" and the *unification* of the masculine and feminine aspects or personas of God. Like the alchemist's *solve et coagula* (which itself may have its origins in the Kabbalah[5]) the kabbalistic view of redemption involves a dynamic of separation and unification. This dynamic involves the separation and disencumbrance of divine energy leading to an erotic unification within the Godhead. All other symbols and theories of *Tikkun*, including, among others, overcoming of the exile of the *Shekhinah*, the reunification of the trees of life and knowledge, the mitigation of judgment by kindness, and the raising of the sparks, participate in this separation/unification dynamic. Each, we will see, can be understood as moments in a drama in which the world itself undergoes a cosmic alienation and is liberated through a release of divine energy leading to the erotic unifications of male and female divine principles. These unifications symbolize the dialectical union of such "opposites" as male and female, good and evil, being and nothingness, creation and destruction, self and other, past and present, mind and world, material and spiritual, etc. By uniting such apparently opposing principles the Lurianic conception of *Tikkun ha-Olam* brings us beyond a purely intellectual dialectic, into a dialectic of mind, heart, and spirit. Indeed it is the overcoming of such contradictions that is the mystical *and* practical essence of *Tikkun ha-Olam*.

We will see that the dual metaphors of separation and unification are integrated within the Lurianic Kabbalah in a single world-restoring act, where humanity, in disencumbering and raising the sparks of divine light (a separation), encourages, and actually participates in, the divine *zivvug* (erotic coupling and unification). This process reverses the uncoupling, destructive process that, as we saw in Chapter Seven, began with the cosmic event known as the "Breaking of the Vessels."

THE SYMBOLS OF *TIKKUN*

The Kabbalists made use of a wide array of symbols in their understanding of *Tikkun ha-Olam*. As with the other aspects of their theosophy, they held that

---

5. See Sanford Drob, *Kabbalistic Metaphors*, Chapter 8.

a notion as broad and significant as the restoration and redemption of the entire world could not be encompassed via a single image or idea. Among the symbols and notions relevant to *Tikkun* are the "unification of God and His *Shekhinah*," "the raising of the sparks," the transition from exile to redemption, the discovery of the "roots" of one's soul, development in the womb of the Celestial Mother, the modulation of emotion by thought, the integration of the *Sefirot*, the mitigation of judgment by kindness, the taming of the evil impulse, the dilemma of Adam and the Tree of Knowledge, the "inner" and "outer" aspects of all things, and the Hasidic notions of "worship through corporeality" and "the descent for the purpose of ascent."

We will discuss each of these symbols in turn, linking them to other ideas, including *Tzimtzum* (concealment or contraction), the *Sefirot* (luminaries, dimensions, spheres), and *Shevirat ha-Kelim* (the Breaking of the Vessels), which as we have already seen, play a pivotal role in Lurianic thought.

THE UNIFICATION OF GOD AND HIS *SHEKHINAH*

The notion of an erotic union between the masculine and feminine aspects of God is an important kabbalistic symbol, which predates the concept of *Tikkun ha-Olam* and that was eventually incorporated into it. The Zohar holds that such a union is necessary because of the "exile of the *Shekhinah*," the exile of God's feminine aspect and presence on earth from God's masculine aspect.[6] According to the Zohar, the main goal of religious life is to restore the unity of the masculine divine principle with the *Shekhinah*, a unity that was broken by the sins of mankind, the exile of the Jewish people from the land of Israel, and the hold of the evil powers of the "Other Side." For the Zohar, it is only through the observance of the *mitzvot* and prayers directed toward heaven that the exile of the *Shekhinah* can be overcome and she can be reunited with "the Holy One Blessed Be He."

The *Shekhinah*, which literally means "presence," "resting," or "indwelling," was identified by the sages of the Talmud simply as the "presence of God" or even as God himself. The medieval philosophers went further in regarding the *Shekhinah* as an independent created entity, which serves as an

---

6. Zohar II, 189b; Sperling and Simon, *The Zohar*, Vol. 4, p. 139; Zohar II, 216b; Sperling and Simon, *The Zohar*, Vol. 4, p. 235.

intermediary between God and man and appears as "God's glory" to the prophets. The Kabbalists were critical of this view, adopting a position that identified the *Shekhinah* as the final *Sefirah*, an aspect of God that is conceptually distinguishable from Him but ultimately contained within the divine essence. For the Kabbalists, the *Shekhinah* came to be understood as the divine power closest to the world, the divine principle within the people of Israel, and, because of its proximity to the world and man, as the "battleground" between good and evil. The Kabbalists, however, in holding that the *Shekhinah* is in exile and that it can commune with the masculine *Sefirah*, *Tiferet*, came close to the philosophical view that the *Shekhinah* is indeed distinct from the Godhead.

In identifying the *Shekhinah* with the tenth *Sefirah*, *Malchut*, the Kabbalists, beginning with *Sefer ha-Bahir*, developed the view that the *Shekhinah* is a feminine receptacle who passively receives the divine influx from each of the higher *Sefirot*, but who is completely empty and lacking in being in and of herself. In receiving the divine influx from the ninth *Sefirah*, *Yesod*, which was identified with the phallus of the Primordial Man, the *Shekhinah* was understood as a cosmic princess, daughter, and mother, who acts as the vehicle for the transmission of divine creativity and revelation to earth. The proper flow of divine energy cannot be sustained unless the *Shekhinah* is conjugally united with the ninth *Sefirah*, *Yesod*, and, especially, the sixth *Sefirah*, *Tiferet*.[7]

The Zohar distinguishes between the "lower *Shekhinah*," identified with the *Sefirah Malchut*, and an "upper *Shekhinah*," identified with the third *Sefirah*, *Binah* (Understanding).[8] The latter must also unite with a masculine principle, the *Sefirah Chochmah* (Wisdom), thus providing the basis for the view that the erotic unification within the Godhead is symbolic of a cognitive unification between wisdom and understanding.

Each of these ideas are adopted and provided with an extraordinarily complex elaboration in the Lurianic theory of *Tikkun*. According to Luria and Vital, the Breaking of the Vessels results in numerous erotic separations (between *Sefirot*, *Partzufim*, divine names, etc.) that must be rectified in the process of *Tikkun ha-Olam*. These separations or "turnings back to back"

---

7. *Tiferet* is the masculine principle uniting all six of the lower *Sefirot* from *Chesed* to *Yesod*. As the masculine aspect of God, it is "The Holy One Blessed Be He" and the *Partzuf Zeir Anpin*, the "Short-Faced" or "Impatient" one.

8. The *Sefirot Chochmah* and *Binah*, as we have seen in earlier chapters, are in turn identified with the *Partzufim Abba* (Father) and *Imma* (Mother).

(*acher b'acher*) evolved directly from the Zoharic doctrine of the *Shekhinah*'s exile. However, in Luria and Vital the entire divine order is reinterpreted in sexual/erotic terms and the *Tikkun* or correction of all the world's disharmonies is understood as contingent upon various *coniunctios* in the upper worlds.

God's unification with his *Shekhinah* can be understood as a reunification of the divided aspects of the cosmos, or in psychological terms as a reunification of a divided self. Carl Jung understood the Kabbalist's divine-wedding symbolism as a metaphor for the unification of the masculine and feminine aspects of the human psyche, or between the ego (persona) and the repressed (shadow). According to Jung, the Kabbalists, like the alchemists who followed them, projected the work of unifying a divided self onto the idea of unifying matter (the alchemists) or God (the Kabbalists).

THE TREES OF LIFE AND KNOWLEDGE

The "exile of the *Shekhinah*" is provided a moral interpretation in the *Midrash HaNeelam* in the Zohar, where it is explained as follows. The *Sefirot* (the ten dimensions or aspects of Godliness) were revealed to Adam in the form of the twin trees of Life and Knowledge. By failing to maintain their primal unity Adam placed a division between life and knowledge that has had far-reaching implications.[9] According to the Zohar this division resulted in a fissure in both God and the world and prompted Adam to worship the tenth *Sefirah* (the *Shekhinah*, God's manifestation on earth) without recognizing its unity with higher, more spiritual forms. Adam's sin is the origin of crass materialism and other shortsighted and incomplete worship in man.

The Zohar's interpretation of the fall of Adam can be understood if we remember that the final *Sefirah*, whether spoken of as *Malchut* (Kingship) or the *Shekhinah* (dwelling), refers to God's presence in space and time, and is the *Sefirah* most closely identified with the material world. By worshipping the *Shekhinah* and failing to understand its unity with the other *Sefirot*, Adam became attached to the temporal, material world as opposed to the values that world instantiates or represents. In this way he worshipped the Tree of Knowledge (of good and evil) and ignored the "Tree of Life" (the sefirotic values embodied in the Torah).

---

9. Scholem, *Major Trends*, p. 232.

The fissure between life and knowledge, like that between God and His *Shekhinah*, can only be healed, according to the Kabbalists, through the observance of Torah, *mitzvot* (commandments), and *avodah* (worship). This, again, is the Zohar's foundation for the later kabbalistic concept of *Tikkun ha-Olam*. In studying Torah, performing the *mitzvot*, and worshipping God (*avodah*), the Jew is able to reattach himself to the *Sefirot* (Godly values) and hence effect a reunification of God and His *Shekhinah*. In so doing mankind undertakes to reunite the source of all values with the material world. The erotic union between God and His *Shekhinah* is, on this interpretation, a union that permits values and meaning to flow freely between God to man. It is for this reason that the Zohar often identifies the *Shekhinah* with *Knesset Yisrael*, the community of Israel. The ethical man, as part of an ethical community, acts as a conduit through which value or godliness is realized on earth. In this way *Tikkun ha-Olam* becomes the realization of spiritual, intellectual, ethical, aesthetic, and natural values, the very values embodied in the heavenly *Sefirot*.[10]

In the Zohar we thus have a concept of the world's redemption in which an erotic metaphor is the vehicle for a spiritual goal. In effect, according to the *Midrash HaNeelam*, man must turn from a purely corporeal view of life (symbolized by the Tree of Knowledge) in order to effect a holy erotic union between God and the world. This is another example of kabbalistic *coincidentia oppositorum*. Here a corporeal, sexual union is used to symbolize its opposite, i.e., a turning away from the corporeal and an embracing of the spiritual.

THE RAISING OF THE SPARKS (*NETZOTZIM*)

The "raising of the sparks" is the most important and powerful of the "separation" metaphors of *Tikkun ha-Olam*. The symbol of a divine spark encased in earthly matter and in man is an ancient Gnostic symbol, which also appears in the Kabbalah of seventeenth-century Safed. Nothing quite comparable to this symbol is present in the Zohar, and its appearance in Luria

---

10. According to the Kabbalists, this is accomplished primarily through participation in the Jewish way of life. (See Sanford Drob, "Judaism as a Form of Life.") Whether other forms of ethical, spiritual, and intellectual endeavor promote the restoration of the world is an issue that, as far as I can tell, is not specifically addressed by the Kabbalists.

(along with the *Tzimtzum* and the *Shevirah*) defines the Lurianic Kabbalah and sets it apart from all prior expressions of Jewish mysticism.

It is instructive to compare the conception of the "sparks," as it appears in the Lurianic Kabbalah, with this symbol's earlier expression in the second-century Gnostic systems of Valentinus and Basilides.[11] In the Gnostic version, a divine spark is entrapped in a world that is conceived of as completely alien and evil. This world, according to the Gnostics, was created by an ignorant demiurge who has no knowledge of the true "Father," the infinite pleroma. However, creation causes a divine spark to be imprisoned in the soul of man. According to the Gnostics, it is the individual's divinely appointed task to obtain knowledge (Gnosis) of the spark within himself and thereby liberate it from this world. Once this is achieved the Gnostic adherent, having no further use for this world, abandons his corporeal self and returns to join the infinite pleroma.

Like the Gnostics, Luria held that divine sparks are entrapped in both matter and man. And like the Gnostics, Luria urged man to liberate the sparks contained within his own soul. However, in contrast to the Gnostics, Luria held that when the spark of divine light is freed, the world is reintegrated and restored, rather than escaped and discarded.

As we have seen, the Lurianists believed divine sparks to be imprisoned by the evil forces of this world. These sparks were immersed in the "Other Side" when the vessels that were meant to contain God's light were shattered. As a result of the Breaking of the Vessels, much of the light that was destined for the seven shattered *Sefirot* returned to its origins in *Ein-Sof* and was reorganized into a series of five "Visages" (*Partzufim*) that embody the sefiriotic qualities in "character types," which reflect basic aspects of both God and mankind. This reorganization of divine light is the beginning of *Tikkun ha-Olam*, the restoration of the world. However, not all of the light contained by the *Sefirot* was capable of returning to the Infinite God. Shards from the shattered vessels fell through the metaphysical void, trapping within themselves sparks (*netzotzim*) of divine light, in much the same manner as oil clings to the shards of a shattered vessel that had contained it. These entrapped shards or "Husks" (*Kelippot*) come to rest in an alien, evil realm known as the *Sitra Achra* or "Other Side." The *Kelippot*, sustained in their

---

11. For an in-depth comparison of Gnosticism and the Kabbalah, see my book, *Kabbalistic Metaphors: Jewish Mystical Themes in Ancient and Modern Thought*, Ch. 5.

very life and existence by the divine light that they enclose, give rise to both matter and evil. Through proper ethical and spiritual conduct humanity can free the holy light from the *Kelippot* that contain them, thus permitting this light to return to its source and assist in the completion of *Tikkun ha-Olam*.

According to the Lurianists, it is through the performance of the precepts of the Torah, and the proper intentions (*Kavvanot*) during prayer (and not simply through gnosis), that the Kabbalist is able to liberate the sparks of both the world and his soul, returning some sparks to their source in *Ein-Sof*, and others to the "worlds" where they assist in the restoration of the cosmic order. In a bold combination of the separation and unification metaphors, the Lurianists held that the liberation of the sparks by mankind is for the purpose of providing the *mayim nukvim* (female waters) for divine intercourse and the unification of male and female *Partzufim*. Such unification is the crux and fulfillment of the *Tikkun* that restores and redeems the material world. Thus, in contrast to the Gnostics, the Lurianists developed an essentially "this-worldy" theory of raising the sparks.[12]

The doctrine of the "raising of the sparks" brought an *immediacy* to the concept of *Tikkun ha-Olam*, which had not hitherto been present in the Kabbalah. The Kabbalists of Safed, and particularly the Hasidim, believed sparks of divine light to be contained in all things and they held that each individual has an opportunity to engage in *Tikkun ha-Olam* in each and every one of his activities, from the most mundane to the most spiritual. There is, according to the Lurianic point of view, something of value, something Godly in all things, and it is incumbent upon mankind to discover, highlight, and, as it were, bring out the value in the material world, thus transforming that world into a spiritual realm.[13] *Tikkun ha-Olam*, the restoration of the

---

12. However, this is not to say that there are no "quietistic" elements within the Kabbalah and Hasidim. Indeed, Schatz-Uffenheimer has provided such a quietistic interpretation of the entire Hasidic movement, in which the ascetic tendencies of the Lurianists were translated into a doctrine of prayer and behavior, in which the avowed goal of the adherent was to raise himself into a blessed union with the deity, abandoning world and self in the process. See Rifka Schatz-Uffenheimer, *Hasidism As Mysticism*. Such a Gnostic escapism, as I have pointed out in Chapter One, appears to conflict with the activist, this-worldly traditions of Judaism, and creates a major challenge to the Kabbalah, and particularly the Hasidim, which can only be resolved through an application of the doctrine of *coincidentia oppositorum*. This topic is provided a fuller discussion in Chapter Four of my *Kabbalistic Metaphors*.

13. This, the Kabbalists explain, is why so many of the *mitzvot* involve operations on the material world. To take one example: in building a sukkah the

world, will be complete when all of the sparks have been raised and the entire world has been informed with spiritual meaning and value.

Among the Hasidim the doctrine of the holy sparks became the key to personal as well as world redemption. As will be seen later in this chapter, for the Hasidim a man's life came to be understood as a providential journey in which the people, places, and events that he encounters contain precisely those sparks that only he can redeem. As such, every moment in a man's life provides the opportunity for raising the sparks of divine redemption, or, conversely, for plummeting the world even further into the grip of the "Other Side."

THE TRANSITION FROM EXILE TO REDEMPTION

According to Scholem,[14] the Kabbalists transformed the biblical theme of *galut* (exile) and *ge'ulah* (redemption) into a mystical metaphor for *Tikkun ha-Olam*. The exile of Adam and Eve from the garden of Eden and the exile of the Jewish people in Egypt, Babylonia, and later throughout the world were each understood as manifestations or symbols of a cosmic process reflecting "the exile of the *Shekhinah*" and the "Breaking of the Vessels." At various points in history (the Sinaitic revelation being the most prominent among them) *Tikkun ha-Olam* was almost complete. However, on those occasions the Jewish people failed in their mission, choosing to align themselves with the forces of the "Other Side" (for example, in the incident of the golden calf) and world harmony was not restored. Still, every Jew has it within his or her own power to raise the sparks of his own soul and environment and in the process move the world closer to the messianic, "restored" age. Indeed the purpose of the Jewish Diaspora is for Jews to collect sparks from all over the world.[15] When this occurs, exile on the historical as well as the cosmic levels will be overcome, the Jewish people will

---

observant Jew takes common natural materials, e.g., wood and leaves, and transforms or spiritualizes them into objects of divine service. The same transformation occurs when ordinary building materials are fashioned into and dedicated as a Jewish home or when an artisan molds silver or brass into objects of religious devotion.

14. Gershom Scholem, *The Messianic Idea in Judaism and Other Essays on Jewish Spirituality* (New York: Schocken, 1971), p. 45.

15. See Schochet, "Mystical Concepts," p. 892, Schochet refers to *Sefer Etz Chayyim*, 3: 6, 19: 3, 26: 1 and Schneur Zalman, *Tanya* I, Chapter 49.

return to Israel and be redeemed there, and the light entrapped by the forces of the "Other Side" will return to its source in the infinite God.

We should note that the entire Lurianic theosophy can be interpreted in exilic terms. Even the initial act of *Tzimtzum*, whereby *Ein-Sof* withdraws or conceals himself to make room for creation, is understood as an act of exile, and a portent of all things to come.[16] Creation itself is conditioned by an exile or alienation, and Luria's dialectic is one in which exiles (*Tzimtzum, Shevirah*) alternate with redemptions (*Sefirot, Tikkun*) in the evolution of both God and the world.

DISCOVERING THE ROOTS OF ONE'S SOUL

The Zohar (to *Shir ha-Shirim*, The Song of Songs) had posited four paths to wisdom:

> One way is to contemplate the mystery of His Master. Another is to know one's self. Who am I? How was I created? Where do I come from, where am I going? How is the body fixed to function? How must I give an account of myself before the Ruler of All? A third way is to know the secrets of souls. What is this soul within me? Where does it come from? Why did it come into this body made of a stinking drop? A fourth way is to know and contemplate the world one is in. What is its purpose? And then to seek to know the supernal mysteries of the higher worlds and to know one's Master. All of these paths of contemplation are within the mysteries of the Torah . . . [17]

The Kabbalists of Safed developed the idea that these paths, particularly those that involve knowledge of the roots of one's own soul, were necessary in order to achieve one's personal *Tikkun*. According to Luria, the Breaking of the Vessels resulted in the imprisonment of sparks not only from the *Shekhinah* (God's "presence") but also the sparks of human souls as well. Indeed it was his view that the souls of all men and women are comprised of sparks from Adam's soul, most of which have been imprisoned in the

---

16. See Scholem, *Major Trends*, p. 261, and Jacobs, "The Uplifting of the Sparks in Later Hasidism."

17. Zohar, Song of Songs 18, quoted in R. Shalom Buzalgo, *Mikdash Melech*, in Meltzer, *The Secret Garden*, p. 188.

Kelippot as a result of Adam's fall. It is the task of each Jew to discover these sparks or roots within himself and through a process of extraction or disencumbrance (*birur*) perform his or her own personal *Tikkun* or restoration. This task is described as follows by Chayyim Vital: "When a man is born his soul must liberate those sparks that are his share and which had fallen into the *Kelippot* . . . because of Adam's sin."[18] According to the Kabbalist Moses Zacuto: "it behooves every man to inquire diligently and to know the roots of his soul as to be able to perfect it and restore it to its origin which is the essence of his being."[19] Here the process of self-perfection is essentially one of self-discovery.

It is important to distinguish the self-discovery of the Kabbalists from self-discovery as it is understood today in the context of popular psychology. Discovering the roots of one's soul, performing the act of *birur*, and achieving one's personal *Tikkun* is not a process that leads to the enhancement of one's ego and the fulfillment of one's personal desires, per se. Rather, it is a process through which one discovers his or her unique spiritual task in life. The raising of the sparks of one's own soul leads to the realization of one's "Godly self"[20] and to the transformation of the individual into a conduit for God's values and God's will. The individual who seeks guidance from a kabbalistic master or Hasidic rebbe does not seek psychotherapy, but rather guidance in discovering the manner of serving God and his fellow man that is uniquely suited to his personality and life circumstance. If successful in this pursuit he will indeed achieve a great sense of personal fulfillment, but this is not his goal. His goal is *Tikkun ha-Olam* through the actualization of God's values on earth.

DEVELOPMENT IN THE WOMB OF THE CELESTIAL MOTHER

Among the most difficult and seemingly opaque aspects of the Lurianic Kabbalah is its treatment of *Partzufim* (Visages). As discussed in Chapter

---

18. *Sefer Etz Chayyim* 50: 3.

19. M. Zacuto, commentary on Zohar I, 78a in Shalom b. Moses Buzalgo, *Mikdash Melech*, as quoted and translated by Scholem, *Sabbatai Sevi: The Mystical Messiah*, pp. 41–42.

20. The concept of the "Godly self" or "Godly soul" is elaborated in Zalman, *Likutei Amarim-Tanya*, Ch. 2ff.

Four, like the *Sefirot*, the *Partzufim* are ideational or spiritual structures that are regarded as aspects of the deity and as intermediaries between God and creation.[21] The Lurianists frequently spoke as if the *Partzufim* emerged spontaneously as a result of the Breaking of the Vessels.[22] These *Partzufim* or "faces of God" are said to reorganize within themselves the divine light that had originally been destined for each shattered *Sefirah*.

The creation of the *Partzufim* is the initial phase of *Tikkun ha-Olam*. Each *Partzuf* represents a specific stage in the process of divine reconstruction, acts as a medium for the reception and transmission of divine influx from the upper worlds, and serves as an archetype for the union of the masculine and the feminine aspects of God, symbolized in their "looking face to face."[23]

However, the *Partzufim*, and *Tikkun ha-Olam* itself, must be completed by man. One *Partzuf*, *Zeir Anpin* (the "short-faced" or "impatient" one), is, according to the Kabbalists of Safed, integrally connected with the phase of *Tikkun* that involves the efforts of mankind. *Zeir Anpin* is said to organize within itself qualities of six of the ten *Sefirot*, precisely those that were completely shattered in the *Shevirah*, including the "moral" *Sefirot* of *Chesed* (Kindness), *Din* (Justice), and *Rachamim* (Mercy). The Zoharic metaphor of "the unification of The Holy One Blessed Be He with His *Shekhinah*" is paralleled in the Lurianic writings by the metaphor of the union between "Zeir Anpin" and "Rachel." Each, as a symbol of *Tikkun*, refers to the union of Godly values with each other and their instantiation on earth.

Of greater relevance to our understanding of the nature of *Tikkun*, however, is the fact that two of the *Partzufim*, *Zeir Anpin* and *Nukva*, are themselves described as developing within the womb of another *Partzuf*, *Imma*, the Celestial Mother, creating, according to Scholem, what appears to be a myth of "God giving birth to Himself."[24] In their development, *Zeir Anpin* and *Nukva* are said to progress through five distinct stages: *ibur* (conception), lidah (pregnancy), *yenikah* (birth), *katanot* (childhood), and *gadolot* (maturity). The final stage, *gadolot*, is reflective of mankind's own intellectual and moral maturity. According to Vital these *Partzufim* require

---

21. Schochet, "Mystical Concepts," p. 884.

22. Scholem, *Kabbalah*, p. 140.

23. Ibid., p. 142. Scholem says that together the *Partzufim* "constitute the final figure of *Adam Kadmon* as it evolves in the first stages of *Tikkun*."

24. Scholem, *Major Trends*, p. 271.

the final "three stages of development to become complete—gestation, suckling, and mental development."[25]

Of significance is the fact that the *Partzuf Imma*, within which this development takes place, is identified with the *Sefirah Binah*, Understanding.[26] Before the six moral or emotional *Sefirot* (the six that are embodied in *Zeir Anpin*) can fully participate in *Tikkun ha-Olam* they must undergo a developmental process through which they come under the guidance of intellect and understanding. Similarly, before man can properly perform his own individual *Tikkun*, he too must undergo a developmental maturing process that leads not only to self-understanding but also to the integration of his emotions and intellect.

THE INTEGRATION OF THOUGHT AND EMOTION

The integration of mind and passion is not, according to the Kabbalists, easily achieved. It involves the study of religious texts and the constant application of one's intellect to the problems of personal, community, and religious life that such study entails. Chabad (Lubavitch) Hasidism, which sees itself as embodying the spirit of the Lurianic Kabbalah, places a great emphasis on the modulation of the emotions by the intellect as the key to *Tikkun*. The author of the classic Hasidic work *Tanya*, Schneur Zalman of Lyadi (the first Lubavitcher rebbe), held that the reason why animals are rooted in *Tohu* (the fragile imperfect world that existed before creation was perfected), while humans are rooted in *Tikkun*, is that only man's emotions are modulated by *Chabad* (a Hebrew acronym for *Chochmah* [Thought] *Binah* [Wisdom], and *Da'at* ([Understanding]).[27]

This doctrine that in *Tikkun* the "lower" *middot* (traits, values, emotions) are mitigated by the influence of the "higher" or intellectual *middot* is important to any comparison between Hasidism and contemporary psychology. Freud's famous dictum "where id was, there ego shall be,"[28] which

25. Vital, *Sefer Etz Chayyim* 1:1, p. 33; Menzi and Padeh, *The Tree of Life*, p. 112.

26. Scholem, *Major Trends*, p. 271.

27. Schochet, "Mystical Concepts," p. 885, note 3, referring to Schneur Zalman's *Likutei* Torah II 37cff.

28. Sigmund Freud, *New Introductory Lectures on Psychoanalysis* (New York: W. W. Norton, 1965) (originally published in 1933), p. 80.

refers to the process through which emotions and instincts come to serve the goals of the rational self, comes close to the Chabad Hasidic formulation, as does the psychoanalytic view that the sublimation of one's instincts in intellectual, aesthetic, and spiritual pursuits is the foundation for all civilization and culture.[29]

THE INTEGRATION OF CONFLICTING VALUES AND IDEAS

As we have seen, kabbalistic thought is dialectical in nature, inasmuch as its basic conceptual categories are opposites, even apparent contradictories, that give rise to one another or are blended together in new syntheses.[30] In the Lurianic scheme, the initial impetus to *Tikkun ha-Olam*, the restoration of the world, is an act of *destruction*, the Breaking of the Vessels (*Shevirat ha-Kelim*). *Tikkun* does not restore the world to its condition prior to the *Shevirah*, but rather the world prior to the *Shevirah* was itself in need of restoration; and the Breaking of the Vessels, in true dialectical fashion, was not only destructive but was also a creative act. As we shall see, the dialectical blending of opposites is in other respects an important part of the concept of *Tikkun ha-Olam* and informs several metaphors that represent the restoration process, including the integration of the *Sefirot*, the mitigation of judgment by kindness, and the taming of the evil impulse.

THE INTEGRATION OF THE *SEFIROT*

According to Luria and his followers, the original "flaw" in creation that led to the Breaking of the Vessels was the condition in which the *Sefirot* were completely separate and unrelated. In the primordial world of *Tohu*, the *Sefirot* did not interpenetrate one another, and thus the values they represented failed to come under the rational guidance of *Chochmah*, *Binah*, and *Da'at*. The result was that the *Sefirot* in this earlier world opposed one

---

29. Other Hasidim placed a far greater emphasis on man's passion and will in the process of *Tikkun*. These two views (one calling for the modulation of emotion by intellect, the other celebrating the intensity of passion) reflect an essential controversy and dialectic within the Hasidic movement.

30. See Scholem, *Kabbalah*, p. 143.

another and were not able to assist each other in containing the light of the Infinite God.[31] With the advent of *Tikkun*, the *Sefirot* became completely integrated, and, like reeds that are made stronger by being bonded together, these integrated *Sefirot* are capable of containing the light of the infinite God and thereby maintaining harmony within the cosmos.

On a psychological level, the Kabbalists held that it was only the integration of the sefirotic traits (*middot*) within the individual's own personality that brings about his or her personal *Tikkun*. Not only must the "emotional" *middot* or values (kindness, judgment, beauty, endurance, foundation, and splendor) be modulated by the intellectual (*ChaBad*) *middot*, but values must themselves be integrated with each other.

These ideas came to be embodied in the doctrine of the interpenetration of the *Sefirot*, a doctrine that holds that in the world as it develops toward *Tikkun ha-Olam*, each of the last seven *Sefirot* contains within itself an element of each of the others, so that *Chesed* (Kindness) for example, is composed of the Kindness of Kindness, the Judgment (*Din*) of Kindness, the Beauty (*Tiferet*) of Kindness, the Endurance (*Netzach*) of Kindness, etc. From a moral and psychological point of view this doctrine implies that the development of an individual's character consists of work on all forty-nine possible combinations of the seven moral/emotional *Sefirot*. Only when an individual has developed each of these forty-nine character traits to their fullest potential can it be said that his personal *Tikkun* is complete. The impact of this doctrine can be observed in the practice of many Jews during the forty-nine-day period between *Pesach* and *Shavuot*, (the so-called period of the *Sefirah* or counting) during which one day is assigned to the development of each of these moral traits, up until the fiftieth day when the individual is finally deemed ready to symbolically receive the Torah, just as his/her ancestors did on *Shavuot* at Mount Sinai.

THE MITIGATION OF JUDGMENT BY KINDNESS

One moral dichotomy, the conflict between *chesed* (kindness) and *din* (judgment), was singled out by the Kabbalists for special consideration. Indeed, the importance of mitigating judgment by kindness is apparent throughout Jewish literature, even in sources that are quite remote from the

---

31. Schochet, "Mystical Concepts," p. 884.

Kabbalah. For example, in his commentary on the commandment to reprove the unjust acts of one's neighbor Maimonides warns: "A person who rebukes another, whether for offenses against the rebuker himself or for sins against God, should administer the rebuke in private, speak to the offender gently and tenderly and point out that he is speaking only for the wrongdoer's own good."[32] Thus, even in our judgment (*din*) of another we must show the trait of *chesed* (kindness). This temperance of judgment by kindness (and vice versa) is the foundation of the character trait *rachamim* (mercy, compassion), which Jewish tradition equates with the third moral *Sefirah*, *Tiferet* (Beauty). This is because like beauty, mercy or compassion involves a harmonious blending of opposite currents and trends. The third *Sefirah* also came to be known as the masculine aspect of God, "The Holy One Blessed Be He," and came to play another prominent role as the *Partzuf Zeir Anpin*, in the Lurianic theosophy.

The Midrash teaches that the worlds that God created and then destroyed were created through the principle of *din* or strict divine justice and could thereby not be sustained.[33] The Kabbalists felt, however, that a world created through unmitigated *chesed* or kindness would also self-destruct. This is because kindness that is distributed without regard to the receiver's merit would overwhelm mankind and actually lead to serious injustice. Our present world is sustained by a balance between kindness and judgment and is, in this sense, dominated by the *Sefirah Tiferet* (*Rachamim*). It is the pursuit of a balance between kindness and judgment (a balance that according to the Kabbalist Cordovero must be weighted slightly in the direction of kindness)[34] that leads to the individual's personal *Tikkun* and his contribution to the restoration of the world.

THE DIALECTIC OF GOOD AND EVIL AND THE TAMING OF THE EVIL IMPULSE

As we have seen in Chapter Eight, one of the most startling passages in Jewish mystical literature is to be found in the second book of the Zohar. "In

---

32. *Mishneh Torah* I, 6: 7, translated by Moses Hyamson, *The Code of Maimonides* (Jerusalem: Boys Town, 1965).

33. *Genesis Rabbah* 3: 7, 9: 2 See also 12: 15, and *Pesikta Rabbati* 40.

34. Schochet, "Mystical Concepts," p. 842, citing Moses Cordovero, *Pardes Rimonim* 8: 2, 9: 3.

fact," the Zohar tells us, "there can be no true worship except it issue from darkness, and no true good except it proceed from evil."[35] How, we must ask, can evil, which by definition is diametrically opposed to good, at the same time be the latter's source and foundation? The answer to this question goes to the very essence of *Tikkun ha-Olam.*

Recall that, according to the Kabbalists of Safed, if *Tikkun* is to be achieved, the sparks of divine light (*netzotzim*) that had been alienated from their source must be liberated from the Husks (*Kelippot*), which entrap them in the dark world of the "Other Side." The extraction of the divine light, referred to in the Kabbalah as the act of *birur*, is, metaphysically speaking, the process of *Tikkun ha-Olam* and the essence of "the good" as it can be achieved by mankind. It should, however, be apparent that because the *Kelippot* (which are sustained by the sparks of divine light that they contain) are the source and substance of both matter and evil, the process of extraction (and thus the very process of *Tikkun*) requires a sojourn into the realm of evil. *Tikkun,* the "raising of the sparks," proceeds, as it were, out of the "Other Side," and as such there is no goodness, i.e., no liberated light, except that which issues forth from the evil realm.

We must, however, emphasize that for the Kabbalists, this dialectic of good and evil was no mere play of words or metaphysical sophistry. What was true for them on the metaphysical level was true on the psychological and moral level as well. The Kabbalists held that the good that an individual is capable of in his personal life issues forth from his evil impulse. The Kabbalists of Safed and, particularly, the Hasidic masters who further adapted their philosophy to the concerns of psychology, held that the *Kelippot* (Husks) manifest themselves in the individual as drives for sex and power. Unmodified, these drives, embodied in the *yetzer hara,* "the evil impulse," lead to an exaltation of pleasure and self over all other earthly and Godly values. However, like the Freudian libido (to which it bears a remarkable resemblance), the energy of the *yetzer hara* can be modified and redirected in the service of good. In a process that is hinted at by the psychoanalytic term "sublimation," the evil impulse in man is placed in the service of Godly commandments, and is ultimately redirected in the service of *Tikkun ha-Olam.* However, unlike sublimation, which leaves the libido redirected but essentially unchanged, the redirection implied by the processes of *birur* and *Tikkun* actually elevates and transforms the evil impulse into the *yetzer*

---

35. Zohar II, 184a; Sperling and Simon, *The Zohar*, Vol. IV, p. 125.

hatov, the impulse for good. At bottom, in the deepest level of the subconscious, the Kabbalists (unlike modern psychoanalysis) held the soul to be essentially "good."[36] When the evil impulse is redirected, the divine sparks within the soul are liberated and return to their source in God. The individual whose energy is placed in the service of Torah and *mitzvot* does not act so much as an animal whose energy has been redirected and put to good use, but rather as a being created in God's image whose Godly soul can now act unencumbered by the forces of material desire. "The perfection of all things," our passage in the Zohar continues, "is attained when good and evil are first of all commingled, and then become all good, for there is no good so perfect as that which issues out of evil."[37]

THE SIGNIFICANCE OF HUMAN FREEDOM

One of the great mysteries of the Kabbalah concerns the origins of the *Shevirah*, the Breaking of the Vessels. Why did the *Shevirah* occur at all? Was there some accidental flaw in creation as it was originally conceived or was the Breaking of the Vessels somehow a part of God's plan, a necessary phase in the world's ultimate perfection? While one source of the *Shevirah* doctrine is an old midrashic tradition to the effect that God created many worlds before our own, which he destroyed simply because they did not please him,[38] the overwhelming opinion of the Kabbalists themselves was that the original "flaw" in creation was an important, even logically necessary, part of the divine plan.

In Chayyim Vital's *Sefer Etz Chayyim* we find the doctrine that God created the original imperfect world of ten *Sefirot* in order to allow for the possibility of evil.[39] The Breaking of the Vessels, which resulted in the exile of divine light to the "Other Side," brought evil into the world and made possible the process by which mankind could exercise his freedom to choose between evil and good.

Evil exists only *in potentia* within *Ein-Sof*, the infinite God. Its archetype is expressed in the creation of the *Sefirah* of Judgment (*Din*), and its reality is assured when this and the other *Sefirot* are shattered and their light

---

36. Alter Metzger, personal communication.
37. Zohar II, 184a; Sperling and Simon, *The Zohar*, Vol. IV, p. 125.
38. Genesis Rabbah 3: 7, 9: 2.
39. Vital, *Sefer Etz Chayyim* 2: 4.

entrapped in the *Kelippot* that serve as the foundations for the material world. As we have seen, the Kabbalists held, in true dialectical fashion, that it is only as a result of the existence of evil that there can be any possibility of meaningful good. One reason for this, provided by the Kabbalists themselves, is that freedom to choose between good and evil is a necessary postulate for responsibility and morality.[40] Similarly, free choice is a necessary postulate for *Tikkun ha-Olam*, which, as we have seen, is the realization of values on earth. This is because there are indeed many values that cannot exist apart from human choice and decision. We cannot hold an individual morally account-able for acts, regardless of their good or bad consequences, if that individual did not intend or choose to perform them. As such there could not be true kindness, righteousness, self-sacrifice, etc., apart from man's freedom of choice.

THE TREE OF KNOWLEDGE OF GOOD AND EVIL

Earlier we considered the Zohar's view that *Tikkun* involves a reintegration of the Tree of Knowledge with the Tree of Life. Here I will consider the kabbalistic view that the Tree of Knowledge is integrally connected with *Tikkun* because it is a symbol of man's freedom. Indeed, it is because freedom of choice is central for the realization of significance and value that the predicament of Adam and the Tree of Knowledge of Good and Evil is an important metaphor for *Tikkun ha-Olam*. By placing the Trees of Life and Knowledge in the middle of the garden, and commanding Adam not to eat therefrom, Adam was faced with the archetypal human dilemma. The Kabbalists held that Adam's choice is not only a metaphor for the original *Shevirah*, and hence for the crystallization of evil on earth, but also a metaphor for all subsequent human decision. Like Adam, we all stand between the paths of *Tikkun* and life on the one hand and *Kelippah* and wickedness on the other. Adam's sin was catastrophic precisely because it was an act of free choice, and for this reason it increased the power of the "Other Side." Similarly, the Kabbalists regarded the later sins of Israel, the worship of the Golden Calf, the "causeless hatred" (which resulted in the destruction

---

40. See Nissan Mindel, *The Philosophy of Chabad*, Vol. 2, p. 72. See also Martin Buber, *Hasidism*, p. 68. Buber, the existentialist, was attracted to Lurianic Kabbalah and its Hasidic variant in part because of the absolute moral freedom implied by their doctrines.

of the second temple), etc., as expressions of the Breaking of the Vessels, which reversed previous rectifications and strengthened the power of the *Sitra Achra*. Such acts were evil because they were freely chosen by those who performed them.

TIKKUN, EROS, AND REBIRTH: THE DOCTRINE OF *TIKKUN* IN *SEFER ETZ CHAYYIM*

There is a decidedly sexual and erotic aspect to the Lurianic conception of *Tikkun ha-Olam*. Vital, for example, provides a description of the world's restoration that involves the divine in a surfeit of erotic and sexual activity. His account, which is exceptionally baroque, involves the erotic coupling of no less than six pairs of *Partzufim* (male and female "Visages" or personas of God) and the eventual rebirth of the seven kings (representing the seven broken vessels) who died in the womb of *Binah*, the Celestial Mother. According to Vital, the lights or energies from each of the shattered vessels are the "feminine waters" (*mayim nukvim*) that stimulate the coupling of the Celestial Mother and Father.

Vital explains that this renewed coupling and pregnancy of the Celestial Mother restores the entire world of *Atzilut*, and prompts another *Partzuf*, *Attik Yomim* (the "Ancient of Days"), to engage in a coupling with its own feminine counterpart. According to Vital, couplings (*zivugim*) then proceed down the chain of being in the same direction (top down) as the uncouplings occurred after the Breaking of the Vessels. Eventually, there is an erotic coupling between the *Partzuf Zeir Anpin* and his feminine counterpart, *Nukvah*. It is through this final coupling, which is spoken of liturgically as the union between "the Holy One Blessed Be He" and His bride or *Shekhinah*, that all of the worlds are restored.

In his enthusiasm for the erotic Vital spreads the sexual activity comprising *Tikkun* to the "names of God," which are sometimes regarded as equivalents to the *Partzufim*, but which, according to Vital, have their own function in the *Tikkun* process. Vital even interprets biblical events and themes in terms of conjugal events on high. According to Vital, the holy city of Jerusalem, which is the center point and foundation of the entire world, is represented by the *Partzuf Rachel*, which is itself derived from the final *Sefirah*, *Malchut*, and therefore identified with the feminine divine presence, the holy *Shekhinah*. This identification is, of course, completely consistent with the talmudic tradition that the divine (feminine) presence contracts itself and spreads itself over the temple and city of Jerusalem. According to Vital, the mystical secret of the biblical verse "three times each year all your males will be seen in Jerusalem" is that the presence of the males (and not the females) in Jerusalem on the festivals of Passover, Shavuot, and Sukkoth, is designed to cause a supernal conjunction between masculine and feminine aspects of the Godhead.

SIGNIFICANCE OF THE SEXUAL METAPHORS

Psychoanalysts and, particularly, Jungians can find much of theoretical interest in all of these sexual pairings between various archetypal images. The main *Partzufim* correspond almost perfectly with key Jungian archetypes. *Attik Yomim* (the "Ancient of Days") correspond's with Jung's Senex (old man), *Zeir Anpin* (the Impatient One) with Jung's *Puer* (impulsive youth), *Abba* and *Imma* with the Jungian archetypes of Mother and Father, and *Nukvah* (the female) with Jung's *anima* (the feminine aspect of the psyche). These couplings and the resultant pregnancies would, for Jung, be symbolic of the "coincidence of opposites" that characterizes the development of the human psyche and "Self." Jung, in spite of a genuine interest in the Kabbalah, was, for the most part, unaware of this Lurianic *"coniunctio"* material. Had he been aware of it I am certain he would have regarded this material as constituting significant support for his theory in *Mysterium Coniunctionis* that mystical and mythological thinking involves a resolution of antinomies through the imagery of celestial sexuality.[41]

It is not hard to understand why sexuality becomes such an important theological and theosophical principle in the Lurianic Kabbalah. The sexual is an extremely important archetype that gains metaphorical power from a variety of sources. The first of these is that the sexual is the paradigm of passion, desire, and action with one's whole being and soul. Second, as the source of human procreation, the sexual literally involves a unification of opposites and the resultant development of a new being. Finally, sexuality is the archetype for relatedness to an other. In erotic unification, the individual has the power to move beyond his own narcissism and relate to an "other." Each of these elements—desire, creation, unification of opposites, and

---

41. Jung, *Mysterium Coniunctionis.*

relatedness to an "other"—are fundamental kabbalistic themes. That the sexual not only serves as a symbol of these themes but is also understood as their actual fulfillment should come as no surprise. The eroticization of the cosmos, is, on this view, actually reflective of the world's essential nature.[42]

TIKKUN AND PSYCHOANALYSIS

As explained in earlier chapters, the kabbalistic metaphors of *Shevirah* (the Breaking of the Vessels) and *Tikkun* are structurally isomorphic to basic concepts in psychoanalytic theory. While such isomorphism might lead to speculation (as per Jung) that the Lurianic understanding of God is a projection of the human psyche, it can also lead to the conclusion that both psychoanalysis and the Kabbalah reflect a structural pattern that is common

---

42. We are, perhaps, entitled to offer a slightly different interpretation, one that sees the Kabbalah (and the cosmic hierarchy represented in Kabbalistic thought) as expressing genuinely sexual themes, which either consciously or unconsciously are designed to overcome some of the basic distinctions, particularly the gender distinctions, in human life. We have already seen (in Chapter Four) how the Zohar explains that the apparently incestuous conjugal relations among the *Sefirot* and *Partzufim* actually reflect the fact that such earthly prohibitions are transcended in the celestial order. We might further postulate that the distinctions between young and old, male and female, even birth and death, are likewise overcome in the upper worlds. Indeed, such distinctions, however "natural," are often experienced as a source of great philosophical perplexity and existential anguish, and it is equally "natural" that mankind should engage in various scientific, mythological, and even "perverse" efforts aimed at overcoming them. We might say that the pervert who delights in sadomasochism, transsexualism, pedophilia, etc., as well as all those who achieve erotic gratification in an experience that they describe as akin to death, are participants in mythological dramas in which the basic antinomies of human existence are revealed and at least temporarily overcome. Similarly, the apparently perverse insertion of seven dead kings into the womb of the feminine *Partzuf, Imma,* or the identification of God's bride with a masculine "king" in the Lurianic Kabbalah, involve a transcendence of these distinctions in the service of a higher, mystical end: an experience of the union of opposites in an absolute Self. That such a union of opposites is basic to a wide range of mythological traditions is evident from the work of Jung in psychology and Levi-Strauss in anthropology. That such a union is a *prerequisite* for an experience and comprehension of the unity of self and cosmos is one esoteric meaning of the fluidity of age, gender, and birth/death in the Lurianic Kabbalah.

to both the cosmos and man, and hence equally fundamental for both theology and psychology.

The restorative acts of *Tikkun ha-Olam* parallel the therapy of psychoanalysis, inasmuch as in both *Tikkun* and psychoanalytic therapy a split-off or repressed sexual energy is disencumbered and made available both for erotic coupling and the sublimation in creative activity. However, the fact that in the Kabbalah this "psychoanalytic" process occurs in a worldly as opposed to psychic arena assures that *Tikkun ha-Olam* will not, in Philip Rieff's terms, become a "triumph of the therapeutic,"[43] but will rather result in an active encounter not only with man's psyche but with his world as well. The Kabbalists, and especially the Hasidim, affirmed that all meaningful, value-making activity serves the process of *Tikkun*. While *Tikkun ha-Olam* certainly involves a rediscovery and, in a sense, "therapy" of the self, it is, as its very name implies, first and foremost a repair and reintegration of the world.

LANGUAGE AND MEANING AS THE VEHICLE OF *TIKKUN*

According to the Lurianists the world as it will be restored in *Tikkun* will be one filled with meaning and significance. Vital explains that the lights that constitute the restored *Sefirot* of *Tikkun*, instead of shining through a variety of *Adam Kadmon*'s orifices, are now emanated via a single orifice, the mouth,[44] which emits phonemes and letters. These lights are emanated through a "single channel" in order to emphasize that they are bound together in significance.[45] Vital uses an interesting metaphor to describe how the lights or letters emanating from the mouth of *Adam Kadmon* come to be united in the formation of Vessels (*Kelim*) in the World of *Tikkun*. As the letters rush out of the mouth of *Adam Kadmon* they strike and bump into each other, and from this striking their results a fusion that gives birth to the existence of the restored vessels. Vital tells us that each letter, as we know: "is

---

43. Phillip Rieff, *The Triumph of the Therapeutic*.

44. In other places Vital says that these lights are emanated from the forehead of *Adam Kadmon*.

45. The lights and vessels emanated in *Tikkun* are completely connected with one another. They are called *Akudim* (striped or bound together), alluding to Jacob's dream of "striped, spotted and blotched sheep." The Torah uses the word *Akudim* to mean both striped and bound.

a dead or meaningless entity, but you put them all together and there is light and significance."[46] In the World of Points (the "formless" world prior to *Tikkun ha-Olam*) the units of meaning (*Sefirot*, letters) are completely separate from one another and are thereby devoid of significance. In the World of *Tikkun* they are united in meaningful discourse. The process of *Tikkun* (which is the province of man) is one in which the world is rendered meaningful.

Vital provides a second image that illustrates the interconnectedness, and hence the significance, of the *Sefirot* in the World of *Tikkun*. According to Vital, in the restored world order the *Sefirot* are emanated from the forehead of *Adam Kadmon* and, in the process, the *Partzufim*, Visages of God, spread downward below the navel to the feet of *Adam Kadmon*. As a result of the interpenetration of the *Sefirot*, these *Partzufim* come to clothe (*malbush*) one another in such a manner that the higher *Partzufim* become "souls" to the lower ones. The result of this process is that in contrast to the World of Points, the *Partzufim* in the World of *Tikkun* are composed of vessels that are larger, more integrated (endressed) and meaningful. As such these *Partzufim* can tolerate the light emanating into them from *Ein-Sof* without shattering.

THE *TIKKUN* OF THE DIVINE "NAMES" AND LETTERS

To fully comprehend the linguistic aspects of *Tikkun* it is necessary to recall the complex Lurianic theory of divine names, which was discussed in Chapter Five. We should also recall that in *Etz Chayyim*, Vital divides the *Partzufim* into sublevels according to the system of *ta'amim* (musical notes), *nekudot* (vowel marks), *tagim* (crowns or embellishments of the letters), and *otiyot* (the letters themselves). Each metaphysical level is composed of letters, but these letters, in turn, are made up of "subatomic" notes, vowels, crowns, and further letters.

According to Vital as a result of the coupling of *Chochmah* and *Binah*, the supernal Father and Mother, a new "45"-letter name of God is produced. This name, abbreviated as MaH, is in effect a "reborn" aspect of the Godhead

---

46. Chayyim Vital, *Sefer Etz Chayyim* 2: 2, The Breaking of the Vessels. (Translations from sections 2: 2, 2: 3 and Gate 50 of *Sefer Etz Chayyim* in this chapter are from working notes of my study of this work with Rabbi Joel Kenney.)

that plays an important role in *Tikkun ha-Olam*. Vital informs us that through the raising of the *Mayim Nukvim*, the fallen lights, into the *Sefirah Binah*, there is a coupling of an aspect of "*'Havayeh*" (God's name). This aspect is 'aB (Ayin Bet), or the so-called "72-letter name." 'aB couples with the "*ta'amim*" (musical notes) of SaG (the 63-letter name), which because of their level on par with *Binah* were not broken during the *Shevirah*. The conjunction of 'aB and SaG produces "a new light," the 42-letter name of God, MaH, which itself is composed of the dimensions of *Taamim, Nekudot, Tagin*, and *Otiyot*, the musical notations, vowel points, embellishments, and characters that are the elementary linguistic particles that comprise and modify the letters of the Hebrew alphabet. This name of God, MaH, emanates from the forehead of *Adam Kadmon* and brings about *Tikkun ha-Olam*.

In this account, as a result of supernal *coniunctios*, the lights of *Tikkun* are radiated from the forehead of *Adam Kadmon* in the form of one of the names of God. We have here another fusion of the sexual, light, and linguistic metaphors that are so common in the Kabbalah.

Vital's linguistic-sexual metaphors become quite complex. MaH, as we have seen in Chapter Five, is created when God's name, YHVH, is spelled out using the Hebrew letter *aleph*. With the birth of MaH these *alephs* go forth and purify those aspects (the *Nekudot* or vowel points) of its mother, SaG, which had been nullified or blemished by the *Shevirah*. These "points" from SaG are removed and join MaH. For reasons that are somewhat unclear this activity makes MaH masculine and SaG feminine. Apparently the removal of an aspect of SaG creates a feminine "lack" in this name. The name MaH is said to perform a *birur* or extraction of the impure aspects of SaG, leading to its *Tikkun*. This, and what follows, amounts to an incestuous conjunction between mother and son. Vital tells us that because SaG becomes the feminine counterpart of MaH it is transformed and gets yet another name, BoN, in which the *millui* or letters that spell out the divine name YHVH consists of *Hehs* (Hs), resulting in this name having a numerical value of 52.

In his discussion of the divine names, Vital plays with the concepts of masculine and feminine in such a manner as to make them virtually unrecognizable. For example, he relates that the connection between SaG and MaH is such as to make the vowel points (restored by MaH) feminine and this is why they are called *Malchut* (Kings)! What Vital seems to be suggesting is that these vowel points or *Nekudot* become feminine on the principle that whatever is transferred from one level to another is feminine. The paradigm of the feminine in the Kabbalah is the last *Sefirah*, the

Shekhinah, which is God's feminine presence, and these *Nekudot* now become identified with the *Shekhinah*, which, as we have seen, is also called *Malchut*, Kingship. Therefore, on Vital's view, these vowel points *are* kings (which is, of course, masculine). Indeed the very fact that the tenth *Sefirah* is alternately spoken of as the *Shekhinah* and kingship suggests a fluidity in gender that illustrates the principle that with *Tikkun ha-Olam* the masculine and feminine aspects of the Godhead, which had been severed by the Breaking of the Vessels, are reunited and even fused.

MAN'S *TIKKUN*

Vital could not be more explicit with respect to the role of man in the redemption of evil. He says:

> When a person is born his soul must purify (*birur*) the sparks which reach his portion, that fell through the sin of the first man (*Adam ha Rishon*) on *Kelippot Nogah*. This is the reason for a person being born in this world. Understand this well. Through the *mitzvot* (divine commandments) one extracts the good from those portions that were damaged and fell.[47]

We should not lose sight of the significance of this idea for the subsequent development of Judaism. Not only the Kabbalists but generations of Hasidim have lived their lives according to this theory: that the divinely appointed mission of each individual is to free the light, and hence raise the sparks of those *Kelippot* that reside within his own soul or that come his way in the course of a lifetime. It is in this manner that man is able to turn darkness into light, the bitter into the sweet, and perform his part in *Tikkun ha-Olam*.

According to the Lurianists, the erotic unifications that constitute *Tikkun ha-Olam* involve mutual male and female orgasms, spoken of as male and female "waters." The male waters flow from above, but the female waters are supplied by mankind through the raising of the sparks, which constitutes a liberation of the libidinous energy inherent in these *netzotzim*. Mankind, in effect, provides the feminine aspect of the *zivvug*, or sacred marriage.

The task of *Tikkun ha-Olam* originally rested on the shoulders of *Adam haRishon*, the first man. As we have seen, had Adam performed the one commandment intended for him (refraining from eating of the Tree of

---

47. Vital, *Sefer Etz Chayyim*, 2: 3, *Tikkun*.

Knowledge of Good and Evil), *Tikkun* would have been complete and all the worlds set aright and restored. However, this was not to be. By partaking of the fruit, Adam caused a second cosmic catastrophe, a repetition and deepening of the Breaking of the Vessels. With his fall, Adam's soul, which had originally contained all the souls of humanity, itself shattered, splintering into a multitude of "soul-sparks," which now must be uplifted by the individual men and women who are vivified by them. There were now, according to Vital, three types of sparks: "cosmic sparks" from the original shattered vessels; sparks from the *Shekhinah*, which had been exiled as a further result of the *Shevirah*; and "soul sparks" from the fragmentation of Adam's soul. Mankind must, according to Vital, participate in the liberation of all three kinds of sparks, though as we shall see, each individual is charged particularly with the uplifting of those sparks that correspond to his own "soul root."[48]

By what process are the sparks reclaimed and restored to their proper place? As we will see, this is a question that occupied later generations of Hasidim. For Vital, the process begins with the rejection of evil, through obedience to the negative precepts of the Torah. However, certain sparks, those entrapped in the *Kelippah Nogah*, the ambiguous realm between light and darkness, good and evil, are restored by man's redirecting his natural bodily instincts in the service of God. As a result of this process the potentially holy sparks of *Kelippah Nogah* are absorbed into the realm of the sacred, with the further result that the impure objects that had been parasitic on these sparks are deprived of their vitality and annihilated.[49]

According to the Lurianists, every precept of the Torah is directed toward the reclamation of sparks, and, specifically, toward the restoration of one or another aspect of the various *Partzufim*. Every good deed not only reclaims sparks but causes beneficial impulses to ascend to create harmony among the *Sefirot*. (On the other hand each sin causes the *Kelippot Nogah*, the "potentially redeemable," to be further absorbed among the impure *Kelippot* of the "Other Side."[50])

According to the Kabbalists (though not for the Hasidim), the performance of *mitzvot* is only fully efficacious for *Tikkun ha-Olam* if it is accompanied by the proper *Kavvanot*. These are mystical contemplations

---

48. Louis Jacobs, "The Uplifting of the Sparks," p. 107.
49. Schochet, "Mystical Concepts," p. 891.
50. Ibid., p. 891.

that map the various precepts onto the realm of the *Partzufim* and intend the unification of the various masculine and feminine aspects of the divine. Hence, for the Lurianists, knowledge of kabbalistic theosophy is an essential ingredient to the restoration of the worlds and the perfection of God.

AFTER *TIKKUN*

Man's *Tikkun* has the ultimate effect of restoring our world, *Assiyah*, to a higher spiritual plane, and removing it from the realm of the *Kelippot*. This will, according to Scholem, bring about a state of blissful union between man and God that will be permanent and immune from disruption by the "Other Side."[51]

It is unclear, however, whether this union is "permanent" or even fully comprehensible in our own terms. For the Lurianists, our present historical era is one in which *Tikkun* is underway, but not yet complete. However when *Tikkun* is complete, Vital tells us, the situation will be reversed, and there will be a return of the world to *Tohu* and *Bohu* (Chaos and Nothingness). Vital alludes to the talmudic dictum that two thousand years of chaos and void will be followed by two thousand years of Torah and two thousand years of *Tikkun*, and, finally, a thousand years of destruction. There is thus a hint within the Kabbalah of what Nietzsche was later to call the "myth of the eternal return."

THE *TZELEM*

Man's role in *Tikkun* is facilitated by the nature of his inner psyche. The Kabbalists spoke of the inner psyche as the *Tzelem*, the divine image that accompanies each individual at birth, and which serves as the fixed and determinate essence of his being. The *Tzelem* or "self-image" was equated by the Kabbalists with the individual's "form," which is nonetheless separable from him and is on occasion perceived by a man as a spiritual guide, "astral body," or personal "angel." On some interpretations the *Tzelem* is concealed within the depths of a man's personality.[52] The *Tzelem* is also the individual's

---

51. Scholem, *Kabbalah*, p. 143.
52. Gershom Scholem, "Tselem: The Concept of the Astral Body," in *On the*

"perfected nature," the person he could be if all of his or her potentialities were fully actualized. Two traditions regarding the origin of the *Tzelem* are present in the Zohar. In one tradition the *Tzelem* is a garment of the soul that exists prior to the individual's birth; in another it is a garment woven out of a man's good deeds on earth, which accompanies him after death.[53]

The Kabbalists sought to make contact with the *Tzelem* in their meditative and ecstatic practices. Vital, in his *Sha'arei Kedushah*, tells us: "There are people whose own souls, when they have become utterly purified, appear to them and guide them in all their ways."[54]

In *Sefer Etz Chayyim*, Vital connects the *Tzelem* to the merits of a child's parents, whose good deeds draw down a particular soul from the upper worlds for their offspring. The individual is, according to Vital, not born into the world with a "naked" soul but rather with an image that reflects the moral qualities of his progenitors. The particular *mitzvot* performed and excelled in by his parents determines the nature of the *Tzelem* or spiritual garment that envelops the child at birth. The parents actually extract specific sparks from *Kelippot Nogah*, which are woven together to form the *Tzelem* garment.[55]

DEVELOPMENT OF THE SELF

The creation of the child's *Tzelem* is only the beginning of the development of the adult self. While the *Tzelem* may reflect the child's potentially perfected nature, the child is soon corrupted by extraneous forces that, owing to the sin of Adam, inevitably latch onto a man's soul. While a male's circumcision on the eighth day after birth has the effect of removing an aspect of *Kelippah* ("covering," "foreskin") this does not completely prevent the growth and development of negative forces within the child.

However, when the child is 13, the age of *bar mitzvah*, the *Chasadim*, the "angels" of *Kelippot Nogah* (the Tree of Knowledge), which had long been repressed, are now revealed. As Vital puts it, these "servants in the realm of the *Kelippot* escape to freedom." It is at this point that the child receives

---

Mystical Shape of the Godhead, trans. Joachim Neugroschel (New York: Schocken, 1991), p. 254.

53. Ibid., p. 264.
54. Ibid., p. 317.
55. Vital, *Sefer Etz Chayyim* 50: 3.

his adult knowledge and becomes obligated in the commandments of the Torah. It is also at this point that the child is able to perform his own acts of *birur* and becomes a vehicle for *Tikkun ha-Olam*.

The soul of adulthood does not, according to Vital, enter into the person all at once, but rather develops gradually according to the individual's good deeds and merits. The completion of one's soul is occasioned by the individual's participation in *Tikkun ha-Olam*. Interestingly, Vital holds that a person is completed only when *both good and evil* have entered into him: "With the entry of the Evil Impulses which is from *Gevurah*, the soul of *Gevurah* enters in, and with the entry of the Good Impulses, the soul of *Chesed* enters in . . ."[56] Only with both of these souls is the individual considered complete. According to Vital, "the Good Impulse and the Evil Impulse are both angels,"[57] and the adult human soul is endressed within these two angels. The demons (*Shadim*) of the Evil Impulse become angels when they are sweetened by the acts of kindness involved in an individual's performance of *mitzvot*.

Vital tells us: "It is also possible that a person, in his whole life cannot complete his soul, because he did not perform the commandments that would purify his garment in *Nogah* and the soul is not able to enter in(to) him."[58] It is for this reason that some souls must be reborn.

GILGUL: THE TRANSMIGRATION OF SOULS

Gilgul or reincarnation plays a significant role in the Kabbalist's understanding of *Tikkun*. Classical, rabbinic Judaism knows nothing of the concept of reincarnation. However, beginning with *Sefer ha-Bahir*, the notion of transmigration of souls became accepted doctrine in the Kabbalah. Originally transmigration was restricted to those, for example, who died childless or who failed to perform some other critical *mitzvah* in their lifetime. However, the Zohar expanded the concept of *gilgul* (the "wheel," denoting the soul's movement from one incarnation into another) to include the righteous who return in a new body for the good of the world. Eventually, the notion of *gilgul* came to be regarded as a universal law, and chains of migration, tracing

---

56. Vital, *Sefer Etz Chayyim* 2: 2.
57. Vital, *Sefer Etz Chayyim* 50: 3.
58. Vital, *Sefer Etz Chayyim* 2: 2

individuals to the soul roots of historical and biblical figures, were intuited by kabbalistic visionaries.

The thirteenth century also saw the development of the kabbalistic theory of "soul sparks," in which one soul is thought to subsequently inform many others, just as a single flame can light many candles.[59] The idea also arose that a given individual can acquire sparks from various prior souls, and that *parts* of a person can be reincarnated and mixed with other partial souls in the creation of a new individual. Sparks from an old soul are said to retain what they previously learned in their new incarnation.

The transmigration of souls was frequently connected to individual human development and the *Tzelem*, or divine image, which each man must realize within his own psyche. The Kabbalists held that this *Tzelem* was broken and distorted by the sin of the first man, making it incumbent upon each of Adam's descendants to restore and perfect the *Tzelem* within his own being. This restoration is achieved through the 613 *mitzvot*, each of which corresponds to a "limb" or "sinew" in the body, and hence to an aspect of the divine image that dwells, or is reflected, in the body of man. As we have seen, if a man fails to achieve the completion of his "divine image" within a single lifetime, he becomes subject to the wheel of transmigration.[60]

The process of perfecting one's soul succeeds in drawing down a *ruach* or *neshamah* (higher souls) from heaven, to complement the lower soul or *nefesh* with which each individual is born.[61] Later Kabbalists held that an individual can be "impregnated" with an additional soul later in life, which will assist him in the performance of a certain *mitzvah*, or in the resolution of a personal or spiritual crisis. The Kabbalists reserved the term *gilgul* for transmigrations that occur at conception and birth, and used the term *ibbur* (impregnation) for the entry of souls into a person later in life. Vital, in his works on reincarnation, makes reference to the concept of an evil or wicked impregnation. This conception of an evil *ibbur* was later fused with the Yiddish notion of a *dibbuk* (attachment from outside forces), which is the Jewish folk concept of possession by an evil spirit.

The Safedian Kabbalists developed the idea that all souls on earth were

---

59. See Scholem, *Kabbalah*, p. 143.

60. Gershom Scholem, "Gilgul: Transmigration of Souls," in *On the Mystical Shape of the Godhead*, p. 218ff.

61. David M. Wexelman, *The Jewish Concept of Reincarnation and Creation: Based on the Writings of Rabbi Chaim Vital* (Northvale, NJ: Jason Aronson, 1999), pp. 13–15.

originally part of the great cosmic soul of *Adam Kadmon*. Expanding upon a notion first articulated in *Tikkunei ha-Zohar*, they developed the idea that the process of transmigration in man parallels the emanation and descent of the *Sefirot* in God. Just as the one light of *Or Ein-Sof* passed through Adam and was articulated into a vast array of *Sefirot*, Worlds, *Partzufim*, and sparks, the single divine image passed through Adam and was transformed and broken into a vast number of human souls and soul-sparks. The process of *Tikkun* in which God and the world are restored after the Breaking of the Vessels is according to *Tikkunei ha-Zohar*, a *gilgul*, or reincarnation of divine thought. This signifies that the fluidity and movement of souls within man is the very process through which the divine sparks are restored and reassembled to complete and perfect God.

Scholem points out that the Kabbalists of Safed relied upon an ancient Midrash,[62] one that was somehow ignored by the earlier Kabbalists, to support their conception of *gilgul* from the soul of Primordial Man:

> While Adam was yet lying lifeless (as a *golem*), the Holy One, blessed be He, showed him all the righteous who would come from his seed. There were those who hung from the head of Adam, those who hung from his hair, those from his throat, those from his two eyes, those from his nose, those from his mouth, and those from his arms.[63]

This image is used by the Safedian Kabbalists as a prooftext for their view that all the Jews in all generations, and not just the righteous, are derived from the cosmic soul of the original Adam. Such a view, of course, follows from the Kabbalists' metaphysics, which holds that *all* levels of existence, in each of the five worlds, are derived from Primordial Man. The Lurianists held that just as each individual man must be restored limb by limb, sinew by sinew, via the 613 *mitzvot*, the Cosmic Adam, who has been divided into 613 major soul roots, must metaphorically be restored limb by limb, sinew by sinew as well.[64]

According to the Lurianists, with the fall, Adam was reduced from cosmic to earthly dimensions. Many of his cosmic limbs were said to have fallen off his body with the soul sparks attendant to these limbs falling into the "Other Side." In this way the "Adam of holiness" became mixed with the

---

62. Exodus Rabbah 40: 3; Tanchuma, Ki Tissa, 12.
63. Scholem, "Gilgul: Transmigration of Souls," p. 229.
64. Ibid., p. 230.

ungodly Adam, *Adam Belia'al*. According to Vital, the soul sparks from Adam combine with the cosmic sparks (the so-called sparks of the *Shekhinah*) that fell into the cosmic void with the Breaking of the Vessels. All of these sparks are exiled, awaiting redemption through Torah and *mitzvot*.

The notion that all souls ultimately derive from *Adam Kadmon* gave rise to the concepts of soul roots and soul families. Scholem points out that R. Solomon Alkabez (ca. 1550) and his disciple, R. Moses Cordovero, developed the idea that the souls of certain individuals have a familial connection that is completely independent of those individuals' biological familial status.[65] Parents and children, for example, are rarely from the same soul root. These Kabbalists held that the Cosmic Adam originally fragmented into 613 major soul roots, corresponding to the 613 *mitzvot* and the 613 organs in a man's body. These soul roots further divided into a multitude of "minor roots," each of which is referred to as a "Great Soul." The Great Soul further subdivides into individual souls and sparks.[66] According to Solomon Alkabez all of the sparks derived from a Great Soul are controlled by a law of sympathy,[67] suffering with one another and benefiting from each other's good deeds. A righteous individual (*tzaddik*) for example, is capable of restoring sparks within (but only within) his own soul family.

Many of these ideas are clearly presented by Chayyim Vital in his *Sefer ha-Gilgulim* and other works. Vital expands upon the traditional kabbalistic image of the "cosmic tree" in order to clarify the relationship between individual souls and their "roots" in a higher realm. When such individual souls "descend into this world to become invested in bodies of flesh, they have their roots cleaving to the main root from which they were hewn."[68] The trees roots are in the upper worlds and are called *mazalim* (stars) and further roots and branches extend downward into the souls of individuals on earth. The major roots are connected with the souls of various *Tzadikkim*, e.g., Abraham, Jacob, Moses.[69] Originally all souls were contained as one in *Adam ha-Rishon*, but with the sin of Adam they were fragmented into at least 613 "soul roots," each of which is itself composed of 613 "sparks,"

---

65. Ibid., p. 224.

66. Ibid., p. 235.

67. Ibid., p. 233.

68. Chayyim Vital, *Shaarey Kedushah*, selections trans. by Zalman Schachter, in Meltzer *The Secret Garden*, p. 188.

69. Ibid., p. 188.

corresponding to the total number of positive and negative Torah command-ments.[70]

In addition, each individual human soul "has countless roots in different worlds"; all the roots of a person's soul in a given world, e.g., *Assiyah*, "make up one's whole soul of Assiyah." When an individual commits a particularly grievous sin this can have the effect of cutting him off from his soul roots, like the cutting of a branch from a tree. On the other hand meritorious deeds have the effect of "raising" and uniting all of one's soul roots, an action that helps to complete the *Tikkun* of one's soul on earth. The full *Tikkun* of an individual soul requires the performance of all 613 commandments, some-thing that is not possible in a single lifetime. This is the reason for *gilgul*, the reincarnation of human souls.

Each of the major "soul roots" or "Great Souls" is like a tree unto itself, and each are comprised of a variety of different individual souls, great ones corresponding to fruits, and lesser souls, i.e., ordinary individuals, corre-sponding to the branches and leaves.[71] The *Tikkun* and destiny of each individual soul of a major "soul root" is bound up with each of the others, so that the destiny of the soul root of even a *Tzaddik* as great as Abraham is bound up with those of evildoers and men of low value.[72]

An individual, by turning off the flow of daily thoughts and desires, has the power to turn in "the direction of upper worlds, into the direction of one of the roots of [one's] soul," thereby drawing supernal light into our world.[73] This can take the form of an angel that addresses the individual, and can also result in a type of prophesy.

Vital utilizes these notions in the service of another kabbalistic theme, the *coincidentia* of good and evil. According to Vital, many of the *tzaddikim* or great men of later generations derive from the soul root of Cain, and hence were spiritual participants in the world's first (and archetypal) homicide.[74] In a transmutation of values which rivals that of Nietzsche, Vital informs us that with the advent of *Tikkun ha-Olam*, Cain will be elevated above Abel, the sinner above the victim. This view gives concrete expression to the kabbalistic idea that the creation and vicissitudes of the world are designed not simply for

---

70. Chayyim Vital, *Sefer ha-Gilgulim*, selections trans. by Yehuda Shamir, Meltzer, *The Secret Garden*, p. 196.
71. Vital, *Sefer ha-Gilgulim*, Shamir trans., p. 196.
72. Ibid., p. 197.
73. Vital, *Shaarey Kedushah*, Shamir trans., p. 189.
74. Scholem, "Gilgul: Transmigration of Souls," p. 236.

the manifestation of the good, but also for the manifestation of evil, in order that, through *Tikkun*, evil can be sweetened and transformed into good. Indeed, the transformation of evil to good is the highest manifestation and perfection of the good itself. In Vital, the process of reincarnation becomes a major vehicle for this transformation.

THE SIGNIFICANCE OF *GILGUL*

Let us consider the philosophical meaning and significance of the doctrine of *gilgul*, the transmigration of souls, as it is expressed in the Kabbalah. First, we must remember is that the Kabbalists' view of the world is phenomenological and idealist as opposed to naturalistic and material. As we have seen in relation to their doctrine of the *Sefirot*, underlying the Kabbalists' myths and theories is an assumption that the constituent elements of reality are the phenomena, ideas, emotions, and values that present themselves to human consciousness. On this view, a man's emotions, the values that move him, the ideas that his mind entertains, and the "personalities" of those with whom he is acquainted, are as real or even more real than the material objects that he encounters in his daily life. By extension, the true nature of human personality is itself to be discovered in the ideas, emotions, values, style, etc., which inform human behavior, rather than the corporeal body that expresses it. Indeed, the personality of an individual can be preserved, for example, in his paintings or writings, his spoken words and his "memory" long after his corporeal self has decomposed. To use an analogy we presented earlier in relation to the *Sefirot*: what is unique and essential about an individual is the "software" that informs his bodily self, rather than the "hardware," or the body itself.

It is an assumption of the Kabbalah that two individuals who are completely unrelated physically (from different families, nations, and even religions and race) can be extremely close in their personal "essence." Two people who have met for the first time even late in their lives can instantly discover that they are "soul mates," precisely because there is something in the depths of their experience, emotions, values, style, etc., which resonates between them. Those who have had such an experience can hardly doubt that the perception that two such individuals are from the same "soul root" is phenomenologically real.

It is such a "Platonic" yet nonetheless "commonsense" view of the human soul and personality that underlies the Kabbalists' speculations regarding the transmigration of souls. The idea that the human personality is logically independent from the human body informs the Kabbalist's notions of metempsychosis and reincarnation (*gilgul*). It also plays a vital role in their concepts of the "soul root," the possibility of more than one personality entering the same individual ("impregnation" or *ibbur*), and the possibility that a man's good deeds can draw down an extra soul from heaven, etc. I believe we can understand such ideas within the realm of experience and need not posit the existence of a Cartesian "soul-substance," which enters into a relationship with the material substance of the human body. The "soul" or personality of man or woman can at least be partly understood as a particular arrangement of values, ideas, emotions, styles, and information, which must be expressed in a "material vessel," but which is not essentially bound up with any vessel in particular. Like the software that describes a computer's algorithm or program, the human personality or soul can move from one "machine" to another without being altered in its essential aspects; and the software describing several personalities, or at least aspects of those person-alities, can all be run on a single "machine" or bodily vessel.

Neither do the *methods* of "soul transmission" have to be understood in any occult sense. We are all familiar with actors who are able to, at least in a limited sense, "reincarnate" a historical or contemporary personality within their own being. What I am saying here is that the phenomenon of reincarnation need not be posited as occurring only via the process of birth. The processes of cultural transmission, including imitation, oral and written language, art, music, myth, and any other vehicle through which information can be encoded and transmitted (including the process of genetics and human memory), can facilitate the appearance of at least aspects of a living or historic personality's soul in the person of another individual and contribute to the "restoration of the world." The Hasidim are, as we shall see, insistent upon the idea that everything a person comes in contact with or experiences in a lifetime is meant to be part of his own personal *Tikkun* (restoration process) as well as part of the *Tikkun* of the world at large. That an individual meets certain people, reads certain books, and performs certain tasks and projects, is all part of the process through which he or she has an opportunity to "raise the sparks" that are uniquely his or her own, and bring to light some aspect of the divine plenum that had hitherto been shrouded in the world of *Kelippot*. If he or she is a scholar or a *tzaddik* (righteous individual), for example, then perhaps the personality of a great scholar or saintly individual of the past comes alive within him to guide him in his or her own personal *Tikkun*. Likewise, the contemporary scholar or *tzaddik*, through being inspired by and internalizing the dead person's words and deeds, actually reincarnates an aspect of the deceased's personality and enables the old soul to continue the process of its own *Tikkun*. It is certainly not unusual, for example, for a contemporary author or scholar to believe that a deceased author, upon whom he devotes a lifetime of research and study, can reemerge within and guide him in the mission of his own life. We might say that a contemporary scholar, by bringing the old author's works to light for a new generation, is able to thereby help in the completion of the old soul's mission of *Tikkun*. That individuals throughout the generations have thusly reincarnated the biblical personages of Abraham, Abel, David, and Moses is an axiom of kabbalistic and Hasidic thought. What I am suggesting here is that such reincarnations or *Gilgulim* are neither occult happenings nor mere figures of speech, but are, at least in some cases, phenomenologically and interpersonally very real.

Of course the "reincarnation" of a particular combination of human traits, values, ideas, and emotions need not occur with any awareness on the part of the individual who has "received" the incarnation. As there may be dozens, hundreds, or even thousands of individuals currently alive who each of us would recognize as a "soul mate" should we meet and get to know them, there likely are many individuals who have existed in the past whose sefirotic or personality structure was similar enough to our own to justify the view that their personality has been essentially, or at least in part, reincarnated in our own being. Such a view need not be an offense to our own sense of individuality or uniqueness. That "I" exist in a different time and circumstance than any former or parallel "self" is sufficient to differentiate me as an individual. At any rate, why such an emphasis in difference? There is an important sense in which the birth of any child is a "reincarnation" of all humanity: as the psychiatrist Harry Stack Sullivan once put it, each of us, after all, "are more human than otherwise." For the Kabbalists, all human souls ultimately derive from the original soul of the Primordial Man (*Adam Kadmon*). Indeed, it is only the result of the *Tzimtzum*, an obscuring or concealment of the fullness of knowledge, that we each ultimately come to regard ourselves as distinct and separate selves. In the phenomena of "soul mates" and "reincarnation" we experience moments in which we can catch a glimpse of our common humanity and transcend the alienated and exiled condition of our individual lives.

In this section I have tried to, as it were, bring the kabbalistic and Hasidic notion of reincarnation down to earth, to relate it to aspects of everyday experience, and thereby perhaps place this experience in a new more "ensouled" light. That other, perhaps more metaphysical interpretations of these phenomena of personality, soul, and metempsychosis are possible, I have no doubt. My own view, however, is that the notion of a transmutable soul substance that exists in a quasi-spatio-temporal framework called heaven, for example, arises out of a desire to make the spiritual as much like the material as possible, i.e., to import the categories of space, time, physical energy, and substance into the spiritual realm, a tendency that the Kabbalists warned directly against. Soul, it seems to me, exists in the domain of thought, values, feeling, style, etc., a domain that has its own structure and rules, which, however intertwined with the material world, is essentially different from it. Like the world of numbers, ratios, and equations of mathematics, which exists outside of space, time, and energy, the world of the spirit, of personality and soul, need not be emblazoned with the torch of corporeality for it to be real. To think otherwise is to fall victim to the naturalism and materialism that systems of thought such as the Kabbalah are meant to transcend.

It is true, of course, that the Kabbalists believed that a person's soul, and souls in general, pre-exist the appearance of the human body and persona. This is to say no more or less than that a particular combination of *Sefirot* (ideas, values, emotions, etc.) exists in the realm of "thought" in the same way that a particular "proof," for example, exists in the realm of "ideas" prior to its being discovered.

We are of course, entitled to speculate what place the realm of spirit, values, and ideas has in the world understood as a physical system. In Chapter Four, for example, I briefly entertained the notion that the ideas and values of the sefirotic realm are the six dimensions held by "super-string theory" to have contracted in on themselves with the "big bang." Such speculation, may, for some, provide a handle on what one might otherwise regard to be the *miracle* of reincarnation, or other apparently "occult" processes. My own view is that such processes are no more (and no less) a miracle than the very existence of the world (nature, ideas, consciousness, and value) itself.

HASIDIC CONCEPTS OF *TIKKUN*

Among the Hasidim the doctrine of *gilgul* was utilized to articulate the role and purpose of individual man, and further elaborate the concept of *Tikkun*.

According to the Hasidim, a man's psyche not only exists in sympathy with other individuals who are derived from the same Great Soul, but it is also connected to those aspects of his environment that contain sparks belonging to his soul root. The Hasidim developed the beautiful doctrine that a man's life presents him with a series of opportunities to raise the sparks that only *he* can redeem, and that the people and objects a man encounters in the course of his lifetime are presented to him precisely in order that he can liberate the spiritual energy within them and, in so doing, also liberate the sparks within his own soul. There is thus a spiritually intimate, redemptive relationship between a man and his possessions and all things he encounters, and a person should take care to respect the objects and experiences in his or her life as divinely ordained occurrences for his own destiny and *Tikkun*. When an object changes hands it means that there are no longer any sparks within it that are sympathetic to its original owner. When a man is inexplicably moved to travel to a distant corner of the world it is more than likely that there are soul sparks in that place that only he can redeem.[75] Louis Jacobs has pointed out that such a view reflects the Hasidim's emphasis on the unique importance of the individual. Even today the Hasidim hold that their "rebbe" is somehow capable of peering into the soul of each of his followers in order to advise them to undertake a marriage, job, or journey that is uniquely suited to the individual Hasid's mission in life, and which places him in contact with those aspects of the world that are sympathetic to his own soul root.

THE REDEMPTION OF MATTER:
AVODAH B'GASHMIYUT

In contrast to the Kabbalists, who frequently took an ascetic attitude toward the world, the Hasidim by and large regarded man's engagement in the world as an important vehicle for redeeming the holy sparks. The world of food, drink, and material pleasures, which had been largely shunned by the Lurianists, became, at least for some Hasidim, the very arena of personal and world redemption. While for many Hasidim only a rebbe or *tzaddik* could redeem holy sparks encountered in the material world, others held that the

---

75. Louis Jacobs, "The Uplifting of the Sparks," p. 117.

path of *avodah b'gashmiyut*, "worship through corporeality," was virtually open to all.

Baruch of Medzhibozh, the grandson of the Baal Shem Tov (the founder of Hasidism), went so far as to hold that a *tzaddik* was not only permitted, but was actually obliged, to engage in opulent food, drink, and commerce in order to redeem the holy sparks inherent in these objects. He is said to have even regarded such activity as superior to the study of Torah and the performance of the *mitzvot*.[76] Another Hasidic rebbe, Abraham Joshua Heschel, the Apter Rebbe (d. 1825), was said to have consumed colossal meals because of his obsession with the idea of redeeming the holy sparks in food.[77] Other Hasidim sought, through incessant smoking, to redeem the sparks inherent in tobacco, a practice that embodied both the "sparks" and "extraction" *Tikkun* metaphors. On some views tobacco was thought to be a gift of God, containing the subtlest of sparks to be redeemed just prior to the final redemption.

While it is obvious that the doctrine of "worship through corporeality" was subject to considerable abuse, its thrust, as Schatz-Uffenheimer has maintained, was completely, if dialectically, spiritual.[78] For the Hasidim it is not man who seeks out the sparks in his quest to repair and restore the upper worlds, but rather the divine sparks themselves, present in the material world, which cry out to man and long to be redeemed. It is for this reason that man must not ignore the concrete and material.

Furthermore, the redemption of the material is dialectically its negation, for the redeeming power of man is his intellect, which negates the concrete in favor of the abstract, thereby lifting the material into the realm of the spiritual. One eats, drinks, has intercourse, etc., "for the sake of heaven," and in so doing spiritualizes the world and elevates the holy sparks in matter. There is no pleasure and happiness in the material world per se, but rather one's immersion in the concrete and material is always with a view toward its negation in the universal and spiritual. This is the doctrine of *Yeridah le-zorekh 'aliyah*, "the descent in behalf of the ascent." The confrontation with evil in its own (material) realm results in its transformation into the good.[79] Or, better, this doctrine, along with the concept of "worship

---

76. Ibid., p. 118.
77. Ibid., p. 118.
78. Rifka Schatz-Uffenheimer, *Hasidism As Mysticism*, p. 58.
79. Ibid.

through corporeality," confers a dialectical union between good and evil, and between the spiritual and the material.

But how is this to be achieved? Schatz-Uffenheimer interprets the Besht's famous dictum, "A man should desire a woman to so great an extent that he refines away his material existence in virtue of the strength of his desire," not as a warrant for fulfilling one's desires physically but rather for exhausting them without realizing them.[80] However, the Besht's words say nothing about exhausting one's desire, but rather make reference to a spiritualization that occurs by virtue of the intensity of the desire itself. The actualization spoken of here may be more like an intensification of passion, delight, and desire that elevates one to the delight and desire of the Primal Will itself. Perhaps one who knows burning passion is one who also knows God. As Martin Buber has put it, "One shall not kill 'the evil impulse,' the passion, in oneself, but one shall sense God *with* it."[81] The act of corporeal desire itself enables one to realize the spiritual within oneself. These ideas suggest something of a "romantic" spirit in Hasidism. Indeed, the Hasidic clash with the traditional halakhic authorities parallels the then-contemporary secular romantic revolt against classicism in art and philosophy.

THE ANNIHILATION OF "SOMETHINGNESS"

The views we have just considered certainly give the lie to the proposition that for the Hasidim *Tikkun* is a purely "otherworldly" ideal. For them it is not sufficient that a man raises his own spark(s) and returns to a unity with the absolute. Rather the entire world, or at least those aspects that are part of his "soul root," must be redeemed with him. Nevertheless, there is a quietist trend within Hasidism, one that does seek, in effect, to annihilate the material world, and with it the individual's ego. There developed within Hasidic circles the notion of *bittul ha-Yesh*, the nullification of "somethingness,"[82] a doctrine that held that the purpose of religious activity and prayer is the nullification of the world and self in favor of a complete unity with God. Indeed, the annihilation of the personal ego became such an important Hasidic ideal that it was common for their leaders to hold that a man's

---

80. Ibid., pp. 58–59.
81. Buber, *Hasidism*, p. 71.
82. Louis Jacobs, *Hasidic Prayer* (New York: Schocken Books, 1973), p. 21.

petitions to the Lord should not be understood as a prayer for personal prosperity or even relief from suffering, but rather as referring to the welfare and suffering of the *Shekhinah*, that aspect of God that has been exiled into, and suffers along with, the world.[83]

"STRANGE THOUGHTS"

We might ask, however, if the Hasidic nullification of the world is really equivalent to the Gnostics' escape from it. In order to answer this we must remember that for the Kabbalists and Hasidim the entire universe, from the heights of the world of *Adam Kadmon* down to the realm of the Husks and the "Other Side," is an expression and actually a part of God. The possibility of transcending the world in the Gnostic sense of "escape" is impossible in the Kabbalah precisely because the world itself is considered holy and therefore in as much need of redemption as the adherent. It is for this reason that such doctrines as "worship through corporeality," the "descent on behalf of the ascent," etc., could develop within Hasidic thought. The world cannot be ignored; it must be made an integral part of the spirit. The early Hasidim even went so far as to hold that one must therefore even spiritualize one's "strange thoughts,"[84] those thoughts that intrude upon one's prayers and consist, for example, of the desire for an illicit sexual encounter, or the abandonment of Torah. The manner in which such thoughts are elevated is to mentally attach them to their sefirotic point of origin (for example, illicit passion, like all love, originates in the *Sefirah Chesed*). Some Hasidic masters went so far as to hold that one should concentrate on the various *Sefirot* in order to elicit such "strange thoughts," which could then be sublimated and

---

83. Carried to its logical conclusion this view does not obligate the Hasid to behave in a manner different from what traditional Judaism had prescribed. This is because, to pray for the *Shekhinah* is, in effect, to pray for the world, inasmuch as this aspect of God, exiled as it is into the corporeal world, is completely coextensive with material reality. The difference is simply that the Hasid, in praying for his own welfare, or, for example, in earning his livelihood, is conscious of the fact that in doing so he is "raising sparks," i.e., redeeming an aspect of *Ein-Sof*. It is for this reason that R. Jacob Joseph of Polonnoye could show his concern for *this* world by holding that a man must verbally pronounce his prayers, because it is only speech that can serve as a vessel for drawing down divine grace into the material world.

84. Jacobs, *Hasidic Prayer*, p. 104ff.

elevated into the spiritual realm. Like the doctrine of "worship through corporeality," the concept of "elevating strange thoughts" was either abandoned or ignored by the later Hasidim. Nevertheless it serves to illustrate that the Hasidim, even in their so-called transcendence of the material world, went very far in an effort to include and ultimately spiritualize those aspects of the world that are normally rejected by quietists. The Hasidim, operating within a framework of kabbalistic panentheism, held the world to be a sacred place, and all things an opportunity for an encounter with God.

KAVVANOT AND DEVEKUT

An important aspect of the Hasidic doctrine of *Tikkun* involves the state of mind that an adherent must have while performing commandments and during prayer. While the Kabbalists had formulated a complex series of *kavvanot* (intentions) directed toward the restoration and unification of the heavenly *Sefirot* and *Partzufim*, the Hasidim recommended the much simpler procedure of *devekut*, a simple "cleaving" to God. Indeed, the Hasidim held that the complex intentions of the Kabbalists could actually interfere with all but the greatest *tzaddik*'s attachment to God, and they eliminated even study of the complex kabbalistic theosophy in favor of a much simpler faith. It is for this reason that kabbalistic theosophy is presented in much simplified, and even superficial, form in the writings of the Hasidim. To be sure Hasidism, in contrast to the Kabbalah, is a doctrine intended for the masses, and the masses cannot be expected to understand a complex work such as the *Etz Chayyim*. For the average man the doctrine of the holy sparks, for example, is best rendered synonymous with a recognition of the presence of divinity in all created things.[85] Yet Hasidism is not a mere popularization of the Kabbalah. The Hasidim valued a certain simplicity for its own sake, and further held that an immersion in complex theosophy detracted from one's participation in the world. In spite of certain quietistic tendencies, in Hasidism the "raising of the sparks" becomes a metaphor for engagement as opposed to escape from the world. The Hasidim divested the notion of *Tikkun* of its final traces of Gnosticism and asceticism, thereby refocusing its adherents on the immediate relations among man, the world, and God.

---

85. Ibid., p. 124.

BUBER ON *TIKKUN*

The twentieth-century Jewish philosopher Martin Buber has provided an interpretation of Hasidism, which, although it has been criticized from many quarters, can assist us in our contemporary reading of *Tikkun*. Buber was, for example, the first to recognize the relationship between the Hasidic conception of *Tikkun* and the psychoanalytic concept of sublimation: "The psychoanalysis of our day has again taken up the Hasidic view in the form of the theory of the 'sublimation of the libido,' according to which the stimuli can be diverted, and carried over into the realm of the spirit, therefore changing so to speak their form of energy."[86] But, as Buber points out, the psychoanalytic notion is purely intrapsychic while the Hasidic concept of redemption involves the world at large: " 'Sublimation' takes place within man himself, the 'raising of the sparks' takes place between man and the world."[87] Buber provides what amounts to an existentialist interpretation of the Hasidic "sparks" doctrine: "all the more existence in reality is recognizable as an unbroken chain of encounters each of which demands the whole person for what can be accomplished by him, just by him and only in this hour."[88] For Buber the Hasidic commandment is for man "to do all that he does with the whole of his being."[89]

Buber emphasized those aspects of the theory of *Tikkun* that see humanity as a receptacle for God's fate in the world. Man, therefore, has a great responsibility, which can only be realized through the exercise of his free will. According to Buber, it is "for the sake of the chooser," for the existence of free will, that the world itself was created, for only through a free exercise of choice can the values of the Godhead be made real.

THE "INNER" AND THE "OUTER" ASPECTS OF ALL THINGS

The doctrine of *Tikkun ha-Olam* is a surprisingly psychological doctrine. This is surprising because unlike the religions of the East, Judaism is often referred

---

86. Buber, *Hasidism*, p. 34.
87. Ibid., p. 55.
88. Ibid., p. 58.
89. Ibid., p. 59.

to as a *historical religion*, a religion that places great emphasis on concrete historical acts, on the historical fate of a people, and on this people's relationship to a particular land. Particularly in modern times, Jews have been a politically conscious people and with the rise of the modern state of Israel this political focus has become stronger, perhaps, than at any time in the past. It is thus surprising and perhaps even a bit disconcerting that the Jewish doctrine of *Tikkun ha-Olam*, the restoration of the world, is not a blueprint for tangible, political action. Why, we might ask, is there an emphasis upon the psychological in the Kabbalah at the seeming expense of the political?

In order to answer this question we must momentarily recall a basic dichotomy within kabbalistic theosophy, one that is expressed in the controversy over whether *Chochmah* (Thought, Wisdom) or *Keter/Ratzon* (Will, Desire) is the highest of the *Sefirot*. The Lurianists, at least, all agree that there is a progression in the Absolute, *Ein-Sof*, as it estranges itself within a world of matter and time and then returns to itself via the spiritualization of that world through *Tikkun*. However, on one interpretation of this progression,[90] there is a focus upon the intellectual aspects of this dynamic, in which divine estrangement (and hence, creation) is understood as the instantiation of universal ideas and values in particular actions and events, and *Ein-Sof*'s return to itself is understood primarily as an act of gnosis or knowledge. On this view, the very contemplation of the various theosophical events and unifications in the upper worlds, i.e., a thoroughgoing knowledge of the kabbalistic system, is the major factor in bringing about the restoration of the cosmos.[91]

We have also, however, considered a second point of view within kabbalistic theosophy,[92] one in which the estrangement of *Ein-Sof* is energic or emotional rather than intellectual; and the corresponding return via *Tikkun* is one in which divine *energy*, alienated in the realm of the Husks,

---

90. Which accords with the notion that the highest *Sefirah* is *Chochmah* (Wisdom).

91. Such a view is embodied in the Lurianic notion of *Kavvanot*, the view that man must engage in theosophical contemplation to bring about *Tikkun*. This perspective is quite Hegelian, inasmuch as Hegel held that the return of the Absolute to itself occurs precisely (and most completely) in thought.

92. This perspective is in accord with the notion that *Keter* (as Will {*Ratzon*} and Delight {*Tinug*}) is the highest *Sefirah*, and hence the most exalted manifestation of the divine.

is extracted, uplifted, and transformed to complete the world's restoration and repair. This view, which finds its fullest expression in the Hasidic concept of *Tikkun*, calls for the redirection of man's baser, "evil" impulses in the service of the divine. It also accords well with the Lurianic notion that *Tikkun* results from the erotic unification of the feminine and masculine aspects of God. Such a perspective on kabbalistic theosophy is, in contemporary terms, psychoanalytic as opposed to philosophical, libidinal as opposed to cognitive.

How are we to understand this dichotomy between the intellectual and emotional perspectives upon *Tikkun*? First, we should note that it is a dichotomy that is not exclusive to the Kabbalah. Rather it reflects a basic duality in human life, between thought and affect, reason and emotion, "classicism" and "romanticism," and even between philosophy and psychology. That the kabbalistic theosophy is broad and flexible enough to reflect each of these dual traditions in equal measure is, in my view, a tribute to its own completeness.

The key, however, to understanding this dichotomy between *Chochmah* and *Keter*, Reason and Eros, intellect and emotion, etc., is, I believe, to be found in the Kabbalist's insistence that *Tikkun* must rest upon *action and performance* as well as upon thought and feeling. Both philosophy and psychology, we might observe, are on one side of the divide of another great dichotomy, that between the *inner* and the *outer* aspects of things; the inner being man's thoughts and emotions, and the outer being man's behavior, his actual engagement in the world. The Kabbalah, by its very nature as an esoteric mystical doctrine, focuses upon the "inner," but it holds, as it does for all such dichotomies, that these two great aspects of the world are dialectically interdependent. On the one hand, the measure of *Tikkun*, regardless of one's philosophy and regardless of whether one has achieved gnosis within one's own soul, is action and behavior. However, the Kabbalists held that the outer aspects of things (such as human action and *mitzvot*) are themselves dependent upon the inner and the spiritual, for without such inwardness, the outer acts would be devoid of meaning. Meaning is a function of the inner life of man, which for the Kabbalists depends upon man's reaching up toward God through good intentions and prayer. In short, while the Kabbalists recognized the overwhelming significance of meritorious deeds, one aspect of which constitutes political action, they saw the efficaciousness of these deeds as dependent, in large measure, upon the inner state of those who performed them. Indeed, there are passages in the

Lurianic writings that imply that man can only be concerned with the inner (conceived as lower) aspects of *Tikkun*; the outward *Tikkun* to be completed by lights concealed in the highest *Partzuf, Attika Kaddisha,* which are to be revealed only in messianic times.[93] For example, man's *Tikkun* could not be dependent upon a return of the Jewish people to *Eretz Yisrael* per se, but only upon the alteration in the balance of (inner) "good" and "evil" for which this return is merely a (very important) sign or consequent.

To put it in starker terms, what is truly valuable and good in this or any conceivable world cannot be something so "geopolitical" as the location of certain physical bodies collectively referred to as the Jewish people. Rather what is of value is the making manifest of the Godly values of kindness, justice, mercy, righteousness, etc., with which these people have presumably been entrusted. Man's true freedom consists not in his ability or lack of ability to be victorious in a particular war, or achieve a given political end (however, important these may be), but rather in his ability to choose righteousness and act with good intentions, however powerful or powerless these may be in their effects. The Jews who cried *Ani Maamin* ("I believe") as they were marched to the chambers in Auschwitz were just as significant for *Tikkun ha-Olam* as the soldiers who were victorious in the Six-Day War. In the end, it is only the confluence of right mind *and* meritorious action that brings about *Tikkun ha-Olam.* The result of this confluence is that humanity will merit the divine grace that is essential to its ultimate redemption.

THE SIGNIFICANCE OF *TIKKUN HA-OLAM* TODAY

The symbol of *Tikkun ha-Olam* provides us with a call to pluralism and a celebration of the great diversity that exists within the human and natural worlds. According to Vital:

> Everything was created for the purpose of the Highest One, but all do not suckle in the same way, nor are all the improvements (*tikkunim*) the same. Galbanum (an ingredient in incense, which by itself has a foul odor), for example, improves the incense in ways that even frankincense cannot. That is why it is necessary for there to be good, bad, and in-between in all these worlds and why there are endless variations in all of them.[94]

---

93. Scholem, *Kabbalah,* p. 143.
94. *Sefer Etz Chayyim* 1: 1, p. 32; Menzi and Padeh, *The Tree of Life,* p. 102.

We have already seen how according to Rabbi Aaron Ha-Levi it is fundamental to the divine purpose that the world should be differentiated in all its
plurality, but still be united in an infinite source.[95] According to Rabbi Aron:

> . . . the essence of His intention is that his *coincidentia* be manifested in
> concrete reality, that is, that all realities and their levels be revealed in
> actuality, each detail in itself, and that they nevertheless be unified and
> joined in their value, that is, that they be revealed as separated essences, and
> that they nevertheless be unified and joined in their value.[96]

The metaphors and concepts which taken together comprise the concept
of *Tikkun ha-Olam* also provide the basis for what might be called a
"spiritual" or "ethical" psychology. For the individual, the essential message
of *Tikkun ha-Olam* is that one's goal in life is to actualize the self in the
singular service of spiritual and particularly ethical ends. This message is
particularly significant in the context of what might be described as the
contemporary division of the soul. In our time the human soul has been
divided into a series of separate spheres, one the province of psychology,
another of religion, a third of ethics, a fourth of politics, etc. The theory of
Tikkun is a theory that encompasses all of these "disciplines" and integrates
them into a total perspective on man. Like "psychology" it provides a theory
of human development, emphasizes the resolution of intrapsychic conflict
and the integration of conflicting personality trends, and attempts to enhance
human freedom; like "religion" it offers an experience of spiritual union with
God; like "ethics" its chief concern is with the realization and implementa-
tion of "values"; and like "politics" the doctrine of *Tikkun ha-Olam* is, as its
very name implies, concerned with the betterment of the world. For the
Kabbalah, each of these goals is dependent upon and in a sense *identical* with
the others. The "raising of the sparks" is *at once* a psychological, spiritual,
ethical, and political event. One cannot be "religious" from the standpoint of
the Kabbalah without at the same time devoting energies to one's psychological, ethical, and political self. The individual who comes to think, feel, and
act through his Godly soul achieves his own personal *Tikkun*, becomes
psychologically integrated, spiritually fulfilled, ethical in his conduct, and
will devote himself to the service of a better world. Put in another way, it is

---

95. As discussed in Chapter Two. See Elior, "Chabad," p. 165.
96. Ibid., p. 167.

the achievement of these seemingly diverse goals that taken together, from his unique standpoint in life, constitute his or her personal *Tikkun*, contribution to the "restoration of the world" and participation in the perfection of God.

References

Ariel, David. *The Mystic Quest*. Northvale, NJ: Jason Aronson, 1988.

Bakan, David. *Sigmund Freud and the Jewish Mystical Tradition*. Boston: Beacon Press, 1971. Originally published in 1958.

Berkowitz, Eliezer. *God, Man, and History*. Middle Village, NY: Jonathan David, 1959.

Bettelheim, Bruno. *Freud and Man's Soul*. New York: Vintage Books, 1984.

Biale, David. *Gershom Scholem, Kabbalah and Counter-History*. 2d ed. Cambridge, MA: Harvard University Press, 1982.

———. "Gershom Scholem's Ten Unhistorical Aphorisms on Kabbalah: Text and Commentary." *Modern Judaism* 5 (1985): pp. 86–87.

Birnbaum, David. *God and Evil*. Hoboken, NJ: Ktav, 1989.

Blackman, Philip, trans. *Tractate Avoth: The Ethics of the Fathers*. Gateshead, England: Judaica Press, 1985.

Bloom, Harold. *Kabbalah and Criticism*. New York: Continuum, 1983.

———. "The Pragmatics of Contemporary Jewish Culture." In *Post-Analytic Philosophy*, ed. John Rajchman and Cornel West. New York: Columbia University Press, 1985.

Book Bahir. Trans. Joachim Neugroschel. *The Secret Garden: An Anthology in the Kabbalah*, ed. David Meltzer. Barryton, NY: Stanton Hill, 1998.

Buber, Martin. *The Eclipse of God: Studies in the Relation between Religion and Philosophy*. New York: Harper & Brothers, 1952.

————. "God and the World's Evil." In *Contemporary Jewish Thought*, ed. Simon Noveck. New York: B'nai B'rith, 1963.

————. *Hasidism*. New York: Philosophical Library, 1948.

Cassirer, Ernst. *The Philosophy of Symbolic Forms*. Vol. 1–3. Ralph Manheim, trans. New Haven: Yale University Press, 1953, 1955, 1957. Originally published in Berlin, 1923, 1925, 1929.

Cordovero, Moses. *The Palm Tree of Deborah*. Trans. Louis Jacobs. New York: Hermon Press, 1974.

Covits, Joel. *Visions of the Night*. Boston: Shambhala, 1990.

Culler, Jonathan. *On Deconstruction Theory and Criticism After Structuralism*. Ithaca, NY: Cornell University Press, 1982.

Dan, Joseph. *Gershom Scholem and the Mystical Dimension of Jewish History*. New York: New York University Press, 1987.

————, ed. *The Early Kabbalah*. Texts trans. by Ronald C. Kieber. New York: Paulist Press, 1966.

De Leon, Moses. (From) *The Doctrine of the Ether*. Trans. George Margoliouth. In *The Secret Garden: An Anthology in the Kabbalah*, ed. David Meltzer. Barrytown, NY: Station Hill Arts, 1998.

Derrida, Jacques. *Margins of Philosophy*. Trans. Alan Bass. Chicago: University of Chicago Press, 1982.

Drob, Sanford. "Antinomies of the Soul." *Jewish Review* 3.

————. *Are Mental Acts Myths?* Doctoral Dissertation, Boston University, 1981.

————. "Foreword." In David Birnbaum *God and Evil*. 4th ed. Hoboken, NJ: Ktav, 1989.

————. "Judaism as a Form of Life." *Tradition* 23 (4) (Summer 1988): 78–89.

————. "Jung and the Kabbalah." *History of Psychology*, 2 (2) (May 1999): 102–118.

————. "The Kabbalistic Art of Jan Menses." *Jewish Review* 2.

————. *Kabbalistic Metaphors: Jewish Mysticism, Ancient Religion, and Modern Thought*. Northvale, NJ: Jason Aronson, 2000.

————. "The Metaphors of Tikkun Haolam: Their Traditional Meaning and Contemporary Significance." *Jewish Review*, 3:6 (June 1990).

————. "The *Sefirot*: Kabbalistic Archetypes of Mind and Creation." *Crosscurrents* 47 (1997): 5–29.

————. "Tzimtzum: A Kabbalistic Theory of Creation." *Jewish Review*, 3:5 (April–May 1990).

Eigen, Michael. "The Area of Faith in Winnicott, Lacan and Bion." *International Journal of Psychoanalysis* 62 (1981): 413–433.

Elior, Rachel. "Chabad: The Contemplative Ascent to God." In *Jewish Spirituality: From the Sixteenth-Century Revival to the Present*, ed. Arthur Green. New York: Crossroads, 1987.

———. "The Concept of God in Hekhalot Mysticism." In *Binah: Studies in Jewish Thought*, ed. Joseph Dan. New York: Greenwood Publishing Group, 1989.

———. *The Paradoxical Ascent to God: The Kabbalistic Theosophy of Habad Hasidism*. Trans. J. M. Green. Albany: State University of New York Press, 1993.

Feyerabend, Paul. *Against Method*. London: NLB, 1975.

Filoramo, Giovanni. *A History of Gnosticism*. Trans. Anthony Alcock. Cambridge: Basil Blackwell, 1990.

Findlay, J. N. *The Discipline of the Cave*. London: Allen & Unwin, 1966.

———. *Plato: The Written and Unwritten Doctrines*. London: Routledge & Kegal Paul, 1974.

———. *The Transcendence of the Cave*. London: Allen & Unwin, 1966.

Fine, Lawrence. "The Contemplative Practice of Yihudim in Lurianic Kabbalah." In *Jewish Spirituality: From the Sixteenth-Century Revival to the Present*, ed. Arthur Green. New York: Crossroads, 1987.

Fluegel, Maurice. *Philosophy, Qabbala and Vedenta*. Baltimore: H. Fluegel & Company, 1902.

Frankl, Victor. *From Death Camp to Existentialism*. Trans. Ilsa Lasch. Boston: Beacon Press, 1959.

Freud, Sigmund. *Civilization and Its Discontents. The Standard Edition of the Complete Works of Sigmund Freud*, ed. James Strachey. Vol. 21. London: Hogarth Press, 1955–1967.

———. *New Introductory Lectures on Psychoanalysis*. New York: W. W. Norton, 1965. Originally published in 1933.

Gikatilla, Joseph. *Sha'are Orah* (The Gates of Light). Trans. Avi Weinstein. San Francisco: HarperCollins, 1994.

Goodman, Lenn E., ed. *Neoplatonism in Jewish Thought*. Albany: State University of New York Press, 1992.

Graetz, Heinrich. *Popular History of the Jews*. 5th ed. New York: Hebrew Publishing, 1937.

Handelman, Susan. *Fragments of Redemption: Jewish Thought and Literary Theory in Benjamin, Scholem, and Levinas*. Bloomington and Indianapolis: Indiana University Press, 1991.

Heller-Wilinsky, Sarah. "Isaac ibn Latif—Philosopher or Kabbalist." In *Jewish Medieval and Renaissance Studies*, ed. Alexander Altmann. Cambridge, MA: Harvard University Press, 1967.

Hesse, Mary. "The Cognitive Claims of Metaphor." In *Metaphor and Religion*, ed. J. P. Van Noppen. Brussels: 1984.

Hillman, James. "Anima Mundi: The Return of the Soul to the World." *Spring* (1982): 71–93.

———. *Re-visioning Psychology*. New York: Harper & Row, 1976.

Hoffman, Edward. *The Way of Splendor: Jewish Mysticism and Modern Psychology*. Northvale, NJ: Jason Aronson, 1981.

Husserl, Edmund. *The Crisis In European Philosophy and Transcendental Phenomenology*. Trans. Davis Carr. Evanston, IL: Northwestern University Press, 1970.

Hyamson, Moses, trans. *The Code of Maimonides*. Jerusalem: Boys Town, 1965.

Idel, Moshe. *Hasidism: Between Ecstasy and Magic*. Albany: State University of New York Press, 1995.

———. "Jewish Kabbalah and Platonism in the Middle Ages and Renaissance." In *Neoplatonism and Jewish Thought*, ed. Lenn E. Goodman. Albany: State University of New York Press, 1992.

———. *Kabbalah: New Perspectives*. New Haven: Yale University Press, 1988.

———. *Language, Torah and Hermeneutics in Abraham Abulafia*. Trans. Menahem Kallus. Albany: State University of New York Press, 1989.

———. *Messianic Myths*. New Haven: Yale University Press, 1998.

Jacobs, Louis. *Hasidic Prayer*. New York: Schocken Books, 1973.

———. "The Uplifting of the Sparks in Later Jewish Mysticism." In *Jewish Spirituality: From the Sixteenth-Century Revival to the Present*, ed. Arthur Green. New York: Crossroads, 1987.

Janowitz, Naomi. *The Poetics of Ascent*. Albany: State University of New York Press, 1989.

Jung, Carl Gustav. *Aion: Researches Into the Phenomenology of the Self. The Collected Works of C. G. Jung*, Vol. 9, Part II. Trans. R. F. C. Hull. Princeton, NJ: Princeton University Press, 1969.

———. *Alchemical Studies. The Collected Works of C. G. Jung*, Vol. 13. Trans. R. F. C. Hull. Princeton, NJ: Princeton University Press, 1967. Articles originally published 1929–1945.

———. "Gnostic Symbols of the Self." In *Aion: Researches Into the Phenomenology of the Self. The Collected Works of C. G. Jung*, Vol. 9, Part

II. Trans. R. F. C. Hull. Princeton, NJ: Princeton University Press, 1969.

———. *Letters.* Vols. 1 and 2. Ed. Gerhard Adler. Princeton, NJ: Princeton University Press, 1975.

———. *Mysterium Coniunctionis. The Collected Works of C. G. Jung,* Vol. 14. Trans. R. F. C. Hull. Princeton, NJ: Princeton University Press, 1963.

———. *Psychology and Alchemy. The Collected Works of C. G. Jung,* Vol. 12. Trans. R. F. C. Hull. Princeton, NJ: Princeton University Press, 1968.

Kant, Immanuel. *Critique of Pure Reason.* Trans. Norman Kemp Smith. New York: St. Martin's, 1965.

Kaplan, Aryeh. *The Bahir: Illumination.* York Beach, ME: Samuel Weiser, 1989.

———. *Chasidic Masters.* New York: Maznaim, 1984.

———. *Jewish Meditation: A Practical Guide.* New York: Schocken, 1985.

———. *Meditation and Kabbalah.* York Beach, ME: Samuel Weiser, 1982.

———. *Sefer Yetzirah: The Cook of Creation.* Rev. ed. York Beach, ME: Samuel Weiser, 1997.

Kaplan, Mordecai. *Judaism as a Civilization.* New York: Macmillan, 1934.

Katz, Steven T. "Utterance and Ineffability in Jewish Neoplatonism." In *Neoplatonism in Jewish Thought,* ed. Lenn E. Goodman. Albany: State University of New York Press, 1992.

Klagsbrun, Francine. *Voices of Wisdom.* New York: Pantheon, 1980.

Kuhn, Thomas S. *The Structure of Scientific Revolutions.* Chicago: University of Chicago Press, 1970.

Lerner, Michael. "Neo-Compassionism." *Tikkun,* Vol. 2, (1987) No. 5:9–13.

———. "Tikkun: To Mend, Repair and Transform the World." *Tikkun,* Vol. 1, (1986) No. 1:7–13.

Levi-Strauss, Claude. *Structural Anthropology.* Trans. Claire Jacobson and Brooke Grundfest. New York: Basic Books, 1963.

Liebes, Yehuda. *Studies in the Zohar.* Trans. A. Schwartz, S. Nakuche, and P. Peli. Albany: State University of New York Press, 1993.

Luzzatto, Moses. *General Principles of the Kabbalah.* Trans. Phillip Berg. Jerusalem: Research Centre of Kabbalah, 1970.

Luzzatto, Moses Chayyim. *Derech Hashem* (The Way of God). Trans. Aryeh Kaplan. Jerusalem and New York: Feldheim, 1977.

MacIntyre, Alasdair. "Myth." *The Encyclopedia of Philosophy,* Vol. 5. Ed. Paul Edwards. New York: Macmillan, 1967.

Maimon, Shelomo. *Shelomo Maimon, An Autobiography.* Trans. Clark Murray. London, 1888.

Maimonides. *The Guide For The Perplexed.* Trans. M. Friedlander. New York: Dover, 1956.

Meltzer, David, ed. *The Secret Garden: An Anthology in the Kabbalah.* Barrytown, NY: Stanton Hill, 1998.

Menzi, Donald Wilder, and Zwe Padeh, trans. *The Tree of Life: Chayyim Vital's Introduction to the Kabbalah of Isaac Luria.* Northvale, NJ: Jason Aronson, 1999.

Mindel, Nissan. *The Philosophy of Chabad*, Vol. II. Brooklyn, NY: Kehot, 1973.

Moore, Thomas, ed. *A Blue Fire: Selected Writings of James Hillman.* New York: Harper & Row, 1989.

Neumann, Erich. *The Origins and History of Consciousness.* Trans. R. F. C. Hull. Princeton, NJ: Princeton University Press, 1970.

Nozick, Robert. *Philosophical Explanations.* Cambridge, MA: Harvard University Press, 1981.

O' Regan, Cyril. *The Heterodox Hegel.* Albany: State University of New York Press, 1994.

Otto, Rudolph. *The Idea of the Holy.* London: Oxford University Press, 1970. Originally published 1923.

Piaget, Jean. *Genetic Epistemology.* New York: W. W. Norton & Co., 1970.

———. *Psychology and Epistemology.* New York: Viking, 1971.

Rajchman, John, and Cornel West. *Post-Analytic Philosophy.* New York: Columbia University Press, 1985.

Renou, Louis, ed. *Hinduism.* New York: Braziller, 1962.

Rieff, Phillip. *The Triumph of the Therapeutic.* Chicago: University of Chicago Press, 1966.

Robinson, Ira. *Moses Cordovero's Introduction to Kabbalah: An Annotated Translation of His Or Ne'erav.* Hoboken, NJ: Ktav, 1994.

Rorty, Richard. *The Linguistic Turn: Recent Essays in Philosophical Method.* Chicago: University of Chicago Press, 1967.

———. "Unfamiliar Noises: Hesse and Davidson on Metaphors." In Richard Rorty, *Objectivism, Relativism and Truth: Philosophical Papers.* Vol. I. Cambridge: Cambridge University Press, 1991.

Rotenberg, Mordecai. *Dialogue with Deviance.* Lanham, MD: University Press of America, 1993.

Rudolph, Kurt. *Gnosis: The Nature and History of Gnosticism.* Trans. R. M. Wilson. San Francisco: Harper and Row, 1987.

Schaefer, Peter. *The Hidden and Manifest God: Some Major Themes in Early*

Jewish Mysticism. Trans. Aubrey Pomerantz. Albany: State University of New York Press, 1992.

Schatz-Uffenheimer, Rifka. *Hasidism as Mysticism: Quietistic Elements In Eighteenth-Century Hasidic Thought.* Trans. Jonathan Chipman. Jerusalem: Hebrew University, 1993.

Schochet, Immanuel. "Mystical Concepts in Chasidism," In Schneur Zalman, *Likutei Amarim-Tanya.* Brooklyn, NY: Kehot, 1983.

Scholem, Gershom. "Adam Kadmon." *Encyclopedia Judaica 2: 248.*

———. "Colours and Their Symbolism in Jewish Tradition and Mysticism." *Diogenes* 109 (1980): 64–76.

———. "The Four Worlds." *Encyclopedia Judaica*, Vol. 16, pp. 641–642.

———. "Gilgul: Transmigration of Souls." In Gershom Scholem, *On the Mystical Shape of the Godhead.* Trans. Joachim Neugroschel. New York: Schocken, 1991.

———. *Jewish Gnosticism, Merkabah Mysticism and Talmudic Tradition.* New York: Schocken, 1965.

———. *Kabbalah.* Jerusalem: Keter, 1974.

———. *Major Trends in Jewish Mysticism.* New York: Schocken, 1941.

———. "The Meaning of the Torah in Jewish Mysticism." In Gershom Scholem, *On the Kabbalah and Its Symbolism.* New York: Schocken, 1969.

———. The *Messianic Idea in Judaism and Other Essays on Jewish Spirituality.* New York: Schocken, 1971.

———. "The Name of God and the Linguistic Theory of the Kabbala." *Diogenes* 79 (1972): 59–80; *Diogenes* 80 (1972): 164–194.

———. *On the Kabbalah and Its Symbolism.* Trans. Ralph Manheim. New York: Schocken, 1969.

———. *On the Mystical Shape of the Godhead.* Trans. Joachim Neugroschel. New York: Schocken, 1991.

———. *Origins of the Kabbalah.* Trans. R. J. Zwi Werblowski. Princeton, NJ: Princeton University Press, 1987. Originally published 1962.

———. *Sabbatai Sevi: The Mystical Messiah.* Trans. R. J. Zwi Werblowski. Princeton, NJ: Princeton University Press, 1973.

———. "Sitra Ahra: Good and Evil in the Kabbalah." In *On the Mystical Shape of the Godhead.* Trans. Joachim Neugroschel. New York: Schocken, 1991.

———. "Tselem: The Concept of the Astral Body." In *On the Mystical Shape of the Godhead.* Trans. Joachim Neugroschel. New York: Schocken, 1991.

————. "Yezirah, Sefer." *Encyclopedia Judaica*, Vol. 16:782ff.

Schweid, Eliezer. *Judaism and Mysticism According to Gershom Scholem: A Critical Analysis and Programmatic Discussion*. Trans. David Weiner. Atlanta: Scholars Press, 1983.

Segal, Robert A., ed. *The Gnostic Jung*. Princeton, NJ: Princeton University Press, 1992.

Soloveitchik, Joseph. *Halakhic Man*. Trans. Lawrence Kaplan. Philadelphia: Jewish Publication Society, 1984.

————. "The Lonely Man of Faith." *Tradition* 7:2 (Summer 1965): 5–67.

Sperling, Harry, Maurice Simon, and Paul Levertoff. *The Zohar*. London: Soncino Press, 1931–1934.

Spiegelberg, Herbert. *The Phenomenological Movement*. The Hague: Martinus Nijhoff, 1971.

Staten, Henry. *Wittgenstein and Derrida*. Lincoln: University of Nebraska Press, 1984.

Steinsaltz, Adin. "The Mystic as Philosopher." *Jewish Review* 3: 4 (March 1990): 14–17.

————. *The Long Shorter Way: Discourses on Chasidic Thought*. Northvale, NJ: Jason Aronson, 1988.

————. *The Thirteen-Petalled Rose*. Trans. Yehuda Hanegbi. New York: Basic Books, 1980.

————. "Worlds, Angels and Men." In Adin Steinsaltz, *The Strife of the Spirit*. Northvale, NJ: Jason Aronson, 1988.

Tishby, Isaiah, and Fischel Lachower. *The Wisdom of the Zohar*. Trans. David Goldstein. Vols. 1, 2, and 3. Oxford: Littman Library of Jewish Civilization, 1989.

Verman, Mark. *The Books of Contemplation: Medieval Jewish Mystical Sources*. Albany: State University of New York Press, 1992.

Vital, Chayyim. *Sefer ha-Gilgulim*. Selections trans. by Yehuda Shamir. In *The Secret Garden: An Anthology in the Kabbalah*, ed. David Meltzer. Barrytown, NY: Station Hill Arts, 1998.

————. *Shaarey Kedushah*. Selections trans. by Zalman Schachter. In *The Secret Garden: An Anthology in the Kabbalah*, ed. David Meltzer. Barrytown, NY: Station Hill Arts, 1998.

Waskow, Arthur. *These Holy Sparks: The Rebirth of the Jewish People*. San Francisco: Harper & Row, 1983.

Weiner, Herbert. *9½ Mystics: The Kabbalah Today*. New York: Macmillan, 1986.

Wexelman, David M. *The Jewish Concept of Reincarnation and Creation:*

Based on the Writings of Rabbi Chaim Vital. Northvale, NJ: Jason Aronson, 1999.

Wittgenstein, Ludwig. *Notebooks.* Oxford: Basil Blackwell, 1961. Originally written in 1914–1916.

———. *Philosophical Investigations.* Trans. G. E. M. Anscombe. New York: Macmillan, 1953.

———. *The Tractatus Logico-Philosophicus.* Trans. D. F. Pears and B. F. McGuinness. London: Routledge and Kegan Paul, 1961.

Wolfson, Elliot R. *Along the Path: Studies in Kabbalistic Myth, Symbolism and Hermeneutics.* Albany: State University of New York Press, 1995.

———. *Circle in the Square: Studies in the Use of Gender in Kabbalistic Symbolism.* Albany: State University of New York Press, 1995.

———. "Crossing Gender Boundaries in Kabbalistic Ritual and Myth." In Elliot R. Wolfson, *Circle In The Square: Studies in the Use of Gender in Kabbalistic Symbolism.* Albany: State University of New York Press, 1995.

———. *Through a Speculum That Shines: Vision and Imagination in Medieval Jewish Mysticism.* Princeton, NJ: Princeton University Press, 1994.

———. "Woman—The Feminine as Other in Theosophic Kabbalah: Some Philosophical Observations on the Divine Androgyne." In *The Other in Jewish Thought and History: Constructions of Jewish Identity and Culture*, ed. L. Silberstein and R. Cohen. New York: New York University Press, 1994.

Yalom, Irwin. *Existential Psychotherapy.* New York: Basic Books, 1983.

Zaehner, R. C. *The Dawn and Twilight of Zoroastrianism.* London: Weidenfeld and Nicolson, 1961.

———, ed. *Hindu Scriptures.* Rutland, VT: Charles E. Tuttle, 1966.

Zalman, Schneur. *Likutei Amarim-Tanya.* Bilingual edition. Brooklyn, NY: Kehot Publication Society, 1981.

Zimmer, Heinrich. *Philosophies of India.* Princeton, NJ: Princeton University Press, 1971.

Index

About the Author

Sanford L. Drob is Director of Psychological Assessment and the Senior Forensic Psychologist at Bellevue Hospital in New York. He holds doctorate degrees in Philosophy from Boston University and in Clinical Psychology from Long Island University. In 1987 he co-founded, and for several years served as editor-in-chief of, the *New York Jewish Review*, a publication addressing the interface between traditional Judaism and contemporary thought. In addition to numerous publications in clinical, forensic, and philosophical psychology, Dr. Drob's articles on Jewish philosophy have appeared in such journals as *Tradition, The Reconstructionist*, and *Cross Currents*. His philosophical and psychological interests originally led him to the study of Chassidus. For the past fifteen years he has engaged in intensive study of the Kabbalah, the problems of God, Mind, and Evil, and the relationship between Jewish Mysticism and other traditions in the history of Western and Eastern thought. Contact Sanford Drob at www.newkabbalah.com.

Recommended Resources

The Alef-Beit: Jewish Thought Revealed through the Hebrew Letters
by Yitzchak Ginsburgh   1-56821-413-8

**Ascending Jacob's Ladder: Jewish Views of Angels, Demons,
and Evil Spirits**
by Ronald H. Isaacs   0-7657-5965-9

In the Beginning: Discourses on Chasidic Thought
by Adin Steinsaltz   1-56821-741-2

**Demystifing the Mystical: Understanding the Language and Concepts
of Chasidism and Jewish Mysticism—A Primer for the Layman**
by Chaim Dalfin   1-56821-453-7

**The Fundamentals of Jewish Mysticism: The Book of Creation
and Its Commentaries**
by Leonard R. Glotzer   0-87668-437-1

Inner Rhythms: The Kabbalah of Music
by DovBer Pinson   0-7657-6098-3

Jewish Mystical Leaders and Leadership in the Thirteenth Century
by Moshe Idel and Mortimer Ostow   0-7657-5994-2

The Jewish Mystical Tradition
by Ben Zion Bokser   1-56821-014-0

Jewish Mysticism and Ethics
by Joseph Dan   1-56821-563-0

Jewish Mysticism: Volumes 1-4
by Joseph Dan   Vol. 1   0-7657-6007-X
                                       Vol. 2   0-7657-6008-8
                                       Vol. 3   0-7657-6009-6
                                       Vol. 4   0-7657-6010-X

The Long Shorter Way: Discourses on Chasidic Thought
by Adin Steinsaltz, translated by Yehuda Hanegbi   1-56821-144-9

Magic, Mysticism, and Hasidism: The Supernatural in Jewish Thought
by Gedalyah Nigal, translated by Edward Levin   1-56821-033-7

Reflections on Infinity: An Introduction to Kabbalah
by Raoul Nass   0-7657-6062-2

Sefer Yetzirah: The Book of Creation
translated and with a commentary by Aryeh Kaplan   1-56821-503-7

The Sefirot: Ten Emanations of Divine Power
by Y. David Shulman   1-56821-929-6

The Sustaining Utterance: Discourses on Chasidic Thought
by Adin Steinsaltz   1-56821-997-0

Ten and Twenty-Two: A Journey through the Paths of Wisdom
by Michael Jacobs   1-56821-988-1

The Thirteen Petalled Rose
by Adin Steinsaltz, translated by Yehuda Hanegbi   0-87668-450-9

The Tree of Life, Vol. I: The Palace of Adam Kadmon
(Chayyim Vital's Introduction to the Kabbalah of Isaac Luria)
translation and introduction by
Donald Wilder Menzi and Zwe Padeh   0-7657-6011-8

The Unifying Factor: A Review of Kabbalah
by Nekhama Schoenburg   1-56821-562-2

Available at your local bookstore, online at www.aronson.com,
or call toll-free 1-800-782-0015